THE ULTIMATE RESOURCE 2

Other Books by Julian L. Simon

POPULATION ECONOMICS

The Effects of Income on Fertility (1974)
The Economics of Population Growth (1977)
The Ultimate Resource (1981)
Theory of Population and Economic Growth (1986)
The Economic Consequences of Immigration (1989)
Population Matters: People, Resources, Environment, and Immigration (1990)
Population and Development in Poor Countries: Selected Essays (1992)
Scarcity or Abundance?: A Debate on the Environment (with Norman Myers, 1994)

OTHER

How to Start and Operate a Mail-Order Business (1965; fifth edition, 1993)
Patterns of Use of Books in Large Research Libraries (with Herman H. Fussler, 1969)
Basic Research Methods in Social Science (1969; third edition with Paul Burstein, 1985)
Issues in the Economics of Advertising (1970)
The Management of Advertising (1971)
Applied Managerial Economics (1975)
Resampling: The New Statistics (1975; 1993)
Effort, Opportunity, and Wealth (1987)
Good Mood: The New Psychology of Overcoming Depression (1993)
Economic Essays of Julian L. Simon (1996)

EDITED BOOKS

Research in Population Economics: vol. 1 (1978); vol. 2 (1980) (with Julie daVanzo); vols. 3 (1981) and 4 (1982) (with Peter Lindert)
The Resourceful Earth (with Herman Kahn, 1984)
The State of Humanity (1995)

THE ULTIMATE RESOURCE 2

Julian L. Simon

PRINCETON UNIVERSITY PRESS   PRINCETON, NEW JERSEY

Copyright © 1996 by Princeton University Press
Published by Princeton University Press, 41 William Street,
Princeton, New Jersey 08540
In the United Kingdom: Princeton University Press,
Chichester, West Sussex

Library of Congress Cataloging-in-Publication Data

Simon, Julian Lincoln, 1932–
The ultimate resource 2 / Julian L. Simon.
p.   cm.
Includes bibliographical references and index.
ISBN 0-691-04269-1 (alk. paper)
1. Population.   2. Natural resources.
3. Economic policy.   I. Title.
HB871.S573   1996
333.7—dc20   95-39586   CIP

This book has been composed in Berkeley Book

Princeton University Press books are printed
on acid-free paper and meet the guidelines
for permanence and durability of the Committee
on Production Guidelines for Book Longevity
of the Council on Library Resources

Printed in the United States of America
by Princeton Academic Press

10   9   8   7   6   5   4   3   2   1

Multitudes of people, necessity, and liberty, have begotten commerce in Holland.
   (*David Hume, "Of the Rise and Progress of the Arts and Sciences,"*
   1744–1777)

The development of science . . . requires . . . freedom of the spirit which consists in the independence of thought from the restrictions of authoritarian and social prejudices.
   (*Albert Einstein,* Ideas and Opinions, *1954*)

Contents

Analytical Contents _____

Figures

Tables

Preface _____

THIS BOOK originated in my interest in the economics of population. When (starting about 1969) my studies showed that population growth does *not* hinder economic development or reduce the standard of living, critics asserted that adding more people to the planet causes natural resource scarcities and environmental decay. Hence, I was forced to broaden my inquiries. That's how the first edition of this book came to be written.

Ironically, when I began to work on population studies, I assumed that the accepted view was sound. I aimed to help the world contain its "exploding" population, which I believed to be one of the two main threats to humankind (war being the other). But my reading and research led me into confusion. Though the then-standard economic theory of population (which had hardly changed since Malthus) asserted that a higher population growth implies a lower standard of living, the available empirical data did not support that theory. My technical 1977 book, which is the predecessor of this volume, is an attempt to reconcile that contradiction. It arrived at a theory implying that population growth has positive economic effects in the long run, although there are costs in the short run.

The all-important point in this personal history: It was the facts that changed my mind about population growth away from the conventional belief. It was not some wider, preexisting set of beliefs that brought me to the point my work is now at. Indeed, the facts and my new conclusions about population economics altered my wider set of beliefs, rather than the converse.

About This Author and His Values

One spring day about 1969, I visited the U.S. AID office on the outskirts of Washington, D.C., to discuss a project intended to lower fertility in less-developed countries. I arrived early for my appointment, so I strolled outside in the warm sunshine. Below the building's plaza I noticed a road sign that said "Iwo Jima Memorial." There came to me the memory of reading a eulogy delivered by a Jewish chaplain over the dead on the battlefield at Iwo Jima, saying something like, How many who would have been a Mozart or a Michelangelo or an Einstein have we buried here?[1] And then I thought: Have I gone crazy? What business do I have trying to help arrange it that fewer human beings will be born, each one of whom might be a Mozart or a Michelangelo or an Einstein— or simply a joy to his or her family and community, and a person who will enjoy life?

I still believe that helping people fulfill their desires for the number of children they want is a wonderful human service. But to persuade them or coerce them to have fewer children than they would like to have—that is something entirely different.

The longer I have read the literature about population, the more baffled and distressed I have become that one idea is omitted: Enabling a potential human being to come into life and to enjoy life is a good thing, just as protecting a living person's life from being ended is a good thing. Of course a death is not the same as an averted life, in large part because others feel differently about the two. Yet I find no logic implicit in the thinking of those who are horrified at the starvation of a comparatively few people in a faraway country (and apparently more horrified than at the deaths by political murder in that same faraway country, or at the deaths by accidents in their own country) but who are positively gleeful with the thought that a million or ten million times that many lives will never be lived that might be lived.

Economics alone cannot explain this attitude, for though the economic consequences of death differ from those of non-life, they are not so different as to explain this difference in attitude. So what is it? Why does Kingsley Davis (one of the world's great demographers) respond to U.S. population growth during the 1960s, "I have never been able to get anyone to tell me why we needed those [additional] 23 million"?[2] And why does Paul Ehrlich say, "I can't think of any reason for having more than one hundred fifty million people [in the U.S.], and no one has ever raised one to me."[3] By 1991 he and Anne Ehrlich had even lowered the ceiling: "No sensible reason has ever been given for having more than 135 million people."[4]

I can suggest to Davis and Ehrlich more than one reason for having more children and taking in more immigrants. Least important is that the larger population will probably mean a higher standard of living for our grandchildren and great-grandchildren. (My technical 1977 and 1992 books and a good many chapters in this book substantiate that assertion.) A more interesting reason is that we need another person for exactly the same reason we need Davis and Ehrlich. That is, just as the Davises and Ehrlichs of this world are of value to the rest of us, so will the average additional person be of value.

The most interesting reason for having additional people, however, is this: If the Davises and Ehrlichs say that their lives are of value to themselves, and if the rest of us honor that claim and say that our lives are of value to us, then in the same manner the lives of additional people will be of value to those people themselves. Why should we not honor their claims, too?

If Davis or Ehrlich were to ask those twenty-three million Americans born between 1960 and 1970 whether it was a good thing that they were born, many of them would be able to think of a good reason or two. Some of them might also be so unkind as to add, "Yes, it's true that you gentlemen do not *personally* need any of us for your own welfare. But then, do you think that we have greater need of you?"

What is most astonishing is that these simple ideas, which would immediately spring to the minds of many who cannot read or write, have never come into the heads of famous scientists such as Davis and Ehrlich—by their own admission. And by repeating the assertion in 1991, Ehrlich makes it clear that he does not consider the above ideas, which I suggested to him earlier, to be "sensible."

The absence of this basic value for human life also is at the bottom of Ehrlich's well-known restatement of Pascal's wager. "If I'm right, we will save the world [by curbing population growth]. If I'm wrong, people will still be better fed, better housed, and happier, thanks to our efforts. [All the evidence suggests that he is wrong.] Will anything be lost if it turns out later that we can support a much larger population than seems possible today?"[5]

Please note how different is Pascal's wager: Live as if there is God, because even if there is no God you have lost nothing. Pascal's wager applies entirely to one person. No one else loses if she or he is wrong. But Ehrlich bets what he thinks will be the economic gains that we and our descendants might enjoy against the unborn's very lives. Would he make the same sort of wager if his own life rather than others' lives were the stake? (Chapter 39 has more to say about the morality of betting other people's lives.)

I do not say that society should never trade off human life for animals or even for nonliving things. Indeed, society explicitly makes exactly this trade-off when a firefighter's life is lost protecting a building or a forest or a zoo, and neither I nor hardly anyone else says it should not be so. And I have no objection in principle to the community taxing its members for the cost of parks or wilderness or wildlife protection (although a private arrangement may be better) any more than I object to taxes for the support of the poor. But according to my values, we should (1) have a clear quantitative idea of the trade-offs we seek to make, rather than make them on some unquantified principle such as "the loss of a single human being [or of a single nonhuman species or animal] is obscene," implying that the costs of saving that entity should not be reckoned; (2) recognize that economic science does not show that a greater number of human beings implies slower economic development or a lower standard of living in the long run; and (3) understand that foregoing the births of additional human beings is costly according to the value systems of some other human beings.

Changes in the Intellectual Environment since the First Edition

Most of the above appeared in the preface to the first edition. The common attitude toward the environment in the past decade, however, impels me to add the following personal note.

People who call themselves environmentalists sometimes say to people like me, "You don't appreciate nature." Such remarks often are made knowing little of the other person. Given the personal nature of such attacks, perhaps a few words of information are in order for at least this one representative person.

I'll bet I spend more hours of the year outdoors than any staff member of an environmental organization whose job is not specifically outdoors. I'm outside about nine hours a day perhaps 140 days a year—every day that it is not too cold for me to work. On average, only about one afternoon a year is too hot for me to be outside; shirtless and in shorts, with a fan blowing and a ridiculous-looking wet napkin on top of my head, I am comfortable outside if the temperature is less than 95 or even 100 degrees. Does this not show some appreciation of the out-of-doors?

Two pairs of binoculars are within reach to watch the birds. I love to check which of the tens of species of birds that come to sup from the mulberry tree behind our house will arrive this year, and I never tire of watching the hummingbirds at our feeder. I'll match my birdwatching time with just about any environmentalist, and I'll bet that I've seen more birds this spring than most of your environmental friends. And I can tell you that Jeremy Rifkin is spectacularly wrong when he writes that a child grows up in the U.S. Northeast without hearing birds sing nowadays. There are more different birds around now than there were forty-five years ago, when I first started watching them. (The mulberry tree is a great attraction, of course.)

As to my concern for other species: I don't like to kill even spiders and cockroaches, and I'd prefer to shoo flies outside of the house rather than swat them. But if it's them versus me, I have no compunction about killing them even if it is with regret.

The best part of my years in the Navy were the sunsets and sunrises at sea, the flying fish in tropical waters, the driving rain and high waves, too, even at the cost of going without sit-down meals. And being aboard a small ship near the eye of a killer typhoon (knowing it to be the same spot where thirteen U.S. ships foundered and sank in a typhoon a decade earlier) was one of the great experiences of my life. There is no more compelling evidence of the awesome power of nature.

When I was a Boy Scout I delighted in the nature study merit-badge learning. I loved building bridges over streams using only vines and tree limbs, and I was proud of my skill at making fires with flint and steel or Indian-style with bow-and-drill and tinder.

The real issue is not whether one cares about nature, but whether one cares about people. Environmental sympathies are not in dispute; because one puts the interests of one's children before the interests of the people down the street does not imply that one hates the neighbors, or even is uninterested in them. The central matters in dispute here are truth and liberty, versus the desire to impose one's aesthetic and moral tastes on others.

What's New in the Second Edition?

What's new in this second edition? The most important and best additions are new data that enable us to measure and state quantitatively phenomena that earlier could only be described qualitatively or with few data. For example, in the first edition I could only report that one could see further in London than in years past; now there are excellent data on the number of hours of sunshine on winter days and on the amount of smoke in the air. In the end, the data constitute the entire difference between the case I present here and the case of the doomsters, just as it was data that entirely changed my mind from agreeing with them in 1966. So please bear with the heavy load of graphs and numbers, all of which make the case even stronger than it was in the first edition.

There also are new ways that others and I have developed to explain the topics treated here. And there is a new offer of a wager that confronts the doomsters' predictions in a more complete and testable fashion than before. Some new problems that have come to the fore since the first edition are also addressed, even though they had earlier been discussed by specialists—for example, acid rain, species extinction, household waste disposal, and a variety of chemical substances—all of which need attention but none of which turns out to be of a different nature than other issues discussed in the previous edition.

This book may best be read in conjunction with my edited 1995 book, *The State of Humanity*, which contains a great deal of additional data, as well as discussions of these trends by a wide variety of thoughtful writers.

This second edition has benefited enormously from the ease of writing with the computer and word processor. But this process has produced a new problem. The old edition was scanned electronically to produce the files from which I worked. The scanning did not reproduce quotation marks in most cases. I trust that I have properly identified and marked most if not all of those old quotations. But it is possible that one or more quotes now appears without quotation marks, an apparent plagiarism. This worries me, and I hope that if it has happened, the interpretation will be kindly, considering this as honest error rather than intentional theft. The scanning also did not always catch ellipses in quotations. This was even tougher to check than quotation marks. I hope that where they were omitted and the error not caught, the meaning was not altered.

Some passages have been taken directly from various of my other books without the use of quotation marks or footnotes, because my work on these subjects is an integrated entity that has grown organically over the years, rather than a set of separate special topics. I hope that no one is troubled by these repeated unattributed statements (some sentences surviving unchanged since 1968).

You may notice that certain ideas in the book are repeated, even several times. And you may find that even after I have defined something, I repeat the definition later. This is because I sympathise with those people who, like me, forget certain things quickly, and don't like (or are often too lazy) to check back to see if or where the matter is mentioned earlier. The repetition also increases the chance that the basic ideas in the book will reach those people who may dip in here or there, rather than reading sequentially from beginning to end.

The course of the public's thinking on these matters over the past decade or so has caused in me alternate hope and despair. On the one hand, opinion has reached the point where it seems that everything I pick up has the obligatory reference to "exploding" population or "plundered" Earth. And these ideas are simply taken for granted, unexamined, by journalists, a process which works the ideas ever more deeply into the grain of the public's thinking, and makes them ever harder to challenge successfully. On the other hand, more and more people have come to recognize the unsound theoretical nature of Malthusian thinking, often because they have seen how the plain facts of history and our present state of living contradict those ideas.

The book is called *The Ultimate Resource 2* rather than a revised edition because so much has been added to the content of the original. (For example, there are now more than twice as many citations as in the first edition, I regret to say.) But with a single minor exception (so labeled in the book), every one of the ideas contained in the original remains unchanged. This is the opposite from Malthus's experience with his famous book, whose second and subsequent editions were utterly different in conclusions from the original, but did not indicate that there was a major change.

The chapters on the politics and financing of the population-control movement have been deleted to save space, and because it was a very big job to bring them up to date. The conclusions of those chapters are summarized in the current introduction, however.

This book is friendly to the environment. It has the welfare of poor people at heart. And nothing that I write is inconsistent with, or antagonistic to, direct tax transfers from the rich to the poor of as large a proportion of the society's resources as a democracy deems appropriate. Any critic contemplating an ad hominem attack on my knowledge and experience with the environment and with the poor might usefully check out my origins and my life's activities.

It's a shame to have to begin a book this way. But there is an unfortunate tendency for purveyors of majority thinking and members of popular organizations to indict everyone who does not agree with them as callous to human suffering, lacking compassion for poorer persons, and indifferent to nature. And this is a successful ploy, as shown by the fact that I feel forced to open the second edition of this book with these defensive remarks.

The saddest aspect of that ploy is that it damages the very people and causes that it purports to benefit. Poor people, as well as property of high social value such as natural habitats and valuable species, stand to gain the most from the public's being aware of the facts and concepts contained in this book, and from the policies of freedom and enterprise under the rule of wise laws that are the heart of the book's prescriptions.

The common assertions that resources are growing more scarce, that environmental conditions are worsening, and that the poor suffer from economic freedom are the gravest danger to the poor and the environment. And many of the government interventions that are predicated on these false assertions constitute fraud because they benefit only the well-off and the vested interests that many constricting regulations protect from competition for a good life of cheap, high-quality housing and consumer goods, easy access to wilderness, and upward mobility in society.

Message to Future Generations

When I began my population studies in the 1960s, I was in the midst of a depression of unusual duration (whose origins had nothing to do with population growth or the world's predicament). As I studied the economics of population and worked my way to the views I now hold—that population growth, along with the lengthening of human life, is a moral and material triumph— my outlook for myself, for my family, and for the future of humanity became increasingly more optimistic. Eventually I was able to pull myself out of my depression, and it has never recurred. This is only part of the story, but there is at least some connection between the two sets of mental events—the happy outcomes of my population studies brightened my personal outlook. Because my statement to this effect in the first edition has been misinterpreted by some—albeit only by those who damned the book—I'd like this to be crystal-clear: my mental outlook did not affect my studies; rather, my studies affected my mental outlook. And I believe that if others fully recognize the extraordinarily positive trends that have continued until now, and that can reasonably be expected to continue into the future, it may brighten their outlooks, too.

Consider this anecdote:

The local newspaper in the Indiana town where I was teaching last year ran a contest for schoolchildren. The students were to create a one-frame cartoon on any topic. . . . A sample of the winning entries revealed a common theme.

A girl in Grade 2 drew a sad-faced planet Earth, with the caption, "I am weary. I am tired. Please quit wasting me!" . . . A girl in Grade 3 depicted a number of crying animals looking at a house under construction with some smokestacks in the background; the caption read, "We want our homes back!!!". . .

My college freshmen classes are regularly populated by young adults who are convinced that no solutions are possible and so it's useless to try.[6]

My message to these young people—who are representative of many others, as the polls in chapter 14 show—certainly is not one of complacency. In this I agree with the doomsayers: Our world needs the best efforts of all humanity to improve our lot. I part company with the doomsayers in that they expect us to come to a bad end despite the efforts we make, whereas I expect a continuation of humanity's successful efforts. And I believe that their message is self-fulfilling, because if you expect your efforts to fail because of inexorable natural limits, then you are likely to feel resigned, and therefore to literally resign. But if you recognize the possibility—in fact the probability—of success, you can tap large reservoirs of energy and enthusiasm.

Adding more people to any community causes problems, but people are also the means to solve these problems. The main fuel to speed the world's progress is our stock of knowledge, and the brake is our lack of imagination. The ultimate resource is people—skilled, spirited, hopeful people—who will exert their wills and imaginations for their own benefit as well as in a spirit of faith and social concern. Inevitably they will benefit not only themselves but the poor and the rest of us as well.

A last, very personal word. Because of the fighting words in this preface and elsewhere, I may seem to be feisty or even tough, and able to take care of myself in this argument. But I am not very feisty in person. I have been trying—mostly unsuccessfully—to get a hearing for these ideas since 1969. Although times have changed somewhat, the difficulties of espousing this unpopular point of view do get to me, until recently they were near the point of shutting me up and shutting me down. If there weren't a handful of editors like Sandy Thatcher, then of Princeton University Press, you wouldn't hear from me at all. Some others hold a point of view similar to mine. But there are far too few of us to provide mutual support and comfort. So this is a plea for love, printer's ink, and research grants for our side. All contributions gratefully accepted.

Acknowledgments for the First Edition———————————

THIS BOOK appears at the time and in the form that it does because of the professional and personal qualities of Sanford Thatcher, formerly assistant director of Princeton University Press. Sandy suggested the present order of the topics, which I believe makes the book much better than it was before even if it asks more of the reader; he also advised wisely about where and how to cut a draft which was too long to be publishable or readable. He made sure that the book promptly got at least a fair shake in the process of editorial evaluation. And it was my faith in his word, based on the trust he built between us during the publication of my previous book, that gave me the heart to revise the long early draft even without any commitment from him, and while I had reason to doubt that anyone else would want to publish this controversial material.

The book has greatly benefited from, and I have delighted in, the help of two skilled copy editors. Richard Palmer policed the documentation and the syntax, and in the process improved the prose as much as I would let him; he also gave me the benefit of many amusing asides, some of which I appropriated. William Hively worked the book (and me) over sentence by sentence. He straightened, tightened, and sharpened the language, and detected troublesome errors in writing; he also contributed a good many helpful thoughts from his large stock of general knowledge. And with care and diligence he kept the book on track and away from dangerous derailings while in press. In a better job market for academics, these two talented men would be working on their own writings rather than my book; as the beneficiary, however, I can't help feeling grateful for this circumstance, and for the opportunity of getting to know them in the process.

Michael Aronson of Harvard University Press and Colin Day of Cambridge University Press helped me with their sound editorial judgments about the overall design of the book. Harold Barnett, Allen Chase, and Thomas Mayer generously read through most of the text and gave me copious, useful notes; where I did not take their advice, I hope they will forgive me. The anonymous referees also improved the revision. Stanley Trollip helped me choose the book's title. And James L. Smith read and made important corrections in the energy chapters. Alvin Weinberg also was kind enough to read several chapters and to comment upon them.

Douglas Love assisted in much of the data collection and computer work; he served intelligently and faithfully. James Bier created the excellent figures. And typists Phyllis Stout and Susan Walker contributed high skill and diligence to the making of the book.

The roots of this work go back to William Petty, Adam Smith, and Friedrich Engels; to Jules Verne and H. G. Wells; and to others who have, in their forecasts for the economy and society, given full weight to man's imagination and creative powers of solving the problems of people and resources. But it was in the more recent work of Simon Kuznets, Harold J. Barnett together with Chandler Morse, A. V. Chayanov, and Ester Boserup that I found this idea and was inspired by it.

My wife Rita strengthened me by agreeing with my point of view, just as my children David, Judith, and Daniel strengthened me by saying that my arguments about the topics of this book make sense, despite their not knowing the details of the arguments and in the face of having been told exactly the opposite by the newspapers and television.

Lastly, though I am not accustomed to dealing with organizations as if they have personalities or characters, I am happy to recognize that Princeton University Press has treated this book—and me—the way every author dreams of being treated but seldom is. The experience of having a book published usually feels to me like walking at snail's pace through a mine field; if I get through with most vital organs, I can count on losing at least a few joints of major appendages, plus a big bunch of nerve endings, to what appear to be senseless, arbitrary blasts. Instead, during the publication of this book I have felt like a member of a partnership in which all partners work together enthusiastically toward a common goal, this has been a great joy, indeed.

I am grateful for all your help.

Urbana, Illinois
September 5, 1980

Acknowledgments for the Second Edition _____

HELP WITH THIS second edition came from many. Elizabeth Sobo valiantly battled resistant bureaucrats and wielded the Freedom of Information Act to dig up valuable information about government operations. Carl Gosline sent many useful newspaper reports out of his volunteer clipping service. Donald Bishop drew my attention to the poem about Lincoln which ends the book.

Editor Jack Repcheck sponsored this edition at Princeton University Press and has been effective and generous in his treatment of it. Will Hively again edited the book, this time widening his role to split chapters that were too long, moving some material from place to place, and organizing the logistics of editing and typing. Karen Verde did such a good job as copy editor for a previous book that I asked for her again, and she excelled herself. Beth Gianfagna is a cheerful, efficient, and forceful production editor. Kathy Rochelle did a spectacular job of word (and paragraph and endnote) processing, managing to step around pitfall after pitfall of bad handwriting and confusing instructions. Helen Demarest continues to be the world's best secretary; what more can I say? Rebecca Boggs came along as a summer intern at the Cato Institute when the graphs were desperately disorganized and badly labeled, and with stupendous diligence and great good sense, in a few days relieved me of much work and great anxiety. Guenter Weinrauch helped prepare many of the figures, and was as competent a research assistant as I have ever seen; if he didn't know how to do something, he said he would learn how, and did so—an attitude I always admire greatly.

I would like to thank the Cato Institute for its support of my research and this book. Ed Crane and David Boaz of Cato are as steadfast as people can be in their commitments to liberty and truth; these ends are their only agenda, and they are exceedingly effective in promoting them. I appreciate their help and their comradeship in these happy battles.

I am grateful for extensive comments and generous editorial suggestions by Kenneth Elzinga about the note on Shakespeare's sonnet in chapter 19. I also appreciate useful readings of that section by Jim Cook, Stephen Louis Goldman, Stephen Miller, and Jack Stillinger. Cal Beisner enlightened me about the parable of the talents.

When the first edition was written, there had been few other works that discussed critically the unfounded prophecies of doom about resources, the environment, and population—mainly books by Barnett and Morse (a classic which was one of the pillars on which this book rests), Beckerman, Clark (who almost alone carried the flag of truth about population growth for many years), Kahn and associates, Maddox, Weber, and long before, Mather. There also existed—though I did not know about it until he contacted me about my 1977 book because it provided empirical evidence for ideas he had held for half a century but had never published because they ran counter to the supposed data—Hayek's remarkable *The Constitution of Liberty* (1960). Its chapters on resources analyze the issues in astonishing breadth and depth, in the more general context of his vision of modern society and economic progress, which I have come to find more fundamentally sound and important than any book I have ever read, and with which I agree in almost every detail. And of course the studies of Boserup, Kuznets, and Schultz and some other great predecessors were in print, but did not aggressively confront the Malthusian doomsters.

The volume of available data and analysis—although not the volume of usable theory, I regret to say—has skyrocketed since the first edition, especially concerning the environment, pollution, and conservation. A confirmed doomsayer would extrapolate that we will soon be crowded out of existence by this trend. I do not worry about that, but I do wish to note both the blessings and the burdens that this has imposed on the creation of this second edition.

The welcome outpouring of books on these subjects constitutes most of those that are listed with asterisks in the references at the end of the book. The existence of all these books makes it possible for me to refer to their detailed treatment of such topics as nuclear waste, carbon dioxide emissions, and the ozone layer. Hence, I can reduce my treatment of these topics.

Unlike Malthus, when he published a second edition of his book on population, I have no need to change the first-edition conclusions; everything in the first edition of this book can stand as written. This edition mainly adduces new data and brings the old data series up to date (though this also makes it nearly twice as long).

It is now possible to better document many of the statements made in the first edition. But it is much harder to present enough material so that the reader feels comfortable that I have done the necessary homework. Should there be another edition, the scope of the volume probably will need to be curtailed to allow for the increase in supporting material. The first volume was able to be sufficiently comprehensive to serve as something of a handbook. This volume may still serve somewhat in that role. But in the future no one-author volume can do that job.

It is a bit ironic that the volume of literature about the effects of population growth has not grown nearly so much. The direct economic effects of population growth were and are my central interest, and the only reason that I wrote this book was because the profession ignored my technical articles and 1977 technical book on the subject; I hoped to reach the public directly, and the profession indirectly through the public's interest, with this book. And the only reason that I wrote about the environment, conservation, pollution, and related topics is that whenever I would talk about the direct economic effects, people would say, "Yes, maybe that's true, but what about the effects on pollution? On the wilderness? What about crime and war?" They would keep moving down the ladder of possible negative effects, becoming ever less important, but providing an endless change of objections—quibbles—and each has to be addressed. Now the tail wags the dog, if we measure topics by the space devoted to them.

I cannot claim that I have done well enough in coping with this deluge of material. But I have worked hard at the task. My concurrent editing of the volume *The State of Humanity* has been a big help in keeping me apprised of developments of the past few years. And that volume should serve as the handbook that this book cannnot be. Yet now I feel it appropriate to quote Hayek (1960) as follows:

> It is perhaps inevitable that the more ambitious the task, the more inadequate will be the performance. On a subject as comprehensive as that of this book, the task of making it as good as one is capable of is never completed while one's faculties last. . . . I will merely claim that I have worked on the book until I did not know how I could adequately present the chief argument in briefer form.

THE ULTIMATE RESOURCE 2

Introduction _____

What Are the *Real* Population and Resource Problems?

IS THERE a natural-resource problem now? Certainly—just as always. The problem is that natural resources are scarce, in the sense that it costs us labor and capital to get them, though we would prefer to get them for free.

Are we now "in crisis" and "entering an age of scarcity"? You can see anything you like in a crystal ball. But almost without exception, the relevant data (the long-run economic trends) suggest precisely the opposite. The appropriate measures of scarcity (the costs of natural resources in human labor, and their prices relative to wages and to other goods) all suggest that natural resources have been becoming *less* scarce over the long run, right up to the present.

How about pollution? Is this not a problem? Of course pollution is a problem. People have always had to dispose of their waste products so as to enjoy a pleasant and healthy living space. But we now live in a more healthy and less dirty environment than in earlier centuries.

About population now: Is there a population problem? Again, of course there is a population problem, just as always. When a couple is about to have a baby, they must prepare a place for the child to sleep safely. Then, after the birth of the child, the parents must feed, clothe, protect, and teach it. All this requires effort and resources, and not from the parents alone. When a baby is born or a migrant arrives, the community must increase its municipal services—schooling, fire and police protection, and garbage collection. None of these are free.

For the first decades of its life, an additional child certainly is a burden not only on its parents but also on others. Brothers and sisters must do with less of everything except companionship. Taxpayers must cough up additional funds for schooling and other public services. Neighbors hear more noise. During these early years the child produces nothing material, and the income of the family and the community is spread more thinly than if the baby had not been born. And when the child grows up and first goes to work, jobs are squeezed a bit, and the output and pay per working person go down. All this clearly is an economic loss for other people.

Just as surely, however, an additional person is also a boon. The child or immigrant will pay taxes later on, contribute energy and resources to the community, produce goods and services for the consumption of others, and make efforts to beautify and purify the environment. Perhaps most significant for the more-developed countries is the contribution that the average person makes to increasing the efficiency of production through new ideas and improved methods.

The real population problem, then, is not that there are too many people or that too many babies are being born. The problem is that others must support each additional person before that person contributes in turn to the well-being of others.

Which is more weighty, the burden or the boon? That depends on the economic conditions and institutions, which we shall discuss at some length. But also, to a startling degree, the decision about whether the overall effect of a child or migrant is positive or negative depends on the values of whoever is making the judgment—your preference to spend a dollar now rather than to wait for a dollar-plus-something in twenty or thirty years, your preferences for having more or fewer wild animals alive as opposed to more or fewer human beings alive, and so on. Population growth is a problem, but not *just* a problem; it is a boon, but not just a boon. So your values are all-important in judging the net effect of population growth, and deciding whether there are too many or too few people.

From the economic point of view an additional child is like a laying chicken, a cacao tree, a computer factory, or a new house. A baby is a durable good in which someone must invest heavily long before the grown adult begins to provide returns on the investment. But whereas "Travel now, pay later" is inherently attractive because the pleasure is immediate and the piper will wait, "Pay now, benefit from the child later" is inherently problematic because the sacrifice comes first.

You might respond that additional children will *never* yield net benefits, because they use up irreplaceable resources. We shall see that additional persons produce more than they consume in the long run, and natural resources are not an exception. But we can agree that there is still a population problem, just as there is a problem with all good investments. Long before there are benefits, we must tie up capital that could otherwise be used for immediate consumption.

Please notice that I have limited the discussion to the *economic* aspect of investing in children—that is, to a child's effect on the material standard of living. If we also consider the nonmaterial aspects of children—their meaning for parents and for others who enjoy a flourishing of humanity—then the case for adding children to our world becomes even stronger. And if we also keep in mind that most of the costs of children are borne by their parents rather than by the community during the child's early years, whereas the community (especially in developed countries) gets the lion's share of the benefits later on, the essential differences between children and other investments tend to improve rather than weaken the social economics of children.

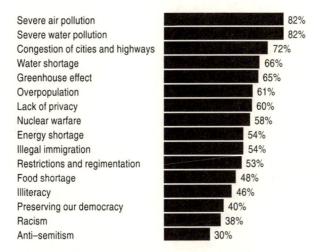

Severe air pollution	82%
Severe water pollution	82%
Congestion of cities and highways	72%
Water shortage	66%
Greenhouse effect	65%
Overpopulation	61%
Lack of privacy	60%
Nuclear warfare	58%
Energy shortage	54%
Illegal immigration	54%
Restrictions and regimentation	53%
Food shortage	48%
Illiteracy	46%
Preserving our democracy	40%
Racism	38%
Anti–semitism	30%

Figure I-1. Public Opinion about "Serious Problems Expected 25–50 Years from Now"

Whether or not there is cause to believe that population, resources, and the environment are worse "problems" than in the past, the public believes them to be so. It has surprised me to learn, when preparing the second edition of this book, that the nexus of issues treated here is nowadays seen by the public as by far the most pressing set of problems facing society (see fig. I-1).

Preview of the Book

Here follow some of the main conclusions of the book. At the time of the first edition they seemed far-fetched to most readers, and they still shock many. But events since then have without exception confirmed the forecasts implicit in the trends and analyses made here.

Food. Contrary to popular impression, food production per capita has been increasing for the half-century since World War II, the only decades for which we have acceptable data. We also know that famine has progressively diminished for at least the past century. Average height has increased in developed countries in recent centuries, a sign that people are eating better. And there is compelling reason to believe that human nutrition will continue to improve into the indefinite future, even with continued population growth.

Land. Agricultural land is not a fixed resource. Rather, the amount of agricultural land has been increasing substantially, and it is likely to continue to increase where needed. Paradoxically, in the countries that are best supplied with food, such as the United States, the quantity of land under cultivation has been *decreasing* because it is more economical to raise larger yields on less land than to increase the total amount of farmland. For this reason, among others, the amount of land used for forests, recreation, and wildlife has been increasing rapidly in the United States—hard to believe, but substantiated beyond a doubt.

Natural resources. Hold your hat—our supplies of natural resources are not finite in any economic sense. Nor does past experience give reason to expect natural resources to become more scarce. Rather, if history is any guide, natural resources will progressively become less costly, hence less scarce, and will constitute a smaller proportion of our expenses in future years. Population growth is likely to have a long-run beneficial impact on the natural-resource situation.

Energy. Grab your hat again—the long-run future of our energy supply is at least as bright as that of other natural resources, though government intervention can temporarily boost prices from time to time. Finiteness is no problem here either. And the long-run impact of additional people is likely to speed the development of cheap energy supplies that are almost inexhaustible.

Pollution. This set of issues is as complicated as you wish to make it. But even many ecologists, as well as most economists, agree that population growth is not the villain in the creation and reduction of pollution. And the key trend is that life expectancy, which is the best overall index of the pollution level, has improved markedly as the world's population has grown. This reflects the enormous decline during the past couple of centuries in the most important pollutions—diseases borne by air and water.

The standard of living. In the short run, additional children imply additional costs, though the costs to persons other than the children's parents are relatively small. In the longer run, however, per capita income is likely to be higher with a growing population than with a stationary one, both in more-developed and less-developed countries. Whether you wish to pay the present costs for the future benefits depends on how you weigh the future relative to the present; this is a value judgment.

Human fertility. The contention that poor and uneducated people breed without constraint is demonstrably wrong, even for the poorest and most "primitive" societies. Well-off people who believe that the poor do not weigh the consequences of having more children are simply arrogant, or ignorant, or both.

Future population growth. Population forecasts are published with confidence and fanfare. Yet the record of even the official forecasts made by U.S. government agencies and by the UN is little (if any) better than that of the most naive predictions.

For example, experts in the 1930s foresaw the U.S. population declining, perhaps to as little as 100 million people well before the turn of the century. In 1989, the U.S. Census Bureau forecast that U.S. population would peak at 302 million in 2038 and then decline. Just three years later, the Census Bureau forecast 383 million in 2050 with no peaking in sight. The science of demographic forecasting clearly has not yet reached perfection.

Present trends suggest that even though total population for the world is increasing, the density of population on most of the world's surface will decrease. This is already happening in the developed countries. Although the total populations of developed countries increased from 1950 to 1990, the rate of urbanization was sufficiently great that population density on *most* of their land areas (say, 97 percent of the land area of the United States) has been decreasing. As the poor countries become richer, they will surely experience the same trends, leaving most of the world's surface progressively less populated, astonishing as this may seem.

Immigration. The migration of people from poor to rich countries is as close to an everybody-wins government policy as can be. Countries in North America and Western Europe thereby advance just about all their national goals— higher productivity, a higher standard of living, and an easing of the heavy social burdens caused by growing proportions of aged dependents. And of course the immigrants benefit. Even the sending countries benefit on balance from the remittances that immigrants send back, and from improved ties between the countries. Amazingly, immigration does not even increase native unemployment measurably, even among low-income groups. This topic, discussed briefly in the first edition, now constitutes a separate book.[1]

Pathological effects of population density. Many worry that mental health is worse in more densely populated areas. This idea was reinforced by research on animal populations. But this putative drawback of population growth has been falsified by psychological studies of humans.

Similar "common sense" convinces many people—including the powers-that-be in the CIA—that population growth increases the likelihood of wars. The data show otherwise.

World population policy. The first edition documented that tens of millions of U.S. taxpayers' dollars are being used to tell the governments and people of other countries that they ought to reduce their fertility. The long-time head of the Population Branch of the U.S. State Department Agency for International Development (AID)—for many years the single most important U.S. population official—publicly said that the United States should act to reduce fertility worldwide *for the country's own economic self-interest*. And a secret policy assessment issued by the National Security Council in 1974 (U.S. National Security Council 1974; Sobo 1991b)—finally declassified in 1989, but with many pages still blacked out—specifies population-control activities for U.S. governmental agents to carry out in various countries, especially Africa; this includes twisting the arms of foreign governments in a variety of ways to ensure "cooperation." But economic data and analyses do not justify this policy. Furthermore, might not such acts be an unwarranted (and resented) interference in the internal affairs of other countries?

Domestic population activities. The first edition also documented that other millions of public dollars go to private organizations in the population lobby whose directors believe that, for environmental and related reasons, fewer Americans should be born. With these funds they propagandize the rest of us to believe—and act—in ways consistent with the views of such organizations as the Population Crisis Committee, the Population Reference Bureau, the Worldwatch Institute, and the Association for Voluntary Sterilization.

Still other tens of millions of U.S. tax dollars target the fertility of the poor in the United States. The explicit justification for this policy (given by the head of Planned Parenthood's Alan Guttmacher Institute) is that it will keep additional poor people off the welfare rolls. Even if this were proven—which it has not been, so far as I know—is this policy in the spirit or tradition of America? Furthermore, there is statistical proof that the public birth control clinics, which were first opened in large numbers in the poorer southern states, were positioned to reduce fertility among blacks.

Involuntary sterilization. Also shown in the first edition: Tax monies are used to involuntarily sterilize poor people (often black) without medical justification. As a result of the eugenics movement, which has been intertwined with the population-control movement for decades, there were (when last I checked) laws in thirty states providing for the involuntary sterilization of the mentally defective. These laws have led to many perfectly normal poor women being sterilized without their knowledge, after being told that their operations were other sorts of minor surgery.

In the chapters to come, you will find evidence documenting these and many other surprising statements about resources, population, environment, and their interconnections. You will also find a foundation of economic theory that makes sense of the surprising facts. And you will find an offer to back with my own hard cash my forecasts about the things we can bet about—not only natural resources, health, and cleanliness of the environment, but also all other measures of human welfare. If you believe that scarcities or more pollution are in the offing, you can take advantage of my offer and make some money at my expense. (My winnings go to finance research on these and other topics.)

You may wonder why the tone of this book is overwhelmingly positive whereas that of most popular writings is so negative. The most important explanation, I think, is the nature of the comparisons that are made. The comparisons in this book mostly compare now with earlier times. The comparisons others make often show one group versus another, or contrast how we are versus how we think we should be or would like to be—situations that guarantee a steady flow of depressing bad news.

As you reflect upon the arguments of the doomsters with which this book takes issue, you may notice a peculiar contradiction: On the one hand, the doomsters say that there are too many of us; on the other hand, they warn that we are in danger of most of us being wiped out.[2] Usually, a larger number of members of a species is greater protection against being wiped out. Hence, there is an apparent contradiction.

The doomsters reply that because there are more of us, we are eroding the basis of existence, and rendering more likely a "crash" due to population "overshoot"; that is, they say that our present or greater numbers are not sustainable. But the signs of incipient catastrophe are absent. Length of life and health are increasing, supplies of food and other natural resources are becoming ever more abundant, and pollutants in our environment are decreasing.

In reply, the doomsters point to vaguer signs of environmental disruption. I confess that I see none of the signs that they point to except those that have nothing to do with the "carrying capacity" of the Earth—I do see profound changes in society and civilization, most of which can be interpreted as either good or bad, and which are entirely within our own control. But you the reader will decide for yourself whether those claims of the doomsters are convincing to you in light of the issues that we can discuss objectively, and that are taken up in the book.

Numbers, Writers, and Believability

There are many numbers and diagrams in the text. Bear with me, please; the arguments depend on them. If my conclusions were not backed with hard data as proof, some would be laughed away because they violate common sense, and others would be rejected instantly because they starkly contradict the main body of popular writings about population and resources.

You may look skeptically at some of the data, such as the statistics showing that world food production and consumption per capita are going up even in poor countries, year by year. You may ask, "But what about the evidence that supports what everyone 'knows'—that the world is headed toward starvation and famine?" There simply are no other data. The food data are from the UN and U.S. government, the only data there are. If UN and U.S. officials often make statements inconsistent with these data, it is because they have not checked the evidence or are purposely disregarding it. Some of the other data are more subject to argument. I have tried to give you an honest shake on the data, but you must be the judge.

If you read the book and still doubt the general theme that conditions have been getting better, I pray that you answer this question: What data would you cite to contradict the proposition that the material conditions of life have been improving? And if you cannot cite any data, ask yourself: what *imaginable* data could conceivably convince you? You will find that most relevant data are contained either in this book or in my forthcoming book, *The State of Humanity*. (If there are still other data that you might seek in this connection, please write me.) But if there is *no conceivable set of data* that might convince you to the contrary, then there is no scientific way to address your reservations. If no data could falsify your belief, then your position is a matter of metaphysical belief, on the same intellectual footing as theology rather than science.

I invite you to research for yourself the assertion that the conditions of humanity have gotten worse. Stop at the nearest library and inspect the two basic reference books: the Bureau of the Census's *Statistical Abstract of the United States* and *Historical Statistics of the United States*. Look in the index under "Pollution: Air," and "Pollution: Water," and examine the data for various years. Then do the same for world food production per person, and then for worldwide availability of natural resources, as measured by their prices. While you're at it, check the amount of space per person in our homes, and the presence of such amenities as telephones and indoor toilets, year by year. Most important, inspect life expectancy and the incidence of death. You will find that just about every single indicator of the quality of life shows improvement rather than the deterioration that the doomsayers claim has occurred. And things have gotten better for the poor as well as the rich, even through the 1980s.

But even based on first-hand evidence of your own senses—such as the improved health and later ages at which acquaintances die nowadays as compared with the past; the material goods that we now possess; the speed at which information, entertainment, and we ourselves move freely throughout the world—it seems to me that a person must be literally deaf and blind not to perceive that humanity is in a much better state than ever before.

The trend toward a better life can be seen in most of our own families. I'll dramatize the matter with an anecdote: I have mild asthma. As an overnight guest in a home where there was a dog, in the middle of the night I woke with a bad cough and shortness of breath caused by the dog dander. So I took out my twelve-dollar pocket inhaler, good for 300 puffs, and took one puff. Within ten minutes my lungs were clear—a small miracle. A few decades ago I would have been sleepless and miserable all night, and I would have had to give up the squash playing that I love so much because exercise causes my worst asthma in the absence of an inhaler. And diabetes: If your child had diabetes a hundred years ago, you had to watch helplessly as the child went blind and died early. Nowadays injections, or even pills, can give the child as long and healthy a life as other children. And eyeglasses: Centuries ago you had to give up reading when your eyes got dim as you got to be 40 or 50. Then when spectacles were finally invented, only the rich could afford them. Now anyone can afford plastic magnifiers at the drugstore for nine dollars. And you can even wear contact lenses for eye problems and keep your vanity intact. Is there not some condition in *your* family that in earlier times would have been a lingering misery or a tragedy, that nowadays our increasing knowledge has rendered easily bearable?

Travel to poor countries, but leave the capital cities and venture into rural areas. Ask farmers about their standard of living, present and past. You will find improvement everywhere, in all respects—tractors, roads to the market, motorbikes, electric pumps for wells, schools where there were none before, and children going to university in the city.

The Role of Political Economy

Here we must address a crucial but touchy element in the economics of resources and population—the extent to which the political-social-economic system provides personal freedom from government coercion. Skilled persons require a framework that provides incentives for working hard and taking risks, enabling their talents to flower and come to fruition. The key elements of such a framework are economic liberty, respect for property, and fair and sensible rules of the market that are enforced equally for all.

The world's problem is not too many people, but lack of political and economic freedom. Powerful evidence comes from pairs of countries that had the same culture and history and much the same standard of living when they split apart after World War II—East and West Germany, North and South Korea, Taiwan and China. In each case the centrally planned Communist country began with less population "pressure," as measured by density per square kilometer, than did the market-directed economy. And the Communist and non-Communist countries also started with much the same birthrates. But the market-directed economies performed much better economically than the centrally planned economies. This powerful demonstration cuts the ground from under population growth as a likely explanation of poor economic performance.

The role of government is discussed much more in this edition than in the first edition, and usually the discussion is critical of government intervention. This shift in emphasis is partly due to greater understanding of the issues through further study (especially the works of Friedrich Hayek, who in turn took advantage of the empirical findings about population in this and my preceding technical book to support his own research into long-run effects of population growth), partly a result of more research by others into the economic results of governments' population and environmental activities, partly a result of more information becoming available about the situations in Eastern Europe and China, and partly a result of an increase in government activities.

The State of the Argument

To sum up the argument of the book: In the short run, all resources are limited. An example of such a finite resource is the amount of attention that you will devote to what I write. The longer run, however, is a different story. The standard of living has risen along with the size of the world's population since the beginning of recorded time. There is no convincing economic reason why these trends toward a better life should not continue indefinitely.

Many people find it difficult to accept this economic argument. Dwindling resources, increasing pollution, starvation and misery—all this seems inevitable unless we curb population growth or otherwise cut back consumption of natural resources. Thomas Malthus reached this conclusion nearly two centuries ago in his famous *Essay on the Principle of Population*, and popular thinking is now dominated by his gloomy theory (not widely accepted in Malthus's own day).

The new theory that is the key idea of the book—and is consistent with current evidence—is this: Greater consumption due to an increase in population and growth of income heightens scarcity and induces price run-ups. A higher price represents an opportunity that leads inventors and businesspeople to seek new ways to satisfy the shortages. Some fail, at cost to themselves. A few succeed, and the final result is that we end up better off than if the original shortage problems had never arisen. That is, we need our problems, though this does not imply that we should purposely create additional problems for ourselves.

The most important benefit of population size and growth is the increase it brings to the stock of useful knowledge. Minds matter economically as much as, or more than, hands or mouths. Progress is limited largely by the availability of trained workers.

In the long run the basic forces influencing the state of humanity and its progress are (a) the number of people who are alive to consume, but also to *produce* goods and knowledge; and b) the level of wealth. Those are the great variables which control the advance of civilization.

Wealth is far more than assets such as houses and cars. The essence of wealth is the capacity to control the forces of nature, and the extent of wealth depends upon the level of technology and the ability to create new knowledge. A wealthy world can find remedies for a new disease more quickly than can a poor world, because the wealthy world possesses stocks of knowledge and skilled persons. That's why wealthier groups live longer, with better health and fewer accidental deaths. A key characteristic of a wealthy society is a well-developed set of legal rules. Wealth both creates such rules and depends upon them to produce the conditions of freedom and security that progress requires. This subject is not developed in this volume; I hope that I will soon produce a proper treatment of it, in connection with population size and growth.

*   *   *

That is the *science* of the matter. It was as far as the first edition could go. But now there is an important new element. The consensus of scholars of these subjects is on the side of the view which I just gave you. This is now quite the opposite of a single lone voice.

The good news mentioned earlier about *agriculture* and *resources* represents the long-time consensus of economists in those fields. Every agricultural econ-omist knows that the world's population has been eating ever-better since World War II. Every resource economist knows that all natural resources have been getting more available rather than more scarce, as shown by their falling prices over the decades and centuries. And every demographer knows that the death rate has been falling all over the world—life expectancy almost tripling in the rich countries in the past two centuries, and almost doubling in the poor countries in just the past four decades. All that has been true right along. And by now even the Environmental Protection Agency acknowledges that our air and our water have been getting cleaner rather than dirtier in the past few decades.

The biggest news is that the consensus of *population economists* now also is not far from the views expressed in this book. In 1986, the National Research Council and the National Academy of Sciences published a monograph on population growth and economic development prepared by a prestigious scholarly group. This "official" report reversed almost completely the frighten-ing conclusions of the previous 1971 NAS report. "The scarcity of exhaustible resources is at most a minor constraint on economic growth," it said. It found that additional people bring benefits as well as costs. Even the World Bank, for many years a major institutional purveyor of gloom-and-doom notions about population growth, reported in 1984 that the world's natural resource situation provides no reason to limit population growth.

A host of review articles by distinguished economic demographers since the mid-1980s have confirmed that this "revisionist" view (a label I am not fond of) is indeed consistent with the scientific evidence, even if only some population economists go as far as I do in emphasizing the *positive* long-run effects of population growth. The consensus is more toward a "neutral" judgment: population growth neither helps nor hinders economic growth. But this is a huge change from the earlier consensus that population growth is detrimental. By now, anyone who asserts that population growth damages the economy must turn a blind eye to both the scientific evidence and the relevant scientific community.

It is to be expected that you will begin by believing that population growth and density drag down economic development and foul the environment, both because the Malthusian argument makes excellent common sense and also because you have read and heard this idea all your life. Indeed, almost all scholars who have eventually come to see that population growth is not mainly a negative force began by believing the conventional Malthusian wisdom. In chapter 30 you will read how one early modern economist (Richard Easterlin) who made discoveries in the field describes the intellectual transit of another (Allen Kelley) as "representative . . . of many of us who have tried to look into the arguments and evidence about the 'population problem.'" In chapter 34 you will read how journalist-anthropologist Richard Critchfield began "in the early 1960s reporting the seemingly hopeless crisis of people surplus and food scarcity in India and China" and gave up his beliefs in doom and gloom only after he revisited villages all over the world that he had studied earlier, and saw how they had progressed along with a growing population. "[T]here is a much happier ending than I ever expected to write when I set out ten years ago."[3]

I, too, began work in this field in the late 1960s believing that rapid population growth was a major threat to the world's economic development—along with all-out war, one of the two fearsome threats to humankind and civilization. So I enlisted in the effort to combat this threat. By 1970, however, my reading had led me into confusion. Newly available empirical studies did not agree with the standard theory. I was shaken by the contradiction between the bare theory and the bare facts. I ask that you, too, keep an open mind, and be willing to believe scientifically sound evidence based upon statistical data rather than remain transfixed by dramatic television pictures and newspaper anecdotes that are not in fact representative of the aggregate.

One story I cannot detail for you is of a television journalist who began making a documentary about population growth with the conventional fears, but then altered her/his ideas in the course of gathering research to the extent that the program—though "balanced" in presenting the "sides"—left an impression not very different than this book. But the journalist is so afraid of being thought to espouse this viewpoint that I am sworn not to identify her/ him.

It may well be that the state of thought about the effect of population on the environment is at the same sort of intellectual juncture reached by thought about the effect of population on the standard of living one or two decades ago. The evidence is now available, and fair-minded scholars are beginning to change their views on environmental changes. Indeed, chapter 17 discusses how William Baumol and Wallace Oates began by believing that the environment was deteriorating, but their detailed long-term statistical studies brought them to doubt their original view.

To repeat, every forecast of the doomsayers has turned out flat wrong. Metals, foods, and other natural resources have become more available rather than more scarce throughout the centuries. The *Famine 1975* forecast by the Paddock brothers that we would see famine deaths in the United States on television was followed by gluts in agricultural markets. After Paul Ehrlich's primal scream—"What will we do when the [gasoline] pumps run dry?"— gasoline became cheaper than since the 1930s. The Great Lakes are not dead; instead they offer better sport fishing than ever. The main pollutants, especially the particulates which have killed people for years, have lessened in our cities.

Although events have been entirely kind to the arguments made in the book, there has been little change in public opinion in past decades. Yes, a good many books have been written containing data and arguments concerning population, resources, and the environment consistent with the ideas in this book; some of the best are so annotated in the bibliography at the back. Yes, several "think tanks" have devoted some or all of their attention to rebutting false propositions about the environment, and offering market solutions to environmental problems (such as the marketing of pollution rights, which has now become public policy). Yes, there are now some sympathetic and knowledgeable journalists. Yes, we have even seen the 1986 National Academy of Science report on population. But the content of everyday newspaper and television reporting on these matters remains almost as one-sidedly doomsaying, with urgent calls for government intervention, as it was two decades ago.

The doomsayers' credibility with the press, or their command over the funding resources of the federal government, has not lessened. The very persons who were entirely wrong in the 1960s and 1970s, and who should have been entirely discredited by the total failures of their forecasts, continue to have the same credibility and prominence as before. That's life, I suppose.

The situation of the anti-population-growth environmentalists today bears much resemblance to the situation of Malthus and his followers. The predictions in Malthus's first edition in 1798 were as wrong as any forecasts could be. The great historian of economic thought, Schumpeter, explains Malthus's error of "pessimism" by saying about the vision that underlay the theory and predictions: "The most interesting thing to observe is the complete lack of imagination which that vision reveals. Those writers lived at the threshold of the most spectacular economic developments ever witnessed. Vast possibilities matured into realities under their very eyes. Nevertheless, they saw nothing but cramped economies, struggling with ever-decreasing success for their daily bread."[4]

We, too, are at a moment when the world is creating new resources and cleaning up the environment at an ever-increasing rate. Our capacity to provide the good things of life for an ever-larger population is increasing as never before. Yet the conventional outlook—perhaps because of a similar lack of imagination—points in exactly the opposite direction.

When the doomsayers hear that oil can be obtained from various kinds of crops, they say, "Yes, but it costs much more than fossil fuels." They do not imagine the cost reductions from increased efficiency that will inevitably take place in the future, and they do not foresee that the total cost of energy, already a very small part of our economy, will become even smaller in the future. And when they hear that the rich countries are becoming cleaner and less polluted with each decade, the doomsayers say, "But what about the poor countries?" They do not imagine that the poor countries, when they become richer, will also eventually turn to becoming cleaner rather than dirtier, as the now-rich countries have done. Again and again they do not imagine the adjustments that individuals and communities make that create more resources, invent better technologies, and overcome environmental problems.

Now let's see if my facts and arguments persuade you of the claims I have made.

A Historical Afternote _____

THE WORLD and therefore the United States have never been in better shape at any time in history, by all the measures discussed in this book and in my forthcoming *State of Humanity*, most especially because the Cold War is over and the threat of nuclear holocaust has receded. The environment in Eastern Europe will be improving now that socialism is disappearing there. Yet there is much assertion to the contrary, and much hankering for the supposedly better times in the past. Let's put this in perspective. This comes from an Assyrian tablet written many millennia ago:

> Our earth is degenerate in these latter days; bribery and corruption are common; children no longer obey their parents; every man wants to write a book, and the end of the world is evidently approaching.[5]

And this from the Romans:

> You often ask me, Justus Fabius, how it is that while the genius and the fame of so many distinguished orators have shed a lustre on the past, our age is so forlorn and so destitute of the glory of eloquence that it scarce retains the very name of orator.[6]

Franklin Pierce Adams put it nicely: "Nothing is more responsible for the good old days than a bad memory."[7]

About the time that Great Britain was beginning to thrive as no country had before, and was taking world leadership economically and politically, William Petty noticed a spate of public lament and doomsaying. He responded as follows:

> But notwithstanding all this (the like whereof was always in all Places), the Buildings of London grow great and glorious; the American Plantations employ four Hundred Sail of Ships; Actions in the East-India Company are near double the principal Money; those who can give good Security, may have Money under the Statute-Interest; Materials for building (even Oaken-Timber) are little the dearer, some cheaper for the rebuilding of London; the Exchange seems as full of Merchants as formerly; no more Beggars in the Streets, nor executed for Thieves, than heretofore; the Number of Coaches, and Splendor of Equipage exceeding former Times; the publique Theatres very magnificent; the King has a greater Navy, and stronger Guards than before our Calamities; the Clergy rich, and the Cathedrals in repair; much Land has been improved, and the Price of Food so reasonable, as that Men refuse to have it cheaper, by admitting of Irish Cattle; And in brief, no Man needs to want that will take moderate pains. That some are poorer than others, ever was and ever will be: And that many are naturally querulous and envious, is an Evil as old as the World.

These general Observations, and that Men eat, and drink, and laugh as they use to do, have encouraged me to try if I could also comfort others, being satisfied my self, that the Interest and Affairs of England are in no deplorable Condition.[8]

Consider the situation as of George Washington's Seventh Annual Address to the Congress, which his biographer tells us was awaited with "anticipations often sadistic" because many believed that everything was going wrong. So Washington said:

> I have never met you at any period when more than at the present the situation of our public affairs has afforded just cause for mutual congratulation; and for inviting you to join me in profound gratitude to the Author of all good for the numerous and extraordinary blessings we enjoy. . . . Is it too much to say that our country exhibits a spectacle of national happiness never before surpassed if ever before equaled?[9]

But as Washington said, "the restless mind of man cannot be at peace." So instead of comparing their situation in 1796 with what it had been, say, fifteen years before, when the country was in a desperate struggle for its independence, and instead of heeding Washington's call that Americans "unite our efforts to preserve, prolong, and improve our immense advantages," people focused on the existing problems, and sought out new ones. So it is today, it seems to me. This anecdote about Adam Smith is amusing as well as instructive:

> One day Sinclair brought Smith the news of the surrender of Burgoyne at Saratoga in October 1777, and exclaimed in the deepest concern that the nation [Great Britain] was ruined. 'There is a great deal of ruin in a nation' was Smith's calm reply.[10]

David Hume suggested that the propensity to find signs of crisis has a genetic explanation, being rooted in "human nature" (see the headnote to the conclusion).

There is a long history of agricultural experts and others being overly pessimistic in their assessments of current and future productivity. The great British agricultural historian Arthur Young traveled throughout Great Britain in the years before 1774, and found that agricultural productivity had been rising rapidly. His good news was greeted with disbelief and derision. This was his response in the introduction to his book:

> I am very sensible that throughout these calculations I have taken the unpopular side of the question. A work (unless conducted with uncommon abilities) rarely succeeds, whose principal aim is to persuade a nation to be easy and satisfied under present circumstances; and to convince them that they have almost every reason to be pleased: such a task has nothing in it that flatters the multitude—you run counter to public prejudice, and all the reward you can hope for, is the approbation of a few sensible individuals.[11]

Adam Smith noticed this bad-news syndrome:

The annual produce of the land and labour of England . . . is certainly much greater than it was, a little more than a century ago, at the restoration of Charles II. Though, at present, few people, I believe, doubt of this, yet during this period, five years have seldom passed away in which some book or pamphlet has not been published, written too with such abilities as to gain some authority with the public, and pretending to demonstrate that the wealth of the nation was fast declining, that the country was depopulated, agriculture neglected, manufactures decaying, and trade undone. Nor have these publications been all party pamphlets, the wretched offspring of falsehood and venality. Many of them have been written by very candid and very intelligent people; who wrote nothing but what they believed, and for no other reason but because they believed it.[12]

Young also came to think that it was necessary that he provide a sound theoretical base for his evidence:

The observations I made in my journies through the kingdom, fixed my opinions concerning population—the inclosure and division of landed property—the prices of the earth's products, &c. I found the language of plain facts so clear, that I could not but listen and be convinced, and I laid the facts before the world on which I founded my opinions: In opposition to these facts, those writers have offered reason upon reason, argument upon argument, and have given elaborate disquisitions on subjects which demanded facts alone. This has occasioned my shewing in the present treatise how the facts I before gave are consistent with, and even naturally arising from first principles.[13]

As did Young, in this edition I have placed more emphasis than before on the theoretical and institutional framework that explains the fundamental facts.

Part One

TOWARD OUR BEAUTIFUL RESOURCE FUTURE

Necessity is the mother of invention.
  (Richard Franck, Northern Memoirs, *1694)*

1

The Amazing Theory of Raw-Material Scarcity

The Great Toy Shortage
Forget it, Virginia. Santa won't be leaving a "Star Wars" R2-D2 doll under the tree this year—just an I.O.U. promising you one at some vague time between February and June. Don't count on a Mego Micronaut kit for building your own robot either, or a Milky the Marvelous Milking Cow, which drinks water when its tail is pumped, moos plaintively and squirts a tiny pailful of cloudy white "milk" from a detachable pink udder. . . .

Not since the Grinch stole Christmas has there been such an unseasonable shortage.

(Newsweek, *December 19, 1977*)

Niels Bohr is said by Richard Feynman to have said: [A]nybody who is not shocked by the theory hasn't understood it.

(*Introduction to Richard Feynman*, Six Easy Pieces, *1994*)

[T]he difficulty really is psychological and exists in the perpetual torment that results from your saying to yourself, "But how can it be like that?" which is a reflection of uncontrolled but utterly vain desire to see it in terms of something familiar.

(*Richard Feynman*, The Character of Physical Law, *1994*)

THE "GREAT TOY SHORTAGE" of 1977 clearly was a freak event. We don't worry that a scarcity of Hula-Hoops, pencils, dental care, radios, or new musical compositions will last. And we don't fear that a larger population will reduce the supply of these goods; manufacturers will make more. Yet people do worry about an impending scarcity of copper, iron, aluminum, oil, food, and other natural resources.

According to a typical pronouncement by Paul Ehrlich, the best-known contemporary doomster, "In the early 1970s, the leading edge of the age of scarcity arrived. With it came a clearer look at the future, revealing more of the nature of the dark age to come."[1] That we are entering an age of scarcity in which our finite natural resources are running out, that our environment is becoming more polluted, and that population growth threatens our civilization and our very lives—such propositions are continually repeated with no more evidence than that "everyone knows" they are true.

Is there a fundamental economic difference between extractive natural resources and Hula-Hoops or dental care? Why do people expect that the supply of wheat will decline but the supplies of toys and drugs will increase? These are the questions that this chapter explores. The chapter draws examples from the metallic raw materials, which are relatively unencumbered by government regulations or international cartels and which are neither "burned up" like oil nor grown anew like agricultural products. Energy, food, and land will be given special treatment in later chapters.

Between Pig Copper and Dentistry

There is an intuitive difference between how we get Hula-Hoops and copper. Copper comes from the earth, whereas a Hula-Hoop does not seem to be a "natural" resource. Copper miners go after the richest, most accessible lodes first. Therefore, they dig into lodes bearing successively lower grades of ore. If all else were equal, this trend would imply that the cost of extracting copper from the ground must continually rise as poorer and less accessible lodes are mined.

Hula-Hoops and dental care and radios *seem* different from copper because most of the cost of a radio, a Hula-Hoop, or dental care arises from human labor and skill, and only a small part arises from the raw material—the petroleum in the plastic hoop or the silver in the tooth filling. For good reason we do not worry that human labor and skill comes from progressively less accessible reservoirs.

But all this neat theorizing about the increasing scarcity of minerals contradicts a most peculiar fact: Over the course of history, up to this very moment, copper and other minerals have been getting less scarce, rather than more scarce as the depletion theory implies they should. In this respect copper follows the same historical trend as radios, undershirts, and other consumer goods (see fig. 1-1). It is this fact that forces us to go beyond the simple theory and to think more deeply about the matter.

At the end of this confrontation between theory and fact, we shall be compelled to reject the simple Malthusian depletion theory and to offer a new theory. The revised theory will suggest that natural resources are not finite in any meaningful economic sense, mind-boggling though this assertion may be. The stocks of them are not fixed but rather are expanding through human ingenuity. There is no solid reason to believe that there will ever be a greater scarcity of these extractive resources in the long-run future than now. Rather, we can confidently expect copper and other minerals to get progressively less scarce.

What Do We Mean by "Scarcity"?

Here we must pause for an unexciting but crucial issue, the definition of "scarcity." Ask yourself: If copper—or oil or any other good—were much scarcer

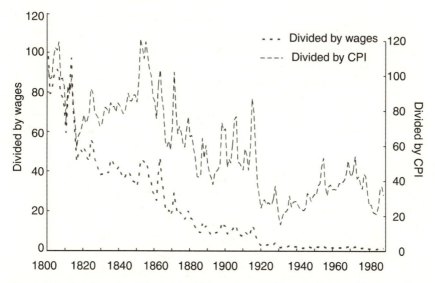

Figure 1-1. The Scarcity of Copper as Measured by Its Prices Relative to Wages and to the Consumer Price Index

today than it actually is, what would be the evidence of this scarcity? That is, what are the signs—the criteria—of a raw material being in short supply?

Upon reflection perhaps you will not expect a complete absence of the material as a sign of scarcity. We will not reach up to the shelf and suddenly find that it is completely bare. The scarcity of any raw material would only gradually increase. Long before the shelf would be bare, individuals and firms—the latter operating purely out of the self-interested drive to make profits—would be stockpiling supplies for future resale so that the shelf would never be completely bare. Of course the price of the hoarded material would be high, but there still would be some quantities to be found at *some* price, just as there always has been some small amount of food for sale even in the midst of the very worst famines.

The preceding observation points to a key sign of what we generally mean by increasing scarcity: a price that has persistently risen. More generally, cost and price—whatever we mean by "price," and shortly we shall see that that term is often subject to question—will be our basic measures of scarcity.

In some situations, though, prices can mislead us. Governments may prevent the price of a scarce material from rising high enough to "clear the market"—that is, to discourage enough buyers so that supply and demand come to be equal, as they ultimately will be in a free market. If so, there may be waiting lines or rationing, and these may also be taken as signs of scarcity. But though lines and rationing may be fair ways of allocating materials in the short run, in the longer run they are so wasteful that every sort of society tends to avoid them by letting the price rise enough to clear the market.

So increased scarcity of a raw material implies a higher price. But the converse need not be true; the price may rise even without a "true" increase in scarcity. For example, a strong cartel may successfully raise prices for awhile, as OPEC did with oil in 1973 even though the cost of producing oil remained unchanged. This suggests that, in addition to the price in the market, we should sometimes consider production costs as an index of scarcity.

There are still other reasons why price does not tell the full story about scarcity and our welfare. A product may be readily available, as measured by its price being low, yet there may still be a problem. For example, a daily ration of vitamin X may be very cheap, but if people are not getting enough of it there is a problem. On the other hand, caviar may be unusually high-priced and scarce this year, but few would consider that to be a problem for society. Similarly, the price of a staple food such as grain may be higher than in a previous year, but this may not indicate a problem—if, for example, the price rises because of an increase in income and a resulting increase in the amount of grain fed to animals to produce meat. So, though the prices of food and social welfare are often connected, they are not identical.

A more personal, but often relevant, test of scarcity is whether you and I and others feel that we can afford to buy the material. That is, the relationship between price and income may matter. If the price of food stays the same but income falls sharply, then we feel that food is more scarce. By a similar test, if our wages rise while the price of oil remains constant, our fuller pockets lead us to feel that oil is getting less scarce.

A related test of scarcity is the importance of the material in your budget. You are not likely to say that salt has gotten appreciably more scarce even if its price doubles, because it accounts for an insignificant share of your expenditures.

So price, together with related measures such as cost of production and share of income, is the appropriate operational test of scarcity at any given moment. What matters to us as consumers is how much we have to pay to obtain goods that give us particular services; from our standpoint, it couldn't matter less how much iron or oil there "really" is in the natural "stockpile." Therefore, to understand the economics of natural resources, it is crucial to understand that the most appropriate *economic* measure of scarcity is the price of a natural resource compared to some relevant benchmark.

Future scarcity is our interest. Our task, then, is to forecast future prices of raw materials.

What Is the Best Way to Forecast Scarcity and Costs?

There are two quite different general methods for forecasting costs of any kind: the economist's method and the technologist's (or engineer's) method.[2]

The engineering method is commonly used in discussions of raw materials, but I shall argue that the conclusions about costs reached with it are usually quite wrong because it is not the appropriate method.

With the technical engineering method, you forecast the status of a natural resource as follows: (1) estimate the presently known physical quantity of the resource, such as copper in the earth that's accessible to mining; (2) extrapolate the future rate of use from the current use rate; and (3) subtract the successive estimates of use in (2) from the physical "inventory" in (1). (Chapter 2 discusses technical forecasts in greater detail.)

In contrast, the economist's approach extrapolates trends of past costs into the future. My version of the economist's method is as follows: (1) ask whether there is any convincing reason to think that the period for which you are forecasting will be different from the past, going back as far as the data will allow; (2) if there is no good reason to reject the past trend as representative of the future as well, ask whether there is a reasonable explanation for the observed trend; (3) if there is no reason to believe that the future will be different than the past, and if you have a solid explanation for the trend—or even if you lack a solid theory, but the data are overwhelming—project the trend into the future.

Given the wide disparity between the engineering and economic approaches, it behooves us to consider the conditions under which each is likely to be valid. The forecasting situation is analogous to that of a businessperson who wishes to estimate costs of some piece of construction or production for the firm. Making sound cost estimates is the businessperson's bread and butter, the difference between solvency and bankruptcy. The choice between the economic or the engineering method depends largely on whether the business has much or little experience with the type of project whose costs it wants to assess. Examples of jobs with which the organization already has a great deal of experience are (a) a construction firm preparing a bid on a small parking lot like many others that the firm has done, and (b) a chain franchising operation estimating the cost of adding another hamburger shop. In such cases the firm will, as a matter of course, estimate costs directly from its own records. In the case of the new hamburger shop, the estimate may simply be the average total cost of shops recently built, as already computed by the firm. In the case of the parking lot, the construction firm may be able to estimate with good accuracy the amounts required of the main components—labor and machine time— and their current prices.

It is only when the firm does not have direct experience with the type of project being costed that it must and will make an engineering analysis of the project, together with estimates of the requirements for each element of the job. But the businessperson, and the academic analyst of natural resources, too, should turn to engineering cost estimates only in the unfortunate absence of reliable data from the past, because engineering estimates are much harder

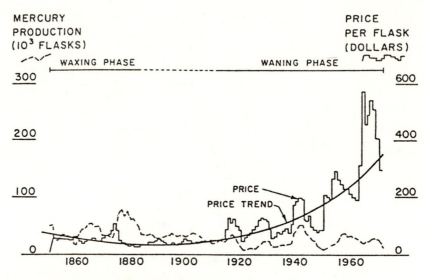

Figure 1-2. Engineering Forecast for Mercury
On opposite page:
Figure 1-3a (*top and center*). Mercury Reserves, 1950–1990
Figure 1-3b (*bottom*). Mercury Price Indexes, 1850–1990

to make accurately, for a variety of reasons. An analogy may help. In forecasting the speed of a three-year-old race horse, would you rely more on a
veterinary and anatomical inspection of the horse's bones and organs, or on
the results of its past races?

The history of mercury prices is an example of how one can go wrong with
a nonhistorical, engineering forecast. Figure 1-2 shows a forecast made in
1976 by natural scientist Earl Cook. He combined a then-recent upturn in
prices with the notion that there is a finite amount of mercury on the Earth's
surface, plus the mathematical charm of plotting a second-degree polynomial
with the computer. Figures 1-3a and 1-3b show how the forecast was almost
immediately falsified, and price continued its long-run decline. (Figure 1-3
also shows that reserves of mercury have increased rather than decreased over
the years, just the opposite of naive, "finitist" doomster ideas).

Fortunately, we don't have to rely on such arbitrary guesswork. Considerable data showing trends in raw-material prices for a century or two, or longer,
are available, as seen in various chapters of this book. Costs of extractive materials clearly have fallen over the course of recorded price history. The economist's first-approximation forecast is that these trends toward less scarcity
should continue into the foreseeable future unless there is some reason to
believe that conditions have changed—that is, unless there is something
wrong with the data as a basis for extrapolation.

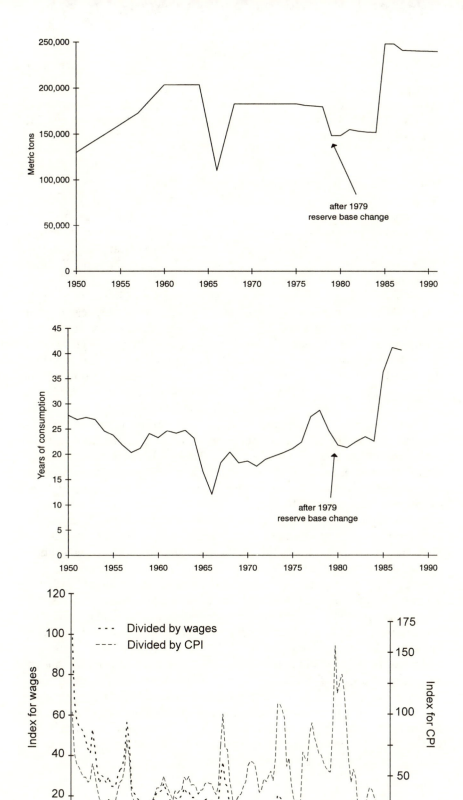

In brief, the economist's and businessperson's approach to price trends is to learn by experience—relevant experience. As P. T. Bauer put it, "It is only the past that gives us any insight into the laws of motion of human society and hence enables us to predict the future."[3]

Will the Future Break with the Past?

Some people believe that we are now at a long-run turning point, and the past is not a guide to the future. Therefore we ask, "How should one judge whether a historical trend is a sound basis for a forecast?" Specifically, how can we judge whether the data from the many decades in the past showing declines in raw-material costs are a good basis for prediction?

This question is a problem in scientific generalization. A sound principle is that you should generalize from your data if you can reasonably regard them as a fair sample of the universe about which you wish to draw conclusions. But prediction is a special type of generalization, a generalization from past to future. Prediction is always a leap of faith; there is no scientific guarantee that the sun will come up tomorrow. The correctness of an assumption that what happened in the past will similarly happen in the future rests on your wise judgment and knowledge of your subject matter.

A prediction based on past data is sound if it is sensible to assume that the past and the future belong to the same statistical universe, that is, if you can expect conditions that held in the past to remain the same in the future.[4] Therefore, we must ask, "Have conditions changed in recent years in such manner that the data on natural resources generated over the many past decades are no longer relevant?"

The most important elements in raw-material price trends have been (1) the rate of movement from richer to poorer ores and mining locations, that is, the phenomenon of "exhaustion"; and (2) the continued development of technology, which has more than made up for exhaustion.

Is the rate of development of such new technology slowing up? To the contrary: the pace of development of new technology seems to be increasing. Hence, if the past differs from the future, the bias is likely to be in the direction of *understating* the rate at which technology will develop, and therefore underestimating the rate at which costs will fall.

The fall in the costs of natural resources, decade after decade and century after century, should shake us free from the idea that scarcity must increase *sometime*. And please notice that current prices do not mislead us about future scarcities. If there is reason to judge that the cost of obtaining a certain resource in the future will be much greater than it is now, speculators will hoard that material to obtain the higher future price, thereby raising the present price. So current price is our best measure of both current *and* future scarcity (more about this later).

Figure 1-1 and others in the book show the fundamental economic facts about natural resources. The costs and prices of most natural resources have been going down rather than up since at least 1800. But as noted earlier, cost and price can be slippery ideas and therefore require technical discussion in an afternote to this chapter. Here I'll say but a few words on the matter.

The basic measure of the cost of, say, copper, is the ratio between the price of copper and the price of another product. One such measure—the most important measure—of the terms of trade is the price of copper *relative to wages*, as shown in figure 1-1. This price has declined very sharply. This means that an hour's work in the United States has purchased increasingly more copper; from 1800 to the present its purchasing power has increased about 50-fold!. The same trend has almost surely held throughout history for copper and other raw materials.

Consider a very different measure of cost: the decreasing price of copper *relative to nonextractive products*. This means that it now takes smaller quantities of haircuts or underwear to buy a ton of copper than it did a century ago. The relative price between copper and other products is like a price that has been adjusted for the cost of living. We must remember that these other, nonextractive items also have been produced progressively more cheaply over the years. Yet minerals have declined in price *even faster* than have the other products.

Still another way to think about the cost of natural resources is the proportion of our total income we must pay to get them. This measure also reveals a steady decline in cost. The absolute physical quantities of natural resources extracted have been rising, decade after decade, century after century, and the kinds of resources used have been increasing in number. But our expenditure on them has been falling as a proportion of total expenditures. "The gross value of extractive output [including agriculture, oil, and coal] relative to value of national product has declined substantially and steadily from 1870 to the present. In 1890, the extractive share was nearly 50 percent. By the turn of the century, it had fallen to 32 percent, and, by 1919, to 23 percent. In 1957, the figure was 13 percent and still trending downward";[5] by 1988 the figure had fallen all the way to 3.7 percent. In 1988, minerals plus energy (but excluding food) accounted for only 1.6 percent of the U.S. GNP,[6] and minerals alone (excluding energy sources) accounted for less than half a percent of total extractive value, or only about an amazing 0.0002 (a fiftieth of a percent of GNP).[7] This trend makes it clear that the cost of minerals—even if it becomes considerably higher, which we have no reason to expect—is almost irrelevant to our standard of living, and hence an increased scarcity of minerals is not a great danger to our peacetime standard of living.

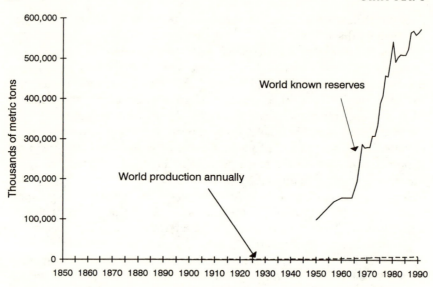

Figure 1-4a. Copper Annual World Production and World Known Reserves, 1880–1991

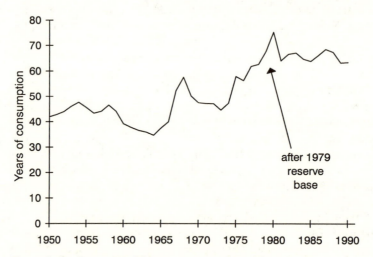

Figure 1-4b. Copper World Reserves/Annual World Production

A vivid illustration of the changing role of natural resources is a floppy computer disk: with a standard word processing program on it, it sells for $450. It embodies only a cent's worth of petroleum and sand.[8]

This is the closest-to-home indicator of changing raw-materials costs. Every measure leads us to the same conclusion, but these calculations of expenditures for raw materials as a proportion of total family budgets make the point most strongly. Raw materials have been getting increasingly available—less scarce—relative to the most important element of life, human time.

Another piece of evidence confirms the price data. Figure 1-4 shows the total world "known reserves" of copper, and the ratio of reserves to total production. The figures show that reserves not only do not go down, they even go up—just as the "reserves" in your pantry go up when you are expecting company. The explanation for this anti-commonsensical trend may be found in chapter 2.

Taken together, the various data suggest the anti-intuitive conclusion that, even as we use coal and oil and iron and other natural resources, they are becoming less scarce. Yet this is indeed the appropriate economic way of viewing the situation. (To further explore these measures of price and scarcity, see afternote 1 to this chapter.)

In lectures on the foregoing section, I commonly ask the audience to raise their hands to indicate whether they think natural resources have been getting more or less scarce. Then I show the price data. One woman responded that I had "tricked" the audience by drawing their attention away from the *physical* aspects of depletion. But it is the inappropriate concepts of physical science that have "tricked" this woman and many of the prominent doomsters. Like Cook predicting a scarcity of mercury, they are led into error by the seductive but unsound theory of "natural" physical limits that draws their attention away from the experience of falling raw-material prices throughout history.

A Challenge to the Doomsdayers to Put Their Money Where Their Mouths Are

Some respond that these price data are "old" and do not reflect what happened last year or last week, and that the long-term trends no longer hold. There is no way of conclusively proving them wrong. But the long, sad history of alarming analyses that run against previous long-term trends shows the alarms to be wrong far more often than simple extrapolations of the long-term trends.

Speaking bluntly, talk is cheap, especially scare talk that gets newspaper attention and foundation grants. Where I come from, when we feel that someone is talking without taking responsibility for the results, we say, "Put your money where your mouth is." I am prepared to back my judgment with my own cash. If I am wrong about the future of natural resources, you can make money at my expense.

If mineral resources such as copper will be more scarce in the future—that is, if the real price (netting out inflation) will rise—you can make money by buying the minerals now and selling them later at the higher prices. This is exactly what is done by speculators who believe that the prices of commodities will rise (although for convenience' sake, they really buy contracts for the commodities, or "futures," rather than physical stocks).

Please notice that you do not have to wait ten or twenty years to realize a profit, even if the expected changes in supply and demand will not occur for ten or twenty years. As soon as information about an impending scarcity becomes known and accepted, people begin buying the commodity; they bid up the present market price until it reflects the expected future scarcity. Current market prices thus reflect the best guesses of professionals who spend their lives studying commodities, and who stake their wealth and incomes on being right about the future.

A cautionary example is how Japan let itself be panicked by fears of future scarcities in the wake of the OPEC oil embargo and the resulting general price rise in 1973.

> The Japanese, and above all Japanese officialdom, were seized by hysteria in 1974 when raw materials shortages were cropping up everywhere. They bought and bought and bought [copper, iron ore, pulp, sulfur, and coking coal]. Now they are frantically trying to get out of commitments to take delivery, and have slashed raw materials imports nearly in half. Even so, industrial inventories are bulging with high-priced raw materials.[9]

Japan began paying heavily for this blunder.*

* The wasteful abuses of security-justified stockpiling can be seen in the vast hoards of diamonds that the Defense Logistics Agency was selling as of 1993. "DLA proposes to offer approximately 1,000,000 [carats] of diamond stones of near gem to gem quality" in the open market (*Washington Post*, April 11, 1993, F1). There is huge direct loss to the public from holding these stones into a time when synthetic diamonds can perform any industrial task that real diamonds can, plus the potential loss from theft and other fraud that such a stockpile invites.

Ninety other types of materials are stockpiled along with the diamonds, including such materials as quinine that have been replaced by better materials. The overall costs of the stockpiling program for the ninety materials were stated in the newspaper by the Administrator of the Defense National Stockpile Center to be about $12 billion. But that is simply the arithmetic sum of the outlays, some as far back as 1946. When the year-by-year expenditures for this purpose are reckoned as one would calculate the costs of any ordinary investment, taking into account the time value of the money, I found that at an average cost of capital of 6 percent (which would seem reasonable for the government over the decades from the 1950s to the 1990s), the present value in 1993 of the expenditures for the asset stockpile was about $72 billion. The Administrator said that in the past sales had been made taking in $10 billion, which would be worth more than that in 1993, and the market value of the remainder in inventory is $6 billion. The exact loss is not

Latin America also suffered from false Malthusian scares about resource depletion which led to forecasts of rising resource prices. Starting in the early 1970s, Mexico and Venezuela borrowed heavily to finance the development of oil, and other South American countries contracted debt in expectation of high prices for their agricultural exports. But the price index of Latin American exports sank sharply from about 110 in 1974 to about 75 by the late 1980s, vastly exacerbating the debt crisis of the 1980s.[10] As the federal Reserve Bank of Dallas wrote about two of the problem countries: "Mexico and Venezuela could not sell oil at the high prices they had anticipated."[11]

False scares are not costless and benign; far from it.

So now it is time for me to put my money where my mouth is. Will the doomsdayers who say that minerals and other raw materials will get more scarce do the same?

The first edition of the book contained this statement: This is a public offer to stake $10,000, in separate transactions of $1,000 or $100 each, on my belief that mineral resources (or food or other commodities) will not rise in price in future years, adjusted for inflation. You choose any mineral or other raw material (including grain and fossil fuels) that is not government controlled, and the date of settlement.[12]

Offering to wager is the last recourse of the frustrated. When you are convinced that you have hold of an important idea, and you can't get the other side to listen, offering to bet is all that is left. If the other side refuses to bet, they implicitly acknowledge that they are less sure than they claim to be.

In 1970 Paul Ehrlich wrote, "If I were a gambler, I would take even money that England will not exist in the year 2000."[13] In an exchange with him in 1980 I offered to take that bet or, more realistically, wager (as above) that natural resources would become cheaper rather than more expensive. Professor Ehrlich and two colleagues said they would "accept Simon's astonishing offer before other greedy people jump in." And he said that "the lure of easy money can be irresistible."[14] They chose five metals—copper, chrome, nickel, tin, and tungsten—and a ten-year period.

At settling time in September 1990, not only the sum of the prices, but also the price of each individual metal, had fallen. But this is not surprising. The odds were all against them because the prices of metals have been falling throughout human history. From my point of view, the bet was like shooting

---

calculable from the available information, but it is clear that if the government had, instead of purchasing the materials, simply not borrowed the expenditures from the public in the form of ordinary government bonds, the national debt in 1993 would be less by many, many billions of dollars.

That is, the program of stockpiling strategic materials is one more testament to the human propensity not to trust the workings of markets and to only feel comfortable when one has control of resources—especially when someone else is paying the bill. The result of this propensity is that the public pays a pretty penny for the folly.

fish in a barrel. Of course I offered to make the same bet again, at increased stakes, but the Ehrlich group has not taken up the offer.

In chapter 9 on land you will read the outcome of another bet I offered to make.

A common reaction of critics was, "We knew it all the time."* These critics then shift the argument and say, "You're ignoring the important issues."* William Conway, General Director of the New York Zoological Society, challenged me in the *New York Times* to "bet on the decline of living habitat or the increase of extinctions."

Okay, I accept the challenge. Here's the new expanded offer for this second edition: I'll bet that just about any environmental and economic trend pertaining to basic human material welfare (though not, of course, the progress of this group compared to that one) will show improvement in the long run. Will the doomsdayers now put their money where their mouths are? (Don't hold your breath until they do. I've made this offer in a good many periodicals since 1990, and have had no takers except for one demographer, and he won't stake real money because of religious principle.) As in the past, my winnings will go to supporting basic research.

This offer includes betting on any explicit or implicit prediction made in this book—and there are plenty of them—about the rate of species extinctions; whether the Earth's forested area is increasing or decreasing; possible ill effects of any ozone-layer depletion and greenhouse warming and infant mortality and lots, lots, more.**

It is true that life expectancy has been falling in Eastern Europe as of the time of writing. We are certainly capable of doing ourselves in with faulty political decisions; and again and again societies show that we do so. But I consider the odds to be against such bad outcomes continuing into the future. And I'm only offering to *bet*; I do not *guarantee* a rosier future in all respects as a sure thing.

* For example, with excellent hindsight columnist Jessica Mathews in *The Washington Post* (who also is a vice president of the environmentalist World Resources Institute) wrote that "Ehrlich didn't need to be an economist to have seen how long the odds were against winning." But then she reverses field and rejects the basis of the argument given here, saying that the idea that "the planet's resources are infinite" is "palpable nonsense." The bottom line: she won't bet that the supposedly finite resources will become more scarce.

"If he's interested in betting on more meaningful measures than today's prices, though, I'd consider it," Mathews wrote.

** This offer does not refer to the progress of particular *physical* conditions such as the ozone layer, because I'm not an atmospheric scientist and also because there are always some physical characteristics moving for a while in directions that worry people. But I will bet on *aspects of human welfare* connected with these physical changes—for example, the trend in skin-cancer deaths or any other health evil thought to result from decreased ozone. The same is true with respect to global warming; I'll bet on the course of agricultural production, which is the main way that the climate affects us. I'll even bet that overall life expectancy continues to rise over the next decade or so in countries where AIDS is now most worrisome.

Summary

The costs of raw materials have fallen sharply over the period of recorded history, no matter which reasonable measure of cost one chooses to use. These historical trends are the best basis for predicting the trends of future costs, too.

It is paradoxical that cost and scarcity decrease as more of a material is used. The following two chapters dispel the paradox, focusing on a couple of crucial theoretical matters that explain the puzzle: first, a definition of resources as the services they provide rather than as stocks of materials, and second, an analysis of the concept of finiteness.

Afternote 1 _____

The "True" Cost (Price) of Natural Resources

THIS CHAPTER discussed why the cost (or the price) of a given resource falls or rises. But we have skimmed past the questions of the meaning of the price of a good and of how best to gauge its cost. Now let's address those questions.

We may measure the cost of a ton of copper by measuring the amount of workers' time necessary to produce it. But there are obvious difficulties with this approach. Capital equipment may be substituted for labor in order to economize on the use of workers' time; no allowance is made in this approach for the cost of the equipment. And some workers' time is more expensive than others'; an hour of a college-trained technician's time might be worth more in the market than that of a pick-and-shovel man.

A better method is to compare the market price of a ton of copper to the market price of some other good that seems to be unchanging—say, the price of grain. But the cost of producing grain (and most other things) has also been changing over the years owing to changes in seeds, fertilizers, technology, and so on. So if the cost of grain has been falling, then the cost of copper would be falling even if the relationship between the two prices—the terms of trade—had remained the same over the years.

Another good method would be to compare the price of copper to the price of a good that has had little technological change for a long time—say, a haircut. But the wages of barbers have gone up, as can be seen from the fact that a barber in the United States now has a much higher standard of living than did a United States barber 100 years ago—because the wages of people in other occupations have risen owing to gains in technology and education. So this comparison, too, does not give us a "true" or "absolute" measure of changes in the price of copper.

Yet another method is to examine the price trend of the source of the raw material—the price of farmland instead of the price of grain, for example, or the price of copper mines instead of the price of copper—relative to some other goods.[15] But the price of the source will rise if there is an improvement in production methods even if there is no change in the "scarcity" of the product; the price of good farmland in the United States rises when crop yields go up or when new machinery is introduced (though the price of poor farmland falls because it is no longer profitable to use such land at all, and the price of mines can fall when the lodes play out).

As yet we have said nothing about inflation. Allowing for price changes in a commodity due to changes in the general price level raises a host of difficult questions.

What to do? We must accept the inevitable: There can be no "true" or "absolute" measure of cost or price. Rather, different measures of cost give different sorts of information, useful for different purposes. But this we can say with assurance: The average cost of all consumer goods taken together—an index of consumer prices—has fallen over the years in more-developed countries, measured in terms of what an unskilled worker can buy; this is proven by the long-run increase in the standard of living. Therefore, if a raw material has not risen in price compared to the average of goods, its "real" cost has fallen. In fact the price of mineral natural resources has declined even more sharply than has the average price of other commodities. Furthermore, all other measures of mineral costs have also declined over the long run. Hence, we can be quite sure that the cost of mineral natural resources has declined substantially, by any reasonable test.

Afternote 2

The Ultimate Shortage

THERE IS ONE resource that has shown a trend of increasing scarcity rather than increasing abundance—the most important of all resources—human beings. Yes, there are more people on Earth now than ever before. But if we measure the scarcity of people the same way that we measure the scarcity of other economic goods—by how much we must pay to obtain their services—we see that wages and salaries have been going up all over the world, in poor countries as well as in rich countries, throughout preceding decades and centuries. The amount that you must pay to obtain the services of a driver or a cook has risen in India, just as the price of a driver or cook—or economist—has risen in the United States. This increase in the price of people's services is a clear indication that people are becoming more scarce even though there are more of us.

Indeed, crude evidence of the shortage is found in the complaints of business people that "we just can't get help now," by which they mean that they can't find people to hire at former wages. "We are now running out of people," reports the business editor of the *Baltimore Sun*.[16] "Scarcity of Workers Is Kindling Inflation" headlines the *Wall Street Journal*, continuing, "A scarcity of skilled workers and declines in young people entering the work force are threatening to put the squeeze on corporate profits in many sectors."[17] There is no reason to believe that the increase in the price of people's work time will not continue indefinitely.

A related concept of scarcity is the labor cost per unit of raw-material output. Labor cost, in constant dollars per unit of output of copper and other metals, has declined sharply although wages (labor costs per unit of labor) have risen markedly. If we calculate the outputs of copper and other metals per hour of labor input, we find a breathtaking decline in the cost of natural resources over the years.[18]

2

Why Are Material-Technical Resource Forecasts So Often Wrong?

THE MOST-PUBLICIZED forecasts of long-run natural-resource scarcity made by natural scientists and engineers disagree sharply with economic forecasts of the sort given in this book. And the engineering forecasts usually have been utterly wrong. This chapter explains this consistent error.

Can sound engineering (or "technical") forecasts be based on physical principles alone? Do economic and material-technical forecasts necessarily contradict each other? The answer is no to both questions.

Some of the best-informed technical forecasters agree strongly with the optimistic economic extrapolations discussed in chapter 1 and disagree with the pessimistic material-technical forecasts. That is, the variation among material-technical forecasts is as great as the differences between technical and economic forecasts, though the pessimistic technical forecasts have always gotten much more attention than the optimistic ones.

This chapter delves into the bases of agreement and disagreement among forecasts of raw-material availability. The next chapter explains why the forces that produced the long-run decrease in scarcity are likely to continue indefinitely, contrary to engineering assumptions. (The specific case of energy is discussed in chapters 11–13.)

The Nature of Material-Technical Forecasts: Explaining the Paradox

The historical evidence in chapters 1, 5, 8, 10, and 11 that natural-resource costs have fallen, as measured by all reasonable concepts of cost, sharply contradicts the notion that diminishing returns must raise costs and increase scarcity. This cries out for explanation. The explanation is quite counterintuitive, however. At first it affronts "common sense."

The approach of the engineering analysts who rely on physical principles is as follows. They estimate quantities and "qualities" of resources in the Earth, assess the present methods of extraction, and predict which methods of extraction will be used in the future. With those estimates they then calculate the amounts of resources that will be available in future years, at various costs of extraction (in the better forecasts) or just at the present cost (in the less-thoughtful forecasts).

At the root of this material-technical view of natural resources is the assumption that a certain quantity of a given mineral "exists" in the Earth and that one can, at least in principle, answer the question: How much (say) copper *is* there?*

What do we mean by a "resource" in the Earth? If we mean a physical quantity, we have no instrument to measure the quantity of copper or iron or oil in the Earth. And even if we did, we probably would not be able to agree on just what ought to be counted as a "resource"—for example, whether the copper salts dissolved in the sea should be included in the measurement of copper.

There is an almost insuperable difficulty in the definition of available "copper," "oil," and so on, because there are many different grades of each resource in places that vary in difficulty of extracting the resource, and because (as seen in table 2-1) the amounts at low concentrations (such as the quantities of metals on the sea bottom and in seawater) are extraordinarily large in contrast to the quantities we usually have in mind (the "proven reserves"). What's more, we constantly create new supplies of resources, in the sense of discovering them where they were thought not to exist. (In the past, the U.S. Geological Survey and others thought that there was no oil in California or Texas.) Often, new supplies of a resource come from areas outside the accustomed boundaries of our system, as resources from other continents came to Europe in past centuries and as resources may in the future be brought from the sea or from other planets. New supplies also arise when a resource is created from other materials, just as grain is grown and nuclear fuel is "bred." (Here we must avoid getting hung up on the word "natural," as in "natural resources.")

Most people do not at first feel comfortable with this point of view. The philosophy of scientific definitions may help. Consider the definition of the potential supply of oil that is implicitly or explicitly used by many people: the amount that would be recorded if someone conducted an exhaustive survey of all the Earth's contents. This quantity apparently is fixed. But such a definition is not operational, because such a survey is impossible. The operational supply of oil is that which is known today, or that which we may forecast as being known in the future, or that which we estimate will be sought and found under varying conditions of demand. These latter two quantities are decidedly not fixed but rather are changeable, and they are the ones relevant for policy decisions. (The next chapter will explore in greater depth the counterintuitive idea that supplies are not "finite.")

But there are other ways of adding to our raw-material supplies besides exploration. We must constantly struggle against the illusion that each time

---

* But the question of how much of a resource is "really" in the Earth is like the question, "Is there a sound in the forest when a tree falls but no one is nearby to hear it?" The question as stated opens a Pandora's box of semantic confusion (as do many statements that contain the word "is").

TABLE 2-1
Number of Years of Consumption Potential for Various Elements

	Known Reserves ÷ Annual Consumption (as of 1990 unless noted)	U.S. Geological Survey's Estimates of "Ultimate Recoverable Resources" (= 1% of Materials in Top Kilometer of Earth's Crust) ÷ Annual Consumption	Amount Estimated in Earth's Crust ÷ Annual Consumption (in millions)
Copper	91	340	242
Iron	958	2,657	1,815
Phosphorus	384	1,601	870
Molybdenum	65 (as of 1970)	630	422
Lead	14	162	85
Zinc	59	618	409
Sulphur	30 (as of 1970)	6,897	n/a
Uranium	50 (as of 1970)	8,455	1,855
Aluminum	63	68,066	38,500

Sources: Nordhaus 1974, p. 23; Simon, Weinrauch, and Moore 1994.

we take a pound of copper from the Earth there is less left to be used in the future. Too often we view natural resources as we view the operation of a single copper mine: dig some ore, and less is left. We must constantly remember that we create new mines and replenish the inventory of copper. The new "mines" may be somewhat different from the old ones—recycled metal from dumps, for example—but the new sources may be better rather than worse, so quality is not a necessary cause for concern. In exactly the same way that we manufacture paper clips or hula-hoops, we create new supplies of copper. That is, we expend time, capital, and raw materials to get them. Even more important, we find new ways to supply the services that an expensive product (or resource) renders, as we shall see shortly.

The common morally charged statement that the average American uses (say) ninety times as much X as does the average Asian or African (where X is some natural resource) can be seen as irrelevant in this light. The average American also *creates* a great deal more of "natural" resource X than does the average African or Asian—on average, by the same or greater proportion as the resource is used by Americans compared with Asians and Africans.

I realize that this approach probably still seems so anti-commonsensical as to be beyond belief, but please read on. Like many other important complex questions, this one can be understood only by coming to see the sense in what seems at first to be pure foolishness. Of course this requires a struggle, and a willingness to be open to radical rethinking of paradoxical propositions. Real understanding, however, often requires paying this price.

The Difficulties of Material-Technical Forecasting

The most common forecasts simply divide the "known reserves" by the current rate of use and call the result "years of consumption left." This procedure is discussed more fully later in the context of oil and energy, but a few words and data will be useful here.

The concept of known (or "proven") reserves is useful as a guide to the decisions a business firm must make about whether it is profitable to search for new deposits, just as a running inventory of a retail store tells the manager when to reorder. But known reserves are a thoroughly misleading guide to the resources that will be available in the future; see table 2-1, which compares known world reserves with two other measurements of available resources. In figure 1-3 we saw how the known reserves of mercury have *increased* rather than decreased. Figure 2-1 shows the total world "known reserves" of copper and other raw materials; almost all known reserves have increased since 1950 as demand for the materials increased—just the way a store inventory often increases because the store's sales volume grows. And table 2-1 shows the ratios of reserves to total production; this is the measure that many writers have used to forecast exhaustion, relying on the simple calculation that if we have (say) only fifteen years of present consumption in "reserves," the cupboard surely will be bare fifteen years from now. But the graphs show that reserves not only do not go down, they even go up—not only in total, but also as a ratio of rising consumption. The explanation for this anti-commonsensical trend may be found in chapter 3. This should be strong proof, even for the doubting reader, that forecasts using the known-reserve concept—which includes most forecasts, especially the doomsday type—are so misleading as to be worse than useless.

The ratio of U.S. reserves to U.S. production also has generally increased. The metals data cited by Earl Cook were, for 1934 and 1974, respectively: copper, 40 years and 57 years; iron ore, 18 and 24 years; lead, 15–20 and 87 years; zinc, 15–20 and 61 years.[1] But these U.S. data are much less relevant than are the world reserves data shown above, because these materials are sold freely in world markets.

To understand the concept of known reserves we must inquire into other concepts of physical reserves, including total crustal abundance and ultimate recoverable reserves, expressed in terms of years of consumption at the current consumption rate. Proven reserves are a ridiculously pessimistic floor for forecasting. At the other end—a ridiculously optimistic ceiling—is the total amount of a material that exists in the Earth's crust. The most economically relevant measure is that of "ultimate recoverable resources," which the U.S. Geological Survey presently assumes is one hundredth of 1 percent (.0001) of the amount in the top kilometer of the Earth's surface; these are the figures given in the middle column of table 2-1, to be compared with proven reserves

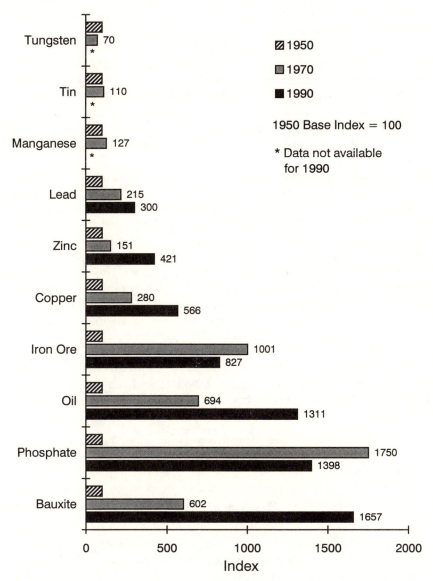

Figure 2-1. Known World Reserves of Selected Natural Resources, 1950, 1970, 1990

and total crustal abundance in the other columns. Even this "ultimately recoverable" estimate will surely be enlarged in the future when there are improvements in mining techniques or if prices rise.[2]

A second difficulty with material-technical forecasts stems from an important property of natural resource extraction. A small change in the price of a mineral generally makes a very big difference in the potential supplies that are economically available—that is, profitable to extract. Yet many forecasts based on physical principles are limited to supplies of the resource available at current prices with current technology. Given that the most promising lodes will always be mined first, this approach inevitably suggests a rapid exhaustion of "reserves" even though the long-term trend is *decreasing* scarcity because of the added incentive to find new lodes and invent better methods of extraction.

A third difficulty with material-technical forecasts: the methods that go beyond the "known reserves" concept necessarily depend on more speculative assumptions than does the economic approach. Material-technical forecasts must make very specific assumptions about discoveries of unknown lodes and about technologies that have yet to be developed. Making the "conservative" (read "unimaginative") assumption that future technology will be the same as present technology would be like making a forecast of twentieth-century copper production on the basis of eighteenth-century pick-and-shovel technology. (Indeed, we must be wary of a tendency of experts in a given field to underestimate the scope of future technological changes and their impact on the economy. As Simon Kuznets said, "Experts are usually specialists skilled in, and hence bound to, traditional views and they are, because of their knowledge of one field, likely to be cautious and unduly conservative.")[3] In contrast, the economic approach makes only one assumption, to wit, that the long-run trend of declining costs will continue.

Fourth, the technical inventory of the Earth's "contents" is at present quite incomplete, for the very good reason that it has never been worthwhile to go to the trouble of making detailed surveys. Why should you count the stones in Montana when you have enough to serve as paperweights right in your own backyard?

> We do not know the true extent of the resources that exist in, and can ultimately be recovered from, the earth. Nor will we know in the next two years or ten years. The reason why we do not know the absolute limits of the resources we have is simple and does not even require recourse to elaborate arguments about the wonders of technology. We do not know because no one has as yet found it necessary to know and therefore went about taking an accurate inventory.[4]

All these difficulties in forecasting resource availability are well known to geologists, even though they are left out of popular discussions. To illustrate, figure 2-2 shows the place of known reserves in the overall scheme of total resources.

What would be the ideal technical forecast if it were possible? All would agree, I believe, that we want to know how much of the raw material could and would be produced at each possible market price for each year in the future. The estimate for each future year 199? or 20?? must depend on the amount of the resource used in years prior to 199? or 20?? Thus on the one hand, if more was extracted in previous years, there will be less high-quality

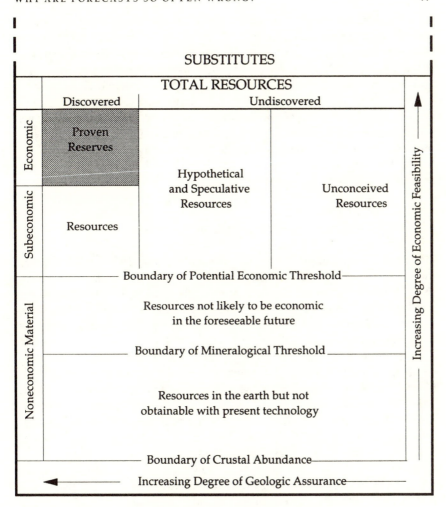

SUBSTITUTES

TOTAL RESOURCES		
Discovered	Undiscovered	
Proven Reserves	Hypothetical and Speculative Resources	Unconceived Resources
Resources		

Boundary of Potential Economic Threshold

Resources not likely to be economic in the foreseeable future

Boundary of Mineralogical Threshold

Resources in the earth but not obtainable with present technology

Boundary of Crustal Abundance

◄──── Increasing Degree of Geologic Assurance ────

(left axis, top to bottom: Economic / Subeconomic / Noneconomic Material)

(right axis: Increasing Degree of Economic Feasibility ▲)

SOURCES OF SERVICES

Figure 2-2. Concepts of Raw-Material Supplies—McKelvey's Box Expanded

material left to extract, which tends to raise the price in 199? or 20?? But on the other hand, greater use in previous years leads to more exploration and more development of advanced technology, which in turn tends to lower the price. On balance, I'd guess that greater use in years prior to 199? or 20?? means a lower rather than a higher price in 199? or 20??, respectively.

This idealized scheme paves the way to an answer to a most troublesome question: Among the wide range of technical forecasts and forecasters, which make the most sense? As we discuss this question, however, please remember my general advice on these matters: Prefer economic trend forecasts, if available, to any and all material-technical forecasts.

Among material-technical forecasters, the best are those who come closest to the ideal of a price-dependent supply schedule that sensibly takes prior use into account. This immediately disqualifies most forecasters because they do not make their predictions conditional on various prices. More specifically, this criterion knocks out all forecasts based solely on the concept of known reserves. Among forecasts that do make the estimate conditional on price, you must judge a forecaster on how well he or she reasons about future technological developments with respect to resources in the land, ocean bottom, and sea. This is a difficult judgment for any layperson to make.

The Vast Differences among Technical Forecasts

Despite those reservations about technical forecasting, I shall briefly survey the results of some of the forecasters, mostly in their own words. My aim is to show that even with relatively "conservative" guesses about future extraction developments, many of the best-qualified forecasters report enormous resource availabilities—in contrast to the scare stories that dominate the daily newspapers. The central difficulty again is: Which expert will you choose to believe? If you wish, you can certainly find *someone* with all the proper academic qualifications who will give you as good a scare for your money as a horror movie. For example, geologist Preston Cloud has written that "food and raw materials place ultimate limits on the size of populations . . . such limits will be reached within the next thirty to one hundred years,"[5] and, of course, not too many years ago the best-selling book by Paul and William Paddock, *Famine—1975!*, told it all in the title.

We begin with the assessment of the raw-materials situation by Herman Kahn and associates. Examining the evidence on the twelve principal metals that account for 99.9 percent of world and U.S. metal consumption, they classify them into only two categories, "clearly inexhaustible" and "probably inexhaustible," finding none that are likely to be exhausted in any foreseeable future that is relevant to contemporary decisions. They conclude that "95 percent of the world demand is for five metals which are not considered exhaustible."[6]

Many decades ago, the great geologist Kirtley Mather made a similar prescient forecast:

> Summing it all up, for nearly all of the important nonrenewable resources, the known or confidently expected world stores are thousands of times as great as the annual world consumption. For the few which like petroleum are available in relatively small quantities, substitutes are known or potential sources of alternative supply are at hand in quantities adequate to meet our current needs for many thousands

of years. There is no prospect of the imminent exhaustion of any of the truly essential raw materials, as far as the world as a whole is concerned. Mother Earth's storehouse is far more richly stocked with goods than is ordinarily inferred.[7]

In a comprehensive 1963 survey of natural and technological resources for the next 100 years, Harrison Brown—a well-known geochemist who would not be described as a congenital optimist by anyone who knows Brown's work—nevertheless looked forward to a time when natural resources will become so plentiful that "mineral resources will cease to play a main role in world economy and politics."[8] (I think that that time has already arrived.)

In an article sufficiently well regarded that it was the first article from the physical sciences ever republished in the *American Economic Review*, H. E. Goeller and A. M. Weinberg explored the implications of possible substitution in the use of raw materials that are essential to our civilization, with this result:

> We now state the principle of "infinite" substitutability: With three notable exceptions—phosphorus, a few trace elements for agriculture, and energy-producing fossil fuels (CH2)—society can subsist on inexhaustible or near-inexhaustible minerals with relatively little loss of living standard. Society would then be based largely on glass, plastic, wood, cement, iron, aluminum, and magnesium.[9]

As a result of that analysis of "infinite" substitutability, they arrive at an optimistic conclusion:

> Our technical message is clear: dwindling mineral resources in the aggregate, with the exception of reduced carbon and hydrogen, are per se unlikely to cause Malthusian catastrophe. . . . In the Age of Substitutability energy is the ultimate raw material. The living standard will almost surely depend primarily on the cost of prime energy.[10]

Are those quotations from far-out voices? Hardly. Vincent McKelvey, then-director of the U.S. Geological Survey, said in an official *Summary of United States Mineral Resources*: "Personally, I am confident that for millennia to come we can continue to develop the mineral supplies needed to maintain a high level of living for those who now enjoy it and raise it for the impoverished people of our own country and the world."[11]

You may be startled by the discrepancies between these assessments and those that you read in the daily newspapers. The best-known doomsday forecast in the last few decades was *The Limits to Growth*. It sold an astounding nine million copies in twenty-nine languages.[12] But that book has been so thoroughly and universally criticized as neither valid nor scientific that it is not worthwhile to devote time or space to refuting its every detail. Even more damning, just four years after publication it was disavowed by its sponsors, the Club of Rome. The Club said that the conclusions of that first report are not correct and that they purposely misled the public in order to "awaken" public concern.

With respect to minerals, Dennis Meadows (an author of *Limits to Growth*) predictably went wrong by using the known-reserves concept. For example, he estimated the world supply of aluminum to be exhausted in a maximum of forty-nine years. But aluminum is the most abundant metal in the Earth's crust, and the chance of its supply becoming an economic problem is nil. (Meadows also made the error of counting only high-grade bauxite, while lower grades are found in much greater abundance.) The price history of aluminum in figure 2-3 shows how aluminum has become vastly more available rather than more scarce since its early development in the nineteenth century. And in the two decades since *Limits to Growth*, price has continued to fall, a sure sign that the trend is toward lesser rather than greater scarcity.

The complete failure of the prophecies of *Limits to Growth*, and even the repudiation by its sponsor, have had little visible effect on the thinking of those who made the false prophecies. In 1990, Meadows was still saying, "We showed that physical growth will stop within the lifetime of those being born today. . . . The underlying problem has not changed one iota: It is the impossibility of sustaining physical growth in a finite world."[13] (The next chapter discusses why finiteness is a destructive bogeyman, without scientific foundation.) And in 1992, there appeared *Beyond the Limits*, which says the same old things while attempting to wiggle out of the failures of past predictions by saying that they just had the dates of the forecasts wrong. (See the afternote to chapter 34 for more discussion of the two *Limits* volumes.)

Forecasts made by government agencies attract much attention, and many naive persons put special credence in them. But the inability of government agencies to predict resource trends, and the ill effects of such "official" but badly made forecasts, would be amusing if not so sad. Consider this episode:

After a sharp price rise in the late 1970s, timber prices in 1983 fell about three-quarters, causing agony for lumber companies that had contracted to cut government timber at the high prices. Industry trade groups then argued that the government owed the industry help because its forecasts had led to the bidding disaster. In the late 1970s [an industry spokesman] says, government economists predicted timber shortages and helped to fan the bidding.[14]

Even economists can be influenced by physical considerations into focusing on too-short-run price series, thereby making wrong forecasts. For example, in 1982 Margaret Slade published an influential analysis of trends in commodity prices based on a theoretical model including grades of ores. Her series ran from 1870 or later through 1978. She fitted quadratic concave-upwards curves to the data and concluded that "if scarcity is measured by relative prices, the evidence indicates that nonrenewable natural-resource commodities are becoming scarce."[15] If she were to conduct the same analysis with data running to 1993, and using data before 1870 where available, she would arrive at quite the opposite conclusion.

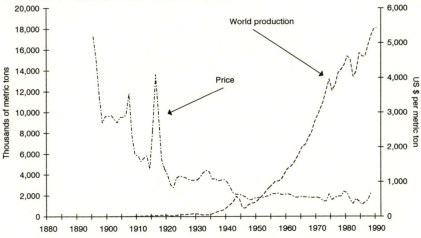

Figure 2-3a. Price and World Production of Aluminum, 1880–1990

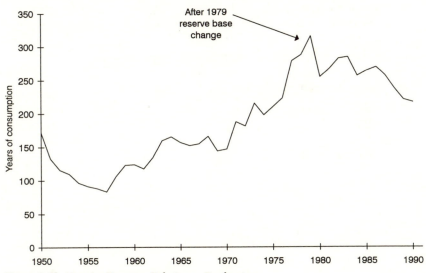

Figure 2-3b. Bauxite Reserves Relative to Production

Summary

The potential supplies of all the important minerals are sufficient for many many lifetimes, on the basis of almost any assumption about these minerals' abundance on Earth. This material-technical assessment is entirely consistent with the historical economic evidence of falling prices relative to wages for all raw materials, showing a trend of increasing availability and declining scarcity, as discussed in chapters 1, 5, 8, 10, and 11.

Material-technical forecasts of resource exhaustion often go wrong for two reasons. (1) No matter how closely defined, the physical quantity of a resource in the Earth is not known at any time, because resources are sought and found only as they are needed; an example is the increase in the known supplies of such resources as copper, as shown in table 2-1 and figure 2-1. (2) Even if the physical quantities of particular closely defined natural resources were known, such measurements would not be economically meaningful, because we have the capacity to develop additional ways to meet our needs: for example, by using fiber optics instead of copper wiring, by developing new ways to exploit low grades of copper ore previously thought not usable, and by developing new energy sources such as nuclear power to help produce copper, perhaps by extracting it from seawater. Thus, the existing "inventory" of natural resources is operationally misleading; physical measurements do not define what we will be able to use as future supplies.

As one wise geologist put it:

> Reserves are but a small part of the resources of any given commodity. Reserves and resources are part of a dynamic system and they cannot be inventoried like cans of tomatoes on a grocer's shelf. New scientific discoveries, new technology, and new commercial demands or restrictions are constantly affecting amounts of reserves and resources. Reserves and resources do not exist until commercial demand puts a value on a material in the market.[16]

Afternote to Investors _____

PERSONS interested in securities investments sometimes get impatient when I say that raw-materials prices will fall "in the long run." Well, to ensure that you understand that the subject of this book is quite practical, and just to lighten up a bit, here is a hot tip: Shun like the plague any investments in mutual funds that deal in commodities. They are sure losers in the long run. Here is a letter I wrote to a newspaper on this subject:

To the Editor:

The Commodity Index fund Goldman-Sachs has just announced [*Wall Street Journal*, July 22, 1991] is the worst investment this side of a Brooklyn Bridge deal. Raw materials have consistently fallen in price over the decades and centuries relative to consumer goods. That is, natural resources have been becoming less scarce rather than more scarce throughout history. The classic *Scarcity and Growth* by H. Barnett and C. Morse documents this trend for the period 1870 to 1957, and my own work does the same for periods up to the present and going back as far as 1800 (where the data are available). G. Anders, W. P. Gramm (now Senator), S. C. Maurice, and C. W. Smithson assessed the investment records of commodities between 1900 and 1975, and showed that the investor would have lost spectacularly by buying and holding commodities; AAA bonds produced a rate of return 733 percent higher than holding resources.

Goldman-Sachs may be able to show that over some selected short period of time commodities do better. But such a showing is either scientific foolishness—the error of relying on an inadequate sample from a short period of time, rather than looking at the long-term record—or outright fraud. There is no other possibility.

And yes, I'll be delighted to take a position on the other side of the investment, selling what they buy.

This misadventure demonstrates the importance of taking a long historical view rather than being seduced by short blips in a time series.

Sincerely,

Julian L. Simon

3

Can the Supply of Natural Resources—
Especially Energy—Really Be Infinite?
Yes!

A professor giving a lecture on energy declares that the world will perish in
seven billion years' time because the sun will then burn out. One of the audience
becomes very agitated, asks the professor to repeat what he said, and then,
completely reassured, heaves a sign of relief, "Phew! I thought he said
seven million years!"
  (Sauvy 1976)

[My economic analyses rest on] some principles which are uncommon, and which
may seem too refined and subtile for such vulgar subjects. If false, let them be
rejected. But no one ought to enter a prejudice against them, merely because
they are out of the common road.
  (David Hume, Essays, 1777 [1987])

[I]t is necessary for the very existence of science that minds exist which do not
allow that nature must satisfy some preconceived conditions.
  (Richard Feynman, The Character of Physical Law, 1994)

Few arguments are more dangerous than the ones that "feel" right but can't be
justified.
  (Stephen Jay Gould, The Mismeasure of Man, 1981)

CHAPTER 2 showed that natural resources, properly defined, cannot be measured. Here I draw the logical conclusion: Natural resources are not finite. Yes,
you read correctly. This chapter shows that the supply of natural resources is
not finite in any economic sense, which is one reason why their cost can
continue to fall indefinitely.

On the face of it, even to inquire whether natural resources are finite seems
like nonsense. Everyone "knows" that resources are finite. And this belief has
led many persons to draw unfounded, far-reaching conclusions about the future of our world economy and civilization. A prominent example is the *Limits
to Growth* group, who open the preface to their 1974 book as follows.

Most people acknowledge that the earth is finite. . . . Policy makers generally assume
that growth will provide them tomorrow with the resources required to deal with

today's problems. Recently, however, concern about the consequences of population growth, increased environmental pollution, and the depletion of fossil fuels has cast doubt upon the belief that continuous growth is either possible or a panacea.[1]

(Note the rhetorical device embedded in the term "acknowledge" in the first sentence of the quotation. It suggests that the statement is a fact, and that anyone who does not "acknowledge" it is simply refusing to accept or admit it.) For many writers on the subject, the inevitable depletion of natural resources is simply not open to question. A political scientist discussing the relationship of resources to national security refers to "the incontrovertible fact that many crucial resources are nonrenewable."[2] A high government energy official says that views that "the world's oil reserves . . . are sufficient to meet the worlds' needs" are "fatuities."[3]

The idea that resources are finite in supply is so pervasive and influential that the President's 1972 Commission on Population Growth and the American Future (the most recent such report) based its policy recommendations squarely upon this assumption. Right at its beginning the report asked,

> What does this nation stand for and where is it going? At some point in the future, the finite earth will not satisfactorily accommodate more human beings—nor will the United States. . . . It is both proper and in our best interest to participate fully in the worldwide search for the good life, which must include the eventual stabilization of our numbers.[4]

The assumption of finiteness indubitably misleads many scientific forecasters because their conclusions follow inexorably from that assumption. From the *Limits to Growth* team again, this time on food: "The world model is based on the fundamental assumption that there is an upper limit to the total amount of food that can be produced annually by the world's agricultural system."[5]

The idea of finite supplies of natural resources led even a mind as powerful as Bertrand Russell's into error. Here we're not just analyzing casual opinions; all of us necessarily hold many casual opinions that are ludicrously wrong simply because life is far too short for us to think through even a small fraction of the topics that we come across. But Russell, in a book ironically titled *The Impact of Science on Society*, wrote much of a book chapter on the subject. He worried that depletion would cause social instability.

> Raw materials, in the long run, present just as grave a problem as agriculture. Cornwall produced tin from Phoenician times until very lately; now the tin of Cornwall is exhausted. . . . Sooner or later all easily accessible tin will have been used up, and the same is true of most raw materials. The most pressing, at the moment, is oil. . . . The world has been living on capital, and so long as it remains industrial it must continue to do so. This is one inescapable though perhaps rather distant source of instability in a scientific society.[6]

Nor is it only noneconomists who fall into this error (although economists are in less danger here because they are accustomed to expect economic adjustment to shortages). John Maynard Keynes's contemporaries thought that he was the cleverest person of the century. But on the subject of natural resources—and about population growth, as we shall see later—he was both ignorant of the facts and stupid (an adjective I never use except for the famously clever) in his dogmatic logic. In his world-renowned *The Economic Consequences of the Peace*, published just after World War I, Keynes wrote that Europe could not supply itself and soon would have nowhere to turn:

> [B]y 1914 the domestic requirements of the United States for wheat were approaching their production, and the date was evidently near when there would be an exportable surplus only in years of exceptionally favorable harvest. . . .
>
> Europe's claim on the resources of the New World was becoming precarious; the law of diminishing returns was at last reasserting itself, and was making it necessary year by year for Europe to offer a greater quantity of other commodities to obtain the same amount of bread. . . . If France and Italy are to make good their own deficiencies in coal from the output of Germany, then Northern Europe, Switzerland, and Austria . . . must be starved of their supplies.[7]

All these assertions of impending scarcity turned out to be wildly in error. So much for Keynes's wisdom as an economist and a seer into the future. Millions of plain American farmers had a far better grasp of the agricultural reality in the 1920s than did Keynes. This demonstrates that one needs to know history as well as technical facts, and not just be a clever reasoner.

Just as in Keynes's day, the question of finiteness is irrelevant to any contemporary considerations, as the joke at the head of the chapter suggests. Nevertheless, we must discuss the topic because of its centrality in so much contemporary doomsday thinking.

The argument in this chapter is very counterintuitive, as are most of the ideas in this book. Indeed, science is most useful when it is counterintuitive. But when scientific ideas are sufficiently far from "common sense," people will be uncomfortable with science, and they will prefer other explanations, as in this parable:

> Imagine for the moment that you are a chieftain of a primitive tribe, and that I am explaining to you why water gradually disappears from an open container. I offer the explanation that the water is comprised of a lot of invisible, tiny bits of matter moving at enormous speeds. Because of their speed, the tiny bits escape from the surface and fly off into the air. They go undetected because they are so small that they cannot be seen. Because this happens continuously, eventually all of the tiny, invisible bits fly into the air and the water disappears. Now I ask you: "Is that a rational scientific explanation?" Undoubtedly, you will say yes. However, for a primitive chief, it is not believable. The believable explanation is that the spirits drank it.[8]

But because the ideas in this chapter are counterintuitive does not mean that there is not a firm theoretical basis for holding them.

The Theory of Decreasing Natural-Resource Scarcity

People's response to the long trend of falling raw-material prices often resembles this parody: We look at a tub of water and mark the water level. We assert that the quantity of water in the tub is "finite." Then we observe people dipping water out of the tub into buckets and taking them away. Yet when we re-examine the tub, lo and behold the water level is higher (analogous to the price being lower) than before. We believe that no one has reason to put water into the tub (as no one will put oil into an oil well), so we figure that some peculiar accident has occurred, one that is not likely to be repeated. But each time we return, the water level in the tub is higher than before—and water is selling at an ever cheaper price (as oil is). Yet we simply repeat over and over that the quantity of water must be finite and cannot continue to increase, and that's all there is to it.

Would not a prudent person, after a long series of rises in the water level, conclude that perhaps the process may continue—and that it therefore makes sense to seek a reasonable explanation? Would not a sensible person check whether there are inlet pipes to the tub? Or whether someone has developed a process for producing water? Whether people are using less water than before? Whether people are restocking the tub with recycled water? It makes sense to look for the cause of this apparent miracle, rather than clinging to a simple-minded, fixed-resources theory and asserting that it cannot continue.

Let's begin with a simple example to see what contrasting possibilities there are. (Such simplifying abstraction is a favorite trick of economists and mathematicians.) If there is only Alpha Crusoe and a single copper mine on an island, it will be harder to get raw copper next year if Alpha makes a lot of copper pots and bronze tools this year, because copper will be harder to find and dig. And if he continues to use his mine, his son Beta Crusoe will have a tougher time getting copper than did his daddy, because he will have to dig deeper.

Recycling could change the outcome. If Alpha decides in the second year to replace the old tools he made in the first year, he can easily reuse the old copper and do little new mining. And if Alpha adds fewer new pots and tools from year to year, the proportion of cheap, recycled copper can rise year by year. This alone could mean a progressive decrease in the cost of copper, even while the total stock of copper in pots and tools increases.

But let us for the moment leave the possibility of recycling aside. Consider another scenario: If suddenly there are not one but two people on the island, Alpha Crusoe and Gamma Defoe, copper will be more scarce for each of them this year than if Alpha lived there alone, unless by cooperative efforts they can devise a more complex but more efficient mining operation—say, one man getting the surface work and one getting the shaft. (Yes, a joke.) Or, if there are two fellows this year instead of one, and if copper is therefore harder to get and more scarce, both Alpha and Gamma may spend considerable time looking for new lodes of copper.

Alpha and Gamma may follow still other courses of action. Perhaps they will invent better ways of obtaining copper from a given lode, say a better digging tool, or they may develop new materials to substitute for copper, perhaps iron.

The cause of these new discoveries, or the cause of applying ideas that were discovered earlier, is the "shortage" of copper—that is, the increased cost of getting copper. So increased scarcity causes the development of its own remedy. This has been the key process in the supply of natural resources throughout history. (This process is explored for energy in chapter 11. Even in that special case there is no reason to believe that the supply of energy, even of oil, is finite or limited.)

Interestingly, the pressure of *low* prices can also cause innovation, as in this story:

> [In the] period 1984 to 1986 . . . the producer price of copper hovered around 65 cents per pound. In terms of constant dollars, this was the lowest price since the great depression of the 1930s. . . . [S]ome companies . . . analyzed what needed to be done to be profitable even if the price of copper remained low. . . .
>
> Major copper companies have found ways of reducing their costs. Phelps Dodge . . . will improve the efficiency of its transportation of rock by use of computer monitoring and by installing an in-pit crusher. . . . [It] has improved the efficiency of its copper concentration process by employing analytic instrumentation, including x-ray fluorescence. The most effective move . . . has been to install equipment that permits inexpensive . . . production of pure copper from leachates of wastes and tailings.[9]

Improved efficiency of copper use not only reduces resource use in the present, but effectively increases the entire stock of unused resources as well. For example, an advance in knowledge that leads to a 1 percent decrease in the amount of copper that we need to make electrical outlets is much the same as an increase in the total stock of copper that has not yet been mined. And if we were to make such a 1 percent increase in efficiency for all uses every year, a 1 percent increase in demand for copper in every future year could be accommodated without any increase in the price of copper, even without any other helpful developments.*

* Baumol compared a reasonable expected increase in the rate of productivity and a reasonable expected increase in population and calculated that the stock of resource services would grow faster than the demand, suggesting that resources would be available indefinitely (1986).

Discovery of an improved mining method or of a substitute such as iron differs, in a manner that affects future generations, from the discovery of a new lode. Even after the discovery of a new lode, on the average it will still be more costly to obtain copper, that is, more costly than if copper had never been used enough to lead to a "shortage." But discoveries of improved mining methods and of substitute products can lead to lower costs of the services people seek from copper.

Please notice how a discovery of a substitute process or product by Alpha or Gamma benefits innumerable future generations. Alpha and Gamma cannot themselves extract nearly the full benefit from their discovery of iron. (You and I still benefit from the discoveries of the uses of iron and methods of processing made by our ancestors thousands of years ago.) This benefit to later generations is an example of what economists call an "externality" due to Alpha and Gamma's activities, that is, a result of their discovery that does not affect them directly.

If the cost of copper to Alpha and Gamma does not increase, they may not be impelled to develop improved methods and substitutes. If the cost of getting copper does rise for them, however, they may then bestir themselves to make a new discovery. The discovery may not immediately lower the cost of copper dramatically, and Alpha and Gamma may still not be as well off as if the cost had never risen. But subsequent generations may be better off because their ancestors Alpha and Gamma suffered from increasing cost and "scarcity."

This sequence of events explains how it can be that people have been cooking in copper pots for thousands of years, as well as using the metal for many other purposes, yet the cost of a pot today is vastly cheaper by any measure than it was one hundred or one thousand or ten thousand years ago.

Now I'll restate this line of thought into a theory that will appear again and again: More people, and increased income, cause resources to become more scarce in the short run. Heightened scarcity causes prices to rise. The higher prices present opportunity and prompt inventors and entrepreneurs to search for solutions. Many fail in the search, at cost to themselves. But in a free society, solutions are eventually found. And in the longrun *the new developments leave us better off than if the problems had not arisen.* That is, prices eventually become lower than before the increased scarcity occurred.

It is all-important to recognize that discoveries of improved methods and of substitute products are not just luck. They happen in response to an increase in scarcity—a rise in cost. Even after a discovery is made, there is a good chance that it will not be put into operation until there is need for it due to rising cost. This is important: Scarcity and technological advance are not two unrelated competitors in a Malthusian race; rather, each influences the other.

Because we now have decades of data to check its predictions, we can learn much from the 1952 U.S. governmental inquiry into raw materials—the President's Materials Policy Commission (the Paley Commission), organized in response to fears of raw-material shortages during and just after World War II. Its report is distinguished by having some of the right logic, but exactly the wrong forecasts.

> There is no completely satisfactory way to measure the real costs of materials over the long sweep of our history. But clearly the man hours required per unit of output declined heavily from 1900 to 1940, thanks especially to improvements in production technology and the heavier use of energy and capital equipment per worker. This long-term decline in real costs is reflected in the downward drift of prices of various groups of materials in relation to the general level of prices in the economy.
>
> [But since 1940 the trend has been] soaring demands, shrinking resources, the consequences [being] pressure toward rising real costs, the risk of wartime shortages, the strong possibility of an arrest or decline in the standard of living we cherish and hope to share.[10]

The commission went on to predict that prices would continue to rise for the next quarter-century. However, prices declined rather than rose.

There are two reasons why the Paley Commission's predictions were topsy-turvy. First, the commission reasoned from the notion of finiteness and used a static technical analysis of the sort discussed in chapter 2.

> A hundred years ago resources seemed limitless and the struggle upward from meager conditions of life was the struggle to create the means and methods of getting these materials into use. In this struggle we have by now succeeded all too well. The nature of the problem can perhaps be successfully over-simplified by saying that the consumption of almost all materials is expanding at compound rates and is thus pressing harder and harder against resources which whatever else they may be doing are not similarly expanding.[11]

The second reason the Paley Commission went wrong is that it looked at the wrong facts. Its report placed too much emphasis on the trends of costs over the short period from 1940 to 1950, which included World War II and therefore was almost inevitably a period of rising costs, instead of examining the longer period from 1900 to 1940, during which the commission knew that "the man-hours required per unit of output declined heavily."[12]

Let us not repeat the Paley Commission's mistakes. We should look at trends for the longest possible period, rather than focusing on a historical blip; the OPEC-led price rise in all resources after 1973 and then the oil price increase in 1979 are for us as the temporary 1940–1950 wartime reversal was for the Paley Commission. We should ignore them, and attend instead to the long-run trends which make it very clear that the costs of materials, and their scarcity, continuously decline with the growth of income and technology.

Resources as Services

As economists or as consumers we are interested, not in the resources themselves, but in the particular services that resources yield. Examples of such services are a capacity to conduct electricity, an ability to support weight, energy to fuel autos or electrical generators, and food calories.

The supply of a service will depend upon (a) which raw materials can supply that service with the existing technology, (b) the availabilities of these materials at various qualities, (c) the costs of extracting and processing them, (d) the amounts needed at the present level of technology to supply the services that we want, (e) the extent to which the previously extracted materials can be recycled, (f) the cost of recycling, (g) the cost of transporting the raw materials and services, and (h) the social and institutional arrangements in force. What is relevant to us is not whether we can find any lead in existing lead mines but whether we can have the services of lead batteries at a reasonable price; it does not matter to us whether this is accomplished by recycling lead, by making batteries last forever, or by replacing lead batteries with another contraption. Similarly, we want intercontinental telephone and television communication, and, as long as we get it, we do not care whether this requires 100,000 tons of copper for cables, or a pile of sand for optical fibers, or just a single quarter-ton communications satellite in space that uses almost no material at all.[13] And we want the plumbing in our homes to carry water; if PVC plastic has replaced the copper that formerly was used to do the job—well, that's just fine.

This concept of services improves our understanding of natural resources and the economy. To return to Crusoe's cooking pot, we are interested in a utensil that one can put over the fire and cook with. After iron and aluminum were discovered, quite satisfactory cooking pots—and perhaps more durable than pots of copper—could be made of these materials. The cost that interests us is the cost of providing the cooking service rather than the cost of copper. If we suppose that copper is used only for pots and that (say) stainless steel is quite satisfactory for most purposes, as long as we have cheap iron it does not matter if the cost of copper rises sky high. (But as we have seen, even the prices of the minerals themselves, as well as the prices of the services they perform, have fallen over the years.)*

Here is an example of how we develop new sources of the sources we seek.

---

* Here is an example of how new developments increase the amount of services we get from a given amount of ore: Scientists have recently rediscovered the "superplastic" steel used in ancient Damascus blades. This causes a large reduction in the amount of scrap that is left over in machining parts, and hence a large decrease in the amount of material needed, as well as the amount of energy used, in metal fabrication processes (*Chemecology*, March 1992, p. 6).

Ivory used for billiard balls threatened to run out late in the nineteenth century. As a result of a prize offered for a replacement material, celluloid was developed, and that discovery led directly to the astonishing variety of plastics that now gives us a cornucopia of products (including billiard balls) at prices so low as to boggle the nineteenth-century mind. We shall discuss this process at greater length in the context of energy in chapter 11.

Are Natural Resources Finite?

Incredible as it may seem at first, the term "finite" is not only inappropriate but is downright misleading when applied to natural resources, from both the practical and philosophical points of view. As with many important arguments, the finiteness issue is "just semantic." Yet the semantics of resource scarcity muddle public discussion and bring about wrongheaded policy decisions.

The ordinary synonyms of "finite," the dictionary tells us, are "countable" or "limited" or "bounded." This is the appropriate place to start our thinking on the subject, keeping in mind that the appropriateness of the term "finite" in a particular context depends on what interests us. Also please keep in mind that we are interested in material benefits and not abstract mathematical entities per se. (Mathematics has its own definition of "finite," which can be quite different from the common sort of definition we need here.)*

* The word "finite" is frequently used in mathematics, in which context we all learn it as schoolchildren. The definition of "finite" used in this book, however, applies not to mathematical entities but rather to physical entities. Therefore, arguments about the mathematical entities and the mathematical definition of "finite" are not germane here, even though the notion of infinity may be originally of mathematical origin.

In the first edition, I wrote that even in mathematics the word "finite" can be confusing. (I appreciate a discussion of this point with Alvin Roth.) For example, consider whether a one-inch line segment should be considered finite. The *length* of a one-inch line is finite in the sense that it is bounded at both ends. But the line within the endpoints contains an infinite number of points which have no defined size and hence cannot be counted. Therefore, *the number of points* in that one-inch segment is not finite. My point, as I wrote, was that the appropriateness of the term "finite" depends upon what interests us. This paragraph elicited much criticism, and because it is not necessary to the argument, I leave it out this time.

When I wrote about a line's finiteness in the first edition, I did not intend to suggest that the supply of copper should be considered to be not finite because it could be subdivided ever more finely; however, what I wrote caused some confusion. I meant to say that if we cannot state *how to count* the total amount of a resource that could be available in the future, it should not be considered finite. But in one important sense the notion of subdivision *is* relevant. With the passage of time and the accumulation of technical knowledge, we learn how to obtain a given amount of service from an ever-smaller amount of a resource. It takes much less copper now to pass a given message than a hundred years ago. And much less energy is required to do a given amount of work than in the past; the earliest steam engines had an efficiency of about 2 percent, but efficiencies are many times that high now.

The quantity of the services we obtain from copper that will ever be available to us should not be considered finite because there is no method (even in principle) of making an apporpriate count of it, given the problem of the economic definition of "copper," the possibility of using copper more efficiently, the possibility of creating copper or its economic equivalent from other materials, the possibility of recycling copper, or even obtaining copper from sources beyond planet Earth, and thus the lack of boundaries to the sources from which "copper" might be drawn. That is, one cannot construct a working definition of the total services that we now obtain from copper and that can eventually be obtained by human beings.[14]

This is easier to see now than ever before. After centuries of slow progress and the use of mostly the familiar materials such as stone, wood, and iron, science is attaining undreamed-of abilities to create new materials. This includes syntheses of known compounds and also "materials that do not exist in nature. . . . Instead of trying to modify existing materials, scientists now are learning to assemble atoms and molecules systematically into new materials with precisely the properties they need for designs too demanding for off-the-shelf resources."[15] The first auto engine parts made of silicon and carbon—water-pump seal rings—are now being installed in Volkswagens, and engines could soon be made of silicon carbide, cutting weight and emissions in addition to replacing metals.[16] Palladium instead of platinum can now be used in auto exhaust emission systems.[17] Organic plastics can now be blended with glass to yield a material as strong as concrete but flexible and much lighter.[18] And a feasible way has been found to make heat-resistant plastics using gallium chloride.[19] Ceramics engineering is exploding with new knowledge, finally putting an end to past generations' worries about running out of metals.

Plastics are now made only from fossil fuels or oils from plants grown in fields, but researchers have recently found ways to convert such agricultural products as potatoes and corn into direct sources of plastics by inserting special plastic-producing genes into them.[20]

In light of these extraordinary developments—which continue the line of discoveries since humankind thousands of years ago found a way to convert iron into a resource by learning how to work with it—concern about running out of materials such as copper seems ever less sensible.

Consider this remark about potential oil and gas from an energy forecaster. "It's like trying to guess the number of beans in jar without knowing how big the jar is." So far so good. But then he adds, "God is the only one who knows—and even He may not be sure."[21] Of course he is speaking lightly. but the notion that some mind *could* know the "actual" size of the jar is misleading,

---

This sort of gain in efficiency fits with Baumol's line of thought, discussed above, that an improvement in productivity not only reduces resource use in the present, but increases the future services from the entire stock of resources.

because it implies that there is a fixed quantity of standard-sized beans. The quantity of a natural resource that might be available to us—and even more important the quantity of the services that can eventually be rendered to us by that natural resource—can never be known even in principle, just as the number of points in a one-inch line can never be counted even in principle. Even if the "jar" were fixed in size, it might yield ever more "beans." Hence, resources are not finite in any meaningful sense.

The entire notion of the nonfiniteness of resources such as copper, energy, and living space may so boggle the mind of some readers as to turn them away from the rest of the book. If this is so for you, please notice that one can reach the same practical conslusions from current data and economic theory, without making the stronger argument about infinite resources, as long as one accepts that it is silly to worry now about any implications of the proposition that energy will run out in (say) seven billion years. If the notion of finitude is quite irrelevant for you, as it is for me, please skip the rest of the discussion on the subject. But for some other, I cannot leave out discussion of the issue, because it is the basis of their thinking.

Well-wishers have advised me to "admit" that resources are limited to the capacities of the planet, thinking that this will keep me from "losing credibility." And I seem pigheaded to them when I do not follow their advice. But this is why I continue to argue that these quantities are not finite: The rhetorical difficulty is that as soon as one would "admit" that there are only (say) seven billion years of energy, some doomsters begin to work backward to argue that the sun's measurable size and rate of energy output means that the supply of energy is finite for next year. But that's physical estimate—it's not an economic definition of "energy," any more than copper atoms in the Earth's crust is a useful *economic* definition of "copper."

Objections to the notion of nonfiniteness often come from a mathematical background. Yet there is ample justification even within mathematics itself for taking the point of view that I do, and mathematical statisticians such as Barrow and Tipler affirm this. As Tipler puts it, "The laws of physics do not forbid perpetual economic growth."[22]

I continue to stand on the ground of nonfiniteness because I have found that leaving that ground leads to more bad arguments than standing on it, even though it seems so strange to many. and I doubt that many people's judgment will be affected by what I write on this particular issue. Hence there is little temptation to trim my sails to this wind, and do that which is offensive to me—to "admit" something that I do not believe is so.

But what if I am wrong? Certainly it is possible that the cosmos has a countable amount of mass/energy. How should we continue with that line of thought?

We have seen that even if energy is the relevant constraint for fabricating new kinds of "raw" materials, one would need to take into account, at the very least, all the mass/energy in the solar system. This amount is so huge relative to our use of energy, even by many multiples of the present population and many multiples of our present rates of individual use, that the end of the solar system in seven billion years or whenever would hardly be affected by our energy use now. This should be reason enough to ignore the issue of finitude.

Even if human population and the rate of using energy and materials should increase vastly so as to controvert the previous paragraph, there is the possibility that humans will come to exploit the resources of other parts of the cosmos, which is so huge relative to the solar system as to render calculations irrelevant under any conceivable rates of growth. If so, further discussion would see frivolous.

Physicist Freeman Dyson, in his book, *Infinite in All Directions*, takes this mode of thought much further and theorizes that even if the world were to get progressively colder forever, it would be possible for human beings to adapt in such fashion as to stay ahead of the cooling; consequently, he writes, "Boiled down to one sentence, my message is the unboundedness of life and the consequent unboundedness of human destiny."[23] And physicist Frank Tipler argues, on the basis of the established body of contemporary knowledge of physics, that the ultimate constraint is not energy but rather information. Because we can increase the stock of information without limit, there is no need to consider our existence finite.* Of course these arguments are exceedingly abstract, and far from contemporary concerns. I cite these ideas not as proof that the future of humanity is not finite, but rather as showing that the doomsayers' arguments from physics that human existence is *not* finite are not consistent with a solid body of reasoning by physicists.

To restate: A satisfactory operational definition—which is an estimate—of the quantity of a natural resource, or of the services we now get from it, is the only sort of estimate that is of any use in policy decision. The estimate must tell us about the quantities of a resource (or of a particular service) that we can expect to receive in any particular year to come, at each particular price,

---

* The amount of knowledge would not be finite in any meaningful sense, because the stock of knowledge can grow at a faster rate than the stock of energy can decline, which would eventuate in a cushion much greater than necessary to accommodate the possible growth in human population. (I do not give the specifics of such a calculation because doing so would be a waste of time.)

In order to show that we ought to take account of finitude, one would first have to show that the previous issue—the eventual domination of knowledge rather than energy—is wrong. Then one would have to show that the probabilities of a nonfinite universe and the future exploitation of the cosmos outside the solar system are very low, then show some reasonable basis for saying that events beyond (say) a thousand or million or more years, all the way to seven billion years, would matter for our economic choices now, then show that the likelihood is low that our present understanding of the mass/energy relationship is wrong, then show that there is little likelihood that it is possible to get our needs serviced with ever-smaller amounts of energy. Without some reasonable argument about *every link* in that chain, discussion of the finitude of energy that will be available to humans seems misplaced.

conditional on other events that we might reasonably expect to know (such as use of the resource in prior years). And there is no reason to believe that at any given moment in the future the available quantity of any natural resource or service at present prices will be much smaller than it is now, let alone nonexistent. Only one-of-a-kind resources such as an Arthur Rubinstein concert or a Michael Jordan basketball game, for which there are no close replacements, will disappear in the future and hence are finite in quantity.

The term "finite" is not meaningful when applied to resources because we cannot say with any practical surety where the bounds of a relevant resource system lie, or even if there are any bounds. The bounds for Crusoes are the shores of their island, and so it was for early humans. But then Crusoes find other islands. Humankind traveled farther and farther in search of resources—finally to the bounds of continents, and then to other continents. When America was opened up, the world, which for Europeans had been bounded by Europe and perhaps by Asia too, was suddenly expanded. Each epoch has seen a shift in the bounds of the relevant resource system. Each time, the old ideas about "limits," and the calculations of "finite resources" within those bounds, were thereby falsified. Now we have begun to explore the sea, which contains amounts of metallic and perhaps energy resources that dwarf any deposits we know about on land. And we have begun to explore the moon. Why shouldn't the boundaries of the system from which we derive resources continue to expand in such directions, just as they have expanded in the past? This is one more reason not to regard resources as "finite" in principle.

Why do we become hypnotized by the word "finite"? That is an interesting question in psychology, education, and philosophy. One likely reason is that the word "finite" seems to have a precise and unambiguous meaning in any context, even though it does not. Second, we learn the word in the context of simple mathematics, where all propositions are tautologous definitions and hence can be shown logically to be true or false. But scientific subjects are empirical rather than definitional, as twentieth-century philosophers have been at great pains to emphasize. Mathematics is not a science in the ordinary sense because it does not deal with facts other than the stuff of mathematics itself, and hence such terms as "finite" do not have the same meaning elsewhere that they do in mathematics.

Third, much of our daily life about which we need to make decisions is countable and finite—our salaries, the amount of gas in a full tank, the width of the backyard, the number of greeting cards you sent out last year, or those you will send out next year. Since these quantities are finite, why shouldn't the world's total possible salary in the future, or the gasoline in the possible tanks in the future, or the number of cards you ought to send out, also be finite? Though the analogy is appealing, it is not sound. And it is in making this incorrect extension that we go astray in using the term "finite."

I think we can stop here. I'm sorry to have taken up your time with this unless you were seriously worried beforehand about what will happen seven billion years from now.

Summary

A conceptual quantity is not finite or infinite in itself. Rather, it is finite or infinite if you make it so—by your own definitions. If you define the subject of discussion suitably, and sufficiently closely so that it can be counted, then it is finite—for example, the money in your wallet or the socks in your top drawer. But without sufficient definition the subject is not finite—for example, the thoughts in your head, the strength of your wish to go to Turkey, your dog's love for you, the number of points in a one-inch line. You can, of course, develop definitions that will make these quantities finite, which shows that the finiteness inheres in you and in your definitions rather than in the money, love, or one-inch line themselves. There is no necessity either in logic or in historical trends to state that the supply of any given resource is "finite," and to do so leads into error.

Someone coined the label "cornucopians" for those who believe that the natural resources are available in practically limitless abundance, to contrast with "doomsters." But the stream of thought that I represent here is not cornucopian. I do not suggest that nature is limitlessly bountiful. Rather, I suggest that the possibilities in the world are sufficiently great so that with the present state of knowledge—even without the additional knowledge that human imagination and human enterprise will surely develop in the future—we and our descendants can manipulate the elements in such fashion that we can have all the raw materials that we desire at prices ever smaller relative to other goods and to our total incomes. In short, our cornucopia is the human mind and heart, and not a Santa Claus natural environment. So has it been throughout history, and therefore so is it likely to be in the future.

Afternote 1

A Dialogue on "Finite"

THE NOTION of nonfinite natural resources is sufficiently important to this entire book, and sufficiently difficult to think through, that it is worth taking the time for an imaginary dialogue between Peers Strawman (PS) and Happy Writer (HW).

> PS: Every natural resource is finite in quantity, and therefore any resource must get more scarce as we use more of it.
>
> HW: What does "finite" mean?
>
> PS: "Finite" means "countable" or "limited."
>
> HW: What is the limit for, say, copper? What is the amount that may be available in the future?
>
> PS: I don't know.
>
> HW: Then how can you be sure it is limited in quantity?
>
> PS: I know that at least it must be less than the total weight of the Earth.
>
> HW: If it were only slightly less than the total weight of the Earth, or, say a hundredth of that total weight would there be reason for us to be concerned?
>
> PS: You're getting off the track. We're only discussing whether it is theoretically limited in quantity, not whether the limit is of practical importance.
>
> HW: Okay. Would you say that copper is limited in quantity if we could recycle it 100 percent?
>
> PS: I see what you're saying. Even if it is limited in quantity, finiteness wouldn't matter to us if the material could be recycled 100 percent or close to it. That's true. But we're still talking about whether it is limited in quantity. Don't digress.
>
> HW: Okay again. Would copper be limited in quantity if everything that copper does could be done by other materials that are available in limitless quantities?
>
> PS: The quantity of copper wouldn't matter then. But you're digressing again.
>
> HW: We're talking about scarcity for the future, aren't we? So what matters is not how much copper there is now (whatever the word "is" means) but the amounts in future years. Will you agree to that?
>
> PS: That I'll buy.
>
> HW: Then, is copper limited for the future if we can create copper from other materials, or substitute other materials for copper?
>
> PS: The size of the Earth would still constitue a limit.
>
> HW: How about if we can use energy from outside the Earth—from the sun, say—to create additional copper the way we grow plants with solar energy?
>
> PS: But is that realistic?

HW: Now it's you who are asking about realism. But as a matter of fact, yes, it is physically possible, and also likely to be feasible in the future. So will you now agree that at least *in principle* the quantities of copper are not limited even by the weight of the Earth?

PS: Don't make me answer that. Instead, let's talk realism. Isn't it realistic to expect resources such as copper to get more scarce?

HW: Can we agree to define scarcity as the cost of getting copper?

[Here an extended dialogue works out the arguments about scarcity and price given in chapter 1. Finally PS says "okay" to defining scarcity as cost.]

HW: Future scarcity will depend, then, on the recycling rate, on the substitutes we develop, on the new methods we discover for extracting copper, and so on. In the past, copper became progressively less scarce, and there is no reason to expect that trend to change, no matter what you say about "finiteness" and "limits," as we just agreed. But there is more. Do you really care about copper, or only about what copper does for you?

PS: Obviously what matters is what copper can do for us, not copper itself.
[Now you know why the name is Strawman].

HW: Good. Then can we agree that the outlook for the services that copper provides is even better than for copper itself?

PS: Sure, but all this *can't* be true. It's not natural. How can we use more of something and have it get less scarce?

HW: Well, this is one of those matters that defies common sense. That's because the common-sense view applies only when the resource is arbitrarily limited—for example, limited to the copper wire in your cellar. But that quantity is only fixed as long as you don't make another trip to the hardware store. Right?

PS: I may be Strawman but my patience is limited.

And so we close

Afternote 2

The "Law" of Diminishing Returns

"BUT the law of diminishing returns must come to bear *sometime*," people often say, meaning that eventually the cost of extracting mineral resources must rise, even if the cost will not rise in the near future.

Happily, there is no "law" that compels cost to rise eventually. The concept of diminishing returns applies to situations where one element is fixed in quantity—say, a given copper mine—and where the type of technology is also fixed. But neither of these factors applies to mineral extraction in the long run. New lodes are found, and new cost-cutting extraction technologies are developed. Therefore, whether the cost rises or falls in the long run depends on the extent to which advances in technology and discoveries of new lodes counteract the tendency toward increasing cost in the absence of the new developments. Historically, as we have seen, costs have consistently fallen rather than risen, and there is no empirical warrant for believing that this historical trend will reverse itself in the foreseeable future. Hence, no "law" of diminishing returns is appropriate here.

I hazard this generalization: In economic affairs, there are always diminishing returns in the small scale, but increasing returns in the large. For example, taking oil from one oil well will gradually increase the cost of successive barrels from that well. But taking oil from *all* the wells will eventually lead to lower cost for energy taken as a whole. This is partly because the oil is used in the growth of an economy that then has a greater capacity to develop cheaper energy sources, and partly because people have an incentive to find new sources of energy (or whatever) when aggregate supplies are affected significantly. Eventually the new source turns out to be cheaper than the old one.

We see evidence for this generalization in the "envelope curve" of the transition from the use of one technique to another for providing the same service, an example of which may be seen in figure 3-1. This phenomenon also explains why, as Kuznets and others have noted (see chapter2), experts tend to be pessimistic about progress in their fields; they think in terms of the particular technology they know—that's why they are experts—and not of the movement from technique to technique.

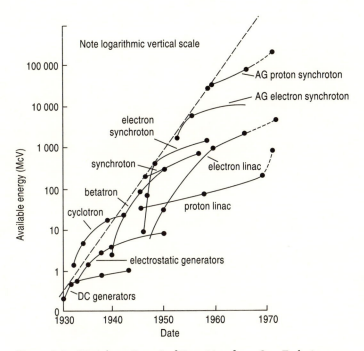

Figure 3-1a. "Envelope Curve" of Transition from One Technique to Another: Energy Machines

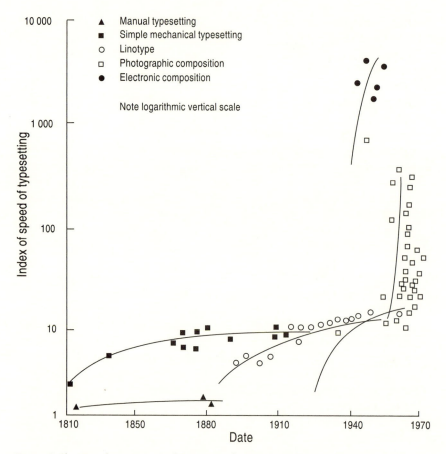

Figure 3-1b. "Envelope Curve" of Transition from One Technique to Another: Typesetting

4

The Grand Theory

THE FIRST THREE chapters offer a mind-boggling vision of resources: The more we use, the better off we become—and there's no practical limit to improving our lot forever (or for at least seven billion years). Indeed, throughout history, new tools and new knowledge have made resources easier and easier to obtain. Our growing ability to create new resources has more than made up for temporary setbacks due to local resource exhaustion, pollution, population growth, and so on. Is there some fundamental reason why this should be so?

After I investigated case after case of phenomena which the doomsters said were getting worse because of increasing scarcity and population growth, and found instead that they were getting better—as you will see in the chapters to come—it came to seem no accident. I even began to be rather sure in advance that I would find improvement rather than deterioration, and though I knew I had to check out each case, I began to worry that I might fall into error by assuming that a mere coincidence is a general rule. So I began to wonder whether there is a deep connection, a general theory that embraces all these phenomena. And I believe that there is.

Let us begin by going beyond the trends in particular resources. The greatest and most important trend, of which these particular trends are a part, is the trend of this Earth becoming ever more livable for human beings. We see the signs of this in our longer life expectancy, improved knowledge of nature, and greater ability to protect ourselves from the elements, living with ever more safety and comfort.

But though this larger trend buttresses the particular resource trends, it still provides no *causal* explanation of the phenomenon we seek to understand. Evolutionary thinking, however, and (more specifically in economics) the sort of analysis suggested by Friedrich Hayek, offers an explanation of the observed long-term trend. Hayek (following upon Hume) urges upon us that humankind has evolved sets of rules and patterns of living which are consistent with survival and growth rather than with decline and extinction, an aspect of the evolutionary selection for survival among past societies. He assumes that the particular rules and living patterns have had something to do with chances for survival—for example, he reasons that patterns leading to higher fertility and more healthful and productive living have led to groups' natural increase and hence survival—and therefore the patterns we have inherited constitute a machinery for continued survival and growth where conditions are not too different from the past. (This is consistent with a biological view of humankind as having evolved genes that point toward survival. But no such genetic evolution is presupposed by Hayek, in part because its time span is too great for us to understand it as well as we can understand the evolution of cultural rules. It may be illuminating, however, to view mankind's biological nature as part of the long evolutionary chain dating from the simplest plants and animals, a history of increasing complexity of construction and greater capacity to deal actively with the environment.)

Let us apply Hayek's general analysis to natural resources. Such resources of all sorts have been a part of human history ever since the beginning. If humankind had not evolved patterns of behavior that increased rather than decreased the amounts of resources available to us, we would not still be here. If, as our numbers increased (or even as our numbers remained nearly stationary), our patterns had led to diminished supplies of plants and animals, less flint for tools, and disappearing wood for fires and construction, I would not be here to be writing these pages, and you would not be here to be reading them.

What are the key patterns that maintained us and increased our numbers? Certainly the evolved cultural patterns include voluntary exchange between individuals, and the market that humankind has evolved to provide resources in increasing quantities; institutions, such as schools that pass on knowledge; libraries and legends and storytellers that store knowledge; and monasteries and laboratories and R&D departments that produce knowledge. The evolved biological patterns include the hunger signals we get when we lack food, and the attention that we focus on apparent regularities in nature, such as the annual cycle of seasons, when they appear before us. But ignorance of these cultural and biological patterns is not devastating for us, and such ignorance ought not to be surprising, given the complexity of these patterns and the difficulty of any one person seeing much of any pattern. Belief that our evolved history is, as I suggest, toward being creators rather than destroyers may be strengthened by some evidence that such evolution spontaneously occurs independently within most human groups, as a result of the conditions of natural life that humankind faces. People build shelters from sun, rain, and snow. The exchange mechanism evolves everywhere as a way of handling differences in abilities among persons, in order to improve our capacities to construct and create new goods as well as to distribute existing goods. Chiefs of work gangs somehow assume their roles to enable constructive tasks to be carried out efficiently. Communities reward creators of community projects in a variety of ways that they do not reward destroyers of community resources. (Warriors against other groups are not exceptions to this proposition. But perhaps it deserves mention as an exception that songs are written about such destroyers as the James Gang as well as about such creators as John Henry.) Mothers probably everywhere ooh and ah about their children's sand castles, and reprimand the children when they kick over other children's sand castles. And though I have no evidence and feel no need to consult anthropologists on the matter, I'd bet that early tribes gave greater honor to persons in dry climates who tended to find water than to those who polluted water sources, and greater honor to those who tended to find food effectively than to those who showed considerable ability to consume food supplies.

Our whole evolution up to this point shows that human groups spontaneously evolve patterns of behavior, as well as patterns of training people for that behavior, which tend on balance to lead people to create rather than destroy. Humans are, on net balance, builders rather than destroyers. The evidence is clear: the civilization which our ancestors have bequeathed to us contains more created works than the civilization they were bequeathed.

In short, humankind has evolved into creators and problem solvers. Our constructive behavior has counted for more than our using-up and destructive behavior, as seen in our increasing length of life and richness of consumption.

This view of the average human as builder conflicts with the view of the average human as destroyer which underlies the thought of many doomsdayers. From the latter view derive such statements as "The U.S. has 5 percent of the population, and uses 40 percent of resources," without reference to the *creation* of resources by the same U.S. population. (Also involved here is a view of resources as physical quantities waiting for the plucking, rather than as the services that humankind derives from some combination of knowledge with physical conditions.)* If one notices only the using-up and destructive activities of humankind, without understanding that constructive patterns of behavior must have been the dominant part of our individual-cum-social nature in order for us to have survived to this point, then it is not surprising that one would arrive at the conclusion that resources will grow scarcer in the future.

Paradoxically, rules and customs that lead to population growth rather than to population stability or decline may be part of our inherited capacity to deal successfully with resource problems in the long run, though the added people may exacerbate the problems in the short run. Such rules and customs probably lead to long-run success of a society in two ways. First, high fertility leads to increased chances of survival of the group, ceteris paribus;* the Parsis in India seem doomed to disappear in the long run due to restrictive marriage and fertility patterns, though individually they have been very successful economically. Second, high fertility leads to resource problems which then lead

---

* Many writers have commented on the fact that natural phenomena such as copper and oil and land were not resources until humans discovered their uses and found out how to extract and process them, and thereby made their services available to us. Hence resources are, in the most meaningful sense, *created*, and when this happens their availability increases and continues to increase as long as our knowledge of how to obtain them increases faster than our use of them, which is the history of all natural resources.

* This key idea comes from Hayek.

to solutions to the problems which usually leave humanity better off in the long run than if the problems had never arisen. Third, in a more direct chain of events, rules and customs leading to high fertility fit together with the positive effect of additional people on productivity, both through the demand for goods and through the supply of ingenious minds, that I discuss at length in recent books.

However, even if one accepts that humankind has evolved into a creator rather than a destroyer, it is certainly not unreasonable to wonder whether there have been changes in conditions, or one or more "structural changes" in patterns of social behavior, that might point to a change in the positive trend, just as there might have been environmental changes in the case of the dinosaurs or structural changes among some human groups that have disappeared.

Change in natural conditions sometimes has affected cultural evolution. But possible "internal contradictions" in a society or economy are more relevant to the present context. This concept represents the intuitive notion that, because of our population size and growth rate, and because of the way we produce goods and are organized socially, our civilization is unwieldy, and hence must collapse of its own weight—by, for example, nuclear destruction, or the failure of a single all-important crop.

Many who are pessimistic about the outcome of the present course of civilization suggest that the externalities of pollution are such an "internal contradiction" that will do us in. Some political organizations and devices have evolved to deal with the matter, and we have both public and private cleanup and collection of various kinds of garbage, as well as laws that regulate pollution behavior. But the possible changes in pollutions, and the recency of the onset of regulatory activities, certainly leave room to wonder whether we have yet evolved reliable patterns of dealing with pollution problems.

Intergenerational relationships with respect to resources are another frequently mentioned possible "internal contradiction," that is, one generation exploiting a resource and leaving too little for the next generation. Futures markets, both those that buy and sell the resources themselves and those that sell and buy the shares of resource-supplying firms, have evolved to protect against this potential danger. And we have had a long enough history by now to be confident that this evolved mechanism is reliable and satisfactory for the purpose.

In conclusion, I am suggesting that humankind has evolved culturally (and perhaps also genetically) in such a manner that our patterns of behavior (with social rules and customs being a crucial part of these patterns) predispose us to deal successfully with resource scarcity. This view of human history is consistent with the observed long-term trend toward greater resource availability, and with the positive (and growing) preponderance of our creative over our exploitational activities. This view provides a causal foundation for the observed benign resource trends. It argues against our being at a turning point in resource history now, and thereby buttresses the technique of simply extrapolating from past trends that produces forecasts of increasing rather than decreasing resource availability. That is, our evolved patterns have given us greater rather than less command over resources over the centuries. The market system is part of that evolution, of course. But it is not the whole of it. The story of Robinson Crusoe (which has been badly twisted by economists, who make it a story of allocation when it is really a story of ingenuity and the use of the knowledge that he brought with him) also illustrates this point, for example, that by this time we have developed a body of knowledge and a set of patterns which allow us to improve our resource situation rather than make it worse, even as we use resources and even in the absence of an exchange mechanism.

Thus, I think we can with confidence expect to observe greater rather than less availability of resources with the passage of time, whether it be arable land or oil or whatever, just as we observe in the trends in the past. If I am correct, we now have systematic grounds to believe that we are not at a turning point in resource history caused by man's propensity to destroy rather than create. Rather, humankind is on balance creator rather than destroyer.

Here we return to figure 1-2, and ask how Earl Cook went wrong with respect to forecasting the price of mercury. Cook did exactly what I recommend—he looked at the longest possible data series. But that did not save him from error. In contrast, why did my predictions for metals prices succeed? Part of the explanation is that he paid attention to a short-run reversal in the trend. But in addition to the data, it can help to bear a general vision—a theory, if you like. My general vision is stated just above—that on balance we create more than we use. Cook's general vision is Malthusian, that resources are finite and eventually must run out—the same vision that inspired *Limits to Growth*. The very different success records of Cook's and *Limits to Growth*'s and my own forecasts provide some basis for judging which general vision is more helpful.

Entropy and Finiteness: The Irrelevant Dismal Theory

Concepts of physics are frequently misused by those who become intoxicated by casual acquaintance with them. After Einstein discovered the principle of special relativity, college sophomores and trendy preachers cited the principle as "proof" that "everything is relative." And after Heisenberg discovered the uncertainty principle, social scientists, humanists, and theologians seized on it to "prove" that certain kinds of human knowledge are impossible.

The concept of entropy and the associated second law of thermodynamics have a long history of abuse—even by physicists, who should know better. Nonsensical ideas hitched onto the second law—including the concept of "energy accounting," which is discussed in the afternote to chapter 12—are still with us, today perhaps more strongly than ever. The cover of a paperback named *Entropy* says, "Entropy is the supreme law of nature and governs everything we do. Entropy tells us why our existing world is crumbling."[1] And persons (such as I) who assert that there is no known ultimate limit to population growth and human progress are said by energy accountants to err because of our supposed ignorance of these laws of physics.

The second law of thermodynamics asserts that in a *closed system* (please note those crucial two words), the random disorder of energy-charged particles must increase over time. The faster the particles move, and the more energy that is used in movements and collisions, the faster the movement away from order and toward disorder. If, for example, you start with some pattern of molecules—say, two gases at opposite ends of a box—they will increasingly mix with each other and spread more uniformly throughout the box.

The doomsters extrapolate from this simple idea to the belief that the more fuel that humans use in current decades, the sooner our species must come to an end for lack of energy to maintain a patterned existence. (And let there be no doubt that they envision an eventual demise.) The concept of the second law underlies a vision of the human condition as inexorably sliding toward the worse in the long run. Ours is a closed universe, they assume, and within such a closed system entropy necessarily increases. Nothing can avail against this tendency toward decreasing order, increasing disorder, and a return to chaos—to the formless and shapeless void described in the first words of Genesis.

This vision is emphasized in the frequent appearance of the term "finite" in the literature of the environmental-cum-population-control movement. The vision is set forth well by the noted mathematician Norbert Weiner, who at least viewed the grim future with an attitude of Whitmanesque nobility rather than of panic.

> [W]e are shipwrecked passengers on a doomed planet. Yet even in a shipwreck, human decencies and human values do not necessarily vanish, and we must make the most of them. We shall go down, but let it be in a manner to which we may look forward as worthy of our dignity.[2]

This vision is embodied in the policy recommendations for our everyday political life offered by Nicholas Georgescu-Roegen with the approval of Paul Samuelson, and of Herman Daly, who urge that we should budget our energy and other resources with an eye to optimum allocation over the eons until the system runs down.[3]

The accompanying political agenda implies greater central planning and governmental control. It is not clear whether a desire to impose more control leads people to believe that the second law is the appropriate model for human activity or whether doomsters tend to be people who fear disorder in the first place and therefore concern themselves with constructing methods of controlling aspects of our social world so as to fight such disorder. Whichever is so, the same persons consistently invoke both sorts of ideas.

The common estimated date of the fearsome end of our cosmos is seven billion years or so from now. The doomsters say that we should therefore be taking steps right now to defer the supposed grim end. (Yes, you read right. And yes, so help me, they are serious.)

The concept of entropy is unquestionably valid and relevant for a closed container in the laboratory. It may also be relevant for any larger entity that can reasonably be considered a closed system. But it is quite unclear where the boundary should be drawn for discussions of the quantity of energy, or if there is any relevant boundary. It is clearly wrong to say that "as to the scarcity of matter in a closed system, such as the earth, the issue may, in my opinion, prove in the end more critical than that of energy";[4] the Earth is not a closed system because both energy (from the sun) and matter (cosmic dust, asteroids, debris from many planets) constantly rain down on the Earth. Perhaps the solar system will prove to be an isolated system for some period in the future, conceivably for the entire life of the human species. But even then it will last perhaps seven billion years. And the chances would seem excellent that during that span of time humans will be in touch with other solar systems, or will find ways to convert the matter on other planets into the energy we need to continue longer. So with respect to energy there is no practical boundary surrounding any unit of interest to us. And without such a boundary, the notion of entropy in the large is entirely irrelevant to us.*

At the conceptual level of the universe—and there is no reason to discuss any smaller entity in the present context of discussion—it is quite unclear whether the concept of increasing entropy is relevant. Stephen Hawking, as eminent a student of these matters as there is in the world, has gone back and forth in his thinking on whether entropy would eventually increase or decrease.[5] His judgment hangs on such matters as whether the universe is finite and/or bounded. His present view is that space-time is finite but the "boundary condition of the universe is that it has no boundary." And he underlines the uncertainty of our knowledge by writing that "I'd like to emphasize that this idea that space and time should be finite without boundary is just a *proposal*."[6] And in any case, he concludes that the nature of our "subjective sense of the direction of time . . . makes the second law of thermodynamics almost

---

* There is in me a pixy-ish (or quixotic) propensity to make it even more difficult than necessary for you to believe the ideas herein. In that spirit: Paul Samuelson, the first American Nobel Prize winner in economics, called Georgescu-Roegen "a scholar's scholar, an economist's economist" in an admiring foreword to a 1966 book of Roegen's that Samuelson says is "a book to own and savor." In my view, this just shows how great talents can swear to nonsense when the nonsense is framed in the "difficult art" (Samuelson's phrase) of mathematical economics.

trivial." These considerations, together with his assessment that "the total energy of the universe is zero"[7] because of the balance of positive and negative energies, added to Hawking's portrayal of the state of thought in physics as thoroughly unsettled on all these cosmological questions (and which may stay unsettled forever because of the difficulty of knowing how many universes there are), would seem more than enough reason to make it ridiculous for us to concern ourselves with saving energy now to stave off for a few hundred years the possible winking out of civilization seven billion years from now.

Roger Penrose, another eminent English physicist, says, "We do not know whether the universe as a whole is finite or infinite in extent—either in space or in time—though such uncertainties would appear to have no bearing whatsoever on physics at the human scale."[8] Other physicists argue in journals about whether it is possible for life to continue forever.[9]

These comments by Hawking and Penrose should be sobering to the many persons who would like government to regulate our daily behavior on the basis of what they believe are the laws of physics. The frequent assertion that *of course* our resources are finite is quite inconsistent with the fact that present scientific knowledge of our physical world is extraordinarily incomplete (and probably always must be). One must wear very tight blinders not to be humbled by reading such accounts in the press as that recent discoveries in astronomy "have punctured almost flat the leading theories on how the first stars and galaxies were born." According to Stephen Maran, a spokesman for the American Astronomical Society, "The field is in disarray. All the leading theories are wrong."[10] Yet an economist and a theologian[11] are sure enough of their understanding of the universe that they advise the government to pressure us to ride bicycles now to budget energy for the next seven billion or so years. Boggles the mind.

Though I earlier quoted Hawking in the service of my argument, I also wish to indicate an inconsistency in his thought which makes my argument even stronger. He insists firmly that "the real test [of science] is whether it makes predictions that agree with observation."[12] But whereas the second law implies decreasing order, from the point of view of human beings all our observations record a long-term increase rather than a decrease in disorder, no matter what quantities we look at. The increases in complexity of living things throughout geological time, and of human society throughout history, are the most important examples, of course. Biologically—as is suggested by the very word "evolution"—the Earth has changed from a smaller number of species of simple creatures toward a larger number of complex and ordered creatures. Geologically, the activities of human beings have resulted in a greater heaping up of particular materials in concentrated piles, for example, the gold in Fort Knox and in gold jewelry compared to the gold in streams, or the steel in buildings and junk piles compared to the iron and other ores in the ground. The history of human institutions describes ever more complex modes of organization, a more extensive body of law, richer languages, a more ramified corpus of knowledge, and a greater range of human movement throughout the universe. All this suggests more order rather than less order in the human environment with the passage of time, and hence contradicts theories of increasing entropy.

The finitists assert that this empirical evidence is irrelevant because it describes only a temporary "local" increase in order, superimposed on the long-term decrease that they say *must* be taking place. And the basis for their "must" is their assumption about the operation of the second law. But again, all the empirical evidence shows an increase in order—which is consistent with the idea that Earth is not a closed system. Hence, Hawking's definition of science implies the conclusion that entropy will continue to decrease rather than increase in the human environment—Earth and any other planets we may choose to inhabit—as long as the laws of physics that are presently operative continue to hold.

The situation resembles a couple of ants sitting on the jungle floor, hesitating to eat a leaf lest by doing so they hasten the disappearance of the forest. One of them says, "We're only two small ants, and the forest is so large," but the other replies, "Yes, but what if all the ants thought that way?" and he carries the day. Indeed, the ants' actual knowledge of the life cycle of the forest may not be much inferior to humans' present knowledge of the life cycle of the set of universes that may exist (a set which may include only ours, of course).

The entropy conservers assume that others do not agree with them either due to simple ignorance of physics and the second law, or because of willful and dishonest disregard of it. Any other possibility seems unimaginable to them. As Garrett Hardin wrote to me, "I am appalled at your omission, misunderstanding, or denial of the second law of thermodynamics, conservation laws, the idea of limits."[13] And Paul Ehrlich writes, "One wonders if Simon could not at least find a junior high school science student to review his writings."[14] Perhaps the problem is that these biologists' own scientific armamentarium is based on the physics that is taught in "junior high school"—the state of the scientific art several decades ago, stripped of all subtlety and complexity.

The concept of entropy simply doesn't matter for human well-being. Our earthly island of order can grow indefinitely within the universal sea of chaos. Life could even spread from Earth to other planets, other galaxies, and so on, incorporating an increasing portion of the universe's matter and energy. What happens at the end of time is anybody's guess: the universe may or may not be bounded. Who cares? That's well beyond the lifetime of our sun. Logically, we should worry much more about the death of our own sun than the supposed limits imposed by entropy and the "laws" of physics.

I urge recognition of other intellectual possibilities. Even if the second law is correct—it's only a century or so old—there is left to humanity a period perhaps 50,000,000 times that long to discover new principles before the sun runs out. But as Hawking demonstrates, cosmologists are in controversy even about whether the universe should be viewed as closed or as open and expanding, which would seem to imply lack of agreement about the validity of the entropy viewpoint held by those who would have us conserve energy to forestall the universe's doom. Can it be sensible to proceed as if our present ideas will forever remain unchanged and unimproved?

Here it might be wise for the entropists to keep in mind the famous blunder of the great British physicist Lord Kelvin (of the Kelvin temperature scale, and presumably the namesake of Kelvinator refrigerators), who asserted at the turn of the century that just about every major principle of physics worth discovering had already been discovered; all that was left was to refine the measurements of the constants. At that time, just as now, it would not have been possible to "guarantee" that great new discoveries would be made. But the spectacular discoveries of the past century do not mean that there are fewer great discoveries in store for the next century (or for the next seventy million centuries). Discoveries, like resources, may well be infinite: the more we discover, the more we are *able* to discover.

The case of gravity is similar to entropy here. With a bit of schooling one can predict the course of an object released within a closed airless container in the laboratory; this has been known for hundreds of years, and we can act safely on the basis of this knowledge. But predicting the trajectory of, say, three objects in space, or the fate of anything in a black hole, still confounds the most learned physicists, and it would be foolish to make major policy decisions on the basis of such controversial assessments.

(Those who view some body of knowledge as unshakeable might keep in mind the amusing and not-so-amusing switches in scientific views that have occurred historically. A few examples: theories of the shape of the Earth, medical doctrine about leeching, belief that the elements are inviolate and that one metal cannot be transmuted into another, derision heaped on the microorganism theory of disease, and the shift within just a few years from dentists advising hard toothbrushes in an up-and-down motion to advising soft brushes in a horizontal motion.)

Indeed, a casual reading of lay science magazines shows that physicists are manufacturing new and competing theories of the cosmos at a very rapid rate. Just a few stray snippets: "For more than a decade now, the nascent field of particle astrophysics has grown like a garden gone wild."[15] Or "Astronomers Go Up Against the Great Wall: The discovery of this huge structure could undermine 'cold dark matter' theory of galaxy formation; but what is the alternative?"[16] And physicist David Layzer "argues that there is an indeterminacy set down in the order of things. He formulates what he calls the 'strong cosmological principle' against starker interpretations of the second law, arguing that even at the origin of the universe indeterminacy played an essential role. . . . Evolution becomes then an open rather than a closed system, offering always the possibility of freedom and surprise. Layzer's conclusion is optimistic: 'The new scientific worldview . . . assures us that there are no limits to what we and our descendants can hope to achieve and to become.'"[17]

Conclusion

Evolution, not entropy, is the appropriate theory for human development. The following chapters in Part One look at particular resources, documenting case after case of the general rule.

5

Famine 1995? Or 2025? Or 1975?

> Launcelot (*to Jessica*) [about her becoming a Christian and marrying Lorenzo]:
> We were Christians enow before; e'en as many as could well live, one by another.
> This making of Christians will raise the price of hogs; if we grow all to be pork eaters
> we shall not shortly have a rasher on the coals for money.
>   Jessica (*to Lorenzo*): He says you are no good member of the commonwealth; for
> in converting Jews to Christians, you raise the price of pork.
>   (*William Shakespeare*, The Merchant of Venice)

> Fraud, luxury, and pride must live,
> While we the benefits receive.
> Hunger's a dreadful plague, no doubt.
> Yet who digests or thrives without?
>   (*Bernard Mandeville*, Fable of the Bees)

THE INTRODUCTION noted that there has been a major shift in the consensus of economic scholars about population growth's effects in the past decade. But there has been no shift with respect to the subject of this chapter—the potential for food production. Rather, the overwhelming consensus of respected agricultural economists has *for many decades* been extremely optimistic.

The public has acquired a very different impression from reading the popular press and watching television, however. A small handful of doomsters, in conjunction with willing journalists, have managed to preempt so much attention that the upbeat mainstream scientific view about food has been subverted and obscured. On the rare occasion when the press reports the outlook as positive, it treats the matter as unexpected and amazing—even though the agricultural economists have been saying it all along. For example

> The world is producing more food than was ever before believed possible. Countries that a decade ago were thought incapable of feeding themselves are doing just that today. The entire world of agriculture is standing on the edge of unprecedented production explosion.[1]

It dismays one to find that respected publications such as the *New York Times* and the *Washington Post* consistently publish material which not only is quite wrong but opposes the mainstream scientific views. When I lived in

Champaign-Urbana, Illinois, I would read on the front page of the local *News-Gazette* about an "overpopulated" world running out of food, drawn from the *New York Times* wire service. Then on the *News-Gazette* farm page I would read of falling prices and farmers worrying about an international food glut. Journalistic schizophrenia.

Food is the gut issue (pun intended) in any book on resources and population. It has been so at least since Malthus. Even people who do not worry about the effect of economic growth or population growth on other resources worry about food. Indeed, such worry is commonsensical, just as it was commonsensical for Launcelot to worry (though in jest) about the scarcity of pork if Jews converted to Christianity. But common sense notwithstanding, this worry is quite misplaced and can be very damaging.

No matter how the food situation changes or how much information we have about it, no matter what the state of our knowledge about food productivity, the public view of food prospects is quite the same. To set the stage for the discussion, here are some quotations mostly from the late 1970s, when the first edition of this book was written. Though I collected a juicy crop then, I could as easily collect a crop now or from earlier eras; the ideas remain eerily the same.

One after the other, official and unofficial forecasts about the future food supply were frightening. In the 1970s, the UN Economic and Social Commission for Asia and the Pacific had predicted "500 million starvation deaths in Asia between 1980 and 2025."[2] And the head of the UN Food and Agriculture Organization (FAO) had said that "the long-term trends in the food production of developing countries remain alarmingly inadequate."[3]

A book-length survey by the staff of the *New York Times* had arrived at these purple-prose conclusions:

> From drought-besieged Africa to the jittery Chicago grain market, from worried Government offices in Washington to the partly-filled granaries of teeming India, the long-predicted world food crisis is beginning to take shape as one of the greatest peace-time problems the world has had to face in modern times.
>
> While there have always been famines and warnings of famine, food experts generally agree that the situation now is substantially different. The problem is becoming so acute that every nation, institution, and every human being will ultimately be affected.[4]

Population/Environment Balance* paid for a full-page advertisement in leading newspapers, signed by such dignitaries as author Isaac Asimov, presidential adviser Zbigniew Brzezinski, author Malcolm Cowley, ecologist Paul Ehrlich, editor Clifton Fadiman, oilman J. Paul Getty, Time Inc. executive

---

* Then called The Environmental Fund.

Henry Luce III, poet Archibald MacLeish, Nobel prize winner Albert Szent-Gyorgyi, *Reader's Digest* founder DeWitt Wallace, U.A.W. President Leonard Woodeock, and many others, saying:

> The world as we know it will likely be ruined before the year 2000 and the reason for this will be its inhabitants' failure to comprehend two facts. These facts are
> 1. World food production cannot keep pace with the galloping growth of population.
> 2. "Family planning" cannot and will not, in the foreseeable future, check this runaway growth.[5]

C. P. Snow used the novelist's art to dramatize the matter: "Perhaps in ten years, millions of people in the poor countries are going to starve to death before our very eyes. We shall see them doing so upon our television sets."[6] And the School of Public Affairs of Princeton was offering a course on "Problems of World Hunger" based on the premise that "Hunger has never been known on such a world-wide scale as today."[7]

Similar examples of widely publicized alarming forecasts could be multiplied by the dozens. Perhaps the most influential was the opening of Paul Ehrlich's best-selling 1968 book, *The Population Bomb*: "The battle to feed all of humanity is over. In the 1970's the world will undergo famines—hundreds of millions of people are going to starve to death."[8]

Even schoolchildren "know" that the food situation has been worsening and that the world faces an impending crisis. If you doubt it, ask a few children of your acquaintance. A book for children puts it thus:

> When man first began to farm, there were fewer than 5 million people on earth, and it took more than a million years for the population to reach that figure. But populations increase geometrically—that is, they double (2, 4, 8, 16, 32, etc.). Food supplies, in contrast, increase only arithmetically, a much slower process (2, 4, 6, 8, 10, 12, etc.). . . .
>
> If the population continues to explode, many people will starve. About half of the world's population is underfed now, with many approaching starvation.[9]

Many writers think the situation is so threatening that they call for strong measures to restrict population growth, "compulsion if voluntary methods fail," as Ehrlich puts it.[10]

Some influential people even urge "triage—letting the least fit die in order to save the more robust victims of hunger."[11] The 1967 book by William and Paul Paddock (*Famine—1975!*) applied this World War I medical concept to food aid, resulting in such judgments as

Haiti	Can't-be-saved
Egypt	Can't-be-saved
The Gambia	Walking Wounded

Tunisia	Should Receive Food
Libya	Walking Wounded
India	Can't-be-saved
Pakistan	Should Receive Food[12]

This was Ehrlich's assessment in 1972:

> Agricultural experts state that a tripling of the food supply of the world will be necessary in the next 30 years or so, if the 6 or 7 billion people who may be alive in the year 2000 are to be adequately fed. Theoretically such an increase might be possible, but it is becoming increasingly clear that it is totally impossible in practice.[13]

This tiny sample should be plenty to establish that frightening food forecasts have dominated the mass media.

Happily, none of these terrible events has occurred. Instead, people have been increasingly better fed, and lived longer and longer lives, since those forecasts were made.

The record of food production entirely contradicts the scary forecasts. The world trend in recent decades shows unmistakably an increase in food produced per person, as seen in figure 5-1.

Progress in food production has not been steady, of course. The first draft of this material, for publication in my technical 1977 book,[14] was written in 1971 and 1972, when food production was having its worst time in recent decades. And some countries' experiences have been tragically different from the general trend, usually because of politics and war. (More about these

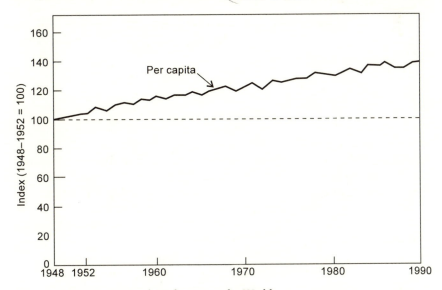

Figure 5-1. Per Capita Food Production in the World

special cases later.) Yet there has been no year, or series of years, so bad as to support a conclusion of long-term retrogression.

A person who sees figure 5-1 sometimes asks, "Where are the other data?" When I ask, "Which other data?" the questioner may reply, "The data the other folks quote to support their worried forecasts."

There simply are no other data. The starting date of the series shown here is the earliest given in the basic sources, chosen by them and not by me; this should reassure you that the starting date was not chosen arbitrarily so as to rig the results. (Such rigging, however, is not unknown in these discussions, as we shall see in chapter 7.) The data shown in figure 5-1 were published by the U.S. Department of Agriculture and the United Nations and were collected by the UN from individual countries. Of course the data are far less reliable than one would like; economic data usually are. But these are the only official data. Standard data that would show a worsening trend in recent decades do not exist. If you doubt it, write to the authors of frightening forecasts, to the UN, or to the USDA. Or even better, go to your local library and examine such basic reference sources as *Statistical Abstract of the United States* and the United Nations Food and Agricultural Organization's *Production Yearbook*.

Indeed, figure 5-1 understates the extent of the improvement in world food supply. Because it shows food *production*, it does not take into account the increase in the amount of food that actually reaches *consumers* due to lower losses over the years as a result of improvements in transportation and storage. It should also be remembered that production could immediately be enlarged if the United States were to stop paying farmers to idle their land instead of planting crops.

Let's examine the very long-run price trends for food, just as we did for copper in chapter 1. Figure 5-2 shows that the real price of wheat—the market price adjusted for inflation—has fallen over the long haul despite the great increase in demand due to both a growing world population and rising incomes. The rise in food output was so great as to cause grain to become cheaper despite the large increases in demand. More startling still, figure 5-2 shows how the price of wheat has fallen by another measure—relative to wages in the United States.

How did total output, and productivity per worker and per acre, gain so fast? Food supply increased because of agricultural knowledge resulting from research and development that was induced by the increased demand, together with the improved ability of farmers to get their produce to market on better transportation systems. (These sentences are a lightning-fast summary of forces that take many books to document well.)

This all-important historical trend toward cheaper food, which probably extends back to the beginning of agriculture, implies that real prices for food will continue to drop—a fact that dismays American farmers and causes them to tractorcade to Washington.

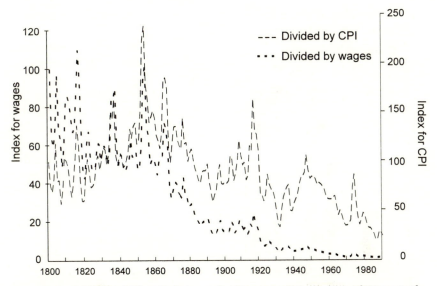

Figure 5-2. The Price of Wheat Relative to the Consumer Price Index and Wages in the United States

Despite the mass-media consensus that we are heading toward agricultural crisis, and though (as we saw in chapter 3) earlier on even famous economist John Maynard Keynes[15] entirely misunderstood the long-run economics of agriculture because he was misled by the idea of diminishing returns, the mainstream view among agricultural economists has for decades been that the trend is toward improvement in the food supplies of almost every main segment of the world's population. For example, D. Gale Johnson could say in an authoritative review (even in 1974):

> [T]he increase of the food supply has at least matched the growth of population in the developing countries, taken as a group, for the past four decades. This has been a period of very rapid population growth in the developing countries. . . . Thus the recent achievement in expanding food supplies in the developing countries has been a significant one. . . .there has been a long term gradual improvement in per capita food consumption over the past two centuries.[16]

And in a 1975 "compendium," the agricultural economists spoke nearly in a single voice, "The historical record lends support to the more optimistic view."[17]

The consensus of agricultural-economic projections confuted the popular doomsday beliefs with calm assessments even at the height of the poor harvests and food worries in the early 1970s. (Since then, conditions have improved even more sharply.)

**The [misleading] disproportions
of people and food**

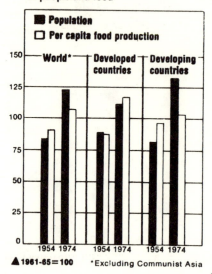

Figure 5-3a. Typical Misleading Diagram
on Food Supply

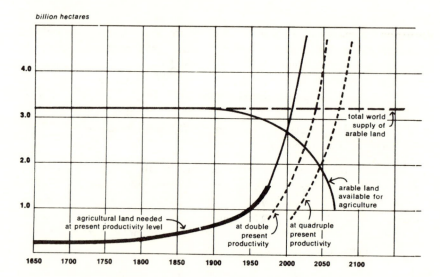

Figure 5-3b. Typical Misleading Diagram on Food Supply

It is a simple fact, then, that the world food supply has been improving. But it is also a fact that people resolutely ignore this silver lining and instead try harder to find the cloud. Consider, for example, this statement from a technical article: "During the last 25 years or so the average rate of increase of world food production has steadily deteriorated . . . it fell from 3.1 percent in the 1950's to 2.8 percent in the 1960's and 2.2 percent in the first half of the 1970's."[18] The apparent changes may not even have been statistically meaningful, but leave that aside. The word "deterioration" suggests that the world food situation was getting worse. But the data tell us only that the gain—the *improvement*—was greater in the 1950s than later. That is quite different than things getting worse.

Consider also figure 5-3, taken from *Business Week*. At first glance it seems to show population growing faster than food. That would imply a fall in food per capita, a bad sign. But on close inspection we see that food per capita has increased, a good sign. It is thoroughly misleading to put a total figure (population) next to a per-capita figure (food per capita). Why is it done? People apparently want to believe, and want to tell others, that the world food situation is getting worse even though it is really getting better. (And journalists get more mileage out of bad-news stories.)

Famines

A famine report written around 1317:

> Because nothing but weeds grew in the fields, and provisions in the town were all consumed, many people sickened and died of starvation. They lay in the streets surrounded by so many dead that in Erfurt the carts were halted so that the cadavers could be loaded on to them and conveyed to Schmiedistedt where sundry graves had been prepared, and here the survivors buried them.[19]

That sort of Malthusian famine happily is long gone. Yet fear of famine is rife—as it has been since the beginning of agriculture.

The historical trend of famines is another important index of how well the world's food supply has been doing. Famine is difficult to define and measure operationally, however, because when nutrition is poor, many people die of diseases and not directly of starvation. Traditionally, historical research on famine simply counts as a famine an event that people living in a particular time referred to as a famine. Though that is skimpy evidence, there is no reason to believe that such accounts have been affected by a bias that would distort the long-term record. Therefore, historians' studies of the occurrence of famines would seem to have considerable validity for our purposes.

Johnson summarizes the incidence of famines as follows, as of the early 1970s:

> Both the percentage of the world's population afflicted by famine in recent decades and the absolute numbers have been relatively small compared with those occurring in those earlier periods of history of which we have reasonably reliable estimates of famine deaths.
>
> There has been a rather substantial reduction in the incidence of famine during the past century. During the last quarter of the nineteenth century perhaps 20 million to 25 million died from famine. [Despite the much larger population now.] For the entire twentieth century to the present, there have been probably between 12 million and 15 million famine deaths, and many, if not the majority, were due to deliberate governmental policy, official mismanagement, or war and not to serious crop failure. . . .[20]
>
> While there have been some deaths due to famine in the third quarter of the 20th century, it is highly unlikely that the famine-caused deaths equal a tenth of the period 75 years earlier.
>
> There has not been a major famine, such as visited China and India in the past, during the past quarter century. There have been some near misses, such as in India in 1965–66, and the current sad situation in Africa should not be ignored because a relatively small population is involved. But the food supply has been far more secure for poor people during the past quarter century than at any other comparable period in the last two or three centuries.[21]

Since the above passage was written, evidence has come to light that perhaps seven million Ukrainians (plus other Soviet citizens) died of famine in the early 1930s,[22] and perhaps 30 million Chinese died of famine from 1958 to 1961.[23] I suggest you read again the numbers in the previous sentence and try to grasp their enormity. The death rate in China jumped from around 11 per thousand in 1957 and 1958 to over 25 per thousand in 1960, and then fell immediately back to 11 or below by 1962 and thereafter,[24] due to the fall in calories from above 2000 per person in 1957 to below 1500 in 1960; food consumption then rose again to its previous level.[25]

The evidence is overwhelming and transparent that those famines were caused by government policies—deliberate murder in the case of Stalin, and wrong-headed economics in the case of China. Most conclusive is the large increase in food produced in China immediately after policies changed toward economic freedom in agriculture, as seen in figure 5-4. As soon as the Chinese government allowed the transformation of agriculture to essentially private enterprise at the end of the 1970s—the largest rapid social change in all of history, involving perhaps 700 million people—production soared.

All throughout China's history, even when the population was only a fraction of what it is now, Chinese food production has struggled to just suffice. But now, production is so great that in response to agriculture failure in the

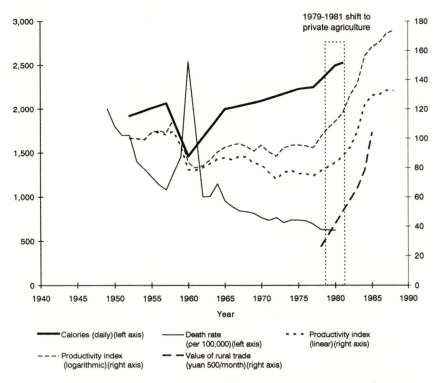

Figure 5-4. Economic System, Productivity, Mortality, and Nutrition in China, 1952–1988

Soviet Union, in 1991 China shipped grain and meat to the Soviets.[26] More about Chinese and Soviet food production in chapter 7.

The irony of the food shipments from China to Russia, and the tragic famines of the past in China and the Soviet Union, reinforce the general conclusion that humanity need never again suffer from peacetime famine caused by natural conditions. Rather, modern famine will take place only in a society that abolishes individual farmers and puts farms under government ownership and the control of bureaucrats.

Do you wonder how these optimistic trends can be reconciled with the pictures of starving children you have seen in national magazines, and with the longstanding myth that "a lifetime of malnutrition and actual hunger is the lot of at least two-thirds of mankind"? This much-quoted FAO statement was made by the FAO director in 1950, within a year of the organization's founding and in the aftermath of World War II, on the basis of no data at all. (The claim soon became the children's-book cliche that "about half of the world's population is underfed now, with many approaching starvation.")[27] After some research the UN reduced its estimate of people in "actual hunger" to

10–15 percent of mankind. But even this estimate was (and is) far too high. Furthermore, the term "malnutrition" is sufficiently vague that it could include the diets of any of us.[28]

Casual as the original FAO conjecture was, a large amount of study has been required to lay it to rest in a scientific cemetery. Yet even now the original statement comes back again and again in current discussion.

But—"The death of a single human being from starvation is an unspeakable human tragedy." That common expression implies that even if the food supply is improving, it would be better to reduce the world's population so that *no* person would die from starvation. The value judgments that underlie this idea will be analyzed in chapters 38 and 39. Here, let us note that if death from starvation is an "unspeakable human tragedy," then death from an auto accident or a fire must also be the same sort of tragedy. But what are the implications for social action? The only way to avoid all such deaths is to have no people. Surely that cannot be intended. Hence this sort of phrase, heartfelt though it may be, really tells us nothing about what should be done.

Paradoxically, greater population density apparently leads to *less* chance of famine. A concentrated population builds better roads and transportation, and better transportation is the key factor in preventing starvation. Consider a reporter's account of the 1970s famine in the Sahel in West Africa.

> "Sure, the food is pouring in," observed British Red Cross liaison officer George Bolton, "but how the hell are we going to get it to the people who need it? There isn't a tarred road within a thousand miles of Juba." Bolton wasn't exaggerating. While I was in Juba, I witnessed the arrival of 5,000 gallons of cooking oil, which had been diverted from the nearby state of Rwanda. Since the rickety old ferry was not strong enough to carry the oil shipment across the White Nile so it could be distributed to the needy in the interior, the oil was promptly unloaded on the riverbank and stored in Juba.
>
> And this was not an isolated incident. I saw warehouses in Juba overflowing with millet, dried fish, cooking utensils, agricultural tools and medical supplies—all useless because nothing could be delivered to the people who needed it.[29]

The Sahel is a classic case study of food, population, and public relations. *Newsweek*, on September 19, 1977, asserted that "more than 100,000 West Africans perished of hunger" between 1968 and 1973 due to drought. Upon inquiry, writer Peter Gwynne informed me that the estimate came from a speech by UN Secretary-General Kurt Waldheim. I therefore wrote to Waldheim asking for the source of the estimate. A remarkable packet of three documents came back from the UN Public Inquiries Unit: (1) Waldheim's message, saying, "Who can forget the horror of millions of men, women and children starving, with more than 100,000 dying, because of an ecological calamity that turned grazing land and farms into bleak desert?" (2) A two-page excerpt from a memo by the UN Sahelian Office, dated November 8, 1974, saying, "It is not possible to calculate the present and future impact of this tragedy, on the populations. . . . Although precise figures are not available indeed unobtainable . . . certainly there has been an extensive and tragic loss of life. . . ." (3) One page by Helen Ware, a respected Australian expert on African demography and a visiting fellow at the University of Ibadan in March 1975, when her memo was written specifically for the UN. Ware calculated the normal death rate for the area, together with "the highest death rate in any group of nomads" during the drought. Her figures made nonsense of the other two documents. She figured that "at an absolute, and most improbable, upper limit a hundred thousand people who would not otherwise have died, succumbed to the effects of famine. . . . Even as a maximum [this estimate] represents an unreal limit."

Ware's figures, which flatly gave the lie to the UN secretary-general's well-publicized assessment, were on page one of a document written for, and sent out by, the UN itself well before the UN Desertification Conference was held and Waldheim's message was publicized. Apparently, it was the only calculation the UN had. But it was ignored. Later, UN press releases retreated to the more modest, but still unprovable, assertion that "tens of thousands" died.[30] Ware's comment, "The problem with deaths in the Sahel is precisely that there was so little evidence of them—rather like the photograph of the dead cow which kept turning up in illustrations to every newspaper story."[31]

As the first edition of this book was in press (July 10, 1980), the Associated Press was crediting the UN with asserting that a forthcoming "permanent food crisis will be deeper than the 1972–74 drought, when 300,000 or more died in Ethiopia and the Sahel belt south of the Sahara."[32] Since then even more inflated numbers have appeared.

(When in 1980 I first wrote about this event in *Science*, I was criticized for writing in an unflattering fashion about such a great man as Kurt Waldheim. Readers said that they simply could not disbelieve a statement coming from such a credible source. Since then Waldheim has been proven an enthusiastic member of the Nazi party, an army officer involved in war crimes, and a liar about his personal history. So much for his greatness and his credibility.)

One might keep the Sahel-Waldheim incident in mind when reading accounts of current famines in Africa. Luckily, even the press has finally gotten the word—which the entire profession of agricultural economics has known for many decades. As *Science* headlined the story in 1991, "Famine: Blame Policy, Not Nature." The most influential scientific journal in the world asked, "Only one region of the world still suffers from widespread famine—Africa. Why is that?" It then breathlessly announced the finding that "the conventional wisdom holds that the answer is a combination of droughts, deforestation, and war." But "a new 4-year study" concludes that "the responsibility for pushing poor people over the edge into starvation lies largely with a network of social and political factors."[33]

This item is typical of African famines of our era:

While They Starve

The Government of Ethiopia has so severely restricted emergency relief operations in the country's north, a region ravaged by both drought and war, that as many as two million people are out of reach of any known system of food distribution, aid officials and Western diplomats say.

Because of the restrictions, these officials say, hundreds of thousands of tons of donated food are piling up at ports and may never reach those in need. Agricultural seeds, too, are not being distributed. This means that farmers who must soon plant crops cannot do so, which could lead to even greater problems next year.[34]

The press still hasn't grasped the core of the issue. The *Science* story quoted just above goes on to recommend "rural public works projects," "improved seeds, fertilizers, and agricultural extension services" and the like. That is all good stuff. But the key is much simpler: economic freedom, meaning private ownership and free agricultural markets. Without that, the improved seeds and fertilizers will end up wasted, just as in Russia.

Conclusions

This chapter does not suggest that complacency about the food supply is in order, or that hunger is not a problem. Some people are starving. And, although not starving, most people would like to be able to purchase a more expensive diet than they now enjoy (though for many of us a more expensive diet could be a less healthy one). But as we have seen, food has tended in the long run to become cheaper decade after decade, whether measured relative to the price of labor or even relative to consumer-goods prices.

6

What Are the Limits on Food Production?

As WE SAW in chapter 5, the cost of food has been declining in recent decades—which means that world food supplies have grown faster than human population, despite the well-publicized dire predictions. What about the future?

The Short-Run Outlook

It is not necessary or useful to discuss whether there is an "ultimate" limit to the supply of any natural resource, including food (as discussed in chapter 3). We know for sure that the world can produce vastly more food than it now does, especially in such low-income countries as India and Bangladesh, even with conventional methods. If India were to produce only at the high present productivity of Japan and Taiwan (which have much less land and a shorter growing season), and if Bangladesh were to produce only at the rate of Holland (which has similar flooding problems and a much shorter growing season), food production would increase dramatically in India and Bangladesh (see fig. 6-1).

More generally, with present technology and without moving toward the much higher yields found under experimental conditions, the world can more than feed any foreseeable population increase. There are a host of already well-proven techniques that could boost production immediately, including better storage facilities that would cut the perhaps 15–25 percent loss to pests and rot every year; improved production devices such as vacuums that suck up bugs instead of killing them with pesticides; and the host of individually small innovations that one can read about every month in farm magazines. Widespread adoption adds up to steady improvement, and yields seem to be accelerating rather than tapering off. An example of the long-term increases in productivity is shown in figure 6-2.

Of course, an increase in consumption imposes costs in the short run. But in the long run, population pressure reduces costs as well as improves the food supply in accord with the general theory, which I'll repeat again: More people, and increased income, cause problems of increased scarcity of resources in the short run. Heightened scarcity causes prices to rise. The higher prices present opportunity, and prompt inventors and entrepreneurs to search for solutions. Many fail, at cost to themselves. But in a free society, solutions are eventually

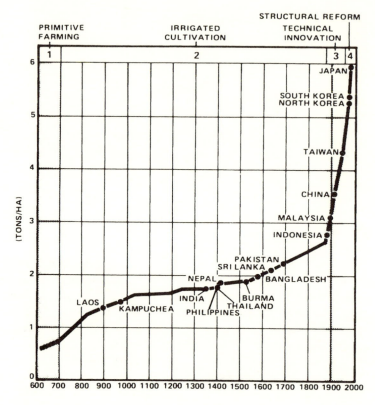

Figure 6-1. Current Rice Yields in Selected Asian Countries, with Japanese History of Yields

found. And in the long run the new developments leave us *better off than if the problems had not arisen.* That is, prices end up lower than before the increased scarcity occurred, which is the long-run history of food supply.

Some people wonder whether we can be *sure* that food production will increase, and whether it would be "safer" to restrict population growth until the increase is realized. But food production increases only in response to demand; farmers will not grow more food until the demand warrants it— either the number of mouths in a subsistence household, or the price in the market. Furthermore, one can predict with great confidence the *average* yields a few years hence in such countries as the United States by looking at the *record* yields for the present year; historically, the average catches up to the record yields only several years later.

The twin keys to this advancement in the agriculturally productive countries are twofold: (1) The existence of new knowledge, and educated people to take advantage of it. (2) Economic freedom. The ability of the world to increase production when there is a profitable opportunity to do so is amazing.

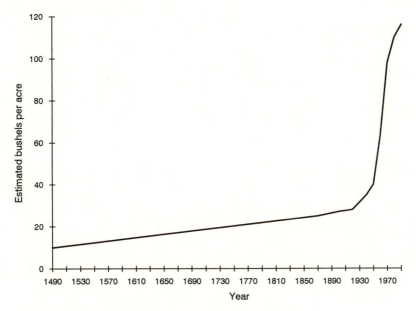

Figure 6-2a. North American Corn Yields, 1490–1990

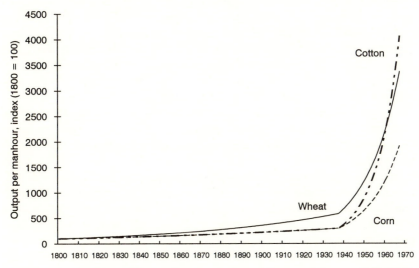

Figure 6-2b. U.S. Farm Labor Productivity in Corn, Wheat, and Cotton, 1800–1967

The Long-Run Outlook

In addition to the already-proven methods of raising output, there are many promising scientific discoveries at the research stage. In the first edition of this book a decade ago, these methods included such innovations as (a) orbiting giant mirrors that would reflect sunlight onto the night side of the Earth and thereby increase growing time, increase harvest time, and prevent crop freezes,[1] (b) meat substitutes made of soybeans that produce the nutrition and enjoyment of meat with much less resource input, and (c) hydroponic farming as described in the next paragraph. Such ideas may seem like unrealistic science fiction. But we should remember that tractors and wheeled irrigation pipes, which are making enormous contributions today, seemed quite unrealistic a hundred or fifty years ago. Furthermore, nowadays we have the capacity to estimate the chances of successful new developments much more accurately than we did in the past. When scientists predict that a process will be commercially successful within a given number of years, the likelihood of it being so is rather good.

Some radical improvements for the long run have already been well tested, and are not just a desperate last resort. In the environs of Washington, D.C., where I now live, there are a dozen or so small farms that raise vegetables hydroponically and sell them through supermarkets at premium prices because of their high quality. And this is commercially viable without subsidies from the government or from other divisions of a large firm. That is, this is not futuristic stuff, but right-now technology. You can read the names of the firms on the produce at the local supermarket. In fact, hydroponics is sufficiently practical that at least one supermarket has built a 10,000-square-foot vegetable garden inside its store to provide the freshest possible vegetables to its customers.[2] If the scarcity of farmland—as measured by the price of farmland—were to increase greatly, the potential production by hydroponic farming is enormous.

In the brief time since the first edition, the capacity of food-factory production has expanded to a degree almost beyond belief. On a space of perhaps 36 *square meters*—that is, a "plot" six meters or 18 feet on each side—with the use of artificial light, enough food can be raised to supply the calories for a single person, day in and day out.[3] (A less conservative estimate is that a plot 10 feet square will suffice. That is, a large bedroom in an ordinary U.S. house, 20 feet by 20 feet, would contain enough area to feed a family of four.)

You might think that though this is possible in a laboratory, practical development might be far in the future, or might never become practical—the way people think of fusion energy now. But farming at almost this level of land efficiency is already in commercial operation. In DeKalb, Illinois, Noel Davis's PhytoFarm produces food—mainly lettuce and other garden vegetables—in a factory measuring 200 feet by 250 feet—50,000 square feet, one acre, 0.4 hectares, 1/640 of a square mile—at a rate of a ton of food per day, enough to completely feed 500 or 1,000 people. This is not substantially below the experimental laboratory rates stated above. And PhytoFarm now does this without government subsidies.[4]

As a bonus, PhytoFarm produce is more attractive to chefs than other produce. It is unbruised, looks good, tastes good, and is more consistent day after day than crops grown in fields, especially in months when the produce must be brought from long distances.

Energy for artificial light is the key raw material in state-of-the-art hydroponics. Even at present electricity costs, PhytoFarm is profitable, and its food prices are affordable at ordinary American incomes. With improved power production from nuclear fission—or from fusion—costs will certainly drop in the future.

But let's go even further. With only a minor boost from artificial light—perhaps by a quarter of the total energy used by the plants—greenhouse tomato production in New Jersey is sufficiently profitable that only about a fiftieth of an acre is sufficient to feed a person fully.[5] This is about a tenth or twentieth as efficient as PhytoFarm, but still would allow food for the entire U.S. population to be produced on about a hundredth of present arable land, which is itself only a fraction of total U.S. land area. And if grain were raised instead of lettuce and tomatoes—which are now more profitable—much less space would be needed to supply the necessary nutrition.

This illustration makes irrelevant the assertion of some biologists that our food supplies are limited by the amount of sunlight falling on green plants.[6] They claim that 40 percent of the sunlight's "net primary production" is "used, co-opted, or foregone as a direct result of human activity" such as logging, farming, or paving over land in urban areas. Those calculations seem to suggest that humans are already at the margin of existence, since we must share the remaining 60 percent of the sun's "net primary production" with millions of other species. But as we have seen, not only can humans get by with very little agricultural space, if needed, but sunlight is not an ultimate constraint, because of the availability of nuclear or even non-nuclear power to make light. Right now, green plants capture less than 1 percent of the solar energy that strikes the Earth's surface. If we indeed "co-opt" 40 percent of that 1 percent, we could give it *all* back to the plants and still draw plenty of "natural" energy from sources like solar cells, wind, ocean currents, and other reservoirs of the untapped 99 percent.

To dramatize the findings a bit (and without worrying about the exact arithmetic because it does not matter), we can imagine the matter thusly: At the current efficiency of PhytoFarm, the entire present population of the world can be supplied from a square area about 140 miles on a side—about the area of Massachusetts and Vermont combined, and less than a tenth of Texas. This represents only about a thousandth as much land as is needed for agriculture at present (give or take a factor of four; for illustrative purposes greater exactitude is unnecessary). And if for some reason that seems like too much space, you can immediately cut the land space by a factor of ten: just build food factories ten stories high, which should present no more problems that a ten-story office building. You could economize even more and build a hundred stories high, like the Empire State Building or the Sears Tower. Then the surface area needed would be no more than the space within the corporate limits of Austin, Texas, to pick the first alphabetically among the many U.S. cities large enough.

PhytyoFarm techniques could feed a hundred times the world's present population—say 500 billion people—with factory buildings a hundred stories high, on 1 percent of present farmland. To put it differently, if you raise your bed to triple bunk-bed height, you can grow enough food on the two levels between the floor and your bed to supply your nutritional needs.

Does this surprise you? It hasn't been front-page news, but the capacity to feed people with an ever smaller small land surface has been developing rapidly for decades. In 1967 Colin Clark estimated that the minimum space necessary to feed a person was 27 square meters, a then-optimistic figure that had not been proven in commercial practice or even large-scale experiment.[7] Now a quarter of a century later there is commercial demonstration of land needs only a fifth or a tenth that large. It is most unlikely that this process of improvement will not continue in the future.

Only 200 years ago, half of the diet of Sauk and Mesquakie Native Americans came from hunting, and "It took 7,000 acres to support one human."[8] Phytofarm's one acre, which supports 500 or 1,000 people, represents an increase in productivity per acre a million times over compared with the Native Americans (see fig. 6-3).

Nor is this any "ultimate" limit. Rather, these gains are just the result of research over the past few decades, and there is no reason to think that future research in the next century or the next seven billion years could not greatly multiply productivity. It is likely that before the world gets to 500 billion people, or even to 10 billion, the maximum output per acre will be increased much beyond what PhytoFarm achieves now. The discussion so far does not take account of such existing technology as bovine growth hormone, which has no proven effect on humans yet greatly increases the yield of milk products.[9] Nor does the above assessment reflect such innovations as genetically engineered plants, which will surely produce huge commercial gains in the next century.[10] For example, rapeseed output can already be boosted 15 to 30 percent with genetic engineering.[11]

The possibilities already shown to be feasible are astounding. For example, one might insert into a potato genes from a moth that affect the potato's

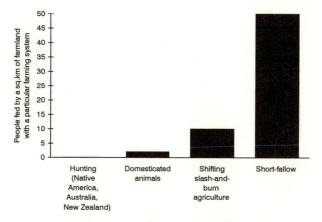

Figure 6-3a. Number of People Fed by a Square Kilometer of Land under Primitive Food-Production Systems

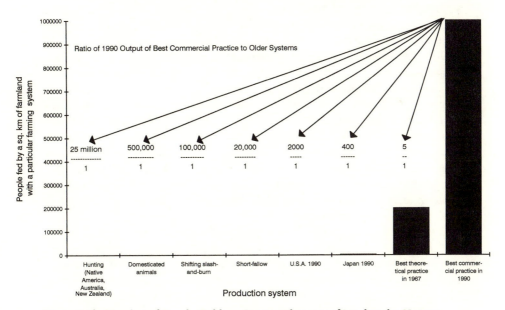

Figure 6-3b. Number of People Fed by a Square Kilometer of Land under Various Food-Production Systems

coloring.[12] Other genes might make proteins in a potato with the full comple-
ment of amino acids that humans need—giving the benefits of meat and potatoes by eating the potatoes alone. Please keep in mind that this technology has
been developed after only a few decades of work on the topic, and only a little
more than a century after the first scientific knowledge of genetics. Potential
progress in the future—even within the next few decades and centuries—is
awesome. Doomsaying forecasts about population growth outstripping the
food supply that take no account of these possibilities surely are seriously
inadequate.

Food from Fish

Fish crops are not fundamentally different from field crops. Based on a few
years of data, the *Global 2000 Report* issued the influential forecast that the
world fish catch had hit its limit—"leveled off in the 1970s at about 70 million
metric tons a year."[13] But by 1988 the catch had reached 98 million tons a
year, and it is still rising rapidly.[14]

No limit to the harvest of wild varieties of seafood is in sight. Yet fish farms
have begun to produce at or near competitive prices. A newspaper in the
1990s in Washington, D.C., advertised perch fillets from the North Atlantic
for $2.99, while aquacultured Tilapia and catfish were $3.99 and $4.99 re-
spectively. The aquacultured products sell well enough at these prices to be
displayed prominently. And there is every reason to believe that with additional experience, aquaculture costs and hence prices will fall. Indeed, the
main obstacle to a rapid increase in aquaculture is that wild fish are too cheap
to invite more competition. The price of cultured catfish has fallen greatly
already. Farm-grown salmon has been so successful that it "has produced a
glut of massive proportions, which has brought down the wholesale price of
a gutted fish from $7 a pound to $4."[15] By 1992, the price to the fish farmer
was only 60 cents a pound.[16]

Aquaculture capacity can be expanded almost indefinitely. Land is a small
constraint, as catfish farming in Mississippi shows; present methods produce
about 3,000 pounds of fish per acre, an economic return far higher than for
field crops.[17] (The biggest obstacle to a large increase in catfish farming in
Texas is the federal subsidy to rice farmers that keeps them producing that
product instead of shifting the land to fish farming.)[18] And now systems that
raise fish intensively by piping in the necessary nutrients and piping out the
waste products, akin to hydroponic cropping, are being developed. The process goes on year-round indoors under controlled temperature conditions,
and can provide fish to restaurants and stores only hours after the catch.[19]

New technology can also expand the supply of seafood by producing artificial substitutes. Imitation lobster, made of Alaska pollock plus artificial lobster

flavor and almost indistinguishable from the real thing, sells for $4.00 per pound—vastly less than the price of real lobster. The same is true of artificial crab.

Why Is the Food Outlook Made to Seem Gloomy?

The reasons why we hear and believe so much false bad news about resources, environment, and population are so many and so complex that they require another volume to discuss (forthcoming soon, I hope). But a couple of comments about food in particular are needed.

It is puzzling why competent biologists go so wrong in their assessments of the food situation. They charge that people like me who are not biologists are by training disqualified from writing such material as this. But why is this so? What is it that they know (or don't know) that makes them believe that they understand the situation better than the rest of us, and that our calculations are not sound? An explicit explanation by one of them would be helpful.

Another curiosity is that even people who should know best about the wonderful long-run prospects for food production often fail to see the larger picture. Typically, Noel Davis of PhytoFarm—which makes land almost irrelevant as a factor of food production—comments that "each year the United States is losing an area of farmland greater in size than the state of Rhode Island."[20] Chapter 8 documents what nonsense this is. Of course, such an alarming assertion may be given as justification for the need to invest in one's own new technology. But still it reflects some belief in the conventional wisdom—which Davis's own work belies.

Still another cause of the common belief that food is a looming problem is the propensity for the news media to put a bad-news twist on even the best news. Catfish farming has been so successful in the United States in the 1980s that prices have fallen rapidly. This is a great boon to consumers, and is additional evidence of the long-run potential of fish farming. But the falling prices have naturally hurt the least efficient producers. So a front-page headline is "Fish Farms Fall Prey to Excess,"[21] and the story contains no suggestion that the overall impact is beneficial to American citizens and to all humanity.

Conclusions

The notion that we are facing a long-run food shortage due to increased population and a Malthusian shortage of land is now scientifically discredited. High-tech methods of producing vastly more food per acre will not be needed for decades or centuries. Only after population multiplies several more times will there be enough incentive to move beyond the present field cropping systems used in the more advanced countries. But beyond the shadow of a doubt, the knowledge now exists to support many times the present world's population *on less land than is now being farmed*—that is, even without expanding beyond our own planet.

Malthus might be rephrased thusly: Whether or not population grows exponentially, subsistence grows at an even faster exponential rate (largely but not entirely because of population growth). And capacity to improve other aspects of the standard of living, beyond subsistence, grows at a still faster exponential rate, due largely to the growth of knowledge.

The main reason why more food has not been produced in the past is that there was insufficient demand for more food. As demand increases, farmers work harder to produce crops and improve the land, and more research is done to increase productivity. This extra work and investment imposes costs for a while. But as we saw in chapter 5, food has tended in the long run to become cheaper decade after decade. That's why production and consumption per capita have been rising.

Will a "population explosion" reverse these trends? On the contrary. Population growth increases food demand, which in the short run requires more labor and investment to meet the demand. (There is always some lag before supply responds to additional demand, which may mean that some will suffer.) But in the foreseeable long run, additional consumption will not make food more scarce and more expensive. Rather, in the long run additional people actually cause food to be less scarce and less expensive.

Once again, the basic process portrayed in this book, applied to food: More people increase scarcity of food for a while. The higher prices prompt agronomical researchers and farmers to invent. The solutions that are eventually found cause food to be more available than before. (The population theme will be developed in Part Two.)

This conclusion presupposes a satisfactory social and economic system that will not prevent progress. The next chapter discusses which social and economic conditions will promote the fastest growth of food supplies.

Afternote

Monocropping

DURING the past ten thousand years of agriculture, humans have concentrated their farming efforts on only a few descendants of the many wild varieties that were formerly eaten. As of the 1970s, the annual production (millions of metric tons) of the top crops was: wheat, 360; rice, 320; maize ("corn" in U.S.), 300; potato, 300. Barley, sweet potato, and cassava were below 200 tons, and no other crop was more than 60 tons.[22] From this data, Jack Harlan and others inferred that the food situation had become more fragile than earlier in history, more vulnerable to catastrophic disaster with the failure of a single crop. This worry became one of the cliches of the 1970s, thrown at anyone who pointed out that nutrition had been improving in the world.

The idea that fewer crops means more fragile food supplies is contradicted by many centuries of human experience: the data show that famine mortality has fallen rather than risen. And when we examine the proposition analytically, it seems unwarranted. First, we notice that though the world's foods have become more concentrated in fewer varieties over the centuries, this does not imply the same for local consumption. The diet of an Indian villager is surely more diverse now than in the past (when a single locally grown crop constituted the overwhelming proportion of every person's diet), because villagers now have access to foods from outside the village, and income to purchase them. Indeed, one need only consider one's daily intake to see how much the sources of our food are much more diversified from all over the world than in past centuries, largely because of the improvement of transportation and of storage techniques such as refrigeration. The data on the size of grocery stores and the number of products carried in them belie the assertion that "the supermarket and quick-food services have drastically restricted the human diet in the U.S."[23]

Because of everyone's greater access to more widespread sources of food, chances are that even if *two* of the top four crops were completely wiped out for an entire year, there would be less effect upon people's nutrition than if only one crop had been wiped out in a past century, if only because a large proportion of our grains are fed to animals and could be redirected to humans. Reduction in agricultural variety would seem to be just one more false scare, which may have arisen simply because people cannot believe that such good things can happen without our having to pay nature a penance for our blessings.

In a telling observation, the same excellent scholar who produced the data adduced above but worried about reduction in variety noted that "Weeds are species or races that thrive in man-made habitats," and "[W]hat species thrives in man-made habitats better than *homo sapiens*? We are the weediest of all"[24] Just so. And our weedlike survival capacities increase from generation to generation rather than diminish, despite (or because of) such changes as reduction in the number of species cultivated in the world.

7

The Worldwide Food Situation Now:
Shortage Crises, Glut Crises,
and Government

Were we directed from Washington when to sow, & when to reap, we should soon want bread.
   (*Thomas Jefferson* in The Works of Thomas Jefferson, *1904*)

CHAPTER 6 took the long and broad view of food production—decades and centuries, for all of humanity—and found continuous improvement with no end in sight. But what about the short-run food alarms that we read about from time to time, often pertaining to particular countries or areas? What creates these real or apparent problems if the long-run trend shows continuous improvement?

In this chapter, we'll look first at the biggest problem agriculture faces—not natural disaster, but politics. Then, after discussing worldwide ups and downs in the food supply, and the special case of stockpiles, we'll examine the U.S. "crisis" of the early 1970s, and finally consider some other important countries.

Government Intervention

Which regime of political economy increases food supplies fastest? The first edition said that "almost all economists agree that a system of individual land-owning farmers operating in a politically stable free market, without price controls, leads to larger food production than does any other mode of organization," but I added, "Little about this can be known for certain." By 1993 enough evidence has accumulated to state: *We now can be perfectly certain* that the earlier assessment is entirely correct. Any country that gives to farmers a free market in food and labor, secure property rights in the land, and a political system that ensures these freedoms in the future will soon be flush with food, with an ever-diminishing proportion of its work force required to produce the food. In the United States, for example, less than 3 percent of the population now works in agriculture, down from (50 percent) a century and a half ago (see fig. 7-1).

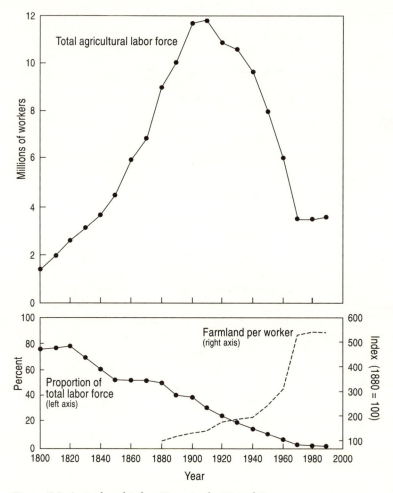

Figure 7-1. Agricultural Labor Force in the United States

Government intervention, however, is a very old story. In every era officials have sought to cleverly manipulate agriculture for one purpose or another, always under the guise of helping the public, but these intellectually arrogant schemes—illustrations of what Hayek calls the "fatal conceit" that rulers can increase production by central planning—always harm the public, and usually most harm the poor. For example, the Roman Emperor Julian imposed price ceilings on grain for the sake of the poor, which resulted in the rich getting even richer by buying up the available supplies on the cheap, and the poor having less food than before.[1]

Communal farming—another very old idea—was tried in America in Plymouth Colony. This was the aftermath:

All this while [during the communal raising of corn] no supply was heard of, neither knew they when they might expect any. So they began to think how they might raise as much corn as they could and obtain a better crop than they had done, that they might not still thus languish in misery. At length, after much debate of things, the governor (with the advice of the chief among them) gave way that they should set corn, every man for his own particular, and in that regard trust to themselves; in all other things to go on in the general way as before. And so [was] assigned to every family a parcel of land, according to the proportion of their number, for that end, only for present use (but made no division for inheritance), and ranged all boys and youth under some family. This had very good success, for it made all hands very industrious, so as much more corn was planted than otherwise would have been by any means the governor or any other could use, and saved him a great deal of trouble and gave far better content. The women now went willingly into the field, and took their little ones with them to set corn, which before would allege weakness and inability, whom to have compelled would have been thought great tyranny and oppression.

The experience that was had in this common course and condition, tried sundry years and that among godly and sober men, may well evince the vanity of that conceit of Plato's and other ancients applauded by some of later times—that the taking away of property and bringing in community into a commonwealth would make them happy and flourishing, as if they were wiser than God. . . . Let none object this is men's corruption, and nothing to the course itself. I answer, seeing all men have this corruption in them, God in His wisdom saw another course fitter for them.[2]

Another early American example was tobacco production in colonial Virginia.[3] When tobacco prices went up, immigration increased; more families arrived to establish new farms and grow more tobacco, which pushed output up and prices down for a while. So as early as 1629–1630 a control scheme arose. The authorities restricted to two thousand the number of tobacco plants that each family could cultivate.

The outcome was not quite as planned, however. Because they could not plant as much as they wanted, families spent their extra effort in growing *bigger* plants. This led them to break new ground near streams. But these plots were further away from their homes, and therefore at increased risk of Indian attack. This required that one-third of the workers had to stand guard, a high extra cost which reduced profit. And tensions with nearby Indians were raised.

Furthermore, prices fell anyway. The combination of lower prices and higher costs meant that the planters were losing money by 1639. So the authorities tried crop destruction schemes, which caused new problems. And so it has gone throughout human history.

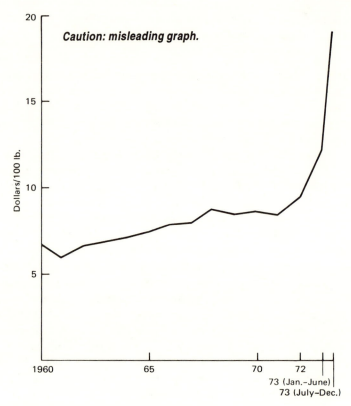

Figure 7-2a. How Brown's Short-Run Data Can Mislead: World Rice Prices, 1960–1973

Cycling between Glut and Shortage

Chapter 1 argued that price (and the cost of production, which is close to price over the long haul) is the most relevant index of scarcity for natural resources. By that test, the sharp rise in food prices in 1972–1973 indicated an increasing food scarcity. Figure 7–2 shows how the situation looked then to doomster Lester Brown. This sudden increase in price was indeed interpreted as a bad sign by a great many consumers, who saw it as a harbinger of a great crisis to come.

For better understanding of the causes and meaning of the sharp rise in food prices in the early 1970s, however, look at the longer historical perspective in figure 5-2a. The 1970s price jump was just another fluctuation. The intellectual practice of focusing on a very short period which runs against the long-term trend—but which fits with one's preconceptions—has been the

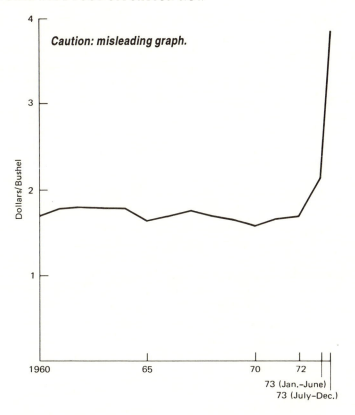

Figure 7-2b. How Brown's Short-Run Data Can Mislead: World Wheat Prices, 1960–1973

most frequent cause of error in understanding the relationship of natural resources to population growth and human progress.

The real price of wheat—the market price adjusted for inflation—clearly has fallen over the long haul. This price decline surprises many people, especially in light of the great increase in demand over the decades and centuries due both to world population increases and to world income increases. Yet the rise in food output was so great as to cause grain to become cheaper despite the large increases in demand. The even more amazing figure 5-2b shows how the price of wheat has fallen by an even more important measure—relative to wages in the United States.

(Supply, measured by total output and by productivity per worker and per acre, increased so fast because of agricultural knowledge gained from research and development *induced by* the increased demand, together with the increased ability of farmers to get their produce to market on improved transportation systems. These sentences are a lightning-fast summary of chapter 5 and of the forces that take many books to document in satisfactory detail.)

Despite the long-run trend, fluctuations in food prices are inevitable. And though short-run price changes carry little or no information about future long-run trends, it is useful to analyze, at least briefly, some short-run price movements, because they scare so many people.

The sharp price rise in the early 1970s was caused by a chance combination of increased Russian grain purchases to feed livestock, U.S. policies to reduce "surpluses" and get the government out of agriculture, a few bad world harvests, and some big-business finagling in the United States.

Though those high food prices alarmed the public, agricultural economists (with notable exceptions such as Lester Brown) continued to be optimistic. Even the UN World Food Conference called in 1974 to talk about the "crisis" produced rather unalarming forecasts. But there was no way to reduce public concern. When I passed on to my classes the prediction that these high prices would soon lead to increased supply, students asked, "How can you be sure?" Of course neither I nor anyone else could be *certain*. But we could rely on all of agricultural history and economic theory for optimistic predictions.

The evidence of history and economic theory proved correct, of course. Farmers in the United States and elsewhere responded to the opportunity with record-breaking crops.

Food Stockpiles

When after 1974 I showed people newspaper reports of a fall in grain prices— a clear indicator of increasing supplies—people said "Yes, but aren't food stockpiles dangerously low?" Indeed, food stocks were then lower than they had been for some time. Figure 7-3 shows the history of food stockpiles in the past few decades. It also includes the misleading truncated graph that Lester Brown published at a time when the recent data seemed frightening. But in fact stocks were not *dangerously* low. Rather, granaries—that is, U.S. and Canadian government-held stocks, which had originally been organized "as a means of holding unwanted surpluses off the market and thus sustaining farm prices"[4]—had come to be considered too large by those governments; that is the main reason why stocks had come down.

Large grain stocks—"excess" in the eyes of farm policy makers—had accumulated in the 1950s and early 1960s, threatening to knock grain prices down sharply. Therefore, between 1957 and 1962, government policies cut back sharply the grain acreage in the United States, and stocks fell as a result.[5] Then new free-market policies took effect in the United States and India, and stocks inexorably began to rise again—a bittersweet harvest for U.S. farmers. Again the U.S. secretary of agriculture became "pessimistic" because of the record harvests and the "surplus" of wheat.[6] Prices were so low that farmers were

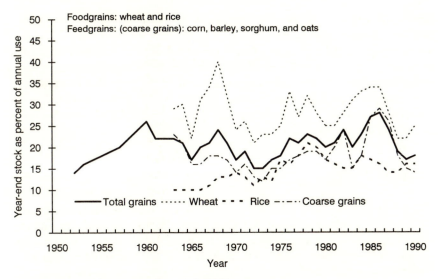

Figure 7-3. World Grain Stocks, 1952–1990

reluctant to sell, and newspaper stories reported that "huge grain crops trigger [a] need for bins as on-farm storage spreads in Midwest."[7] Manufacturers of storage bins said, "sales are booming [and] demand for metal bins is up 40% to 50%."[8]

Like investment scams—where the same old rackets reappear to cheat people generation after generation—the grain stockpile scam is back again. In 1988, *Newsweek* headlined "The Threat of a Global Grain Drain," citing Lester Brown's warning that "grain reserves needed to feed the world will fall from 101 days to 54 days by the beginning of 1989."[9] In late 1989, the *Washington Post* headline was "World's Grain Reserves Called Dangerously Low," citing Brown and using a sixty-day number—"a threshold of danger."[10] In 1991, MIT's *Technology Review* carried an article warning that "In 1989, for the third year in a row, the world consumed more food than it produced. . . . In 1986, the reserves [were] enough to feed the world for 101 days . . . [now] world food reserves would last only 30 days."[11]

Look for yourself at figure 7–3. The comparison in the last quotation above is to the all-time high, a time when reserves were undoubtedly too high by any measure, the results of government subsidies. By any historical standards, the 1987–1989 reserves were not low.

Furthermore, the stocks of food that are necessary to supply a given margin of safety against famine become smaller as transportation improves. In the past, every isolated family and village had to maintain its own stock against a shortfall in the harvest. But now food can be moved quickly from areas of plenty to areas of shortfall. The ship, then the train, and then the truck (and even the airplane for emergencies) drastically reduced the total stocks that need be maintained. (Bruce Gardner in correspondence, July 23, 1993, suggests that market improvements in hedging and forward contracting have also been important in enabling on-farm stocks to be reduced, as have crop insurance and disaster payments.) Reduction in inventories is a sign of efficiency, just as small supply inventories in Japanese factories are a sign of industrial efficiency. (It's called the "just-in-time" supply system.) If the world errs with respect to stockpiles of food, the error is almost surely by governments holding stocks that are too large.*

What Next?

What will happen next? The most likely danger is not a "shortage" due to inability of farmers to produce. Rather, the likely danger is from government-imposed incentives *not* to produce—such as subsidies to keep land out of production—and then rising prices as production falls, prompting price controls (which further discourage production). Such policies have been enacted in the United States in one form or another since the 1930s, and one can expect similar policies to be suggested again and again. Such moves to reduce production might well set the stage for another round of the sort of crisis that the world experienced in the early 1970s, because the United States exercises a crucial role in making up unexpected shortfalls in places where storage facilities are not available to carry over much food from one year to the next. The result might be a greater tragedy than last time, not because of physical limits to food production, but because of economic and political policies.

Indeed, American agriculture has become increasingly involved with the government. One sign of this in the past few decades is the increased numbers of articles about government programs in farm journals, relative to the number on how to farm better. To receive benefits under these programs, farmers must obey regulations. For example, to be eligible for crop insurance, farmers must file soil conservation programs, marketing plans, field surveys, and crop rotation reports with the local Soil Conservation Office;[12] if SCS does not approve the program (a matter which may involve personal politics), SCS can demand another plan, or have the benefits cut off.[13] A typical 1991 story: "[A] Nebraska farmer was prohibited from pasturing a 15-acre stalk field on highly erodable land. Local ASCS officials explained that the 350 steers using the

* Bruce Gardner (1979) constructed a thoughtful analysis of optimal storage levels for grains which takes account of the social benefits of avoiding shortfalls, and came up with an estimate of about 10 percent of normal production (p. 159). But because of the absence of integrated international markets and storage agreements, it makes sense for the United States to consider its own program separately. Gardner suggested an upper limit of 400 million bushels of grains, with government subsidizing private owners to hold perhaps 200 million bushels; the rest could be expected to be held privately without subsidy (p. 160). This recommended level is much below stocks of the past; for example, in the year prior to Gardner's publication, storage was about three times the recommended level (1.2 million tons; p. 159).

field as a winter exercise yard were causing excessive erosion by destroying too much crop residue."[14] Plain and simple, the federal government is telling farmers how to manage their farms—or else. And the "or else" means getting (say) $1.80 per bushel for your corn instead of the subsidized $3.00.

Superficially it might seem that farmers benefit from the overall government program because of the subsidies. But close analysis shows that most of the subsidies finally come to rest in the hands, not of the cultivators, but of the owners of the land—banks and absentee owners heavily represented—in the form of proceeds from land sales at prices made high by the value the subsidies confer.

Another set of beneficiaries of government programs are the government officials. There is about one Department of Agriculture employee for each full-time farmer. These workers are compensated sufficiently well, and there are enough other expenditures, that "the department's annual budget was $51 billion last year [1988]—more than the total net income of American farmers."[15] These officials, whose reason for being and whose natural inclination is to tell farmers what to do—in unholy alliance with environmentalists who want farmers to farm in the ways that environmentalists think is good for the world (and which supposes that farmers are too stupid to take care of their own land)—eventually tie the hands of the farmers, and make them welfare dependents of the government.

Not only do the cultivators themselves benefit little from the subsidy programs, but American agriculture itself suffers by being made less competitive on world markets and hence losing sales to farmers abroad, as has happened in the soybean market. And the land set-aside program, which reduces total output, opens the door to a shortfall in supply—a "crisis"—in a year when the weather is bad. Around and around the scam goes.

The devices that the nexus of government and farmer organizations invent to manipulate production and prices are never-ending. Fruit below a certain size is prohibited from sale, as a way of keeping out fruit from other countries as well as restricting domestic sales. Because of bountiful harvests in California in 1992, the minimum legal sizes were raised for such fruits as peaches, nectarines, and plums, resulting in tens or hundreds of millions of pounds of fruit dumped and left to rot;[16] the Department of Agriculture estimates 16 to 40 million tons are dumped each year.[17] In the long run these policies are bad for everyone, even for the farmers.

This topic is discussed well and at great length by many writers.[18] I'll spare you further depressing details.

The U.S. Drought of 1976–1977

The drought of 1976–1977 is an interesting case study in modern food supply, the sort of episode that tends to recur.

Throughout 1976 and 1977 there were news stories of droughts in various parts of the United States and also worldwide. In fact, dry years are nothing new. "Drought conditions similar to the one of 1977 faced Illinois farmers in 1956. Subsurface moisture was nil, wells were going dry, the weather forecast was gloomy"—in February 1977 just as in 1956.[19] Yet harvests were at or near record levels both in 1977 and in 1956. How could this be?

One reason that harvests were large despite the droughts is people's increased capacity to overcome adverse natural conditions. To illustrate, one of the most publicized droughts was in southern California.

> To thousands of Okies who fled the Midwestern dust bowl in the 1930s, California's San Joaquin Valley was the land of plenty. Aided by irrigation systems they laid down, the valley produced everything from grapes to almonds. But now the nation's most productive stretch of farmland lies parched by its second year of drought, and its farmers, many of them dust-bowl immigrants or their children, are in danger of losing their land again.[20]

The southern California drought did not end. Yet by August of that year the newspaper headlines said, "California Crop Yields Are Surprisingly Good Despite Long Drought." The explanation was that "California farmers, the nation's most productive, have been so successful at finding more water, and making wiser use of what they have, that California crop production is surprisingly strong despite the drought. Statewide cotton and grape crops are expected to set records, and many fruit, nut, and vegetable crops are up from last year. . . ."[21] The California farmers drilled new wells and substituted water-conserving sprinkler systems or trickle irrigation for flood irrigation.

Clearly it was not just luck that brought the public safely past the 1976–1977 drought, but rather hard-won knowledge and skills, which were themselves products of countless earlier natural crises and of population-induced demand.

Another reason why such droughts have had so little ill effect is that they simply are not as severe as they are usually reported to be. A drought in one country or state is dramatic and makes news; the excellent growing conditions in the next state or country seldom get reported. "So huge is American farm geography [even more is this true of world farm geography] that it can absorb pockets of severe loss and still produce bountiful harvests."[22] Furthermore, people often assert that there is a drought when there has not yet been rain and people are worrying about it. This was the case in Illinois in 1977. But later, "Above-average rainfall during August wiped out previous moisture deficits. . . . Despite a year-long drought followed by downpours that delayed harvest, Illinois farmers in 1977 grew a record 327 million bushels of soybeans and led the nation in production of both beans and corn."[23] And in California there was so much rain by the end of the "drought" year that "beleaguered state officials in Sacramento set up emergency relief—and quickly changed the name of the Drought Information Center to the Flood Control Center."[24]

Modern technological capacities in league with modern transportation capacities, harnessed to farmers' ingenuity when offered a chance to make money, have vastly reduced the likelihood of a major disturbance in our food supplies. In the short run as in the long run, worldwide drought, like worldwide famine, is a receding rather than an approaching danger.

The Situation in Some Other Countries

Sometimes a global picture obscures important parts of the world where the situation is quite different. Therefore, let's briefly consider a few countries of special interest.

India

Paul Ehrlich wrote in *The Population Bomb*: "I have yet to meet anyone familiar with the situation who thinks India will be self-sufficient in food by 1971, if ever." He went on to quote Louis H. Bean, who said, "My examination of the trend on India's grain production over the past eighteen years leads me to the conclusion that the present 1967–1968 production is at a maximum level."[25] Yet, "net food grain availability" in kilograms per capita per year has been rising since at least 1950–1951. By September 1977, there was an "Indian grain reserve buildup of about 22 million tons, and U.S. grain exports to India . . . [had] waned."[26] India thus faced the problem of soaring stocks "that overflowed warehouses and caused mounting storage costs" so that the excess grain would not be ruined by rain or eaten by predators.[27] In fact, many experts—people whom Ehrlich apparently had not met—have *always* said that India has a vast potential to increase food production. And nutrition and food production—not just total production, which was enough to confound the Ehrlich-Bean statement cited above, but also production per person—continued to improve through the 1980s, despite some difficult weather conditions (UNFAO *Production Yearbook*).

The cause of India's improved food situation is straightforward. It is not an agronomic miracle but a predictable economic event: Price controls on food were lifted in the mid-1970s, and price supports were substituted for the controls. Indian farmers had a greater incentive to produce more, so they did. For example:

Hari Mohan Bawa, a marginal farmer of [a] village 100 miles north of New Delhi, is richer by $300 this year. "I can marry off my daughter now," he said as he counted the money paid by the Food Corporation of India, a government agency that bought all his rice crop. "Maybe I will pay off part of my debts, or I will buy a new pair of bullocks."

Beginning last year the Food Corporation offered a minimum support price that guaranteed profits. Banks and Government agencies came forward with loans to buy fertilizer and seeds. Mr. Bawa installed a tube-well that freed him of dependence on the monsoon rains.[28]

Is increased economic incentive to Indian farmers too simple an explanation? Simple, but not too simple. And not simple *enough* for India's government to have removed price controls much earlier.

Indian farmers increased production mostly by working longer hours and also by planting more crops a year, on more land, and by improving the land they have.

You may wonder how Indian farmers, who are popularly thought to live in a country with an extraordinarily high population density, can find more land to cultivate. Contrary to popular belief, India (and Pakistan) are not densely populated compared with, say, Japan, Taiwan, and China. (Figure 29-4 shows the data.) And India's rice yield per acre is low compared to those countries. Ultimately, land shortage will never be a problem, as we saw in chapter 6.

China

Older people remember 1940s movies of Chinese starving in the streets, and emaciated rickshaw men. Now the visitor sees food everywhere in Chinese cities—tasty abundance in cheap restaurants; lots of men and women pedaling bicycles, hauling wagons full of meats and vegetables on their way to sell in the market; lush outdoor (covered) vegetable markets; and street corner vendors of finger food.

What happened? Is the abundance now due to Communist collective efficiency? Just the opposite. China is history's greatest proof of the economic principles set forth in this chapter. When I wrote the first edition, China's agriculture was in horrible shape. There had been little or no improvement in nutrition since the 1950s. And around 1960 occurred the worst famine in human history, when perhaps 30 million human beings died—the world's record (for what that's worth). The death rate rose incredibly, from ten per thousand in 1957 to twenty-five per thousand in 1960, then returning again to ten or below within two years.[29] The death rate in the countryside jumped from 14.6 in 1959 to 25.6 per thousand people in 1960,[30] and every economic indicator showed a disastrous downturn. For example, the value of total industrial output fell from 163.7 billion rmb (no sensible dollar equivalent is possible) in 1960 to 92 billion in 1962.[31]

The cause of the famine, plain and simple, was China's policy of collective agriculture. The farmers had small incentive to work hard; rather, they had large incentive to work as little as possible in order to save their strength in the

absence of sufficient calories to nourish themselves. Nor were there management incentives that would encourage sound choices of crops and of cultivation and marketing methods.

China's agriculture limped along until the late 1970s, as can be seen in the
data on productivity in figure 5-4. Then the largest social movement in history
took place, in an unprecedentedly short time. China's agriculture became
mainly private between 1978 and 1981.[32] The result may be seen in the productivity increase since then in figure 5-4. And the effect on consumption may
be seen in the data on caloric availability.[33]

Now when you visit the countryside (if you can manage to evade the bureaucrats who want to keep you from getting out of the cities and their control), you see flourishing and beautifully kept (though tiny) farms. You are
struck by the new houses. "[H]ousing space per capita for peasants for 1957
and 1978 indicate a decline from 11.3 square meters . . . to 10.2 square
meters." Then "the amount of living space per capita almost exactly doubled"
from 1978 to 1987.[34] More generally, "between 1978 and 1987 . . . real consumption levels of farm people roughly doubled."

The contrast to the situation in cities, where the government still controls
most of the economy, is obvious in the urban buses, for example, which are
jam-packed because the government won't allow private transportation enterprise such as now is allowed in rural areas.

The same sort of turnaround in the food situation could happen in Africa,
which is less densely populated than China. Too many governments in Africa
have adopted the Chinese collective ideas, and/or the old Stalinist taxation of
agriculture. (Western countries' subsidies to their own farmers make matters
worse: Western exports of food undercut the incentive of African farmers to
increase their output.)

Perhaps the most amazing and ironic development was an offer in 1990 by
the Chinese government to send food aid to the Soviet Union. For centuries
people thought that China's agricultural problem was lack of land. And the
Soviet Union is as land-rich as a country can be. Yet here was China sending
surplus food to a hungry Soviet Union, which practiced collective agriculture.

The Former USSR

The food future of the then-USSR is the one implicit prediction in the first
volume of this book that went wrong. I did not recognize that the Soviet
system was as resistant to change as it is, and that the system as a whole would
fall apart as it did. (I found out, when visiting a collective farm in 1987, the
strength of the resistance against shifting to market agriculture. The director
of the collective was exceedingly hostile when I cited the Chinese experience
to him.) I counted on improvements in technology to produce some increases

in production despite all the obstacles of central planning and collective farming. In fact, the USSR's food production deteriorated. (Indeed, until the
breakup of the USSR one could not get a decent meal in the Soviet Union,
even as a rich tourist.) This proves once again—with devastating weight of
evidence—that the only barrier to plenty of food for all is an unsound political-economic system.

Bangladesh

When Bangladesh became independent after the devastating war in 1971, U.S.
Secretary of State Henry Kissinger called it "an international basket case." Over
the next few years the food supply was sometimes so bad that some writers
advocated "letting Bangladesh go down the drain," whatever that arrogant
phrase might mean. Other persons organized emergency relief operations. A
1972 newspaper advertisement from the New York Times is shown in figure 7-4.

As early as December 1976, however, there was reason for optimism,
largely because of an improved food supply from "two record annual harvests
in a row. Storehouses [were] full, and food imports [had] been reduced." And
since then Bangladesh has made progress in nutrition as well as in life expectancy, contrary to popular impression. Life expectancy in Bangladesh rose
from 37.3 years at birth in 1960 to 47.4 years in 1980[35] to 55 years in 1984.[36]
Compare this actual long-term result with the pessimistic predictions in Lester
Brown's 1978 The Twenty Ninth Day, where he heads a section "The Tragic Rise
in Death Rates," and puts into a table data that show increasing mortality in
one area of Bangladesh from 1973–1974 to 1974–1975, and in three areas of
India from 1971 to 1972.[37] On the basis of just those two one-year reversals
in the long-run trend, Brown built a prediction of decreasing life expectancy.
It is hard to imagine less prudent scientific procedures and less well-founded
forecasts, and yet the outcome does not discredit Brown and his co-workers,
who are surely the most-quoted "experts" on food supply in the United
States.*

Another important long-run trend for Bangladesh is the decline in the proportion of the labor force in agriculture, from 87.0 percent in 1960 to 74.0
percent in 1980[38] to 68.5 percent[39] in 1990. These are truly amazing gains in
such a short period.

What about Bangladesh's future? "The land itself is a natural greenhouse,

---

* Mahbubul Alam of Dhaka wrote me that "In 1960s a day-labourer could be hired by providing only two meals and no money. At present it will require two meals as well as money ranging
from taka 25 to taka 100 (taka 40 = $1 US)." The price of servants has risen greatly, too, he says,
illustrating how not only the better-off classes but also the poorest classes have progressed since
the 1960s (Alam, letter, July 25, 1992).

Figure 7-4. How Bangladesh's Food Situation Looked to Some in 1972

half of the cultivated 22 million acres is suitable for double cropping, and some could raise three crops a year."[40] But yields per acre are low. One reason is that "growing more than one crop required irrigation during the dry winter season, and only 1.2 million acres are irrigated."[41]

Why is so little land irrigated, and why are yields so low? "Most farmers seem reluctant to grow much more rice than they themselves need. . . . They cite the high price of gasoline needed to run the [irrigating] pumps and the low price paid for their rice. The low price of rice is mostly due to the recent bumper harvests and the government's success in stopping massive smuggling of rice to India."[42] That reporter's analysis makes sense economically. It's the same old story: Government interference with markets reduces the incentive for farmers to increase their crops, so production is constrained. If and when Bangladesh's farmers are unshackled and enabled to take advantage of market opportunities, agriculture will take off just as it has in China.

Bangladesh and Holland are both very low to the sea, though Bangladesh has a much better climate for agriculture. If the Dutch were in Bangladesh for a quarter of a century and applied their skills in farming and in keeping the sea at bay, or if Bangladeshis had the same institutions and educational level as the Dutch, Bangladesh would soon be rich, as Holland is.

Africa and the Cocoa-Producing Countries

Data from the cocoa-producing countries help us understand the situation in Africa. During the past few decades, most countries have had heavy government control over agriculture—especially in the form of marketing boards, which set prices that farmers get for their crops far below market prices, while holding prices for fertilizer artificially high and enforcing collectivized agriculture. In Togo and the Ivory Coast, free-market countries as of 1982, "prices [of cocoa were] two or three times as high as government procurement prices in [controlled] Ghana."[43] It was economically rational for Ghanaian farmers to smuggle their cocoa over the border if they lived near the border, or else quit raising cocoa.

Figure 7-5 shows the course of cocoa production in three African countries plus Brazil. The two non-Socialist countries clearly have done much better than the two Socialist countries. This explains why the bulk of Africa's agriculture has done so poorly.

What Would Be the Best Foreign Aid for Agriculture?

We in the West flatter ourselves by making compassionate sounds about wanting to help the poor countries, especially their agriculture. But every bit

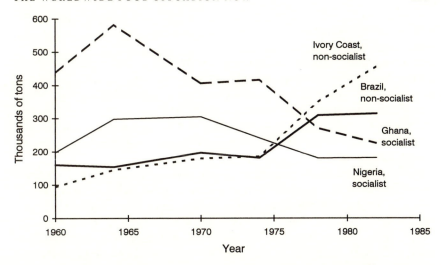

Figure 7-5. Effect of Economic System on Production of Cocoa Beans, 1960–1982

of assistance we give with one hand—shipments of food and technical assistance—we more than offset with the other hand which destroys their farmers' incentives by giving subsidies to our own farmers. These domestic policies in North America and Europe raise food production artificially and hence reduce world prices. They induce "mountains of butter" and "lakes of olive oil," and then dumping of the surpluses in poor countries at market-destroying prices. Hence, poor-country farmers have less incentive to produce more food more efficiently.

Our subsidies to our own farmers go hand-in-hand with the policies of African governments which steal from their farmers by forcing them to accept below-market prices. Together these pincers wreak enormous damage on poor-country agriculture. If we *truly* wish to help poor countries, we should (a) cut our domestic subsidies, and (b) negotiate for elimination of the "market boards" and other devices that control prices in poor countries as the quid pro quo for our aid. Those policies could lead to the sort of extraordinary jumps in production, and elimination of poor nutrition, that were seen in India in the 1970s and China in the 1980s.*

* Sen (1987) and others have pointed out that the cause of poor nutrition among poor people is their shortage of purchasing power rather than lack of world food production. Certainly this is true. But some infer from this that the "solution" is to have fewer poor people. In the short run it is undeniable that one can eliminate poverty by eliminating people. But in the longer run there is no logical or empirical basis for this idea; it is learned nonsense. The only way to eliminate poverty-caused hunger is by economic growth, which enables the rich to redistribute to the poor, at little cost to themselves, more than enough income to buy food; that is the case nowadays in the rich countries of the world, which have gotten rich by means of economic freedom.

Conclusions

Here we go again, it seems. There is a glut of food. Farmers—especially in the United States—are, as always, pushing for increased subsidies to reduce food production, and the U.S. government expanded those subsidies in the 1980s. Are we just at the top of another self-induced cycle, with a food crisis—real or imagined—at the bottom, just a few years away? If it happens, the main villain won't be population growth or physical limits, but rather the blundering of human institutions.

Under which political-economic conditions will food supplies increase fastest? In the first edition I stated that "little about this can be known for certain," although "almost all economists agree that a system of individual land-owning farmers operating in a politically stable free market, without price controls, leads to larger food production than does any other mode of organization." By 1996, enough evidence has accumulated that we now can be perfectly certain that this judgment is entirely correct.

Some lessons cannot be learned permanently, it seems. For four thousand years, governments have tried to increase food supply to the poor by imposing price controls, which instead have reduced the flow of food.[44] And for hundreds of years, "social engineers" have dreamed of increasing food production by "rationalizing" it through central planning and collective farming, taking advantage of supposed economies of scale, with the results seen in the USSR and Africa in the 1980s.

How long will it be before the most recent examples of China and the Soviet Union and Africa are forgotten, just as that of Plymouth Colony was, and clever intellectuals again gain the power to control agriculture in some countries, perhaps leading to disaster on a scale greater than ever before?

8

Are We Losing Ground?

THE MOST IMPORTANT fact about the world's agricultural land is that less and less of it is needed as the decades pass. This idea is utterly counterintuitive. It seems obvious that a growing world population must need larger amounts of farmland. But the title of a remarkably prescient 1951 article by the only economist to win a Nobel Prize for agricultural economics, Theodore Schultz, tells the true story: "The Declining Economic Importance of Land."

Consider these countries, and try to guess which one(s) is (are) rich and which poor: (1) Landlocked, mountainous, almost no oil or metals or other extractive resources, little flat farmland, high population density. (2) So flat and low that it is in constant danger of being flooded by the ocean (which has happened many times in its history), high population density, no natural resources. (3) Fastest population growth rate, and largest rate of immigration, in the world in the past half century, very high population density, no natural resources (not even fresh water). (4) Low population density, huge stores of natural resources, much fertile farmland.

In order, the first three countries are Switzerland, Holland, and Hong Kong. The fourth country might be most of the countries in Africa or South America. The first three are among the richest and most economically vibrant countries on Earth; many of the fourth group are dirt poor.

The reduced economic importance of land is shown by the long-run diminution in the proportion of total tangible assets that farmland has represented in various countries (see fig. 8-1).

Productivity of food per unit of land has grown much faster than has world population in recent decades (see chapter 5), and there is sound reason to expect this trend to continue; this implies that there is less and less reason to worry about the supply of land. Nevertheless, let us address the supposed problem of land shortage.

The title for this chapter comes from the 1976 book by Erik P. Eckholm, *Losing Ground*. That book was written "with the support and cooperation of the United Nations Environment Program," and contains a laudatory foreword by Maurice F. Strong, the executive director of the UN Environment Program. I draw attention to the auspices of Eckholm's book because it was (and is) representative of the "official" position of the interlinked world community of environmental and population organizations.

The thesis of Eckholm's book is that the world's farmland is deteriorating. In the language of Strong's foreword, "our delicately balanced food systems are

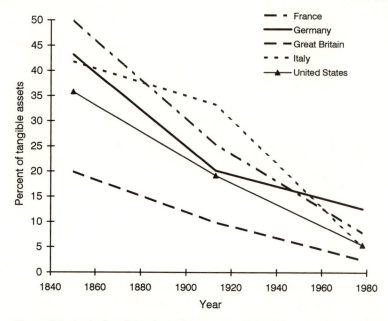

Figure 8-1. Agricultural Land as a Percentage of Tangible Assets, 1850–1978

being ecologically undermined through deforestation, overgrazing, soil ero-sion and abandonment, desertification, the setting of irrigation systems etc."[1] As a *New York Times* headline about the book put it, "Fertile Land Areas Dwin-dling in Poor Countries Despite Aid."[2] And, in conjunction with the appear-ance of Eckholm's book, the UN convened a conference on "desertification." Front-page headlines in the *New York Times* reported "14 Million Acres a Year Vanishing as Deserts Spread Round Globe."[3] *Newsweek's* headline to a full-page story was "Lethal Spread of the Sands."[4] Children's books tell this story in simple terms: "Our Soil Wasted and Lost."[5] The clear implication of these frightening statements is that the world's supply of arable land is decreasing.

Not true. The world is not "losing ground" on a net basis, as this chapter shows. Of course, arable land in some places is going out of cultivation be-cause of erosion and other destructive forces, as well as because productivity elsewhere is increasing and the land is no longer needed (for example, in Wisconsin and the southeastern states of the United States). But taken as a whole, the amount of arable land in the world is increasing year by year, in flat contradiction to the clear implications of the statements quoted above. In-deed, Eckholm now says—and it is good to hear—"My book did not assert that the world as a whole is losing arable land on a net basis, nor did I intend to imply that,"[6] though as the quotations above show, journalists and environ-mentalists (and I) did read a clear net-loss message in Eckholm's book.

The soil-erosion scare goes back a long way—to the story of the Spanish Conquest destroying native cultures by introducing cultivation practices that led to destructive erosion. Now research shows that erosion was as bad before Columbus as afterwards, and going back thirty-five hundred years; indeed, erosion may have declined after the Spaniards because of reduced population due to disease.[7] (At the rate that myth-shattering new information is becoming available, I may never finish this book; it accumulates faster than I can chronicle it.)

How can it be that agricultural land is becoming less important? Let us first step back and specify the questions to address, which are never easy to formulate. We should first ask: What is the present trend in the supply of arable land? Next we ask: What is the effect of increasing affluence on the supply of agricultural land? And last: What is the effect of population growth on the supply of agricultural land and recreational land? The first two questions are answered in this chapter; the third is answered in chapter 29.

As to the meanings of "arable" and "suitable for crops": Here again, economics cannot be separated from semantics. At one time most of Europe could not be planted, because the soils were "too heavy." When a plow was invented that could farm the heavy soil, most of Europe suddenly became "arable" in the eyes of the people who lived there. Most of Ireland and New England originally were too hilly and stony to be farmed, but with backbreaking toil stones were removed and the land became "suitable for crops." In the twentieth century, bulldozers and dynamite have pulled out stumps that kept land from being cropped. And in the future, cheap water transportation and desalination will transform more of what are now deserts into "arable" lands (just as happened with much of California). The definitions change as technology develops and the demand for land changes. Hence, any calculation of "arable" land should be seen for what it is—a rough temporary assessment that may be useful for a while but has no permanent validity.

"You can even make agricultural land out of Mount Everest, but it would cost a fortune to do so," is a common reply to such optimism by those who worry that we are running out of land. But in many parts of the world, new land can be bought and cleared right now for amounts that are considerably below the purchase price of good developed land. Furthermore, the cost of acquiring and clearing land nowadays is less than it was in the past, when tree cutting, stump pulling, and irrigation-ditch digging had to be done by hand or with animal power. New areas are made habitable for agriculture as well as for urban activity with air conditioning.*

---

* The entire South of the United States was rendered much more habitable with air conditioning. The first commercial building west of the Mississippi River to be air conditioned was the Federal Reserve Bank of Dallas in 1920 (Dallas Fed 1991 Annual Report, p. 8). With this device, the effective land area of the United States was greatly increased.

The Trend of Arable Land: Losing Ground?

The quantity of farmland is not a crucial issue, as we saw in chapter 6. In fact (as chapter 29 documents), some African officials contend that Africa has *too much* land—at the same time that the U.S. State Department's AID is wringing its hands and pushing policies in Africa intended to reduce the people/land ratio.

Using technology that is in commercial use to raise food in hydroponic artificial-light factories like PhytoFarm (see chapter 6), the entire population of the world can be fed using only the land area of Massachusetts plus Vermont, or Netherlands plus Jamaica. And the area necessary can be reduced to a tenth or a hundredth of that by producing the food in ten- or hundred-story buildings. Nevertheless, doomsters spook the public with fears that we are losing the quantity that now exists. Hence we need to examine the data in order to reassure you.

Eckholm and others provide frightening anecdotes aplenty about how the world is "losing land" to deserts, dust, overgrazing, woodcutting, and salting due to irrigation—often the stories are travelers' impressions and other casual evidence. But statistics they do not give. "Ideally, a book on the ecological undermining of food-production systems would include detailed national statistics. Unfortunately, such comprehensive data are not available," Eckholm says. But in fact comprehensive data *are* available. And these data contradict the picture suggested by the anecdotes.

Joginder Kumar laboriously collected and standardized the first set of data on land supply and use throughout the world. His finding: Nine percent more total arable land in 1960 than in 1950 in the eighty-seven countries for which he could find data; these countries account for 73 percent of the total land area of the world.[8] More details on this impressive gain of almost 1 percent per year may be found in the top panel of table 8.1. Some of the places where the quantity of cultivated land is going up may surprise you—India, for example, where the amount of cultivated land rose from 1,261,000 to 1,379,190 square kilometers between 1951 and 1960.[9]

The trend that Kumar found from 1950 to 1960 still continues. The UNFAO now has collected data back to the 1960s showing that there was a rise in "arable and permanent cropland" in the world as a whole during the period 1961–1965 to 1989 from 10.41 percent to 11.03 percent of Earth's dry-land area, which represents an increase of 5 percent in arable area for the roughly twenty-five-year period (see table 8-1); the data for agricultural (arable plus pasture) are comparable, as the bottom panel of table 8-1 shows. Furthermore, the gain in the developing countries is particularly significant and heartening.

We begin, then, by taking notice of the fact that the amount of arable land

TABLE 8-1

Changes in Quantities of the World Arable and Agricultural Land, 1961–1965 to 1989

Arable Land as a Percentage of Total Area		
Area	1961–1965	1989
Africa	6.28	6.17
Middle East	6.25	6.83
Far East	18.50	18.77
U.S. and Canada	11.50	12.19
USSR (now CIS)	10.24	10.29
Latin America	5.64	8.77
Western Europe	27.21	24.38
ALL REGIONS	10.41	11.03

Agricultural Land (Arable and Pasture Land) as a Percentage of Total Area		
Area	1961–1965	1989
Africa	32.88	35.56
Middle East	Data appear to be unreliable	
Far East	37.41	42.34
U.S. and Canada	26.10	26.38
USSR (now CIS)	26.83	26.86
Latin America	29.56	36.71
Western Europe	46.35	42.34
ALL REGIONS	33.13	35.71

Sources: Data for 1961–1965 are from FAO *Production Yearbook 1976*. Data for 1989 are from FAO 1990, except those for Western Europe. The Western Europe statistics are from FAO 1986 and represent numbers for 1985.

in the world—and especially in the poor and hungry countries—is increasing, rather than decreasing as the popular press would have it. Nor should we worry about diminishing returns in the long run due to successively poorer land being brought into use, because average yields per acre are increasing.

Where Is the Amount of Cultivated Land Declining?

The amount of cultivated land certainly is going down in some places. But this decline is not necessarily a bad sign. In the United States, the trend is downward, as can be seen in figure 8-2. This has happened because both the total agricultural output and average yields per acre have been going up sharply in the United States. This high output is obtained in large part with huge farm

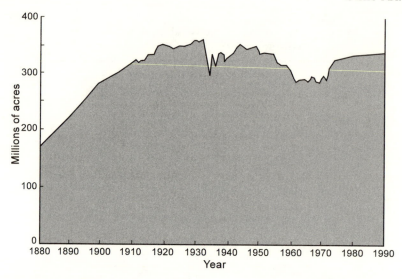

Figure 8-2. Cropland Harvested in the United States (48 states)

machines that require flat land for efficiency. The combination of increased productivity per acre of good land, and increased use of equipment adapted to flat land, has made it unprofitable to farm some land that formerly was cultivated. For example, in New Hampshire between 1860 and 1950, the tillable area declined from 2,367,000 acres to 451,000 acres.[10]

There are, however, places where, for negative reasons—usually wars, or fights about land tenure—good land that was formerly cultivated is no longer farmed. Mexico in the 1970s was a typical example. Frustrated by the slow pace of agrarian reform, Mexican peasants began seizing land. In fear of more seizures, the big estates then cut their investments. "The agrarian unrest has interrupted agricultural production and investment at a time of economic crisis—Sonora's farmers, who grow more than half the country's wheat, complain that their 1977 production will be reduced as much as 15%, or 220,000 tons, because of the unrest."[11]

Even the persons who worry about the "loss" of land acknowledge that it is in our own power to have more land if we will work for it. Eckholm wrote, "Today the human species has the knowledge of past mistakes, and the analytical and technical skills, to halt destructive trends and to provide an adequate diet for all using lands well-suited for agriculture."[12]

When confronted by these aggregate data, the loss-of-land worriers bring up the supposed "desertification," especially in the Sahara region. This has been hard to disprove until recently. But once again the anecdotal claim is confounded by scientific evidence when it can be gathered:

Despite the widely held impression that the sands of the Sahara are relentlessly expanding, consuming villages and contributing to famine in Africa, a new analysis of satellite images . . . shows the greatest desert on Earth has stopped growing and is now shrinking.

For years, researchers and agencies have assumed the Sahara's advance was implacable, but scientists who examined 4,500 satellite pictures taken over the past decade say it is clear the Sahara essentially reversed its expansion in 1984, and has since contracted dramatically.[13]

The story goes on to quote Compton J. Tucker and Harold Dregne as saying that the previous belief in Sahara expansion was "simply assumed," and that expansion and contraction seem to be natural. Trying "to stop the natural process probably would be fruitless."

Desertification certainly can occur in some circumstances. For example, recent satellite evidence shows that in the western United States, "hundreds of millions of acres are being degraded" by cattle. But this degradation is taking place on public lands, where individuals do not have a stake in maintaining the value of the land assets and where the prices they pay for grazing rights may be too low, leading to overgrazing. Where the land is privately owned, the satellite apparently did not report degradation. So desertification is not the result of population growth but rather of faulty economic arrangements. Unfortunately, however, many biologists and environmentalists focus on the physical rather than the social systems, making such forecasts as "Future desertification is likely to be exacerbated by global warming and to cause significant changes in global biogeochemical cycles."[14]

Indeed, even in the Sahel, private ownership can cause land to be improved rather than degraded. Figure 8-3 shows an area of private agricultural land in the Sahel; its borders sharply demarcate the green zone within from the brown area outside.

Nor is the problem of "sustainability" the bogey it is made out to be. Land can be used indefinitely, even on an intensive basis, without loss of fertility. This may be seen in the Morrow Plots at the University of Illinois, the oldest experimental agriculture station in the United States (my favorite place to take visitors in the years I taught there). Starting in 1876, corn has been planted every year without any fertilizer, and the yields are visibly scrawny. But land that has been planted every year but rotated among corn and other crops retains excellent fertility, the corn towering over the no-fertilizer-no-rotation yields, with no observable loss of soil fertility. Crops using commercial and organic fertilizer both do as well as the rotation crops. And crops using both rotation and fertilizer do best of all.[15]

Now we proceed to our second question, leaving the third question, about the effects of population growth, for chapter 29.

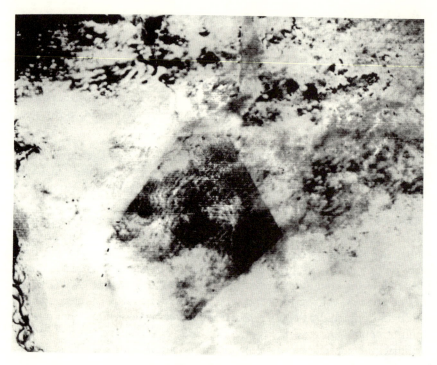

Figure 8-3. Private Agricultural Land in the Sahel

Is Land Different from Other Resources?

Many people consider land to be a special kind of resource. But like other natural resources, land is the result of the human creative process, as discussed in chapters 1–3. Though the stock of usable land seems fixed at any moment, it is constantly being increased—at a rapid rate in many cases—by the clearing of new fields or the reclamation of wasteland. Land also is constantly being enhanced by increasing the number of crops grown per year on each unit of land, and by increasing the yield per crop with better farming methods and with chemical fertilizer.

Last but not least, land is created anew where there was none. For example, much of Holland originally belonged more to the sea than to the land. "According to strict geographical determinism, one would expect to find there nothing but a fever-ridden delta and lagoons, the undisputed domain of sea fowl and migratory birds. Instead, we find a prosperous and densely-peopled country, with in fact the highest densities of population in Europe."[16] The new land was won by diking and draining. "This is essentially a triumph of human will, it is the imprint of civilization on the landscape."[17] A hundred years ago someone said of the Netherlands, "This is not soil, it is the flesh and blood and sweat of men."[18]

Modern Japan is applying the lesson of Holland. When land around Tokyo becomes scarce and extraordinarily expensive, the Japanese build an artificial island in Tokyo Bay and contemplate large floating structures, including perhaps an airport. And Hong Kong is planning to build a new airport on reclaimed land just off one of its islands.[19]

Holland was created by muscle power. But the potential for creating new land has increased as new power sources and our knowledge and machinery have developed. In the future, the potential for creating new and better land will be even greater. We will make mountains where there now is water, learn new techniques of changing the nature of soils, and develop our ability to transport fresh water to arid regions.

Extending the process into a third dimension which Holland demonstrated in two dimensions, the capacity to grow food in multilevel structures with the use of artificial light (see the discussion of Phytofarm in chapter 6) means that the supply of effective agricultural land can be expanded without limit—that is, it is not finite. This is no pipedream, but a demonstrated reality that is economic even at current prices.

The role of landbuilding in population history became clear to Malthus, who said of the Germans in Roman times,

> [W]hen the return of famine severely admonished them of the insufficiency of their scanty resources, they accused the sterility of a country which refused to supply the multitude of its inhabitants, but instead of clearing their forests, draining their swamps, and rendering their soil fit to support an extended population, they found it more congenial to their martial habits and impatient dispositions, to go in quest of "food, of plunder, or of glory," into other countries.[20]

The cooperative interrelationship among landbuilding, irrigation, population growth, and prosperity in prehistoric times is also well understood by historians of the ancient Middle East.

> In the great alluvial valleys of the Nile, the Tigris-Euphrates, and the Indus system collective effort had created artificial environments. The organized exploitation of lands reclaimed from swamp and desert was yielding unprecedented supplies of corn, fish and other foodstuffs.[21]

But once built, land can be lost through neglect and depopulation, as happened in the same Tigris-Euphrates area. "Many of these districts have not been settled or cultivated in a thousand years or more, and have been deeply and cleanly scoured by wind erosion during that interval."[22] One can see, under the sand, traces of the old abandoned *ghanats*—irrigation systems—when flying over the desert.

Investment in land is as important in the modern world as it was in the ancient world. The key idea is that land is made by people, just like other inputs to farm production. "The productive capacity of a farm is the cumulative result of what has been done to the land in the past and is largely the result of investment. The more progressive agriculture becomes, the smaller is its dependency on the natural endowments."[23]

Furthermore, whether land deteriorates or improves depends on its treatment by farmers. Land owned in common tends to deteriorate because no one has a property stake in maintaining it; in contrast, private farm owners improve their land because it raises the value of their investment. Reports about increasing soil erosion in various countries should be seen in this context.[24]

The extent of land improvement on subsistence-agriculture farms can be very great, depending on needs. Much agricultural investment has always come from the additional labor done by farmers during the off-season. For example, in agriculturally primitive Rapitok Parish in New Britain, "men of working age invest one-quarter of their manpower per year in the formation of new agricultural assets such as cocoa and coconut trees. This is a longterm agricultural investment."[25]

In Champaign-Urbana, Illinois, where our family lived two decades in the midst of some of the most valuable corn and soybean farmland in the world, townpeople are surprised to learn that before the pioneer farmers applied their labor and sweat (and lives) in developing this land, it was a malarial swamp. Though the area is flat, it was also waterlogged and therefore unproductive. "Until white settlers drained the prairie, Champaign County was very marshy. Early settlers noted that the Indians built platforms high in the trees to escape the mosquitoes."[26] The schoolchild imagines a vast, untapped prairie frontier where the white man, if he was brave enough to stand up to the Indians, needed only to drop seeds in the earth to have a bountiful crop. This is simply a myth.

Nor is landbuilding a thing of the past, even in Illinois. In Champaign County, Harold Schlensker is a retired farmer whose farmholdings, which his sons work, are worth perhaps a million dollars. Much of the increase in the value of his land came from reclamation. "Pointing out the back window of his house, Schlensker indicated a drainage ditch that was one of his first improvements to try to upgrade a plot of land he characterized as 'just swampland.' He said, 'I put that ditch in and some tile, and brought it up to good productive land.'"[27]

In various parts of the United States, new cropland is being created at the rate of 1.25 (or another estimate, 1.7) million acres yearly by irrigation, swamp drainage, and other techniques. This is a much larger quantity of land than the amount that is converted to cities and highways each year, as we shall see in the next chapter. Compare this with the nightmarish *Limits to Growth* view that land is fixed in quantity and that agricultural capacity is being "lost" to cities and highways.

The United States was blessed with an endowment of land and water that long made irrigation unprofitable. But now, with an increased demand for food and new technological advances, irrigation has become important in creating new land. California's San Joaquin Valley illustrates the miracle: "A century ago it was desert, but today a Rhode Island-size tract in California's arid San Joaquin Valley known as the Westlands Water District contains some of the richest farmland in the world—the product mainly of multi-billion-dollar Federal reclamation projects that irrigated the parched valley floor with water from government dams."[28]

Center-pivot irrigation is a landbuilding innovation so promising that it deserves special attention. (Those are the huge circles you see below you as you fly west from Ohio to the West Coast.)

> In its natural state, the land along the Columbia River in eastern Washington and Oregon is a forbidding expanse of shifting sand, sage brush and Russian thistle, and only the hardiest of farmers or ranchers would try to wrest a living from it. The region is so desolate that the Navy uses some of the land as a bombing range. But for all this, the mid-Columbia region is one of the most thriving new agricultural areas in the world. Thanks to a remarkable new system of irrigation, the desert along the river is blooming. . . . With pivot irrigation, the water is pumped from the river to the center of a round field a half mile in diameter. A giant arm of 6-inch pipe a quarter-of-a-mile long pivots around the center of the field like the hand of a clock, making one revolution every 12 hours. Since much of the land is almost pure sand, it must be continuously fertilized, and here too the sprinkler system is used by feeding the appropriate nutrients into the water.[29]

By the 1970s, irrigation had begun to appear even in fertile areas such as Champaign County, Illinois, whose corn-and-soybean land is as rich as any in the world even without irrigation. And in areas where water is too scarce or saline for ordinary irrigation, and where labor is scarce, the Blass system of drip irrigation (also called "trickle irrigation") multiplies yields.[30]

There are vast barren areas of the planet that may be brought into cultivation when energy, together with desalination and irrigation technology, become cheaper. To fly over the Nile River in Egypt is an amazing experience. A beautiful verdant strip surrounds the river. But beyond a few thousand meters from the river the rest of the country is entirely brown. That narrow green strip supports 56 million Egyptians (1990). Irrigation and desalination could make the rest of the country green, too.

Then there is outer space and the planets. Science fiction? Many respected scientists see potential there.

> Making plans so bold that they seem almost unbelievable, many of the nation's leading scientists are calling for immediate steps to begin colonizing space. Their goal is to make the vast reaches of space the natural habitat of man with Mother Earth remembered as the "old world." Peering into their crystal balls at the recent meeting

of the American Association for the Advancement of Science, the scientists concluded that space colonization is inevitable—and sooner than we think.[31]

As with other resources, the demand for land lessens when new substances are found to substitute for agricultural products. For example, "In India in 1897 nearly two million acres were used for cultivating indigo plants." Along came the German chemical industry and synthesized an indigo dye that was cheaper than the natural product. The two million acres were no longer needed for indigo.[32]

In high-tech farming, *knowledge* substitutes for land. Chapter 6 described how hydroponic farming can produce as much in one acre as conventional agriculture in a hundred or a thousand acres. And of course high-rise buildings greatly economize on surface area used for living.

Conclusion

I do not preach complacency about the supply of land. I am not suggesting that we cease to care about our agricultural fields, worldwide or regionally. Just as homeowners must take care of their lawns lest they go to ruin, farmers must continually protect and renew their acreage so the stock of good land is increased and improved.

The message of these land data is that there is no ground for the panic into which anecdotal accounts can throw us when they are not balanced by the larger picture of accurate figures. And there is no basis in these figures for opposition to continuing economic and population growth. (The wisdom of such growth with respect to land, as opposed to the feasibility, will be discussed in chapter 29.)

The hoaxes (by now old and tired) about "urban sprawl" and soil erosion wasting the farmland of the United States are exposed in the next chapter, along with a discussion of the newer concern about loss of wetlands.

9

Two Bogeymen:
"Urban Sprawl" and Soil Erosion

THIS CHAPTER tells at length the saga of the most conclusively discredited environmental-political fraud of recent times.

Since the 1970s, many well-intentioned people have worried that population growth produces urban sprawl, and that highways pave over "prime farmland" and recreational land. This fear proved to be groundless. The purpose in giving so much detail here is that this case may serve as a model for many similar issues about which the full story has not come to light, and in which there is not a confession by the official agency involved that the original scare was entirely false.

The heart of the matter is that many, in the name of "environmentalism" and under the guise of preventing future food shortage, want to prevent people from building houses on farmland. They are again mobilizing the powers of government to attain their private goals. That is, it may well be that the famine-protection claims are simply a smoke screen for property owners who want a bucolic view. But whatever the motives, this phony scare campaign steals taxpayers' money and prevents young couples from getting the housing they want.

Three 1990s examples:

March 6, 1991: A *Washington Post* editorial comments approvingly on a bill coming before the Maryland General Assembly that will prevent "suburban sprawl" in the name of "protecting farmland."

March 28, 1991, front page banner headline in the *Press Enterprise*, Bloomsburg, Pennsylvania: "Farm Preservation: $100M Mistake?" The State of Pennsylvania is spending $100 million to "purchase development rights to prime farmland in an effort to shield it from development."

September 10, 1992, *Washington Post* (pp. Md 1, 7): "State Preservation Program Stems Loss of Farmland to Development. . . . The easement program was enacted . . . not only to curb development . . . but also to help keep the state partially self-sufficient in food production. . . . Loss of farming . . . also means more food must be imported from out of state, which can drive prices up." By this point in the book, the reader should be aware that these arguments in support of the preservation program are the worst sort of economic nonsense.

These and similar programs in seventeen other states are founded on the assumption that the United States is losing farmland at an unprecedented rate,

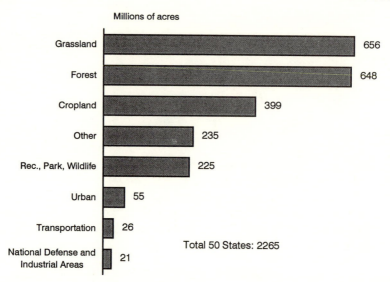

Figure 9-1. Major Uses of Land in the United States

and that the farmland is needed to stave off hunger in the future. Both those assertions have now been wholly disproven—and acknowledged to be so by the U.S. Department of Agriculture, which originally raised the alarm. That is, even the original purveyors of the false facts about the "vanishing farmland crisis" agree that the widely reported scare was without foundation.[1]

The relevant data are as follows:

Figure 9-1 shows that of the 2.3 billion acres in the United States as of 1987, all the land taken up by cities, highways, nonagricultural roads, railroads, and airports amounts to only eighty-two million acres—just 3.6 percent of the total.[2] Clearly there is very little competition between agriculture on the one side, and cities and roads on the other.

Concerning the trends: from 1920 to 1987, land in urban and transportation uses rose from 29 million acres to 82 million acres—a change of 2.3 percent of the total area of the United States.[3] During those fifty-seven years, population increased from 106 million to 243 million people. Even if this trend were to continue (population growth has slowed down), there would be an almost unnoticeable impact on U.S. agriculture, just as in past decades (see fig. 9-2).

Concerning the notion that the United States is being "paved over," as of 1974, the U.S. Department of Agriculture's official view was that "we are in no danger of running out of farmland."[4] But then there occurred a bizarre incident in which the failure of the press and television is undeniable and inexcusable. Even the original purveyors of the false facts have 'fessed up and now agree that the widely reported scare was without foundation.

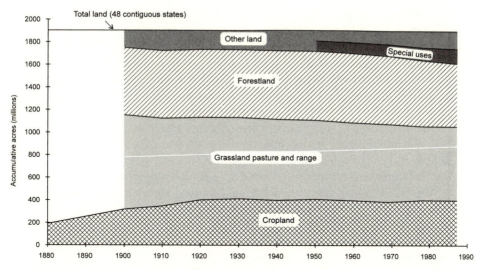

Figure 9-2. Trends in Land Use in the United States

Headlines like these began to appear in the newspapers about 1980: "The Peril of Vanishing Farmlands" (*New York Times*) and "Farmland Losses Could End U.S. Food Exports" (*Chicago Tribune*). "Vanishing Farmlands: Selling Out the Soil" (*Saturday Review*), and "As World Needs Food, U.S. Keeps Losing Soil to Land Developers" (*Wall Street Journal*). They asserted that the urbanization-of-farmland rate had jumped by a multiple of three from the 1960s to the 1970s, from less than one million acres per year to three million acres per year. This assertion was wholly untrue, as we shall see.

Several scholars—including Fischel, Luttrell, Hart, and me—found that the three-million-acres-a-year rate was most implausible in light of data from other sources, and given the nature of the surveys from which the estimate was drawn by the National Agricultural Lands Study (NALS), an organization set up by the Department of Agriculture together with other existing government entities. We also got help from H. Thomas Frey, a geographer who had been the keeper of the urbanization and other land-use data for the Economic Research Service of the USDA for many years. Everyone agreed that in 1967 the total urban and built-up area in the United States (excluding highways, railroads, and airports) was between 31 and 35 million acres. It was also agreed that the rate of urbanization was slower in the 1960s than in the 1950s. Yet NALS said that over the ten years from 1967 to 1977, there was a 29-million-acre increase in urban and built-up land.

That is, over the course of more than two centuries, in the process of reaching a population of about 200 million people, the United States built towns on between 31 and 35 million acres. NALS asserted that suddenly in the course of another ten years, and with a population increase of only 18 million people, the urban and built-up areas increased by 29 million acres (almost none of it due to transportation)—a near-doubling.

To put it differently, the long-run trend in the decades up to 1970 was about one million acres of total land urbanized per year, and constant or slowing down. The Soil Conservation Service in conjunction with NALS asserted that the rate then jumped to between two and three million acres yearly from 1967 to 1975 or 1977 (depending on which version you read).

There were two bases given for the publicized three-million-acre number; NALS shifted from one to the other when either was criticized: (1) A small-sample re-survey of part of the 1967 sample "inventory" of farms, done by the Soil Conservation Service. (A similar inventory had been done in 1958.) (2) The 1977 sample inventory. Seymour Sudman, an expert in research design, joined me in a technical analysis showing that there were so many flaws in both the 1975 re-survey and the 1977 survey that both should be considered totally unreliable. The flaws included an incredible boo-boo that put the right numbers in the wrong columns for big chunks of Florida.

Various government agencies were mobilized to rebut our criticisms. USDA had claimed that farmland was decreasing, to support the idea that farmland was being urbanized. But we showed that farmland was in fact increasing.

NALS then got the Census bureau to produce a similar adjustment for the United States as a whole. The result: "The latest data show a national decline of 88 million acres in land in farms between 1969 and 1978—an annual rate of 9.8 million acres," as published in *The Journal of Soil and Water Conservation*.

Analysis of the adjustment showed it to be as full of holes as Swiss cheese. And eventually the Census of Agriculture revealed detailed data on the appropriate adjustment showing that land in Illinois farms and in cropland had, as we said, indeed increased from 1974 to 1978.

After publication of these results, the scare seemed to die down a bit, but not before the private American Farmland Trust was organized in 1980 from former employees of NALS. It spends a couple of million dollars annually to "protect" the United States from the danger of vanishing farmland.

In 1984, the Soil Conservation Service issued a paper by Susan Lee that completely reversed the earlier scare figures and confirmed the estimates by our side. And the accompanying press release made it clear that the former estimates were now being retracted. "[T]he acreage classified as urban and built-up land was 46.6 million acres in 1982, compared to 64.7 million acres reported in 1977." Please read that again. It means that whereas in 1977 the SCS had declared that 64.7 million acres had been "lost" to built-upon land, just five years later SCS admitted that the actual total was 46.6 million acres. That is, the 1977 estimate was fully *50 percent too high*, a truly amazing error for something so easy to check roughly as the urbanized acreage of the United States.

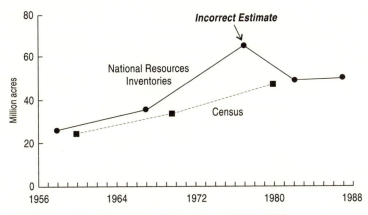

Figure 9-3. Official Estimates of Urban Area, 1958–1987

With unusual candor, the USDA press release added, "The 1982 data, which correlate closely with data from the 1980 U.S. Census of Population [the census was not available at the time of the argument described above, but later fully corroborated Frey's estimates based on prior data] are considered accurate because of the availability of better maps, more time for data collection, many more sample points, and better quality control." The press release continued: "The 1977 estimate thus appears to have been markedly overstated."

A Congressional Research Service report summarized the outcome: "National Agricultural Lands Study indicated that almost three million acres of agricultural land was annually converted to relatively irreversible nonfarm uses between 1967 and 1975. . . . Subsequent analyses and more recent empirical evidence have not supported these results. . . . In conclusion, the most recent reliable information indicates that the conversion of farmland to urban and transportation uses occurred at about half the rate indicated in the National Agricultural Lands Study. . . . The putative figure of 3 million acres per year from the NALS has been repudiated by subsequent analyses and more recent empirical evidence."[5] This report completely confirms the criticisms that others and I have leveled at the NALS claims. Figure 9-3 shows a revealing graph drawn from a recent official publication; the falsity of the 1977 National Resources Inventory estimate is immediately apparent.

The demolition of the NALS estimates—and the conclusion that urbanization of farmland is not a social problem—is not welcomed by either environmentalists or by "specialists" in the field. William Fischel wrote the following after a 1988 conference on the subject:

It is not a matter about which reasonable people can differ. . . .

The argument was advanced orally at the conference that the NALS data ought to be regarded merely as the "high estimates" of the amount of farmland conversion, so that the truth is somewhere in between. This is not acceptable. One does not average the results of scientific studies when one knows that some of the studies used invalid methods.[6]

It is relevant that the press did nothing to uncover the scam. The press-release reversal and "confession" did not evoke coverage; yet the original scare story was a front-page headliner for the *Chicago Tribune* and a cover story for news magazines.

Nor did the farmland crisis then vanish for lack of factual support. The false news continues to reverberate.

Did the false bad news matter? Following upon NALS publicity, in 1980 Congress provided a tax break to owners who will attach a "conservation easement" to their land which will keep the land out of development and in agriculture in perpetuity. And to ease the owners even more, some states have programs to recompense the owners the difference between the current market value and the value after the easement. That is, as usual the public purse is being tapped to further the purpose of the special interest group. And in 1981, the Farmland Protection Policy Act was enacted by Congress. Hundreds of state and local laws restricting farmland conversion also were passed. And the American Farmland Trust's 1985 Annual Report brags that in that year "Congress adopted . . . a Conservation Reserve . . . conceived and championed by AFT" as part of the 1985 Farm Bill. In June 1994, the final regulations implementing the 1981 Farmland Protection Policy Act were published in the Federal Register (*Washington Post*, July 5, 1994, p. A13), and will henceforth govern agriculture in the United States. All this legislation was based on wrong information, with no reasonable prospect of doing good for the nation but with much prospect of causing harm to individuals and damage to the nation. So it goes in America.

The false bad news continues to reverberate in another way, too. As of 1994, some rich landowners with million-dollar homes individually have filed to pay the federal Farmers Home Administration (FmHA) their delinquent loans of as much as $15 million. And the government does not press the loan abuse because officials say that "most delinquent borrowers are victims [note that word] of a mid-1980s decline in crop prices, farm income and farmland values." The farmland values fell when the land price bubble burst—the very bubble to which the government contributed with false publicity about vanishing farmland.[7]

The entire "crisis" was hokum. This was not a regrettable yet understandable exaggeration of a real problem, but a nonproblem manufactured by the Department of Agriculture and some members of Congress out of whole cloth under the guise of concern about food production for the starving world. The crisis was created for the benefit of (a) the environmentalists, and (b) people who own homes that abut on areas which might be developed into housing developments, and whose vistas and ambience might thereby be affected.*

As discussed in chapter 6, increasingly efficient production methods are the major factor enabling the United States to "ensure our domestic food and fiber needs" and yet use less land for crops—not because land is being "taken" for other purposes, but because it is now more efficient to raise more food on fewer acres than it was in the past.

But what about the *fertility* of the land used for human habitation and transportation? Even if the total quantity of land used by additional urban people is small, perhaps the new urban land has special agricultural quality. One often hears this charge, as made in my then-home town in the 1977 City Council election. The mayor "is opposed to urban sprawl because 'it eats up prime agricultural land.'"[8]

New cropland is created, and some old cropland goes out of use, as we have seen. The overall effect, in the judgment of the U.S. Department of Agriculture, is that between 1967 and 1975 "the quality of cropland has been improved by shifts in land use . . . better land makes up a higher proportion of the remaining cropland."[9]

The idea that cities devour "prime land" is a particularly clear example of the failure to grasp economic principles. Let's take the concrete (asphalt?) case of a new shopping mall on the outskirts of Champaign-Urbana, Illinois. The key economic idea is that the mall land has greater value to the economy as a shopping center than it does as a farm, wonderful though this Illinois land is for growing corn and soybeans. That's why the mall investors could pay the farmer enough to make it worthwhile for him or her to sell. A series of corny examples should bring out the point.

If, instead of a shopping mall, the corn-and-soybean farmer sold the land to a person who would raise a new exotic crop called, say, "whornseat," and who would sell the whornseat abroad at a high price, everyone would consider it just dandy. The land clearly would be more productive raising whornseat than corn, as shown by the higher profits the whornseat farmer would make as compared with the corn-and-soybean farmer, and as also shown by the amount that the whornseat farmer is willing to pay for the land.

A shopping mall is similar to a whornseat farm. It seems different only because the mall does not use the land for agriculture. Yet economically there is no real difference between the mall and a whornseat farm.

The person who objects to the shopping mall says, "Why not put the mall on inferior wasteland that cannot be used for corn and soybeans?" The mall owners would love to find and buy such land—as long as it would be equally convenient for shoppers. But there is no such wasteland close to town. And

* The connection between the farmland scare and prevention of housing construction has been documented for California by Frieden 1979.

"wasteland" far away from Champaign-Urbana is like land that will not raise whornseat—because of its remoteness it will not raise a good "crop" of shoppers (or whornseat or corn). The same reasoning explains why all of us put our lawns in front of our homes instead of raising corn out front and putting the lawn miles away on "inferior" land.

Of course, the transaction between the mall investors and the farmer does not take into account the "external disutility" to people who live nearby and who hate the sight of the mall. On the other hand, the transaction also does not take account of the added external "utility" to shoppers who enjoy the mall. Some of this externality is reflected in changes in property values; some individuals will suffer and others benefit. But neither a market system nor any other system guarantees that everyone is made better off by every transaction. Furthermore, this consideration is a long way from our original concern about the loss of prime agricultural land.

Both ignorance and mysticism enter importantly into conventional thinking about farmland. For example, one hears that "once it's paved over, it's gone for good." Not so. Consider the situation in Germany, where entire towns are moved off the land for enormous stripmining operations. After the mining is done, farmland is replaced, and the topsoil that is put down is so well enriched and fertilized that "reconstituted farmland now sells for more than the original land." Furthermore, by all measures the area is more attractive and environmentally pure than before.[10]

Soil Erosion

Soil erosion is a related and exactly parallel story. The scare that farmlands are blowing and washing away is a fraud upon the public similar to the urbanization fraud.

In the early 1980s there was a huge foofarah about the terrible dangers of farmland being ruined. In a January 11, 1983 speech to the American Farm Bureau Federation, the President of the United States said, "I think we are all aware of the need to do something about soil erosion." The headline on a June 4, 1984 Newsweek "My Turn" article typified how the issue was presented: "A Step Away from the Dust Bowl." (It may or may not be coincidence that the soil-erosion scare began just about the time that the paving-over scare seemed to peter out in the face of criticism.) More recently we have such statements as that of Vice President Albert Gore, Jr., about how "eight acres' worth of prime topsoil floats past Memphis every hour," and that Iowa "used to have an average of sixteen inches of the best topsoil in the world. Now it is down to eight inches."[11]

It is important to put such isolated claims into context. A tiny proportion of cropland—3 percent—is so erosive that no management practices can help

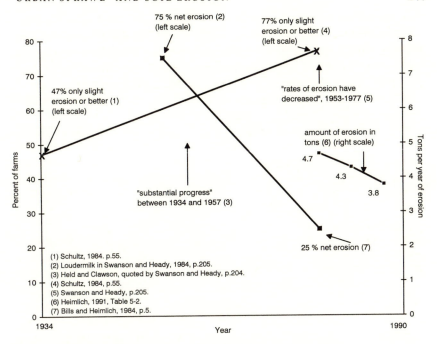

Figure 9-4. Trends in Soil Erosion in the United States, 1934–1990

much. Seventy-seven percent of cropland erodes at rates below five tons per acre each year—the equilibrium rate at which new soil is formed below the surface, that is, the "no net loss" rate. Only 15 percent of U.S. cropland "is moderately erosive and eroding about a 5-ton tolerance. Erosion on this land could be reduced with improved management practices," though this does not necessarily mean the land is in danger or is being managed uneconomically.[12]

In short, the aggregate data on the condition of farmland and the rate of erosion do not support the concern about soil erosion. What's more, the data suggest that the condition of cropland has been *improving* rather than worsening. Theodore W. Schultz and Leo V. Mayer both wrote very forcefully that the danger warnings were false. Schultz cited not only research but also his own life-time recollections starting as a farm boy in the Dakotas in the 1930s. Figure 9-4 shows data from soil surveys which make clear that erosion has been lessening rather than worsening since the 1930s. But even a Nobel laureate's efforts (Schultz's) could not slow the public-relations juggernaut that successfully co-opted the news media and won the minds of the American public.

The USDA press release of April 10, 1984 contained a second quiet bombshell: "The average annual rate of soil erosion on cultivated cropland dropped from 5.1 tons per acre to 4.8 tons per acre." That is, erosion was *lessening rather than getting worse*, exactly the opposite of what NALS claimed. But newspapers and television either did not notice or did not credit these criticisms. Even after the USDA admitted that the newer data clearly show that the danger was not as claimed, nothing appeared in print (to my knowledge) to make the public aware of this new nondanger and of how the public was misled. (Ask a few of your acquaintances their impressions about farmland urbanization and cropland erosion.)

The main bad effect of soil erosion is not damage to farmland but rather the clogging of drainage systems, which then need costly maintenance; the latter is many times as costly as the former.[13]

Afternote

How Environmental Con Artists Work
Their Scams

THOSE WHO perpetrated the "vanishing farmland crisis" followed the usual evasion strategies when confronted with the facts. Perhaps this example will help expose the usual warning signs of a scam artist at work and make such hoaxes harder to accomplish in the future.

When I wrote about the sorry "vanishing farmland crisis" fraud for the *Washington Journalism Review*, my basic assertion that the three-million-acre figure was at least twice too high was attacked frontally in that journal by Robert Gray, head of the American Farmland Trust and former head of NALS. My reply was as follows:

> Robert Gray has done us a large favor in his reply by committing himself explicitly to the statement that "3 million acres of rural land were lost to non-agricultural uses annually," meaning urbanization, roads, and the like. This enables me to make the following offer: I will wager ten thousand dollars with him that 1 million acres is a more appropriate figure than the 3 million he asserts. If I lose, the money will come from my pocket; if I win, the money will go to a University of Maryland foundation for research.
>
> The bet could be judged by a committee of (say) 5 ex-presidents of the American Statistical Association and the American Agricultural Economics Association, or by an expert committee selected by those associations, with the Washington Journalism Review holding the stakes. If Mr. Gray does not accept the bet, the offer is open to anyone else—journalists included, of course.
>
> Whether or not Mr. Gray accepts the wager should be a fair test of whether what I write is "false," as he says it is. If he does not accept the wager, perhaps his members and donors might consider whether NALS and the American Farmland Trust constitute a scam, as I say they are, for promulgating the phony figure of 3 million acres.
>
> Of course this bet is like shooting fish in a barrel, because even the USDA has retreated from the 3 million acre figure, as stated in the article. The interesting aspect of Gray's repetition of that figure is that he expects readers to believe him anyway.
>
> I am also prepared to make a cash wager on the validity of just about any of the hundreds of other statements about resources, environment, and population growth that I have made in my books and articles over the decades. There certainly must be factual and theoretical errors, but luckily none of importance have come to light, which gives me confidence. So how about it, you who shout "lies, damned lies, and

statistics" when someone says that resources have become more available rather than more scarce, and that the U.S. air we breathe and the water we drink have been getting less polluted and safer rather than dirtier and more dangerous? Care to put your money where your mouths are?

Please forgive the harshness of an offer to wager. It is, however, the last remaining device to bring the doomsayers to book on the statements that they make.

Gray was not, of course, willing to bet, but simply equivocated by offering to debate. So my response was:

To Mr. Gray: I will be happy to "debate" you under the following conditions: (1) The judges to be a panel of persons both scientifically eminent and expert in a related discipline—for example, five ex-presidents of the American Statistical Association or of the American Agricultural Economics Association, or such persons as those associations designate. (2) You and I submit in writing full scientific documentation of our positions.

This is the same offer I made before. I will not insist on a wager. The wager was simply to get you to put up or shut up. Unfortunately, you have done neither.

You have another possibility open to you: I have written that this matter is a scam, and that your organizations have been involved in the responsibility. You could sue if you believe that I have spoken falsely in this regard.

Hey readers: Can this fellow Gray really get away with avoiding the issue by crude name-calling like "trivializing," "theatrics," and "unprofessional"? When he is talking to newspeople, will no one "hold his feet to the fire," as you people put it?

The continued disinterest of most journalists to this story of purposeful distortion of fact by a government agency and environmental organizations is disheartening. The editor has received only two letters in response, both denouncing me. I have received just one call from a journalist who thinks the matter newsworthy and wishes to pursue it, Howard Banks of *Forbes*. What does this, and the events chronicled in my original article, say about the disinterested search for truth when the facts make the environmental movement and the press look bad?

10

Water, Wood, Wetlands—and What Next?

PUBLIC CONCERN about resources, the environment, and population growth constantly shifts its target. When those who are worried about loss of farmland run out of arguments with which to rebut the data that land is growing less scarce, they are wont to say, "But what about water? If we run out of water, the amount of land won't matter." Worry about the "loss" of forests is another old bugaboo that has again become fashionable. Earlier in this century, people worried that timber would become scarce as forests were cut for lumber, yet wood is now in greater supply than ever. (Another concern about forests—their availability as recreational land and as habitat for wildlife—is addressed in chapter 29.) And now even wetlands, formerly known as swamps, have come to share the environmentalists' spotlight.

Let's begin by briefly discussing the supposedly worsening water shortage, a topic that there was no need to address at the time of the first edition. The ridiculousness of such "conservation" measures as not putting water on the tables of restaurants or not flushing the toilet every time it is used is discussed in chapter 20.

Nature of the Problem

Water does not change into something else, as do fossil fuels that are burned. Rain and seawater come back to us in the same form in which we originally used them, unlike (say) raw copper. And water never languishes in a dump, as scrap iron does. Furthermore, the quantity of water in the oceans is huge by any criterion. The only possible water problems, then, are that (a) there is not enough water in a place that it is wanted at a given moment, and hence the price is too high; and (b) the available water is dirty.

Usable water is like other resources, however, in being a product of human labor and ingenuity. People "create" usable water, and there are large opportunities to discover and utilize new sources. Some additional sources are well known and already in partial use: transport by ship from one country to another, deeper wells, cleaning dirty water, towing icebergs to places where water is needed, and desalination. But there also are entirely new possibilities, about some of which there already are hints, and about others which—inevitably—nothing is known.

An important example of a newly discovered source is the aquifers in areas where the underlying rock has large faults. In the past, geologists had assumed that the water in these large watersheds does not flow easily from place to place, and especially, does not flow vertically. But scuba divers have been able to map the movement of the water in these aquifers, and to demonstrate that it does move vertically. In this fashion, huge new supplies of groundwater have been found in the Red Sea Province of eastern Sudan, Florida, and elsewhere.[1]

This new method has also revealed that massive watersheds are in greater danger of being polluted by ground water than had previously been known. The direction is thereby pointed to pollution prevention.

Consumer Water Issues

For perspective on modern consumer water issues, consider that in a typical poor area in South Africa in the 1990s—which is how it also used to be only a century or so ago in what is now the rich world—the average household spends about three full hours of labor each day hauling water from the source to the house in order to supply its water needs. In comparison, typical households in middle class areas can pay for a day's worth of water with the pay from perhaps one or two minutes of work. And the price of water brought to the house by a water carrier in poor areas of South Africa is perhaps twenty-five or thirty times the price of water in a modern middle-class area in South Africa.[2] So the long-run trend, as with all other natural resources, has been toward a much greater abundance of water, rather than toward greater scarcity. This illustrates the basic theory of this book, the process by which new problems eventually leave us better off than if the problems had not arisen. The opposite view—that we are exploiting the future and that retribution will inevitably destroy civilization—is discussed in chapter 37.

We can immediately simplify our subject by noting that water for residential use will never be a long-run problem in itself because even at the cost of the most expensive means of production—desalination—the cost of water used by households is small relative to household budgets in rich countries. Let's say that an acre-foot of desalinated water—that is, 325,851 gallons—costs $700 or $1,900 in 1992 dollars (depending on how you figure), as in Santa Barbara, California.[3] The average household in that affluent area uses perhaps 7,500 gallons per month (about the same as in the suburbs of Washington, D.C.), or 90,000 gallons ($500 worth) a year.[4] Even if the price of water in Washington, D.C., rises at the source from zero to $1,900 per acre-foot, the increase per household would only be about $500 yearly. This is not an insignificant amount, to be sure, but it represents the greatest possible increase; desalinated water will be available forever at a maximum of this price, so population can grow indefinitely without pushing the price of water beyond the desalinated cost. The desalinated price probably will be much less as technology improves and the price of energy falls; for example, a desalination plant that uses waste heat from an existing power plant produces water for only about half of the cost cited above.[5] (The present price of water at the source is not zero, either; in southern California the wholesale price of water is about $500 per acre-foot.)[6] Furthermore, homes reduce their use of water as the price goes up. In areas where water is metered even though not expensive, water use is only about half what it is per home as in areas where water is purchased at a flat monthly rate.[7] Figures 10-1a and 10-1b show how the amount of water used is responsive to the price.

The most important fact for consumer water supply is that most water is used in agriculture. For example, irrigation takes 80 percent of the water used in Utah and 90 percent in New Mexico.[8] And the amount of water used in agriculture is very sensitive to the price. The reason that there are cases of absolute shortage and rationing is that price is not allowed to respond to market conditions, but rather is fixed at a low subsidized price in many agricultural areas. For example, farmers near Fresno, California pay $17 for an acre-foot of water, while according to the U.S. General Accounting Office the "full cost" is $42 a foot. In some areas in California farmers pay $5 per acre-foot, whereas the Los Angeles water authorities pay $500 per acre-foot.[9] Such subsidies encourage farmers to plant crops that use water heavily, which diverts water from urban areas.

Another difficulty is that agricultural and municipal rights to use water from rivers are complex legal structures that often do not fit modern needs. Water economists are agreed that if governments stop subsidizing water to farmers, and allow water rights to be bought and sold freely, water shortages would no longer appear. But bureaucratic government restrictions often prevent those who have rights to more water than they need from selling their water rights to those who are willing to pay for the water; the bureaucrats fight a free market tooth and nail to protect their own powers, and the results are amazing stories of governmentally caused inefficiency and true scarcity leading to rationing.[10]

The typical endpoint of this irrational structure of overcontrol, miscontrol, and price-fixing by government is "drought police" or "water cops" in California cities who ticket people for activities such as illegal lawn watering.

For more information, see Terry Anderson's article (1995). As to the cleanliness and purity of the water that we drink, see chapter 17.

Lumber

Lumber is an agricultural product. As such it fits more neatly into this chapter on water and land use than into a chapter about energy, even though wood has been the main source of fuel in most places in the past.[11]

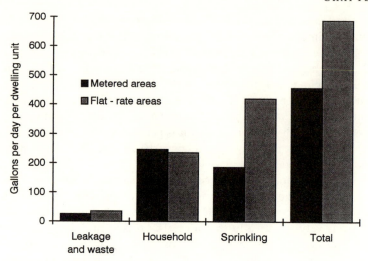

Figure 10-1a. Comparison of Metered versus Flat-Rate Use of Water

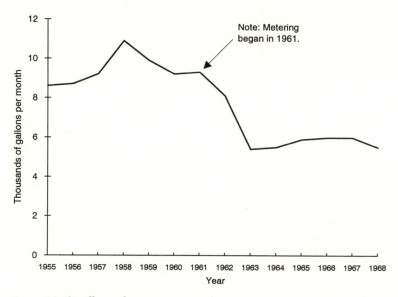

Figure 10-1b. Effects of Metering on Total Water Consumption per Dwelling, Boulder, Colorado, 1955–1968

Americans have long worried about a lumber shortage. In 1905, President Roosevelt said that "a timber famine is inevitable," a statement that culminated a national worry dating from as early as 1860. There was special concern over such woods as hickory. And under titles like "Tree Slaughter," a typical commentator today laments the "nightmare of splintered stumps and ravaged land." With too-typical disregard for the facts, that author talks about how the national forests are "now the great remaining repository of high quality softwood timber," when in fact privately owned forests are the overwhelmingly important source of sawtimber, and growing more so with every year, as figure 10-2 shows.

In the first edition, I said that despite the heavy use of wood since Teddy Roosevelt's time, the picture was quite different in the 1970s than it was then. I quoted a report that a "glut of low grades of factory lumber exists [and] a lack of market opportunities continues to set severe limitations on improvement of state and national forests. . . . [By 1951] hickory trees were taking over the eastern hardwood forest. In spite of expanded uses of timber for pulp and paper, we are [in 1971] probably growing more cubic feet of wood annually than we were in 1910."[12]

As the Council on Environmental Quality explained, "trends in net annual timber growth [total annual growth less mortality] show that the net annual growth of softwoods and hardwoods combined increased by 18 percent between 1952 and 1962 and another 14 percent between 1962 and 1970. This increase is a result of expanded programs in forest fire control, tree planting, and other forestry measures."[13] Since then, the amount of lumber being grown has continued to rise (see fig. 10-3).

Data on the trends in quantities of trees growing in various size classes of hardwoods and softwoods show the basis for both the fears of the environmentalists and the reassurances of the forest industry. The largest and oldest trees—the Douglas firs and other softwoods of the Pacific Northwest—were cut at an extraordinary rate from the 1960s to the 1980s. (The rate of cutting may have been increased by fear of coming regulations, one of the side effects of regulation.) But the quantity of trees in just about every other category has been increasing rapidly. and the rate of removal of the old growth in the Pacific Northwest has slowed almost to a crawl.

Data on reforestation are shown in figure 10-4. And 86 percent of that reforestation is private, only 14 percent being done by government—testimony again to the role of private incentives in creating both wealth and ambiance. Many trees are planted in order to be cut down—especially for paper. Indeed, "87 percent of all paper in the United States is produced from trees planted and grown for that purpose by the paper industry."[14] Hence, regretting the cutting of trees for paper is like lamenting the cutting of corn in cornfields.

Figure 10-5 shows data on the decline in losses to wildfire—again, good news for tree lovers.

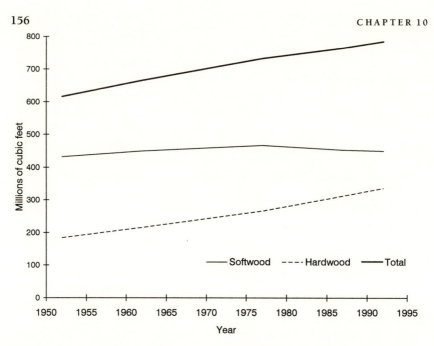

Figure 10-2. Volume of Timber on U.S. Timberland by Wood Type, 1952–1992

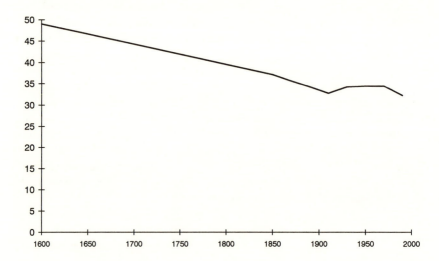

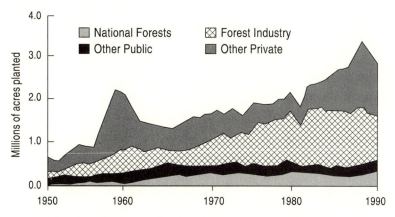

Figure 10-4. Tree Planting in the United States, 1950–1990

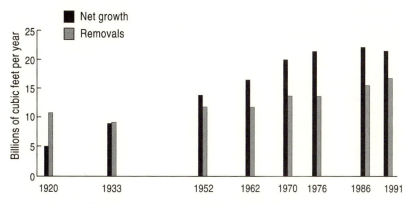

Figure 10-5. Timber Growth and Removals, 1920–1991

Despite the improving situation, as of the first edition, the data did not show a long-run decline in the price of wood—unlike all other natural resources.* But by 1992, the price data show that the same pattern of price decline is taking place as with other natural resources. The present situation is captured in a headline in a timber industry publication: "Bad News: Timber Prices Are Not Rising as Fast as Inflation Rate." The decline in prices occurred for each of the eight kinds of sawtimber and pulpwood (including hardwood), for the entire U.S. South.[15]

* The first edition erred in referring to the "heavy use" of timber at the turn of the century. Johnson and Libecap 1980 have shown that the investment rate of return on timber was about the same then as for railroad bonds, and that the price of wood increased at much the same rate throughout the nineteenth century and into the 1930s. This suggests that wood did *not* become more scarce for awhile around the turn of the century. If such a "famine" had really occurred, prices and returns on investment would have been abnormally high then.

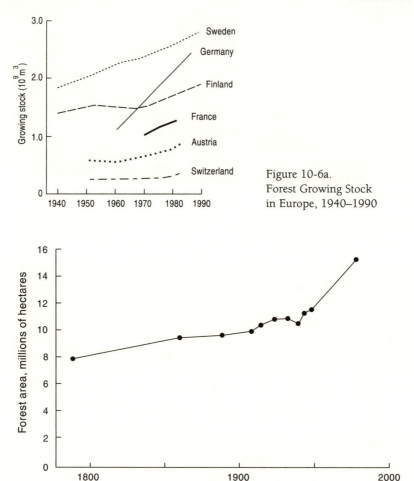

Figure 10-6a.
Forest Growing Stock
in Europe, 1940–1990

Figure 10-6b. Forest Area in France since the Late Eighteenth Century

   The situation in Europe is much the same. Forest resource surveys, which
provide fairly reliable data, show that for Austria, Finland, France, Germany,
Sweden, and Switzerland, there has been "a general increase of forest resources" in recent decades[16] (see fig. 10-6). Estimates for other European
countries based on less accurate methods indicate that "all countries reported
an increase of growing stock between 1950 and 1980."[17]
   These data are at odds with assertions that European trees have been adversely affected by air pollution. The forestry specialists reporting in *Science*
therefore adjudge that "the fertilization effects of pollutants override the adverse effects at least for the time being." In fact, the rate of growth of tree size

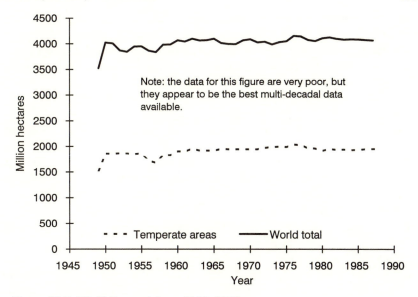

Figure 10-7. World Forested Area, 1949–1988

in Europe has been faster in more recent years than earlier in the century. Of course there have been some cases of forest decline due to pollution, such as the five kilometers around a smelter at Kola in northwestern Russia. The damaged areas total perhaps two thousand square kilometers in the former Soviet Union, and a total maximum of eight thousand square kilometers in Europe, less than 0.5 percent of the total.[18]

Why does the public believe that forests in Europe are declining when they are really increasing? Part of the explanation is that researchers invalidly infer general effects from partial biological data. For example, in an earlier issue of *Science* there appeared an article entitled "Air Pollution and Forest Decline in a Spruce Forest" in which the author inferred the conclusion of an overall decline. What he had actually observed were "symptoms of forest decline of spruce in Europe range from needle yellowing and loss to tree and stand mortality," to which he added theories about the effects of various gaseous pollutants.[19] Logical? Perhaps. Correct? No. That has too often been true of environmental scares.

Even taking the world as a whole—which includes poor countries that are still in the phase of deforesting (they will reforest when they become more affluent)—the total quantity of forests shows no evidence of declining, as seen in figure 10-7.

The confounding of predictions, and the shift from an apparently impending "timber famine" to actual glut was not fortuitous. It resulted from responses to perceived need. One response was that more timber was purposely planted. Another response has been higher productivity, so that an increasing number of trees grow on a shrinking area.[20] Perhaps most important have been conservation efforts due to higher prices, and research on wood and wood substitutes. We see the results in our homes—plastic bags substituted for paper bags; and newsprint made thinner and yet stronger, as in airmail editions of overseas newspapers. Perhaps wood will not even be used for paper in the future.

Kenaf and other plants show promise as alternative sources of newsprint. Kenaf grows to a height of 12–15 feet in five months, and yields "about 12 tons of dry plant per acre . . . roughly nine times the yield of wood" per year.[21] It has disadvantages, such as a high cost of transportation that makes it necessary that the farms be close to the mill. But the quality of paper made from it is better than paper from wood. And it is already being used in the Far East. Ironically, greater use of kenaf would reduce the demand for trees to be grown, which outdoorspeople might regret.

Just as with food, fears in the past about running out of wood have not been realized. And there is no reason to believe that the trends of earlier decades will suddenly reverse their direction. (Of course, we value forests for more reasons than timber. The extent of forests in the United States and in the world as an amenity for people and as an environment for other species is discussed in chapter 29.)

Wetlands

The preservation of "wetlands"—up to recent decades, known as "swamp ground"—is a remarkably clear-cut case of an activity having nothing to do with food production. The prevention of urbanization is justified (wrongly) as saving land for food production in the future, but wetlands preservers make very clear that keeping land available for agriculture is not their reason. "If the price of soybeans gets high enough, there's no reason why the owner wouldn't sell them [wetlands] or convert them [to crops]" says Louisiana's chief habitat biologist. The aim is to keep these lands out of production. (Actually, the preservationists need not worry about agricultural encroachment, because the price of soybeans is likely to be dropping rather than increasing in future years, just as it has for all other foodstuffs; see chapter 5).[22]

If our society deems it worthwhile to keep some lands wet or unurbanized or desertlike for the sake of the ambiance, or for the sake of animals, the economist can make no judgment about the wisdom of the policy. If we want to have arid Gila National Forest in New Mexico the way that "forest biologists [think] the range should look," as the ranger in charge put it,[23] or because, as the county executive in Montgomery County, Maryland, where I now live, said about farmland, "Most people find it attractive. It has good ambiance,"[24] that is a public choice. Or as a Wilderness Society official says, we should "protect the land not just for wildlife and human recreation, but just to have it there."[25]

Of course, if we want parks, or even land that no one will use or visit, we should be prepared to pay for them. We can also ask that the judgment be made on the basis of sound facts and analysis. And civil libertarians can raise reasonable questions about whether private owners of these lands should have their property rights taken away without compensation.

Conclusions

Concerning water, there is complete agreement among water economists that all it takes to ensure an adequate supply for agriculture as well as for households in rich countries is that there be a rational structure of water law and market pricing. The problem is not too many people but rather defective laws and bureaucratic interventions; freeing up markets in water would eliminate just about all water problems forever.

Ever cheaper desalination and water transportation—in considerable part because of declining energy prices in the long run—will ease supply in the future. In poor, water-short countries the problem with water supply—as with so many other matters—is lack of wealth to create systems to supply water efficiently enough. As these countries become richer, their water problems will become less difficult and more like those of the rich countries today, irrespective of population growth.

11 _____

When Will We Run Out of Oil? Never!

> If I say they behave like particles I give the wrong impression; also if I say they behave like waves. They behave in their own inimitable way, which technically could be called a quantum mechanical way. They behave in a way that is like nothing that you have ever seen before. Your experience with things that you have seen before is incomplete.
>
> *(Richard Feynman*, The Character of Physical Law, *1994)*

> The so-called theories of Einstein are merely the ravings of a mind polluted with liberal, democratic nonsense which is utterly unacceptable to German men of science.
>
> *(Dr. Walter Gross, Nazi Germany's official exponent of "Nordic Science," in Cerf and Navasky 1984)*

> The theory of a relativistic universe is the hostile work of the agents of fascism. It is the revolting propaganda of a moribund, counter-revolutionary ideology.
>
> *(Astronomical Journal of the Soviet Union, in Cerf and Navasky 1984)*

> What will we do when the pumps run dry?
>
> *(Paul and Anne Ehrlich,* The End of Affluence)

Energy, the Master Resource

Energy is the master resource, because energy enables us to convert one material into another. As natural scientists continue to learn more about the transformation of materials from one form to another with the aid of energy, energy will be even more important. Therefore, if the cost of usable energy is low enough, all other important resources can be made plentiful, as H. E. Goeller and A. M. Weinberg showed.[1]

For example, low energy costs would enable people to create enormous quantities of useful land. The cost of energy is the prime reason that water desalination now is too expensive for general use; reduction in energy cost would make water desalination feasible, and irrigated farming would follow in many areas that are now deserts. And if energy were much cheaper, it would be feasible to transport sweet water from areas of surplus to arid areas far away. Another example: If energy costs were low enough, all kinds of raw materials could be mined from the sea.

On the other hand, if there were to be an absolute shortage of energy—that is, if there were no oil in the tanks, no natural gas in the pipelines, no coal to load onto the railroad cars—then the entire economy would come to a halt. Or if energy were available but only at a very high price, we would produce much smaller amounts of most consumer goods and services.

The question before us is: What is the prospect for oil scarcity and energy prices? Here is the summary—at the beginning rather than at the end of the chapter to provide guideposts for your foray into the intellectual jungle of arguments about energy.

1. Energy is the most important of natural resources because
    a. the creation of other natural resources requires energy; and
    b. with enough energy all other resources can be created.

2. The most reliable method of forecasting the future cost and scarcity of energy is to extrapolate the historical trends of energy costs, for reasons given in chapters 1 and 2.

3. The history of energy economics shows that, in spite of troubling fears in each era of running out of whichever source of energy was important at that time, energy has grown progressively less scarce, as shown by long-run falling energy prices.

4. The cause of the increasing plenty in the supply of energy has been the development of improved extraction processes and the discovery of new sources and new types of energy.

5. These new developments have not been fortuitous, but rather have been induced by increased demand caused in part by rising population.

6. For the very long run, there is nothing meaningfully "finite" about our world that inevitably will cause energy, or even oil in particular, to grow more scarce and costly. Theoretically, the cost of energy could go either up or down in the very long run. But the trends point to a lower cost.

7. Forecasts based on technical analyses are less persuasive than historical extrapolations of cost trends. Furthermore, the technical forecasts of future energy supplies differ markedly among themselves.

8. A sure way to err in forecasting future supplies is to look at current "known reserves" of oil, coal, and other fossil fuels.

9. An appropriate technical forecast would be based on engineering estimates of the amounts of additional energy that will be produced at various price levels, and on predictions of new discoveries and technological advances that will come about as a result of various energy prices.

10. Some technical forecasters believe that even very much higher prices will produce only small increases in our energy supply, and even those only slowly. Others believe that at only slightly higher prices vast additional supplies will be forthcoming, and very quickly.

11. Causes of the disagreements among technical forecasters are differences in
    a. scientific data cited,
    b. assessments of political forces,
    c. ideology,

    d. belief or nonbelief in "finiteness" as an element of the situation, and
     e. vividness of scientific imagination.

    12. The disagreement among technical forecasters makes the economic extrapolation of decreasing historical costs even more compelling.

Now let's fill in this outline.

Because energy plays so central a role, it is most important that we think clearly about the way energy is found and used. This is the common view:

> Money in the bank, oil in the ground.
> Easily spent, less easily found.
> The faster they're spent, the sooner they run out.
> And that's what the Energy Crisis is about.[2]

But this jingle omits the key forces that completely alter the outcome. We shall see that, with energy just as with other raw materials, a fuller analysis produces an entirely different outlook than does this simplistic Malthusian projection.

The analysis of the supply of mineral resources in chapters 1–3 identified four factors as being important: (1) the increasing cost of extraction as more of the resource is used, if all other conditions remain the same; (2) the tendency of engineers to develop improved methods of extracting the resource in response to the rising price of the resource; (3) the propensity for scientists and businesspeople to discover substitutes—such as solar or nuclear power as substitutes for coal or oil—in response to increasing demand; and (4) the increased use of recycled material.

The supply of energy is analogous to the supply of other "extracted" raw materials with the exception of the fourth factor above. Minerals such as iron and aluminum can be recycled, whereas coal and oil are "burned up." Of course this distinction is not perfectly clear-cut; quarried marble is cut irreversibly and cannot be recycled by melting, as copper can. Yet even cut marble can be used again and again, whereas energy sources cannot.

The practical implication of being "used up" as opposed to being recyclable is that an increased rate of energy use would make the price of energy sources rise sharply, whereas an increased use of iron would not affect iron prices so much because iron could be drawn from previously used stocks such as dumps of old autos. This may seem to make the energy future look grim. But before we proceed to the analysis itself, it is instructive to see how energy "shortages" have frightened even the most intelligent of analysts for centuries.

The English Coal Scare

In 1865, W. Stanley Jevons, one of the nineteenth century's greatest social scientists, wrote a careful, comprehensive book proving that the growth of

England's industry must soon grind to a halt due to exhaustion of England's coal. "It will appear that there is no reasonable prospect of any relief from a future want of the main agent of industry," he wrote. "We cannot long continue our present rate of progress. The first check for our growing prosperity, however, must render our population excessive."[3] Figure 11-1 reproduces the frontispiece from Jevons's book, "showing the impossibility of a long continuance of progress." And Jevons's investigation proved to him that there was no chance that oil would eventually solve England's problem.

What happened? Because of the perceived future need for coal and because of the potential profit in meeting that need, prospectors searched out new deposits of coal, inventors discovered better ways to get coal out of the earth, and transportation engineers developed cheaper ways to move the coal.

This happened in the United States, too. At present, the proven U.S. reserves of coal are enough to supply a level of use far higher than the present consumption for many hundreds or thousands of years. And in some countries the use of coal must even be subsidized because though the labor cost per unit of coal output has been falling,[4] the cost of other fuels has dropped even more. This suggests that not enough coal was mined in the past, rather than that the future was unfairly exploited in earlier years. As to Jevons's poor old England, this is its present energy situation: "Though Britain may reach energy self-sufficiency late this year or early next, with its huge reserves of North Sea oil and gas lasting well into the next century, the country is moving ahead with an ambitious program to develop its even more plentiful coal reserves."[5]

The Long-Running Running Out of Oil Drama

Just as with coal, running out of oil has long been a nightmare, as this brief history shows:

> 1885, U.S. Geological Survey: "Little or no chance for oil in California."
> 1891, U.S. Geological Survey: Same prophecy by USGS for Kansas and Texas as in 1885 for California.
> 1914, U.S. Bureau of Mines: Total future production limit of 5.7 billion barrels, perhaps ten-year supply.
> 1939, Department of the Interior: Reserves to last only thirteen years.
> 1951, Department of the Interior, Oil and Gas Division: Reserves to last thirteen years.[6]

The fact that the gloomy official prophesies of the past have regularly been proven false does not prove that every future gloomy forecast about oil will be wrong. And forecasts can be overoptimistic, too. But this history does show that expert forecasts often have been far too pessimistic. We therefore should

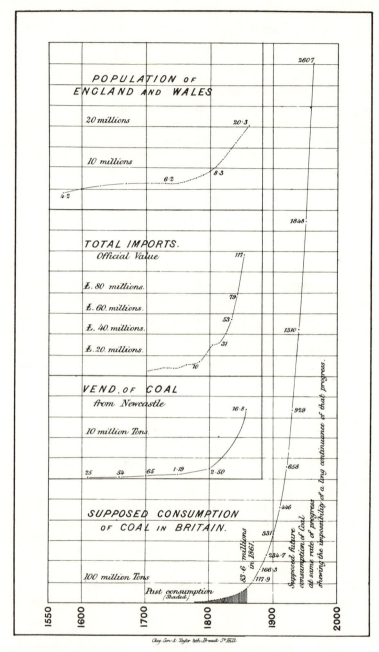

Figure 11-1. Jevons's View of Coal and of England's Future, as of 1865

not simply take such forecasts at face value, because of the bad record as well as because they are founded on an unsound method of proven reserves, as discussed in chapter 2.

The Long-Run History of Energy Supplies

The statistical history of energy supplies is a rise in plenty rather than in scarcity. As was discussed at length in chapter 1, the relevant measures are the production costs of energy as measured in time and money, and the price to the consumer. Figures 11-2, 11-3, and 11-4 show the historical data for coal, oil, and electricity. Because chapter 1 discussed the relationship of such cost and price data to the concepts of scarcity and availability, that discussion need not be repeated here. Suffice it to say that the appropriate interpretation of these data is that they show an unambiguous trend toward lower cost and greater availability of energy.*

The price of oil fell because of technological advance, of course. The price of a barrel (42 gallons) fell from $4 to thirty-five cents in 1862 because of the innovation of drilling, begun in Pennsylvania in 1859. And the price of a gallon of kerosene fell from fifty-eight cents to twenty-six cents between 1865 and 1870 because of improvements in refining and transportation, many of them by John D. Rockefeller. This meant that the middle class could afford oil lamps at night; earlier, only the rich could afford whale oil and candles, and all others were unable to enjoy the benefits of light.[7]

The price history of *electricity* is particularly revealing because it indicates the price to the consumer, at home or at work. That is, the price of electricity is closer to the price of the *service* we get from energy than are the prices of coal and oil, which are raw materials. And as discussed in chapter 3, the costs of the services matter more than the costs of the raw materials themselves.

The ratio of the price of electricity to the average wage in manufacturing (fig. 11-4) shows that the quantity of electricity bought with an hour's wages has steadily increased. Because each year an hour's work has bought more rather than less electricity, this measure suggests that energy has become ever less troublesome in the economy over the recorded period, no matter what the price of energy in current dollars.

In short, the trends in energy costs and scarcity have been downward over the entire period for which we have data. And such trends are usually the most reliable bases for forecasts. From these data we may conclude with consider-

---

* An interesting and revealing incident in which Ehrlich et al. asserted that the trend had changed before 1970, but their judgment was based on a single observation which turned out to be a typographical error, is discussed briefly in the Epilogue, and at more length in Simon (1990), selection 3, or in Simon (1980b).

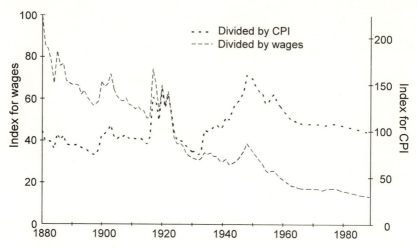

Figure 11-2. The Price of Coal Relative to the Consumer Price Index and Wages in the United States

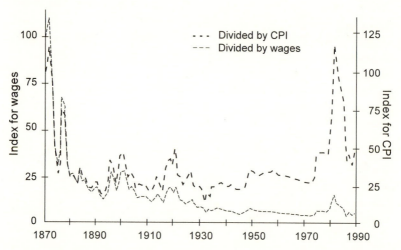

Figure 11-3. The Price of Oil Relative to the Consumer Price Index and Wages in the United States

able confidence that energy will be less costly and more available in the future than in the past.

The reason that the cost of energy has declined in the long run is the fundamental process of (1) increased demand due to the growth of population and income, which raises prices and hence constitutes opportunity to entrepreneurs and inventors; (2) the search for new ways of supplying the demand for

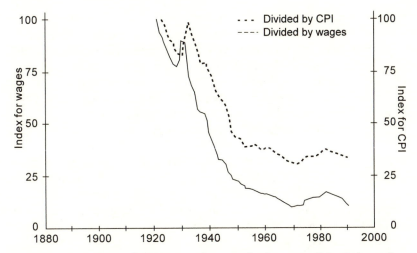

Figure 11-4. The Price of Electricity Relative to the Consumer Price Index and Wages in the United States

energy; (3) the eventual discovery of methods which leave us better off than if the original problem had not appeared.

An early illustration of the process: In 300 B.C.E., so much wood was being used for metal smelting that the Roman Senate limited mining. (Using the coercive power of government, instead of the creative power of the market, is a very old idea.)[8] Almost two millennia later, in England, the shortage of wood for use as charcoal in the casting of iron became so acute—it was affecting the building of naval ships—that in 1588 Parliament passed a law against cutting trees for coke in iron making, and then banned the building of new foundries in 1580.[9] Though the use of coal in place of charcoal had been known, there were technical difficulties—impurities that affected the quality of the iron. This time, the wood shortage exerted pressure that led to the development of coal as well as blowing machines to be used in smelting, a keystone in the upcoming Industrial Revolution.

Jumping Off the Eiffel Tower

You may object that extrapolating a future from past trends of greater and greater abundance is like extrapolating—just before you hit the ground—that a jump from the top of the Eiffel Tower is an exhilarating experience. Please notice, however, that for a jump from the tower we have advance knowledge that there would be a sudden discontinuity when reaching the ground. In the case of energy and natural resources, there is no persuasive advance evidence for a negative discontinuity; rather, the evidence points toward positive discontinuities—nuclear fusion, solar energy, and discoveries of energy sources that we now cannot conceive of. Historical evidence further teaches us that such worries about discontinuities have usually generated the very economic pressures that have opened new frontiers. Hence, there is no solid reason to think that we are about to hit the ground after an energy jump as if from an Eiffel Tower. More likely, we are in a rocket on the ground that has only been warming up until now and will take off sometime soon.

More appropriate than the Eiffel Tower analogy is this joke: Sam falls from a building he is working on, but luckily has hold of a safety rope. Inexplicably he lets go of the rope and hits the ground with a thud. Upon regaining consciousness he is asked: "Why did you let go of the rope?" "Ah," he says, "it was going to break anyway." Analogously, letting go of all the ropes that support the advance of civilization—for example, turning our backs on the best potential sources of energy—is the advice we now receive from energy doomsters and conservationists.

The Theory of Future Energy Supplies

Turning now from trends to theory, we shall consider our energy future in two theoretical contexts: (1) with income and population remaining much as they are now, (2) with different rates of income growth than now. (The case of different rates of population growth than now will be discussed in chapter 28.) It would be neatest to discuss the United States separately from the world as a whole, but for convenience we shall go back and forth. (The longer the time horizon, the more the discussion refers to the world as a whole rather than just to the United States or the industrialized countries.)

The analysis of energy resembles the analysis of natural resources and food, but energy has special twists that require separate discussion. With these two exceptions, everything said earlier about natural resources applies to energy: (1) On the negative side, energy cannot easily be recycled. (But energy can come much closer to being recycled than one ordinarily thinks. For example, because the fuel supply on warships is very limited, heat from the boilers is passed around water pipes to extract additional calories as it goes up the smokestack.) (2) On the positive side, our energy supplies clearly are not bounded by the Earth. The sun has been the ultimate source of all energy other than nuclear. Therefore, though we cannot recycle energy as we can recycle minerals, our supply of energy is clearly not limited by the Earth's present contents, and hence it is not "finite" in any sense at all—not even in the nonoperational sense.

Furthermore, humanity burned wood for thousands of years before arriving at coal, burned coal about three hundred years before developing oil, and burned oil about seventy years before inventing nuclear fission. Is it reasonable and prudent to assume that sometime in the next seven billion years—or even seven hundred or seventy years—humanity will not arrive at a cheaper and cleaner and more environmentally benign substitute for fission energy?

But let us turn to a horizon relevant for social decisions—the next five, twenty-five, one hundred, perhaps two hundred years. And let us confine ourselves to the practical question of what is likely to happen to the cost of energy relative to other goods, and in proportion to our total output.

The Bogeyman of Diminishing Returns Again

First let us dispose of the "law of diminishing returns" with respect to energy. Here is how Barry Commoner uses this idea:

> [T]he law of diminishing returns [is] the major reason why the United States has turned to foreign sources for most of its oil. Each barrel [of oil] drawn from the earth causes the next one to be more difficult to obtain. The economic consequence is that it causes the cost to increase continuously.[10]

Another environmentalist explains her version of the "law of diminishing returns" with respect to oil:

> We must now extract our raw materials from ever more degraded and inaccessible deposits. This means that ever more of our society's precious investment capital must be diverted to this process and less is available for consumption and real growth. Fifty years ago, getting oil required little more than sticking a pipe in the ground. Now we must invest several billion dollars to open up the Alaska oilfields to deliver the same product. *Economists, if they understood this process as well as physical scientists,* might call it the declining productivity of capital [law of diminishing returns].[11]

All these quotes are just plain wrong; it costs less today to get oil from the ground in prime sources than it cost fifty years ago to get it from the ground in prime sources. (The second afternote to chapter 3 explains how there is no "law" of diminishing returns in general, and hence why this line of thinking is fallacious.)

In brief, there is no compelling theoretical reason why we should eventually run out of energy, or even why energy should be more scarce and costly in the future than it is now.

The Best—and Worst—Ways to Forecast Future Energy Availability

The best way to forecast price trends is to study past price trends, if data are available and if there is no reason to believe that the future will be sharply different from the past. (The reasoning that supports this point of view is set forth at length in chapter 2.)

For energy there are plenty of past price data available, as we have seen in figures 11-2, 11-3, and 11-4. And there is no convincing reason to believe that the future will break completely from the past. Therefore, extrapolation of the trends in those figures is the most reasonable method of forecasting the future of energy supplies and costs, on the assumption that price has been close to cost in the past and will continue to be so in the future. This method of economic forecasting envisions progressively lower energy costs and less scarcity.

Geologists and engineers, however, rely on technical rather than price-trend data in their forecasts of energy supplies. Because their forecasts have had so much influence on public affairs, we must analyze their methods and meanings.

We must first dispose of the preposterous but commonly accepted notion that the energy situation can be predicted with the aid of "known reserves." This notion is an example of the use of misleading numbers simply because they are the only numbers available. We briefly considered the uselessness of this concept of "reserves" in chapter 2 with respect to mineral resources. Now let us discuss it with respect to oil.

"Known reserves" means the total amount of oil in areas that have been prospected thoroughly, quantities that geologists are quite sure of. Individuals, firms, and governments create known reserves by searching for promising drilling areas long in advance of the moment when wells might be drilled—far enough ahead to allow preparation time, but not so far ahead that the investment in prospecting costs will not obtain a satisfactory return. The key idea here is that it costs money to produce information about known reserves. The quantity of known reserves at any moment tells us more about the expected profitability of oil wells than it does about the amount of oil in the ground. And the higher the cost of exploration, the lower will be the known reserves that it pays to create.

"Known reserves" are much like the food we put into our cupboards at home. We stock enough groceries for a few weeks or days—not so much that we will be carrying a heavy unneeded inventory that bulges the cupboard and ties up an unnecessary amount of money in groceries, and not so little that we may run out if an unexpected event—a guest or a blizzard—should descend upon us. The amount of food in our cupboards tells little or nothing about the scarcity of food in our communities, because as a rule it does not reveal how much food is available in the retail stores. Similarly, the oil in the "cupboard"—the quantity of known reserves—tells us nothing about the quantities of oil that can be obtained in the long run at various extraction costs.

This explains why the quantity of known reserves, as if by a miracle of coincidence, stays just a step ahead of demand, as seen in figure 11-5. An elderly man commented to me in the 1970s that, according to the news stories about known reserves, "we've been just about to run out of oil ever since I've

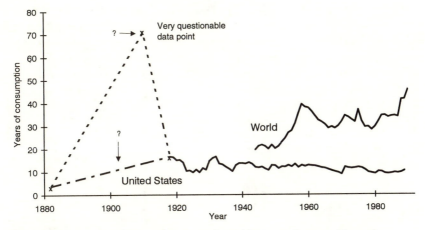

Figure 11-5. Crude Oil, United States and World Known Reserves/Annual Production

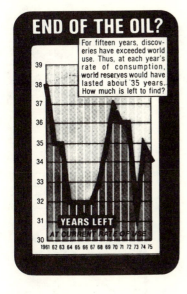

Figure 11-6. The Confusion of the Proven-Reserves Concept

been a boy." Yet most discussions of the oil and energy situation—among laymen and also among the most respected journalists—still focus on known reserves. Figure 11-6, taken from *Newsweek*, is typical. The graph apparently shows that the world's proven reserves have been declining, leading to the rhetorical threat above the picture "End of the oil? . . . How much is left to find?"

Even more misleading is a graph of proven reserves in the United States alone, as in figure 11-7. As the United States turns to imports because they are

STILL IN THE GROUND
America's proven reserves of oil and gas are on the decline, but geologists estimate there may be a total of 1.6 trillion barrels of oil and potentially astronomical amounts of gas still to be found. The hitch: how much will it cost?
YEARS SUPPLY OF PROVEN RESERVES AT CURRENT RATES OF USE
U.S. RESERVES
NATURAL GAS
CRUDE OIL
1966 1967 1968 1969 1970 1971 1972 1973 1974 1975 1976

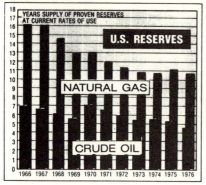

Figure 11-7. More Confusion

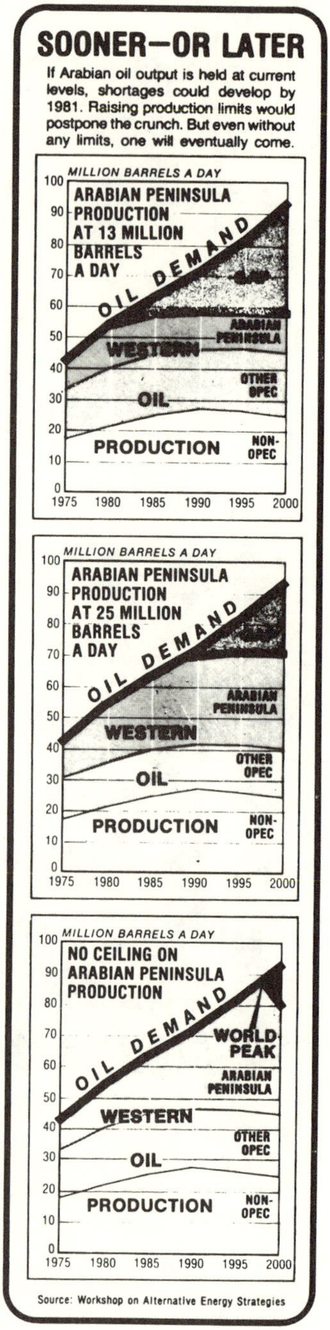

SOONER—OR LATER
If Arabian oil output is held at current levels, shortages could develop by 1981. Raising production limits would postpone the crunch. But even without any limits, one will eventually come.
MILLION BARRELS A DAY
ARABIAN PENINSULA PRODUCTION AT 13 MILLION BARRELS A DAY
OIL DEMAND
ARABIAN PENINSULA
WESTERN
OTHER OPEC
OIL
PRODUCTION
NON-OPEC
MILLION BARRELS A DAY
ARABIAN PENINSULA PRODUCTION AT 25 MILLION BARRELS A DAY
OIL DEMAND
ARABIAN PENINSULA
WESTERN
OTHER OPEC
OIL
PRODUCTION
NON-OPEC
MILLION BARRELS A DAY
NO CEILING ON ARABIAN PENINSULA PRODUCTION
OIL DEMAND
WORLD PEAK
ARABIAN PENINSULA
WESTERN
OTHER OPEC
OIL
PRODUCTION
NON-OPEC
Source: Workshop on Alternative Energy Strategies

Figure 11-8. Another Form of Hokum

cheaper than the home product, its proven reserves inevitably will fall. If one were to draw a graph of U.S. proven reserves of aluminum or gold, they also would appear tiny. So what?

A more "sophisticated"—and even more misleading—approach is to project present growth in demand, assuming the price will remain constant, and then compare that projection to known reserves, thereby indicating that demand will apparently outstrip supply very soon. This approach may be seen in figure 11-8. Even assuming that the growth in demand at present prices is reasonably estimated—and this would be difficult to do well—all that such a calculation would show is that price must rise in order to lower the demand and raise the supply until demand and supply meet. This basic economic way of looking at supply and demand is totally missing from figure 11–8.

Equally misleading is the assumption underlying figure 11-8 that there will be no developments in oil production or in other energy sources that will make future energy costs lower than they would be with the present state of technological knowledge.

Better Technical Forecasting Methods

If one insists on making a technical forecast of the energy supply—even though such a forecast is likely to be inferior to extrapolations of past economic trends—how should it best be done? That is, how might one make a sound material-technical forecast for oil and energy in the near term—say over the next ten or twenty years? (See chapter 2 for a general discussion of material-technical forecasts of resource supply.)

During the next decade or two, increases in income and population in the United States and in the world may be assumed to be known. Therefore, they can be taken into account as data rather than treated as imponderables. In addition, forecasts of the production of energy in the near-term future utilize two other kinds of information: (1) engineering estimates of the cost of extracting fuel from such currently unexploited sources as shale oil and wind power with available technology, based on calculations of the engineering inputs required for each type of energy source; and (2) economic estimates of how many conventional new oil wells and coal mines and nuclear reactors will be developed at various prices higher and lower than the present energy prices, based on past data about the extent to which energy-producing firms respond to changes in market prices.

Engineering estimates must play the dominant role in forecasts of the place of nuclear energy, shale oil, solar power, wind power, and other energy sources for which there are considerable uncertainties about technical processes and costs due to a lack of experience with these sources. But where an energy source is currently being employed sufficiently to produce a large body of data about the process of extraction and about producer behavior, as is true of the fossil fuels, empirical economic estimates of supply response to price changes should have the dominant role. The best overall energy forecast, therefore, would be a blend of both the economic and engineering approaches.

There is great variety, however, in the estimates of engineers and scientists about the future costs of developing such energy sources as shale oil and nuclear power. Technologists also differ greatly in their guesses about the dangers to life from the various processes. And economists differ considerably in their estimates of the responsiveness of the energy industry to various price levels. For example, in 1977 the supply of natural gas became a very contentious political issue. These were some of the resulting supply estimates: (1) A predecessor agency of the Department of Energy, the Energy Research and Development Administration (ERDA), made three production estimates within three months, varying by a factor of three![12] President Carter offered an even lower estimate than the lowest of those three, that there was only "10 years supply . . . at 1974 technology and 1974 prices."[13] (2) The American Gas Association said that there is enough gas "to last between 1,000 and 2,500 years at current consumption." And the newspaper story continued that "Experts in ERDA have been trying to tell the White House [this] too."[14] The difference between this and the estimate in (1) above boggles the mind—ten years' supply versus a 1,000–2,500 years' supply! (3) A later "official" estimate, made in the midst of the congressional debate on energy in the same year 1977, by Dr. Vincent E. McKelvey, who was then director of the U.S. Geological Survey, was that "as much as . . . 3,000 to 4,000 times the amount of natural gas the United States will consume this year may be sealed in the geopressured zones underlying the Gulf Coast region."[15] But this estimate ran contrary to what the White House was saying, and within two months McKelvey was fired from his job as director—after six years as director and thirty-seven years at the Geological Survey, and after being nominated for the director's job by the National Academy of Sciences. As the *Wall Street Journal* put it, "Dr. McKelvey did not know enough to keep his mouth shut!"[16] Such enormous variation can arise simply as a result of political fiddling with the figures.

A more recent sober estimate by the "International Gas Union Committee on World Gas Supply and Demand estimates that even by the year 2000, the static lifetime of world gas reserves will be 112 years"[17]—and that does not include future discoveries of gas, of course.

With respect to still-undeveloped sources such as shale oil and artificial gas, the variation in estimates is greater yet.

Why do estimates of supply response to price changes differ so widely? There are a host of reasons, including (a) vested interests—for example, the oil companies have a stake in low gas prices paid to gas suppliers so that fewer gas wells will be drilled and more oil will be sold, and hence they want lower estimates of the responsiveness of natural gas supplies to changes in price; in contrast, gas companies have a stake in higher (unregulated) prices, and hence want higher estimates of gas supply responsiveness; (b) basic beliefs about the "finiteness" of potential supplies and about the likelihood of the human imagination to respond to needs with new developments; (c) differences in the scientific imaginations of the engineers and geologists making the estimates; and (d) professional differences among engineers and among economists due to differences in technical approaches.

Every month, it seems, we read of new ways to get more energy. Item: Three-dimensional seismic exploration methods have produced large new oil discoveries at very low cost. In Nigeria and Oman, Shell "has found new oil reserves at costs of less than 10 cents a barrel."[18] Item: Lumps of methane hydrate on the ocean floor could constitute "a potential fuel reserve that may dwarf all the fossil fuel deposits on land combined."[19]

In my view, the data and theory continue to support a forecast made years ago by Herman Kahn and associates. "Energy costs as a whole are very likely to continue the historical downward trend indefinitely. . . . Except for temporary fluctuations caused by bad luck or poor management, the world need not worry about energy shortages or costs in the future."[20]

What about the Very Long Run?

Chapter 3 alluded to the increase in efficiency in energy use over the decades and centuries. An analysis by William Baumol mentioned there shows that such increases in efficiency have huge effects. The key idea is that an improvement in productivity not only reduces resource use in the present but, even more important, also increases the future services of the entire stock of unused resources. This alone could mean that the future supply will never run out.

This process may be seen in figure 11-9, where the amount of coal required to move a ton of freight by sea fell to about a tenth of its 1830 value by 1890. That is a greater proportion of increase in efficiency than was the increase in population over those years. The transition to oil represented an increase in economic efficiency (or it would not have taken place). And there is no reason why that process should not continue indefinitely, with ship surfaces getting smoother, and so on. Of course nuclear power can replace coal and oil entirely, which constitutes an increase in efficiency so great that it is beyond my powers to portray the entire process on a single graph based on physical units.

Much the same occurs with electricity in figure 11-9. A generator converts the heat from fuels or the power of falling water into electrical energy. One

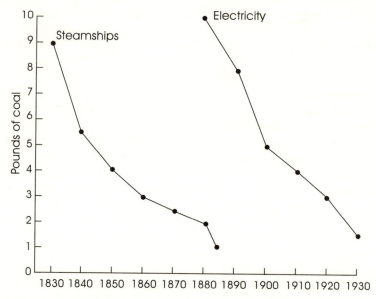

Figure 11-9. Energy Utilization over the Long Term, 1830–1930

cannot extract more energy from a generator than one puts in, but in addition to increasing efficiency in generation, there is increasing efficiency in end-use products such as refrigeration, heaters, and appliances.

The process is even more extraordinary with respect to the input of human energy (no matter how human energy is measured). A handful of humans can now move hundreds of thousands of tons of freight across an ocean in a single ship, many fewer people per ton than in centuries past. And measured in ton-miles per day, the increase in efficiency is even greater.

The Nonfiniteness of Oil

You may wonder whether "nonrenewable" energy resources such as oil, coal, and natural gas differ from the recyclable minerals in such a fashion that the nonfinite arguments in earlier chapters do not apply. Eventually we'll burn all the coal and oil that powered these impressive advances, you may be thinking. But our energy supply also is nonfinite, including oil as an important example. That was not a misprint. In chapter 3, I showed that it is necessary to say how one would count the amount of a resource if one is to meaningfully say that the resource is finite. Therefore, let's consider the following sequence of difficulties with respect to counting the amount of oil. As with other resources, careful thinking leads to the conclusion that the potential amount of oil—and even more, the amount of the services that we now get from oil—is not finite.

1. The oil potential of a particular well may be measured, and hence it is limited (though it is interesting and relevant that as we develop new ways of extracting hard-to-get oil, the economic capacity of a well increases). But the number of wells that will eventually produce oil, and in what quantities, is not known or measurable at present and probably never will be, and hence is not meaningfully finite.

2. Even if we unrealistically assume that the number of potential wells in the Earth might be surveyed completely and that we could arrive at a reasonable estimate of the oil that might be obtained with present technology (or even with technology that will be developed in the next one hundred years), we still would have to reckon the future possibilities of shale oil and tar sands—a difficult task.

3. But let us assume that we could reckon the oil potential of shale and tar sands. We would then have to reckon the conversion of coal to oil. That, too, might be done, but the measurement is becoming increasingly loose, and hence less "finite" and "limited."

4. Then there is the oil that we might produce, not from fossils, but from new crops—palm oil, soybean oil, and so on. Clearly, there is no meaningful limit to this source except the sun's energy (land and water are not limits—see chapters 6 and 10). The notion of finiteness is making ever less sense as we proceed.

5. If we allow for the substitution of nuclear and solar power for oil—and this makes sense because what we really want are the services of oil and not oil itself—the notion of a limit is even less meaningful.

6. Of course the sun may eventually run down. But even if our sun were not as vast as it is, there may well be other suns elsewhere.

The joke at the head of chapter 3 makes the point that whether there is an "ultimate" end to all this—that is, whether the energy supply really is "finite" after the sun and all the other planets have been exhausted—is a question so hypothetical that it should be compared with other metaphysical entertainments such as calculating the number of angels that can dance on the head of a pin. As long as we continue to draw energy from the sun, any conclusion about whether or not energy is "ultimately finite" has no bearing upon present policy decisions.

About energy from the sun: The assertion that our resources are ultimately finite seems most relevant to energy but yet is actually more misleading with respect to energy than with respect to other resources. When people say that mineral resources are "finite," they are invariably referring to the Earth as a bounded system—the "spaceship Earth" to which we are apparently confined just as astronauts are confined to their spaceship. But the main source of our energy even now is the sun, no matter how you think of the matter. This goes far beyond the fact that the sun was the prior source of the energy locked into the oil and coal we use. The sun is also the source of the energy in the food we eat, and in the trees that we use for many purposes.

In coming years, solar energy may be used to heat homes and water in many parts of the world. (As of 1965, much of Israel's hot water had been heated by solar devices for years, even when the price of oil was much lower than it is now, although I remember that the showers you got with this water were at best lukewarm unless you used a backup electrical system to boost the temperature.) If the prices of conventional energy supplies were to rise considerably higher than they now are, solar energy could be called on for much more of our needs, though this price rise seems unlikely given present technology. And even if the Earth were sometime to run out of sources of energy for nuclear processes—a prospect so distant that it is a waste of time to talk about it—there are energy sources on other planets. Hence, the notion that the supply of energy is finite because the Earth's fossil fuels or even its nuclear fuels are limited is sheer nonsense. And this discussion has omitted consideration of any energy sources still to be discovered.

Conclusions

Energy differs from other resources because it is "used up," and cannot be recycled. Energy apparently trends toward exhaustion. It seems impossible to keep using energy and still never begin to run out—that is, never reach a point of increasing scarcity. But the long-run trends in energy prices, together with the explanatory theory of induced innovation, promise continually decreasing scarcity and cost—just the opposite of popular opinion. At worst, the cost ceiling provided by nuclear power guarantees that the cost of electrical power cannot rise far above present energy costs, political obstacles aside.

The historical facts entirely contradict the commonsensical Malthusian theory that the more we use, the less there is left to use and hence the greater the scarcity. Through the centuries, the prices of energy—coal, oil, and electricity—have been decreasing rather than increasing, relative to the cost of labor and even relative to the price of consumer goods, just as with all other natural resources. And nuclear energy, which at present costs much the same as coal and oil,[21] guarantees an inexhaustible supply of energy at declining cost as technology improves.

In economic terms, this means that energy has been getting more available, rather than more scarce, as far back as we have data. This implies that the rate at which our stocks of resources increase, or the increasing efficiency of use over time, or a combination of the two forces, have overmatched the exhaustion of resources.

Another way to look at the matter: Energy has become less and less important as measured by its share of GNP. This is the same story as revealed by all other natural resources.

The reason that the prices of energy and other natural resources decline even as we use more is the advance of technology. Nevertheless, just as with land and copper, there are other forces at play which make it possible for us to have increasing amounts of the services we need even as we boost the demands we make upon the supplies of those resources.

One saving grace is improved techniques of use. Consider the steam engine, which when first invented operated at 1 percent efficiency. Engines nowadays operate perhaps thirty times more efficiently. That is, they use a thirtieth as much energy for the same result. The invention of the microwave oven immediately meant that only 10 percent as much energy was necessary to cook a meal as before.[22] When someone finds a way to increase the efficiency of using a resource, the discovery not only increases the efficiency of the energy we use this year, but it also increases the effective stocks resources that are known or are as yet undiscovered. And this process could continue for a long time, perhaps indefinitely.

Also important are increases in energy supply. We learn how to dig deeper, pump faster. And we invent new sources of energy—aside from coal, shale, oil, tar sands, and the like. We can also "grow" oil substitutes as long as there is sunlight to raise plants. (See chapter 6 on hydroponic farming using fresh water. And production of oil-seed crops that grow with salt water, which allows agriculture with irrigation of the desert, is now entering commercial development in Saudi Arabia.)[23] Also, nuclear fission power will be available at constant or declining costs practically forever.

After our sun runs out of energy, there may be nuclear fusion, or some other suns to take care of our needs. We've got seven billion years to discover solutions to the theoretical problems that we have only been able to cook up in the past few centuries of progress in physics. It's reasonable to expect the supply of energy to continue becoming more available and less scarce, forever.

12

Today's Energy Issues

[G]iving society cheap abundant energy at this point would be equivalent to giving an idiot child a machine gun.
(*Paul Ehrlich*)

Low Oil Prices Are Bad, Some U.S. Experts Say
(New York Times, *March 12, 1991, quoted by Charles Krauthammer,* Washington Post, *March 15, 1991*)

[G]asoline is too cheap. Everyone knows it. None dares say it.
(*Jessica Mathews*, Washington Post, *May 19, 1992*)

KEYNES'S famous remark, "In the long run we're all dead," was remarkably foolish. A charitable guess is that his love of a clever line overcame his better judgment (although we saw in chapter 3 that his judgment about the future of raw materials also was entirely wrong-headed). In any case, the remark expresses a common preoccupation with the present and the immediate future. So let us now talk about current energy issues.

Energy generally, and oil in particular, raises emotional temperatures. Figure 12-1 shows that the percentage of the public that says energy is the "most important problem facing the nation" jumped from 3 percent in September, 1973, to 34 percent in January 1974, and then quickly fell back down to 4 percent. Then it went sharply up and then down again in 1977, and then up once more in the summer of 1979, following the price rise by OPEC, and then down once more.[1] Fully 82 percent in 1979 said that "the energy situation in the United States" is "very serious" or "fairly serious,"[2] but another series of polls also showed that public concern quickly dropped in the 1980s (see fig. 12-1). These swift changes in the public's thinking illustrate the volatility of concern about energy and oil. And since the public has no first-hand experience of energy supply, other than changes in gasoline prices (which show no increased scarcity in the long run), these poll results also suggest that the public's concern derives from how the press and television describe the situation.

Our true energy situation can be seen in the price data for coal, oil, and electricity shown in figures 11-2, 11-3, and 11-4. These figures cover a long span of time, however, and they could obscure important changes in the recent past. Therefore, let us analyze the recent course of energy costs, with

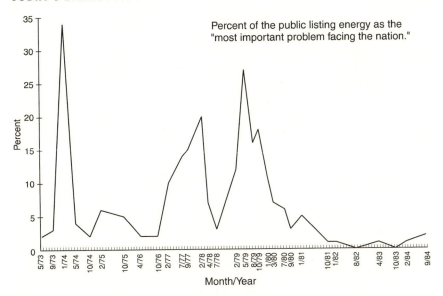

Figure 12-1. Energy as the "Most Important Problem"

emphasis on the proximate cause of concern—oil. The chapter will also touch on "alternative" sources of energy. (Chapter 13 examines special issues of nuclear power.)

The key short-run issue is government policy with respect to energy. Persons who worry most about energy supply in the immediate future tend to call for various government interventions. In contrast, those who conclude that energy supply should not worry us at all—I am among them—tend to believe that just about every likely government intervention in energy markets will be both costly to the public and damaging to the supply of energy.

The programs called for by environmentalists combine support for "alternative" sources of energy such as wind and solar, taxation of fossil fuels to reduce their use, and raising all possible obstacles to the use of nuclear power. These actions would have the following effects: (1) increase the number of deaths, because nuclear power is much safer to produce than coal or oil, and because lightweight autos are less safe than heavy ones; (2) limit the rise in the standard of living and the creation of jobs by raising energy costs to enterprises, and by hampering the efforts of energy producers; (3) raise costs to consumers and hence lower the purchasing power of their incomes; and (4) enmesh the economy in regulations that fritter away the energies of entrepreneurs.

The reasons that activists desire these programs are complex. Consumer welfare certainly is not the only or even the preeminent motive, as seen in the arrogant epigraphs—by Ehrlich that people who have plentiful energy are dangerous, and by Mathews that "gasoline is too cheap" (stated in the original context without any explanation). One motive is energy activists' belief that economic growth is bad in itself, as is seen in the Ehrlich quote above, and in the quotation from Herman Daly on page 202. This motive is hostile to *every* reasonably efficient energy source, including nuclear, oil, and coal. An official of the World Resources Institute says, "Coal burning is a fundamental threat to life on this planet. We'll eventually have a fight over every coal-powered electric plant."[3] It's harder to be against such options if you worry about supplying enough energy for growing public demand.

First Some Facts

Energy in general, and oil in particular, are topics about which it is most difficult to find agreement. But let us see how far we can get. Let us briefly note which facts scholars agree on, which matters are in dispute, and how the energy situation is tangled with conflicting interests, politics, and ideology.

Agreed-upon facts about oil. (a) Enough oil to supply the world for several decades can be produced in the Middle East at perhaps fifty *cents* per barrel (1992 dollars), to be compared with a market price of about twenty *dollars* per barrel. (b) Transportation from the Middle East to the United States and elsewhere costs $2 to $4 per barrel.[4]

Apparently, few speculators believe that the price of oil will sharply and continually go up in the future. If anyone really did believe that, it would make sense to buy and stockpile oil for long-term appreciation, even with the cost of storage. But no one does so (though South Africa is said to have a seven-year supply because of its political-military situation).

Much of the world has not been explored systematically for oil. This may be seen in the numbers of wells that had been drilled in various parts of the world up to 1975, and the number of producing wells as of 1989, respectively: United States—2,425,095 and 603,365; USSR—530,000 and 145,000; Latin America—100,000 and 17,500; Canada—100,000 and 38,794; Australia and New Zealand—2,500 and 1,024; Western Europe—25,000 and 6,856; Japan—5,500 and 368; Africa and Madagascar—15,000 and 5,381; South and Southeast Asia—11,000 and 9,900; China—9,000 and 1,944; and the Middle East—10,000 and 6,827.[5] The reason so much more exploration and drilling have been done in the United States than elsewhere is not that the United States has so much greater potential for oil production but rather that it has had a high *demand* for oil, plus plenty of production know-how, trade protection against imported oil for many years, and political stability.

Estimates of crude-oil reserves are highly sensitive to the definition of crude oil. The U.S. Geological Survey uses a definition that includes only oil that will come to the surface at *atmospheric pressure*. If one also includes oil that can be

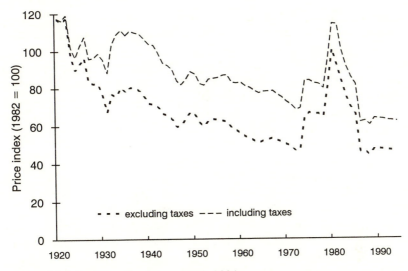

Figure 12-2. Real Gasoline Prices, 1920–1994

forced to the surface under pressure, plus naturally nonliquid oil in shale and tar sands and other sources, the estimate would be considerably greater.[6]

The most important long-run fact about oil is the decline in the price of crude since it was first discovered. The most important short-run fact is the decline in the price of gasoline—the key petroleum product—so that the price now is lower than ever in our history, despite the activities of the OPEC cartel (see fig. 12-2).

Agreed-upon facts about coal. (a) There are known quantities of coal in the United States and elsewhere that are vast compared with the known quantities of oil. (b) Coal is expensive to transport. (c) In energy yield at 1990s market prices, coal is cheaper than oil or gas.[7] (d) The use of coal creates air pollution that can raise coal's total social cost above that of oil. (e) Most important, coal's damage to health due to mining risks as well as air pollution is much worse than even the most *pessimistic* estimates of the possible risks from nuclear power, and *dwarfs* any *likely* damage from nuclear power.

Agreed-upon facts about oil substitutes. In addition to shale rocks, tar sands, coal, and methane from coal seams, oil substitutes can be derived from a wide variety of agricultural crops. Aside from methanol—which may be viable commercially even at present—none of these substitutes can presently be produced at a price which is competitive with fossil oil (perhaps $15 to $20 per barrel in 1992 dollars). But if the price of fossil oil were to rise considerably, there would be much greater incentive for research on reducing the costs of gasoline substitutes, and the prices of some substitutes—perhaps liquid fuel made from tar sands and coal are the likeliest possibilities—would undoubtedly fall considerably.

The cost of fuel from cane sugar, corn, biomass (such as hardwood), or municipal solid waste is presently about three times the cost of gasoline from petroleum.[8] Lowering that cost substantially would require large gains in agricultural productivity that probably would take several decades at least, though the speed of progress can often surprise us. Many are attracted to the idea of home-grown alternatives to fossil fuels, but forced reliance on such fuels can run into self-made disasters. Brazil, for example, heavily subsidized ethanol from its cane sugar (aided by a big subsidy from the World Bank), and many autos converted to that fuel. But when the world price of sugar went up, Brazil could not buy raw material, and motorists therefore could not obtain fuel.[9]

Wind power, geothermal sources such as geysers, and solar energy may be viable alternatives in some places, but the chance that any of them will gain a large share of the market without heavy government subsidy is almost nil.

Even at the present high costs of substitutes, however, a modern society such as the United States or Europe or Japan would not be affected much if it had to turn to such substitutes. Oil accounts for a sufficiently small part of total expenditures that such a cost increase would therefore not much affect total costs or, consequently, people's consumption.

The market price of oil affects the market price of other fuels. For example, as soon as OPEC increased the price of oil in 1973, the price of coal and uranium jumped, apparently because the owners of those commodities perceived greater demand for them. On the other hand, investment in coal and nuclear power is made risky by the possibility that oil prices might fall due to a collapse of the OPEC cartel, which would make investment in coal and nuclear power a financial disaster.

Agreed-upon facts about nuclear power. The physical supply of nuclear fuel is awesomely large and inexhaustible on any human scale.

Electricity can be produced from uranium at perhaps half or two-thirds the 1992 price of oil—if the burden of regulation does not greatly lengthen the period over which plants are constructed, and does not complicate design and construction.[10] This is shown by experience in France, and in earlier decades in the United States.[11]

If nuclear power is cheaper than oil, it is therefore *much* cheaper than other, non-fossil-fuel energy sources. Perhaps the most revealing statement is a compilation by the pro-solar and pro-wind-power group Worldwatch Institute. They estimated that the number of persons employed in the energy-producing industries per thousand gigawatt-hours per year in the United States is: nuclear, 100; geothermal, 112; coal, 116; solar thermal, 248; wind, 542.[12] They presented these data as being *favorable* to solar and wind because they "create

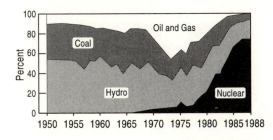

Figure 12-3a. French Electricity Generation According to Source

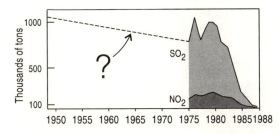

Figure 12-3b. Releases of SO_2 from EDF Power Plants

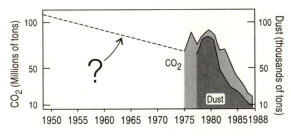

Figure 12-3c. Releases of CO_2 and Dust from French Power Plants

more jobs," apparently without recognizing that the amount of labor required is the most basic measure of a good's social cost. Using a spade "creates" more jobs than using a bulldozer, but working only with spades dooms us to near-subsistence living. (This is apparently what is meant by the phrase "sustainable economy.") It is the same view of the world as held by members of the Glass Bottle Blowers Association, who "for many years had an unwritten law that after a member of the union finished a bottle of beer, it was his duty to break the bottle and so provide employment for the bottle blowers."[13]

Nuclear fission creates radioactive wastes that raise storage and disposal problems. (This point will be discussed further in chapter 13.)

Shifting to nuclear power greatly reduces the emission of all important by-products of fossil fuel combustion, including carbon dioxide (a possible problem in connection with global warming) and dust particulates (the most dangerous pollutant). Data on the reduction in emission of these and of sulfur dioxide and nitrogen-oxygen compounds that accompanied the increase in nuclear power and decline in fossil fuels are shown in figures 12-3a–c.

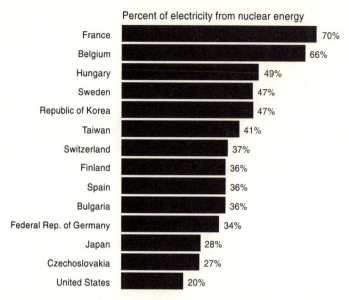

Figure 12-4. Selected Countries, Use of Nuclear Energy, 1993

Other countries have made nuclear power their main source of electrical power—to a much greater degree than the United States (see fig. 12-4).

Nuclear fusion, as distinct from fission, would be relatively clean with respect to radioactive wastes. Fusion is not yet controllable as an energy source, but it may become an economical source of energy.

The following matters are in dispute:

How much future supply of petroleum remains. Some geologists tell us that at present prices and rates of consumption, production of oil will peak sometime soon and then decline. Other geologists confidently predict that vast new sources of oil will be found when sought. The official spokespersons for various organizations with different interests in the matter put forth a cacophony of different views.

Also in dispute are the amounts of oil and other fossil fuels that people can safely burn without creating excessive atmospheric levels of carbon dioxide—the "greenhouse effect."[14] All now agree that the 1980s forecasts of the sea rising many inches or feet due to global warming are nonsense.

The future supply of natural gas. The 1970s saw extraordinary confusion and contradiction in the estimates that various politicians and experts put forth about the future of natural gas (see chapter 11). That scare ended toward the end of 1978 when the official views of the U.S. government had flip-flopped sufficiently so that the secretary of energy announced, "DOE is encouraging industries and utilities that now burn oil to switch, not to coal, but to gas." So much for another energy panic.

Whether the "alternative" energy sources are practical. Tidal power, ocean thermal power, geothermal power, wind power, fuel cells, conventional solar power, or geopressurized methane and alcohol might be able to compete with oil in the near or not-so-near future if the price of oil were to remain at the present level. On the other hand, these sources might not be important even if the price of energy were to double, triple, or quadruple.[15] Tidal power may be the best bet of the lot, especially in Great Britain where a variety of devices that the sea compresses or bumps to convert its movements into electricity are well into the testing stages.[16] There is considerable dispute whether shale oil, available in vast quantities in the United States and elsewhere, could be profitable at present energy prices even with considerable research and development.

Also an open question are the potentials of a variety of new and radical ways to harness solar power, some of which promise energy at remarkably low costs if they are developed. One such idea is launching huge orbiting satellites to convert solar rays into electrical energy which would then be transmitted to Earth by microwaves.[17] Another plan is to build mirrors in space that would turn night into day for agricultural areas and hence increase food productivity as well as the productivity of solar-heating systems. A third possibility is new forms of solar cells.[18] These alternatives—and others, too—are backed by solid scientific evidence that they can work in principle, and by considerable engineering support that they might be practical in the foreseeable future.

The fundamental—and unchangeable—difficulty with solar power is that the energy is so dilute. That is, the amount of sunlight that falls on any square meter of ground is only about 1,300 watts.

It now seems unlikely that during the next few decades any source of energy other than fossil fuels and nuclear power will be available over a wide geographic area at a price low enough to serve a large proportion of the total demand. (It would take many chapters to provide the necessary details to properly support this statement.) If this forecast should be falsified by some great new scientific discovery—which is unlikely in the near future, despite the frequent overly optimistic forecasts that have been made since the 1960s—that would be marvelous. And good luck to those who enjoy testing their wits and their muscles by racing sun-powered two-horsepower automobiles across Australia, or crossing the English Channel in a pedal-powered airplane; even if such endeavors do not pan out economically, they often produce useful new knowledge, as well as entertainment. But they are most unlikely to make a difference in the energy outlook.

The role of oil conservation. Some informed persons argue that it is possible to increase greatly the efficiency of energy use—that is, to waste less of it. Other informed persons doubt that there is great potential or great benefit. Raising the price of fuels such as gasoline to very high levels could affect consumption considerably, of course, but whether this makes economic sense is also in dispute, as chapter 20 discusses.

A commonly heard idea is that "[I]t's cheaper to save energy than to create it,"[19] and "The cheapest way to cut oil dependence is by conservation."[20] That notion is not logically wrong. It is equally correct—and equally nonsensical— to say that the cheapest way to save on food is to stop eating. If a given individual chooses to keep the house cooler in the winter and warmer in the summer to save on fuel bills in order to spend more on artwork or vacations—fine. But that has nothing to do with social policy. If the government *forces* someone to cut oil use, that is quite another matter, and in no logical sense is it true that that is "cheap."

The danger from nuclear energy. The main-line scientific position—expressed in a report of the National Academy of Sciences Committee on Nuclear and Alternative Energy Systems—concluded that "if one takes all health effects into account (including mining and transportation accidents and the estimated expectations from nuclear accidents), the health effects of coal production and use appear to be a good deal greater than those of the nuclear energy cycle."[21]

As to waste disposal, the main-stream scientific consensus is that "risks from the disposal of radioactive waste are less than those of the other parts of the nuclear energy cycle—if appropriate action is taken to find suitable long-term disposal sites and methods."[22] A standard view is that "the task of disposing of the radio-active wastes—is not nearly as difficult or as uncertain as many people seem to think it is."[23] The geoscientist for the American Physical Society's study group on nuclear fuel cycles and waste management says much the same thing: "The problems, including hazards and waste disposal, about which much has been made, are not so serious as commonly pictured."[24] On the other hand, opponents of nuclear energy, such as those associated with the Sierra Club, claim that these assertions about waste-disposal risks are "not true," just "myths."[25] These issues will be addressed briefly in chapter 13.

The Energy Crisis of the 1970s

As so often is the case, government is once again the problem rather than the solution. Typically, "Abandoning its laissez-faire policy of the 1980s, the Energy Department said yesterday that it will conduct an ambitious campaign to promote energy conservation and the use of renewable fuels."[26] Under the guise of "saving" money, governments frequently coerce people to use fuels that are more expensive and less convenient than consumers' free choices. As explained in chapter 21, such interventions are disastrous—designed with good motives, perhaps, but fatally flawed by abysmal ignorance of economic theory and the history of energy supplies.

The sharp rise of crude oil prices in the 1970s provides an illustrative case history of government intervention in the energy market. While the first edition of this book was in production, the price of oil tripled to $30 and even $35 per barrel, and all the conventional "experts" predicted a continued rise— to, say, $3 per gallon for gasoline by 1990. The analysis given in this book led to quite a different conclusion—that in the long run "energy will become more available and less costly." The intervening years have confirmed the latter view, of course (as with just about all other predictions made in the first edition). Hence, from here on the discussion is either the same as in the first edition or is a slight paraphrase of the discussion there.

The 1979 price rise was clearly due to the cartel agreements of the oil-producing countries' association (OPEC)—that is, expensive oil was clearly a result of political power rather than rising extraction costs. Of course the consumer is interested only in the market price of oil, not production cost. But if one is interested in whether there is, or will be in the future, an economic shortage of oil, or if one wants to know about the world's capacity to produce oil, the appropriate indicator is the cost of production and transportation— and for oil that cost remains only a small fraction of the world market price.

During the years of the "energy crisis," the cost of oil production did not rise at all. It remained far less than 1 percent of the selling price of crude—a cost of perhaps five cents to fifteen cents per barrel, in comparison with a selling price of somewhere around $30 per barrel in 1980.[27] For perspective, we should remember that energy prices to the consumer have been falling over the very long haul, as we saw in figures 11-2 to 11-4. Before the OPEC cartel became effective, the price of Iranian oil fell from $2.17 per barrel in 1947 to $1.79 in 1959,[28] and the price of oil at Rotterdam was at its lowest point in 1969; an inflation adjustment would show even more decline. The cost of electricity—and especially electricity for residential use—also had been falling rapidly in the decades prior to 1973 (and continues to fall; see fig. 11-4b). And the overall index of energy prices (weighted by their values and deflated by the consumer price index) fell steadily from 1950 to 1973, as follows: 1950, 107.2; 1955, 103.9; 1960, 100.0; 1965, 93.5; 1970, 85.4; June 1973, 80.7.[29] The index was falling at an ever-increasing rate over this period.

The history and the basic economic theory of cartels square with each other. A cartel such as OPEC, whose members have differing interests, is subject to pressures that make it difficult to maintain whichever price maximizes profit for the cartel as a whole. There is a great temptation for individual countries to sell more than their quotas. Furthermore, a sharp increase in price—as happened when OPEC raised prices in the early 1970s—reduces consumer demand. The result is an oversupply of oil and an underutilization of production facilities—a true "surplus" of oil—and this is exactly what has happened. Even as early as 1974 the press was reporting that

> [I]n the face of a world-wide oil surplus, Saudi Arabia and several other OPEC nations have cut their oil production by 10 percent this month in order to prop up oil prices. Industry sources attribute the decision to cut production to ARAMCO, owned jointly by Saudi Arabia, Exxon, Texaco, Mobil and Standard Oil of California. ARAMCO officials however, blamed "weather conditions" for the slash.[30]

By March 1975, the reports were, "Growing oil glut . . . sagging Western demand for oil has forced OPEC members to cut production sharply to maintain the current high price of crude.[31] By 1976, the price of fuel oil and gasoline had apparently fallen in real terms (adjusted for inflation).[32] And the OPEC members were fighting among themselves about whether to raise prices. At the beginning of 1978, OPEC decided not to raise prices at all, despite inflation, which meant a fall in the relative price of oil. Newspaper headlines again referred to an "oil glut."[33] The executive director of the International Energy Agency, though choosing not to speak of a glut, foresaw that OPEC and oil-producing countries "will face a slight overcapacity problem all the way into 1981–82 . . . [due to] inadequate demand for [OPEC's] oil for some years."[34]

Then came a huge price jump in 1979. Yet the first edition of this book asserted that "even if the present price of oil should rise even higher, the costs of oil, and of energy in general, are not likely to be so high as to disrupt Western economies.[35] In the long run, however, it is reasonable to assume that economic forces will drag the market price of oil down closer to the cost of production, which implies a lower world-market oil price."

And so it turned out. The price of oil in 1996, adjusted for inflation, is close to its low point in history. Even the Persian Gulf War of 1991 did not boost price for more than a very short time. The analysis of the first edition of the book has been completely vindicated. And there is more reason than ever to extrapolate the same trends of falling price and increasing supply into the indefinite future.

Curiously, the oil situation of the 1970s produced the strange spectacle of an "illiterate" person teaching at the Hebrew University of Jerusalem. In 1974 or 1975, a poll of the Israeli public asked such questions as the name of the prime minister, and whether respondents were familiar with the world's "energy crisis." Those who gave the "wrong" answers to such questions were labeled "illiterate." I declared that I was not familiar with the "energy crisis," because in fact there was none; the concept was a fiction of the press. Ergo I was illiterate—while professoring.

Another costly lesson about government intervention in energy markets was taught (though unfortunately, few learn from it) during the late 1970s under the Carter administration when there was much fear about running out of natural gas. In response, laws were passed prohibiting the use of gas in power plants and restricting use in industry. The supply of gas was not increased by producers, and prices rose. Then in the 1980s prices were decontrolled and power-plant use allowed.[36] As a result, supply increased vastly, and price fell sharply.

Still another economic waste due to false energy scares was the $15 billion thrown away on the development of synthetic fuels.[37]

There is no great secret for predicting the energy future with considerable accuracy. Simply predict that, as with all other raw materials, the trends in the future will resemble the very-long-run trends of the past—toward lower prices. One must simply avoid being seduced by Malthusian theories of "finite" resources and the exponential growth of demand. Here I repeat my offer to wager on this forecast, as discussed in chapter 1.

Politics and the Current Energy "Crisis"

The energy scares of the 1970s led to a web of U.S. government interventions which (as predicted by economists) aggravated the situation. The policies and arguments were so tangled that it would take a whole book to sort them out. The system of energy regulation was sufficiently complex that even a professional economist could not understand it without much study.

In the crude-oil market, for example, the price that oil producers were allowed to charge depended upon the date the well had been drilled; this device was an attempt to (a) keep "old" oil wells from obtaining a windfall gain due to the rise in the world oil prices since 1973, but at the same time (b) provide an incentive to producers to keep drilling new wells. Different amounts of taxes had to be paid for "new" and "old" oil to equalize the market price. Then there were "entailments" that refiners got for purchasing old or new oil, allowing them to make other products of oil of different "ages"; these "entailments" could be bought and sold. This system was a patchwork crazy quilt that hid from view the actual facts of oil supply.

George Stigler once remarked that a business firm is a collection of devices to overcome obstacles to profit. The energy market nicely illustrated the remark. For example, the price of gas for interstate delivery was controlled far below the price of oil for an equivalent amount of thermal energy, but gas prices were not controlled in intrastate commerce. The regulatory structure in which energy firms operated was a mine field of such obstacles to profit. Each obstacle, however, provided an opportunity to some firms just as it blocked others; it was an invitation to finagle. And sure enough, the finagling had not only begun by the time of the first edition, it had already been discovered and was a huge scandal.

The government-induced energy scams would have been amusing if the corruption had not been so damaging to business morals as well as to energy production. Furthermore, the government's price-regulation system had the effect of supporting the OPEC cartel's price-fixing power and subsidizing member countries' operations. Adding insult to injury, consumers had to wait in long lines at gasoline stations. The United States may have been the only country where there were lines, because it was the only country stupid enough to attempt to control the price of gasoline.

Here is a sample of the news stories that had surfaced by the time of the first edition about these government-created crimes against both the laws of the nation and the laws of economics governing the supply of energy:

> July 21, 1978: Continental Oil Co. is under criminal investigation for alleged violations of federal oil-pricing rules. According to government sources, Continental, the nation's ninth largest oil company, is the first major oil company to face possible criminal charges in a new crackdown by the Energy and Justice departments on improper oil-pricing practices during the years immediately following the 1973 Arab oil embargo. . . .
>
> In separate cases, also in Texas, federal investigators are considering seeking indictments soon against several smaller companies that resell oil bought from major producers. The smaller concerns are suspected of participating in a criminal scheme to sell lower-priced "old" crude oil at the higher prices that apply to "new" oil.[38]
>
> August 14, 1978: The Florida case involves a so-called "daisy chain" scheme during late 1973 and 1974. The government alleges that five oil companies sold fuel oil back and forth to raise their paper costs and, thus, the allowable price under federal regulations, before selling it to the buyer, Florida Power Corp. . . . [The government lawyers admitted that] the oil pricing rules they are trying to apply may have been too confusing and vague.[39]
>
> December 11, 1978: "Possible Misconduct within Energy Unit Is Charged in Study of Oil-Pricing Cases." Washington—Energy Department officials failed to move swiftly against suspected massive oil-pricing frauds in recent years and thus may have been guilty of serious, even criminal misconduct, a congressional report charged.[40]
>
> February 9, 1979: "Kerr-McGee to Settle U.S. Oil-Price Claims, Firms to Refund $46 Million in Alleged Overcharges from 1973 through 1978."[41]
>
> July 28, 1979: "Tenneco Inc. pleaded guilty of concealing the transportation of natural gas from federal regulation officials."[42]
>
> November 9, 1979: "U.S. Is Accusing Nine Major Oil Concerns of $1.1 Billion in Consumer Overcharges."[43]
>
> February 15, 1980: "Mobil Oil Ordered to Pay $500,000 Fine on Criminal Charges Involving Gas Sales," and "Indiana Standard Settles Price Case for $100 Million."[44]
>
> February 25, 1980: [L]eading domestic oil refiners have agreed to pay a total of

$1 billion to settle charges of overpricing brought by the Department of Energy. Last week, DOE announced the biggest single settlement yet: a $716 million package arranged with Standard Oil Co. of Indiana.[45]

August 13, 1980: [The Energy Department] has filed some 200 actions accusing the 15 top oil companies of violations amounting to more than $10 billion since 1973, and seeking restitution.[46]

Who benefits from the various government interventions into energy markets? The politicians and bureaucrats tout every policy change as benefiting the consumer. But even those policies which are intended to transfer funds directly from business to consumers—such as the price controls of the 1970s on oil and gas—inevitably harm the consumer by causing short-run shortages and long-run diminished supply. And the myriad other actual and potential interventions—such as requirements that cargo be carried in American ships, and oil import taxes—inevitably have huge benefits for some segment of the industry.

The first edition gave readers insight into the pulls and tugs on government policy made for the benefits of various segments of the industry—the owners of "old" and "new" wells, international oil firms, nuclear plant construction firms, the merchant seamen's union, and so on—by imagining the thought processes of each group. In each of these economic-political roles you find yourself fabricating reasons why your type of energy should not have its price controlled while the others' prices ought to be controlled, and why the government should finance research on your type of energy but not on others. One excellent all-purpose reason that you find, of course, is that the "supplies" of the other sorts of energy will soon run out, which makes your sort of energy deserving support as the best hope. And you tie your arguments to expected economic and population growth, which will make the other fuels run out faster and make the need for yours that much greater.

Is it any wonder, then, that the rhetoric about energy is so impassioned and hard to untangle? It should also be clear why population growth is dragged into the discussion by all sides as posing an immediate threat to our supply of energy, and as being a reason for special treatment of each particular industry.

This situation breeds not only tortured arguments and frightening forecasts, but also (as we saw earlier) scams on a vast scale. One more example: Prior to 1973, Westinghouse contracted to sell large quantities of uranium to nuclear power plants, uranium that it planned to buy from the producers at market prices. When OPEC boosted the price of oil in 1973, the price of uranium began a jump from $8 to as much as $53 a ton within three years.[47] This meant that Westinghouse might accrue losses of perhaps $2 billion. Along the way, Gulf Oil (a producer of uranium) got together with the Canadian government and other producers of uranium to keep the price of uranium high—which in the United States is illegal price-fixing, of course—so that Gulf and the others would profit from the final purchases of all consumers of nuclear electricity, and, incidentally, from Westinghouse. Sweet. The matter tied up the courts for years.

Toward a Sound U.S. Energy Policy

What is the best U.S. policy with respect to energy? Before anything else, let us take up the question of national security, because the rest is easy in principle—and, for that matter, in principle the national security problem is not very difficult either.

If the United States has a large enough stockpile of oil—say, a year's worth—no foreign nation can exert much economic leverage or endanger U.S. military security with the threat of an oil shut-off. And there is no reason why the United States should not have such a stockpile, as apparently exists now.

With national security taken care of, importing oil and gas poses little more threat than importing television sets or tourist services. The balance of payments is not a worry; economics teaches that importing whatever buyers want and can get cheapest abroad maximizes economic welfare.

There are always, however, hands outstretched for government funds with the claim of benefiting the public by developing one or another form of energy—subsidies for solar-powered homes, tax credits for research into hydropower and coke-gas equipment, development programs for shale oil.

Which sources of energy should the U.S. government promote? The appropriate reasoning was stated clearly as "the least cost principle" by the Paley Commission decades ago. "This Commission believes that national materials policy should be squarely founded on the principle of buying at the least cost possible for equivalent values. . . . [W]e cannot afford to legislate against this principle for the benefit of particular producer groups at the expense of our consumers and foreign neighbors, and ultimately with prejudice to our own economic growth and security."[48]

That is, the economic mechanism that hews most closely to the least-cost principle is a free market. No government decision maker can match the efficiency of millions of individual buyers and investors who go comparison shopping among gas, oil, coal, and so on.

If the solution is so simple, why is there a multi-billion-dollar Department of Energy supporting hundreds of experts working on other kinds of schemes? Answer that for yourself.[49]

In addition to the indirect but large costs of misallocation due to government controls, the direct costs of the energy bureaucracy are not trivial.

The Department of Energy had a budget of $12 billion in 1990. This represents:

$633,379 per employee (it employed 18,968 people in 1991),or
$48 for each and every person in the country, or
$1.98 per barrel of petroleum products consumed (1989), or
10 cents for every gallon of gasoline consumed (1989).[50]

A few activities of the Department of Energy may benefit the public, such as collecting useful data. But if DOE were abolished today and its functions assigned to no other government agency, on balance we surely would be better off. To the best of my knowledge, no systematic analysis has shown the opposite. That is, there is no evidence that DOE is on balance a constructive force, and there is much reason to call that proposition into question. We are simply expected to accept on faith that such government agencies are of net benefit. This conclusion is not welcome to those of us who prefer to think well of government agencies and employees. But the older I get and the more evidence I see, the more convinced I have become that such faith is misplaced in many cases—DOE being a leading example.

Conclusions

Government planning and control in the energy and raw-materials markets inevitably raises prices, creates scandals, and reduces rather than increases the supplies of resources; all this the record of the past shows again and again. Chapter 11 provides the data which document that natural resources always become less rather than more scarce in the long run, and chapters 3 and 11 give the theory that explains this anti-intuitive phenomenon. (The supply of energy is not even finite, and its price may be expected to fall forever.) Government controls on resources—such as the price controls on oil and gas of the 1970s—are based on false ideas about diminishing returns and inevitable scarcity.

Governmentally mandated conservation of energy would only be a drag on the progress toward ever cheaper and more plentiful energy.

Afternote 1

Externalities of Energy Use

SOME MORALISTS call for a reduction in energy use because of religious-like beliefs that a return to a "simpler" life would be more "natural" and good for all of us. Others would have us reduce energy use because they believe there is something inherently valuable about energy, and especially fossil fuels. Both groups would have us waste our time and effort, slow the progress of civilization, and cripple our economy in order to mitigate a shortage of energy that they speculate will finish us off starting perhaps seven billion years from now. (See quotations of Lovins, Daly, and Ehrlich below and in chapter 13.) One cannot easily argue about such matters, because they are matters of taste.

Others, however, argue that energy use should be reduced because of purported negative externalities—that is, consumers supposedly do not pay the full cost of the energy that they use while other members of the public pay part of the cost—and that rules of the market should "internalize" these externalities. "Using energy involves potential costs for society that aren't fully reflected in market prices."[51]

This can be a meritorious argument. If a coal furnace deposits pollution on other people's wash, or harms their health, the polluters should pay the cost. If the use of gasoline causes highways to deteriorate, vehicle operators (or owners) should pay for the damage. But large difficulties lie in the assessment of the externalities, and in the choice among policies to internalize them.

Gasoline use makes an interesting brief case study in these difficulties. At first it seems reasonable to charge for road use with a gasoline tax. But then we realize that light vehicles apparently wear out much less road per gallon of gasoline than do heavy vehicles, so this device does not work well. The CAFE standards which dictate the proportion of cars of various weights that the automakers can sell, by way of a requirement for maximum average miles per gallon for the year's output, work even less well because this rule leads to people buying lighter cars and suffering more injuries as a result—somewhere between twenty-two hundred and thirty-nine hundred people dying during the ten-year period following adoption of CAFE in 1975 who would not have died otherwise; nor were there clear-cut economic gains that offset this human loss.* (The main advantage of the CAFE rules over a gasoline tax seems to be that CAFE is political; the cost to consumers is better disguised.) Such alternatives as subsidized mass transit, which go farther and farther afield from the

---

* Crandall and Graham (1989). See chapter 20 for more discussion.

initial problem, enmesh the economy in an ever-thicker web of regulations and cross-forces which are ever more difficult to evaluate; another result is ever-increasing opportunities for special interests to feather their nests. Probably the best system would be a direct toll tax based on the weight of vehicles as well as miles driven; nowadays this is technically possible. My point, however, is the difficulty of choosing an appropriate remedy, rather than any specific suggestion.

The press—of course—focuses on negative externalities because they make good stories. But there also are positive externalities. For example, though offshore oil rigs are anathema to many environmental activists, they provide remarkable habitat for sea life. Working rigs, and the tipped-over carcasses of old rigs, have brought many new species to barren Texas and Louisiana waters, which attract the majority of recreational saltwater fishing trips off Louisiana. One commercial diver said, "These are probably the biggest and best aquariums in the world."[52] And the warm waters that flow from many nuclear power plants constitute remarkable fisheries. When assessing the effects of an energy-providing activity, it is important to make a complete accounting that includes the positive as well as the negative externalities, even though the positive effects are usually much harder to spot.

It is also necessary to take into account the negative effects—some of them large—of energy regulations that force people into activities that they would otherwise not choose. For example, government manipulation of gasoline and public transportation prices in such fashion that people are induced to spend more time commuting than they would with free-market prices can be a very expensive drag upon productivity. A reduction of half an hour in time at the workplace might cause a drop of (say) 8 percent in output, a huge proportion of loss to the economy. These indirect effects are often omitted from consideration when making rules that force energy "conservation." The belief that conservation forced upon others is the "cheapest source of energy" is not just nonsense, it is destructive. (See chapters 20 and 21.)

Afternote 2

Energy Accounting

BECAUSE OF their worry that humanity will eventually run out of energy—even if it be seven billion years from now—some writers assert that we should make our economic decisions on the basis of "energy accounting" rather than on the basis of the theory of value determined by prices that is at the core of standard economics. They write fearfully about an increase in "entropy"—a disappearance of order and a disintegration of all patterns of life into chaos. This flies in the face of the trend over the decades and centuries of energy becoming more rather than less available, just like all other raw materials such as copper and land. Human life becomes better organized rather than more disordered.

The idea of a "currency based on energy units" goes back at least as far as the novelist H. G. Wells in 1905.[53] According to the theory of energy accounting, the value of any good or service should be determined by the amount of energy that goes into making it. For example, a trip by bicycle should be valued more highly by society than the same trip by auto because less total energy is expended in powering the bicycle. Typically, Lester Brown and company recommend the use of bicycles because their "energy intensity" is only thirty-five compared to an index of one hundred for a pedestrian and one hundred for each of two passengers in a light car or 350 in a big car.[54]

In this line of thought, any energy-supplying process that uses more raw energy than it produces is judged to be perverse, and should be avoided. For example, a farming operation that inputs more energy by way of tractor operations than the energy output to human consumers in the food supplies is ipso facto a waste. This kind of thinking is another part of the notion of a "sustainable economy" (see discussions of nuclear and solar power in chapters 12 and 13).

These analyses exclude any other values. The difference in time a traveler expends in going by car rather than by bicycle is assumed irrelevant. And the fact that food produced with the help of a tractor keeps us alive, and with enjoyment, whereas the diesel fuel that powers the tractor cannot provide those benefits, is omitted from the calculation.

Energy accounting has great intellectual charm, just as does Marx's labor theory of value to which it bears close resemblance. But of course if society were to follow an energy-economizing rule, we could not have modern life. Less energy comes out of an electricity-producing operation in the form of electricity than goes in as coal or nuclear fuel. But in the form of power for our appliances, the electricity is more valuable to us than is the raw coal or uranium. The prices we are willing to pay for goods and services express our values for these goods and services; we pay more for a unit of energy as electricity than as a lump of coal. The price system directs economic activity. And it is this price system that enthusiasts wish to replace with energy accounting.

An analogy may help explain the intellectual issues at the root of the discussion. Imagine yourself in a lifeboat marooned at sea after a tropical shipwreck. The supply of water is frighteningly low. Because water is so valuable, you and the other passengers decide to ration the water, allocating a cupful to each person each day. And each of you is likely to drink your ration of water yourself rather than trading it even if another passenger offers to swap you an expensive wristwatch or necklace, because you figure that the watch or jewelry is worthless if you die of thirst. This is the logic of conserving energy irrespective of other values.

Now notice how different is the value of a given amount of water on the lifeboat and ashore. It makes sense to swap a cup of water for a watch where there is plenty of water, and hence the relative values—expressed in trading prices—are different ashore and on a lifeboat. But the energy accountants do not agree that trading prices as set by the market embody the sensible bases for exchange.

Aboard a lifeboat, if the water is at the other end of the boat, you will need to sweat a bit to move to get the water to drink, and the sweat moisture will be borne off you into the air and "lost" to the lifeboat—just as the process of cultivating food mechanically may "lose" energy. But if you don't move to the other end of the lifeboat to get the water, you will die, so it obviously makes sense to do so even though that operation reduces the amount of water in the lifeboat. By the same token, urinating overboard is a loss. But you cannot live without urinating, and hence you do so.

In just the same way, it makes sense for us to spend more energy in producing electricity than is embodied in the electricity we use. If we were suddenly to find ourselves in a situation in which the supply of energy were much more limited than it really is—say, a year's availability instead of at least a seven billion years' supply—it would make sense for us to value energy and other goods and services differently than we now do, and the market would reflect this difference. But to enforce an energy-based theory of value in our present circumstances is simply to doom ourselves to ridiculously impoverished lives. (Anyone who disagrees and believes in energy accounting ought to buy and stockpile supplies of coal and oil for later resale.)

The average American uses about 150 times as much energy as did a Native American before the white man introduced horses to North America. We each employ the equivalent of about fifteen horses' power around the clock every day (which would require a stable of about fifty actual horses), and a horse exerts about ten times as much energy as a human does.[55]

Some would lament this, saying that it shows how expensive human life is, in energy terms. Another way to look at these data is that they show how cheap energy has become; we are now able to afford the benefits of all that help in getting the things that we want.

Marx's labor theory of value is cut from the same cloth as energy accounting. Marx would have us value each good and service by the number of minutes of human time involved in its production, irrespective of whether the time is that of a surgeon or a janitor, a leading soprano or a stagehand, the president of IBM or a shipping clerk. The basis for this valuation scheme is primarily moral rather than economic, however, because the purported scarcity of human life or time is not the issue for Marx, unlike the argument for energy accounting.

Curiously, the leading proponents of energy accounting also assert a moral-theological basis for the use of such a scheme, not dissimilar from the Marxian valuation system. Herman Daly founds his belief in reducing energy use and his opposition to economic growth on an "Ultimate End" which "presupposes a respect for and continuation of creation and the evolutionary process through which God has bestowed upon us the gift of self-conscious life." From this he deduces that "the apparent purpose of growth economics is to seek to satisfy infinite wants by means of infinite production. This is about as wise as chasing a white whale, and the high rationality of the means employed cannot be used to justify the insanity of purpose."[56] That is, the call for energy conservation is involved with the belief that "sanity" requires living more simply—a moral-theological belief that would be imposed on everyone else.*

* Daly and Cobb end their section on energy with a neat dig at this book and this writer: "In sum, all the talk about knowledge and the mind as an ultimate resource that will offset the limits imposed by finitude, entropy, and ecological dependence seems to us to reflect incompetent use of the very organ alleged to have such unlimited powers" (1989, p. 199).

13

Nuclear Power: Tomorrow's Greatest Energy Opportunity

> There is not the slightest indication that [nuclear] energy will ever be obtainable. It would mean that the atom would have to be shattered at will.
> *(Albert Einstein, 1932, in Cerf and Navasky 1984)*

> The energy produced by the atom is a very poor kind of thing. Anyone who expects a source of power from the transformation of these atoms is talking moonshine.
> *(Ernest Rutherford, 1933, after being the first person to split the atom, in Cerf and Navasky 1984)*

NUCLEAR POWER is fundamental to a discussion of energy because it establishes the long-run ceiling to energy costs. No matter how much any other source of energy costs us, we can turn to nuclear power at any time to supply virtually all our energy needs for a very long time. Therefore, to put all other energy issues into a proper long-run perspective, we must discuss the height of that cost ceiling and the practicality of nuclear power—including its dangers.

By now there is sufficient experience—several decades' operation in several countries—to prove that nuclear plants can generate electricity at costs that are of the same order as, or lower than, the present costs with fossil fuels.[1] Whether nuclear power is considerably cheaper (say 80 percent of the cost of fossil fuels), or about the same cost, or somewhat more expensive (say 120 percent of the cost of power from fossil fuels), matters greatly to producer-sellers of electricity. But to the consumer it does not much matter. What does matter is that the calculations do not matter. It will not affect our future lives greatly whether electricity is, say, 20 percent more or less expensive than now. Of course, an electricity bill 20 percent higher than now would not be pleasant. But it would not lower the standard of living noticeably. Nor would an electricity bill 20 percent lower than now make appreciably richer the inhabitants of developed countries. And the longer one looks into the future, the smaller will be the percentage of the total budget devoted to electricity, as our total incomes grow, and the less important to the consumer will be the production cost of in-the-home electricity with nuclear power.

Fission is the source of nuclear power at present. But in the longer run, much "cleaner" nuclear fusion may well be practicable, though physicists cannot yet predict with certainty when—or even whether—fusion will be available.

If fusion becomes practicable, the possibilities are immense. By Hans Bethe's estimate, even if we assume energy consumption a hundred times greater than at present, "the heavy hydrogen supply of the world will be sufficient to give us power for one billion years," at a price perhaps equivalent to that at present for fission power.[2]

Nuclear Power, Danger, and Risk Aversion

The Dangers of Nuclear Power

Because we (luckily) do not have experience with many nuclear mishaps the way a life insurance company has available data on millions of lives, estimating the dangers from a nuclear mishap must derive from scientific and engineering judgment. Hence, laypersons such as you and I can do no better than consult the experts. And there is necessarily some controversy among the experts because of the absence of mishaps which would provide solid statistical evidence.

A section later in this chapter discusses some of the problems that arise in responding sensibly to risks of various kinds.

When evaluating the safety of nuclear power, it is crucial to keep in mind the risks to life and limb that arise in producing energy from other sources—such as drilling accidents at oil wells, mine disasters, and the pulmonary diseases of coal miners.

All would agree that nuclear power's past record has been remarkably good compared with the best alternatives, along with its economic advantages. The extraordinary safety record in nuclear submarines over several decades—no evidence of any damage to human life from radiation despite the very close proximity of Navy personnel to the nuclear power plants—is compelling evidence that nuclear power can be remarkably safe. Furthermore, the safety of nuclear plants has been improving rapidly, as figure 13-1 shows—progress which would not be possible if opponents of nuclear power were able to prevent reactors from operating. Nevertheless, evaluating the risks of nuclear disaster is subject to argument. The contradictory conclusions of the authoritative report from the National Academy of Sciences, and of anti-nuclear critics, were cited in chapter 12.

Though it is not possible to establish their validity without entering into extensive technical analysis, these two assertions can safely be made: First, a nuclear plant cannot explode any more than can a jar of pickles, as physicist Fred Hoyle (with Geoffrey Hoyle) put it. (Chernobyl is no exception: it was not a *nuclear* explosion.) Second, the problem of safeguarding the processed

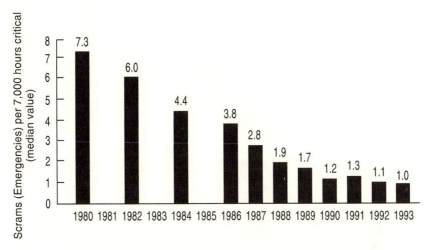

Figure 13-1. U.S. Nuclear Power Plant Safety Performance (Emergencies)

waste from year to year is much less difficult than is safeguarding the national gold supply at Fort Knox, and much less risky than safeguarding against terrorist explosions of nuclear weapons. More about nuclear waste below.

Best guesses about the dangers from various energy sources are shown in table 13-1.[3] There is general agreement, too, that nuclear reactors in the future will utilize now-existing designs that are safer and easier to operate than earlier designs.[4]

The accident at Three Mile Island in 1979 gave many people the impression that nuclear power is more dangerous than previously thought. But that accident would seem to demonstrate quite the opposite: Despite almost every possible error being made, no one suffered any harm. And the Chernobyl accident throws no light on safety in the United States because the reactor design was so different from plants in the West, and the protections provided in the West were not provided there. (More about Chernobyl below.)

The likelihood of injury from radiation continues to be crucial in attitudes toward nuclear power. Of course people can be killed and maimed by nuclear bombs, and children in the womb can be harmed. But the greatest fear—especially in peacetime—is long-run damage, somatically and genetically, from radiation. "When the atomic bombs fell. . . . The tragedy was only beginning, scientists thought."[5] But amazingly, the delayed damage from even the Japanese bomb blasts is either very little in quantity, or nonexistent. In a study of 100,000 people's cancer rate until the late 1980s, about one hundred more have developed leukemia than would be otherwise expected, and about three hundred more than expected have developed solid cancers—a total of four hundred, to be compared to a total of twenty thousand who would have died

TABLE 13-1

Health Effects and Accident Hazards of Different Fuel Cycles[a]
(normalized to the production of 1 GW/yr of electrical energy)

| | (a) Comparison of Health Effects[b] | | | | | |
| | Workers | | Population | | Total | |
Fuel Cycle	Deaths	Diseases	Deaths	Diseases	Deaths	Diseases
Coal	0.1 (5)	1.5 (2)	3 (10)	1000 (20)	3 (10)	1000 (20)
Oil	~0	0.01	3 (10)	1000 (20)	3 (10)	1000 (20)
Gas	~0	~0	~0	~0	~0	~0
Uranium	0–0.2	0–0.2	0–0.1	0–0.1	0–0.3	0–0.3

Note: Best estimates are accompanied by uncertainty factors in parentheses.

| | (b) Comparison of Accident Hazards[c] | | | | | |
| | Workers | | Population | | Total | |
Fuel Cycle	Fatal	Nonfatal	Fatal	Nonfatal	Fatal	Nonfatal
Coal	1.40 (1.5)	60 (1.5)	1.0 (1.5)	1.8 (2.0)	2.40 (1.5)	62 (1.5)
Oil	0.35 (1.5)	30 (1.5)	?	?	0.35 (1.5)	30 (1.5)
Gas	0.20 (1.5)	15 (2)	0.009	0.005	0.21 (1.5)	15 (2)
Uranium	0.20 (1.5)	15 (2)	0.012	0.11	0.21 (1.5)	15 (2)

Notes: Best estimates are accompanied by uncertainty factors in parentheses.

[a] The tables cover the hazards caused by the activities of extraction, processing, transport, conversion to electricity and waste management. They are from W. Paskievici' who reviewed the findings of nineteen different studies dated from 1974 to 1980.

[b] Table 13.1a covers occupational fatalities and diseases, and fatalities and chronic disease in the general population due to normal working conditions and operations.

[c] Table 13.1b covers occupational fatalities and injuries, and fatalities to the general population due to accidents.

of cancer anyway.[6] And there does not seem to be any damage to children not yet conceived at the time of the blast.[7]

New research at the time of writing suggests that "a given dose of radiation is less dangerous than currently believed," because the Japanese survivors at Hiroshima received "considerably more radiation than generally believed."[8]

(Of course an atomic bomb explosion has nothing in common with a nuclear plant accident except that both involve the release of radiation. And of course I am not suggesting that the atomic bomb "is not so bad after all." The reason why the study of the Japanese children was made—and the reason it is mentioned here—is that vastly more radiation was received by the pregnant mothers in Japan than would be received by people in a peacetime accident under almost any conceivable conditions. Yet there was no excess incidence of cancer in the children. Tragedies though Hiroshima and Nagasaki were, we ought not to close our eyes to this useful lesson that they can teach us.)

An "official" report from the American Medical Association gives nuclear power an excellent bill of health, saying it is "acceptably safe."[9] Coal-supplied energy is assessed to cause eighteen times more deaths per unit of electricity than nuclear power, because of both mining and transportation deaths. And solar energy is "less safe" than nuclear power due to construction and maintenance costs.[10] These estimates are consistent with the data in table 13-1 above.

Perhaps the most surprising finding by that AMA report concerns Chernobyl: "[N]o member of the general public received a dose capable of producing radiation sickness," though plant and rescue workers were killed. As to long-run effects, even using rules of thumb, the cancer rate in the surrounding population would increase "by less than 2%, and this effect would be difficult to detect."[11]

An even later report reaches an even stronger conclusion. "Reports that the Chernobyl nuclear accident caused widespread illness are false. . . . The [United Nations multinational research] teams [of 200 experts from 25 countries] did not find any health disorders that could be directly attributed to radiation exposure." And as to long-run dangers, "Radioactivity in drinking water and food was well below levels hazardous to health—in many cases, even below detection limits."[12] I confess that even with my experience of many, many initial scary reports of environmental events later being revealed to be minimal or zero risks, I was shocked to read that Chernobyl was found not to have caused observable damage to the general public. This was not widely reported to the public, however.

A large and solid body of research—culminating in a 1990 National Cancer Institute study—has found "no increased risk of death from cancer for people living in proximity to nuclear installations in the United States. . . . Cancer cluster studies performed in Europe, Canada, and the U.S. over the last ten years have uniformly failed to establish a link between reports of apparent increased cancer incidence and local discharges of radiation."[13] Wing may have found higher-than-expected cancer rates among Oak Ridge workers, contradicting earlier studies on workers in nuclear plants. But even if this turns out to be supported by later studies, the very fact that the increased mortality is so difficult to identify statistically implies that it is small relative to other hazards to life.[14]

Furthermore, it is possible to have *too little* exposure to radiation. There is now a well-established phenomenon called hormesis, which causes people exposed to relatively *heavy* natural levels of radiation to have *increased* longevity rather than shorter lives.[15] This is apparently connected with the fact that "low-level radiations make the cells less susceptible to subsequent high doses of radiation."[16]

Here I interject an editorial remark of the sort that prudent scientists avoid lest readers think that they are less than "objective" and that personal feelings bias their presentations: If the nuclear power industry in the United States had even a touch of courage, it would publicize to the heavens the advantage of nuclear power in saving lives. Instead, they try to sway the public to favor nuclear power by talking about reducing dependence on imported oil—an argument which is bad economics at best, and phony at worst.

Nuclear Power and Risk Aversion

Yet there still remains much public aversion to risk. Let's see the issue from the layman's point of view. Perhaps nuclear energy really is cheap enough to be a viable alternative to fossil fuels in generating electricity. And maybe it has been safer than other sources. But what about the chance of a big catastrophe? Would it not be prudent to stay away from nuclear power to avoid that risk?

This question embodies what economists call "risk aversion"—a reasonable and normal attitude. Risk aversion is evidenced when a person prefers to keep a dollar in hand rather than bet it double or nothing, even when the chance of winning is greater than fifty–fifty. That is, if one were not risk averse, one would accept all gambles when the "expected value"—the probability of winning multiplied by the payoff if you do win—is greater than the amount you must put up to make the gamble. But a risk-averse person would prefer, for example, a one-in-a-hundred chance of winning $10 to a one-in-a-million chance of winning $100,000, even though the "expected value" is the same.

A risk-averse society might well prefer to take many one-in-a-hundred chances of ten persons dying rather than take a single one-in-a-million chance of 100,000 or even 10,000 people dying. That is, the risk of a lot of small likely tragedies might be more acceptable than the risk of a very infrequent and much less probable major catastrophe. If so, that society would eschew nuclear energy. This is the implicit argument against nuclear energy.

It is important, however, that the implicit risk aversion must be enormous if one is to oppose nuclear power. There is practically zero chance of a nuclear-plant catastrophe that would cost tens of thousands of lives. The very outside possibility envisioned by the official committees of experts is a catastrophe causing five thousand deaths. While indeed tragic, that number of deaths is not of a different order from the number of deaths in a dam break, and it is smaller than the number of coal miners that we know *for sure* will die early from black lung disease.

So even risk aversion does not make nuclear energy unattractive. The size of the worst possible catastrophe is of the same order as other social risks that are accepted routinely, and hence we can judge nuclear energy according to the "expected value" of the mortalities it may generate. And according to expected-value calculations, it is considerably safer than other energy alternatives.

Disposal of Nuclear Waste

The Hoyles illustrate the waste-disposal problem from a personal point of view, and they are worth quoting at length.*

> Suppose we are required individually to be responsible for the long term storage of all the waste that we ourselves, our families and our forebears, have generated in an all-nuclear energy economy.
>
> It will be useful to think of waste in terms of the categories of [the table below].

Categories of Nuclear Waste and Their Lifetimes

	Lifetime (years)
High-level	10
Medium-level	300
Low-level	100,000
Very low-level	10 million

> High-level waste is carefully stored over its 10-year lifetime by the nuclear industry. This is done above-ground in sealed tanks. It is not proposed to bury nuclear waste underground until activity has fallen to the medium-level category. Instead of underground burial, however, we now consider that medium-level waste is delivered for safekeeping to individual households.
>
> We take the amount of the waste so delivered to be that which has been generated over the 70 years from 1990 to 2060. . . .
>
> Over this period a typical family of four would accumulate $4 \times 70 = 280$ person years of vitrified nuclear waste, which for an all-nuclear energy economy would weigh about 2 kilograms. Supplied inside a thick metal case, capable of withstanding a house fire or a flood, the waste would form an object of about the size of a small orange, which it could be made to resemble in colour and surface texture—this would ensure that any superficial damage to the object could easily be noticed and immediately rectified by the nuclear industry.
>
> The radioactive materials inside the orange would be in no danger of getting smeared around the house, not like jam or honey. The radioactive materials would stay put inside the metal orange-skin. Indeed the orange would be safe to handle freely but for the γ-rays emerging from it all the time. The effect on a person of the γ-rays would be like the X-rays used by the medical profession. If one were to stand for a minute at a distance of about 5 yards from the newly acquired orange, the radiation dose received would be comparable to a medical X-ray.
>
> Unlike particles of matter, γ-rays do not stay around. Once emitted γ-rays exist only for a fleeting moment, during which brief time they are absorbed and destroyed

* From Hoyle and Hoyle (1980).

by the material through which they pass. Some readers will be familiar with the massive stone walls of old houses and barns in the north of England. If a γ-ray emitting orange were placed behind a well-made stone wall 2 feet thick, one could lounge in safety for days on the shielded side, and for a wall 3 feet thick one would be safe for a lifetime.

Our family of four would therefore build a small thick-walled cubicle inside the home to ensure safe storage of the family orange.

After several generations, the waste inside the orange would have declined to the low-level category when the orange could be taken out of its cubicle and safely admired for an hour or two as a family heirloom. . . .

Such individual tedium would of course be avoided if the waste were stored communally. For 100,000 families making up a town of 400,000 people there would be 100,000 eggs to store. Or since it would surely be inconvenient to maintain a watch on so many objects the town would have the eggs reprocessed into a few hundred larger objects of the size of pumpkins or vegetable marrows. The whole lot could be fitted into a garden-produce shed, except that instead of a wooden wall, the shed would need to have thick walls of stone or metal.

This then is the full extent of the nuclear-waste problem that our own generation is called on to face. If by the mid-21st century it has become clear that nuclear fission is the only effective long-term source of energy, society will then have to consider the problem of accumulating waste on a longer time-scale. For the town of 400,000 people, a shed of pumpkins would accumulate for each 70 years, until the oldest waste fell at last into the very low-level category . . . , when it could be discarded. After 7000 years, there would be a hundred sheds, which could be put together to make a moderate-sized warehouse. In 100,000 years there would be about 15 medium warehouses, which could be accumulated into two or three large warehouses. Thereafter, the problem would remain always the same, with the oldest waste falling into the very low-level category as fast as new waste was generated. Of course, the "warehouses" would be deep underground . . . , and there would be no contact between them and the population of the town. . . .

The risk that each of us would incur, even if called upon to store our own waste, would be insignificant compared with the risks we routinely incur in other aspects of our daily lives.[17]

A shorter and less whimsical description of the nuclear waste problem comes from Petr Beckmann:

The ease and safety of its waste disposal is one of nuclear power's great advantages. Nuclear wastes are 3.5 million times smaller in volume than fossil wastes producing the same electric energy. High-level wastes which contain 99% of the radioactivity, but only 1% of the volume, are the first type of industrial waste in history that can be completely removed from the biosphere. Their volume per person per year equals that of 1–2 aspirin tablets. What is put back into the ground has less radioactive energy than what was taken out. After 100 years, the wastes are less toxic than many ores found in nature. After 500 years they are less toxic than the coal ash produced from the same electricity supply. The artificial and irrational arguments against disposal in stable geological formations ("Prove that they won't . . .) help to perpetuate the present way of disposing of fossil-powered electricity wastes—some of them in people's lungs.[18]

There is complete agreement among scientists about every one of the statements in Beckmann's brief summary above, and those in the Hoyles' analysis.

Still another practical disposal method was suggested by the Nobel-winning physicist, Luis Alvarez, and tested by British engineers: Place the waste in projectile-shaped rust-resistant tubes, and release them from the surface of the ocean where the water is deep. The projectiles will embed themselves one hundred feet deep in the bottom, and will dependably remain there safely for a long time (1987, p. 65).

Most important in thinking about waste disposal: We do not need to think of a very long period such as the next 10,000 years when we consider storing nuclear waste; we only need to worry about a few decades or centuries. Scientists and engineers will be producing a stream of ideas about how to handle the waste even better, and indeed, will probably soon find ways to put the waste to such use that it becomes a commodity of high value. As I am writing this chapter, a biologist has found a way to use jimson weed to reduce the volume of plutonium waste by a factor of 10,000, by stimulating the weed to separate the plutonium from the rest of the sludge in which it is embedded. This makes the waste (or storage) problem immeasurably easier.[19]

The best ways to increase future safety are to increase wealth and increase population now, both of which lead to a greater rate of scientific discoveries.

Conclusions

Energy from nuclear fission is at least as cheap as other forms of energy, and is available in inexhaustible quantities at constant or declining prices. Its safety record in the West shows it to produce energy at a lower cost in lives than any other form of energy, on average. The opposition to it is mainly ideological and political, as indicated by this statement by the noted activist, Amory Lovins: "[I]f nuclear power were clean, safe, economic, assured of ample fuel, and socially benign per se, it would still be unattractive because of the political implications of the kind of energy economy it would lock us into."[20] The aim of such writers as Lovins is not increasing the availability of energy and consumer benefits, but decreasing the use of energy for supposed environmental gains and beliefs about the morality of simple living. This may be seen in the headline, "Improved Fuel Efficiency Negated by Glut of Cars, Trucks."[21]

14

A Dying Planet?
How the Media Have Scared the Public

> The air is polluted, the rivers and lakes are dying, and the ozone layer has holes
> in it.
>
> *(Ann Landers)*[1]

> Most environmental, economic and social problems of local, regional, and global
> scale arise from this driving force: too many people using too many resources at
> too fast a rate.
>
> *(Blue Planet Group)*[2]

ACCORDING TO a CBS News Survey before Earth Day 1990, "The American public has an almost doomsday feeling about the national seriousness of environmental problems."[3] The press, environmental organizations, and the public say that pollution in the United States and the world is not just bad, but getting worse.

One could cite prominent scientists, politicians of every stripe, and religious leaders of every denomination. In 1991, the nation's Roman Catholic bishops "acknowledged that overpopulation drains world resources." They asked Catholics "to examine our lifestyles, behaviors and policies, to see how we contribute to the destruction or neglect of the environment." Even the Pope issued a 1988 encyclical "In Sollicitude Rei Socialisis" and a 1990 New Year's message on this theme of environmental "crisis" and "plundering of natural resources," and "the reality of an innumerable multitude of people." Luckily, the Pope apparently has "gotten religion" and turned back since then.

The environmentalist ideal has suffused the Jewish community, too. Consider a "Consultation on the Environment and Jewish Life" in Washington, intended as "a Jewish communal response to the world environmental crisis." The italicized second paragraph of that invitation letter says: "We appreciate the many important issues on the Jewish communal agenda. But the threat of ecological catastrophe is so frightening and universal that we believe we must mobilize our community's considerable intellectual and organizational resources as soon as possible." The signers of the invitation included just about every big name in the organized Jewish community.

Even grammar-school texts and children's books fill young minds with unsupported assertions that mankind is a destroyer rather than a creator of the environment. A couple of decades ago, parents and schools began to present children with material like this from Golden Stamp Book of *Earth and Ecology.**

Our Dirty Air—The sea of air in which we live—our sky—is no longer sparkling clean. Once the smoke from chimneys was whisked away by winds and soon became lost in a clear sky. Then we believed that the sky could hold all the wastes we could pour into it. By some sort of miracle, we thought, the sky kept itself clean.

Now there are too many chimneys pouring smoke, ashes, and poisonous fumes into our sky. Where the land has been scoured of grass and forests and there are no crops planted to hold the soil, the slightest breeze whips up choking clouds of dust that spill the dirt into the air. Hour after hour, fumes from millions of automobiles' exhausts are spewed into the air. . . .

In many large cities, there are no clear days at all now. Over portions of the earth, there is a haze, darkest where the population is greatest. Each year air pollution becomes worse as we dump greater loads into the sky.

Yet, this is the air we must breathe to live. You can survive for days or even weeks without food, but without air, you will die in only a few minutes. Right now you are probably breathing polluted air. It is air containing poisons. Some of these poisons are kinds that do not kill immediately. They take their toll over the years, and more and more people are becoming victims of respiratory ailments. . . .

No more Clean Waters—Once the United States was a land of pure, sparkling waters. . . . But in the few hundred years since America's discovery, its waters have been almost totally spoiled by pollution. The greatest damage has come in very recent years.

Still, the people in many cities must drink the water from these lakes and rivers. They make it drinkable by loading it with purifying chemicals. But the chemicals make the water taste bad. There is also a point at which the chemicals used to purify water become poisonous to people, too.

Streams in the United States have indeed become open sewers carrying away wastes from industries and dwellings. The wastes are really only moved downstream to the next town or city, where more wastes are added, until the pure stream becomes little more than a sluggish stench.

Now Lake Erie is dead—killed by pollution.

Lake Michigan may be the next of the Great Lakes to be killed by man. Even sooner, a much larger body of water appears to be doomed—the giant Gulf of Mexico![4]

By now we have reached the stage that *50 Simple Things Kids Can Do to Save the Earth* has sold almost a million copies (this book retails meaningless and false information to kids—for example, instructing them to use water-based instead of oil-based paint);[5] *This Planet Is Mine* is another best-seller in this

---

* Adapted from Fichter (1972), used by permission of the publisher.

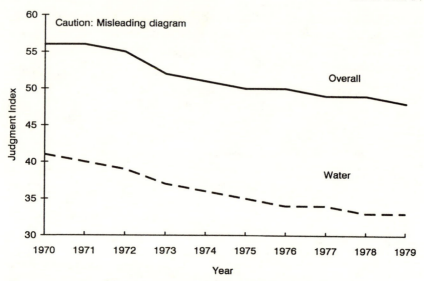

Figure 14-1. National Wildlife Magazine Judgments about Environmental Quality

genre.[6] It is a sign of the times that "more Pennsylvania high school students are taking environmental education classes than physics."[7]

The schools' teachings are having a powerful effect. The consensus view of an informal *Fortune* survey of high-schoolers on this "issue on which almost everyone agreed" was: "If we continue at the pace we're going at now, the environment is going to be destroyed completely."[8] A 1992 poll found that 47 percent of a sample of 6–17 year olds said that "Environment" is among the "biggest problems in our country these days"; 12 percent mentioned "Economy" as a far-distant runner-up. Compare the almost opposite results for their parents: 13 percent "Environment" versus 56 percent "Economy."[9]

Just about all of these assertions of rising pollution are nonsense, as we shall see—but they are dangerous nonsense.

A revealing sequence of events:

From 1970 to 1984, the widely reported Environmental Quality Index of the National Wildlife Federation gave numbers purporting to show that environmental conditions were getting worse, as seen in figure 14-1. In a typical year, the *New York Times* headline for the Index was "Environmental Quality Held Down," and the story began, "The nation's overall environmental well-being declined slightly in 1976. . . ."[10]

Despite the impressive name of the index and its numerical nature, it was, according to the National Wildlife Federation which prepares and disseminates it, "a subjective analysis [that] represent[s] [the] collective thinking of the editors of the National Wildlife Federation Staff." That is, the Environmental Quality Index represented casual observation and opinion rather than statistical facts. It included such subjective judgments as that the trend of "living space" is "down . . . vast stretches of America are lost to development yearly." (Chapter 9 shows the facts on that particular nonpollution issue.) In 1984, as it got harder and harder to reconcile the real facts and the foolish numbers, National Wildlife dropped the numbers and retreated to words only, which are less easy to confute and make ridiculous with the actual data. I hope that my criticism in the first edition helped sink the numerical index by making it seem ridiculous.

Several types of public opinion polls confirm the above anecdotal evidence of rising public concern:

1. People's answers to poll questions about whether environmental conditions have been getting better or worse during (say) the past twenty years show that many more people believe that there has been deterioration than believe that there has been improvement (see fig. 14-2). A 1988 survey found that "eight in ten Americans (81 percent) were convinced that 'the environment today is less healthful than the environment in which my parents lived.'"[11] In 1990, 64 percent said that pollution increased in the past ten years, and 13 percent said it decreased.[12] Another 1990 poll found that when asked, "Compared to twenty years ago, do you think the air you breathe is cleaner today, or more polluted?" 6 percent said cleaner, and 75 percent said "more polluted." With respect to the "water in the lakes, rivers, and streams," 8 percent said "cleaner" and 80 percent said "more polluted," but these polls were taken in the midst of the Earth Day publicity.[13] In 1991, 66 percent of Americans responded "Worse" to "Overall, do you feel the environment has gotten better, gotten worse, or stayed the same over the past 20 years?" and only 20 percent said "better."[14]

2. The trends in proportions of people expressing worry about pollution problems show large increases over recent years. In Harris polls (a) the proportion who said that air pollution by vehicles was "very serious" rose from 33 percent in 1982 to 59 percent in 1990; (b) the proportion who said that "Air pollution from acid rain, caused by sulfur dioxide emissions from power plants" was "very serious" rose from 42 percent in 1986 to 64 percent in 1990; (c) there was an increase from 30 percent in 1986 to 49 percent in 1990 saying "very serious" for "Air pollution by coal-burning electric power plants."[15] (However, a 1991 Roper poll found that people thought that the environment would be cleaner five years hence than at the poll date, unlike a similar comparison in 1980. And people's assessment of the environment "at the present time" was less positive in 1991 than in 1980.[16] Also see figure 14-3.

3. People expect worsening. In 1990, 44 percent said they "expect pollution to increase," and 33 percent expected decrease.[17]

4. A survey of high school students found that "the only interviewees who didn't share the perspective . . . that the environment is going to be destroyed

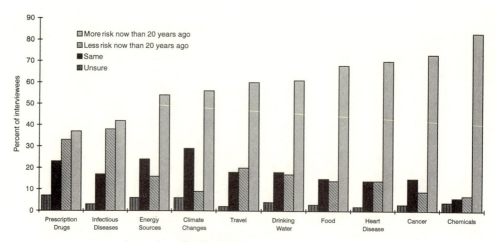

Figure 14-2a. Perceived Risk "Now" versus "20 Years Ago"

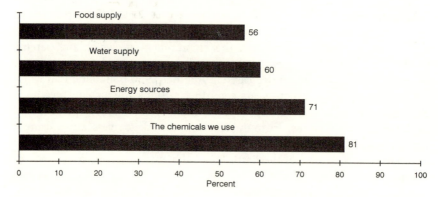

Figure 14-2b. Among Those Who Say There Will Be More Risk in the Future, Which Items Will Present More Risk?

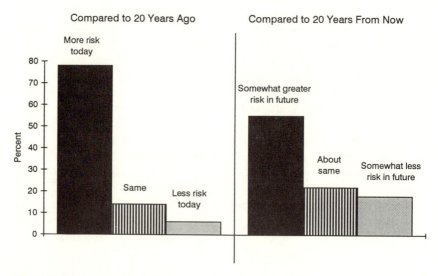

Figure 14-2c. Perceived Risk in Past and Future by U.S. Public

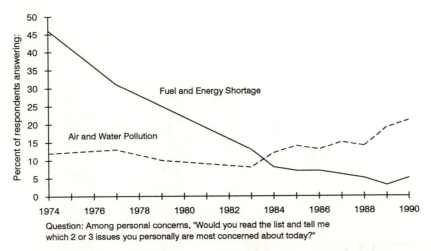

Question: Among personal concerns, "Would you read the list and tell me
which 2 or 3 issues you personally are most concerned about today?"

Figure 14-3. Salience of Environmental Issues: Air and Water Pollution versus Energy

completely . . . were the worst educated of the inner-city youth."[18] This finding is similar to the polls on energy mentioned in chapter 12. It is consistent
with the fact that such powerful abstract thinkers as Bertrand Russell, John
Maynard Keynes (who wrote a famous book on statistical logic in addition to
his work in economics), and several Nobel prize winners in mathematical
economics such as Paul Samuelson, Wassily Leontief, and Jan Tinbergen arrived at exactly the same wrong conclusions as did Malthus about the effect of
population growth on food and natural resource supplies (see chapter 3). In
this subject one will arrive at sound understanding and predictions only if one
pays much attention to historical experience and does not allow oneself to be
carried away by elegant deductive and mathematical constructions such as
exponential growth in a finite system. Education in large quantities would
seem to increase one's propensity to rely on such abstractions. (I hope to write
more on the nature of the thinking involved in these subjects in a coming
book.)

One might wonder whether less-well-educated persons are less responsive
to environmental issues simply because they know less. But surveys that ask
whether "pollution increased in the past ten years," or "decreased," or "stayed
about the same" show that answers are not related to amount of education.
(The only striking difference is that females were more likely than males to say
"increased" and less likely to say "decreased"—72 percent versus 56 percent
and 8 percent versus 19 percent, respectively. There also was a slight gradient
downward in "increased with older groups."[19]

Consider this important piece of conflicting evidence, however: When
asked about the environmental conditions *in their own area*—whose condi-

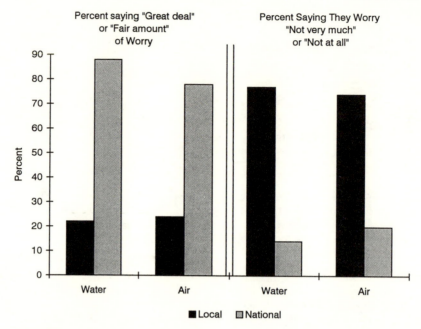

Figure 14-4a. Complaints and Concern about the National Environment versus One's Own Environment

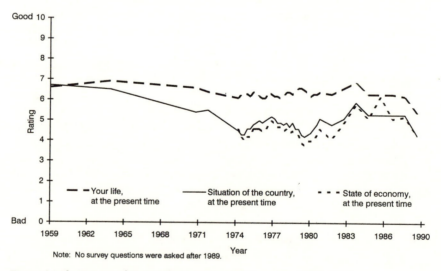

Note: No survey questions were asked after 1989.

Figure 14-4b. Ratings of Own Life, Country, and Economy, 1959–1989

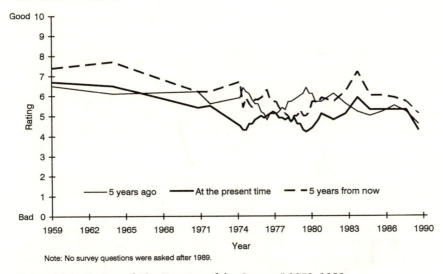

Figure 14-4c. Ratings of "the Situation of the Country," 1959–1989

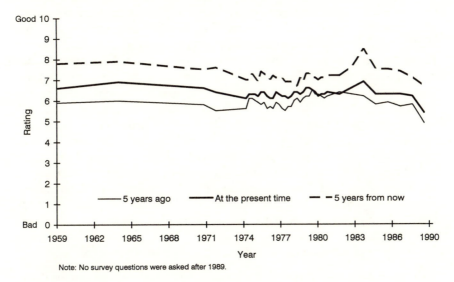

Figure 14-4d. Ratings of "Your Life," 1959–1989

tions they know personally—as well as conditions in the country as a whole, respondents rate the local environment more highly and indicate a much lower degree of worry about it than about the environment in the country as a whole (see fig. 14-4). When asked before Earth Day 1990 whether pollution is "a serious problem that's getting worse" for "the country as a whole,"

84 percent said "serious," but with respect to "the area where you live," only 42 percent said "serious."[20] As the *Compendium of American Opinion* put it, "Americans are primarily concerned about the environment in the abstract . . . most Americans are not worried about environmental problems where they live . . . most Americans do not feel personally affected by environmental problems."[21] In this instance, people feel that the grass is greener on *his or her* side of the street—or more precisely, that the grass is browner on the other person's side of the street which the comparer has never even seen. This cuts the logical ground out from under the abstract aggregate judgments, because they are not consistent with the sum of the individual judgments.

That is, there is a disjunction between public belief and the scientifically established facts that will be shown in the next three chapters. The discrepancy between the public's beliefs about the environment that they know *first-hand*, and about the areas that they *only know second-hand*, is most revealing. The respondents view the situation they know first-hand more positively than the situation at large. The only likely explanation is that newspapers and television—the main source of notions about matters which people do not experience directly—are systematically misleading the public, even if unintentionally. There is also a vicious circle here: The media carry stories about environmental scares, people become frightened, polls then reveal their worry, and the worry then is cited as support for policies to initiate actions about the supposed scares, which then raise the level of public concern. The media proudly say "We do not create the 'news.' We are merely messengers who deliver it."[22] These data show that the opposite is true in this case.

Data that show the interplay of media attention to pollution stories and the public's expressed concern are found in figure 14-5; pollution was no worse in 1970 than in 1965, but the proportion of the population that named it one of the three most important governmental problems rose from 17 percent in 1965 to 53 percent in 1970 (and fell thereafter), marking the media attention to the 1970 Earth Day.[23] Erskine, a long-time student of public opinion, labeled this "a miracle of public opinion," referring to the "unprecedented speed and urgency with which ecological issues have burst into American consciousness."[24]

Consider this question and the answers to it over just five years:

Compared to other parts of the country, how serious, in your opinion, do you think the problem of air/water pollution is in this area—very serious, somewhat serious, or not very serious?[25]

Very Serious or Somewhat Serious

	Air	Water
1965	28%	35%
1966	48%	49%
1967	53%	52%

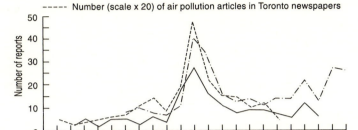

Figure 14-5. Coverage of Pollution Issues in Newspapers and Magazines in the Late 1960s

1968	55%	58%
1970	69%	74%

These data show the speed with which public opinion can change—or really, be changed, because here there is no possibility that the actual conditions changed radically (and indeed, if they changed, if was for the better, as we shall see).

A very strange poll result emerged from a November 1993, poll conducted by the *Los Angeles Times*.[26] Various groups of elites, and the general public, were asked, "I'm going to read you a list of dangers in the world and after I finish, tell me which one of them you think is most dangerous to world stability." Eighteen percent of the public responded "environmental pollution" and 10 percent, "population growth." But of the "science and engineering" members of the National Academy of Sciences, only 1 percent said "environmental pollution"—but an extraordinary 51 percent said "population growth." (The latter is not a typographical error; the percentages add to 100.) The only explanation I can guess at is that many of those NAS members are biologists, whose attitudes toward population growth have long tended to be very negative. (In passing, notice how population growth is simply assumed in the poll to be a danger, which biases the results, of course.)

In the next chapter, we'll look at some facts—as opposed to these whipped-up worries.

Summary

The public believes that pollution in the United States is bad, and has been getting worse. These beliefs can be seen to be connected to writings in the press and statements on television. The poll results showing popular belief

that pollution at large is bad are logically contradicted and thereby undermined by poll results showing that what respondents know best—conditions
in their own areas—are reported as much better than conditions in the nation
at large.

15

The Peculiar Theory of Pollution

ON APRIL 19, 1970, at the time of the first Earth Day demonstrations, the top-of-page headline story in the *Chicago Tribune* was "The Pollution of Earth: 'I'm Scared,'" with the subheadline "Air, Sea and Land—All Being Strangled." The story was typical of headlines all across the country: "I'm scared," said Joseph Sauris, 16, a sophomore at Maine East Township High School, Park Ridge. . . . I don't like the idea of leaving a dead world to my children. That might sound like a cliche, but it may be the truth someday."[1]

Today, a quarter-century later, people still believe that the Earth is being strangled. But what are these deadly substances that are supposedly killing the planet? Almost without exception, the purported pollutions that have most scared the public in the past few decades—Alar, dioxin, acid rain, and a large number of others ranging back to DDT—have turned out to be destructive false alarms (for examples, see chapter 18). Yet the alarms have been much louder than the later all-clears; this contributes to the public's impression that pollution is becoming worse rather than improving.

Let us first distinguish between real, important pollutions and false or trivial claims.

The worst pollutions of the past were diseases caused by microorganisms, and spread by contaminated drinking water and by airborne germs and insects. The following story conveys an aspect of life that was common throughout all of human history until very recently:

> The mystery of death finally came into our household. There had been a fourth child born in the house on the hill—"little Frankie," we always called him—blue-eyed like my father, the sunniest of us all. For weeks one season he lay in the parlor fighting for life—scarlet fever—a disease more dreaded by mothers in those days than even smallpox. Daily I stood helpless, agonized, outside the door behind which little Frankie lay screaming and fighting the doctor. I remember even today how long the white marks lasted on the knuckles of my hands after the agony behind the closed door had died down and my clenched fists relaxed.
>
> Little Frankie died, became a pathetic and beloved tradition in the household. My little sister, who had made a terrible and successful fight against the disease, told me how she could not understand why father and mother cried when they talked of Frankie.[2]

Pollution used to mean such phenomena as human excrement floating in rivers everywhere, as it still does in India and Thailand (and I'm sure many other countries), and as it did in the Hudson River off Manhattan when I was a young man. When I was in the Navy in the 1950s, there were few harbors in the world that were not completely foul, and it was always disgusting to see native kids diving into that mess to fetch the coins the sailors and tourists would throw near the docks for amusement.

In the rich countries we have been so successful in sanitary operations and preventive medicine that infectious diseases are no longer even thought of when pollution is discussed, though in poor countries these diseases still are mass killers.

The next worst pollutions of past and present are dust particulates (and perhaps other smog-making emissions) from burning fossil fuels. These have killed thousands on occasion, and have been systematically associated with the death rate in Great Britain and surely elsewhere.

Finally, there are the trivial pollutions and downright false alarms. To see how far we have traveled from the serious killers, consider that packages of common salt for use in medical laboratories must carry the statement: "WARNING: CAUSES IRRITATION."[3] And a Geiger counter at a landfill in Berkeley, California, set off a major incident when it was triggered by a bit of iodine 131 in the kitty litter of a cat that had been treated for cancer by a veterinarian.[4]

In the poor countries, there are still too many of the age-old pollutions:

> The next morning, we . . . went down to the nearby Ganges. . . . Close by us, a young woman held a tiny baby and washed its face with river water. She opened the baby's mouth and with a bit of the Ganges she massaged its gums with her finger. Eight feet away, the corpse of a dead camel floated by that baby.[5]

The plan for the next few chapters is as follows: (1) Clarify how economics views pollution—as a trade-off between cost and cleanliness. (2) Study the trends in the purity of air and water as income and population have increased in recent decades. (Surprising to many, pollution has decreased, on balance.) (3) Consider which is the best overall measure of environmental purity and pollution. (Life expectancy seems to be the best, and by that measure pollution is decreasing sharply.)

The Economic Theory of Pollution

Economic theory views natural resources and pollution as the opposite sides of the same coin. For example, sooty air is undesired pollution; it may also be thought of as the absence of a desired resource, pure air.

The economic theory of resources, introduced in chapter 1, therefore applies to pollution as well. If the resource in question—pure air—seems to be getting scarcer, that's a sign that society has been using the resource to get richer. And rich societies have more options (as well as more knowledge) for cleaning the air than poor societies. They can install scrubbers in smokestacks, switch to alternative sources of energy, hire researchers to improve technology, and so on. In short, the perceived scarcity of this resource—pure air—generates a public clamor and then economic activity that creates more of the resource than was originally "used up."

The principle behind the long-run increase in our supply of pure air (or any other environmental good) is the same as with minerals, farmland, forests, energy, and other resources discussed in the preceding chapters. And that's why the title to this chapter echoes the title to chapter 1. The "peculiar" theory of diminishing pollution is peculiar only because it runs counter to the prevailing opinion. At first, it seems like common sense to assume that pollution is the inevitable consequence of economic growth. But if we think the problem through, we should expect to see pure air, clean water, and healthier environments in general become less and less "scarce," or easier to obtain, just as raw materials, food, energy, and other resources have become easier and easier to obtain. Our environment should become more and more suitable for human habitation—with no meaningful limit on making it cleaner.

A study of European countries confirms the theory that increased income brings about decreased pollution. Countries with higher per capita income tended to have more laws that control pollution. And during the 1970s and 1980s, the richer countries had significantly greater decreases in carbon dioxide and sulfur dioxide than did the poorer countries (though no statistically significant effect on nitrogen oxides was observed).[6]

The key conceptual difference between a natural resource and pollution is that the goods we call "natural resources" are largely produced by private firms, which have a strong motive—profit—for providing what consumers want. A deal is made through the market, and people tend to get what they are willing to pay for. In contrast, the good we call "absence of environmental pollution" is largely produced by public agencies through regulation, tax incentives, fines, and licensing. These political mechanisms that adjust supply and demand are far less automatic, and they seldom use a pricing system to achieve the desired result.

Another difference between natural resources and pollution is that natural-resource transactions are mostly limited in impact to the buyer and the seller, whereas one person's pollution is "external" and may touch everybody else. This difference may be more apparent than real, however. One person's demand for natural resources affects the price that all pay, at least in the short run; conversely, the price that one person must pay for a resource depends upon the demand of all others for the resource. Much the same would be true for pollution if there were a well-adjusted system by which people had to pay for the privilege of polluting. But such a price system for regulating pollution is not easy to achieve. And hence resources and pollution tend to differ in how "external" they are.

Economics also teaches the habit of searching out unintended, diffuse, and long-run consequences of immediate actions—the way of looking at problems that we may call the "Bastiat-Hazlitt maneuver." This is the central issue in the study of population economics, and of this book. A pollution example: CFCs, chemicals used in refrigerators, are being phased out with the aim of protecting the Earth's ozone layer and reducing skin cancers. Whether this direct effect would occur is itself an open question. But there are indirect and unintended effects that should also be considered. For example, might this ban lead to higher prices of refrigerators and hence lower the use of them in some poor parts of the world? And might this lead to increased spoilage of food and hence increased disease, which would work in the opposite direction from any skin cancer reduction?

Ralph Keeney and Aaron Wildavsky have shown that any government intervention—environmental rule, safety requirement, or conservation regulation—that saves lives at a sufficiently high cost in reduced economic growth would have a more-than-offsetting indirect negative effect on health and mortality, because lower income causes poorer health.[7]

The Bastiat-Hazlitt maneuver insists that when assessing a technology or policy, one should see the benefits as well as the costs, the hidden effects as well as the obvious ones. Automobiles not only cause air pollution and accidents and become junked cars; they also reduce the number of horse carcasses in the streets—15,000 per year in New York City alone at the turn of the century, deaths from horses and runaway carriages—750,000 injuries a year in 1900 when the population was much lower than now—and pollution from manure in the streets—forty-five pounds per day per horse. And one should factor in such matters as the increased personal liberty that autos provide, which enables a person to select from a wider geographic range of jobs and places to shop, and hence lessened control by monopoly employers and merchants.

A third insight from economic theory concerns the different outlooks of engineers and economists. The engineer views all emissions of pollutants as bad, and studies how to get rid of them. Though sensible technical persons do not make this error, many technical analysts set as a goal the total absence of pollution.

The notion of "zero pollution" reminds me of a Simon household discussion comparing the virtues of rinsing a dish from the faucet versus dipping it into a pan of rinse water which fairly quickly is no longer pure. When my children were growing up, I often said to them that the aim in washing dishes is not to get the dishes clean but rather to dilute the dirt to an acceptable degree. This always put them in a tizzy. I pointed out that this is what one necessarily does in managing a swimming pool, and also in purifying a water supply. But no amount of example or logic would budge them when they were young. And they considered it downright immoral on my part that I did not cleave to the ideal of total purity.

Perhaps there is an instinctive esthetic reaction to wastes as there seems to be to snakes or blood. Revulsion to excrement is seen in the use of such words as "crap" for anything we do not like. It may be that this instinct makes it difficult for us to think about pollution in a cool and calculating fashion. Indeed, nowadays washing dishes pertains mainly to esthetics rather than disease, though we "feel" that uncleanness is unhealthy.*

Another relevant analogy is that pollution is like sin; none is the ideal amount. But in economic thinking the ideal amount of pollution is not zero.

It is no easier to wean environmentalists from the ideal of no radiation and no trace of carcinogens than it was to persuade the Simon kids that we should simply dilute the dirt to an acceptable extent. This mind-set stands in the way of rational choice on the path to the reduction of pollution.

In contrast to the technical view, the economist asks about the optimal level of pollution. How much cleanliness are we willing to pay for? At some point we prefer to spend money to buy more police service or more skiing rather than more environmental cleanliness. The problem of pollution for economists is like the problem of collecting a city's garbage: do we want to pay for daily collection, or collection twice a week, or just once a week? With environmental pollution as with garbage, a rational answer depends upon the cost of cleanup as well as our tastes for cleanliness. And as our society becomes richer, we can afford and are prepared to pay for more cleanliness—a trend that we shall see documented in the following chapters.

A "cost-benefit analysis" that weighs and compares the goods and bads of a given pollution control policy implements the economic theory of comparing the overall costs and benefits to society, including the toll in human life of pollution. Though economists have long conducted such analyses, they now are being called for more frequently by policy makers, to the applause of most economists and to the dismay of many noneconomists who feel that it is immoral to put explicit values upon human life, as the analyses usually require.*

An example of this controversial type of cost-benefit analysis is the study of regulations to control volatile organic compounds (VOCs), and to a secondary extent, dust particulates, by Alan Krupnick and Paul Portney. Analyzing the

---

* Thinking rationally about pollution may be difficult in the same fashion as with many of the other counterinstinctive ways in which having a modern civilized life requires us to behave—for example, a public offical having to treat his relatives like other members of the public rather than showing favoritism (see Hayek 1988, on civilization and the suppression of instincts).

* But there are some economists—and I find the argument weighty (especially when the number of persons is at issue) though not necessarily persuasive in every case—who argue that such "utilitarian" analyses are inherently flawed because they require assumptions about inividuals' preferences that cannot be known by the analyst (Hayek 1976, vol. 2, p. 176).

improvements in air quality mandated by the 1990 Clean Air Act, they assessed the costs and benefits—and if the analysis is to be done well, it must include *all* such effects, even effects upon nature that are difficult to appraise in dollars—as valued by the public now and in the future. The analysis showed that "the costs associated with a 35% reduction in nationwide emissions of VOCs in [areas presently violating the law] will be at least $8.8 billion annually by the year 2004 and could be as much as $12 billion. Yet the acute health improvements that we predict to result from these changes are valued at no more than $1 billion annually and could be as little as $250 million."[8]

Krupnick and Portney also applied their analysis of health effects to the especially troubled area of Southern California. They found a similarly unfavorable cost-benefit balance for proposed air pollution control efforts taken as a whole in Southern California, but speculate that the benefit-cost ratio may be favorable for particulates (and could also be affected substantially if effects other than on health were included in the analysis). So this analytic tool can help policy makers sharpen a policy to operate where it is especially needed, thereby gaining benefits to the public and avoiding waste.

The Krupnick-Portney analysis also has the virtue of helping discriminate among subpolicies. For example, they found that though reducing urban ozone gets the most attention from the public, reducing dust particulates has a better cost-benefit health ratio.

Still another virtue of cost-benefit studies is that they help sharpen scientific discussion. Because the Krupnick-Portney calculations are stated objectively, other analysts could a year later present another set of calculations for California's South Cost Air Basin,[9] and make clear which elements of the analysis are the subject of disagreement; this helps researchers and policy makers thrash out differences in a reasonable fashion.

Of course it is crucial that a cost-benefit analysis take into account all the important aspects of the situation—nonmonetary as well as monetary. By making the calculation explicit, however, such studies can highlight these intangible matters which otherwise may be considered in a quantitative fashion.

Conclusion

Pollution is a bad thing—by definition.

Economists conceptualize the reduction of pollution as a social good that can be achieved technologically but costs resources. The question before us is: What is the optimal level of pollution, in light of our tastes for a cleaner environment relative to our desire for other goods?

Afternote

Ecologists' Criticisms of Economics

SOME WHO call themselves "ecologists" severely criticize economists' thinking and its effects on national policy. They even deny that "those who have been trained in modern 'economics' actually deal with economic realities."[10] Among these critics, Paul Ehrlich is noteworthy. He laments the "blunders Simon and other economists of his ilk commit when they attempt to deal with problems of population, resources, and environment."[11] Here is a quote from him in a newspaper article, introduced as follows: "Next to the possibility of war, the danger that concerns Dr. Ehrlich most is economic growth":

> Economists think that the whole world is just a market system, and that free goods are infinitely supplied. They are a discipline built on transparent mistakes, from the point of view of a physicist or a biologist.
>
> Economists are probably the most dangerous single profession on earth, because they are listened to. They continue to whisper in the ears of politicians, all kinds of nonsense. Everybody feels that the economic system is what dominates human affairs, when actually the economic system is hopelessly embedded in the physical and environmental systems. Economists say it's jobs or the environment, when actually if you don't treat the environment right, there will be no jobs. (Steward McBride, "Doomsday Postponed," *The Christian Science Monitor*, Aug. 26, 1980, pp. B10–B11)

From Stephanie Mills, prominent environmental organization person:

> Another impediment to perceiving and acting on overpopulation has been conventional economics, which activist and author Hazel Henderson has called "a form of brain damage." . . . For example, economist Julian Simon, whose work has served as a rationalization for recent U.S. population non-policy, maintains that population growth generates its own solutions." (1991, p. 48)

Neither Mills nor Henderson explains why the theory or facts are in error; calling it "brain damage" is as far as they get.

Robert Goodland, the World Bank's principal ecologist, states that "the most important thing for the environmental movement is to revamp economic thinking." Peter Raven puts it this way: "Perhaps the most serious single academic problem in the world is the training of economists."[12] The ecologists claim to provide a set of larger and more penetrating concepts than the concepts used by economists.

People who have never studied the subject feel qualified to make statements such as "Economic theory was developed at a time when human population was small and the planet was considered an infinite resource."[13] The intellectual basis of such ideas is a mystery.

Regrettably, I have not been able to find much response by economists to this criticism.

Ecologists say that economists omit crucial goods and bads from assessments of policy issues and from calculations of the state of economic welfare from one period to another. Indeed, if these criticisms were valid, economics would fail in its task. Like Oscar Wilde's cynic, to them an economist is a person who knows the price of everything but the value of nothing. But in fact, to be a good economist one must be able to establish a sound valuation—and that means not leaving out any important elements relevant to the valuation. Of course economists often fail, but this is not a failure of the science but of its practitioners.

The question really hinges on what will and will not be included in cost-benefit analyses.

Economists have long taken into account goods other than those that pass through the market when doing cost-benefits analyses of such governmental activities as dam building. Included have been the value to vacationers of boating and other recreational opportunities. At the same time, economists have tried to determine the felt costs to people who would be moved from their homes by the building of a dam. I am not suggesting that these analyses have always been carried out well, but simply that economists have been cognizant of the need to include magnitudes other than those paid for in money. They have mostly proceeded by estimating how much people *would* pay to obtain these goods or to avoid these bads if given the opportunity to do so. In all cases, the magnitudes that have been considered have been *impacts upon human beings*, taking futurity into account with the discounting mechanism in standard economic fashion.

On a macroeconomic level, economists—William Nordhaus and James Tobin early among them—have experimented with factoring some important nonmarket goods and bads into expanded estimates of national economic welfare.[14] They have found that these expansions of the intellectual framework do not change the general impression left by GNP times series, however.

But these widenings of the standard economic measurements have not satisfied many ecologists and a few economists. One major charge is that conventional economics does not take into account a depletion cost of the use of natural resources. But such an entry into the calculation often turns out to be double counting, and assumes that the value of materials extracted will be rising in the future rather than falling, as we have seen (see chapter 2 for materials and chapter 11 for energy).

Another assertion is that the effects of our activities *other than on humans* should also be included in the calculations. That is, eradication of mosquitoes and reduction of malaria might simply be recorded on the positive side of the ledger by economists. Biologists ask that the effect upon the mosquitoes, and upon species in the rest of the ecosystem such as fish that eat the mosquito larvae, also be taken into account. Some who call themselves "ecological economists" have produced graphs that show an "index of sustainable economic welfare"—as a substitute for conventional national income accounting— which is declining in recent years rather than rising.[15] Regrettably, mainstream economists have not dignified this work with solid critique, to my knowledge. I confess that I cannot make head or tail of this writing. A detailed analysis of what seems like metaphysical writing would require considerable space and would go beyond decent bounds for this book.

Ecological economics also tends to have a different concept of the role of future generations in present decisions than does conventional economics. Sometimes it has a very short horizon, quoting "In the long run we're all dead," and sometimes a very long horizon, as in energy accounting where the effects seven billion years from now are treated as of equal value with present effects. Conventional economics discounts the future in a graded way, as do buyers of bonds. (See chapter 10 for more discussion of the matter in the context of conservation of resources; also chapter 4 on humans as long-run creators rather than destroyers.)

This ecological line of thought does not allow for the fact that because knowledge accumulates with time and human effort, the sources of wealth increase with time, and the relative values of natural resources decline—as, for example, the value of farmland declines over time as a proportion of all assets (see figure 8-1). Herman Daly disputes this by saying that "the current 3% figure [the size of the agricultural sector] could soar to 90% in the event of a serious disruption of agriculture."[16] I do not know how to reply to this without resorting to satire.

More generally, people in the future are likely to be richer in every sense— including a cleaner, healthier environment—than people now and in the past, because of the accretion of knowledge. But this is apparently left out of ecological economics.

Economists reverse the charges with a parallel argument. Ecologists accuse economists and human society generally of being free-loaders in using up the world's endowment of natural resources and leaving too little for people in the future. Economists accuse ecologists of being free-loaders in using the knowledge produced by human beings in the past while opposing the addition of more people who will increase the stock of knowledge that will raise the standard of living even more for people in the future, including future ecologists.

Ecologists seem to be calling for an economics-like science based on their own values, which include the points of view of other species. But the science of economics has always been concerned with *human welfare*. To ask that it be otherwise is properly not a criticism of it but rather an assertion of one's own values.

Furthermore, there simply is no way to bring these additional valuations into the standard calculus of economics, nor into any objective science. How could one operationally *value* the loss to individual mosquitoes, to their species, and to other species, of eradication? This goes beyond simply estimating the size of populations—a standard task of ecologists. One can base on objective measurements an analysis of whether the United States is better or worse off economically if, say, cigarette advertising is banned, though even this requires assumptions that some economists regard as improper. And it is possible to make a meaningful cost-benefit analysis of the effects upon humans—including the values *to humans* of the spotted owl—of banning logging in an area where the spotted owl lives. But to include the value of the spotted owl to itself or to other species, or to calculate the loss of a species that humans do not even know about, or the value of an event on another planet that we do not see or hear or feel would require an entirely different sort of calculus. The only calculus that has been suggested so far depends upon specifically religious values deriving from particular religious doctrines, and is not based on measurements that have the basic scientific property of objectivity, and can be repeated by independent observers. This is the thrust of the "ecological economist" Herman Daly mentioned in chapter 12.

Energy accounting has seemed to ecological economists to have the property of objectivity. One can measure the number of units of energy used in various human activities. They then value the activities by their energy inputs. The fundamental flaw in an economics based upon energy accounting is discussed in the afternote to chapter 12.

Though they could not be more critical of conventional economics, these persons have not offered a substitute for criticism in its turn. In the vernacular, you can't beat sump'n with nuttin.

16

Whither the History of Pollution?

SOUND THINKING requires that we consider separately the many forms of pollution rather than just a single, general "pollution." It is useful to classify pollutions as (a) health-related, or (b) aesthetic. We shall concentrate on the health-related pollutions largely because it is easier to talk objectively about them. One person's aesthetic pollution can be another's aesthetic delight—for example, the noise of children at play nearby—which makes such issues complex and difficult.

Pollution and History

In thinking about pollution, as with so many other topics, a key issue is: what is the appropriate comparison?

It is common to compare the present to a hypothetical pristine past. When they hear that pollution has been declining, many people ask: From the beginning of history?

From perhaps the most important point of view—pollution as measured by life expectancy—pollution has been declining since the beginning of the species. The image of the Garden of Eden does not correspond to the available physical evidence.

If, however, one does not consider as pollution human and animal excrement, or the bones cast aside after meals, and instead takes a more restricted point of view and considers as pollutions only the modern pollutions—such as smog from industry, and litter from pop-top soda cans and junked cars—then there certainly is an increase in pollution as societies move from subsistence agriculture toward modernization. But when the society becomes rich enough to put cleanliness high on its list of priorities—as the rich societies do—there is every likelihood that it, too, will move toward less of even the pollutions which come with modernization.

The combination of affluence and improved technology tends toward greater cleanliness.

Contrast a major Western metropolis today with London of 1890:

> The Strand of those days . . . was the throbbing heart of the people's essential London. . . . But the mud! [a euphemism] And the noise! And the smell! All these blemishes were [the] mark of [the] horse. . . . The whole of London's crowded wheeled

traffic—which in parts of the City was at times dense beyond movement—was dependent on the horse lorry: wagon, bus, hansom and "growler," and coaches and carriages and private vehicles of all kinds, were appendages to horses . . . the characteristic aroma—for the nose recognized London with gay excitement—was of stables, which were commonly of three or four storeys with inclined ways zigzagging up the faces of them; [their] middens kept the cast-iron filigree chandeliers that glorified the reception rooms of upper- and lower-middle-class homes throughout London encrusted with dead flies, and, in late summer, veiled with living clouds of them.

A more assertive mark of the horse was the mud that, despite the activities of a numberous corps of red-jacketed boys who dodged among wheels and hooves with pan and brush in service to iron bins at the pavement-edge, either flooded the streets with churnings of "pea soup" that at times collected in pools over-brimming the kerbs, and at others covered the road-surface as with axle grease or bran-laden dust to the distraction of the wayfarer. In the first case, the swift-moving hansom or gig would fling sheets of such soup—where not intercepted by trousers or skirts—completely across the pavement, so that the frontages of the Strand throughout its length had an eighteen-inch plinth of mud-parge thus imposed upon it. The pea-soup condition was met by wheeled "mud-carts" each attended by two ladlers clothed as for Icelandic seas in thigh boots, oilskins collared to the chin, and sou'westers sealing in the back of the neck. Splash Ho! The foot passenger now gets the mud in his eye! The axle-grease condition was met by horse-mechanized brushes and travellers in the small hours found fire-hoses washing away residues. . . .

And after the mud the noise, which, again endowed by the horse, surged like a mighty heart-beat . . . and the hammering of a multitude, of iron-shod hairy heels . . . , the deafening, side-drum tatoo of tyred wheels jarring from the apex of one set to the next like sticks dragging along a fence; the creaking and groaning and chirping and rattling of vehicles, light and heavy, thus maltreated; the jangling of chain harness and the clanging or jingling of every other conceivable thing else, augmented by the shrieking and bellowings called for from those of God's creatures who desired to impart information or proffer a request vocally—raised a din that . . . is beyond conception. It was not any such paltry thing as noise. It was an immensity of sound.[1]

Compare that picture with the results of England's cleanup campaign:

British rivers . . . have been polluted for a century while in America they began to grow foul only a couple of decades ago. . . . The Thames has been without fish for a century. But by 1968 some 40 different varieties had come back to the river.[2]

Now to be seen [in London in 1968] are birds and plants long unsighted here. . . . The appearance of long-absent birds is measured by one claim that 138 species are currently identified in London, compared with less than half that number 10 years ago. . . . Gone are the killer smogs. . . . Londoners . . . are breathing air cleaner than it has been for a century . . . effect of air pollution on bronchial patients is diminishing . . . visibility is better, too . . . on an average winter day . . . about 4 miles, compared with 1.4 miles in 1958.[3]

My aim is to show that if one lifts one's eyes from one's own yard to others', one may see that things are not necessarily better over there.

Life Expectancy and Pollution

What about more recent trends? Is our environment getting dirtier or cleaner? Shifts in the pollutions that attract people's attention complicate the discussion of trends in the cleanliness of our environment. As we have conquered the microorganism pollutions that were most dangerous to life and health— plague, smallpox, malaria, tuberculosis, cholera, typhoid, typhus, and the like—lesser pollutions have come to the fore, along with improvements in technical capacity to discern the pollutants. And some new pollutions have arisen.

Here is an example of dramatically increased pollution: The danger of an airplane falling on your house is *infinitely* greater now than it was a century ago. And the danger from artificial food additives is now many times greater than it was one thousand years ago (though it seems to be a very tiny danger today). You may or may not worry about falling airplanes or food additives, but an alarmist can *always* find some new man-made danger that is now increasing. We must, however, resist the tendency to conclude from such evidence that our world is more polluted now than it was before the existence of airplanes or food additives.

How may we reasonably assess the overall trend of health-related pollutions? It would seem reasonable to go directly to health itself to measure how we are doing. The simplest and most accurate measure of health is length of life, summed up as the average life expectancy. To buttress that general measure, which includes the effects of curative medicine as well as preventive (pollution-fighting) efforts, we may look at the trends in the mortality rate.

After thousands of years of almost no improvement, in the past two hundred years in the rich countries there has been a long upward climb in life expectancy. And in the poor countries, life expectancy has increased extraordinarily sharply during the latter half of this century. The data concerning these all-important facts are shown in chapter 22. Surely this historical view gives no ground for increased alarm about pollution; if anything, it supports the general assessment that pollution has been decreasing. (This view of pollution caused some amusement among critics of the first edition of this book, perhaps because those critics simply put aside the history of environmental disease conquest.)

Of course, the trend could change tomorrow, and we might plunge directly into a cataclysm. But no existing data give reason to believe that this will happen. And despite popular notions to the contrary, life expectancy is still increasing in the United States, especially at the older ages, and even faster than before.[4]

Factors other than reduction in pollutions, such as improved nutrition, also have contributed to the increase in life expectancy. But the decline of the old pollution-caused diseases certainly accounts for much of the increase in length of life. A century ago, most people in the United States died of environmental pollution—that is, from infectious diseases such as pneumonia, tuberculosis, and gastroenteritis. (The extraordinary decline in the great killer tuberculosis may be seen in fig. 16-1. The recent upturn is only a blip due to lax public-health policies.) Humanity's success in reducing these pollutions has been so great that young people today do not even know the names of the great killer pollutions of history—such as typhoid fever, bubonic plague, and cholera.

Nowadays, people die mostly of the diseases of old age, which the environment does not force upon the individual—such as heart disease, cancer, and strokes (see fig. 16-2). And there seems to be no evidence that the increase in cancer is due to environmental carcinogens; rather, it is an inevitable consequence of people living to older, more cancer-prone ages.[5] The sharp decline in accident deaths, despite increased auto use, may also be seen as an improvement in the health environment.[6]

In sum: Life expectancy is the best single index of the state of health-related pollution, though it has the conceptual flaw of being affected by other health-improving forces as well. And by this measure, pollution has been declining very fast for a long time. Hence it is reasonable to say that, taken together, the health-affecting "pollutions" (using that term in its widest and best sense) have been diminishing.

As a comparison to conditions nowadays in rich countries such as the United States, here is a description of environmental conditions in Great Britain a century and a half ago, derived from a social survey:

> At Inverness, the local observer reports, "There are very few houses in town which can boast of either water-closet or privy, and only two or three public privies in the better part of the place exist for the great bulk of the inhabitants." At Gateshead, "The want of convenient offices in the neighborhood is attended with many very unpleasant circumstances, as it induces the lazy inmates to make use of chamber utensils, which are suffered to remain in the most offensive state for several days, and are then emptied out of the windows." A surveyor reported on two houses in London, "I found the whole area of the cellars of both houses were full of night-soil, to the depth of three feet, which had been permitted for years to accumulate from the overflow of the cesspools; upon being moved, the stench was intolerable, and no doubt the neighborhood must have been more or less infected by it." In Manchester, "many of the streets in which cases of fever are common are so deep in mire, or so full of hollows and heaps of refuse that the vehicle used for conveying the patients to the

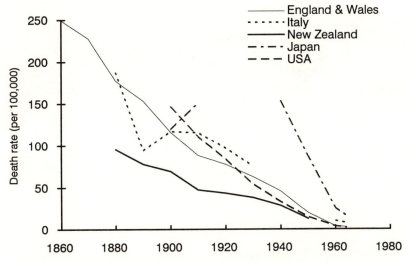

Figure 16-1a. Mortality from Tuberculosis, Standardized Death Rates, 1861–1964

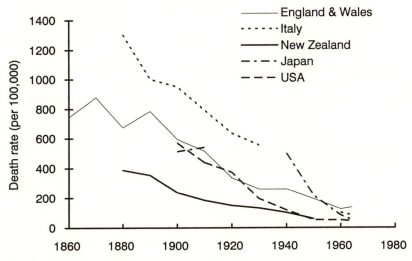

Figure 16-1b. Mortality from Infectious Diseases (except Tuberculosis), Unstandardized Death Rates, 1861–1964

House of Recovery often cannot be driven along them, and the patients are obliged to be carried to it from considerable distances." In Glasgow, the observer says, "We entered a dirty low passage like a house door, which led from the street through the first house to a square court immediately behind, which court, with the exception of a narrow path around it leading to another long passage through a second house, was

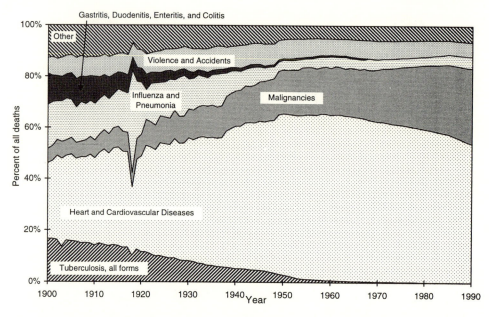

Figure 16-2. Trends in the Leading Causes of Death in the United States

occupied entirely as a dung receptacle of the most disgusting kind. Beyond this court the second passage led to a second square court, occupied in the same way by its dunghill; and from this court there was yet a third passage leading to a third court and third dungheap. There were no privies or drains there, and the dungheaps received all filth which the swarm of wretched inhabitants could give; and we learned that a considerable part of the rent of the houses was paid by the produce of the dungheaps." At Greenock, a dunghill in one street is described as containing "a hundred cubic yards of impure filth, collected from all parts of the town. It is never removed; it is the stock-in-trade of a person who deals in dung; he retails it by cart-fuls. To please his customers, he always keeps a nucleus, as the older the filth is the higher is the price. The proprietor has an extensive privy attached to the concern. This collection is fronting the public street; it is enclosed in front by a wall; the height of the wall is about 12 feet, and the dung overtops it; the malarious moisture oozes through the wall, and runs over the pavement. The effluvia all round about this place is horrible. There is a land of houses adjoining, four stories in height, and in the summer each house swarms with myriads of flies; every article of food and drink must be covered, otherwise, if left exposed for a minute, the flies immediately attack it, and it is rendered unfit for use, from the strong taste of the dunghill left by the flies."[7]

And for comparison with the industrial environment today, consider this description of what the oil industry wrought a century or so ago:

We had lived on the edge of an active oil farm and oil town [in Pennsylvania]. No industry of man in its early days has ever been more destructive of beauty, order, decency, than the production of petroleum. All about us rose derricks, squatted enginehouses and tanks; the earth about them was streaked and damp with the dumpings of the pumps, which brought up regularly the sand and clay and rock through which the drill had made its way. If oil was found, if the well flowed, every tree, every shrub, every bit of grass in the vicinity was coated with black grease and left to die. Tar and oil stained everything. If the well was dry a rickety derrick, piles of debris, oily holes were left, for nobody ever cleaned up in those days.[8]

The growth of knowledge has been crucial in reducing the pollutions of communicable disease, of course. But the wealth generated by successful economies has been all-important, too; increased affluence and good government enabled the United States to afford effective sanitation and safe drinking-water systems, infrastructure which is still far beyond the reach of poor Indian villages where dysentery often spreads because the simple preventive measure of installing a concrete rim around the communal drinking well is made impossible by a combination of poverty and communal strife. The good nutrition that wealth brings also increases resistance against catching diseases and builds greater strength to recover from them.[9]

The extraordinary improvement in the cleanliness of the environment may be discerned from the types of pollutants that Americans now worry about—substances of so little harm that it is not even known whether they are harmful at all. Alar was a notorious false alarm, as was DDT (discussed in chapter 18 on false environmental scares). In 1992 alarm was raised over crabmeat from Canada, and anchovies from California, which supposedly contain an acid that might cause Alzheimer's disease. The substance in question is a natural one, and has always been there. We are only aware of it because, as the New England District Director of the Food and Drug Administration said when commenting on this issue, "There is equipment today that allows you to find a whole lot of nasty things in the food we eat." This does not imply that these substances hurt us. "The U.S. has a zero pathogen tolerance."[10]

The pattern in the poor countries has begun to show the same characteristics as in the rich countries. Smallpox, for example, once a common killer everywhere, now has been wiped out. And cholera, purely a pollution disease, is no longer an important factor in the world.

The only major exception to world trends is Eastern Europe, where mortality has increased and life expectancy has diminished in recent years (see fig. 22-12). And the extent of industrial pollution in Eastern Europe under communism was horrifying, as we will see in chapter 17. Again, there are other contributing causes to the decline in length of life in Eastern Europe. But the concatenation in Eastern Europe of high and increasing pollution, and decline in life expectancy, strengthens the argument for considering life expectancy as the best general index of the state of a country's pollution.

In brief, there has been an extraordinary diminution in the severity of the environmental pollutions we face. But because people are unaware of this history, they react to each new alarm with undiminished fear.

In the next two chapters, we turn to trends in particular pollutions which are the by-products of civilization and progress.

Summary

The public believes that the world is less healthful than decades ago, and that the trend is toward a more polluted environment. This widespread belief is entirely contradicted by the facts.

There are many sorts of pollution. Some have lessened over the years—for example, filth in the streets of our cities, and the pollutants that cause contagious diseases. Others have worsened—for example, gasoline fumes in the air, noise in many places, and atomic wastes. The long-run course of yet others, such as crime in the streets, is unknown. To summarize the direction of such a varied collection of trends is difficult, and can easily be misleading. If one has to choose a single measure of the extent of pollution, the most plausible one—because it is most inclusive—is life expectancy. The expected length of a newborn's life has increased greatly in past centuries, and is still increasing.

After decades of trying unsuccessfully to persuade people by showing them serious analyses and data that our environment is getting cleaner rather than dirtier, I have decided that the only way to deal adequately with the subject of this chapter—and perhaps of the entire book—may be with the sort of satire that P. J. O'Rourke brings to bear. (See epigraph to the next chapter.)

17

Pollution Today: Specific Trends and Issues

> Dr. Ehrlich predicted . . . that the oceans could be as dead as Lake Erie by 1979. Today Lake Erie is palatable, and Dr. Ehrlich still is not.
>
> (P. J. O'Rourke, Parliament of Whores)

AIR POLLUTION caused by human action has long been recognized as a problem. For example, "in about 1300 under Edward I, a Londoner was executed for burning sea coal in contravention of an Act designed to reduce smoke."[1]

Smoke and soot (known technically as "particulates") are the oldest and most dangerous of these pollutions. It has long been known that smoky air can be lethal, as indicated in figure 17-1 for Manchester, England. And recent statistical studies have confirmed the damage of industrial soot particles, even at relatively low levels; Joel Schwartz found that at presently acceptable levels, "as many as 60,000 U.S. residents per year may die from breathing particulates."[2] (The phrase "as many as" can be tricky; studies of other industrial air pollutants do not show nearly so much damage to health.) This study, plus the cost-benefit analysis of Krupnick and Portney discussed earlier, constitute reason to focus on dust particulates.

The history of soot and other air pollutions in the developed countries includes a long period of increasingly dirty air accompanying the growth of industrial activity, and then a decline without observable end, as may be seen in figure 17-2 for London and figure 17-3 for Pittsburgh.

The variety of air pollution measurements are difficult to sort out at first. They fall into the two general groups, (a) emissions,* which can be estimated after the fact by knowledge of industrial activity, but do not reveal how bad the air actually was for human beings; and (b) measurements of air quality, which are relevant but more scarce. There tends to be a general correlation between emissions and airborne concentrations (at least for particulates and sulfur dioxide), as figures 17-4 and 17-5 show, and hence the emissions data are meaningful even in the absence of air quality data. I'll present both sorts of measures for recent decades in the United States, utilizing the series

---

* The reader may wonder why I include data on the emissions of particulates and some other substances, but do not show emissions of carbon dioxide. The reason is that particulates and the other emissions I have shown cause direct harm to human beings. The only postulated ill effects of carbon dioxide are through the purported greenhouse effect; there is no known link to the health of humans.

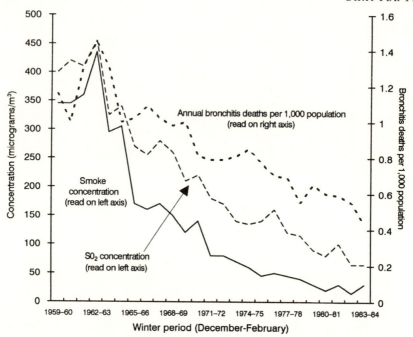

Figure 17-1. Air Pollution and Bronchitis Deaths, Manchester, 1959–1960 to 1983–1984

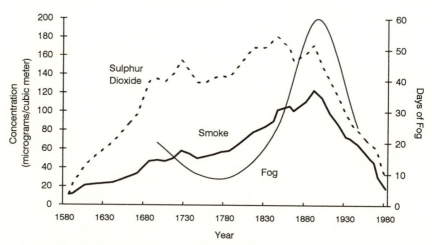

Estimated decadal mean smoke and sulphur dioxide concentrations.

Figure 17-2. Long-Term Trends in London Air Pollution

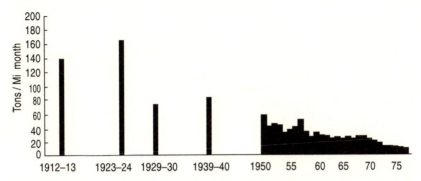

Figure 17-3a. Dustfall in Downtown Pittsburgh, 1912–1913 to 1976

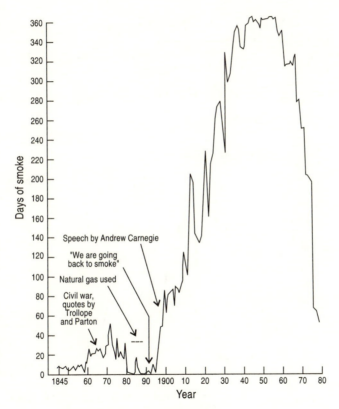

Figure 17-3b. Smoky Days in Pittsburgh

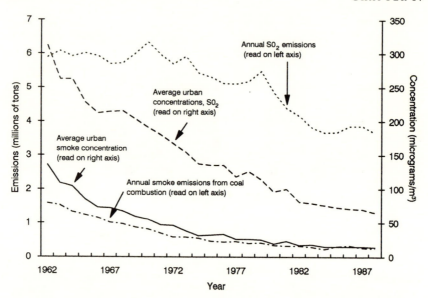

Figure 17-4. Sulfur Dioxide, Smoke Emission, and Soot Concentration, UK, 1962–1988

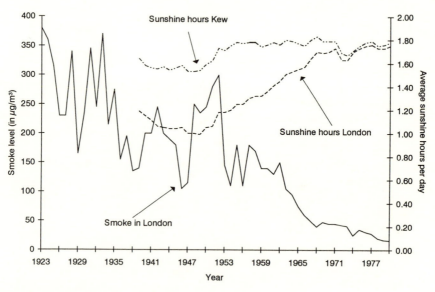

Figure 17-5. Smoke Level and Mean Hours of Winter Sunshine in London

published in the *Statistical Abstract* so that readers can easily update the positive trends for themselves. And I remind you that dust particulates are the most important air pollution, with sulfur dioxide perhaps the second most dangerous.

The official Environmental Protection Agency U.S. data on particulates and sulfur dioxide in recent decades—as seen in figure 17-6—show that emissions have been declining. Lead emission also has declined very sharply, and other pollutant emission also have declined somewhat.[3] And figure 17-7 shows that the quality of the air Americans breathe has been sharply improving rather than worsening—just the opposite of common belief, as indicated in the polls cited in the previous chapter. The data for other pollutants mostly show similar improvement. Figure 17-8 shows data from 1975–1990 for a set of mostly developed countries.

The foregoing graphs make clear that in the rich countries air is getting purer. And the public is being taken to the cleaners by such environmental groups as the National Wildlife Federation, which tell people just the opposite of the facts.

It has been my experience that when these data are presented to people who believe our air and water are getting dirtier, they do not accept the general picture of steady improvement. Often they question the conditions in specific cities. Therefore see figure 17-9 for New York and Los Angeles, the biggest and the most pollution-troubled, respectively.

The extent of air pollution does differ widely within the United States, of course, and among the rich countries. But in just about all places in the West, and with respect to just about all pollutants, the trend is toward diminution and a cleaner world.

Doubters often wonder whether other data series show the opposite, or whether some important measures are being omitted.* For those who will believe that the picture presented here is somehow untruthful, I can only urge that they consult original data sources themselves to check out their suspicions.

A theoretical understanding of the long-term trends seen in the United States and Great Britain will help to predict the future course of air pollution in countries that are now still poor. Technological improvements in fuels and in pollution control undoubtedly contributed to the reversal of rising early pollution levels, though clean natural gas was used for a period during the nineteenth century in Pittsburgh. (The mills later returned to coal.) The ability

* Though this chapter contains many sets of data, the reader may wonder about some that I have left out, and how I decided to include or exclude series. I have included dramatic trends, both positive and negative, when the period covered was fairly long—say, at least two decades. I have not included some series that did not show much of a trend in either direction; often this was because the available series were short or there were too few observations at some part of the time range; examples include shellfish bed closures, oil spills in and around U.S. waters, and phosphorus loadings to the Great Lakes (Council Environmental Quality 1990, pp. 307, 309).

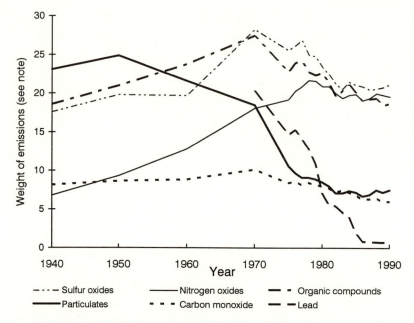

(in millions of metric tons per year, except lead in ten thousands of metric tons per year, and carbon monoxide in 10 million metric tons per year)

Figure 17-6. Emissions of Major Air Pollutants in the United States

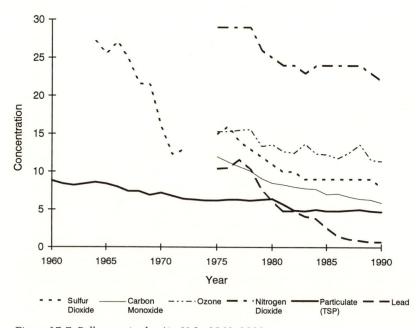

Figure 17-7. Pollutants in the Air, U.S., 1960–1990

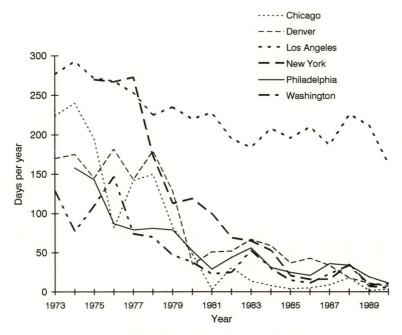

Figure 17-8. Air Quality Trends in Major Urban Areas (number of days greater than the Pollutant Standard Index Level)

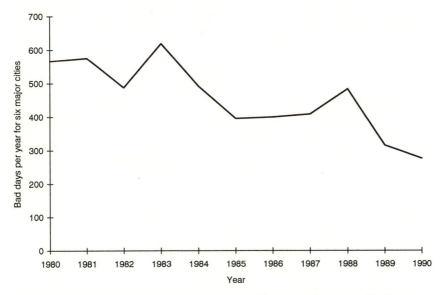

Figure 17-9. Air Quality Trends in United States Urban Areas (number of Pollutant Standard Index days greater than 100)

of new technology to reduce air pollution may be seen in figure 13-3, which shows the dramatic results of the shift to nuclear power in France.

The more important factor, however, is that as wealth increases, one of the goods that people are prepared to buy is a cleaner environment. The demand for a cleaner environment may be expressed through political activity, as was observed centuries ago in Great Britain; citizens clamor for businesses to be held responsible for their noxious emissions, which is entirely consistent with free-market principles; the form of the incentives and sanctions can matter greatly, however, as discussed in chapter 21.

The most horrifying stories of air pollution in recent decades come from Eastern Europe. Western observers spotted some of these disasters years ago. But only in 1988 did the then-Soviet Union admit what had taken place, including some of these sad happenings:

> A top Soviet environmental official said that "50 million people in 192 cities are exposed to air pollutants that exceed national standards tenfold." His term for the situation was "catastrophic pollution."
>
> The gasoline used in autos contains lead.[4]
>
> "Atmosphere haze results in . . . 40% reduced light intensity" in Prague.[5]
>
> In Magnitogorsk, Russia, the coroner said in 1991, "Every day there is some new disaster . . . a worker in his thirties dead from collapsed lungs, a little girl dead from asthma or a weakened heart." He said that "over 90 percent of the children born here suffer at some time from pollution-related illnesses."[6]

The revelations in the 1980s of the terrible air and water pollutions in Eastern Europe have provided powerful evidence of the role of government structure in such matters. Economic theory[7] shows that in socialism the managers of enterprises have an incentive to use large amounts of raw material inputs without penalty for waste, rather than an incentive to economize on inputs as there is in a free-enterprise system. Hence, the ratio of inputs to outputs is much larger in socialism, as seen in figure 17-10. And because factories are part of the government in socialism, and also because consumer protests were squelched by the authorities in Eastern Europe, consumers could not raise the charge that greedy businesspeople were polluting the environment for their own self-interest (although ironically the managers of the state enterprises were doing exactly that). This political system leads to a large volume of waste outputs that must either be controlled or—as was the case in Eastern Europe—simply vented to the environment.

Noise is another product of socialism. Chang shows that the noise in six large Chinese cities is far louder than in London, Madrid, Rome, New York, and Medford, Massachusetts, due largely to industrial activity and construction projects.[8] And to make clear that the cause is not population density or culture, but rather the social system together with the depressed income level it produces, Chang shows that Hong Kong—though it is Chinese and very densely populated—is far less noisy than any other Chinese city.

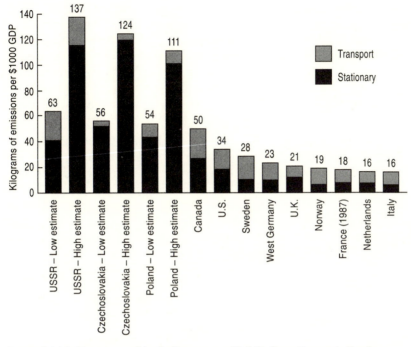

Figure 17-10. Emissions of Air Pollutants per $1,000 Gross Domestic Product, Market and Socialist Economies

Pollution under socialism is further discussed later in connection with water pollution.

Societal devices for dealing with pollutions are compared in chapter 21. But let us tarry here for one example of misguided policies that occur not under socialism, but in a democracy. Such policies are sometimes adopted because of private grabs obtained by political shenanigans, hallowed by the environmentalist label. The original Clean Air Bill proposal in 1990 provided for a 60-cent per gallon subsidy for ethanol as a substitute for gasoline—equal to the entire refinery cost of gasoline at that time. That subsidy would raise the consumer price of gasoline 10 to 15 percent. Seventy-five percent of the production subsidy would go to a single company, Archer-Daniels-Midland, that was very active in lobbying for the bill. The environmental benefits were dubious at best. While ethanol may emit less of some kinds of pollutants than gasoline, it emits more of others, and on balance may make the air more noxious.[9]

So it goes in the developed nations. What about the rest of the world? Assessing air pollution for the world as a whole is difficult, and is not necessarily meaningful. It is clear that the biggest cities in the biggest poor countries—China and India—have horrifying amounts of air pollution (SO_2, smoke, particles) compared to the richer West.[10] But the number of sites worldwide listed by the United Nations shows more sites with improvement on all three measures than deterioration.[11] We can only hope that the poor countries get rich enough soon enough to speed their cleanup operations.

Water Pollution

Concerning the *amount* of water available, see chapter 10 and chapter 20.

The National Wildlife Federation's Index (a "subjective" measure, you may remember from chapter 14) depicted a continuing deterioration in water quality from 1970 until they stopped using numbers, seen in figure 17-11. The facts go in exactly the opposite (and happier) direction, as the official Environmental Protection Agency data show.

The basic measures of water purity found in the *Statistical Abstract of the United States* (for which the reader can easily check future data) are as follows:

1. The proportion of observation sites with high rates of fecal coliform bacteria (an indicator of biologically unhealthy water) fell sharply (see fig. 17-12). This measures the cleanliness of the water with regard to the diseases carried in human excrement. And figure 17-13 shows that the proportion of people in the United States who are served by sewers has risen over the years.

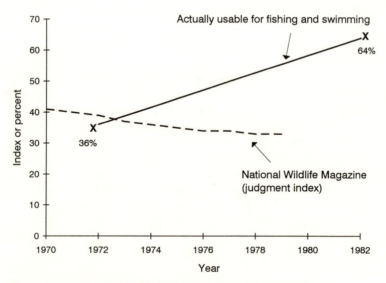

Figure 17-11. National Wildlife Magazine Judgments about Water versus Actual Proportion of United States Streams Usable for Fishing and Swimming, 1970–1982

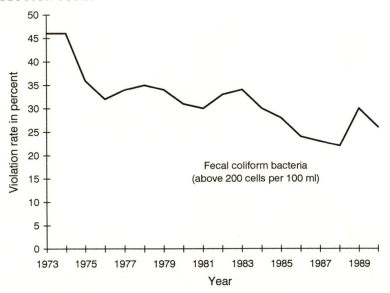

Figure 17-12. National Ambient Water Quality in Rivers and Streams, 1973–1990

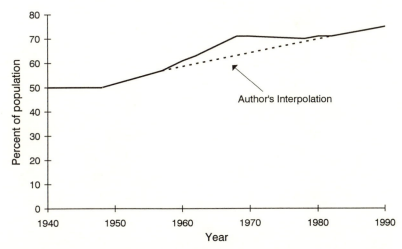

Note: Source of official data changed in 1970, and re-classification took place in 1979. Data for 1973 has been interpolated due to inconsistency with others. Estimates for 1990 have been adjusted by the author.

Figure 17-13. United States Population Served by Sewage Treatment Systems, 1940–1990

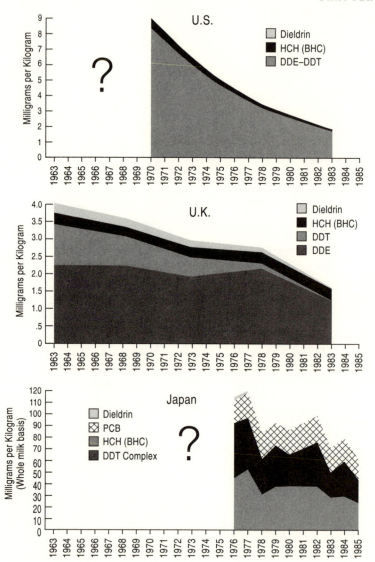

Figure 17-14. Pesticide Residue Levels in Human Adipose Tissue and
Human Milk, U.S. 1970–1983, UK 1963–1983, Japan 1976–1985

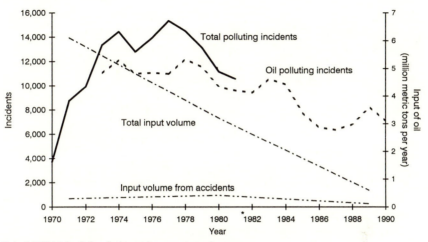

Note: * 1982 total polluting discharges is apparent error in source

Figure 17-15. Oil Pollution in U.S. and World Waters

2. The amounts of various kinds of toxic residues found in humans have been falling in the United States, the United Kingdom, and Japan (see fig. 17-14).

3. The number and amount of polluting incidents in and around U.S. waters fell (see fig. 17-15).

Solid long-run data for water quality are hard to come by. But most students of the subject would probably agree with this assessment by Orris Herfindahl and Allen Kneese:

> Serious deterioration in some aspects of environmental quality did take place between, say, 1840 and 1940. . . .
>
> Since 1940, however, the quality of the environment has in some respects markedly improved. Rivers have been cleaned of their grossest floating materials.[12]

More recent measures indicate improvement in the past few decades. Council of Environmental Quality data show that the proportion of water-quality observations that had "good" drinking water rose from 42 percent in 1961 to 61 percent in 1974. (I have not found consistent data to extend the series to the present; the EPA apparently quit publishing the data because the problem has diminished so greatly.)

Socialist Countries

The Eastern European Socialist countries were for many years paragons of virtue for many in the West. Therefore, it was surprising to some when the first edition included the following notes: "'Blue Only a Memory, The Danube

Is Filthy,'" says a *New York Times* headline. 'A dozen years ago we could swim in the Danube. Today the river is so dangerous it is illegal to swim in it,' said the head of the Czechoslovak Research and Development Center for Environmental Pollution Control. . . . Brastislava [the capital of Slovakia] has the most polluted atmosphere and the worst environment among other European cities."[13]

The ex-Soviet Union, too, was beset with water pollution problems.

> In Russia, a huge chemical plant was built right beside a beloved tourist attraction: Yasnaya Polanya, Leo Tolstoy's gracious country estate. Unmonitored fumes are poisoning Tolstoy's forests of oak and pine, and powerless conservationists can only wince. With equal indifference, the Soviet pulp and paper industry has settled on the shores of Lake Baikal. No matter how fully the effluents are treated, they still defile the world's purest waters.
>
> The level of the Caspian Sea has dropped 8½ feet since 1929, mainly because dams and irrigation projects along the Volga and Ural rivers divert incoming water. As a result, Russia's caviar output has decreased; one-third of the sturgeons' spawning grounds are high and dry. Meanwhile, most municipalities lack adequate sewage treatment plants.[14]

Water pollution continues to be a very grave problem in Eastern Europe as of this edition:

> Half of Poland's river mileage in 1990 was so bad as to be even "unfit for industry . . . it would corrode pipes."[15]
>
> The tap water in then-Leningrad (now St. Petersburg) is dangerous to drink.
>
> The public beaches on the Black, Baltic, and Aral seas were closed because of pollution.
>
> Typhoid outbreaks—the sort of epidemic pollution that the West mostly banished years ago—are common. In 1985 there were 15,000 cases in the Soviet Union, 400 in the United States.
>
> The largest (by volume) fresh-water body in the world, Lake Baikal, is a textbook case of pollution from paper pulp mills.[16]

The explanation for this sad situation is the same as given above for air pollution under socialism.

Poor countries have similar problems, or worse. Some of the rates of pollution are staggering—and I'm talking about the disease pollutions that sicken and kill of people immediately. For example, the rate of fecal coliform bacteria in the Sacramento River (U.S.) was 50 in 1982–1984, and 680 in the Hudson River, whereas in the Sabarmati River at Ahmedabad, India, the rate in 1985–1987 was 1.7 million, down from 5.4 million in 1979–1981, and in the Lema River in Mexico it was 100,000 in 1982–1984. (But by 1985–1987 the Lema rate had dropped to 5,965—real improvement. In other rivers in Mexico and India the rates were much lower to begin with.) The increase in the Sacramento River from 37 in 1979–1981 to 50 in 1982–1984—potential grist for those who churn out scare stories—is entirely irrelevant in the context of such enormous pollutions elsewhere, and is surely just a statistical blip.[17] Other data on access to safe drinking water and sanitation services give some indication of the improving trends in poor countries.

On the Politics of Environmental Hindering

Perhaps because so many people think that the environment is deteriorating where it is really improving, we now have an environmental politics of hindering—of "monkeywrenching," as the Earth First! group calls their strategy—rather than a movement of enabling and creation. The aim is to interfere, stop, and prevent—for example, "gumming up the gas tanks of bulldozers and driving spikes into trees that have been marked for the sawmill"[18]—rather than to build. Instead of "Lead, follow, or get out of the way" it is "Don't lead, don't follow, do whatever you can to get in the way of those who will lead or follow." This spirit can be seen in just a few casually selected environmental policies: preventing the paper industry from choosing how much recycled paper should be included in its products;[19] preventing timber firms from cutting trees (or in some cases, even from planting trees); preventing individuals from building homes even on their own large farms, and firms from building housing and commercial developments; preventing people from raising exotic animals for live sale (such as parrots) or for their products (such as the fur of minks and the ivory of elephants); preventing firms and communities from building nuclear power plants, and incinerators of waste materials, no matter how well tested are the protections for environmental effects of the plants; and on and on. Only a wealthy society which has well satisfied its basic needs can afford this mind-set, of course. But the diffuse and unintended ill effects of this mind-set that are not immediately obvious to the affluent are yet to be reckoned.

An example of unintended consequences: The banning of asbestos was one of the factors in the Challenger shuttle tragedy (see the next chapter), and it also has led to lethal brake-drum failures such as the shard of a truck's drum that flew off and killed a motorist near my home.[20] Of course, the "activists" who fought for the banning of asbestos—which almost surely cannot have any ill effects in the small-volume uses connected with the Challenger's O-ring putty and with brake drums—did not intend these tragedies. And therein lies the point of the argument.

Conclusion

Advanced economies have considerable power to purify their environments. England's top anti-pollution bureaucrat, Lord Kennet, long ago identified the key element precisely. "With rare and usually quickly solved exceptions, there is no contaminating factor in the environment, including noise, that defies a technical solution. All it takes is money."[21] Purification simply requires the will to devote the necessary part of a nation's present output and energy to do the job.

Recent history and current trends illustrate that simple maxim. Many kinds of pollution have lessened in many places—for example, filth in the streets of the United States, buffalo dung in the streams of the Midwest, organic impurities in our foods, soot in the air, and substances that killed fish in the rivers of England.

And here is a U.S. success story:

> Long used for recreational purposes, Lake Washington [an eighteen-mile-long body of fresh water bordered by Seattle on its western shore and a number of smaller communities on its eastern shore] began to deteriorate badly soon after World War II when ten newly built waste treatment plants began dumping some 20 million gallons of treated effluents into its water every day.
>
> Algae thrived on the phosphorous and nitrogen in the sewage discharge, and each time more of the burgeoning aquatic plants died, so did a little bit of the lake—in the form of oxygen lost in decomposition. The lake became cloudy and malodorous, and the fish died along with the algae.
>
> Alarmed, the state legislature in 1958 created a new authority—the Municipality of Metropolitan Seattle—and charged it with sewage disposal for the Seattle area. With the support of local residents, Metro, as the agency soon became known, built a $121 million integrated system that funnels all of the area's effluents far out into Puget Sound. In that way, the wastes are dissipated by tidal action.
>
> Starting in 1963, the system was far enough along for the plants that had been dumping their nutritive wastes into the lake to begin, one by one, to divert their output into the new system and Puget Sound. The results were obvious in the clearer, cleaner water and the return of fish populations. "When the phosphorous levels fell off, so did the algae blooms," says one zoologist, "and so did the pollution." What Lake Washington demonstrates, of course, is that pollution is not irreversible—provided the citizenry is really determined to reclaim the environment, and willing to pay for past years of neglect.[22]

Most astonishing of all, the Great Lakes are not dead—not even Lake Erie! Though the fish catch in Erie fell during the 1960s, it quickly rebounded. By 1977, 10 million pounds of fish were caught there. Ohio beaches on Lake Erie reopened, and "trout and salmon have returned to the Detroit River, the Lake's biggest tributary."[23] For the Great Lakes as a whole, the catch was at its lowest in history in 1965 (56 million tons), but has since rebounded to 73 million tons in 1977, not far from the average since World War I. By 1977, Lake Michigan had become "an angler's paradise . . . the finest fresh-water fishery in the world," a $350-million-a-year sport fishing industry.[24]

What about all the other possible pollutants—PCBs, mercury, global warming, global cooling, and the rest? Because their number is as large as the environmentalist's imagination, it is not possible here or elsewhere to consider, one at a time, all the past, present, and future pollutions; many are briefly mentioned in chapter 18, however. But we should learn a sharp lesson from the recent histories of environmental scares, as briefly discussed in the next chapter. Without important exception, the scares have turned out to be without merit, and many of them have been revealed as not simply a function of ignorance but of fraud.

18

Bad Environmental and Resource Scares

> Perhaps the most disappointing aspect of the [Alaska National Wildlife
> Refuge pollution] debate is the false information being disseminated by
> well-meaning zealots who oppose any human activity on the Coastal Plain.
> Do they believe that their cause is so just that they are above and beyond
> the truth?
>
> *(Walter Hickel, former governor of Alaska, 1991)*

HERE IS the plan for this chapter: First comes a list of the known killers. Next
are mentioned a few phenomena whose effects are in question. Then comes a
long list of threats that scared many people when first made public—and still
frighten many—but which have now been thoroughly disproven. (The refutations are not given here but references are given for most.)

Last is a brief discussion of acid rain, the ozone layer, and global warming.

Known Killers

These are important pollutions that certainly can kill many: plague, malaria
(the worst killer in the nineteenth century into the twentieth century);[1] typhus, tropical yellow fever, encephalitis, dengue fever, elephantiasis, African
sleeping sickness, river blindness, and dozens of other diseases carried by
insects, often through the air; cholera, dysentery, typhoid fever carried by polluted water; leprosy, tuberculosis, smallpox, and other epidemic diseases.
Spoiled food (botulism and other ills) from primitive preparation and lack of
proper storage. Cigarettes (tobacco causes 25–40 percent of all cancer deaths
in the United States).[2] Poor diet (causes perhaps 35 percent of all cancer
deaths in the United States).[3] High doses of medical X-rays. Dust particulates
and smoke from burning coal and wood. Overuse of almost anything—for
example, alcohol and drugs. Guns, autos, ladders. Work-related exposure to
formaldehyde, EDB,[4] Bhopal-type chemical accidents and kepone.[5] Cher-
nobyl-like nuclear accidents due to carelessness and bad design. Coal-mining,
police work, and fire fighting. War, homicide, suicide, forced starvation, and
other deaths caused by human predators.

Possibly Dangerous Threats

These are some phenomena which may be dangerous but whose effects (if any) are not well understood: Too much ozone in Southern California (see chapter 15 concerning Krupnick and Portney). Low-voltage electric and magnetic fields around power lines and appliances.[6] (There is no known evidence of damage to health from either. They are listed in this section only because some reputable scientists are still asking for more research on the subjects, although others say it is a waste of funds.)

Questionable Issues

These are phenomena whose dangers have been alleged. They have not been supported by any solid evidence, but have not yet been conclusively disproven.

1900s–1990s: Global warming.

?–1990s: Ozone layer. See discussion to follow.

1992: "Big Drop in Sperm Count since '38."[7] A Danish study asserts drop of almost 25 percent in human sperm count in past half-century. PCBs are said to be the cause by some "experts." Would anyone care to bet on whether this new scare turns out to be valid?

1992: Chlorinated water causing birth defects. Study finds that among 81,055 births in New Jersey, fifty-six were born with spinal defects, and eight of those were born to women exposed to high levels of chlorine in the water; two or three would have been expected among this group if there were no effect. Since every medicine has side effects, and just about everything "causes" cancer in one fashion or another, it would not be surprising if chlorine does, too. But given the sample size, and the number of such possible effects that are examined by researchers, the odds are very high that this effect will be found not to exist. Yet it occasioned large newspaper stories with headlines such as "Chlorination Byproducts in Water Seen as Risk during Pregnancy."[8] No mention is made in the article of the huge pollution-reducing effects of putting chlorine into the water.

1992: "Study Suggests Electric Razor Use May Raise Risk of Getting Cancer." A study of 131 men who had leukemia. For readers some years in the future, you may test the plausibility of new scares then by checking whether this and other 1992 scares have been validated or disconfirmed by then. (Also, only about three new cases of leukemia are reported per year per 100,000 people.)[9] And consider, too: Are there any dangers from shaving with a straight-edge razor that are avoided with an electric razor?

Definitely Disproven Threats

Earliest history to the present: Land shortage. As nomadic groups grew, land scarcity increased. This led to agriculture. This is just the first in the sequences of technical advances → population increase → new food or land scarcities → new advances described in chapters 5 and 6.

??? B.C.E.: Running out of flint. Worries about running out of resources have been with us since the beginning of time. Shortages surely occurred in many places. Archaeologists studying two Mayan villages in Central America found that about 300 B.C.E. in the village far from plentiful flint supplies, there was much more conservation and innovation by reusing the flint in broken implements, compared to the village with plentiful flint nearby.[10] The Neanderthals could produce five times more cutting edge from a block of flint than could their predecessors. And successors of the Neanderthals increased their efficiency to produce eighty times as much cutting edge per block as the Neandertal's predecessors.[11] Eventually, flint was replaced by metal, and scarcity declined. This is the prototype of all resource scares.

1700 B.C.E.?: Running out of copper. Iron was developed as a replacement for tool manufacture.

1200 B.C.E.?: Tin. New sources were found from time to time. Bronze became increasingly scarce and high priced in the Middle East and Greece because of a tin shortage probably caused by a war-induced breakdown in long-distance trade. Iron-working and steel-making techniques developed in response.[12]

550 B.C.E.?: Disappearing forests. The Greeks worried over the deforestation of their country, in part for lack of wood to build ships. When scarcity became acute, shipbuilders shifted to a new design that required less wood.[13] Greece is well forested now.

1500s, 1600s: Running out of wood for fuel.

1500s to 1700s C.E.: Loss of trees in Great Britain. See chapter 10 for outcome.

Late 1700s: With the invention of lightning rods came fear of *electricity accumulating* in earth (Ben Franklin's time).[14]

1798: Food—the Malthusian mother of all scares that warns: increasing population must lead to famine. Since then there has been continuous improvement in average nutrition (see chapter 5).

1800s: Running out of coal in Great Britain. Jevons's book documented the scare. See chapter 11 for outcome.

1850s and intermittently thereafter: Running out of oil. See chapter 12 for outcome.

1895–1910: Rubber. Wild-grown public-property supplies became exhausted and the price of rubber rose from $0.50 to $3. Plantations were established in response. Price fell back to $0.50 by 1910, and then went further down to $0.20.[15]

1900s: Timber in the United States. See chapter 10 and Sherry Olson (1971).

1922–1925: Rubber again. British-Dutch cartel squeezed supplies, and prices tripled. Increased scarcity provoked conservation in production, increased productivity on plantations, and recycling. Price returned to $0.20 and cartel was broken. Research on synthetics began as a result of the price run-up.[16]

1930s, 1950s, 1980s in the United States, other periods in other countries: Water. See chapters 10 and 17.

1940–1945: Rubber again. War cut supplies. The research on synthetics, induced by the earlier episode, was available for rapid development.

1945: DDT, sensationalized by Rachel Carson in 1962. Said to cause hepatitis.[17] Discontinued in United States in 1972. Known then to be safe to humans (caused death only if eaten like pancakes).[18] Some damage to wildlife under special conditions.[19]

With the aid of DDT, "India had brought the number of malaria cases down from the estimated 75 million in 1951 to about 50,000 in 1961. Sri Lanka . . . reduced malaria from about three million cases after World War II to just 29 in 1964." Then as the use of DDT went down, "Endemic malaria returned to India like the turnaround of a tide." By 1977 "the number of cases reached at least 30 million and perhaps 50 million."

In 1971, amidst the fight that led to the banning of DDT in 1972, the president of the National Academy of Science—distinguished biologist Philip Handler—said "DDT is the greatest chemical that has ever been discovered." Commission after commission, top expert after top Nobel-prize-winning expert, has given DDT a clean bill of health.[20]

1950s: Irradiated foods. Now approved in thirty countries for various uses, approved in United States, 1992.[21]

1957–continues: Fluoridated water. The arguments used against fluoridating water were eerily similar to those later used against nuclear power—but from the other end of the political spectrum.[22]

1960s: PCBs. Banned in 1976.[23] A side effect of banning PCBs is malfunctions in large electrical transformers. One such case caused the July 29, 1990, blackout covering 14 square miles in Chicago, leading to rioting and three deaths.[24]

Early 1960s: Low-level nuclear radiation. Rather than being harmful, this was later shown to produce a beneficial effect called hormesis (see chapter 13).

November 1959: Thanksgiving cranberries and pesticides.

Mid-1960s: Mercury dental fillings. Declared safe in 1993 by U.S. Public Health Service.[25]

Mid-1960s: SST threat to ozone layer; two scientific flip-flops within a few years.[26] (See below.)

1970: Mercury in swordfish and tuna.[27]

1970: Cyclamates banned for causing bladder cancer. Totally cleared in 1985.[28] But ban never lifted.[29]

1972: Red dye #2. One Russian study claimed dye caused cancer. Many subsequent studies absolved the dye. Nevertheless, banned in 1976.[30]

1970s (and earlier): Running out of metals (see chapters 1–3).

1970s: Saccharin causing bladder cancer. Exonerated in 1990s.[31] But warning still required on containers.

Early 1970s: Pesticides aldrin and dieldrin, suspended in 1974.[32] Chlordane and heptachlor. All banned in the 1970s because of belief that they cause tumors in mouse livers. But "[t]here has never been a documented case of human illness or death in the United States as the result of the standard and accepted use of pesticides. Although Americans are exposed to trace levels of pesticides, there is no evidence that such exposure increases the risk of cancer, birth defects, or any other human ailment."[33]

1970s: Acid rain. Shown in 1990s not to harm forests. (See below.)

1970s: Agent Orange (dioxin). Dioxin declared safe by federal court in 1984 when veterans brought suit.[34] August 1991: *New York Times* front-page headline was "U.S. Backing Away from Saying Dioxin Is a Deadly Peril." The story continued, "Exposure to the chemical, once thought to be much more hazardous than chain smoking, is now considered by some experts to be no more risky than spending a week sunbathing." Concerning the Agent Orange case: "Virtually every major study, including a 1987 report by the Centers for Disease Control (CDC), has concluded that the evidence isn't strong enough to prove that the herbicide is the culprit" in the bad health of some Vietnam veterans.[35]

Mid-1970s: Humanity in danger because of a millennia-long *reduction in the number of varieties of plants used for food.* Belied by evidence on famine prior to the 1970s and since then, as explained in the afternote to chapter 6.

1976: Chemical residues at Love Canal.[36] Scare ended 1980; solid scientific consensus is that there was no observable damage to humans from living near Love Canal.

1976: Explosion of PCB plant in Seveso, Italy. The PCBs caused no harm to anyone. (See the statement by Haroun Tazieff on page 573.)

Mid- and late-1970s: Global cooling. By 1980s, replaced by the scare of global warming. (See below.)

1978: Asbestos in schools and other buildings.[37] The ill-considered regulations on the use of asbestos not only are costly, but have had a devastating side effect: the *Challenger* space shuttle disaster. The sealant used to replace the asbestos-based O-ring sealant in the rocket engine that launches space shuttles malfunctioned at the low temperature at which *Challenger* was launched, causing the explosion shortly after launch and deaths of the astronauts. As in many such cases, it is impossible to foresee all the consequences of an environmental regulation, and as David Hume and Friedrich Hayek teach us, we should be extremely wary of altering evolved patterns of behavior lest we make such tragic blunders with our "rational" assessments of what our social interventions may bring about. For more on asbestos, see the 1992 article by Malcolm Ross—a hero in bringing to light the facts about asbestos—and Bennett's 1991 book.

1970s–1980s: Oil spills. The worst cases of oil spills have all been far less disastrous to wildlife than initially feared.

1980s: Radon. Eventually, *too little* radon found dangerous, rather than too much.[38]

1979 Lead ingestion by children lowers IQ. Study by Herbert Needleman led to the federal ban on leaded gasoline. Study entirely repudiated in 1994.[39] No mention of again allowing leaded gasoline has been made, however.

1981: Coffee said to cause 50 percent of pancreatic cancers. Original researchers reversed conclusion in 1986. Also, no connection found between caffeine intake of pregnant women and birth defects.[40]

1980s, 1990s: BST (Bovine somatotropin). Assertion that this growth-promoting element will make cows more liable to infection proven false.[41]

1981: Malathion and medfly threat to agriculture in the West. Malathion found safe in 1981 as a medfly killer, after its use had been threatened.

1982: Times Beach dioxin threat, found to have caused no harm to humans. In 1983 dioxin was cleared of charges. The Centers for Disease Control asserts that the Times Beach evacuation was unnecessary.[42]

1984: Ethyl dibromide (EDB). Banned, though no one harmed. Result: more dangerous pesticides used instead.[43]

Mid-1980s, continues: Ozone hole. No connection found between thinner ozone layer and skin cancer. (See below.)

1986: In November, warning of *lead in drinking water*. In December, retraction by EPA.[44]

1987: Alcohol said to be responsible for 50 percent increase in breast cancers.[45]

1987: Sand from California and other beaches. Silica was listed as a "probable" human carcinogen, and warnings were required by the State of California on containers of sand and limestone. Has been classified as carcinogenic by OSHA and other regulatory agencies.[46]

1989: Red dye #3. This scare came and went in a hurry.[47]

?DES (Diethylstilbesterol): Cattle growth hormone said to cause cervical cancer. Banned.[48] Only cause for fear was finding of vaginal cancer when DES used in large doses as a human drug during pregnancy.[49]

1989: Aflatoxin in corn. Another supposed threat to our food supply.

1989: Alar.[50]

? Nuclear winter: Atom bombs can surely kill us. But this threat to humanity as a whole was soon found to be shoddy science.

1991: Smoke from Kuwait oil fires and global cooling. No global effects found.[51] "Fires in Kuwait Not a Threat to Climate, Federal Study Finds."[52] First reports estimated an "unprecedented ecological catastrophe, the likes of which the world has never seen," with five years required to extinguish all the fires. The last fire was extinguished within six months.[53]

1991: Lefthanded people die earlier. Proved unsubstantiated in 1993.[54] False scare based on faulty age-compositional data.

1993: Cancer caused by *cellular telephones.* This scare is an excellent example of the scare epidemic. A single layman made the charge on a television talk show of a link between his wife's brain tumor and her use of cellular phones. That was enough to produce front-page stories for days, activity in Congress, the Food and Drug Administration, and the National Cancer Institute, plus statements by manufacturers that studies of the matter will be forthcoming. All scientists quoted have stated that there is no evidence of a connection. In the meantime, stock prices of firms in the industry fell substantially—the price of Motorola, the largest manufacturer, fell 20 percent[55]—and many persons became fearful of using their phones.

Given that the human imagination is active, and that there is no sanction for floating such scares but there is a news value in them, there is every reason to expect many, many more false scares to proliferate, each one adding to the impression that the environment is a more and more frightening milieu. Hence a brief digression:

> [I]f you were to wear both a belt and suspenders, the chance of your suffering "coincident failure"—having both snap at once and your pants fall down—is one occurrence every 36,000 years.[56]

Reassuring people about environmental and resource scares is not easy. It is like reassuring a small child that night noises do not imply danger. You can investigate room after room with the child. But the fears reappear later, and are directed to places you did not investigate. Perhaps vague fears are an ineradicable part of our nature, so long as we lack solid knowledge of the actual conditions. But policy makers must try to rise above the childish and primitive thinking of these scares, and to gain the necessary knowledge, so as not to make costly and destructive decisions.

The possibility of a dangerous or unesthetic polluting effect may be raised against almost any substance humans have ever produced or ever will produce. And we cannot immediately rebut any such charge, because it takes much time and research effort to get the facts. It only takes one sentence to accuse a person of murder or a substance of causing cancer, but it may take years and volumes to rebut the charge. It is clear that if we act as if all *possible* dangers from a substance are also *likely* dangers, and if we take seriously all charges even when there is little evidence presented to back them up, we will become immobilized.

May I now introduce a surprise witness whose qualifications in the fight against pollution are formidable? Here is his congressional testimony about sodium azide, which is used in air bags for automobiles. (He was responding to a report that this chemical may cause mutations and cancer.)

Sodium azide, if you smell the gas or taste it, is very, very unsafe. So is gasoline. So are the additives in gasoline. So are battery additives. So are tire wear and tire flakes that get into the air. So are hydrocarbons. So is nitrogen oxide, and so is carbon monoxide.

It strikes me as eroding the credibility of some of these opponents who suddenly become full of such concern for these toxic substances because it happens to be in accord with what certain special industrial interests want, and so unconcerned with the massively more pervasive, massively more poisonous array of chemical substances that we too charitably call pollution.

I also spoke with Dr. Bruce Ames (chairman at the Genetics Department at the University of California-Berkeley). . . . Dr. Ames was merely talking about sodium azide as it is exposed to human contact. He is not talking about sodium azide as it is solidified in pellets, and contained in sealed containers, etc. He does not have any information on that.

The point I want to make is that sodium azide, if it is exposed to acidic contact, will under certain extraordinary circumstances, given the fact that it is a solid pellet, emit a hydrozoic acid gas which is an intolerably pungent gas. If anybody has ever taken the slightest whiff of this gas, they would know it.

In all the crashes which involve air bag equipped cars on the highways, and sodium azide as the inflator, there has been no such reaction.

I don't say that by way of saying that sodium azide should be the inflator. Undoubtedly it is likely that most of the cars with air bags in the '80s will not have sodium azide.

But I do point out that the attempt to sensationalize this product in ways that are not shared by EPA, the Department of Health, Education and Welfare, or OSHA, who know how sodium azide has been used for years in medical laboratories, for example—your attempt to sensationalize it does not receive much credibility given the source of the persons who are doing the sensationalizing.[57]

The irony of this effective defense of sodium azide by Ralph Nader—for that is the identity of my surprise witness—is that the consumer and environmental movements in which Nader is influential have attacked many other substances and conditions in the same way that sodium azide and air bags were attacked, and now the same consumerists were suffering from irresponsible attacks on their own pet safety project, the air bag.

Major Environmental Scares of the 1990s

Acid Rain

The acid rain scare has now been exposed as one of the great false alarms of our time.[58] In 1980, the federal government initiated the huge National Acid Precipitation Assessment Program (NAPAP), employing seven hundred scientists and costing $500 million. The NAPAP study found—to the surprise of most of its scientists—that acid rain was far less threatening than it had been assumed to be at the onset of the study. It is mainly a threat to a few lakes— about 2 percent of the lake surface in the Adirondacks[59]—all of which could be made less acid with cheap and quick liming. Furthermore, before 1860, when forests around those lakes began to be cut and wood burned (which lowers acidity), the lakes were as acid as now. The Clean Air Act of 1990, which will have large economic consequences for the United States, was passed while the NAPAP findings were unknown to most or all of the Congress; the NAPAP director expressed disappointment in 1990 that "the science that NAPAP performed . . . has been so largely ignored."[60] Indeed, the NAPAP findings were systematically kept from public view until the television program "60 Minutes" aired a broadcast on the scandal.

In Europe, the supposed effects of acid rain in destroying forests and reducing tree growth have now been shown to be without foundation; forests are larger, and trees growing more rapidly, than in the first half of this century (see chapter 10).

The acid-rain scare reteaches an important lesson: It is quick and easy to raise a false alarm, but to quell the alarm is hard and slow. The necessary solid research requires considerable time. And by the time the research is complete, many people have a stake in wanting the scientific truth not to be heard— advocacy organizations who gain public support from the alarm; and bureaucrats who have a stake in not being shown to have been in error, and who already have built some empire on the supposed problem.

Global Warming

Along with acid rain and the ozone hole (addressed below), the supposed greenhouse effect and global warming must be mentioned in this book because it is so salient in public thinking. I am not an atmospheric scientist, and I cannot address the technical issues. I can, however, try to put these issues in reasonable perspective.

Given the history of such environmental scares—over all of human history—my guess is that global warming is likely to be simply another transient concern, barely worthy of consideration ten years from now should I then be writing again of these issues. After all, when I first addressed environmental matters in the late 1960s and 1970s, the climatological issue of major public concern was still global *cooling*. These quotations collected by Anna Bray illustrate the prevailing thinking about climate in the early 1970s, only a decade before the hooha about warming began in earnest.[61]

[C]limatologist J. Murray Mitchell, then of the National Oceanic and Atmospheric Administration, noted in 1976: "The media are having a lot of fun with this situation.

Whenever there is a cold wave, they seek out a proponent of the ice-age-is-coming school and put his theories on page one. . . . Whenever there is a heat wave . . . they turn to his opposite number, [who predicts] a kind of heat death of the earth."

The cooling has already killed hundreds of thousands of people in poor nations. It has already made food and fuel more precious, thus increasing the price of everything we buy. If it continues, and no strong measures are taken to deal with it, the cooling will cause world famine, world chaos, and probably world war, and this could all come by the year 2000. (Lowell Ponte, *The Cooling*, 1976)

The facts have emerged, in recent years and months, from research into past ice ages. They imply that the threat of a new ice age must now stand alongside nuclear war as a likely source of wholesale death and misery for mankind. (Nigel Calder, former editor of *New Scientist* and producer of scientific television documentaries, "In the Grip of a New Ice Age," *International Wildlife*, July 1975)

At this point, the world's climatologists are agreed. . . . Once the freeze starts, it will be too late. (Douglas Colligan, "Brace Yourself for Another Ice Age," *Science Digest*, February 1973)

I believe that increasing global air pollution, through its effect on the reflectivity of the earth, is currently dominant and is responsible for the temperature decline of the past decade or two. (Reid Bryson, "Environmental Roulette," *Global Ecology: Readings Toward a Rational Strategy for Man*, John P. Holdren and Paul R. Ehrlich, eds., 1971)

Bryson went so far as to tell the *New York Times* that, compared to the then-recent "decade or two" of cooling, "there appears to be nothing like it in the past 1,000 years," implying that cooling was inevitable.[62]

Indeed, many of the same persons who were then warning about global *cooling* are the same climatologists who are now warning of global *warming*— especially Stephen Schneider, one of the most prominent of the global-warming doomsters.*

It is interesting to reflect on the judgments that would be made in (say) 1996 of past decisions if the world had followed the advice of the climatologists only two decades years earlier who then urged the world to take immediate steps to head off the supposed cooling threat. Should we not be glad that

---

* When described as a former advocate of the cooling view by George Will (*Washington Post*, September 7, 1992, op-ed page) and Richard Lindzen (*Regulation*, vol. 15, no. 2), Schneider violently denied it. He referred to Will's assertion as "false and possibly malicious" (*Washington Post*, September 26, 1991, A19) and objected to Lindzen's statement in a strong "personal note" (*Regulation*, Summer 1992, p. 2), in both places asserting that his earlier book was "relatively neutral" on the subject. Therefore it behooves me to quote this summary from that earlier book in the section entitled "What Does It All Mean?" (1976, p. 90): "I have cited many examples of recent climatic variability and repeated the warnings of several well-known climatologists that a cooling trend has set in—perhaps one akin to the Little Ice Age—and that climatic variability, which is the bane of reliable food production, can be expected to increase along witht he cooling." There is no qualification or rebuttal in the following text.

governments did not listen to the anti-cooling advice they were given in the 1970s? And therefore, is it reasonable now to trust the forecasts of those very scientists who have been systematically wrong in every doomsaying prediction that they have made—as is true of the environmental spokespersons of the past two decades, who are up in arms about global warming?

Curiously, within days after I first wrote the above paragraph, there appeared a newspaper story entitled "Volcano Reverses Global Warming: Scientists Expect Mean Temperature to Drop 1 Degree over 2–4 Years."[63] The event in question was the eruption in June 1991, of Mount Pinatubo in the Philippines. Then within a few days more there appeared a scholarly article finding that smoke particles may lead to cooling rather than warming, as had previously been assumed.[64] Or do I have it backwards? No matter.

Whether the climate models will be right about Mount Pinatubo or not, and about the cooling effect of smoke particles, is in question, of course. The problem here, as with the global warming issue generally, is that our planet contains many forces about which we as yet know very little, and which we can predict little if at all—for example, volcano eruptions. It is an act of hubris and great imprudence to proceed as if we know much more than we do when a single article in a single journal can undermine our basic conclusions.

All that can be done within the scope of the available space and of my nonexpert's knowledge is to give the following quick list of propositions about the issue.[65] Before the "concerned" reader concludes that the following treatment is simply a whitewash, it would be fair to examine the state of one's own knowledge on the subject—what you know about technical facts, and the sources of the supposed information. The basis of most people's thoughts on the subject is simply general newspaper stories that assert that a problem exists. (In the following summary of the facts I rely heavily on Balling's book.)

1. All climatologists agree that there has been an increase in atmospheric carbon dioxide in recent decades. But there is great disagreement about the implications (if any) of the CO_2 trend for global temperature. In the late 1980s the range of thinking ran from those who believed that there will be warming of up to 10 degrees Fahrenheit by the next mid-century to those who argued that the evidence is so mixed that one cannot predict any warming at all; by 1994, the range had come down somewhat at the top, but there is still great disagreement.

2. Even those who predict warming agree that any likely warming would not be great relative to year-to-year variability, and would be swamped by long-run natural variability over the millennia.

The high-end-estimate climatologists have also scaled back their estimates of a possible rise in sea level (due to glacial and polar ice melting) from several feet to at most a few inches.

3. Those who foresee warming rely heavily on computer simulation models. Many of those who foresee little or no warming rely on the temperature data for the

past century. And many of the skeptics of global warming believe that the simulation models lack solid theoretical basis and are built on shaky ad hoc assumptions. Skeptics also point to the absence of correlation between past carbon dioxide buildup and the temperature record.

4. Even if warming will occur, it is likely to be uneven in time and place. More of the effect would be at night than day, more in the low-sun season and less in the high-sun season, and more in the arctic regions than in the tropical parts of the world. It should be noted that these effects are less unwelcome than if the effects were in the opposite parts of the daily cycle and the planet's geography.

5. If there is warming, it will occur over many decades, during which period there will be much time for economic and technical adjustment.

6. Any necessary adjustments would be small relative to the adjustments that we make during the year to temperature differences where we reside and as we travel. A trip from New York to Philadelphia, or spring coming a day or two earlier than usual, is not very different than the temperature gradient for any likely warming within the next century.

7. The necessary adjustments would be far, far smaller than the effects of the advent of air conditioning in any of the places in this world where that device commonly is found. The alterations that air conditioning—let alone central heating—make in the environment in which we spend our hours dwarf any alterations required by any conceivable global warming.

8. If there is warming, and if one is worried about it, the clear policy implication would be the substitution of nuclear fission for the burning of fossil fuels. This would have other benefits as well, of course, especially the lives saved from air pollution and coal mining.

Does this calm assessment differ from the impression you get from the news? One can gauge the effectiveness of the mass media in creating public opinion on global warming and other doomsday subjects by the increase in just a single year in the proportion of the public that were "aware of the global warming issue"—from 59 percent in 1988 to 79 percent in 1989.[66] There is no way that individuals can measure for themselves the extent of global warming. Hence their thinking is labile and easily influenced by television and newspapers. Then the politicians and the environmental activists who give scare stories to the press cite public opinion as a reason to change public policy.

Assessing global warming seems more and more like assessing the likely availability of raw materials: every alarm about scarcity has been a case of speculative theory not fitted to the historical data. The alarm about greenhouse warming seems to come from those who pay attention only to various theoretical models—just as the alarm about global cooling came only from theoretical models in the 1970s (and from some of the same persons who were alarmed then)—whereas those who focus on the historical temperature record seem unconvinced that there have been unusual changes and are quite unworried about the future. With respect to natural resources, the conclusion is inescapable that those who have believed the historical record have been correct, and those who have believed theories without checking them against the record have been in error. Is it not likely that this will be the case with global warming, too?[67]

The Ozone Layer

This unprecedented assault on the planet's life-support system could have horrendous long-term effects on human health, animal life, the plants that support the food chain, and just about every other strand that makes up the delicate web of nature. And it is too late to prevent the damage, which will worsen for years to come.[68]

As with the supposed greenhouse effect and global warming, the loss of protective ozone from the upper atmosphere must be addressed here because it looms large in public thinking. In the 1990s when I tell an audience that population growth does not have the bad economic effects it is commonly believed to have, invariably someone asks: But what about the ozone layer? What about the greenhouse effect? If I simply point out that those questions are nonsequiturs, the audience thinks the questions are being ducked.

The best I can do within the scope of the available space and within my nonexpert's knowledge is to try to put the issue in reasonable perspective with respect to human welfare. Much of the sound thinking about global warming and acid rain also fits the ozone-layer issue. My guess is that this is most likely to be simply another transient concern, barely worthy of consideration in the next edition of this book. As with global warming, there follows a short list of propositions about the issue. For reliable scholarly assessments which provide the full background to these propositions, please see F. Singer (1995).

1. The ozone layer and its "hole" over Antarctica certainly deserve study. But this is very different than recommending action. The best principle might be: "Don't do something. Stand there." As noted above, when scientists recently warned of global *cooling* rather than warming, it is important that the government does not attempt to fix what is not broken.

2. The long-run data on ozone show no trends that square with public scares.

3. Concern about the ozone hole is only recent. There has hardly been time for competent researchers to build a body of reliable evidence on which to judge what is happening.

4. Scares come and go. The likelihood that a scare that is only a few years old will turn out to be a truly difficult problem for society is very low, given the record of scares and subsequent debunkings shown above.

Indeed, the history of one related scare should give special pause to those who are inclined to take action about the ozone layer: the saga of the supersonic transport

(SST) airliners.[69] In 1970 the alarm was raised that SSTs would emit water vapor that would destroy ozone. Research then began, but not before critics of the SST were urging that the planes be banned because of their supposed threat to the ozone layer.

First it turned out that the relevant emission was not water vapor but nitrogen oxides. Then further research showed that, if anything, SSTs would *add* to the amount of ozone in the stratosphere. Along the way the consensus of atmospheric scientists began with a prediction of perhaps 6–12 percent negative effect on total ozone as of about 1975, to a 6 percent positive effect about 1979, to a substantial negative effect again by 1981.[70]

The SST scare is dead and gone, though not without causing damage within the scientific and industrial communities.

5. Just as with SSTs, there is great controversy about the threat to the ozone layer now, with some respected scientists arguing that there is nothing to worry about just as some argue to the contrary. The press tends to report only on those scientists who utter warnings of catastrophe.[71]

6. Volcanic ash and sunspots are cited as possible "natural" influences on the amount of ozone along with the human-produced chlorofluorocarbons (CFCs), which contain ozone-destroying chlorine. It has been noted that CFCs at the peak production level were only a quarter of a percent (.0025) of the amount of chlorine released every year by the sea, which makes the effect of reducing CFCs very questionable.[72]

7. Even if the ozone layer should be thinning right now, it need not be a permanent thinning. If human intervention is causing the change, human intervention can reverse it.

8. Perhaps most important is that even if the ozone layer should be thinning, it need not imply bad effects for humanity. The chief threat seems to be a rise in skin cancers as more of the sun's ultraviolet rays pour through the thinning ozone. But evidence on the geography or the time pattern of skin cancers over the years does not square with the thickness of the ozone layer.[73] And even if a thinner layer implies more skin cancer, all else equal, people can intervene in many ways—even with as simple a remedy as wearing hats more frequently.

There is also the possibility that increased ultra-violet radiation stemming from decreased ozone may have beneficial effects in reducing rickets disease, which results from too little sunlight and lack of vitamin D.[74]

9. Banning CFCs—a family of remarkably useful chemicals, especially as refrigerants—runs the risk of raising the cost of refrigeration enough to put it out of the reach of some people in poor countries. We in rich countries who take refrigeration for granted may not be aware of the huge impact on food safety, on variety of diet, and on reduced effort in cooking that refrigeration makes.[75]

10. In 1992 there was an international agreement to stop producing halon, as a result of its supposed threat to the ozone layer. Halon is used to fight fires, and "no equivalent substitutes for halons have yet reached the American market . . . nothing yet made matches halon's ability to put fires out quickly without hurting nearby

people or causing further property damage," yet firms have begun to dismantle their halon systems.[76] It is hard to even imagine how the amount of halon released from such systems could have any meaningful impact on the atmosphere.

As is too often the case, the unsubstantiated fear of CFCs in refrigeration systems has led to added regulation of private behavior and new police powers. And as of 1993, "the Federal government is offering as much as $10,000 for tips that lead it to air-conditioning scofflaws."[77] That is, people are being invited to inform the authorities about their neighbors. This, of course, is reminiscent of totalitarian regimes.

In the months that this book is being edited, the newspapers are reporting "'Greenhouse Effect' Seems Benign So Far," and similar news about the ozone effect.[78] So much for the two great scares of the early 1990s. The point is not that these stories represent conclusive proof that the scares are wholly unfounded; indeed, between now and the next edition of this book the pendulum could swing back and forth again on these issues, maybe several times. Rather, the point is that it is remarkably imprudent to base any public policies on supposed phenomena whose scientific base is so thin or nonexistent that the consensus of scientific belief can change overnight.

A personal note: While editing and reviewing the material in this chapter, I found myself shocked by the flimsiness of the scientific arguments that have been adduced with respect to many of these issues, the rapidity with which they were falsified (often by equally flimsy research), and the willingness (even avidity) of the media to promulgate the results of such shoddy work. I thought that after a quarter-century of studying these issues and observing this scene I could not still be shocked by incompetence and dishonesty in science. But the record is so bad that I am newly amazed and again saddened.

I find myself wondering whether it is better that the young be unaware of this sordidness so that their faith is not too much lessened, or that they look the truth about human nature (even in science) squarely in the face so that they will know the strength and identity of the enemy. I worry that knowing the extent and the perversity of these happenings will turn them away from science in general—the science which is, after all, not only our best protection against real dangers and our best prospect for true progress, but also one of the great sources of challenge for the human capacities and the human spirit; we cannot afford to forgo these gains and challenges.

Summary

Biologists, engineers, and environmentalists who have warned of pollution problems and then developed methods of abating those problems have performed a great service to humankind. And warnings about the possible dangers from coal, nuclear energy, medicines, mercury, carbon dioxide, and the like can serve a similar valuable purpose, especially in connection with ill effects that do not appear immediately but only after many years. We must keep in mind, however, that it is not possible to create a civilization that is free of such risks. The best we can do is to be alert and prudent. Exaggerated warnings can be counter-productive and dangerous. The epigraph to this chapter by Walter Hickel is worth pondering.

Afternote _____

Healing the Planet

THE PHRASE of the 1990s seems to be "heal the earth" or ". . . the planet." It falls from the lips of Jewish rabbis (the only kind, I suppose), Roman Catholic churchmen, Protestant ministers, as well as environmental activists such as Paul Ehrlich, who so named a book. What means this?

The phrase seems to suggest that the planet is sick or injured. When one inquires in what way, one learns that the "problem" is the difference between the way the Earth is now and the way it "originally" was. The "cure" is to be found in "virgin" woods, wilderness untrammeled by the foot of (modern) woman and man, with all species restored to their numbers before recent times, and without traces of structures built or substances deposited in recent centuries. In short, all evidence of human activity during the last two hundred or two thousand years is to be "healed."

The only way that this could be done, of course, is to restore the number of *human beings* to what it was about ten thousand years ago. And the environmental activists—especially Garrett Hardin and Paul Ehrlich—do not shrink from reducing the numbers of human beings.

The condition of the planet that they call for has nothing to do with its excellence for human health or living standards. The evidence is overwhelming that people now live more healthily and with more of the material goods they desire than ever in the past, and there is no reason to believe that the trend will not continue in the same direction forever. Obviously, then, "healing" will not make human life better in the future. It is to be done for the sake of the planet itself, whatever that means.

It could not be clearer that the view that the planet needs "healing" rests entirely upon one set of values. More generally, the call to "heal" the planet is a feel-good notion, full of sentiment but empty of content, and perhaps motivated largely by selfishness.

19

Will Our Consumer Wastes Bury Us?

> The disposition of mankind, whether as rulers or as fellow-citizens, to impose their
> own opinions and inclinations as a rule of conduct on others, is so energetically
> supported by some of the best and by some of the worst feelings incident to human
> nature, that it is hardly ever kept under restraint by anything but want of power.
> (*John Stuart Mill*, On Liberty)

FUTURE HISTORIANS will surely marvel at the 1990s fear of being overcome by wastes.

Disposable diapers have become a cause célèbre, and at least for a time, Americans considered disposable diapers as "the single most important cause of our solid waste problem."[1] Government agencies have used the estimate that disposable diapers account for 12 percent of total trash, and a poll of attendees at a National Audubon Society meeting produced an average estimate that diapers account for 25 to 45 percent of the volume of landfills. And a Roper poll found that 41 percent of Americans cited disposable diapers as a major cause of waste disposal problems. Yet according to the best available estimate, the diapers constitute "no more than one percent by weight of the average landfill's total solid-waste contents . . . and an average of no more than 1.4 percent of the contents by volume."[2]

Then there was much dispute over whether disposable or washable diapers, foam cups or paper cups, are the more environmentally friendly. And some activities that are being undertaken or suggested are bizarre—being asked to flush our toilets less frequently, for example, and take cold showers and turn off the water when soaping (which may make sense on a Navy ship).

There is similar misunderstanding about fast-food packaging. The Audubon Society meeting poll found an average estimate of 20 to 30 percent of landfills; the actual volume is "no more than one-third of 1 percent."[3]

Yet we must take the fear of throwing things away seriously here, because it has serious effects upon government policy. (See also chapter 21 on government conservation policy.)

A kid's-page article in the Sunday paper purveys such bits of "obvious wisdom" as "It takes more than 500,000 trees to make the newspapers that Americans read on Sunday . . . we're running out of places to put it . . . there aren't very many new places to put [landfills]."[4] The children are not told that trees are grown, and forests are created, in order to make newspaper.

In school, 46 percent of children ages six to seventeen said they had heard about the importance of "solid waste" disposal (36 percent recycling, 15 percent litter, 6 percent garbage/landfills) in school in the 1991–1992 school year.[5] (One wonders what the comparable figures would be for the importance of honesty and hard work.)

The propaganda to the children is effective. A "national survey of children ages 5 through 8 asked these questions: 'What would you do to make your city a better place?' and '. . . America a better place?' A majority of the kids . . . answered 'Clean up'." This finding is significant for what the children *do not* say. There is no mention of "Build schools and parks" or "Go to the moon" or "Help those who are less well-off."

Nor is this childish thinking confined to children. An attorney for the EPA complained to the newspaper that the post office's new self-sticking stamps were "long-term environmental mistakes" because "as everyone knows, there is a solid waste problem in the country," and stamps with plastic "strike me as an incredibly irresponsible use of our limited petroleum resources."[6] The more relevant limited resource is newspaper space, and the editor choosing to print this letter rather than the hundreds of other contenders on serious subjects strikes *me* as "irresponsible."

The wastes that have been the subject of most concern over the years have been industrial pollutants. Some are toxic and others are aesthetic blights; hence the argument for reducing their output is strong. Household wastes are a more complicated matter. Here the issues of pollution and conservation get all mixed together. Household wastes are seldom a true health pollution, except for sewage containing bodily wastes, which carry disease. Household garbage and trash, and even junked vehicles, are not dangerous. Of course eyesores and smelly garbage are an aesthetic pollution, but this is not the same as a threat to life and limb.

So the arguments for reducing or controlling household wastes are different than for dangerous substances. Yet the issues become conflated.

The issues with respect to household waste products in rich countries are twofold: (1) Which resources are necessary to dispose of the wastes, and what is the best way to organize the disposal? and (2) Should people be should given a special inducement to recycle household wastes in order to conserve some resource whose conservation is "in the public's interest"? The latter question boils down to asking about whether waste recycling involves some value that is not reflected in the purchase price of the good.

That is, we must consider both the *bad* side of waste products—the need to dispose of them, even if they are not toxic—and the *good* side, which is their usefulness as a substitute for using more raw materials. The latter issue is addressed in chapter 21 on recycling versus other alternatives.

We will first discuss the quantitative dimensions of the supposed waste problem—amounts and trends. Next comes some "theory" of waste, and its relationship to other categories of economic entities, together with some examples of the conversion of bads to goods. Later, in chapter 21, we will discuss the pros and cons of various public policies toward waste—arrangements and payments, required recycling, and subsidized recycling.

The Dimensions of Our Waste

These are some basic facts about the dimensions of our waste output:

1. An American produces about four pounds of solid wastes per day, on average, with estimates varying from a pound less to a few pounds more.[7]

2. The growth in the quantity of household waste has slowed in recent years; it is less than the growth of GNP, and not much more than the growth in population.[8] Waste per person in New York City at the beginning of this century (excluding ash) was greater than the national average today.

3. The quantity of coal ash generated by homes was almost four pounds per day at the turn of the century.[9] So total waste has declined sharply. (As a young boy I shoveled out the furnace and carried to the curb our house's coal-ash waste. I can testify that the onset of modern fuels such as natural gas not only reduced urban waste but removed an onerous household burden.)

4. The United States is not an extravagant producer of waste. "The average household in Mexico City produces one third more garbage a day than does the average American household."[10]

5. If all the U.S. solid waste were put in a landfill dug one hundred yards deep or piled one hundred yards high—less than the height of the landfill on Staten Island within the boundaries of New York City—the output for the entire twenty-first century would require a square landfill only nine miles on a side.[11] Compaction would halve the space required. Compare this eighty-one square miles to the 3.5 million square miles of U.S. territory. The area of the United States is about forty thousand times larger than the required space for the waste. Nine miles square is a bit less than the area of Abilene, Texas, the first city in the alphabetical list, and a bit more than the area of Akron, Ohio, the second city alphabetically.

If each state had its own landfill, the average state would require only about 1.5 square miles to handle its next century's entire waste. I chose the period of a hundred years because that is ample time for scientists to develop ways of compacting and converting the wastes into smaller volumes and products of commercial value— twice as long as the time since we got rid of household coal ash.

6. The cost of urban recycling programs is typically about twice the cost of landfill disposal, even without including the cost to consumers of separating various kinds of materials (a cost that can be very high to an individual whose time has a high market or personal value.)[12] In New York City the cost of recycling in 1991 dollars "appears to be $400 to $500 per ton," and "in one Midwest city reached $800 per ton," compared to the $25 to $40 per ton costs for landfill disposal.[13]

The cost of recycling tends to rise as more recycling is done, because recycling increases the supply of recycled materials, especially newspaper. This decreases the prices paid for recycled paper. Indeed, the price may fall below zero, and recycling programs then either must pay the recycling facility to accept the paper, or put the paper in a landfill. For example, in 1988, Barberton, Ohio received $30 per ton for its waste paper, but by 1989, the town had to pay $10 per ton to the recycler. Hence, Barberton shut down its recycling program and sold off its equipment.[14]

7. Landfills need not be either noxious or burdensome. Demonstrating the principle to be discussed below, waste can usually be transformed into products of value, or valuable by-products can be derived from them. For instance, Riverview, a Michigan suburb of Detroit, has built a trash mountain 105 feet high, with plans to raise it to two hundred feet.[15] The facility services neighboring communities for a fee, which makes taxes in Riverview lower than elsewhere. And by covering the landfill with clay, it has become a recreation area whose "ski slope has been rated among the best in the Midwest, and serviced 25,000 skiers" in 1990; the skiers would not come if the areas were unpleasant. Enough methane gas is vented from the landfill and then burned to turn turbines which supply electricity to five thousand homes—more than a third of the thirteen thousand population of the city, who have no complaints and only praise for the neighborly dump.

Compare the pleasant ambiance of the Riverview facility with the state of garbage disposal in 1930. Then, "40 percent of [U.S. cities surveyed] still saved their wet garbage for the purpose of slopping—this despite the well-known relationship between trichinosis and garbage-fed pigs."[16] When driving past Secaucus, New Jersey, the across-the-river recipient of New York City's garbage, one had to roll up one's auto windows to avoid the ghastly smell of the pig farms as late as the 1940s. Now the area is parklike, the site of a sports facility.

During the short span of time during which this edition was being prepared, the United States went from a crisis of too much household waste to too little household waste. The typical newspaper headline in 1992 is "Economics of Trash Shift as Cities Learn Dumps Aren't So Full," and the story goes on to present evidence that "overall, the supply of dump space exceeds demand."[17] A huge new high-technology dump in an abandoned Illinois strip mine may close because it cannot get enough business, amid statements that "earlier projections of ever-rising dump fees haven't played out"[18]—just as the theory in chapters 1–3 predicts happens in the long run with all resources. And sure enough, municipalities that face trash "shortages"—getting garbage to keep their dumps filling rapidly enough to be profitable—are now using legal coercion to prevent haulers from trucking trash elsewhere to take advantage of lower prices. The environmental groups see this alleviation of the supposed problem as bad news, too. "Kevin Greene, research director for Citizens for a Better Environment, said availability of more landfill space [in Illinois] will take pressure off government and industry to employ more recycling and waste-reducing measures . . . 'I'm worried about this glut of land-fills', he said."[19]

The glut of landfill space is so severe that the incineration industry is suffering. Waste disposal prices are so low that by 1993 there were too many incinerators in operation.[20]

What happened to abate the landfill crisis? Firms saw an opportunity to earn profits by opening large modern dumps. Presto, shortage relieved. And the new dumps are much safer, cleaner, and more aesthetic than the old ones. Should there be another edition of this book in a few years, the topic will probably not deserve mention any more, and readers will have forgotten that it was ever an issue.

You would think that the proponents of recycling would be abashed and embarrassed by how the issue has developed—going from a public clamor to not let other states send their garbage into our state, to not letting the garbage from our state be taken to other states—all within about two years. But I have not come across a single statement by an official who says that she or he has learned any lesson from all this. Stay tuned for the next nonsensical turn of events.

Here we see again the recurring theme of the book: A problem induced by more people and higher income, a search for solutions, success on the part of some in finding solutions, and a solution that leaves us better off than if the problem had not arisen.

It is crucial to understand that it is not a happy accident that the landfill crisis has dissolved. Rather, it is an inevitable outcome of the process of adjustment in a free society.

Can one guarantee that every crisis will be overcome in such a timely fashion before great damage is caused? No, no more than one can guarantee that a driver will safely negotiate every turn on a road; accidents happen. But accidents decline in frequency, in part because we learn from the accidents that occur. When I was in the Navy, I was taught that every safety device in gun mounts is the result of a fatal accident. That is not a happy thought, but it is a happier situation than one in which bad happenings occur simply at random, without our ability to reduce their frequency by learning from our past tragedies.

The Theory of Waste and Value: Dump on Us, Baby, We Need It

Many "environmentalists" worry that the unintended by-products from humankind's economic activities—the "externalities," in the lingo of economics—are malign even if the direct effects of production and trade are beneficial. But a solid case can be made that even activities which are not intentionally constructive *more often than not* bestow a positive legacy upon subsequent generations. That is, even the unintended aspects of humans' use of land and other raw materials tend to be profitable for those who come afterward.

Hence, population growth that increases the volume of trash may increase our problems in the short run, but improve the legacy of future generations. The pressure of new problems leads to the search for new solutions. The solutions constitute the knowledge that fuels the progress of civilization, and leaves humanity better off than if the original problem had never arisen. That is the history of our species, as we see elsewhere in the book (see especially chapter 4).

Would Robinson Crusoe have been better off if there had preceded him on the island a group of people who had produced, consumed, and left the trash in a dump that Crusoe could uncover? Surely he would. Consider how valuable that dump would have been to Crusoe. If his predecessors had had a low-technology society the trash would have contained sharp stones and various animal remains useful for cutting, binding, and carrying. Or if the preceding society had had high technology, the dump would have contained even more interesting and useful materials—metal utensils, electronics parts, plastic vessels—which a knowledgeable person could have used to get help.

Material that is waste to one community at one time is usually a valuable resource to a later community that has greater knowledge about how to use the material. Consider the "borrow pits" by the sides of turnpikes, from which earth was taken for road-building. At first thought the pits seem a despoliation of nature, a scar upon the land. But after the road is finished the borrow pits become fishing lakes and reservoirs, and the land they occupy is likely to be more valuable than if the pits had never been dug.

Even a pumped-out oil well—that is, the empty hole—probably has more value to subsequent generations than a similar spot without a hole. The hole may be used as a storage place for oil or other fluids, or for some as-yet-unknown purposes. And the casing that is left in the dry well might be reclaimed profitably by future generations. Or even more likely, it will be used in ways we cannot dream of now.

The value of old rigs to ecology and recreation in the Gulf of Mexico and off the coast of California is told in chapter 12.

Humans' activities tend to increase the order and decrease the randomness of nature. One can see this from the air if one looks for signs of human habitation. Where there are people (ants, too, of course) there will be straight lines and smooth curves; otherwise, the face of nature is not neat or ordered.

Manufacturing-like activities bring similar materials together. This concentration can be exploited by subsequent generations; consider lead batteries in a dump, or the war rubble from which Berliners built seven hills which are now lovely recreational spots. The only reason that newspapers are an exception and used newspapers are worth so little now is that businesses have learned how to grow trees and manufacture paper so cheaply. When I was a kid, we collected and sold bundles of old papers to the paper mill at the edge of town. (And then when the mill pond froze in the winter we exploited it as our hockey rink.) But now there is no market for those old papers, and no mill pond (one of the costs of progress).

Another act that some consider as despoiling the land but actually bestows increased wealth upon subsequent generations: Ask yourself which areas in the Midwest will seem more valuable to subsequent generations—the places where cities now are, or the places where farmlands are?

One sees evidence of this delayed benefit in the Middle East. For hundreds of years until recently, Turks and Arabs occupied structures originally built by the Romans two thousand years ago. The ancient buildings saved the late-comers the trouble of doing their own construction. Another example is the use of dressed stones in locations far away from where they were dressed. One finds the lintels of doorways from ancient Palestinian synagogues in contemporary homes in Syria.

So we tell again the important story: Humans have for tens of thousands of years created more than they have destroyed. That is, the composite of what they sought to produce and of the by-products has been on balance positive. This most fundamental of all facts about the progress of civilization is evidenced by (a) the increasing standard of material living enjoyed by generation after generation, (b) the decreased scarcity of all natural resources as measured by their prices throughout history, and (c) the most extraordinary achievement of all, longer life and better health. The treasures of civilization that one generation bequeaths to the next, each century's inheritance greater than the previous one, prove the same point; we create more than we destroy. The core of the inheritance, of course, is the productive knowledge that one generation increments and passes on to the next generation.

If human beings destroyed more they produced, on average, the species would have died out long ago. But in fact people do produce more than they consume, and the new knowledge of how to overcome material problems is the most precious product of all. The more people there are on Earth, the more new problems, but also the more minds to solve those problems and the greater the inheritance for future generations.

Engineers are constantly inventing myriad new ways not only to get rid of wastes but also to derive value from them. "From their one-time reputation as major pollutants, garbage and sewage now seem to be acquiring the status of national resources."[21] Within a year after Connecticut set up a Resources Recovery Authority "to manage a collection and re-use program for the entire state," the authorities could judge that "there are no technological problems with garbage any more. All that is needed is initiative."[22] Seldom does a day pass without news of valuable innovations that turn waste into goods: farmers using recycled paper as beds for animals, poultry, and plants; wood and coal ash substituted for lime; burning old tires to produce electrical energy; recy-cling the steel from discarded cans as an input to the copper mining process; J. R. Simplot, the Montana potato king, feeding the leavings from french-fry production—half of the potato—to livestock.[23]

All this recycling makes economic sense—as proven by the fact that indi-vidals and firms choose to do it because it suits them, and not because they are forced to do it. It is only coerced recycling—the kind that forces people to wash and sort glass and costs hundreds of dollars per ton—that is costy and odious to those who value liberty highly.

The pollution of our living space by junked cars is particulary interesting. Not only can this problem be solved by the expenditure of resources for cleanup,but it also illustrates how resource scarcity is decreasing. Improved iron suppies and steel-making processes have made iron and steel so cheap that junked cars are no longer worth recycling. The old cars—if they could be stored out of sight, say, on the bottom of the Gulf of Mexico as habitats for fish, like old oil rigs—would be a newly created reservoir of "raw" materials for he future. In this important sense, iron is not being used up but is simply being stored in a different form for possible future use, until iron prices rise or better methods of salvage are developed. Much the same is true with many other discarded materials.

Do I have a solution to the used-diaper problem other than burning them for energy? Not at the moment. But there is every likelihood that, as with other wastes created in the past, human ingenuity will find a way to convert them to a valuable resource rather than a costy nuisance. The same is true of nuclear waste, of course (see chapter 13). I just wish I could feel as hopeful about the pollution of human thought and intercourse that we all contribute both in our private relationships and in our public utterances—of which the scare reports about disposable diapers are an example. Now *that's* a problem more worth our attention than the disposition of disposable diapers.

Conclusion

Here is the sound-bite summary: The physical garbage the doomsayers worry about is mostly not a problem. The problems they urge us to worry about are mostly intellectual garbage. The history of humanity is the creation of life, health, and wealth out of what was formerly waste.

20

Should We Conserve Resources for Others' Sakes?
What Kinds of Resources Need Conservation?

I finally got to ask Marla Maples a question. It was at a frenetic press conference
where the 26-year old actress, having pocketed a cool $600,000 for endorsing
No Excuses jeans, was pirouetting for the horde of photographers in a
skintight pair. Was she, I inquired, simply exploiting her notoriety as the
Alleged Other Woman? Au contraire, she said, this was part of her new campaign
to save the environment. When pressed for specifics, Maples said breathlessly,
"I love the ocean."
   (*Howard Kurtz in* Washington Post *magazine, August 19, 1990*)

SHOULD we try to conserve our resources? It depends. Should we try to avoid
all waste? Certainly not. Are the Sierra Club, Friends of the Earth, and other
conservationist groups barking up the wrong tree? Yes and no.

This is a topic so apparently "simple" and "common-sensical" that adults
delight in instructing children in it: "Environmental singer Billy B. sings about
recycling on the stage at Wolf Trap."[1] Children are told to "Cover both sides
of every sheet of paper you use. . . ." (Yes, Einstein did that, but it is disastrous
advice for any office worker at today's paper prices.) They are instructed to
"encourage your family to take part in your community's recycling program,"
implying that the author of the article is prepared to have children induce
guilt in parents she does not know, with needs she cannot discern, for the sake
of her own values.[2] That is the sort of social relationships that recycling programs engender. More about this in the next chapter.

The kids get the message—too well. A Wooster, Ohio seventh-grader writes
to the newspaper: "On Earth Day we think people should restrain from using
aerosol cans [which presumably pollute the atmosphere] and disposable diapers, and they should recycle everything they can."[3]

We can clarify conservation issues by distinguishing among the following:
(1) Unique resources, which are one-of-a-kind or close to it, and which we
value for aesthetic purposes; examples include the Mona Lisa, an Arthur Rubinstein concert, or a Michael Jordan basketball game, and some species of
animals. (2) One-of-a-kind resources that we value as historical artifacts; examples include the original U.S. Declaration of Independence and the Dead

Sea Scrolls, Abraham Lincoln's first log cabin (if it exists), and perhaps the Mona Lisa. (3) Resources that can be reproduced or recycled or substituted for, and that we value for their material uses; examples include wood pulp, trees, copper, oil, and food. Categories 1 and 2 are truly "nonrenewable" resources, but contrary to common belief, category 3 resources (including oil) are all renewable.

This chapter deals mainly with resources in category 3, those we value primarily for their uses. These are the resources whose quantities we can positively influence. That is, these are the resources for which we can calculate whether it is cheaper to conserve them for future use, or use them now and obtain the services that they provide us in some other way in the future. The benefits we get from the resources in the other categories—the Mona Lisa or Lincoln's log cabin—cannot be adequately replaced, and hence the economist cannot determine whether conservation is economically worthwhile. The value of a Mona Lisa or a disappearing breed of snail must be what we as a society collectively decide is the appropriate value, a decision upon which market prices may or may not shed some light.

Conservation of resources and pollution often are opposite sides of the same coin. For example, waste newspapers are a pollution, but recycling them reduces the number of trees that are planted and grown.

The costs and scarcities of resources in category 3—mainly energy and extractive materials—are likely to decline continuously in the future, according to the analyses in chapters 1–3. But this chapter asks a different question: whether as individuals and as a society we should try to use less of these materials than we are willing to pay for. That is, should we make social efforts to refrain from using these natural resources, and hence treat them differently from the consumption of pencils, haircuts, and Hula-Hoops for reasons *other than* their costs? The broad answer is that, apart from considerations of national security and international bargaining power, there is no economic rationale for special efforts to avoid using the resources.

Conservationists perform a valuable service when they alert us to dangers threatening humanity's unique treasures, and when they remind us of the values of these treasures to ourselves and to coming generations. But when they move from this role, and suggest that government should intervene to conserve pulp trees or deer beyond what individuals are willing to pay to set aside the trees or the deer's habitat, they are either expressing their own personal aesthetic tastes and religious values, or else they are talking misguided nonsense. (When the Conservation Trust in Great Britain puts "Re-Use Paper, Save Trees" on an envelope, it is simply talking trash; the paper comes from trees that are planted in order to make envelopes.) And when some famous conservationist tells us that there should be fewer people so that it is easier for him or her to find a deserted stretch of beach or mountain range or forest, she or he is simply saying "gimme"—that is, "I enjoy it, and I don't want to share it." (In chapter 29, we shall see how population growth paradoxically leads to *more* wilderness, however, rather than less.)

Thinking straight about conservation issues is particularly difficult because we must do what we human beings desperately resist doing: Face up to the fact that we cannot have it both ways. We cannot both eat the pie and continue to look at it with pleasure. Grappling with such trade-offs is the essence of microeconomic theory. For example, it is obvious that having the wilderness be pristine and not hearing other human voices when one is there means denying the same experience to others. Many who in principle would like others to be able to have that experience, as well as themselves, do not face up to that inevitability.*

Anthropologists lament the arrival of civilization to the Yonomami Indians of Brazil. But the anthropologists also seek the health and cultural benefits of civilization on behalf of that group. Whichever way it goes they will feel regrets, and both cannot be the case. Or, Jews in Israel yearn for the ingathering of Jews from the Diaspora into Israel, where most immigrants live a healthier life than before. But when the Jews of Yemen leave their ancient home, Israeli Jews lament the passing of the twenty-five-hundred-year-old Yemenite community, despite the present miserable state of that community.

It is natural to want things both ways. When an economist uses quintessential economic thinking to point out that we must accept the necessity for a trade-off and that we cannot usually have our cake and eat it too, the argument is met with denial of any such necessity—say, denial that reserving a forest for spotted owls means fewer jobs and lost income—or with charges that harvesting wood is an "obscenity." This makes it very difficult to think straight about conservation issues.

One possible reason why some people refuse to accept the economist's stricture that trade-offs are necessary is that the economist's motivations somehow are not considered noble. And indeed, the economist does try to focus on matters other than motivations. As Murray Weidenbaum wisely notes, economists "care more about results than intentions."[4] If we can succeed in focusing others' attention on results rather than intentions, too, we will achieve results that people will like better than they will otherwise obtain.

It is useful perspective to go back and re-read the classics of the conservation movement in the United States in the early years of the twentieth century—for example, the great 1910 book by Charles van Hise. There one finds all the themes being sounded today, and expressed very well. There is one great difference between that literature and the present writings, however. In van Hise's day people believed as follows: "What is the purpose of conservation? It is for man."[5] As chapter 38 discusses, humankind's welfare is no longer the only—or even the main—goal for many conservationists.

---

* Garrett Hardin is outstanding among the doomsters in accepting the need for such trade-offs.

Conservation of Replaceable Resources

Should you conserve energy by turning off lights that are burning needlessly in your house? Of course you should—just as long as the money that you save by doing so is worth the effort of shutting off the light. That is, you should turn out a light if the money cost of the electrical energy is greater than the felt cost to you of taking a few steps to the light switch and flicking your wrist. But if you are ten miles away from home and you remember that you left a 100-watt light bulb on, should you rush back to turn it off? Obviously not; the cost of the gasoline spent would be far greater than the electricity saved, even if the light is on for many days. Even if you are on foot and not far away, the value to you of your time is surely greater than the cost of the electricity saved.

The appropriate rule in such cases is that you should conserve and not waste just so far as the benefits of conserving are greater than the costs if you do not conserve. That is, it is rational for us to avoid waste if the value to us of the resource saved is more than the cost to us of achieving the saving—a matter of pocketbook economics. And the community does not benefit if you do otherwise.

Ought you save old newspapers rather than throw them away? Sure you ought to—as long as the price that the recycling center pays you is greater than the value to you of your time and energy in saving and hauling them. But if you—or your community—must pay someone more to have paper taken away for recycling than as trash, there is no sound reason to recycle paper.

Recycling does not "save trees." It may keep some particular trees from being cut down. But those trees never would have lived if there were no demand for new paper—no one would have bothered to plant them. And more new trees will be planted and grown in their place after they are cut. So unless the very act of a saw being applied to a tree makes you unhappy, there is no reason to recycle paper nowadays.

Human beings produce the living raw materials that we value, as long as the economic system encourages it. As Henry George said a century ago, an increase in the population of chicken hawks leads to fewer chickens, but an increase in the population of humans leads to more chickens. Or as Fred Lee Smith, Jr., put it, there is a choice between the way bison and beef cattle were treated in the United States in the nineteenth century; the bison were public property and the cattle were private, so the bison were killed off and the cattle throve.[6]

Consider elephants. If people can personally benefit from protecting elephants, and then selling their ivory and the opportunity to hunt them, the elephant population will grow in that place—as is the case now in Zimbabwe, Botswana, and some other southern African countries, where ownership belongs to regional tribal councils. In Kenya the elephant population had grown so large by 1993 that officials were administering contraceptive injections to combat elephant "overpopulation."[7] But where no one has a stake in the welfare of the elephants because they are owned only by the "public" at large, a ban on the sale of ivory will not prevent the elephant herds from being slaughtered and the size of the herds decreasing—as is the case now in Kenya and elsewhere in East and Central Africa. (Indeed, a ban raises the price of ivory and makes elephants even more attractive targets for poachers.)

There is much confusion between *physical* conservation and *economic* conservation. For example, some writers urge us not to flush our toilets each time we use them, but rather to use other rules of thumb that delicacy suggests not be mentioned here. The aim is to "save water." But almost all of us would rather pay the cost of obtaining the additional water from groundwater supplies or from cleaning the water; hence, to "save water" by not flushing is not rational economics. (You will find discussion of the supply of water in chapters 10 and 17 on resource trends and pollution.)

It is economically rational to systematically replace light bulbs before they burn out so that all the bulbs can be changed at once; this is not a "waste" of light-bulb capacity. To do otherwise is to commit yourself to a lower level of material living, unless the country is a very poor one where the cost of labor is small relative to the cost of a light bulb. (In Russia in the early 1990s, burned-out light bulbs were sold on the street, to be taken to one's place of work and substituted for working light bulbs to be stolen to take home.)

Though a "simpler way of life" has an appeal for some, it can have a surprisingly high economic cost. One student calculated that if U.S. farmers used 1918 agricultural technology instead of modern technology, forswearing tractors and fertilizers in order to "save energy" and natural resources, "We'd need 61 million horses and mules . . . it would take 180 million acres of cropland to feed these animals or about one-half of the cropland now in production. We'd need 26 or 27 million additional agricultural workers to achieve 1976 production levels with 1918 technology."[8]

Conservation—or just nonuse of given materials—is a moral issue for some people, about which it is not appropriate to argue. Todd Putnam, founder of *National Boycott News*, will not wear leather shoes because "that would be cruel to animals; . . . rubber and plastic are also out because they don't recycle well."[9] But there is no more economic warrant for coercing recycling than for coercing other sorts of personal behavior that are moral issues for some— whether people should eat high-fat diets, or pray three times a day, or tell ethnic jokes.

Coercion to conserve is not a joke, though it may seem to be. The community adjoining the one in which I live has an "environmental" television program. On a typical show the theme music is from the crime program "Miami Vice," and the narrator warns that "a recycling violation is in progress" at that moment somewhere in the community.[10]

Because conservation of ordinary resources confers no economic benefits upon the community, each case should be evaluated just as are other private decisions about production and consumption. Misunderstanding on this point leads to foolish suggestions and actions which—though they may have expressive value for some of us—accomplish nothing, and may even have harmful effects for others. For example, there will be no discernible improvement in the food supply of people in poor countries if you do not eat meat. In fact, the opposite may be true; heavy meat eating in the United States stimulates grain planting and harvesting in order to feed cattle; this increased capacity represents an increased ability to handle an unexpected massive need for food. As D. Gale Johnson put it:

> Suppose that the United States and the other industrial countries had held their direct and indirect per capita use of grain to half of the actual levels for the past several decades. Would this have made more food available to India or Pakistan in 1973 and 1974? The answer is clearly no. The United States, and the other industrial countries as well, would have produced much less grain than has been produced. Reserve stocks would have been much smaller than they have been. If U.S. grain production in 1972 had been 125 million metric tons instead of 200 million or more, it would not have been politically possible to have had 70 million metric tons of grain reserves. . . . If the industrial countries had had much lower total grain consumption in the past, the institutions required to handle the grain exports to the developing countries in the mid-1960s or in 1972/73 and 1973/74 would not have been able to do so. International trade in grains would have virtually disappeared.[11]

Nor would the research have been done that led to production breakthroughs if industrial countries had consumed less.

Yet many laypersons, and even some people considered experts by the media (and therefore by government agencies), espouse the "obvious" (though incorrect) short-run view that if we consume less, others in need will have more. Testifying before Congress, Lester Brown—whose forecasts about food and other resources have been more consistently wrong over the years than almost anyone else's, and whose views are at variance with the entire profession of agricultural economics (see, for example, chapter 7 and fig. 7-2)—said that "it might be wise to reduce consumption of meat a few pounds per capita within affluent, over-nourished societies such as the United States."[12] And laypersons say, "Millions of people are dying. . . . It sickens me to think of the money spent in America on food that is unnecessary for our basic nutritional needs. Would a sacrifice be so difficult?"[13] And "We serve tens of millions of pets vast quantities of food that could be used to feed millions of starving people in Asia, Africa, and Latin America—if we would only practice birth control for our pets"![14]

Would it be sound charity to eat less or cheaper food and send the money saved to poor countries? It would indeed be kind for each of us to send money. But why take the money from our food budgets? Why not from our overall incomes? That is, why not reduce whichever expenditures are most comfortable, rather than just reducing our expenditures on food? That would make better economic sense (though it might have less ritualistic meaning to us, which could be a persuasive argument for "saving food").

Energy conservation is another favorite target. We are urged not to eat lobsters because it takes 117 times as much energy to catch a lobster as it does to catch enough herring to yield an equal amount of protein.[15] One of the co-authors of the study that reached this nonsensical conclusion is Jean Mayer, adviser to presidents, president of Tufts University, and perhaps the best-known student of nutrition in the world (but not a student of energy or economics).

Marvelous disputes arise in Washington because everyone is trying to get into the energy-saving act. Any one group's panacea is another group's problem. "Transportation officials are 'outraged' by a Congressional report suggesting that buses, van pools, and car pools may use less energy than mass transit rail systems."[16] And the U.S. Post Office in 1978 issued a postage stamp entitled "Energy Conservation," picturing a light bulb, a gas can, and the sun with an inscrutable face.

Much of the call for conservation would be funny if it did not have serious results—for example, the federal Corporate Average Fuel Economy (CAFE) standards requiring manufacturers to raise average miles per gallon from 18 mpg to 27.5 mpg from 1978 to 1985.[17] These standards increase highway deaths by making cars lighter, and therefore providing poorer protection in collisions—and this would be true even if *all* cars would be smaller; having all football players wear helmets reduces total football injuries. Robert Crandall and John Graham studied the effect on a single cohort of cars and found "1989 model year cars will be responsible for 2,200–3,900 additional fatalities over the next ten years because of CAFE"—an increase in the death rate of somewhere between 14 percent and 29 percent.[18]

The CAFE standards have also cost vast sums of money to consumers, and much damage to the U.S. auto industry, in addition to the much more important increase in mortality. And for what? CAFE proponents who are not economists not only make arguments about the necessity of "saving" oil but also resort to justifying the standards on grounds of "how vulnerable we are to foreign oil" when this undoubtedly was not their objective. And they debase the standards of public debate in the service of their cause by calling "liars" those who point out that lightening cars makes them more dangerous.[19]

Apparently it is an inbred moral intuition that makes us feel that nonconservation is wrong.

Bishop Edward O'Rourke, head of the Peoria diocese of the Catholic Church, and Bruce Hannon, environmentalist and energy researcher in the UI Center for Advanced Computation, attempted to raise the "level of consciousness" of church leaders and laymembers. . . . One solution they cited for the growing problem is for everyone to lead lives that are simpler, more spiritual and less resource consuming. . . .

Even buying a tube of toothpaste is energy wasting. . . . The toothpaste is encased in a cardboard box, which must then be put in a paper bag, with a paper sales receipt—all of these products use wood pulp, and all are usually thrown away and destroyed.

"We are custodians and stewards of God's gifts. The more precious the gifts, such as energy, the more urgent the need to protect them," Bishop O'Rourke reminded.[20]

A Louis Harris poll reveals that

a substantial, 61–23 percent majority thinks it is "morally wrong" for Americans—6 percent of the world's population—to consume an estimated 40 percent of the world's output of energy and raw materials. And, the public indicates it is ready for a number of drastic cutbacks. . . . A 91–7 percent majority is willing to "have one meatless day a week." . . . A 73–22 percent majority would agree to "wear old clothes, even if they shine, until they wear out. . . ." By 92–5 percent the public reports it would be willing to "reduce the amount of paper towels, bags, tissues, napkins, cups and other disposables to save energy and to cut pollution."[21]

I share this moral impulse. I take a back seat to no one in hating waste—unnecessary lights, avoidable errands, trivial meetings. But I try to restrict my waste-fighting to matters where the benefit is worth the cost (though when they were young my children had a different view of my behavior). I try to remember not to waste more additional valuable resources in fighting the original waste than the original waste is worth. And most important, I do not want to legally impose my moral impulse on other people who do not share it.*

This anecdote teaches about the role of conservation in the modern world: During the 1970s I found that the replaceable nibs for the ink pens I wrote with were no longer being sold. Because those nibs, and the pen into which they fitted, were more enjoyable than anything else I had found to write with, I got worried that I might run out sometime, costing me efficiency and pleasure.

I therefore went around to all the offices in my college and collected the old nibs which were tucked away in the backs of the storeroom; no one else continued to use them. I congratulated myself on being set for life.

Then in the early 1980s the personal computer and word processing came along. And there went my need for pen nibs. I was saddled with a lifetime inventory that I would never use and that no one else would use, either.

This typifies how we worry about running out of something, and how the

* The moral element in conservation has been developed at length in a book by Herman Daly and theologian John Cobb (1989), discussed in chapter 12.

worry usually turns out to be wholly misplaced because of technological advance.

When I was collecting the nibs in the 1970s, no one could *guarantee* me that I did not need to worry about a lifetime supply, because no one could guarantee me that a better replacement would be invented. And no one can now make such guarantees for other resources. But it would be foolish for us to assume that the *worst case* will occur—that no substitute will be invented. Proceeding on a worst-case basis may avoid that worst case, but it is likely to impose heavy costs that would not apply if the worst case does *not* occur—as in most cases it will *not*.

Worst-case thinking may be appropriate for safety engineers. But it is not appropriate for most everyday planning. Both of a family's cars may fail to start tomorrow. But you recognize that it would be foolhardy to stockpile two extra cars (or even one) just in case. Instead you recognize that the chance that both will fail to start is very small. And even in that very small eventuality, there are taxis, neighbors, and other solutions—including shank's mare. So it is with other resources. As far as I can trace its intellectual history, the idea that worst-case analysis—which dismisses the cost of taking unnecessary precautions ("What does it matter if we are wrong?")—is appropriate for ordinary decision making seems to be a curse foisted on us by game theorists enamored of its mathematical charms.

The anti-waste, pro-conservation moral impulse sometimes is used to flim-flam the public. Consider the Hunger Project, an offshoot of the est organization. Under the headline "The End of Starvation," a shiny four-color brochure recites a few figures (uncorroborated) about the numbers of children who die of hunger each year, then asks people to (a) fast for a day, and (b) contribute money to The Hunger Project. No explanations are given about how the fast or the money will affect anyone else's hunger. The stated purpose of the fast is "to express and experience my alignment with having the end of starvation be a reality in the world. To express and experience that I am the source of The Hunger Project."[22] Whether this and the rest of the brochure is a masterpiece of communication or of noncommunication I leave for the reader to judge. But for a decade I have offered six pieces of bubble gum to anyone who will explain just how The Hunger Project (as of 1977) would end anyone's hunger except the sponsors', with no takers.

After the first spurt of enthusiasm for conservation and recycling in the 1970s, some people began to calculate that the costs of recommended recycling projects can often exceed the savings.

[A high-school student in Los Angeles] for 18 weeks . . . collected bottles from a restaurant to raise money for a favorite organization. At the end of that time, he had collected 10,180 pounds of glass, driven 817 miles, consumed 54 gallons of gas . . . and used up 153 man-hours of work. It is difficult to estimate the amount of pollution his car threw into the air.[23]

Why do conservationists think people must be pressured to conserve more than what they "naturally" would? Apparently, the conservationists do not believe that consumers will react rationally to changes in resource availabilities and prices. But the reduction in use of electricity per unit of GNP since 1973 is striking evidence of consumers' sensitivities to cost and scarcity. Another striking example is the drop far below the trend in gasoline use in the late 1970s, as gasoline prices rose sharply.

Sometimes coercion is justified on the basis that government subsidizes the activity. For example, the Wetland Law prevents farmers in (say) North Dakota from draining low spots on their land—even though some of these spots sometimes are dry all year—because they can sometimes be a haven for migratory birds. Environmentalists say "the American taxpayer has spent billions on farm subsidies. It seems to me we ought to be able to put some strings on that money."[24] Here we see the ill effects of the entire system of government intervention. The original subsidies induce farmers to produce too much, leading to government stockpile programs which eventually release food and depress prices in less-developed countries, which destroys agriculture in those countries. The overproduction may also lead to the cropping of land which would be better left in other uses. Then the farmers become dependent upon the subsidies and are forced to comply with other regulations which in themselves may be economically counterproductive (such as idling land, or using inefficient cropping practices) lest they lose their subsidies. And perhaps most insidious in the long run, individual actions become subject to politics and decisions by groups of outsiders who have no economic stake in the operation, rather than subject to purely economic calculation based on the market.

Conservation of Animals or People?

Some say that the human population should be stabilized or reduced because we threaten some species of animals. This raises interesting questions. If we assume there is a trade-off between more people and more of species X, then which species should we favor? Buffalo or golden eagles over *Homo sapiens*? If yes, does the same logic hold for rats and cockroaches? And how many people do we want to trade for more buffalo? Should the whole Midwest be made a buffalo preserve, or do we want only to maintain the species just this side of extinction? If the latter, why not just put them in a few big zoos? And do we want to protect malaria-carrying mosquitoes from extinction?

We ought also consider the species of animals whose numbers are increased when the human population increases—chickens, goats, cattle, minks, dogs, cats, laboratory white mice, and canaries. Is this a justification for *increasing* the *human* population? (Here lies a problem for those who are against killing animals for food or clothing. Without humans to consume these products there would be fewer chickens and minks to be killed.) Which way does one prefer to have it from the viewpoint of animal welfare?

My point: Where costs do not settle the issue, the decision about what is conserved, and how much, is a matter of tastes and values. Once we recognize this, the arguments are easier to resolve. There is considerable discussion in chapters 38 and 39 of particular conflicting values relevant to these issues.

Resources and Future Generations

Conservationists and technologists attend to the future, and often properly so. We should conserve, they say, so that there will be "enough" for future generations, even if the value we get from the resource saved is less than what it costs us to achieve the saving.

When we use resources, then, we ought to ask whether our present use is at the expense of future generations. The answer is a straightforward no. If the relative prices of natural resources can be expected to be lower for future generations than for us now—and this seems to be a reasonable expectation for most natural resources, as we have seen earlier—this implies that future generations will be faced by no greater economic scarcity than we are, but instead will have just as large or larger supplies of resources to tap, despite our present use of them. Hence our present use of resources, considered in sum, has little if any negative effect upon future generations. And our descendants may well be better off if we use the resources in question right now to build a higher standard of living instead of refraining from their use. So we need make no ethical judgments with respect to leaving resources to our descendants.

Furthermore, the market protects against overuse of materials that may become scarcer in the future. The current price of a material reflects expected future supply and demand as well as current conditions, and therefore current prices make an automatic allowance for future generations. If there is a reasonable basis to expect prices to rise in the future, investors will now buy up oil wells, coal mines, and copper-mining companies; such purchases raise the current prices of oil, coal, and copper, and discourage their use. Paradoxically, normal market speculation "cannot prevent an unduly *low* rate of consumption, which would leave future generations with more reserves than they need—just the opposite of what conservationists worry about"![25]

But what if the investors are wrong? you may ask. In return I ask you: Are you prepared to believe that your understanding of the matter is better than that of speculators who study the facts full time, who are aware of the information you are aware of, and who earn their livings by not being wrong when they invest their own money?

The storage of fresh fruits throughout the year illustrates how markets and businesses ensure a year-long supply and prevent future scarcity. The example also shows how present price reflects future scarcity, and why it would not make sense to buy oranges in the summer to "conserve" for winter or for future years.

Oranges are harvested in the spring and early summer in various countries such as Italy, Israel, Algeria, and Spain. Naturally the price to consumers is cheapest at harvest time. But fruit dealers also buy at harvest time and store the fruit in warehouses for later sale. The price throughout the winter is roughly the cost at harvest plus the cost of storage (including the cost of the capital tied up in the oranges). The price in the winter therefore is not much higher than at harvest, and there is no reason for consumers to worry about scarcity at any time.

The desire of merchants to make a profit by buying cheap at harvest and selling dear later ensures that prices will not rise precipitously at harvest time. And the competition of other merchants who have the same desire prevents them from pushing the price very high in the winter. Of course any consumer who worries that winter prices will be unbearably high can pay the storage price by stockpiling oranges in the refrigerator. Likewise, these forces work to prevent scarcity or a rapid price run-up in natural resources. Merchants who believe—on the basis of a very full investigation, because their economic lives depend upon it—that future scarcity is not yet fully reflected in present prices will buy raw materials now for future resale. They will do our conserving for us, and we will pay them only if they were right. And the argument is even stronger with respect to metals because they do not require a refrigerated warehouse.

The fact that there will be another orange harvest next year does not make the orange situation different from the copper situation discussed earlier. New discoveries of copper, and new technological developments in the mining and use of copper, are also expected to occur, though the timing of the events is less certain with copper than with oranges. But that just means a wider market for merchant speculators. Hence we need not worry that the needs of future generations are being injured by our present consumption patterns. And please notice that orange prices at harvest time, and present copper prices, too, reflect expected population growth. If consumption is expected to rise due to increased population, merchants with good foresight will take that into account (and merchants with poor foresight do not remain in business for very long).

If the economic situation were different than it is—if technology were fixed and costs of resources were therefore expected to be higher in the future than now, indicating greater scarcity to come—it might be appropriate to make ethical judgments that would differ from the results of a free market. It might then be appropriate to worry that our consumption and fertility (if influenced only by market prices) might have such adverse effects on future generations that a prudent government might intervene to reduce present use of the mineral natural resources. But such intervention is not now necessary or appropriate, because, as Harold Barnett and Chandler Morse put it, "By devoting itself to improving the lot of the living . . . each generation . . . transmits a more productive world to those who follow."[26] It does so by accumulating real capital to increase current income, by adding to the stock of useful knowledge, by making its own generation healthier and better educated, and by improving economic institutions. This is why the standard of living has been rising with successive generations, which is the central fact in all discussions of conservation.

Because we can expect future generations to be richer than we are, no matter what we do about resources, asking us to refrain from using resources now so that future generations can have them later is like asking the poor to make gifts to the rich.

Resources and "International Rape"

Is there need for ethical judgments to supersede market decisions when rich countries buy raw materials from poor countries?

The idea that the rich countries "rape" the poor countries and "pirate" their bauxite, copper, and oil does not rest on a solid intellectual foundation. These resources have no value for home use in a country without a manufacturing industry. But when sold to an industrial country, the resources provide revenue that can aid in development—and, in fact, this revenue may represent a poor country's very best chance of development.

What if the "exploiters" actually stop buying? This is what happened in 1974 in Indonesia:

> Many of those Indonesians who took to the streets only eight months ago to protest alleged Japanese exploitation of their natural resources are now beginning to complain that the Japanese are not exploiting them enough. Because of setbacks in their own economy, Japanese importing companies have had to cut their monthly purchases of 760,000 cubic yards of Indonesian timber by as much as 40%. As a result, Indonesian lumber prices have dropped some 60% and . . . 30 firms have already gone bankrupt, causing widespread unemployment in . . . timber-dependent areas.[27]

Nor are contemporary poor-country people who sell their resources benefiting at the expense of their own future generations. "Saving" the materials for the poor country's future population runs the grave risk that the resources will drop in relative value in the future, just as coal has become less valuable over the past century; a country that hoarded its coal starting a hundred years ago, as so many then advised, would be a loser on all accounts.

Please remember, too, that the United States and other rich countries export large amounts of primary products that poor countries need, especially food. The primary products that the poorer countries produce enable them to trade for the rich countries' primary products, an exchange from which both parties gain. Of course, nothing in this paragraph suggests that the prices at which rich countries buy these resources from poor countries are "fair" prices. The terms of trade are indeed an ethical matter, but one that is likely to be resolved by the hard facts of supply, demand, market power, and political power.

Summary

A public policy of conservation implicitly assumes that the "true" value of the good to be conserved is greater than its price to consumers. But in a well-operating free market the price of a commodity reflects its full social cost. Hence, if an individual or firm refrains from using the product even though its value to the firm or individual is greater than the market price, there is an economic loss without compensating benefit to anyone directly involved (except perhaps the producers of products that compete with the product being "conserved"). For example, saving old newspapers when their market value is far below the cost of your time and trouble to do so may make you feel good, but it lowers the overall productivity of the economy without any long-run benefit to the supply of timber.

Nor is conservation needed to protect future generations in ordinary situations. Market forces and present prices take into account expected future developments, and thereby automatically "conserve" scarce resources for future consumption. Perhaps more important, present consumption stimulates production and thereby increases productivity, which benefits future generations; the use of newsprint today causes forests to be grown for future consumption, and encourages research into how to grow and harvest trees. Only if you suffer pain for the tree itself when it is cut does it make sense for you to recycle newsprint.

Nor does conservation by the rich benefit the poor, domestically or internationally. What the poor need is economic growth. And "economic growth means *using* the world's resources of minerals, fuels, capital, manpower and land. There can be no return to Walden Pond without mass poverty."[28]

21

Coercive Recycling, Forced Conservation, and Free-Market Alternatives

SOME PEOPLE get pleasure from recycling. That's fine, even if the impulse springs from the wrongheaded belief that recycling is a public service. Coercing people to recycle is something very different, however.

Bette Bao Lord's description of forced-labor recycling in China during the "Cultural Revolution" is instructive:

> One of the most frequent duties was to sort the city garbage dump. The job was a big one and we were usually excused from school for the day. We had to sort the trash into piles of paper or leather or scrap steel, etc., which were in turn reprocessed for further manufacture. Another frequent detail was cleaning the streets of used paper and other litter. Each student was given a stick with a nail at one end for spearing and a paper bag for collection. After a day of this type of labor detail, I suffered from a backache. When the school collected all our full bags, it would turn them over to the factory for making new paper to ease the paper shortage.[1]

In poor societies, it may be worthwhile to recycle. But in China people not only recycle because they are poor, they are also poor because they recycle. The recycling mind-set in China in the late 1950s and early 1960s was inimical to economic development. The notion of making progress by forcing people to recycle, when they could be doing more productive things, makes societies poor. This mistake is sometimes compounded by the glorification of primitive production techniques (as Mao tried to do with backyard steelmaking and Gandhi with household textile manufacturing), rather than using the same amount of effort to learn how to do the work more efficiently and to gradually build a more modern system.

The recycling mind-set can also be counterproductive in rich countries. People praise saving trees by recycling newspapers, and they condemn those who cut down trees. But they do not cheer those who *grow* the trees in the first place—trees deliberately planted and grown to make paper. This is like praising people for "saving" a field of wheat by not eating bread, while ignoring the farmers who grow our food. It acts to suppress the creative impulse. (There is a further perversity in thinking here. People are focusing only on harvesting and death, not on planting and growth. It is much the same with respect to population growth—wringing of hands over someone who may die prematurely or unnecessarily, but no cheering of those who create and nurture new life.)

This is not to say that all recycling is misguided. Recycling is one thing when it is economically worthwhile for the person who is doing the recycling, but another thing when it is done purely for symbolic purposes, as now mostly in the United States. Please reflect on the fact that in our kitchens we voluntarily recycle ceramic plates but not paper plates. Would it make sense to require households to recycle paper plates and cups by washing and reusing them? It would make no economic sense whatever (and it's doubtful that the paper could survive washing), though for some it might make symbolic sense—and those people are entitled, of course, to their private rituals.

The logic is the same with community recycling. People voluntarily recycle valuable resources and throw away less valuable items that take more effort to recycle than they are worth. Coercive recycling is actually more wasteful than throwing things away. It wastes valuable labor and materials that could be put to better use—creating new life, new resources, a cleaner environment.

Why Do People Worry So Much about Wastes?

Why do so many people worry so greatly about what seems to be such an easy problem to handle, given time and resources? My best guess is simply that the worriers (1) lack understanding of how an economic system responds to an increased shortage of some resource; (2) lack technical and economic imagination, together; and (3) harbor a moral impulse that says recycling is inherently good, and we should be willing to suffer a bit for it. Let's touch briefly on all three.

Lack of Understanding of How a Market Economy Works

Persons who are not economists—and perhaps especially those persons such as biologists who work with entities other than human beings—may underestimate the likelihood that people and organizations will make characteristically human adjustments to daily life and society. Such persons may then have too little faith in the adjustment capacities of human beings. Concepts that are appropriate for nonhuman organisms—niche, carrying capacity, etc.—are inappropriate for the creative aspect of human beings which is the central element in long-run economic activity. The 1960s and 1970s generalization of the work of Calhoun on Norwegian rats to policy recommendations for human society (see chapter 24) has been a classic example of this muddle.

For example, in regard to the possibility of fusion energy, Paul Ehrlich recycled his quote about energy in general by saying that cheap, inexhaustible power from fusion is "like giving a machine gun to an idiot child."[2] Presumably the pronouncer of such pronouncements arrogates to him/herself greater wisdom than the people being pronounced about. Garrett Hardin says, "People often ask me, well don't you have faith in anything? And I always have the same answer. . . . I have an unshakable [belief] in the unreliability of man. I know that no matter what we do, some damn fool will make a mess of it."[3] This sort of thinking blinds one to the possibility that spontaneously coordinated market responses will deal with the wastes our society generates.

Lack of Technical Knowledge or Imagination

Many people who do not already know a technical answer to a given problem do not try to discover possible solutions, and they do not even imagine that others can dream up solutions. For example, when trains came along, some worried about the problem of providing toilets; where would the wastes go? Then when long-distance buses came along, people again worried, because they knew that the ship and train solution—dump over the side or from the bottom—was not possible on the roads. Then some worried about the same problem in planes. Then when the problem was solved for airplanes, the problem seemed insuperable in spacecraft. Yet in all these cases the problem simply required some diligent thought and engineering skill. And so it is with just about every other waste disposal problem.

"But you are depending on a technical fix," some say. Yes, and why not? A "technical fix" is the entire story of civilization. Yet our solutions are not limited to the physical-technical; new economic-political arrangements can solve problems. How can a community reduce the amount of garbage that people put out? Charge households and businesses by the pound or the liter of waste collected. So it is for other waste problems, too. Imagination and economic-organizational skill are necessary. But there is every reason to believe that once we direct those skills to a waste problem, solutions will be forthcoming.

The combination of technical imagination plus a free-enterprise system constitutes the crucial mechanism for dealing with waste—turning something of negative value into something of positive value. Slag from steel plants was long thought of as a nuisance. Then there arose entrepreneurs who saw the slag as "man-made igneous rock, harvested from blast furnaces," which could be used to provide excellent traction in road surfaces such as the Indianapolis 500.[4] And old railroad ties are not just clumsy chunks of wood to be burned, but now decorate retaining walls for lawns.

The Moral Feeling about Recycling

In a hearing on taxing disposable diapers, California State Senator Boatright pointed to the committee members and said that they "all raised our kids with cloth diapers. And you know, it didn't kill 'em at all. . . . Got your hands a little dirty, maybe, but it didn't kill 'em. It's a hell of a lot more convenient to use disposable diapers, but you know what—you *save a lot of money* when you use cloth diapers."[5] Like a fraternity initiation—I suffered, why shouldn't you?

When I tell my neighbor that I don't want to wash bottles and cans in order to recycle them, he tells me that "it takes practically no time at all." But when I ask him, in light of his assessment, if he would regularly do the job for me, he demurs.

Pros and Cons of Waste Disposal Policies

There are three ways society can organize waste disposal: (a) commanding, (b) guiding by tax and subsidy, and (c) leaving it to the individual and the market. The appropriate method depends on the characteristics of the situation, and depends to a considerable extent on whether there are difficult "externalities"—effects that go beyond the individuals involved and that cannot be "internalized" (a rare situation).

Almost all solid household waste is a perfect case for untrammeled free enterprise. Garbage is one of the easiest of waste disposal problems for society to deal with because there are no externalities that are difficult to deal with.

In Urbana, Illinois, we had the best and cheapest garbage collection I have ever heard of, each homeowner contracting with any one of the private haulers who worked in the area. They gauged their charges according to how much garbage you put out, the standard rate being augmented by special charges for special hauling. If the service was sloppy or unpunctual, you changed haulers at the end of the month. The hauler in turn made a deal with a private landfill operator. The community could be neutral and inactive, and there were no significant externalities. There is no sound reason why such a system cannot operate almost anywhere.

Problems arise when the community gets involved, either through contracting with a single hauler, or the municipality paying the hauler, or the municipality providing the service directly. There is then no incentive for homeowners to reduce the amount of waste they create, which leads to high waste output. And the community becomes subject to voters who have ideological views about waste and recycling, which distorts the best economic choice. And as a result of individuals' political values, together with their ignorance of the facts stated above, communities turn to recycling.

There are two drawbacks to recycling. The first is that it costs the taxpayers more money, as noted below. The second drawback is that it usually injects an element of coercion which is antagonistic both to basic American values as well as to the efficient working of a free-market system. Both will now be discussed.

The Resource Costs of Recycling

Unnecessary recycling and conservation cannot simply be dismissed as a harmless symbolic amusement. There is a major cost in other activities that are foregone. People could be building instead of recycling—building roads, public buildings, parks, even improving their own private shelters and spaces.

People's value for building may have been affected by the role of government. In the eight years that I have lived in a suburb of Washington, D.C., we have had scores of people come to the door soliciting funds. Never once has anyone solicited funds for a building project—never for trees to be planted, a cathedral to be built, or a concert to be given. Almost every solicitation has been for funds to lobby government to do something. And in most cases a large proportion of the funds collected goes toward soliciting more funds to do the same thing. In decades past it was not so. People solicited funds to build private hospitals, and religious and cultural institutions, and other great works for the benefit of the public. But now people expect the government to perform those activities. Hence, funds are solicited mainly to bend the government's will to support people's private interests.

If government did a better job in building and administering, perhaps there would be no grounds for complaint. But we know from much solid evidence that government performs these activities very poorly—at high cost, and with poor service. These are part of the costs of a conservation mentality—of saving whales and Chesapeake Bay.

Another unreckoned cost is the coerced time of private persons. When a town calculates the cost of a recycling program, it ignores the minutes spent by householders in separating types of trash, putting them in separate places, and stocking separate containers, and learning where and when the various kinds of trash must be placed for pickup. These are nontrivial costs.

The Cost in Coercion

As of 1988, six states had mandated household separation of types of waste, and as of 1991, twenty-eight states have recycling or waste reduction "quotas."[6] As of 1990, the District of Columbia—like a large proportion of the twenty-seven hundred communities that have recycling programs[7]—requires recycling of newspapers, glass, and metals in all apartment buildings. Not only does this law require individuals and firms to do what they would not do voluntarily, with fines for offenders, but it invites some of the practices of a totalitarian society wherein people are invited to meddle in their neighbors' lives. The *Washington Post*, one of the three national and international newspapers of the United States, recommends that apartment dwellers first "Try peer pressure" and then "Complain to authorities" if the landlord does not recycle according to law. And there is provision "to report scofflaws to the city's 'trash police,' a team of 10 inspectors hired to search through trash and identify culprits."[8] Not only are such practices odious (at least to me), but police expenditures are a high cost that surely are not included when an account is made of the total burden of recycling.

Zurich, Switzerland has such a system in place. "Inspectors will track down people who don't use the spiffy new sacks and hit them with fines."

> Collectors have instructions to search through any old bags left in the street for evidence that will identify offenders. "An envelope with an address, for example", says Rudolph Walder, the city's garbage-disposal czar. "Then we will hit them with a 100-franc ($67) fine. And if they keep on doing it, we'll inform the police."[9]

Involvement of the government also opens the door to bureaucrats working to protect their own interests against those of the public. For example, "In Loudoun County, Virginia . . . local officials have gone to great lengths to stop one businessman from composting some of the community's yard wastes (decaying them into a rich soil for farming). Public officials have opposed the operation—with regulations, and even by 'sending local government landfill representatives to block the entrance' to the site—on the grounds that it threatened the local government's landfill revenues."[10] One of the sins committed by this operation is that it charges only $10 a ton to take in garbage, whereas landfilling costs $50 a ton.

On a larger scale, the state of Rhode Island prevented a hauler from taking waste out of the state to dumps in Maine and Massachusetts.[11] The state-owned Central Landfill is now the only licensed facility in the state, and its monopoly prices are higher than elsewhere. The state prevented the hauler from going elsewhere so that it would not lose the revenue. If a private firm were to somehow maneuver itself into a similar monopoly position, it could not use the law to keep customers from going elsewhere. Furthermore, the Federal Trade Commission would break up its monopoly. But government can get away with abuses that private enterprises cannot.

The problem of junked abandoned cars is not well handled by the market, however. One knows in principle what should be done: Create proper rules that will compel producers of the waste to pay appropriate compensation to those who suffer from the pollution, either as individuals or as groups, so as to "internalize the negative externalities," as we say in economistese. But crafting and legislating such rules is not easy; Friedrich Hayek asserts that this is the most difficult of intellectual tasks, and the most important. And there often are strong private interests that militate against remedial actions. The outcome of this sort of pollution, then, depends largely on the social will and on political power, as well as upon our wisdom.

Price and Value

The most complex and confusing conservation issues are those that are dollars-and-cents questions to some people, but to other people are matters of aesthetics and basic values. Consider saving old newspapers in this connection. (The waste disposal aspect of newspapers is discussed in chapter 19.) In some cases it makes sense to save and recycle paper because the sales revenue makes the effort profitable. In World War II the price of waste paper rose high enough to make the effort worthwhile for many households. And where shredded newspapers are used as insulation after treatment with fire-retardant chemicals, paper collection can be a fund-raising device for community groups such as Boy Scout troops.[12] But nowadays, in most communities the cost of recycling less the sales price of paper seems greater than the cost of landfill disposal or incineration. (Indeed, the price is now negative; by 1989 the amount of recycled paper had grown so large that communities had to pay $5–25 per ton to have paper brokers take the stuff.)[13]

Here we must consider the economic meaning of the market price of waste paper. That price will roughly equal the price of new paper less the recycling cost of making the old paper like new. In turn, the price of new paper is the sum of what it costs to grow a tree, cut the tree, and then transport and convert the wood to paper. If the cost of growing new trees rises, so will the prices of new and used paper. But if the cost of growing trees goes down, or if good substitutes for trees are developed, the price of used and of new paper, and of wood, will fall. (An increase in recycling also drives the price down.) And that is what has been happening. The total quantity of growing trees has been increasing and their price falling, and the newspapers report the successful development of kenaf as a substitute for paper. So why bother to recycle newspapers?

Conservationists, however, feel that there is more to be said on this matter. They feel that trees should be saved for reasons other than the dollars-and-cents value of pulp or lumber. They argue that it is inherently right to try to avoid cutting down a tree "unnecessarily." This argument is based on aesthetic or even religious values. The conservationists believe that stands of trees are unique national or international treasures just as Westminster Abbey is for Englishmen and as the Mosque of the Golden Dome is for Muslims. Perhaps we can express this by saying that in these cases even the believer who does not directly use the treasure is willing to pay, in money or in effort, so that other people—now and in the future—can enjoy the good without paying the full price of creating it. (Additionally, there is the argument that, even if future generations will be willing to pay the price, they will be unable to do so if we don't preserve it for them.) Some people even impute feelings to nature, to trees or to animals, and they aim to prevent pain to those feelings.

There is no economic argument against a person holding these points of view. But neither is one person's aesthetic taste or religious belief an economic warrant for levying taxes on other people to pay for those preferences.

If one is willing to urge that the community pay in order to recycle, it is useful to know the price that has to be paid. The state of Florida has promised to subsidize firms to produce products out of recycled material and then sell them to the state, which will guarantee to buy the goods. Florida is just one among thirty states that are willing to buy recycled products (mainly paper) that cost 5 percent to 10 percent more than comparable nonrecycled products.[14] For perspective, perhaps three to five years of economic growth are necessary to make up that much of a reversal in progress by way of cost increase and productivity reduction. The governor of Florida calls this a "no-brainer for companies" because it is so easy for them to decide that a guaranteed market makes sense. Sometimes an argument is made for conservation on the grounds of national security and international bargaining. It may well make sense for a country to stockpile enough oil and other strategically sensitive resources for months or even years of consumption. But these political matters are beyond the scope of this chapter and of the usual discussions of conservation.

Conservation and the Government System

Do our treasured resources fare better in a private-enterprise system or a Socialist centrally planned system?

There is no evidence that public officials are better stewards of any class of property—including wilderness and parks—than are private owners. (Witness the state of upkeep of public and private housing.) Consider the private (not-for-profit) case of Ravenna Park in Seattle, Washington, which was a public treasure from 1887 to 1925, selling admission to see the giant Douglas firs at very modest prices. Then the city took it over by legal action. The park fell victim to corrupt tree-cutting for the sale of firewood.[15]

Government ownership permits overuse of resources not only because of common ownership but also because of incompetent management. For example, government often sets the prices too low for such resources as boating use fees, and timber and grazing rights. And as I am writing this I read in the *Washington Post* that "concessionaires at national parks gross millions of dollars using government-owned buildings, from hotels to boat houses. But the U.S. Treasury earns hardly a penny because it charges little or no rent."[16] Low prices encourage heavy use of a government-controlled resource. The private market would not "fail" to charge and collect prices that are appropriately high for access to grazing lands, timber, and so on.

I cannot *prove* that a combination of academics and politicians will never design a social-political economic system that will better conserve nature and produce an aesthetic environment than will an undesigned system that relies upon people's spontaneous impulses and a market system governed only by very general rules. (If any sentence in this book will be widely quoted, it probably will be that one—ungainly and dull as it is.) I cannot even assert that each and every ecological feature would be better served in an undesigned system. It may be that if governments were not to preserve the giant pandas in zoos, the animals would die out. Indeed, no private firm now exhibits pandas for profit (though P. T. Barnum's great museum did this sort of thing).[17] It might well be, however, that if government were not to do so, interested individuals might take steps to preserve the pandas through voluntary organizations.

In the nineteenth century, when hawks were being shot as predators and were in danger of extinction, private individuals created a preserve that is now Hawk Mountain Sanctuary in Pennsylvania, which eventually became not only a preserve but also a center for research on raptors.[18] Nature lovers should not underestimate the likelihood that, in the absence of government action, others like them will act spontaneously to protect the values they hold dear. (Indeed, that was the original nature of such organizations as the Audubon Society before they turned much of their effort to attempting to increase government intervention.) But government activity often drives out private activity, as government intervention in the provision of hospital services has reduced the role of religious organizations that built and maintained hospitals in earlier years in the United States.

The best evidence I can find is the data mentioned in chapter 17, which shows that when the government completely controls (by ownership) the emission of pollution, the pollution is much greater than when the ownership is private, albeit with greater or lesser regulation.

Now follows the general vision which does not promise that every particular aspect of ecology will fare better than a planned system, but which does promise that—taking everything together—humans will prefer the overall outcome to the overall outcome of a system where officials plan and dictate how resources will be treated.

Those who seek to plan our ecology argue that while markets may successfully bring us autos and tennis matches, markets "fail" with respect to wilderness, plant and animal species, and aesthetics of the landscape. In support of their vision of a designed system they point to the slaughter of the buffalo and the passenger pigeon, the befouling of our rivers and lakes for many decades, and ugliness of some inexpensive housing developments. And they argue that humanity changes the planet further and further away from the pure pristine world that they imagine existed before humans became many.

In rebuttal, the free-market environmentalists analyze such regrettable events and argue that the source of the destruction usually is a system lacking property rights that would prevent such events. And they point to countervailing examples—beef cattle preserved by individual ownership, facilitated by the branding system and the barbed wire invented to resolve the problem of common grazing;[19] the growth of elephant herds in Zimbabwe (see chapter 20); the improvement over time in housing quality in most neighborhoods, even those like Levittown that were originally thought "tacky"; the habitat preservation on farms where owners sell the rights to hunt; the beauty of fishing streams in Great Britain which are privately owned or which clubs own fishing rights to;[20] and the well-stocked fish ponds that sell fishing rights in old "borrow pits" by the sides of highways in Illinois, dug by the highway builders to get building materials.

Free-market environmentalists also cite the insults to human dignity and constraints upon individual freedom that planned conservation brings about—"trash police," "water cops," farmers being fined and going to jail for making their farms more productive at the expense of migratory ducks; neighbors and people's own children bringing pressure on homeowners to separate types of trash.

These examples (and the theory behind them, to be discussed below) are compelling, in my view. But as the designed-system advocates offer counterexamples, the issue must also be discussed at the level of the overall vision, and the test is the analogous comparative experience of planned versus free-enterprise economies.

"Common sense" argues that specific planning for particular kinds of outcomes results in a better general outcome than an undesigned system. Yet the evidence is incontrovertible that with respect to ordinary economic matters, an undesigned free-enterprise system does much better than does a planned Socialist system. Investigations of the performance of Socialist economies, and the breakup of communism in the 1980s and 1990s, entirely vindicate the theoretical visions of David Hume, Adam Smith, Karl Menger, Ludwig von Mises, and Friedrich Hayek. And even worse than the economic effects of a planned system are the effects upon human welfare in noneconomic aspects— liberty and health, for example (see chapters 17 and 22).

Telling evidence is found in the economic comparison of North and South Korea, and of East and West Germany, and also of Taiwan and China, discussed in more detail in chapter 21. The Communist countries use(d) much more energy and produce(d) much greater amounts of pollution both per person and per dollar of GNP. One might say that this is because the Communist countries were (are) poorer. But this relative poverty is itself part of the story: centrally controlled economies do less well economically, which is part of the reason they pollute more per unit of GNP, and even per capita. The same sort of result would undoubtedly hold if the investigation were widened to include all countries, as Scully (1988) has done for the effect of state system on per person income.

Before the 1980s there was only anecdotal evidence for the comparative success of market-based decentralized systems versus centrally planned systems, just as there is today with respect to conservation and pollution of the environment. And the same kinds of common-sensical arguments for the advantage of a "rationally" planned system were given in favor of communism— economies of scale, avoidance of duplication, control by the cleverest intellectuals instead of less-educated "ordinary" persons, and so on. But the transformation of countries to a planned command-and-control system based upon this theorizing was demonstrably the greatest human blunder of all time. This is the same vision that leads to such an "activist" command-and-control approach as this suggestion for the Alaskan Wildlife Refuge: "You drive a stake in the ground and say, 'You don't cross the Canning River.'"[21]

It must be said, however, that if one wants a planet the way it was twenty thousand years ago—not just "stop the world I want to get off," but "reverse the world to the way it used to be"—a free society will not move in that direction. The only way to obtain that result is to kill off almost all of humanity, and destroy all libraries so that the few remaining humans cannot quickly learn how to rebuild what we now have. If someone wishes this sort of "conservation," no arguments are relevant.

Some ecologists urge on us a "mixed" system where government only does what is "necessary." It is impossible to disagree with this in principle—the panda being a case in point. But those persons should be aware that in the analogous situation of the "mixed" economy, almost all the activities that were regarded as "necessary"—government-owned steel mills and mines and telephone systems, for example—turned out not to have the desirable properties that in advance they were touted to have. The "mixed system" is mainly a mirage and an intellectual illusion, and sometimes a Trojan horse for wider planning. And the idea that government can manipulate prices to simulate a well-working market has in Eastern Europe been shown conclusively to be a figment of unsound theorizing.

When the first edition was written in the late 1970s, the theoretical ideas discussed in chapter 15 and above, in this chapter, had not yet been adopted by the federal government, and indeed, were anathema to environmental activists. (See the afternote to chapter 15 on ecologists' criticisms of standard economics.) And the first recourse of policy makers is still to command-and-control systems. For example, the state of Maryland plans to reduce air pollution by coercing people to drive less. The mechanism is to require all employers of more than 100 persons to provide "free farecards, grants to buy bicycles, subsidized car pools, flexible work hours or greater opportunities to work at home," along the lines of the 1990 Clean Air Act, and of programs in southern California, Seattle, Phoenix, and other cities.[22]

Since the 1980s, however, there has been growing recognition, even among noneconomists, that direct controls are usually inferior to market-based economic incentives as ways to manage pollution. For example, the law now makes provision for firms such as electrical utilities to buy and sell rights to emit quantities of pollutants. The Chicago Board of Trade even has laid the groundwork for a public market in "smog futures" along the lines of commodity and securities markets, and environmental organizations have approved.[23]

In the 1980s, these economic ideas were refined into a body of applied work. The free market environmentalist writers emphasize the concepts of property rights, and of allowing price rather than command-and-control devices to allocate goods. They discuss "nonmarket government failures" as a counterpart to the "market failures" that many see at the root of pollution problems.[24]

The free-market environmentalists point to the successes of market systems in the cases of conservation mentioned earlier in the chapter. Proven successes with market systems for controlling pollution are less conspicuous. But such conservation cases as private fishing streams may be seen as the opposite side of the coin from the issue of pollution in streams and rivers, where privatization of rights has been shown to be effective.

Conclusion

If you want society to force you to waste effort and money because sacrifice is good for you, mandatory recycling fills the bill. But if you want people to have the best chance to live their lives in the ways that they wish, without imposing waste costs on others, then allowing private persons to deal with their private problems privately should be your choice.

The key question for social decisions is how to get the optimal level of recycling and waste disposal, pollution, and environmental preservation with a minimum of constraint upon individuals and economic activity. Economic incentives working in free markets often are a better system than command-and-control. Aside from the economic costs of inefficient controls, there is usually excessive, overzealous coercion—as in the regulations that eventuated in King Edward executing the man who polluted the air with sea coal mentioned in chapter 17, or the milder coercion of recycling zealots today.

(Additional discussion of this topic may be found in chapter 30—"Are People an Environmental Pollution?")

Part Two _____

POPULATION GROWTH'S EFFECT UPON
OUR RESOURCES AND LIVING STANDARD

As for the Arts of Delight and Ornament, they are best promoted by the greatest
number of emulators. And it is more likely that one ingenious curious man may
rather be found among 4 million than among 400 persons.
   (*William Petty*, Another Essay in Political Arithmetic, *1682*)

Wherever there are most happiness and virtue, and the wisest institutions, there
will also be most people.
   (*David Hume*, Essays, *1777*)

Little else is required to carry a state to the highest degree of affluence from the
lowest barbarism but peace, easy taxes, and a tolerable administration of justice;
all the rest being brought about by the natural course of things.
   (*Adam Smith, in Rae 1965*)

An Author is little to be valued, who tells us nothing but what we can learn from
every coffee-house conversation.
   (*David Hume*, Essays, *1777*)

22

Standing Room Only?
The Demographic Facts

> After performing the most exact calculation possible . . . I have found that
> there is scarcely one-tenth as many people on the earth as in ancient times. What
> is surprising is that the population on the earth decreases every day, and if this
> continues, in another ten centuries the earth will be nothing but a desert.
> *(Montesquieu, in Cerf and Navasky 1984)*

> [T]he population is constant in size and will remain so right up to the end of
> mankind.
> *("Population," L'Encyclopédie, in Cerf and Navasky 1984)*

> The facts of human population growth are simple.
> *(Paul Ehrlich, "World Population: A Battle Lost," in Reid and Lyon 1972)*

SCHOOLCHILDREN "know" that the world's environment and food situation
have been getting worse. And the children's books leave no doubt that population size and growth are the villains. As the *Golden Stamp Book of Earth and
Ecology* says, "Can the earth survive this many people? . . . If the population
continues to explode, many people will starve. About half of the world's population is underfed now, with many approaching starvation. . . . All of the
major environmental problems can be traced to people—more specifically, to
too many people."[1]

This child's text distills into simplest form the popular adults' books and
articles about population and resources. And Herbert London's study of
schoolbooks shows this text to be representative.[2] Indeed, the National Education Association in 1980 published a guide for teachers that says "Food
production is losing the race with the population explosion, and a massive
famine within the next decade seems probable." It then goes on to forecast across-the-board worsening conditions in natural resources and the
environment.[3]

But these propositions that are given to children with so much assurance
are either unproven or wrong. (Indeed, the NEA 1980 forecast has already
been proven incontrovertibly wrong; it would be interesting to know what the
NEA says now.) This chapter deals with the demographic facts. The next

chapter considers various forecasts, and the following chapter examines the dynamics of the birthrate and of population growth, in order to lay the foundation for the economic discussion of these issues in the rest of Part Two.

Population Growth Rates

The demographic facts, to the extent that they are known scientifically, can indeed seem frightening—at first glance. Figure 22-1 is the kind of diagram that, back in 1965, impressed and scared me enough to convince me that helping stop population growth should be my life's work. What we seem to see here is runaway population growth; the human population seems to be expanding with self-generated natural force at an exponential rate, a juggernaut chained only by starvation and disease. This suggests that unless something unusual comes along to check this geometric growth, there will soon be "standing room only."

People have, however, long been doing arithmetic that leads to the prediction of one or another version of "standing room only." In fact, the phrase "standing room only," used so often in recent discussions of population growth, was the title of a book by Edward Ross in 1927, and the notion is found explicitly in both Malthus and Godwin (whose conclusions differed completely, however). Just one among many such colorful calculations is that of Harrison Brown, who worried that humanity might continue increasing "until the earth is covered completely and to a considerable depth with a writhing mass of human beings, much as a dead cow is covered with a pulsating mass of maggots."[4]

One can get absurd results by simple extrapolation of other trends, too— especially short-term trends. The rate of construction of university buildings in the 1960s would soon have covered the entire Earth if the trend continued. Or, the growth of inmates of American prisons from 1980 to 1981 was 10 percent (from 315,974 to 353,674) and from 1981 to 1982 it was 11 percent. For amusement, Calvin Beisner extrapolated a 12 percent growth rate the following year, then 13 percent, and so on, and by only the year 2012 the number of inmates would exceed the entire projected population.[5] Nice arithmetic, but so what?

People have worried about population growth since the beginning of recorded time. The Bible gives us this early story of population exceeding the "carrying capacity" of a particular area: "And the land was not able to carry them . . . and Abram said to Lot: . . . Is not the whole land before thee? . . . If thou will take the left hand, then I will take the right; or if thou take the right hand, then I will go to the left."[6] Euripides wrote that the Trojan War was due to "an insolent abundance of people."[7] And many classical philosophers and historians such as Polybius, Plato, and Tertullian worried about population

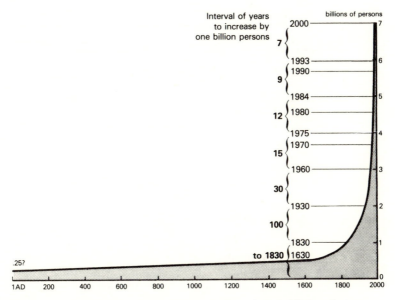

Figure 22-1. How the U.S. State Department Saw the World's Population
Growth

growth, food shortages, and environmental degradation.[8] The Tiberius Grac-
chus in about 100 B.C.E. complained that returned Roman soldiers "have no
clod of earth to call their own."[9] Early in the 1600s, John Winthrop left England for Massachusetts because he considered England so crowded. And
when England and Wales had fewer than five million people, one man expressed the wish for the earlier "times when our Country was not pestered
with multitude, not overcharged with swarmes of people."[10]

In 1802, when Java had a population of 4 million, a Dutch colonial official
wrote that Java was "overcrowded with unemployed."[11] As of 1990, Java had
108 million people[12] and again it is said to be overcrowded, with too much
unemployment.

Just because people have worried about population growth in the past does
not imply that we should *not* be worried now, of course. If a monster really has
been on the loose for a while, the fact that it has not yet done us in is hardly
reason to stop worrying. Therefore we must ask: Is population growth an
unchecked monster, on the loose since the beginning of time but likely to
destroy us in the foreseeable future?

Contrary to the impression given by figure 22-1, population growth has not
been constant or steady over the long sweep of time. Even the broadest picture
of the past million years shows momentous sudden changes. Figure 22-2 indicates that population growth has three times taken off at "explosive" rates.

Another common misleading impression about world population is that a

millions of persons — logarithmic scale

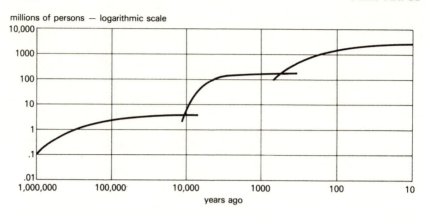

Figure 22-2. Deevey's Logarithmic Population Curve

large proportion of all the people who have ever lived are alive now. Not so. A reasonable estimate is that 77 billion human beings were born from 600,000 B.C.E. to A.D. 1962, twelve billion up to 6000 B.C.E., forty-two billion from 6000 B.C.E. to A.D. 1650, and twenty-three billion from A.D. 1650 to A.D. 1962.[13] Compare this to the five-plus billion who are alive now. Of course many of the people born in earlier years died at young ages. But even so, the number of years of human life lived on Earth in the past was large relative to the present.

The tool-using and tool-making revolution kicked off the rapid rise in population around 1 million B.C.E. The aid of various implements "gave the food gatherer and hunter access to the widest range of environments."[14] But when the productivity gains from the use of primitive tools had been exploited, the rate of population growth fell, and population size again settled down near a plateau.

The next rapid jump in population started perhaps ten thousand years ago, when people began to keep herds and cultivate the earth, rather than simply foraging for wild plants and game. Once again the rate of population growth abated after the initial productivity gains from the new technology had been exploited, and once again population size settled down to a near-plateau, as compared with the rapid growth previously experienced. The known methods of making a living constituted a constraint to further population growth once the world's population reached a certain size.

These two previous episodes of sharp rise and subsequent fall in the rate of population growth suggest that the present rapid growth—which began perhaps 300 or 350 years ago, in the 1600s—may settle down again when, or if, the benefits of the new industrial and agricultural and other technical knowledge that followed the early scientific and industrial revolutions begin to peter out. And population size may again reach a near-plateau and remain there until another "revolution" due to another breakthrough of knowledge again suddenly increases the productive capacity of mankind. Of course the current knowledge-revolution may continue without foreseeable end, and population growth may or may not continue as long as the revolution does. Either way, in this long-term view population size adjusts to productive conditions rather than being an uncontrolled monster. (We should keep in mind, though, that our present, technical knowledge will support vastly larger populations than at present.)

To put the matter another way: This long-run view of demographic history suggests that, contrary to Malthus, constant geometric growth does not characterize human population history. Rather, at each stage a major improvement of economic and health conditions has produced a sudden increase in population, which gradually moderated as the major productive advances and concomitant health improvements were assimilated. Then, after the initial surge, the rate of growth slowed down until the next big surge. In this view, population growth represents economic success and human triumph, rather than social failure.

Deevey's picture of population history (fig. 22-2) still leaves us with the image of population growth as having an irresistible, self-reinforcing logic of its own, though subject to (very rare) changes in conditions. That view is so broad, however, that it can be misleading. The entire world, for example, had a stable population over the seven centuries prior to A.D. 750, as seen in figure 22-3. And if we look more closely, in figure 22-4 we see that even for as large an area as Europe, where local ups and downs tend to cancel out, population growth did not proceed at a constant rate, nor was there always positive growth. Instead, there were advances and reverses. Figure 22-4 shows that population change is a complex phenomenon affected by a variety of forces; it is not an inexorable force checked only by famine and epidemic.

Now let us move to an even greater level of detail—a country or region. Figures 22-5, 22-6, and 22-7 show three histories where a decline in population has been more than a temporary episode. In Egypt, the breakdown of the Roman Empire led to a series of population declines due to disease and bad government, declines that ended only in the nineteenth century. In Iraq's Dyala region (around Baghdad) there were a series of political-economic perturbations that adversely affected irrigation and agriculture; it took years of population growth to overcome such setbacks—only to have another such breakdown occur. And in Mexico, it was the conquest by Cortés that set off a remarkable population decline. In the Spaniards' wake came wars, massacres, political and economic breakdowns among the indigenous civilizations, and new diseases, all of which caused death, desolation, and depopulation.*

* The population estimates for the native American populations in South America are tenuous, and the estimates for North America are even more tenuous. One of the few solid pieces of evidence is that the ratio of the population before the first smallpox epidemic in 1519, compared to the population a century later, was about 20 to 1 in two places in Peru and two in Mexico (*Science* 8, December 1989, p. 1246, discussing work of Henry F. Dobyns).

millions of persons

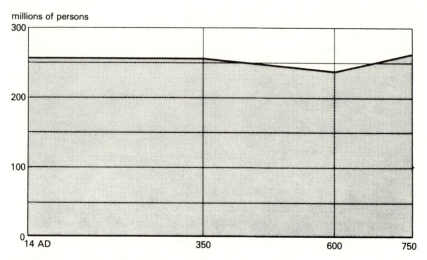

Figure 22-3. The Population of the World, A.D. 14–A.D. 750

millions of persons

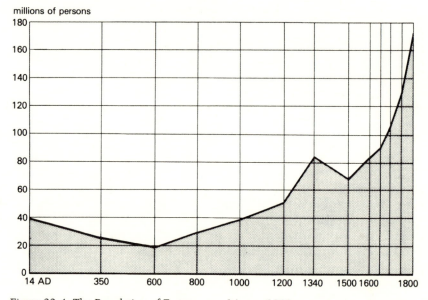

Figure 22-4. The Population of Europe, A.D. 14–A.D. 1800

On opposite page:
Figure 22-5. The Population of Egypt, 664 B.C.–A.D. 1966. *Note:* McEvedy and Jones (1978, pp. 228–29) persuasively suggest that Egypt's population was nowhere near as high as Hollingsworth shows it to be.
Figure 22-6. The Population of Baghdad (Lower Diyala, Iraq) Region, 4000 B.C.–A.D. 1967

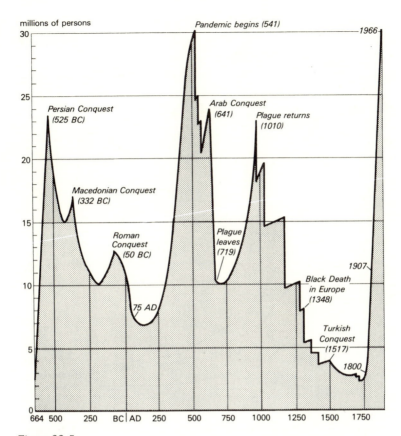

Figure 22-5

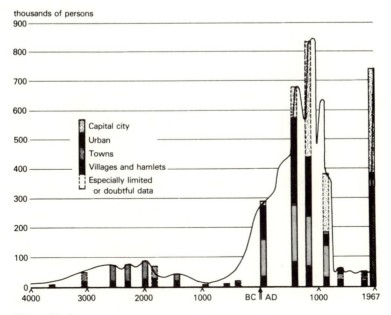

Figure 22-6

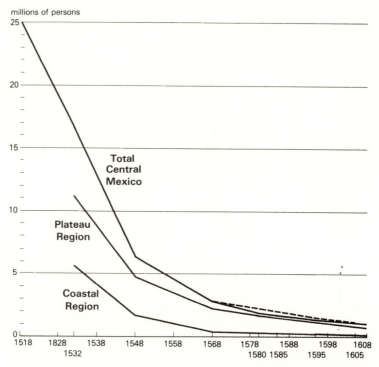

Figure 22-7. The Population of Central Mexico, A.D. 1518–A.D. 1608

A shocking example close to home for Americans is the population decline of native Americans in California from perhaps 310,000 in 1769 to a low of perhaps twenty thousand to twenty-five thousand at the end of the nineteenth century. "The population decline became catastrophic between 1848 and 1860. The number of Indians fell in *twenty years* from 200,000 or 250,000 to merely 25,000 or 30,000."[15]

These historical examples prove that population size and growth are influenced by political and economic and cultural forces, and not only by starvation and plague due to changes in natural conditions.

The Approaching Victory against Premature Death

The main cause of the rapid increase in population during the past two centuries—the most important and amazing demographic fact, and the greatest human achievement in history, in my view—is the decrease in the world's death rate.* It took thousands of years to increase life expectancy at birth from

* One reader of the first edition could not be satisfied that this is broadly true even after two

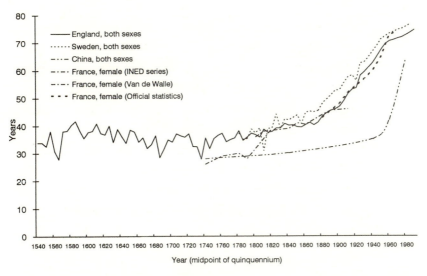

Figure 22-8. Life Expectancy in England, France, Sweden, and China, 1541–1985

just over twenty years to the high twenties. Then in just the past two centuries, the length of life you could expect for your baby or for yourself in the advanced countries jumped from less than thirty years in France, and the mid-thirties in Great Britain, to perhaps seventy-five years today (see fig. 22–8). What greater event has humanity witnessed?

Then starting well after World War II, the length of life one could expect in the poor countries has leaped upwards by perhaps fifteen or even twenty years since the 1950s, caused by advances in agriculture, sanitation, and medicine (see fig. 22-9).

Again, it is this amazing decrease in the death rate that is the cause of there being a larger world population nowadays than in former times. In the nineteenth century the planet Earth could sustain only one billion people. Ten thousand years ago, only four million could keep themselves alive. Now, more than five billion people are living longer and more healthily than ever before, on average. The increase in the world's population represents our victory against death, our advancing march toward life being ended mainly by the diseases of old age.

Most of the decline in the death rate is caused by a decline in disease, interrelated with an improvement in nutrition.[16] But the long-run decline in injuries is also worth noting; an example is seen in figure 22-10.

letters. I thought that this idea must be obvious, but apparently it is not. In lieu of extended argument, I'll cite a solid authority. In the table of contents of *Scientific American* for September 1974, by Ansley Coale, "The History of the Human Population: Its rapid growth results from the decline in death rates over the past 200 years."

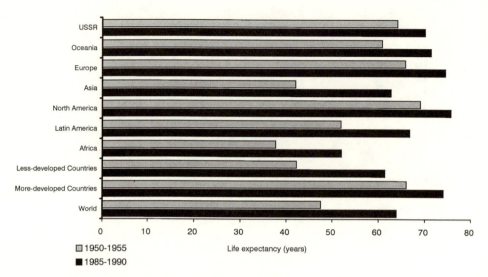

Figure 22-9. Life Expectancy around the World, 1950–1955, 1985–1990

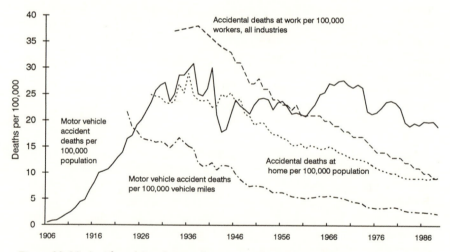

Figure 22-10. Accidental Death Rates by Cause, U.S., 1906–1990

The only places that have suffered a long-run interruption in this advance are (a) some of the inner cities of the United States, where violence and drug-related AIDS have raised the death rate among young black males, and have lowered life expectancy for all black males taken together in the latter 1980s;[17] and (b) the ex-Communist bloc of nations in Eastern Europe, which are suffering a demographic tragedy as a result of bad government and its disastrous effects on pollution (see chapter 17), industrial accidents, medical care, and perhaps even nutrition.[18] Throughout Eastern Europe, male mortality above the age of thirty increased from 1958–1959 to the mid-1980s, at least, as may be seen in figure 22-11. In the Soviet Union even infant mortality rose between the mid-1960s and the mid-1980s. All throughout Eastern Europe, the improvements in the death rate at all ages were far less than in Western Europe[19] (see fig. 22-12).

The standardized total mortality per thousand men of working age was almost twice as high in the USSR in 1987 as in Western "free-market" countries (6.59 versus 3.63), and more than double in all major categories except cancers, including cardiovascular diseases, lung and respiratory diseases, and accidents. For females the differences are not as marked, but still are important.[20]

Leave aside the exceptions, which are surely temporary. One would expect lovers of humanity to jump with joy at the triumph of human mind and organization over the raw killing forces of nature. Instead, many lament that there are so many people alive to enjoy the gift of life. And it is this worry that leads them to approve the Chinese and other inhumane programs of coercion and denial of personal liberty in one of the most precious choices a family can make—the number of children that it wishes to bear and raise (see chapter 39).

Not only do many not consider the successful fight against death to be good news, but many refuse to even recognize the good news. For example, with respect to infant mortality, journalists compare the rates of different groups instead of focusing on the absolute improvement over time. An April 2, 1991 headline was: "Explaining Racial Differences in Infant Death." The article illustrates a painful story about black-white differences with pictures of slavery days and unheated apartments in Harlem. The result of this consistent emphasis on comparative rates rather than long-term trends is grim: Ask any group, "Is the trend of black infant mortality encouraging?"[21] Almost everyone's reaction in the United States—even a group of demographers I asked—is that black infant mortality is a bad situation. But a graph of black and white infant mortality in the United States since 1915 (see fig. 22-13) leaves a different impression. White infant mortality in 1915 was almost 100 deaths per 1,000 births, and black infant mortality was fully 180 deaths per 1,000 births. Both are horrifying. And the rates were even more horrifying in earlier years in some places—up to 300 or 400 deaths per 1,000 births.

Probabilities of Dying by USSR Males, Relative to 1958, in 1964-65, 1969-70, 1984-85

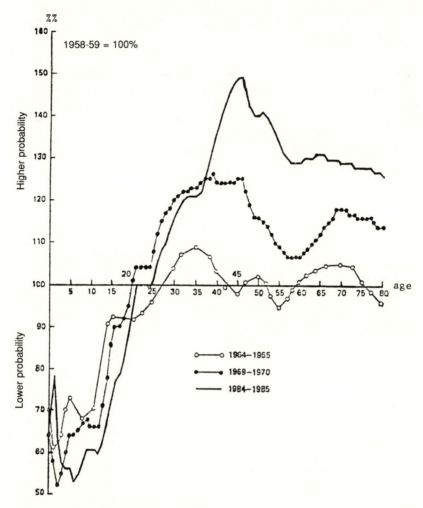

Figure 22-11a. Male Mortality in USSR

Probabilities of Dying by USSR Females, Relative to 1958, in 1964-65, 1969-70, 1984-85

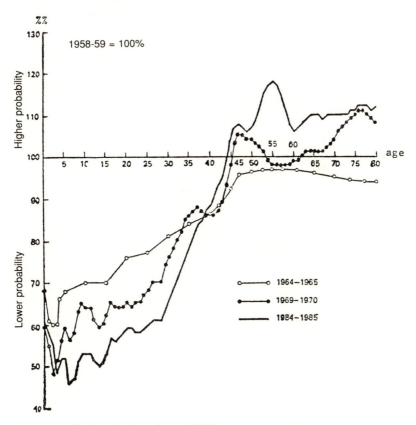

Figure 22-11b. Female Mortality in USSR

Nowadays white infant mortality is about nine per thousand, and black infant mortality is about eighteen per thousand. Of course it is bad that mortality for blacks is higher than for whites. But should we not be impressed by the tremendous improvement for both races—both falling to about 10 percent of what they were—and the black rate coming ever closer to the white rate? Is not this extraordinary gain for the entire population the most important story—and a most happy story? Yet the public has the impression that we should be mainly distressed about the state of black infant mortality.*

* Furthermore, though black infant mortality obviously is a problem the society should address, it is not clear what should be done; it is not a direct effect of poverty—an unusual situation. "Relatively few low-birth-weight births in the U.S. result from undernutrition," studies show (Graham 1991). Government programs to curb malnutrition are not a cure for infant mortality, but rather the behavior of mothers must change.

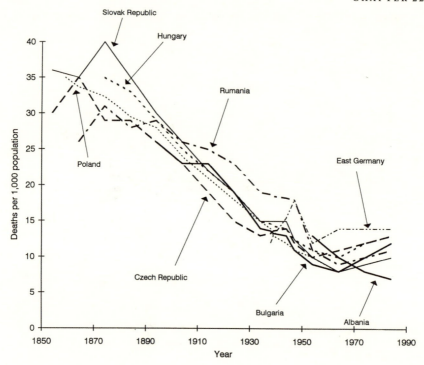

Figure 22-12a. Mortality in Eastern Europe, 1850–1990

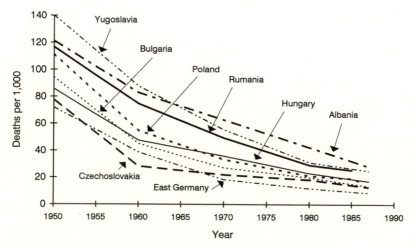

Figure 22-12b. Infant Mortality in Eastern Europe, 1950–1990

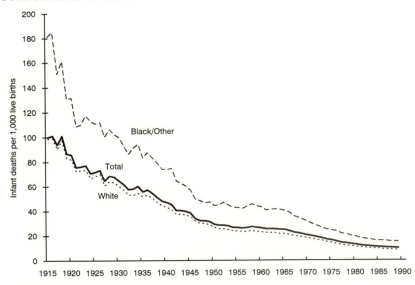

Figure 22-13. Black and White Infant Mortality in the United States, 1915–1990

Summary

This chapter discussed some of the pertinent historical and contemporary facts about population growth. It showed that population growth is neither constant nor inexorable; it is not smoothly geometric, as Malthus thought it to be. Population grows at various rates under various conditions. Sometimes population size shrinks for centuries due to poor political and health conditions. That is, economic, cultural, and political events, and not just catastrophe, control population size. But recently conditions have improved dramatically and population has added another growth spurt—joyous news for humanity.

23

What Will Future Population Growth Be?

WHEN LOOKING AT the demographic facts with an eye to population policy, one wants to know what the future holds—how great the "pressures" of population size and growth will be. Hence governmental agencies and academic researchers make forecasts. The history of demographic predictions calls for humility, however, and teaches caution rather than fear-motivated over-reactive policies.

Voodoo Forecasting

About 1660, with tongue in cheek William Petty extrapolated population trends to show that by the year 1842 the population of London would about equal the population of England.[1]

In the 1930s, most Western countries worried about a *decline* in population growth. The most extensive investigation of the "problem" was undertaken in Sweden by some of the world's best-regarded social scientists. The dotted lines in figure 23-1 show how the future looked to them then. But all their dotted-line hypotheses about the future—intended to bracket all of the conceivable possibilities—turned out to be far below the actual course of population growth, as shown by the solid line; that is, the future turned out far better, from the point of view of those scientists, than any of them guessed it might. It may well be that we are now at an analogous point with respect to the world as a whole, except that now population growth is popularly thought to be too fast rather than too slow.

The Swedes were not alone in making inaccurate "pessimistic" forecasts. A U.S. Presidential Research Committee of eminent scientists reported to Herbert Hoover in 1933 that "we shall probably attain a population between 145 and 150 million during the present century."[2] Figure 23-2 shows a variety of forecasts made in the 1930s and 1940s by America's greatest demographic experts. For the year 2000, none of them forecast a population even as large as 200 million people; in fact, the United States reached 200 million people sometime around the year 1969, and is far beyond that already. A good many of the forecasters actually predicted a decline in population before the year 2000, which we now know is impossible unless there is a holocaust.

The forecasts just mentioned erred by extrapolating the recent past. An-

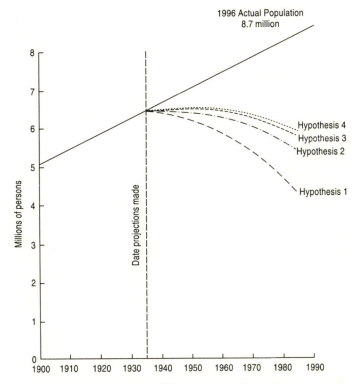

Figure 23-1. The Population of Sweden According to Four
Hypotheses Made in 1935, and the Actual Population in 1979

other blunder is fitting the data to the wrong ideal mathematical form, among
which the logistic curve has been the most dangerously seductive; it assumes
that population will level off. Figure 23-3 shows how Raymond Pearl, one of
the greatest mathematical demographers, went wrong. And the graph is coming to us with the approval of Walker Shewhart, the greatest of quality-control
statisticians.

The accuracy of long-run forecasts has not benefited from the huge errors
of the 1930s. Figure 23-4 shows how forecasters went wrong in 1965; they
extrapolated a large increase for 1990, but a decline actually occurred.

Even as late as the 1970s there were astonishing flip-flops in world population forecasts for the turn of the century—then only three decades away. As of
1969, the U.S. *Department of State Bulletin* forecast 7.5 billion people for the
year 2000, citing the United Nations.[3] By 1974, the figure commonly quoted
was 7.2 billion.[4] By 1976, Raphael Salas, the executive director of the UN
Fund for Population Activities (UNFPA), was forecasting "nearly 7 billion."[5]
Soon Salas was all the way down to "at least 5.8 billion."[6] And as early as 1977,

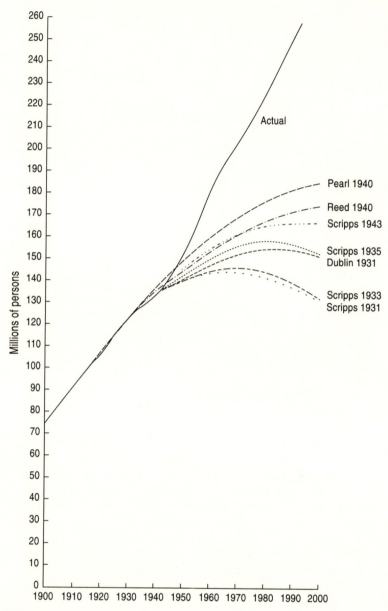

Figure 23-2. U.S. Population Forecasts Made in 1931–1943, and the Actual Population

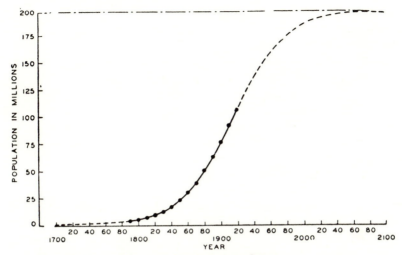

Pearl's 1920 Forecast of Population Growth of the United States

Figure 23-3. How Raymond Pearl Went Wrong Forecasting Population

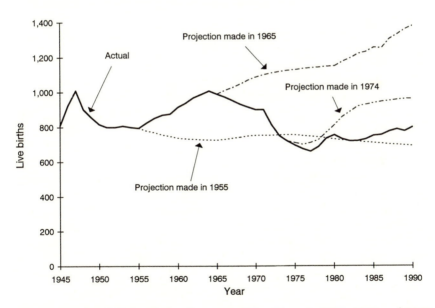

Figure 23-4. How U.K. Population Forecasters Went Wrong in 1955, 1965, and 1974: The Result of Extending Recent Observations

Lester Brown and his Worldwatch Institute (which has a close relationship to the UN) dropped the estimate again, forecasting 5.4 billion people for the year 2000—which was surpassed around 1990 (if the data are sound). This variation in forecasts must be astonishing to laymen—to wit, that a United Nations-State Department forecast for a date then only twenty-three years away, when a majority of the people who would then be living were already living, could be later revised by two billion people, a change of more than a third of the total forecast. By 1992, the latest UN "medium" forecast for the year 2000 was 6.3 million.[7] Does this example of forecasting "science" suggest that we should give credence to long-run population predictions?

And consider this: In 1972, the President's Commission on Population Growth forecast for the United States that "even if the family size drops gradually—to the two-child average—there will be no year in the next two decades in which the absolute number of births will be less than in 1970."[8] How did it turn out? In 1971—the year *before* that forecast by the august President's Commission was transmitted to the President and then published—the absolute number of births (not just the birthrate) was *already* less than in 1970. By 1975, the absolute number of births was barely higher than in 1920, and the number of white births was actually lower than in most years between 1914 and 1924 (see fig. 23-5).

This episode shows once again how flimsy are the demographic forecasts upon which arguments about growth policy are based. In this case the Commission did not even *backcast* correctly, let alone *forecast* well.

Then in 1989, the U.S. Census Bureau forecast that U.S. population would peak at 302 million in 2038 and would thenceforward decline. But just five years later in 1992, the Census Bureau forecast 383 million in 2050 with no peaking in sight; one gives the lie to the other by about fifty million people—a sixth of the 1989 forecast.[9] The science of demographic forecasting clearly has not yet reached perfection.

With a track record this poor, one wonders why official agencies should make any such forecasts at all, especially when they are based on little more than guesses concerning such matters as future immigration policy and people's decisions about how many children to have. We have no experience to rely on for estimating how people will act under the conditions that will prevail in the future.

In short, this history of population forecasts should make us think twice—or thrice—before crediting doomsday forecasts of population growth.

(Actually, demographic forecasting is very easy—even movie actresses can do it. Actress Meryl Streep noted that "men were given more than twice as many roles as women in 1989 movies," and then she forecast that "by the year 2000 we will have 13 percent of roles . . . and in 20 years we will be eliminated from the movies.")[10]

Some trusting persons respond to data on past failed forecasts by saying

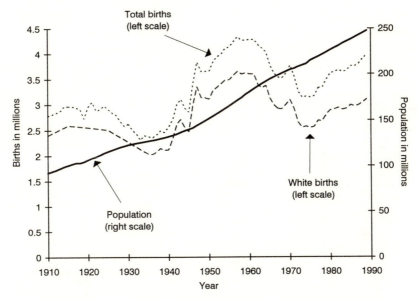

Figure 23-5. Total Births, White Births, and Population in the United States, 1910–1990

that this shows we need better research, and "the government should do something about it." But "official" forecasts made by government agencies—always at very large public expense, of course—have been shown to be no better than the run of private forecasts.[11] And official forecasts have the grave disadvantage that people are more likely to believe them than private forecasts—and then take legal action against the government if the forecasts are wrong, as the timber industry did in the 1980s when an officially predicted tree shortage never occurred.

Not only are methods of population forecasting unreliable, but the base of data used for many countries, and for the world as a whole, is still shockingly weak. In 1992, it was revealed that the populations of several developing countries were much lower than anyone had imagined they could be. Nigeria's population, for example, was said by standard sources to be 122.5 million in 1991. But when the results of the 1991 Census were released—quite likely the best census ever done, by far—the total turned out to be 88.5 million people.[12] Amazing.

Do Current Trends Call for Coercive Policies?

What population size or rate of growth does the long-run future of the world hold in store? No one can be sure. One frequently hears that zero population

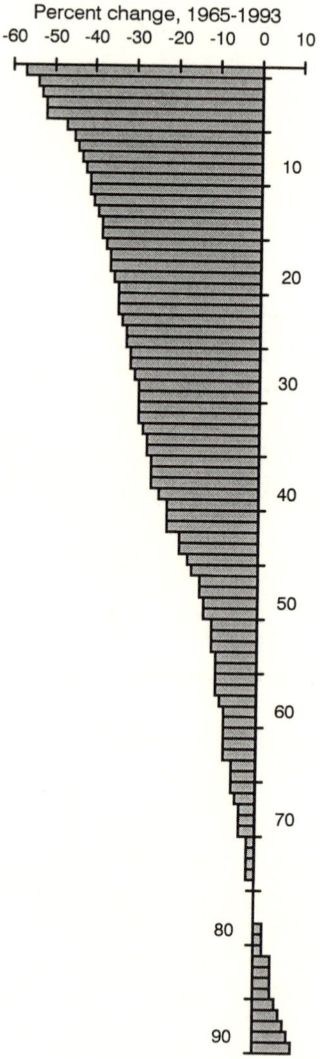

Percent change, 1965-1993
-60 -50 -40 -30 -20 -10 0 10
10
20
30
40
50
60
70
80
90

Crude Birth Rate and Percent Change, 1965-1993

		1965	1975	1993	% change
1	Hong Kong	28	18	12	-57
	Korea, South	35	24	16	-54
	Cuba	34	21	16	-53
	Taiwan	33	23	16	-52
5	Thailand	44	34	21	-52
	China	34	26	18	-47
	Brazil	42	38	23	-45
	Tunisia	45	34	25	-44
	Indonesia	46	40	26	-43
10	Mauritius	36	26	21	-42
	Barbados	27	19	16	-41
	Colombia	44	33	26	-41
	Dominican Rep.	47	38	28	-40
	Sri Lanka	33	27	20	-39
15	Panama	40	31	25	-38
	Korea, North	39	37	24	-38
	Morocco	49	48	31	-37
	Chile	33	23	21	-36
	Trinadad & Tob.	33	23	21	-36
20	Peru	43	42	28	-35
	Costa Rica	41	29	27	-34
	Jamaica	38	30	25	-34
	Mexico	44	40	29	-34
	Malaysia	42	31	28	-33
25	Algeria	50	48	34	-32
	Lebanon	41	40	28	-32
	Figi	36	28	25	-31
	Ecuador	45	45	31	-31
	Kuwait	46	44	32	-30
30	Vietnem, North	42	32	30	-29
	Turkey	41	34	29	-29
	Venezuela	42	37	30	-29
	Vietnam, South	42	41	30	-29
	India	43	36	31	-28
35	Philippines	44	37	32	-27
	Burma	41	40	30	-27
	Egypt	42	35	31	-26
	El Salvador	46	40	34	-26
	Bangladesh	50	49	37	-26
40	Honduras	51	48	39	-24
	Nicaragua	49	46	38	-22
	Rwanda	51	51	40	-22
	Saudi Arabia	50	50	39	-22
	Paraguay	42	39	34	-19
45	Papua New Guin.	43	41	35	-19
	Jordan	48	47	40	-17
	Bolivia	44	44	37	-16
	Mongolia	42	38	36	-14
	Ghana	50	49	43	-14
50	Guatemala	45	43	39	-13
	Khmer/Kampuch.	47	47	41	-13
	Bhutan	45	43	40	-11
	Libyan Arab. Rep.	47	47	42	-11
	Uganda	46	47	51	-11
55	Tanzania	51	48	46	-10
	Nigeria	50	49	45	-10
	Kenya	50	50	45	-10
	Iraq	48	48	45	-10
	Nepal	45	45	41	-9
60	Pakistan	48	47	44	-8
	Senegal	48	47	44	-8
	Sudan	49	49	45	-8
	Madagascar	50	50	46	-8
	Lesotho	38	40	35	-8
65	Syrian Arab. Rep.	48	46	45	-6
	Ethiopia	50	49	47	-6
	Liberia	50	50	47	-6
	Congo	44	45	42	-5
	Togo	51	50	49	-4
70	Haiti	45	45	43	-4
	Zambia	50	50	48	-4
	Cen.African Rep.	45	43	44	-2
	Cameroon	42	41	41	-2
	Chad	45	44	44	-2
75	Burundi	48	48	47	-2
	Guinea	47	46	47	0
	Upper Volta	50	49	50	0
	Niger	52	52	52	0
	Afghanistan	49	49	49	0
80	Zaire	47	44	48	2
	Laos	44	42	45	2
	Mauritania	45	45	46	2
	Angola	49	47	51	4
	Yemen	51	50	53	4
85	Somolia	48	48	50	4
	Mali	50	50	52	4
	Mozambique	43	43	45	5
	Yemen, P.D.R. of	50	49	53	6
	Sierra Leone	45	45	48	7
90	Malawi	49	47	53	8
	Ivory Coast	46	45	53	9

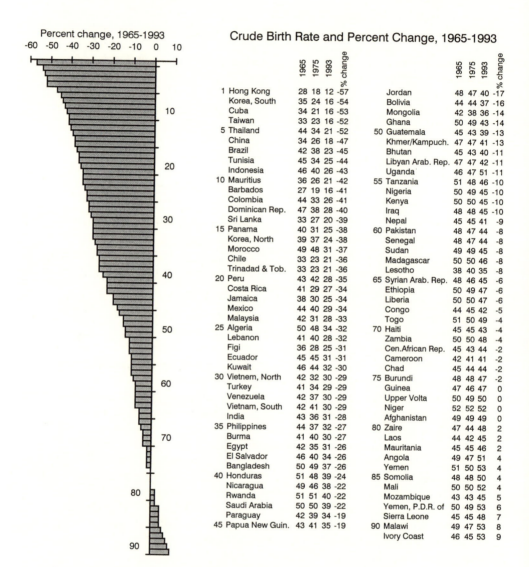

Figure 23-6. Recent Changes in the Birthrate in Developing Countries

growth (ZPG) "obviously" is the only viable state of affairs in the long run. But why? Why shouldn't population get *smaller* instead of staying level if it already is too large? What is sacred about the present population size, or the size that will be attained if it levels off soon? As one writer put it, the concept of ZPG is simply "a careless example of round number preference."[13] As to whether a larger stationary population, or a larger and still growing population, is plausible or desirable in the long run—the whole of Part Two of this book addresses that topic.

The mere recitation of a number like "five and a half billion people" can evoke the reaction that the number is very large, or too large, or unsustainable. But no one says that the numbers of trees or birds or bacteria on our planet are too large, or calculates the number of doublings until their space would run out. Why the difference between birds and people?

Contemporary data show us that the rate of population growth can go down as well as up. In many poor countries, including the largest of them, fertility has been falling—and very rapidly (see fig. 23-6). Many of the countries with the fastest-falling birthrates are small islands, which seem especially quick to respond to new conditions and currents of thought; perhaps it is because they have good communication networks due to their high population density. Hong Kong's crude birthrate fell from thirty-eight to thirty in just the six years from 1960 to 1965.[14] But huge China is no island, and it supports a quarter of all humanity; yet fertility there, too, has apparently dropped sharply in the past decade or two (though the coercion involved makes this case different from other countries).

The supposed inevitability of population leveling off seems to be an implicit assumption of a scenario like Malthus's two postulated growth rates—exponential for humans, arithmetic for food. But this scenario lacks supporting evidence. Humans and wheat are both biological species, and the growth of each is constrained by various forces. There is no a priori reason why the two species should follow different growth patterns.

The recent drops in fertility imply that countries that are now poor and have high fertility rates will sooner or later follow the pattern of the richer countries, whose mortality rates fell years ago and whose fertility rates then likewise fell. This pattern may be seen in figure 23-7, which shows the well-known "demographic transition" as it actually occurred in Sweden.

In the more-developed countries, fertility now is low by anyone's standard. In figure 23-8 we see that the birthrate is far below replacement—that is, below zero population growth—for many of the largest countries in Europe. What if those trends continue? Forecasts of population size require assumptions about the fertility of future couples, and about the fertility of present couples who have begun but not yet finished bearing children. Such assumptions have proven wildly wrong in the past, as we have seen. Yet it is interesting to imagine the implication of assuming that childbearing patterns like

births per 1000 population

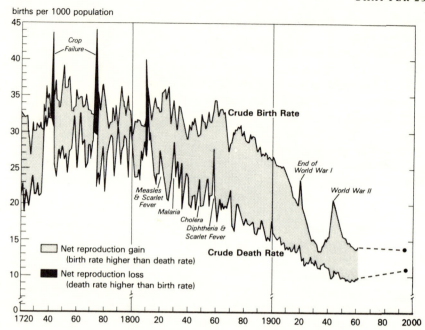

Figure 23-7. Demographic Transition: Birth and Death Rates in Sweden, 1720–1993

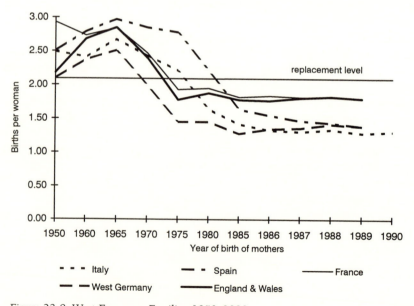

Figure 23-8. West European Fertility, 1950–1990

those practiced at present will continue—population decline in the major Western countries.

Already there is a felt "labor shortage" in the Western countries,* though it may well be that this is a result of short-term ups and downs of the birthrate rather than a result of the long-term rate. And it might be that because of the long-term growth in income, there might be a felt shortage even if population were to continue growing at a substantial rate in rich countries. This squares with the paradoxical idea expressed in chapter 1, afternote 2, that human beings are the only resource whose scarcity is increasing over the decades.

Even if total population continues to grow, there may be declines in some large geographic areas. This is discussed below in the section on population density.

As to the long-run future—again, no one *knows* what will happen. We can expect that people's incomes will rise indefinitely. But how much of that income will people spend on additional children? And what other activities will compete with bringing up children for parents' interest and time? These factors influence population growth, and no one knows well how they will operate. My guess—based on no solid evidence—is that fertility in the rich countries will again begin to be large enough to produce population growth. We can say with confidence, however, that an extrapolation of the last few centuries' world population growth rapidly toward infinity and doom, as seen in the silly figure 22-1, has no warrant in the facts.

Who Will Support Whom? The Dependency Burdens

A key issue in the economics of population is the proportion of persons of working age relative to the proportions of child dependents and of old-age dependents. A fast-growing population contains a large proportion of children, who are an economic burden until they are old enough to earn their keep (just like capital investments while they are being constructed). On the other hand, a population that is growing very slowly or not at all contains a large proportion of persons too old to work but who require that others support them.

The interrelationships among births, deaths, population size, and age distributions have been changing over the years:

1. Figure 23-9 shows that the total number of persons under twenty has risen little in France in over two hundred years, and now is little higher than in 1881. But the total number of persons sixty-five and over has multiplied by a factor more than six.

* The term "labor shortage" has little meaning in technical economic analysis. But the fact that people talk about it has meaning.

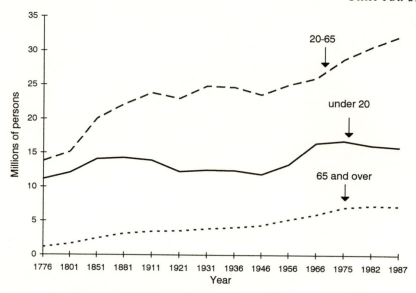

Figure 23-9. Persons by Age Group, France, 1776–1987

2. The total number of deaths each year is no greater than it was in 1950, though the world's population has doubled.[15]

Consider the large differences in the child-dependency burdens from one country to another: In 1985, fully 46 percent of the population of Bangladesh (typical of many countries in Asia and Africa) was younger than fifteen years old, compared with only 17 percent in Switzerland (typical of many countries in Europe); that is, in Bangladesh there were ninety-one children for each 100 working-age persons ages fifteen to sixty-four, while in Switzerland there were twenty-seven children for each 100 persons ages fifteen to sixty-four.[16] The age pyramids for the two countries are shown in figure 23–10.[17] Clearly, the economic effect of such dependency differences is not trivial.

Many draw from these data the conclusion that the standard of living will be higher if the birthrate is lower. For the immediate future this is undeniable; the proposition can be demonstrated by the simplest kind of arithmetic: If income per capita is our measure of economic well-being, then we need only divide gross national product by population to calculate income per person. Adding a nonproducing baby to the population immediately reduces the calculated income per capita; it is that simple.

The *implications* of this simple arithmetic are less simple, however. Another baby means there is less of everything to go around—for the time being. But the squeezes in schooling, feeding, and housing (the extent of which will be

SWITZERLAND

Males
3,152,820

1985 Age Structure

Females
3,317,545

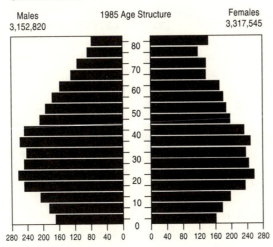

BANGLADESH

Males
52,136,730

1985 Age Structure

Females
49,009,830

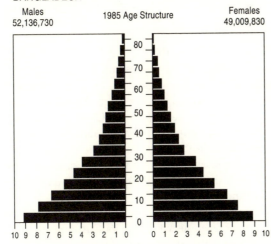

Figure 23-10.
Age-Distribution Pyramids
for Switzerland and
Bangladesh

discussed later) bring forth additional efforts on the part of individuals and
institutions to mitigate the squeezes. Also very important in assessing the impact of an additional child is the issue of who assumes which part of the
burden—the parents or the public. (Later we'll talk more about this, too.)

The story of dependency burdens does not end here, however. A modern
low-mortality society with a low birthrate supports few children. But each
person in the labor force also has a great many old people to support. Consider
these variations. (a) In 1900 in the United States, 4 percent of the population

was over sixty-five.[18] But perhaps 13 percent of the population will be over
sixty-five in 2000, and 17 percent in the year 2020.[19] (b) The proportions of
the male population within the prime labor-force ages of fifteen to sixty-four
were 70 percent in Sweden in 1940, and 52 percent in Bangladesh in 1985[20]
(that is, there were about twice as many workers in Sweden then as in Bangladesh now to support each dependent).

But counting the numbers of people in different age groups does not tell the
whole story. The cost of supporting a retired person is much greater in the
United States than the cost of supporting a child. Least important in a developed society is the difference in food consumption, unlike the situation in a
subsistence-agricultural society. Consider that old people need much more
expensive health care than do children. And old people may travel for twelve
months a year in trailers on public roads, whereas children cannot. Except for
schooling, old people consume much more than do children in almost every
category of expensive goods and services.

This pattern of old-age dependency causes perturbations. The U.S. Social
Security system has already been in severe funding trouble, and financing the
payments is a serious economic and political problem for the federal government. In the future, the burden of Social Security payments will take up an
even larger proportion of a U.S. worker's pay, and of the production of the
economy as a whole.

Even more fundamentally, the deficit in the U.S. government budget,
which troubled so many people so much in the 1980s and beyond, may reasonably be seen as a demographically caused phenomenon. If people were still
dying at the 1900 mortality rate, there would now be no budget deficit, because benefits to the aged would be enormously lower. Or, if couples had
continued having children at the fertility rate of the baby boom, there would
be more working taxpayers now, and the deficit would not exist or at least
would be much lower than it is. (At present, increased immigration is the only
feasible solution which would keep the deficit from growing while avoiding
the pain of decreased benefits or increased taxes.)

Are you now, or will you in the future be, a working person? If so, a lower
birthrate means that you have fewer people who will look to you now for
support. But the same reduction means that there will be fewer people to support *you* when you get older, and you will then be a relatively greater burden
on others.

This two-edged sword involves one of the major themes of this book. The
short-run effect of a given demographic factor is often the opposite of its effect
in the long run. Deciding which demographic pattern you prefer—faster or
slower population growth—requires that you put relative values upon the
long-run and short-run effects. And this, of course, requires that you decide
who is to contribute and who is to receive.

Decreasing Population Density in the Future?

If one divides the number of square miles on the Earth's surface by population size, an increasing population obviously implies a greater density of persons per surface unit.

But this simple calculation is seldom (if ever) a meaningful or appropriate calculation. What matters are the densities that *people experience*.

In the United States, a large proportion of rural counties have lost population in recent decades, and in 1986 the entire state of Iowa had fewer people under the age of five than at any time since before 1900; the number declined by fully a third between 1960 and the 1980s.[21] Rural people move to cities. And the people in Iowa worry about it because the trend feeds on itself; the fewer people there are, the poorer the economic opportunities for those who remain (just the opposite of Malthusian theory), and the greater the incentive for them to leave, too.

The continued concentration of population could mean that the *absolute number* of persons living on (say) 75 percent of the area of the Earth might be declining even as total world population increases, due to the reduction in the total number of persons needed for agriculture as countries grow wealthy. (This is likely to continue indefinitely: see chapter 6.)

Consider this: Between 1950 and 1985 (and surely continuing beyond 1985), the population density on 97 percent of the surface of the United States has been *decreasing*. Here is the calculation that shows this to be so: The total population outside of metropolitan areas fell from about sixty-six million people in 1950 (44.9 percent of total population) to about fifty-nine million people in 1985 (23.4 percent of total population).[22] That is, aside from the (roughly) 3 percent of the area of the United States incorporated within metropolitan areas, the total population has fallen (see fig. 23-11). Those who choose to live in rural areas are experiencing a decline in the density of neighbors. And there is little reason to expect this trend to reverse for a long time, if ever. The total urban area may creep up a bit—say to 6 percent in a century—but in the rest of the country, density may well decline indefinitely, except for vacation uses. The trend is the same for the rest of the developed world, too (see fig. 23–11).

Yes, population density within any given metropolitan area will probably increase. But individuals can choose to live in cities or their surrounding suburbs of whatever density they prefer, and the range of individual choices at any density level will increase in the future.

Even more important than population density per unit of surface area is the amount of living and work space available to an individual. And this is continually increasing, in considerable part due to multi-story buildings, made

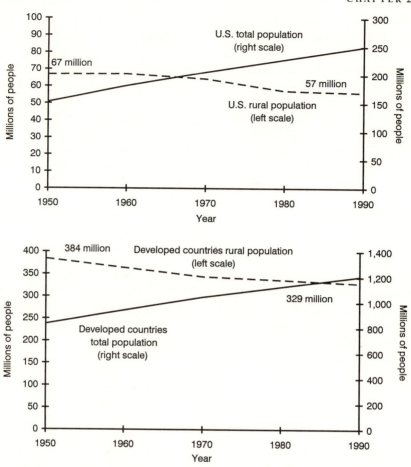

Figure 23-11. Millions of People Living in Rural Areas of Developed Countries and United States, 1950–1990

possible by increasing income as well as greater technology, as discussed in chapter 6.

Of course this line of thinking does not comfort those who call themselves wilderness lovers, and simply want no human beings there—except themselves. "Rivers like the Hulahula and the Kongakut have lost some of their wilderness character," said George Heim of Alaska River Adventures, a group that organizes trips. "You're not getting what you go up there for if you end up sharing the river with 20 other people and jockeying for campsites."[23] One wonders what is the "optimal" number of visitors that authorities should allow—100? 10? 1? 0? And, should Alaska River Adventures be given a monopoly on the trade?

A cute device used to show that a larger population is a bad thing—based just on population numbers alone—is used by Zero Population Growth in their ratings of the quality of life in American cities. The ratings simply *assume* that a larger population is bad. And hence it is not surprising that the smaller cities that have no growth garner such headlines as "Albany, N.Y. Ties for First Place in Measure of Urban 'Livability."[24] And such publicity leads the mayor of Phoenix to be "aggressive about growth-control measures." One wonders how the journalistic staff of such an august newspaper as the *Wall Street Journal* can fall for such simple-minded stuff—unless they desperately wish to believe in it, which leads into the discussion of values in chapters 38 and 39.

Conclusion

The doomsday scenario of "standing room only" suggests a juggernaut inexorably bearing down upon the world, subject to no control. But such forecasts have a very poor track record. The data suggest that not only starvation and disease act to control population size; rather, a variety of economic, political, and social forces are also important. To understand these forces is the task of the following chapter, which will show how such an understanding can help us predict what the future holds in store if we adopt one or another policy toward population growth.

Even when we have the correct data, the gross numbers can sometimes be misleading. Some of the implications of the long-run trends—an increasing "labor scarcity" in the world, and at least for some time a decline in population density in most areas in the developed world, for example—will surely seem strange if stated out of context.

24

Do Humans Breed Like Flies?
Or Like Norwegian Rats?

> If we breed like rabbits, in the long run we have to live and die like rabbits.
> (A. J. Carlson, "Science versus Life," Journal of the American Medical Association, 1955)

> Heavier than air flying machines are impossible.
> (Lord Kelvin, the world's greatest physicist at the time, in 1895, in Cerf and Navasky 1984)

> Man will not fly for fifty years.
> (Wilbur Wright to Orville Wright, 1901, in Cerf and Navasky 1984)

MANY WHO WORRY about population growth in poor countries assert that people breed "naturally." That is, poor people are assumed to have sexual intercourse without taking thought or doing anything about the possible consequences.

In the words of environmentalist William Vogt, whose *Road to Survival* sold millions of copies, population growth in Asia is due to "untrammeled copulation" by Muslims, Sikhs, Hindus, and the rest of "the backward billion."[1] Biologist Karl Sax asserted that "nearly two thirds of the world's people still rely largely on positive checks [death by starvation and disease] to control excessive growth of populations."[2] Or as Robert C. Cook, the long-time population activist and editor of *Population Bulletin*, put it more politely, "Over a billion adults in less developed countries live outside the realm of decision-making on this matter" of family size.[3] This idea goes hand in hand with the view that population growth will increase geometrically until starvation or famines halt it, in the ever-ascending curve shown in figure 22-1.

The same view of human behavior underlies the assertion of Herman Daly and Clifford Cobb that "our current practice [is] allowing new human beings to be unintended by-products of the sexual fumblings of teenagers whose natural urges have been stimulated by drugs, alcohol, TV, and ill-constructed welfare incentives."[4]

The notion of "natural breeding," "natural fertility," and "untrammeled copulation" has been buttressed by the animal-ecology experiments that some biologists offer as analogies to human population growth. Their models include John B. Calhoun's famous Norwegian rats in a pen,[5] hypothetical flies in a bottle or germs in a bucket,[6] and meadow mice or cotton rats,[7] which will indeed keep multiplying until they die for lack of sustenance. Daniel 0. Price, in *The 99th Hour*, gives a typical example of this view.

> Assume there are two germs in the bottom of a bucket, and they double in number every hour. (If the reader does not wish to assume that it takes two germs to reproduce, he may start with one germ, one hour earlier.) If it takes one-hundred hours for the bucket to be full of germs, at what point is the bucket one-half full of germs? A moment's thought will show that after ninety-nine hours the bucket is only half full. The title of this volume is not intended to imply that the United States is half full of people but to emphasize that it is possible to have "plenty of space left" and still be precariously near the upper limit.[8]

It is interesting that a similar analogy was suggested by Benjamin Franklin two centuries ago. In Malthus's words:

> It is observed by Dr. Franklin, that there is no bound to the prolific nature of plants or animals, but what is made by their crowding and interfering with each others' means of substinence. . . . This is incontrovertibly true. . . . In plants and animals the view of the subject is simple. They are all impelled by a powerful instinct to the increase of their species and this instinct is interrupted by no reasoning or doubts about providing for their offspring . . . the superabundant effects are repressed afterwards by want of room and nourishment . . . and among animals, by their becoming the prey of each other.[9]

Perhaps the most nightmarish of the biological analogies came from Alan Gregg, the former director of the Rockefeller Foundation's Medical Division: "There is an alarming parallel between the growth of a cancer in the body of an organism and the growth of human population in the earth's ecological economy."[10] Gregg then asserts that "cancerous growths demand food; but so far as I know, they have never been cured by getting it. . . . The analogies can be found in our plundered planet." Gregg then goes on to observe "how nearly the slums of our great cities resemble the necrosis of tumors." And this "raises the whimsical query: Which is the more offensive to decency and beauty, slums or the fetid detritus of a growing tumor?"[11]

Some demographic facts suggest that humans will increase the number of children when conditions permit. After food supplies and living conditions began to improve in European countries several centuries ago, the birthrate rose. And the same effect has been observed in the poor countries in the twentieth century. "While the data are not so good as to give decisive evidence, it seems very likely that natality has risen over the past generation—certainly in the West Indies, very likely in tropical America, and probably in a number of countries of Africa and Asia."[12]

But we must recognize what Malthus eventually came to recognize. After he published the short simplistic theory in the first edition of his *Essay on Population*, he took the time to consider the facts as well as the theory. He then concluded that human beings are very different from flies or rats. When faced with the limits of a bottle-like situation, people can alter their behavior in the short run so as to accommodate to that limit, and in the long run people usually alter the limit itself.

Unlike plants and animals, people are capable of foresight and may abstain from having children from "fear of misery." That is, people can choose a level of fertility that fits the resources that will be available. As Malthus put it in his later writing, "Impelled to the increase of his species by an equally powerful instinct, reason interrupts his career, and asks him whether he may not bring beings into the world, for whom he cannot provide the means of support."[13]

People can also alter the limit—expand the "bottle" or the "lily pond"—by consciously increasing the resources available. When the town's population has grown enough so that the school is full, the town builds an additional school—usually a better one than the old school. The arithmetic about how many doublings it takes to fill the container is nothing but pretty arithmetic, wholly irrelevant to human issues.

Malthus came to stress the difference between the breeding of animals and of humans, and he decisively rejected Benjamin Franklin's animal analogy: "The effects of this [preventive] check on man are more complicated. . . . The preventive check is peculiar to man, and arises from that distinctive superiority in his reasoning faculties, which enables him to calculate distant consequences."[14] Human beings are different from the animals in that we have much more capacity to alter our behavior—including our fertility—to meet the demands of our environment.

To control fertility in response to the conditions facing them, people must be capable of rational, self-conscious forethought that affects the course of sexual passion—the kind of planning capability that animals apparently do not possess. Therefore, we must briefly ponder the extent to which reason and reasoning have guided the reproductive behavior of individual persons in various societies at different periods in their histories. To put the matter bluntly, we must inquire into the notion—often held by the highly educated—that uneducated people in poor countries tend to breed without foresight or conscious control.

For most couples in most parts of the world, marriage precedes childbearing. It is therefore relevant to a judgment about the amount of reasoning involved in "breeding" that marriages are contracted, in most primitive and poor societies, only after a great deal of careful thought, especially with reference to the economic effects of the marriage. How a marriage match is made in rural Ireland shows the importance of such calculations.

The young lady's father asks the speaker what fortune do he want. He asks him the place of how many cows, sheep, and horses is it? He asks what makings of a garden are in it; is there plenty of water or spring wells? Is it far from the road, he won't take it. Backward places don't grow big fortunes. And he asks, too, is it near a chapel and the school or near town? The Inagh countryman could pause here; he had summarized a very long and important negotiation.

"Well," he went on, getting to the heart of the matter, if it is a nice place, near the road, and the place of eight cows, they are sure to ask 350 fortune [pounds dowry]." Then the young lady's father offers 250. Then maybe the boy's father throws off 50. If the young lad's father still has 250 on it, the speaker divides the 50 between them. So now it's 275. Then the young man says he is not willing to marry without 300— but if she's a nice girl and a good housekeeper, he'll think of it. So there's another drink by the young man, and then another by the young lady's father, and so on with every second drink till they're near drunk. The speaker gets plenty and has a good day.[15]

An astute weighing of economic conditions is also seen to affect marriage in a Southern Italian town that was "as poor as any place in the western world."[16] The young man whose account is given lived in a family of four whose total yearly cash and computed income amounted to $482 in 1955 dollars. Edward Banfield described the courtship and marriage decision.

In 1935 I was old enough to marry. My sisters wanted me to take a wife because they had no time to do services for me.

At that time there was a law that anyone who was 25 years old and not married had to pay a "celibacy" tax of 125 lire. That amount was much, if we recall that to earn it you had to work 25 days. I thought it over and finally decided to marry.

My present wife was at that time working with relatives of my employer. Once I stopped her and asked her to marry me, and she liked the idea too, but I had to tell it before her father. He was happy to accept me, and we talked about what she had to bring as dowry and what I had to do.

He asked me to bring my mother to call so that everything would be fine. The next time I brought my mother, and we had a nice feast. When I wanted to meet my fiancee I had to ask the boss' permission. In 1937 I asked the girl and her family to hasten the marriage before I was 25 years old. The father told me that she was not ready with the dowry. I asked him if at least we couldn't have the civil ceremony on February 6, 1938, two months late, so that I had to pay the tax for that year.

Once my mother and I went to Addo to visit my father-in-law in order to discuss and establish definitely what they were going to give us [in the dowry]. My mother wanted everything to be conveyed through a notary. My father-in-law gave us one tomolo of land and my mother gave the little house, but she reserved for herself the right to use it. Everything was written on official tax-stamp paper by the notary. As soon as my wife was ready with the dowry the church marriage was set for August 25, 1938.[17]

As to reason and self-control *after* marriage, there has been much debate among demographers in recent years about whether in pre-modern societies fertility is or is not "natural"—that is, at a rate equal to the biological limit. As I read that literature, those who reject the "natural fertility" proposition have the better data and analyses,[18] but a conclusive answer is still to come.

In virtually no observed society (except, paradoxically, the very modern Hutterites in the United States and Canada, and a few other such groups) does actual fertility approach women's fecundity (potential fertility). And in many "primitive" societies, fertility is quite low.[19]

The anthropological evidence for fertility control within marriage also seems convincing. Even among the most "primitive" and "backward" of people, fertility seems to be subject to both personal and social constraints. One example is the "primitive" (as of 1936) Polynesian island of Tikopia, where "strong social conventions enforce celibacy upon some people and cause others to limit the number of their offspring,"[20] and "the motive of a married pair is the avoidance of the extra economic liability which a child brings."[21] Another example is the effect of the size of the harvest on marriages in Sweden in the eighteenth century (a backward agricultural country then, but one that happened to keep good vital statistics). When the harvest was poor, people did not marry, as figure 24-1 shows. Birthrates were also responsive to the harvest, and even unmarried procreation was affected by objective economic conditions. This is clear evidence that poor people's sexual behavior is sensibly responsive to objective circumstances.

After an extensive study of the anthropological literature, A. M. Carr-Saunders concluded, "The mechanism whereby numbers may be kept near to the desirable level is everywhere present,"[22] the particular mechanisms being "prolonged abstention from intercourse, abortion, and infanticide."[23] And as a result of a study of "data on 200 societies from all over the world . . . from tropic to arctic . . . from sea level to altitudes of more than 10,000 feet," Clellan S. Ford concluded that "both abortion and infanticide are universally known. . . . It is extremely common . . . to find a taboo on sexual intercourse during the period when the mother is nursing. . . . In nearly every instance, the justification for this abstinence is the prevention of conception."[24] He also found instances of many kinds of contraceptive practices. Some are "clearly magical." Others "are relatively effective mechanical devices [for example] inserting a pad of bark cloth or a rag in the vagina . . . [and] attempts to flush out the seminal fluid with water after intercourse."[25]

In the 1960s there was a widely reported estimate that five million U.S. women lacked access to contraception, but later analysis produced a more solid estimate of 1.2 million women.[26] Surveys document that perhaps 10 percent of children born in the United States in the 1980s were the result of lack of knowledge of or access to contraception and could be said to be "un-

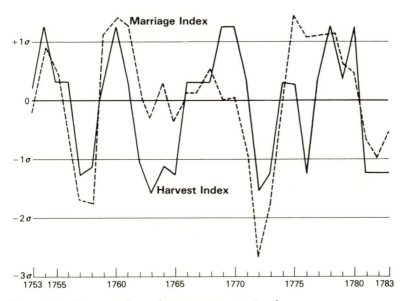

Figure 24-1. Harvest Index and Marriage Rates in Sweden

wanted" by the *mothers* at the time of conception, and many of these mothers later became glad that they had the children.[27] If the definition of "unwanted" included both the mother *and* the father, the proportion of "unwanted" at conception would be much lower yet.

There continue to be some supposed experts and officials of anti-population-growth organizations who, on the basis of discredited anthropological accounts, assert that poor people do not know how babies are made—a notion so silly that it should not be necessary even to mention it. For example, "not only are animals ignorant of the relation between mating and offspring, but even modern man until the last few thousand years was probably equally ignorant. In fact, there were recent reports of primitive tribes in Australia who are similarly unenlightened today."[28]

More to be believed are such stories as the one about a "primitive" tribesman who said to another, "Do you know what I told that white man? I told him I don't know how to make a baby. And—get this—he believed it!" This joke has now been documented in astonishing fashion. Ever since the 1920s, Margaret Mead's *Coming of Age in Samoa* has been considered as great a classic in anthropology as any other book, providing the foundation for an entire ruling theory of human behavior. In 1983 Derek Freeman disproved her account, using a variety of materials. But more recently there emerged incontrovertible evidence that Mead was not only wrong, but had been hoaxed.

> If Mead's conclusion of 1928 had been correct it would have been the most important conclusion of twentieth-century anthropology. It is now known that Mead's long-influential conclusion was wholly false. In 1983 I was able to demonstrate in detail that Mead's extreme conclusion was very definitely not supported by the relevant ethnographic evidence. And since then, there have been even more significant developments.
>
> It had long been a major mystery that Mead's account of Samoan sexual behavior, on which her conclusion rests, is radically at odds with the reports of all other ethnographers. This mystery was solved in 1987, when Fa'apua'a Fa'amu, who is listed in *Coming of Age in Samoa* as one of her principal informants, came forward to confess that in March of 1926, as a prank, she and her friend Fofoa, had completely hoaxed Margaret Mead by telling her, when she questioned them, the antithesis of the truth about Samoan sexual behavior and values.
>
> In Samoa the playing of such pranks, which they call taufa'ase'e, is commonplace . . . when Mead put to Fa'apua'a, who was herself a taupou or ceremonial virgin, the supposition that she was promiscuous, she and Fafoa, with sidelong glances and pinching one another, set about hoaxing her. They had no idea, says Fa'apua'a, that Margaret Mead was an author and that their wild untruths would be published as facts in an immensely influential book.
>
> After Fa'apua'a's testimony had been carefully checked by Leulu Felisi Va'a of the National University of Samoa . . . a sworn deposition by Fa'apua'a Fa'amu has been lodged with the American Anthropological Association in Washington, D.C.[29]

What testimony, then, can we trust? Clear evidence that poor people consider their incomes and economic circumstances when thinking about having children is found in their answers to questions about the disadvantages and advantages of large families. A variety of such surveys in various parts of Africa reveal that economic motivations are indeed important.[30]

Study after study shows that poor people do indeed think about economic circumstances in relationship to fertility. They do not practice "untrammeled copulation" or "breed without limit."

People in developed countries, too, are accustomed to think about how family size fits their incomes.

> GRENOBLE, France—a 29-year-old grade school teacher gave birth yesterday to quintuplets, three boys and two girls. . . . The children's grandfather, a tailor, said, "This certainly creates a lot of problems and you can't say it's really a joyous event because you've got to think about raising the little wolves."[31]

Lee Rainwater interviewed 409 Americans about "their family design." In representative interviews with three pairs of husbands and wives, all men tioned economic factors predominantly, though many other factors were also mentioned, of course.

> "Husband 1: Would [I] prefer two or four children? I guess two because you can give two more than four. You can send them to college. The average family could not give four very much. . . . Two is all we can support adequately.
>
> Wife 1: Two, but if I had loads of money I would want loads of kids. . . . If I had lots of money, enough for full-time help, and plenty of room I would like half-a-dozen or more.
>
> Husband 2: I think two is ideal for the average American family based on an average income of $5,000 [1950 dollars]. I don't see how they could properly provide for more children. Personally I'd take a dozen if I could afford them. I wanted four when we got married or as many as the family income could support.
>
> Wife 3: I think three is ideal because I feel this is all most people are equipped to raise, to give a good education and send them through college.[32]

Another study asked a sample of U.S. wives why their intended family size was not bigger. The first reason given by more than half of the respondents was economic.[33]

In brief, even though income in rich countries is ample to provide a bare subsistence for many more children than the average family chooses to have, people say that their incomes constrain their family size. In all societies, rich or poor, people give much thought to sex, marriage, and childbearing. Fertility is everywhere subject to some rational control, though the degree to which achieved family sizes match the desired size varies from group to group. Couples in some countries plan their family size more carefully and are better able to carry such plans to fruition than are couples in other countries because of differences in contraceptive technology, infant mortality, and communication between husband and wife. But certainly there is strong evidence that people everywhere think rationally about fertility; hence, income and other objective forces influence fertility behavior to a significant degree, everywhere and always.

An interesting example of how home economics affects fertility occurred in East Germany following the introduction in 1976 of incentives to have more children. Prior to that time fertility in East and West Germany had been much the same. But the incentives raised marital fertility at least temporarily (perhaps just having some births occur earlier) and more permanently raised extra-marital fertility, as figure 24-2 shows.

The fact that there are large families in some poor countries does not prove the absence of rational planning in matters of fertility. Behavior that is reasonable in London or Tokyo may well be unreasonable in a Tibetan or African village. The costs of rearing children are relatively less, and the economic benefits of having children are relatively greater, in poor agricultural commu-

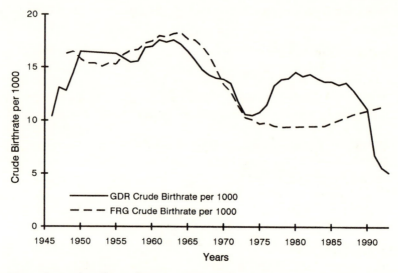

Figure 24-2. The Effects of Family Policies in Germany

nities than in well-off urban places. Therefore, even though the primary motive for having children—in Nigeria as in France—surely is that couples want
children for the satisfactions they give, the economic conditions may differ in
such a manner that the same desire for children that sensibly implies a two- or
three-child family in a city may imply a five- or six-child family in a poor rural
area. The economics of child-rearing involve the amounts of time and money
that people spend on children, on the one hand, and the amounts of work that
children perform and the old-age support they render after they grow up, on
the other hand. It costs more time and money to rear children in urban than
in rural areas, and children in rural areas of poor countries perform more work
than children elsewhere.[34] Hence the larger average size of rural families may
reflect sound economic planning. We see this vividly in the following accounts from the period of very high population growth a decade or two ago.

BABARPUR, India, May 24, 1976—Munshi Ram, an illiterate laborer who lives in a
crude mud hut in this village 60 miles north of New Delhi, has no land and very little
money. But he has eight children, and he regards them as his greatest wealth.

"It's good to have a big family," Mr. Ram explained as he stood in the shade of a
leafy neem tree, in a hard dry courtyard crowded with children, chickens and a
dozing cow.

"They don't cost much, and when they get old enough to work they bring in
money. And when I am old, they will take care of me. . . ."

Mr. Ram, who says he is not likely to have more children, is aware that the Government is now campaigning hard with the birth-control slogan, "Stop at two." But he
has no regrets.

"Children are the gods' gift," he said, as several of his own clustered around him. "Who are we to say they should not be born?"[35]

Here are two more examples, this time through the eyes of an Indian writer.

Let us take a few examples. Fakir Singh is a traditional water carrier. After he lost his job, he remained as a messenger for those Jat families which used to be his Jajmans, barely earning a subsistence living. He has eleven children, ranging in age from twenty-five to four. . . . Fakir Singh maintains that every one of his sons is an asset. The youngest one—aged five or six—collects hay for the cattle; the older ones tend to those same cattle. Between the ages of six and sixteen, they earn 150 to 200 rupees a year, plus all their meals and necessary clothing. Those sons over sixteen earn 2,000 rupees and meals every year. Fakir Singh smiles and adds, "To raise children may be difficult, but once they are older it is a sea of happiness."

Another water carrier is Thaman Singh. . . . He welcomed me inside his home, gave me a cup of tea (with milk and "market" sugar, as he proudly pointed out later), and said, "You were trying to convince me in 1960 that I shouldn't have any more sons. Now, you see, I have six sons and two daughters and I sit at home in leisure. They are grown up and they bring me money. One even works outside the village as a laborer. You told me I was a poor man and couldn't support a large family. Now, you see, because of my large family, I am a rich man."[36]

Hand in hand with the short-run reduction in fertility when times worsen in a poor country is the short-run increase in fertility that accompanies a betterment of conditions. Consider, for example, this report about an Indian village:

In the early 1950's, conditions were distinctly unfavorable. The large influx of refugees from Pakistan was accompanied by severe disruption of economic and social stability. We were repeatedly told by village leaders on the panchayat, or elected village council, that important as all of their other problems were, "the biggest problem is that there are just too many of us." By the end of the study period in 1960 a remarkable change had occurred. With the introduction of more irrigation canals and with rural electrification from the Bhakra Nangal Dam, and with better roads to transport produce to market, improved seed and other benefits of community development, and especially because there were increasing employment opportunities for Punjabi boys in the cities, a general feeling of optimism had developed. A common response of the same village leaders now was, "Why should we limit our families? India needs all the Punjabis she can get." During this transitional period an important reason for the failure of education in family planning was the favorable pace of economic development. Children were no longer a handicap.[37]

Infant mortality is another influence that uneducated villagers take into account very rationally. In 1971 I asked a few men in Indian villages why they have as many or as few children as they do. A common answer came from a man with five children, "Two, maybe three will die, and I want to have at least two that live to become adults." But by the 1990s villagers in most parts of the world know that the infant mortality rate has fallen very fast in recent decades, and they need not have many more babies than the number of children they want to raise to maturity. This change in conditions, and in people's perception of the change, is part of the reason that fertility has fallen rapidly in so many countries, as seen in figure 23-5.

Malthus's theory of population asserts that because fertility goes up if income goes up due to new technical knowledge of agriculture, the extra population eats up the additional income. That is, Malthus asserted a tendency for humankind to be squeezed down to a long-run equilibrium of living at bare subsistence; this is Malthus's "dismal theorem." But when we examine the facts about fertility and economic development (as Malthus himself finally did, after he quickly dashed off his first edition), we find that the story does not end with the short-run increase in the birthrate as income first rises. If income continues to rise, fertility later goes down.

There are two main reasons for this long-run decline in fertility. First, as income rises in poor countries, child mortality falls because of better nutrition, better sanitation, and better health care (though, in the twentieth century, mortality may decline in poor countries even without a rise in income). As couples see that fewer births are necessary to achieve a given family size, they adjust fertility downward. Evidence on response of families to the death of a child buttresses the overall historical data. Several careful researchers have shown that there is a strong relationship between the death of a child and subsequent births in a family.[38] That is, couples produce additional children to "make up for" children who die. If we also consider that families decide to have additional children to allow for deaths that might occur in the future, the relationship between child mortality and fertility shows that childbearing is responsive to the family's circumstances.

A rise in income also reduces fertility in the long run through a cluster of forces set in motion by increased income, including (a) increased education, which improves contraception, makes children more expensive to raise, and perhaps alters people's tastes about having children; and (b) a trend to city living, where children cost more and produce less income for the family than they do in the country.

The decline in mortality and the other forces set in motion by economic development reduce fertility in the long run. This process is the famous "demographic transition." We see it very clearly in the excellent historical data for Sweden shown in figure 23-6; notice how the death rate began to fall *before* the birthrate fell. And we can see the same relationship between income and birthrate in a cross-sectional look at various countries of the world (see fig. 24-3).

From the 1930s through the 1950s, most demographers were convinced that the demographic transition would take place in developing countries in

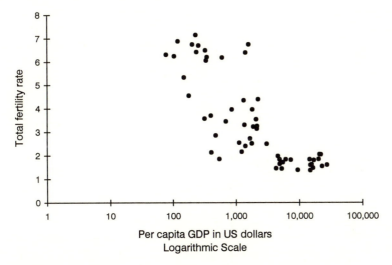

Figure 24-3. Per Capita Gross Domestic Product Plotted against the Crude Birthrate for Selected Nations

the twentieth century, just as it had earlier happened in Europe and North America. Then in the 1960s demographers began to worry that fertility would not fall in poor countries even after mortality fell. But in the 1970s, evidence showed that fertility was indeed falling in at least some developing countries. By the time of the first edition of this book in 1981, I wrote that we could be *reasonably* sure that the European pattern of demographic transition will also appear in other parts of the world as mortality falls and income rises, though there were still many doubters, especially those who run anti-natalist organizations. In the 1990s we can take out the qualifier "reasonably," because the fall has appeared almost everywhere, and in all the countries with large populations, as seen in figure 23-5.

Worth mentioning because many persons believe that teenage childbearing in the United States runs counter to the general pattern, fertility has fall among the fifteen to nineteen age group over the long run, as figure 24-4 shows, though the latter half of the 1980s showed an upturn too brief to be meaningful.

So the foundation is gone from under Malthus's grand theory and his dismal theorem. At the heart of Malthus's theory—quoting from his last edition—is the following: "(1) Population is necessarily limited by the means of subsistence. (2) Population always increases when the means of subsistence increases."[39] The history of the demographic transition and the data in figure 23-8 disprove the second proposition. The first proposition is shown to be false in chapters 5–8.

Contrary to Malthus, people respond to the two major influences on fertil-

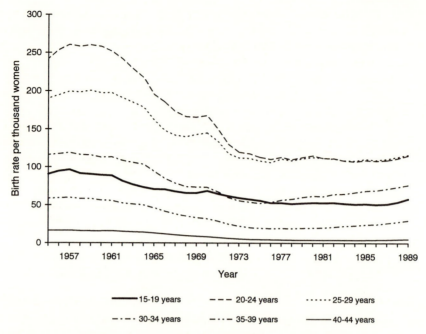

Figure 24-4. Teenage and Other Birthrates, United States, 1955–1989

ity—mortality and level of income—in an economically appropriate fashion. Of course there are delays, especially in the response of society as a whole to changes in the cost of a family's children to other people in the community. But overall, the fertility-adjustment system works in such a fashion that it leads to an optimistic outlook rather than the "dismal" view described by Malthus in the famous first edition of his book, before he changed that view in the second edition.[40]

How many children would families have if material resources presented no constraints at all? That is, what would be the level of fertility if child mortality were as low as in advanced countries now, and if income were very high—say, ten times the level in the United States now? We have little basis for predicting whether population would tend to increase, decrease, or stabilize in the long run in such a case, because there is no experience to learn from. It is clear, however, that where the material conditions of income and child mortality are harsh, fertility adjusts to meet those conditions, even among poor and uneducated people.

But what about the costs that big families impose on society as a whole? Certainly this is a reasonable and important question, because any child does impose some monetary and nonmonetary costs on persons other than the parents. There are two parts to the answer:

1. An additional person causes not only costs but also benefits for others in a variety of ways that we shall discuss later. The central question may be expressed quantitatively: Which are greater in various years following a child's birth, the costs or the benefits to others? Once we know whether these "external" effects are positive or negative in any given year, we must next ask: Are the external effects large or small compared with other costs and benefits in the economy? These matters are discussed in chapters 25 and 34.

2. The burden upon the community of an additional child depends very greatly upon the nature of the economic-political system. In Chinese cities, where housing and transportation systems are owned by the government, an additional child imposes a much larger burden upon others than in the United States, where schooling is the only major cost of a child that the parents do not pay from their own pockets. If the parents pay the full costs of a child, their individual childbearing decisions are likely to be optimal for the community at large.

Summary

At the heart of much of contemporary theorizing about population growth is the belief that, as one widely read author put it, "The Malthusian laws of population are as valid today as when they were formulated" (in the first edition of his *Essay*).* The core of those "laws" is that population increases faster than does the means of sustenance until the standard of living has fallen to bare subsistence. Those who urge this proposition support it with analogies drawn from other forms of life. "The germs of existence contained in this earth, if they could freely develop themselves, would fill millions of worlds in the course of a few thousand years. Necessity, that imperious, all-pervading law of nature, restrains them within the prescribed bounds. The race of plants and the race of animals shrink under this great restrictive law and men cannot by any efforts of reason escape from it."**

* Indeed they are "as valid": invalid then, invalid now.

** The notion of a geometrical (or exponential growth in population has been around a very long time. It was old stuff by Malthus's time. Jefferson (Koch and Peden 1944, p. 327) used it in a matter-of-fact fashion when speaking with satisfaction of the population growth of the United States.

One cannot sensibly say, however, whether or not the experience of humanity evidences such a growth pattern, and hence whether there is a tendency to do so. The rate of growth has been much higher in a few periods than in most other periods (see fig. 22-2), and the rate has tended to increase over the millenia until now, which argues against smooth geometrical growth (but for *faster* than geometrical growth). The variations from any simple pattern are so great, however, that in my view a prudent forecaster would not forecast a future rate on the basis of such a pattern for anything shorter than a period of many millenia.

Nor is the idea of "ideal" geometrical growth useful, I think. One might observe such a pattern for a nonhuman species for a short time in a controlled environment in which nutriment is

Implicit in this statement, and quite explicit in Malthus's first edition and in the writings of many writers today, is the assumption that people—or at least poor people—breed "naturally" and "without limit," due to "untrammeled copulation." But as Malthus came to accept in his subsequent editions, and as is shown with a variety of evidence in this chapter, people everywhere give much thought to marriage, sex, and procreation. The notion of "untrammeled copulation" expresses either ignorance or untruth.

Income affects fertility everywhere. In poor countries, an increase in income leads in the short run to an increase in fertility. But in the longer run, in poor countries as elsewhere, a sustained increase in income leads eventually to a decrease in fertility. Decreased child mortality, increased education, and movement from country to city all contribute to this lowering of the birthrate. This process is known as the "demographic transition." Malthus's early (but still popularly accepted) theorizing—which he himself later rejected—does not fit the facts.

---

continually unlimited. But this is hardly a reasonable basis for drawing conclusions about growth in other environments for nonhuman species, nor for drawing conclusions for humans, who supply their own nutrition in a very systematic feedback manner.

I think one must conclude that this is a classic case of the importation of a concept useful in one field to another field where it has no relevance, simply because of its intellectual power and charm.

Furthermore, if one believed that the exponential model is a good one—that is, if one assumes that population grows exponentially—it would be reasonable to assume that subsistence grows at an *even faster* exponential rate (largely but not entirely because of population growth). And capacity to produce new technical knowledge of subsistence and other aspects of the standard of living grows at a still faster exponential rate, due in large part to the growth of knowledge.

25

Population Growth and the Stock of Capital

THE AMOUNT of physical capital—equipment and buildings—available to a worker influences his or her output and income. Nonphysical capital such as the education, skill, and dedication of the worker—whether at a machine or at a desk—is very important, too, and we shall discuss it shortly. But the availability of machinery, buildings, and other physical capital certainly has a strong effect on the amount of goods and services that a person can produce.

People must save some part of their income in order to build a stock of capital. Therefore, the amount we save from our present incomes influences our future incomes and consumption. And population growth and size may influence the amount of saving.

Population affects our stock of physical capital both positively and negatively. On balance, the effect is positive.

The productivity of the equipment available for purchase at a given moment also is affected by population size. A larger population, and a higher income level, increases the demand for new capital goods to be invented and developed, and a larger population also increases the supply of new inventors, both of which lead to more efficient equipment. So by way of the forces of both supply and demand, a larger population increases the technology of capital goods. More about that in the next chapter.

Simple Theory and Data

Let us start the analysis with a given population of workers and a given supply of physical capital—a given farm acreage, a given number of factories, and a given number of machines. If the number of workers increases, then the supply of capital will be diluted; that is, if there are more workers, there is less capital available for each worker to use. If there is less capital per worker, output (and income) per worker will fall. This Malthusian dilution effect is one of the main liabilities of additional population. The extent of the loss can be calculated easily. Twice as many workers with the same capital implies half as much capital per worker. In a typical modern economy this would reduce each worker's output (and hence income) by about one-third.

Population growth also may reduce the available capital per worker because, in order to build and maintain a stock of capital, people must save part of their incomes. Savings can come directly from individuals and businesses, and some of the money extracted as taxes can also be saved by the government. We shall focus on individual saving, however.

A higher birthrate was long thought to reduce the rate of individual saving simply because an additional child is a burden on the family's income. This line of argument assumes that additional children induce parents to give a higher priority to immediate consumption (baby shoes now) than to later consumption (a trip around the world after retirement). That is, parents with (say) five hungry children were assumed to spend more out of income, and hence save less, than with (say) two children. The basis for this assumption is simply the psychological guess that more children mean more pleas, requests, and demands, pressure that shifts the parents' preferences in such a way that they spend more of their income sooner. But there may also be an opposing effect. More children may induce parents to forego some luxuries in order to save for the children's future needs—for example, a college education.

The former line of argument implicitly (but wrongly) assumes that earning opportunities are fixed, so that a greater number of children cannot induce parents to go out and work more. But to assume that income is fixed, rather than variable in response to the number of children, also is unrealistic. It is well documented that the more children men have, the more they work; so, too, women after their children are no longer young. Assuming income to be fixed is particularly inappropriate for subsistence agriculture; a large portion of agricultural saving—especially the clearing of new land and the construction of irrigation systems—is accomplished through the farmers' own labor, and this is usually added to the labor they expend in raising their crops. Population growth stimulates this extra labor, and hence adds to the community's stock of capital.

The effects of more children on governmental saving may also be important. It is often assumed that in poor countries governments have less power to tax if people have more children, because the competition in the family budget between feeding children and paying taxes is then more acute. One can also reason in the opposite direction, however. If there are more children, governments may be able to extract *more* in taxes, because people recognize a greater need for taxes to buy additional schools and other facilities. The number of children may also affect the kinds of investments that governments make. For example, an increase in children may induce a government to invest more, but much of this increase might be in housing and other "demographic" investment at the expense of the sort of capital investment that will immediately increase the production of goods.

The statistical evidence about the effect of population growth upon the savings rate is as mixed and inconclusive as the theorizing. Taken together, the data suggest that a population increase may slightly reduce the formation of industrial capital, but this is probably not an important effect.[1]

The efficiency of capital, as well as the quantity of it, is also important. And there has recently developed a strong body of evidence showing that capital is used more efficiently in larger communities. For example, less capital is needed for a given amount of productivity per person in larger cities.[2] This jibes with the fact that wages are higher in bigger cities in a sample of countries.[3] Further, interest rates are lower in bigger cities, which implies that capital is cheaper.[4] In sum, the evidence suggests that one can get more output from a given capital investment where there are more people.

When we think about the effect of additional children on the supply of capital, it is crucial that we keep in mind farm capital and social-overhead capital as well as industrial capital. In chapter 28 we shall see that the supply of farm capital—especially arable land—increases when population increases because people respond to the demand for additional food with increased investment, much of which is additional labor to clear trees and stones, dig ditches, and build barns.

The effect of additional persons on the supply of capital is most marked with respect to social-overhead capital such as roads, which are crucial for the economic development of all countries and especially poor countries. Here the effect of population is sharply positive, especially in less-developed countries.

The Transportation Connection

If there is a single key to economic development other than economic liberty, that key is the transportation and communication system. Transportation obviously includes roads and railways and airlines, which carry agricultural and industrial products as well as persons and messages. It also includes irrigation and electrical systems, which transport water and power. There is abundant testimony by scholars of contemporary and historical economic development that "one sure generalization about the underdeveloped countries is that investment in transport and communications is a vital factor."[5]

Enabling farmers and businesses to sell in organized markets, and to deliver output and obtain delivery of inputs at reasonable cost, is crucial to a developing economy. A comparison of the costs of transportation by various methods is illuminating. Examples: (1) Canal transportation cost only 25–50 percent as much as land transportation between cities in England about 1790.[6] (2) "In August 1799 a courier set out from Detroit to deliver U.S. Army muster rolls to headquarters in Pittsburgh [perhaps 200 miles]. His trip took fifty-three days of hard riding."[7] (3) Carrying loads on human backs is seventeen times as expensive as by ship or train, on average[8] (see table 25-1). Such cost differences greatly affect the amounts of merchandise transported, and the prices at various distances from the producer.

TABLE 25-1

Transport Costs in Developing Countries
(expressed as kilograms grain equivalent/ton-kilometer transported)

	Maximum	Median	Minimum
Porterage	12.4 (East Africa)	8.6	4.6 (China)
Wheelbarrow			3.2 (China)
Pack Animals	11.6 (East Africa, donkey)	4.1	1.9 (Middle East, camel)
Wagons	16.4 (18th century, England, milk collection)	3.4	1.6 (U.S.A. 1800)
Boats	5.8 (Ghana 1900)	1.0	0.2 (China 11th century)
Steam boats		0.5	
Railways	1.4 (Australia 1850s)	0.45	0.1 (Chile 1937)
Motor vehicles	12.5 (Basutoland)[a]	1.0	0.15 (Thailand)

Source: Clark and Haswell 1967, p. 189.

[a] This figure hardly seems meaningful.

Lack of a good transportation system presents an enormous barrier against development. In the early nineteenth-century United States, for example, farm products could be transported only where there were natural waterways. As for overland transport, "the cost . . . was so high that even if corn had cost nothing to produce, it could not have been marketed twenty miles from where it was grown. It was cheaper to move a ton of iron across the Atlantic than to carry it ten miles through Pennsylvania." But the Erie Canal reduced freight rates from New York City to the Great Lakes from $100 to $15 per ton.[9] (Similarly in eighteenth-century France, "food would not normally be transported more than 15 kilometers from its place of origin.")[10] Flour that sold for $10 or $20 a barrel on the East Coast cost $100 a barrel in Ohio. Coal cost three or four times as much in Philadelphia as at the mineheads in western Pennsylvania.[11] Such inability to transport food from farms to large markets caused a large difference between at-the-farm prices and market prices, and was responsible for frequent local famines even when food was plentiful a short distance away. My 1977 book gives a variety of other historical and contemporary examples of how improved transportation systems have stimulated agriculture and improved the efficiency of industry in various countries.

Transportation is also important in the flow of information—technical agricultural know-how, birth control, health services, modernizing ideas, and so forth. It makes an enormous difference if a particular village in India can be reached with a truck, or even a jeep or a bicycle, rather than just by a bullock, with which a trip to the big city is out of the question. Most villages in countries such as India and Iran cannot easily be reached by motor transportation. When transportation is improved, radical developmental changes will occur.

There is great room for improvement in poor countries' transportation systems, especially local rural transportation. This may be seen by a comparison between countries with well-developed agriculture and countries where agriculture is less developed.

> In agriculturally advanced Western countries, there are from 3 to 4 miles of farm to market roads per square mile of cultivated land. . . . In India there is only about 0.7 of a mile of road per square mile of cultivated land. In Malaya it is about 0.8 mile and in the Philippines about 1 mile. None of the developing countries that are dependent on agriculture has sufficient rural access roads.[12]

And in industrial areas, too, the low transportation and communication costs in larger cities lead to their higher productivity compared with smaller cities.[13]

The Effect of Population on Transportation Systems

Population density and the system of transporting goods, people, and information influence each other. On the one side, a dense population makes a good transportation system both more necessary and more economical. Having twice as many people in a village implies that twice as many people will use a wagon path if it is built, and twice as many hands can contribute to building the path. This is what happened on the Continent and in England, where "the growth of population made it worthwhile to improve and create transport facilities."[14] On the other hand, a better transportation system brings an increased population,[15] and probably leads at first to higher birthrates because of a higher standard of living. (But later the birthrates drop, as we have seen in chapter 24.) Furthermore, good transportation connections are likely to reduce a village's death rate because the village is less vulnerable to famine.

The opposite condition, population sparsity, makes traveling slow and difficult. This is how it was near Springfield, Illinois, when Abraham Lincoln was a lawyer "riding the circuit" of courts.

> Traveling was a real hardship—so real that the words of old lawyers, describing early days, become fresh and vivid when the circuit is the subject. "Between Fancy Creek and Postville, near Lincoln," wrote James C. Conkling, "there were only two or three houses. Beyond Postville, for thirteen miles was a stretch of unbroken prairie, flat and wet, covered with gopher hills, and apparently incapable of being cultivated for generations. For fifteen or eighteen miles this side of Carlinville, the country was of a similar character, without a house or improvement along the road. For about eighteen miles between South Fork and Shelbyville, there was only one clearing. I have travelled between Decatur and Shelbyville from nine o'clock in the morning until after dark over a country covered with water, from recent rains, without finding a house for shelter or refreshment."[16]

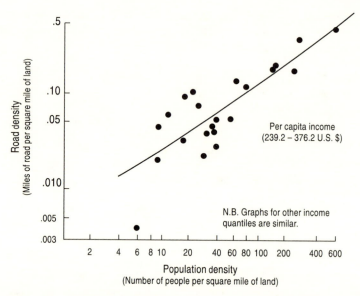

Figure 25-1. Relationship between Road Density and Population Density

Donald Glover and I made a cross-national study of the relationship between road density and population density, and we found that relationship to
be very strong, as figure 25-1 shows. Population growth clearly leads to an
improved transportation system, which in turn stimulates economic development and further population growth. This unexciting but important statistical
finding cannot, of course, match in dramatic appeal the photographs that
purportedly show population growth to be an unmitigated evil. A picture of
an emaciated starving child is surely tragic and compelling, but it conveys no
verifiable information as to why that child is suffering—as likely for the lack
of a good road and the medical attention it could bring as for any other reason.
Though the statistical fact is less exciting, it reveals an irrefutable story—the
enormous social benefits of population growth. Yet it is the picture of the
emaciated child that appears in the popular press and remains in people's
minds.

When roads and other infrastructure become burdened and congested with
an increased population and the traffic that accompanies increased income, a
variant of the basic theoretical process described in this book comes into play:
More people, and increased income, cause problems of strained capacity in
the short run. This causes transportation prices to rise and communities to
become concerned. This same state of affairs also presents opportunity to
businesses and to ingenious people who wish to contribute to society by improving roads, vehicles, and services or inventing new forms of transportation.
Many are unsuccessful, at cost to themselves. But in a free society, new facili-

ties are eventually designed and built. And in the long run the new facilities leave us *better off than if the problems had not arisen.* That is, prices end up lower, and access to transportation becomes greater, than before the congestion occurred.

The development of the Panama Canal passage from the Atlantic to the Pacific illustrates the theory.[17] When the canal was first opened, the locks were considered larger than would ever be needed. By 1939 the locks were too small to handle ships then being built, and the volume of shipping was straining capacity, so the canal was modified. An addition was planned and begun (but halted by World War II). Now the Panama Canal is so inadequate that some ships go around South America at the Straits of Magellan. Hence a new canal probably will be built—and the new one will probably be at sea level rather than using locks to lift ships up and down over the terrain—which will be a great improvement.

Population density brings a similar increase in the efficiency of communications, easily seen in a comparison of cities of very different sizes. For the same price to the reader, the daily newspaper is much larger and supplies much more information in (say) a big city like Chicago than in smaller Illinois cities. There are generally more radio and television programs available to people in larger cities (though cable television has made this more equal). And the price charged an advertiser—whether a department store or an individual seeking employment—is much lower per one thousand readers reached in a large city than in a small city, a clear benefit stemming from a larger population (see fig. 25-2).

Summary

Population growth is responsible for great improvements in the social infrastructure, especially in the transportation and communications systems that are crucial to economic development. Growth also gives a boost to agricultural saving. Population growth may or may not reduce nonagricultural saving; this is still a matter of scientific controversy. For readers who wish more detail, chapters 2, 3, 10, 11, and 12 in my technical 1977 book cover the effects of population growth on capital.

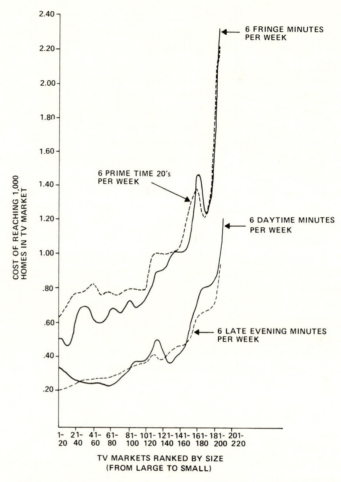

Figure 25-2. Spot TV Costs per 1,000 Homes by TV Market Size

Afternote _____

A Parable of Population Growth, Racquetball, and Squash

THIS PARABLE was written in 1980. Nothing in it has needed change except the last paragraph.

There are twenty-three wonderful handball-racquetball courts on the Urbana campus of the University of Illinois, and seven excellent squash courts, in addition to a batch of old courts. The new racquetball courts are frequently crowded nowadays, though not so badly that people complain a lot. From time to time, however, players worry about the future growth of the university, saying that it is going to be tough to get a racquetball court. And I have heard people argue against increasing the number of students for that reason.

The racquetball court situation exemplifies the country's situation with respect to population growth and the supply of capital. If there come to be more people, there will immediately be an increased demand for the courts. It will also be harder to find parking space, and perhaps a job. That is, the immediate effect of an increase in population is an increase in congestion. The individual suffers because of the greater competition for the good things that are available and because of the greater out-of-pocket costs of providing more of these good things to take care of the added population. This increase in costs is inevitable and undeniable.

But now let us take a slightly longer view. Why are players so lucky as to have twenty-three wonderful racquetball courts and seven squash courts at the University of Illinois? Years ago there were sixteen dingy wrong-size courts to be used for both sports together. But then came a rapid population growth at the university. The superb new facilities were built in response to that population growth—though at a considerable cost to the taxpayers and students at that time.

So players are now reaping the benefits of the rapid population growth in the past and at the same time talking against further population growth so that they do not have to share this stock of capital—the benefits of past population growth—with more people, and so that the taxpayers do not have to cough up the investment necessary for additional population growth. There is nothing illogical about this point of view. As the sage Hillel put it, "If I am not for myself, who will be for me?" But if we see ourselves as part of a longer historical process than this instant of our own consciousness, and if we take into account the welfare of ourselves and our children in the years to come—as people before us took our welfare into account—then we will see that we ought to cooperate and put back as well as take from the pot. As Hillel added, "But if I am for myself alone, what am I?"

Our children may well have more racquetball courts in the future—and better ones—if more children are born year after year than if fewer are born. That is, if the population does grow at the university, more courts and better courts will be built, whereas if the population stabilizes at its present size, no more facilities will be built.

More generally, if farmers had not come to Illinois and developed the land and built up the state so that it could support a university, there would certainly be no courts at all to enjoy now. Central Illinois, with its remarkably productive cornfields, would still be a malarial and unproductive swamp.

Let's consider the squash courts too. One can get into a squash court at any time of the day, except very occasionally at 5:00 in the afternoon, when there are one or two courts too few for all those who would like to play. Most of the day the squash courts are used hardly at all. From one point of view, this is paradise for squash players like me. On the other hand, there are often too few people to play with. Furthermore, there is a slightly depressing air about the squash courts. It seems a bit like a home for the aged, because most of the players are thirty-five and up except for those who have come from England or South Africa. Few young students or faculty members have taken up the game, which is why there is no problem in getting a court. In contrast, there is a vitality around the racquetball courts. There are always people watching and giving advice and jostling a bit and checking out the challenge court to see the newest rising star. The racquetball courts have produced some national-level competitors in a short time. Around the squash courts (but not on them!) it is all very dignified and peaceful. But as I said, it is also a bit depressing.

What about the future? If the population of the university grows, there is a good chance that there will still be plenty of squash courts fifteen years from now—except that the players will be doddering incompetents. And by that time the squash courts will be in rundown condition, whereas chances are that there will be a whole new battery of racquetball courts. The run-down squash courts (and players) will be the cost of having no growth in the population of squash players.

So which do you want? Will you choose the genteel, run-down, peaceful, and slightly depressing no-growth policy, as with the squash courts? Or do you prefer the less-peaceful, slightly jostling population growth that costs you capital for awhile, as with the racquetball courts?

Now, in 1996, at the University of Maryland, I play racquetball, partly because it had gotten too hard to find squash partners.

26

Population's Effects on Technology and Productivity

> But the real and legitimate goal of the sciences, is the endowment of human life with new inventions and riches.
>
> (*Francis Bacon*, Advancement of Learning and Novum Organum, *1944*)

> I think there is a world market for about five computers.
>
> (*Remark attributed to Thomas J. Watson, chairman of IBM, 1943, in Cerf and Navasky 1984*)

> Where a calculator on the ENIAC is equipped with 18,000 vacuum tubes and weighs 30 tons, computers in the future may have only 1,000 vacuum tubes and perhaps only weigh 1½ tons.
>
> (Popular Mechanics, *1949, in Cerf and Navasky 1984*)

IT IS YOUR MIND that matters economically, as much as or more than your mouth or hands. The most important economic effect of population size and growth is the contribution of additional people to our stock of useful knowledge. And this contribution is great enough in the long run to overcome all the costs of population growth. This is a strong statement, but the evidence for it seems very strong.

Many who deprecate the potential contribution of knowledge of additional people, and who would halt population growth, also make little allowance for mind-boggling discoveries yet to be made. They assume that what we now believe is impossible will always be so. Even great scientists (Ernest Rutherford and Albert Einstein in the epigraphs to chapter 13, for example) frequently underestimate the possibilities for useful discoveries, especially in fields they themselves work on. (See chapter 2 for a discussion of experts' tendencies to discount new knowledge.)

This does not imply that a higher standard of living *requires* additional discoveries. As discussed in chapter 11, we now have in our hands the knowledge to provide energy at constant or declining costs forever, and the know-how to produce food in almost inexhaustible quantities (see chapter 6). All other natural resources become less important and a smaller part of the economy with every passing decade. But additional discoveries can certainly be welcome, if only because of the excitement of scientific adventure.

Let us begin weighing the importance of new knowledge with this question: Why is the standard of living so much higher in the United States or Japan than in India or Mali? And why is the standard of living so much higher in the United States or Japan now than it was two hundred years ago? The proximate cause is that the average worker in the United States and Japan now produces X times as much in market value of goods and services per day as does the average worker in India or Mali, or as did the average worker in the United States or Japan two hundred years ago, where X is the ratio of the standard of living now in the United States or Japan to the standard in India or Mali now, or in the United States or Japan then.

Though that answer is almost definitional,[1] it points us to the important next question. Just *why* does the average worker in the United States and Japan now produce so much more? Part of the answer is that she or he has a much larger and better supply of capital equipment to work with—more buildings and tools, and more efficient transportation. But that is only a minor factor; as proof, notice how fast West Germany and Japan were able to regain a high standard of living even after much of their capital was destroyed in World War II. (They had some economic help from the United States and the benefit of being restrained from spending on the military, but these factors were not crucial.) Another part of the difference between then and now (and between rich and poor countries) is due to economies of scope—the straightforward advantages of industry size and market size—which we shall consider in the next chapter.

The most important difference between poor then and rich now, however, is that there is a much greater stock of technological know-how available now, which people are educated to learn and use. The technology and the schooling are intertwined; in both the United States and India now, unlike the United States two hundred years ago, the knowledge is available in books in the library, but without schooling it cannot be adapted to local needs and put to work. The stock of industrial capital is also intertwined with knowledge and with education; the value of many of our capital goods such as computers and jet airplanes consists largely of the new knowledge that is built into them. And without educated workers, these chunks of capital could not be operated and hence would be worthless.

The importance of technological knowledge emerged in two famous studies, one by Robert Solow and the other by Edward F. Denison.[2] Using different methods, each calculated the extent to which the growth of physical capital and of the labor force could account for economic growth in the United States (Solow and Denison) and Europe (Denison). Both found that even after capital and labor are allowed for, much of the economic growth—the "residual"—cannot be explained well by any factor other than an improvement in the level of technological practice (including improved organizational methods). Economies of scope due to larger factory size do not appear to be very important in this context, though in larger and faster-growing industries the level of technology improves more rapidly than in smaller and slower-growing ones (more about this shortly). Of course, this improvement in productivity does not come for free; much of it is bought with investments in research and development (R & D). But that does not alter the importance of the gains in technological knowledge.

Let's illustrate the growth in technical knowledge and skill with a few examples of its benefits:

1. In Roman times, the world's biggest amphitheaters could seat a few— maybe even a score or two—of thousands of people to watch a sport or entertainment. In 1990, an average of 577 million people watched on television each of the fifty-two World Cup soccer matches; a total of perhaps 2.7 billion—half the world's population—watched at least one match.[3] Not only was that enjoyable entertainment for a multitude, but for shut-ins and those in a hospital bed, games on television can be a blessed diversion from pain (a miracle I once experienced, for which I am still most grateful).

If sports and theater do not excite you, consider music. Instead of at most hundreds or thousands who could listen to a soloist or orchestra a few centuries ago—and had to pay high prices—millions and even billions can listen on radio, records, and tape, all at prices that the poorest farmers in the world can now afford. And great performances of the twentieth century will continue to be heard in future centuries and millennia, which today's performers appreciate.

2. Not much more than one century ago—after more than fifty centuries of recorded history and hundreds of centuries of unrecorded history—for the first time people had something better than firelight or an oil lamp to break the darkness after dusk. And the absence of electricity continued almost into the second half of the twentieth century for substantial portions of the population of even the richest country in the world—much of rural Kentucky, for example. Now all of us Americans take Edison's gift for granted, and the rest of the world is rapidly being wired up.

3. Less than two centuries ago there appeared the first land transportation that did not depend entirely on animal muscles. Now we complain about the ubiquity of cars. The increased maximum speed of human transportation in shown in figure 26-1. And the increased capacity to move food rapidly and cheaply is the cause of the extraordinary reduction in famine deaths worldwide (other than those due to stupid and/or murderous governments; see chapter 5). Whereas in all the centuries of human history until the 1800s, commercial overland movement of foodstuff beyond a few score miles was usually impossible, canals, then railroads, and now also roads and trucks put foods from every part of the world on your plate every day.

4. Until the past two centuries the richest potentate could not purchase any anesthetic other than alcohol to provide surcease from the hellish pains of

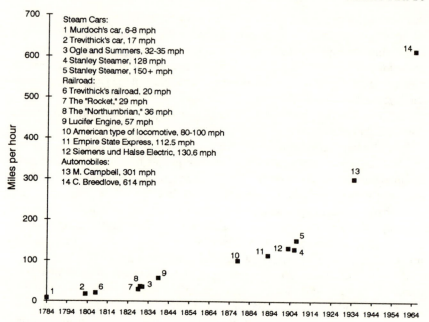

Figure 26-1a. Top Speed of Ground Transport of Humans, 1784–1967

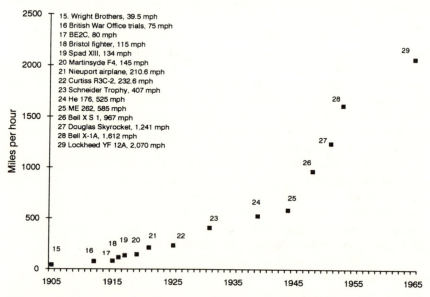

Figure 26-1b. Top Speed of Air Transport of Humans, 1905–1965 (Excluding Space Travel)

medical and dental operations, and of diseases such as cancer, nor was there any relief for women in childbirth who wanted another option besides deep breathing. What new invention in the future could match the discovery of anesthetics? Yes, we now regret the abuse of various painkillers due to low price (legal or illegal), but this marks a shift from the economic problem of boosting productivity of physical goods to other challenges for humanity.

5. The increased availability of raw materials (including food and energy), as measured by their prices relative to the price of labor, is detailed in chapters 1, 5, and 11. Increased production of food per unit of land is detailed in chapter 6. And productivity in all these activities is likely to increase indefinitely. For example, we read every day of such new processes as bacteria eating dissolved low-quality gold ore, and releasing the gold from the dirt,[4] and of plants taking in nuclear waste to speed the disposal problem (see chapter 13).

6. Increased speed of computation is a well-documented story. Typically

[I]n the early 1940s, Nicholas Fattu was the leader of a team at the University of Minnesota . . . on some statistical calculations involving large matrices. . . . He brought about ten people together in a room each of whom was given a Monroematic desk calculator. These people worked full-time for ten months in a coordinated way, carrying out the computations and cross-checking each other's results as they went along. About twenty years later. . . . Professor Fattu redid the calculations on an IBM 704 in twenty minutes.[5]

Nowadays, Fattu's calculation can be done in a fraction of a second on even a desk computer. The speed of calculation has multiplied by *a factor of about ten every seven years* over these decades, with no limit in sight.[6]

Here is an experience of my own: In the early 1970s I did a simulation of the price behavior of two competing firms. My work required tens of thousands of dollars of computer time, hour after hour in the middle of the night using the university mainframe computer, which required constant attendance by technicians. The printed output was so voluminous that it overflowed an entire small storeroom, and I had nowhere to save it. Now in the 1990s, Carlos Puig and I have returned to that work but extended it to three firms, which requires much more extensive calculations. The work is done by letting the computer chug along by itself during the night, on an ordinary desk computer that sells for much less than the cost of one hour of work on the old mainframe. And the entire output can be put onto a few one-dollar floppy disks, and sent by mail in a small envelope.

7. The future gains in productivity that technology has already created are plainly before us. Orbiting space laboratories with conditions of zero gravity already can produce protein crystals that are "much larger and provided much better structural data than those grown on Earth under identical conditions."[7] Growing new human tissues and body parts in space also seems feasible.[8] And

new possibilities of human gene therapy as well as genetic transformations of plant and animal life are reported every day.

Among all these gains in our standard of living, only personal services have not been greatly reduced in price by increased productivity—prostitution being the sharpest example (though modern transportation and communication facilitate even this transaction).

What is the role of population size and growth in the astonishing advance of human know-how? The source of these improvements in productivity is the human mind, and a human mind is seldom found apart from a human body. And because improvements—their invention and their adoption—come from people, the amount of improvement plainly depends on the number of people available to use their minds.

This is an old idea, going back at least as far as William Petty in 1682.

> As for the Arts of Delight and Ornament, they are best promoted by the greatest number of emulators. And it is more likely that one ingenious curious man may rather be found among 4 million than 400 persons. . . . And for the propagation and improvement of useful learning, the same may be said concerning it as above-said concerning . . . the Arts of Delight and Ornaments.[9]

More recently, this benefit of population size has been urged upon us by Simon Kuznets.[10]

In contrast, many of the doomsters completely omit from consideration the possibility that, all else equal, more people implies more knowledge and greater productivity. One wrote, for example, "It is difficult to see how any further growth in world population could enhance the quality of human existence. On the other hand, one can readily envisage ways in which further population increments will diminish our well-being."[11]

It is suggestive, even if the fact cannot be considered solid statistical evidence, that in ancient times high civilizations—that is, civilizations marked by such advances as the discovery of metals and the methods of working with them—did not appear in Australia or in pre-Columbian North America, where populations were few in number and sparsely distributed, in contrast to Europe, Asia, and even South America.[12]

Along about here the question often arises: If more people cause faster discovery of new knowledge, how come populous China and India are not the most advanced countries of all? Quite obviously, China and India do not produce as much new knowledge as the United States right now, because China and India are relatively poor, and hence they are able to educate relatively fewer people.

(It is instructive that despite its poverty, India has one of the largest scientific communities in the world—just because it has such a large population. Put differently, would you bet on Sweden or Holland, say, against Great Britain or Russia, or even India, to produce the great discoveries that will make nuclear fusion practical?)

Then you note that today's rich countries were also poor at one time, and ask: Why did not China and India get rich long ago? More than two centuries ago, David Hume explained clearly why China fell behind Europe. "[I]t is impossible for the arts and sciences to arise, at first, among any people unless that people enjoy the blessing of a free government. . . . An unlimited despotism . . . effectually puts a stop to all improvements, and keeps men from attaining . . . knowledge."[13]

Hume then explained why freedom is necessary: "Though a republic should be barbarous, it necessarily, by an infallible operation gives rise to LAW, even before mankind have made any considerable advances in the other sciences. From law arises security: From security curiousity: And from curiousity knowledge."[14]

Hume then explained why Europe advanced and China did not: "Nothing is more favorable to the rise of politeness and learning [by which he meant the development of the sciences], than a number of neighbouring and independent states, connected together by commerce and policy." His reason why a Europe of independent states should forge ahead in technology and economic development was the braking "which such limited territories give both to *power* and *authority*."[15]

Hume said it over and over again: "[T]he divisions into small states are favourable to learning, by stopping the progress of *authority* as well as that of *power*."[16] He contrasted the progress in Europe with the lack of it in China, which was "one vast empire, speaking one language, governed by one law. . . . This seems to be one natural reason, why the sciences have made so slow a progress in that mighty empire."[17]

Hume's analysis of this (and all other topics in political economy), made in the 1760s and 1770s, has proven right across the board. In the past decade economic historians have come to agree that the institutional and cultural nature of societies is crucial. More specifically, the extent to which individuals are free to pursue economic opportunity, and the extent to which there is protection for the property they purchase and create for both production and consumption, together with the presence of diversity and competition at all levels, seem to make an enormous difference in the propensity of people to develop and innovate. Shepard B. Clough discussed the importance for the "development of civilization" of a social and political organization which will permit individuals to realize their total potential as contributors to civilization.[18] What is implied here is that in a system where social taboos or political restrictions prevent large segments of a culture's population from engaging in types of activity which add most to civilization, the culture cannot attain the highest degree of civilization of which it is capable. Thus the caste system in India, restrictions on choice of occupation in medieval Europe, and the anti-Semitic laws of Nazi Germany curtailed the civilizing process.

This factor seems to be the best explanation of the "European miracle," to use Jones's term, in comparison to the recent centuries' histories of India and

China. And it seems to explain why Hong Kong and Singapore are doing so well, and Africa is doing so poorly, right now.

That is, the modern explanation of why Europe forged ahead with the industrial revolution but China did not is exactly as Hume said: The competition fostered by independence allowed people considerable freedom from monarchs and bureaucracy. This afforded them economic opportunity to use their talents, make advances, and profit from their efforts.

The mode of economic-political organization influences the speed of development of new discoveries and new applications at all levels. Communism in China prevents entrepreneurs from putting jitneys on the road to compete with publicly owned buses (so does regulation in most U.S. cities), and hence innovation is prevented. But even at the micro-level, that is, in units much smaller than nations, economic organization matters. The miners of Cornwall, who have been digging since the Roman occupation, evolved an unusual market system of decentralized decision making and developed great skill in geology because of it. This skill enabled them to dominate mining on four continents in the nineteenth century. The system was as follows:

> Their system of mining, based on "tribute," was perhaps unique in maintaining both production and morale in an industry historically riven by conflict. By this system the mine managers, called captains, marked out the various areas down the mine, and fixed for each one a price per ton for the ore recovered from it. The miners bid for the areas they considered would be most rewarding, and worked them for two months, fixing their own hours and working arrangements. They received no wages, but at the end of the period they received the agreed percentage of the value of the ore they had brought up. The "tributers" among the miners, who did the selection of the places to work, had to become, in effect, practising geologists. They ac quired an unrivalled knowledge of ore bodies and ways of mining them most efficiently.
>
> It was this knowledge and experience which made Cornish miners welcome everywhere they went.[19]

Please note that "technological advance" as used in these examples most definitely does not mean only "science." Scientific geniuses—if that term is meaningful—are just one part of the knowledge process. Much technological advance comes from people who are neither well educated nor well paid—the dispatcher who develops a slightly better way of deploying the taxis in her ten-taxi fleet, the shipper who discovers that garbage cans make excellent cheap containers, the supermarket manager who finds a way to display more merchandise in a given space, the supermarket clerk who finds a quicker way to wrap the meat, the market researcher in the supermarket chain who experiments and finds more efficient and cheaper means of advertising the store's prices and sale items, and so on.

Here is an example, from a local Illinois paper, of inventions coming from "ordinary" people.

Better Idea Results in Drywall Installer

Two area men have combined their respective good ideas to come up with a better idea.

William Vircks of Villa Grove and Harold Propst of 2802 E. California Ave., U, have developed an electric motor-driven drywall installer called "Board Ease." Vircks received the original patent on the machine in 1969, but the model was hand-cranked, not motorized. He said the original machine, which was designed to lift the drywall or ceiling material up and hold it there, was built by his father.

Vircks said his father built the first model, but it "stood for years in the corner" until he began tinkering with it.

He sold about 100 machines throughout the Midwest, and one of the buyers was Propst, a professional drywaller. Propst bought the machine several years ago and developed the motor and electric controls for his own machine. The two men got together last spring through a mutual friend and combined their ideas, and they now hope to market the machine through a national company. Vircks, who works at Tuscola's USI plant, says he's been working on the machine for 12 to 13 years and hopes he'll soon be getting a return on his investment.[20]

Of course, Cornish miners and U.S. drywall installers are just examples—not exceptional, but typical of human minds. The "quality circle" movement in manufacturing, following the Japanese and Swedish leads, is a formalization of the process by which people on production lines can contribute their ideas, based on their day-to-day learning on the job, to improving the production process.

The need for additional producers of knowledge is manifest. Nobel prize winner Hans Bethe tells us that the future cost and availability of nuclear power—and hence the cost and availability of energy generally—would be a rosier prospect if the population of scientific workers were larger. Talking specifically about nuclear fusion, Bethe said, "Money is not the limiting factor. . . . Progress is limited rather by the availability of highly trained workers."[21]

Students of organizational behavior also tell us that, all else being equal, the larger an organization's resources in number of people and amount of money, the more innovations it will come up with. "If any one group of variables may be said to stand out among all others as empirically determined correlates of innovation, it is the group of interrelated factors indicating size, wealth, or the availability of resources." A variety of investigators "all conclude that organizational size and wealth are among the strongest predictors of innovation in the sense of readiness to adopt new patterns of behavior."[22]

There have been many more discoveries and a faster rate of productivity growth in the past century than in previous centuries, when there were fewer people alive. True, ten thousand years ago there wasn't much knowledge to build new ideas upon. But seen differently, it should have been all the easier ten thousand years ago to find important improvements, because so much still lay undiscovered. Progress surely was agonizingly slow in prehistory, however; for example, whereas we read of new metal and plastic materials almost every week, it was centuries or millennia between the discovery and use of, say, copper and iron. It makes sense that if there had been a larger population in earlier times, the pace of increase in technological practice would have been faster. In fact, that is exactly what happened in Britain from the 1500s to the 1800s. The number of agricultural patents filed, and the number of books on agriculture published, were larger when population was larger, and also when the price of food was higher (which is also a result of recent population growth).[23]

Population growth spurs the *adoption* of existing technology as well as the invention of new technology. This has been well documented in agriculture[24] where people turn to successively more "advanced" but more laborious methods of getting food as population density increases—methods that were previously known but not used because they were not needed earlier. This scheme well describes the passage from hunting and gathering—which we now know requires extraordinarily few hours of work a week to provide a full diet—to migratory slash-and-burn agriculture, and thence to settled long-fallow agriculture, to short-fallow agriculture, and eventually to the use of fertilizer, irrigation, and multiple cropping. Though each stage *initially* requires more labor than the previous one, the endpoint is a more efficient and productive system that requires much less labor, as we see in chapters 6 and 28.

This sequence throws light on why the advance of civilization is not a "race" between technology and population advancing independently of each other. Contrary to the Malthusian view, there is no immediate necessary linkage between all food-increasing inventions and increased production of food. Some inventions—the "invention-pull" type, such as a better calendar—may be adopted as soon as they are proven successful, because they will increase production with no more labor (or will enable less labor to produce the same amount of food). But other inventions—the "population-push" type, such as settled agriculture or irrigated multicropping—at first require more labor, and hence will not be adopted until demand from additional population warrants the adoption.[25] The Malthusian invention-pull innovation is indeed in a sort of race between population and technology. But the adoption of the population-push inventions is not in a race at all; rather, it is the sort of process discussed at length in chapters 1–3 on natural resources.[26] The Malthusian view of the dynamic relationship between population growth and the supply of food, and the view urged here, are shown in figures 26-2a and 26-2b.

J. D. Bernal provides additional evidence—case studies of steel; electricity, light, and power; chemistry, bacteriology, and biochemistry; and the theory of heat and energy in the nineteenth century—showing that innovations respond to economic demand. In the case of electricity, for example, "The barrier, or rather the absence of stimulus to advance, was economic. Electricity developed quickly when it paid, not a moment before."[27] And a large pop-

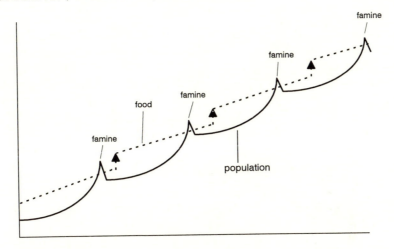

Note: arrow head indicates the effect of lucky spontaneous invention

Figure 26-2a. Malthus-Ehrlich-Newspaper-Television Vision of Population and Food

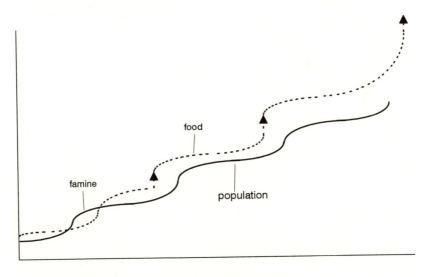

Note: arrow head indicates the effect of lucky spontaneous invention

Figure 26-2b. Barnett-Boserup-Clark-Schultz-Simon Vision of Population and Food

ulation size and density imply higher total demand, ceteris paribus, which is why Edison's first street lighting was in New York City rather than in Montana. It is also clear that countries with more people produce more knowledge, assuming income is the same, for example, Sweden versus the United States. And Bernal shows how the power of final demand works indirectly, too.

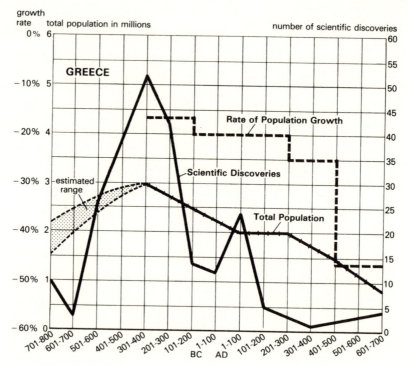

Figure 26-3a. Population and Scientific Discoveries in Ancient Greece

"Once electric distribution on a large scale was proved feasible and immensely profitable, then came a demand for large efficient power sources," leading to the development of turbines. And the development of light bulbs led to advances in creating vacua, after the subject "had stagnated for about two hundred years. . . . Here was another clear case of the law of supply and demand in the development of science and technology."[28]

On the "supply side" there is also much misunderstanding, especially the belief that the number of potential inventors does not matter. One source of this misunderstanding for some is the idea that, to paraphrase, "One need only contrast innovation and creativity in tiny Athens in the Golden Age with monstrous Calcutta" now, or Calcutta with Budapest of the 1930s, to see that more people do not imply more technical knowledge being produced. This argument leaves out the all-things-equal clause; Calcutta is poor. And, underlying this argument is the implied (but unwarranted) assumption that Calcutta is poor *because* it has so many people.

If we make more appropriate comparisons—comparing Greece to itself and Rome to itself during periods with different population sizes and growth rates, or comparing industries of various sizes in different countries now—we find that a larger population is associated with *more* knowledge and productivity,

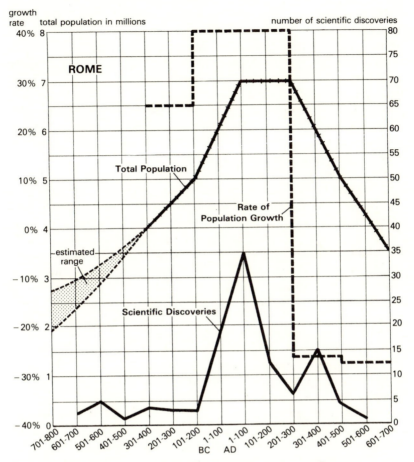

Figure 26-3b. Population and Scientific Discoveries in Ancient Rome

because there are more potential inventors and adopters of new technology. I plotted the numbers of great discoveries, as recorded by historians of science who have made such lists, against population size in various centuries. Figure 26–3 shows that population growth or size, or both, were associated with an increase in scientific activity, and population decline with a decrease. (Of course other factors come to bear, too, and I am exploring the matter in more detail for the whole history of Europe.)[29]

On the related question of whether material well-being can be improved through there being more ordinary persons—not geniuses—who contribute to our knowledge in their everyday work, the story of electricity and power production is again illuminating. Bernal describes the "stumbling progress of the first fifty years from 1831 to 1881 . . . the effort put into the development (1831–1881) . . . was small." The people who made the necessary technical developments "were not geniuses . . . and others no more gifted could have hit upon these ideas earlier if the field had attracted enough workers."[30] As said by Soichiro Honda, the inventor and founder of the Japanese motorcycle and auto firm bearing his name, "Where 100 people think, there are 100 powers; if 1,000 people think, there are 1,000 powers."[31]

If a larger labor force causes a faster rate of productivity increase, one would expect to find that productivity has advanced faster and faster as population has grown. Robert Solow concludes that the yearly rate of increase of productivity doubled, from 1 percent to 2 percent, between the periods 1909–1929 and 1929–1949;[32] and the populations and labor forces of the United States and of the developed world were larger in the latter period than in the earlier period. William Fellner calculated these rates of productivity increase (using two methods of calculation): *1900–1929*—1.8 (or 1.5) percent; *1929–1948*—2.3 (or 2.0) percent; *1948–1966*—2.8 percent.[33] These results are consistent with the assumption that productivity increases faster when population is larger—though of course other factors could explain part of the acceleration.[34] Philip Meguire has calculated, however, that the rate of increase in U.S. productivity has been constant for most of the past century. (Yet productivity *necessarily* was lower in earlier centuries. Otherwise, extrapolating backward would show us to have been producing nothing at all at some time in the past.) And Meguire's analysis shows that the rate of productivity gain has increased over the decades in all the *other* countries that he has analyzed.[35]

Here an important caution is needed: Because of the economic inter-relatedness of all modern countries, we should focus on the population and productivity growth of the entire developed world—or indeed, the world as a whole—rather than any particular country. One country can to some extent ride on the coattails of the developed world as a whole. (This is less likely than is often thought, however, because local research and development is needed to adapt international knowledge to local conditions. For example, high-yielding seeds cannot simply be imported and planted successfully without extensive adaptation to the local sunlight angle, temperature, water and soil conditions, and so on.) So, though our data refer to individual countries or to cross-sections of countries, the unit to which our discussion applies best is the developed world as a whole.

But is it *certain* that the recent acceleration of productivity would not have occurred if population had been smaller? The connections between numbers of scientists, inventors and ideas, and the adoption and use of new discoveries are difficult to delineate clearly. But the links needed to confirm this effect seem very obvious and strong. For example, the data show clearly that the bigger the population of a country, the greater the number of scientists and the larger the amount of scientific knowledge produced; more specifically, as seen in figure 26-4, scientific output is proportional to population size, in countries at the same level of income.[36] The United States is much larger than

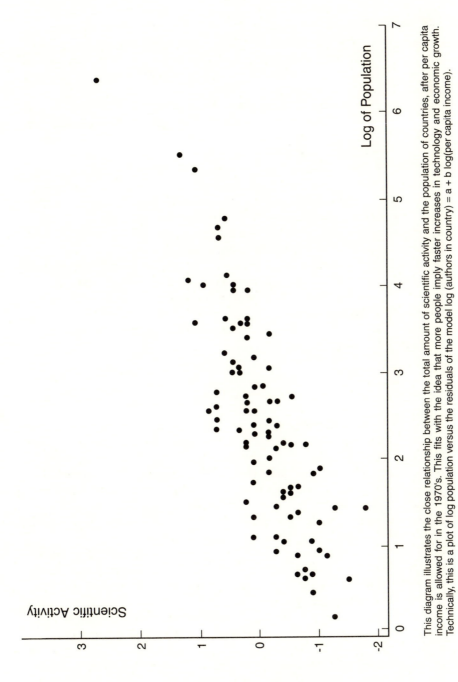

This diagram illustrates the close relationship between the total amount of scientific activity and the population of countries, after per capita income is allowed for in the 1970's. This fits with the idea that more people imply faster increases in technology and economic growth. Technically, this is a plot of log population versus the residuals of the model log (authors in country) = a + b log(per capita income).

Figure 26-4. The Relationship of Scientific Activity to Population Size

Sweden or the Netherlands, and it produces much more scientific knowledge. Sweden and Holland benefit from the larger U.S. population because they "import" much more knowledge from the United States than the United States imports from Sweden and Holland; this can be seen in the references used in Swedish, Dutch, and U.S. scientific writings, and in the number of patented processes licensed from each other.

Additional evidence that more people cause a faster rate of technological advance comes from comparisons of productivity gains in various industries. This evidence is quite compelling, in my judgment. We observe that a given industry grows faster in some countries than in other countries, or than other industries in the same country. Comparisons of faster-growing and slower-growing industries show that, in the faster-growing industries, the rate of increase of productivity and technological practice is highest. This indicates that faster population growth—which causes faster-growing industries—leads to faster growth of productivity. We shall examine this in more detail in the next section. But once more the caution: Our subject is the effect of population upon productivity increase in the developed world as a whole. The discussion of particular countries is only a device to increase the size of the sample.

Formal economic theory has now been developed to link these fundamental ideas with classical economics, and help explain why a larger population—by way of a larger labor force—leads to faster economic growth because of the faster growth of knowledge.[37]

Summary and Concluding Thoughts

Humanity by now enjoys extraordinary advances in communication, transportation, nutrition, health and freedom from pain, and the general standard of living. Can it be doubted that this is a miracle age of liberation from the bonds in which nature has kept us shackled throughout all of our history? The increased size of the human population is a fundamental cause of these gains.

The overall process, which is the main theme of the book, runs as follows: A larger population influences the production of knowledge through both supply and demand mechanisms.

On the supply side, a larger population implies a larger amount of knowledge being created, all else being equal, as a result of there being more people to have new ideas. The data on scientific productivity compared across countries bear out this obvious proposition.

More people, and higher income, cause problems of increased demand for and consumption of resources in the short run. Heightened demand causes prices to rise for awhile. The higher prices present opportunity for businesses to make money and for inventors to gain satisfaction and glory with new inventions, prompting inventors and entrepreneurs to search for solutions.

Many fail, at cost to themselves. But in a free society, solutions are eventually found. And in the long run the new developments leave us *better off than if the problems had not arisen.* That is, prices end up lower than before the increased scarcity occurred. This applies to metals (see chapter 1), energy (see chapter 11), land (see chapter 6), physical infrastructure (see chapter 25), and all other goods.

The reason for forecasting that any *particular* raw material or aspect of material human life will get better is mainly the trend of that particular case—the centuries of decline in the price of copper, for example—together with the theory above that explains how this trend comes about. But in Part One of the book I also forecast with confidence that the same improving trend will take place for *all* natural resources and other aspects of material life even in the absence of data for many of those cases. What is the basis for this set of predictions?

One ground for doing so is simply generalization from the known cases to the unknown—from the metals for which we have data, say, to the few for which such data are lacking. But there is still a stronger ground for this set of forecasts.

The strongest reasons for believing that solutions leave us better off than if the scarcity problems had never arisen is the record of humanity over the millennia becoming both more wealthy in the power to control our environment and make it yield the goods that we want, and our consequent increase in numbers. This implies that, on average, the people in each generation create a bit more than they use up. Not only must this be so for there to have been an increase in our wealth and numbers, but if this were not so—if we used up a bit more than we create, and our assets deteriorated like a many-times-patched tire deteriorates until it is no longer useful, we simply would have become extinct as a species. The essential condition of fitness for survival for our species is that we do create a net surplus each generation on average (or at least break even), and since we have survived and increased, this condition must have been present.

The question then immediately arises: Must not we, like other species, cease our growth when we have filled up our niche—that is, reached the limit of the available resources? One cannot answer this question with assurance, of course, because with each increase of wealth and numbers we proceed into a situation for which we have no prior experience. But as is argued in various chapters (especially those on energy, food, and natural resources), there apparently is no fixed limit for the future. There are limits at any moment, but the limits continually expand, and constrain us less with each passing generation. In this we are quite unlike all other animals.

So, the material history of humanity is a sequence of these population-caused problems, solutions in the form of new technical and organizational discoveries, increased population in part as a result of the largess flowing from the new solutions, new problems caused thereby, and so on. This process was described in some detail for the development of new energy forms in chapter 11. It also describes the evolution of villages into early cities, and the consequent need for new methods of food storage and related new forms of knowledge such as counting[38] and writing, as well as new forms of social organization. These in turn made possible continued growth in total population and city size.

Another example is the improvement of transportation in England—starting in the 1700s with the provision of food to supply growing cities, then industrial raw materials to supply factories making new products, and finally, distribution of the products to consumers at home and abroad—which constitutes an interrelated saga of canals, the coal industry, railroads, the iron and steel industry, bridge building, and steel ships.[39] Each solution to one industry's problem induced new problems—and opportunities—elsewhere, whose solutions moved the economy further forward and led to still more new problems. For a single example, hills are a major obstacle to canals. Putting barges on cradles that traveled on iron rails up and down an inclined slope enabled canals to avoid expensive and slow sets of locks.

Let us end this chapter by repeating an earlier quotation:

[I]t is impossible for the arts and sciences to arise, at first, among any people unless that people enjoy the blessing of free government.[40]

Afternote _____

On the Importance and Origins of
Productive Knowledge

IN 1948, John Bardeen, Walter Brattain, and William Shockley invented the transistor. If a person or a corporation were able to collect the money value of that invention in just a single year now, the net value of the goods made with that invention (a calculation that involves the cost and value of similar products that would have been made with technology that does not utilize the transistor) is greater than the value of all the two billion ounces of gold that now exist in the world, worth now perhaps a trillion (a thousand billion) 1996 dollars.

Furthermore, the salary of Bardeen, in the last year before he retired in the mid-1970s, was $46,500, and in the year when the transistor was invented he earned much much less. The difference between what society pays people like Bardeen, Shockley, and Brattain, and the benefit we get from such people, is a measure of the gain to the rest of us in our standard of living due to the advance in knowledge caused by the growth in population those inventors represent. This example should give some perspective to the rest of this afternote.

The main contribution that additional persons make to society is the new knowledge of all kinds—scientific, organizational, and everyday knowledge such as how to high-jump better—that they create and leave behind them. And to repeat an earlier statement, these gains are the result not only of geniuses but of a great number of work-a-day ingenious people. Understanding the processes underlying the creation and utilization of productive knowledge helps one understand the effect of population growth upon economic growth in the industrialized world. And as we have seen, size of population is interwoven with the creation of knowledge on both the supply side (supply of goods through the supply of knowledge) and on the demand side (demand for industrial goods, extractive products, services, and total output). Hence, we now discuss the nature of the process of knowledge creation.[41]

This section involves a bit more economic theory than does the rest of the book, which is why it comes after the chapter. It is labeled an "afternote" instead of an "appendix" because people seldom read appendices unless their need to do so is desperate. And this section should be read by anyone with a serious desire to understand the effects of population growth.

The Gains from Knowledge Creation

The main difficulty in the economics of knowledge creation is assessing the benefits from advances in knowledge "external" to the producer of knowledge—that is, the difference between the producer's private benefits from the creation of knowledge and the benefits to the economy and society as a whole. It is this positive externality that distinguishes the creation of knowledge capital from investment in physical capital.*

The benefits of knowledge are not fully exploited by its creators even if the knowledge is created as an investment whose profit is realized. Advances in knowledge spill over from the individual creator to other individuals, from the firm that invests in creating new knowledge to other firms, and from one generation to another. And the firm that creates knowledge seldom is able to elicit from consumers all the value of the new knowledge to consumers. Of course the spillover phenomenon can also interfere with knowledge creation, because the smaller the benefits and the greater the costs to the inventor, the less likely is the inventor (or the firm) to invest in the knowledge.

Before going further, we must distinguish between two types of knowledge—"spontaneous" knowledge and "incentive-responsive" knowledge.

Spontaneous Knowledge

It is obvious that not all knowledge creation is influenced by short-term or even long-term economic incentives. That is, economic forces do not account for all new inventions, even technical inventions. Much basic knowledge is created in universities and only distantly influenced by economic needs and priorities. As Friedrich Hayek puts it, "Man has been impelled to scientific inquiry by wonder and by need. Of these wonder has been incomparably more fertile." But Hayek does go on to note that "Where we wonder we have already a question to ask."[42] The needs of the community, interpreted in the widest sense, often raise questions in thinkers' minds.

Other knowledge is created with the aim of boosting efficiency but yet is uninfluenced by any profit calculations, and is produced without explicit expenditure for R & D; this is the sort of improvement in production, marketing,

---

* Technical note: Aside from the wealth that people bequeath to their descendants—which clearly is only a small part of total savings, though we do not know well the total of bequests in our society—all of people's physical wealth created as savings is used up within their lifetimes. Hence bequests do not entirely offset the process by which an additional person (all else equal) lowers the average income of the community by diluting its supply of capital—which is the basic Malthusian population proposition. Only the bequest of knowledge causes the generational balance to be positive.

financing, or other aspect of a business that might arise from an idea of an executive about how to operate more efficiently—for example, Alfred Sloan's idea of decentralizing General Motors, or the idea of using cut-down old detergent boxes as magazine storage units, or a host of developments by ingenious farmers. Additional people increase the stock of this sort of knowledge simply by there being more minds to become curious about some aspect of the world about them, and inventing new ways to understand and change it.

Incentive-Responsive Knowledge

Some incentive-responsive knowledge is produced in universities, and much comes out of R & D programs in industry. Applied knowledge and technical progress also arise out of casual on-the-job discovery by workers of all kinds at all levels, in response to an opportunity to make an enterprise more efficient and more profitable. Additional people increase the growth of this sort of knowledge not only by supplying a larger number of inventive minds, but also by increasing the demand for goods and hence increasing the incentive for people to produce new solutions to problems.

The Beneficiaries of Gains in Knowledge

The Economy as a Whole

If a firm creates knowledge, invests in it, and realizes profits from the project at (say) a 30 percent yearly rate of return, whereas the economy-wide return to invested capital is (say) 20 percent and the break-even project returns (say) 10 percent, then the economy as a whole benefits from the new project that pays back at 30 percent because the resources used in it are producing returns in excess of what they would produce in alternative uses. True, the "profit" goes to the firm, at least at first. But the owners of the firm are part of the economy, and if they are made better off ceteris paribus, then the society is made better off. If everyone owned a firm in such circumstances, then everyone would be made better off by such profits even though the profits are "private."

Furthermore, the benefits from a high-return project that utilizes resources productively go to many other parties in addition to the owners of the firm— to employees as job creation, and higher wages to suppliers, and to the fisc as taxes. So again, even without externalities in the form of knowledge, a high-yielding knowledge project is good for society.

The example of the inventors of the transistor, and its value to society, was given at the start of this section as an indication of the magnitude of the externalities from knowledge. We can extend the illustration a bit. The present value of all the gold that humanity has accumulated since the beginning of time is equal to the income of perhaps one-fifth of the U.S. work force in just one year. And the cause of that income being as large as it is—rather than the mere pittance it would be if the same number of people still worked at a primitive economic level—is the accumulation of knowledge by people who have gone before us, and which we do not pay them for; it is an externality they bestowed upon us.

To repeat, the income of perhaps fifty million Americans equals the worth of all the world's store of gold, due to the knowledge that we possess. In earlier centuries, the stock of gold would have been worth the incomes of many more people. This shows both the diminishing relative value of physical goods such as copper and gold, and the increasing relative value of the knowledge we have gained as an externality of the labors of those who have gone before us. Nor should this be surprising in light of the fact that the proportion of the world's work force that is employed in mining gold or copper—one measure of the relative importance of a good—is minuscule relative to the production of other goods. If there were more people alive now to produce more knowledge, the value of any given number of persons' incomes in any future year would be larger relative to the value of gold than it would otherwise be.

Externalities Realized by Other Firms

The benefit realized by other firms in the same industry from the knowledge created by the knowledge-producing firm is a key element of the economic system. And the benefits external to the innovating firm certainly must be large, relative even to the discount-factor effect mentioned above. That is, the main social benefit from profitable research and development (R & D) probably derives from effects external to the firm investing in the R & D. Firms are able to reduce costs and introduce new products more easily because of research done by others in the industry and in other industries.

Consumer Benefits from the Externalities

There is still another channel through which R & D brings social benefits. At the break-even point on the R & D opportunity ladder, the increased revenue to the firm doing the R & D just balances the added inputs to produce the new knowledge, so there is no net gain to the firm. But when competitors acquire some of the knowledge (almost) free, there will be a lowering of cost and then price throughout the industry, which will be a windfall gain to consumers and to society as a whole.

Furthermore, except under most unusual conditions a firm cannot charge consumers for all of the knowledge benefits they receive. So even if the firm can control its new knowledge so that competitors cannot acquire it, there will still be a net social benefit in the "consumer surplus."

Process and Product Research

Concerning the *size* of the knowledge-creation externalities: Given that year-to-year growth in per-worker output as recorded in the national income accounts is something less than 3 percent per year in most years in most countries, and given that a sizable proportion of this growth is accounted for by inputs of labor and capital (just how sizable depends upon the researcher and upon how you classify inputs),[43] you may wonder how much "residual" there really is that might show the effect of increases in technical progress. But our national income accounts do not directly show the benefits of that very large part of knowledge creation represented by new and improved products. If a pharmaceutical firm introduces a new drug that allows people to leave mental hospitals quickly, thereby saving large sums of money and improving health and life enjoyment, the first impact on the economy is a *reduction* in GNP, because some hospital workers will be out of work until they find new jobs. If a firm finds a new soup recipe that increases the pleasure people get from soup, there is no effect at all on GNP unless sales of the soup change. If a firm invents a contraceptive that is more reliable and pleasant than existing products, there is no effect on GNP unless total expenditures on contraceptives change, and if the price of the new product is the same as the price of old products (per unit of use), there will be no change in GNP.

Yet such new and improved products constitute a large part of the increase in economic welfare from year to year, accounting for increases in life expectancy, physical appearance, sense of well-being, range of activities available to us, and so on.

The proportion of R & D expenditures on new products is very large relative to the proportion that goes into new processes. In a survey of industrial firms, 45 percent said that their "main object" in R & D is to "develop new products," and another 41 percent said they concentrated on "improving existing products"—a total of 86 percent for product research—compared with 14 percent whose R & D aims at "finding new processes" to be used in manufacturing.[44] Of course these figures are sketchy and suggestive at best. And one firm's new products may change another firm's production process, of course. But no matter how unsatisfactory these figures may be, we can certainly rely on them to show that consumer product research is a large proportion of total research. This implies much more impact on consumer welfare by R & D than is shown in any audit of GNP.

Government-supported R & D is another important category of knowledge production that contributes to technical progress. But it is exceedingly difficult to make a reasonable guess about how much of the government's total expenditure on knowledge creation affects productivity.

Probably we wish to exclude weapons research, though it brings some by-product knowledge that contributes to productivity. And probably we wish to exclude "pure" or basic research, though it influences technical progress in a variety of ways. Agricultural research is the best example of the relevant sort of government-supported research. An interesting estimate of "at least 700 percent per year" return on investment in hybrid corn research was arrived at by Zvi Griliches.[45]

Can We Be Sure that Knowledge Will Solve Our Problems?

Perhaps it is useful to reflect as follows: If the past two hundred years brought a great deal of new knowledge relative to all the centuries before that time,[46] and if the past one hundred or even fifty years brought forth more than the preceding one hundred years, and the past twenty-five years brought forth much knowledge compared to the previous quarter century—a sequence of an increasing rate of knowledge creation, it would seem—why should one believe that the next century or millennium or seven billion years will not bring forth knowledge that will greatly enhance human life? To do so is to reject all of human experience.

27

Economies of Scope and Education

More is not always better. We're moving into an era when the less we use,
the better off we will be. Is a 400-pound wife better than a 130-pound wife?
(Television mogul Ted Turner, quoted in "Notable Quotables," 1992)

THE PHENOMENON called "economies of scope" (a related term is "economies of scale")—meaning the greater efficiency of larger-scale production—has been known for centuries. William Petty, a predecessor of Adam Smith, made the point when talking of the advantages of a large city like London over a small city:

> [T]he Gain which is made by *Manufactures*, will be greater, as the Manufacture it self is greater and better . . . each *Manufacture* will be divided into as many parts as possible, whereby the Work of each *Artisan* will be simple and easie; As for Example. In the making of a *Watch*, If one Man shall make the *Wheels*, another the *Spring*, another shall Engrave the *Dial-plate*, and another shall make the *Cases*, then the *Watch* will be better and cheaper, than if the whole Work be put upon any one Man. And we also see that in *Towns*, and in the *Streets* of a great *Town*, where all the *Inhabitants* are almost of one Trade, the Commodity peculiar to those places is made better and cheaper than elsewhere. . . .[1]

The Theory

Economies of scope stem from (1) the ability to use larger and more efficient machinery, (2) the greater division of labor in situations where the market is larger, (3) knowledge creation and technological change, and (4) improved transportation and communication. We shall take up each of these factors briefly at first, then in more detail. Please keep in mind as we proceed that there is no easy and neat distinction between increases in productivity due to increased knowledge and increases in productivity due to economies of scope; they are interdependent, and both are accelerated by population growth.

1. A bigger population implies a bigger market, all else equal. A bigger market promotes bigger manufacturing plants that likely are more efficient than smaller ones, as well as longer production runs and hence lower setup costs per unit of output.

2. A larger market also makes possible a greater division of labor and hence an increase in the skill with which goods and services are made. Adam Smith emphasized the importance of the division of labor and used the famous example of pinmaking. (Petty, quoted above, cited a more vivid example.)

Specialization can also occur with respect to machinery. If the market for a firm's goods is small, it will buy multipurpose machines that can be used in the production of several kinds of products. If its market is larger, the firm can afford to buy more efficient specialized machines for each operation.

Larger markets also support a wider variety of services. If population is small, there may be too few people to constitute a profitable market for a given product or service. In such a case there will be no seller, and people who need the product or service will suffer by not being able to obtain the good they want.

Increased population must be accompanied by an increase in total income if there is to be a bigger market; more babies do not automatically mean a bigger total income, especially in the short run. But under almost any reasonable set of assumptions, when the increment of population reaches the age at which youths begin to work, total income and total demand will be larger than before.

3. Economies of scope also stem from learning. If you are putting your first set of tires onto a car, the second tire goes much faster than the first one. The more airplanes or bridges or television sets that a group of people produces, the more chances they have to improve their skills with "learning by doing"— a very important factor in increasing productivity. The bigger the population, the more of everything that is produced, which promotes learning by doing.

4. A bigger population makes profitable many major social investments that would not otherwise be profitable—for example, railroads, irrigation systems, and ports. The amount of such construction often depends upon the population density per given land area, as is discussed in chapter 25 on population and capital. For example, if an Australian farmer were to clear a piece of land very far from the nearest neighboring farm, he might have no way to ship his produce to market and will have difficulty in obtaining labor and supplies. But when more farms are established nearby, roads will be built that will link him with markets and supplies. Such reasoning lay behind Australia's desire for more immigrants and a larger population, as it did in the American West in the last century. Also, public services such as fire protection often can be provided at lower cost per person when the population is larger.

There may also be diseconomies of increased scale, however, such as congestion. As the number of sellers and activity in, say, a city's wholesale fruit-and-vegetable market increases, transacting one's business may become more difficult because of crowding and confusion. Each additional person imposes some costs on other people by decreasing the space in which the other person can move around and by inflicting his pollution (soot, noise, litter) on other people. Therefore, the more people there are, the less space each person has and the more pollution each suffers from, all else equal. These effects would be felt both in a decreased ease and joy of living, and in higher prices due to the higher costs of production caused by congestion. This sort of diseconomy of scope is very much like the concept of diminishing returns from a given acre of land that is at the heart of Malthusian reasoning. It eventually must occur as long as there is some factor of production that remains fixed in size, be it land for the farmer or the market area for the wholesaler. But if that factor can be increased rather than remaining fixed—by building a bigger market, or by bringing new land into cultivation—then the diseconomies of scale, especially congestion, can be reduced or avoided indefinitely.

The Statistical Evidence

Because there are a variety of forces associated with economic scope that affect activity in opposite directions, and because these factors cannot readily be studied separately, we must examine the overall net effect of greater population and larger markets upon productivity and technological change.

Let's begin with an estimate of the overall effects of population size on productivity in less-developed countries (LDCs). Hollis B. Chenery compared the manufacturing sectors in a variety of countries and found that, all else being equal, if one country was twice as populous as another, output per worker was 20 percent larger. This is a very large positive effect of population size no matter how you look at it.

Moving from the national level down to the industry level, and shifting from LDCs to more-developed countries (MDCs) because most of the available information pertains to MDCs: In every industry, there is some minimum size of operation that must be attained to reach a reasonable operating efficiency— one person for a hot-dog stand, tens of thousands for an auto plant. But though this is the sort of economy of scale that has been most studied in the past (because of its industrial applications), it is not the economy of scale that is most relevant to population questions. Also, the range of feasible plants is very large in many industries—the restaurant industry ranges from firms with one person to firms with thousands—and a small country may bear no disadvantage, or even have an advantage over larger countries in some industries.

More relevant are studies of industries as wholes. As mentioned above, it is an important and well-established phenomenon that the faster an industry grows, the faster its efficiency increases—even compared with the same industry in other countries. Though the best analyses are dated, their data are surely still valid. In figure 27-1 we see comparisons of the productivity of U.S. industries in 1950 and 1963, and of U.K. industries in 1963, with U.K. industries in 1950—and also comparisons of U.S. industries in 1963 with those of

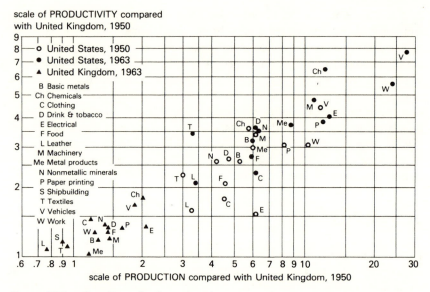

Figure 27-1a. The Effect of Industrial Scale upon Productivity, U.S. versus UK

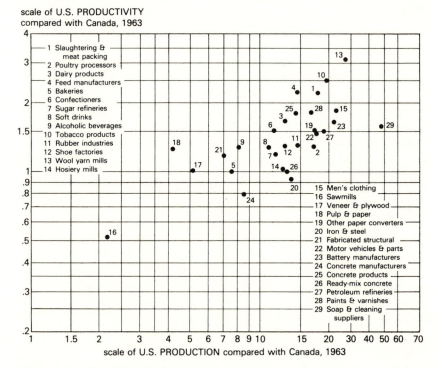

Figure 27-1b. The Effect of Industrial Scale upon Productivity, Canada versus the United States

Canada in the same year. The larger the industry relative to the U.K. or Canada base, the higher its productivity. This effect is very large. Productivity goes up roughly with the square root of output. That is, if you quadruple the size of an industry, you may expect to double the output per worker and per unit of capital employed.

The effect Chenery saw in economies as wholes, together with the effects seen in individual industries, constitute strong evidence that a larger and faster-growing population produces a greater rate of increase in economic efficiency.

The phenomenon called learning by doing[2] is surely a key factor in the improvement of productivity in particular industries and in the economy as a whole. The idea is a simple one: The more units produced in a plant or an industry, the more efficiently they are produced, as people learn and develop better methods. Industrial engineers have understood learning by doing for many decades, but economists first grasped its importance for the production of airplanes in World War II, when it was referred to as the "80 percent curve": A doubling in the cumulative production of a particular airplane led to a 20 percent reduction in labor per plane. That is, if the first airplane required 1,000 units of labor, the second would require 80 percent of 1,000 (that is, 800) units, the fourth would require 80 percent of 800 (that is, 640) units, and so on, though after some time the rate of learning probably slows up. Similar "progress ratios" have been found for lathes, machine tools, textile machines, and ships. The economic importance of learning by doing clearly is great, and the role of a larger population in speeding learning by doing is clear.[3]

The effect of learning by doing can also be seen in the progressive reduction in price of new consumer devices in the years following their introduction to the market. The examples of room air conditioners and color television sets are shown in figure 27-2.

The various studies of productivity discussed earlier automatically subtract costs of congestion from the benefits of scale. Congestion should be reflected more sharply in the cost-of-living data for cities of different sizes. Therefore it may be surprising that no strong relationship between size of city and cost of living is apparent—at most a tiny effect; the largest estimate being a 1 percent increase in the *overall* cost of living for each additional million people, for people living on a high budget; other estimates range downward to no effect at all.[4]

Furthermore, a study of the relationship of city size to the prices of over 200 *individual* goods and services found that although more prices go up with increasing city size than go down, for almost every good or service, workers are found to be *more productive* in the larger cities after the higher wage in bigger cities is allowed for. And the higher incomes in larger cities more than make up for the higher prices, so that the overall purchasing power of a person's labor is greater in the bigger cities.[5] This suggests that the disadvantages

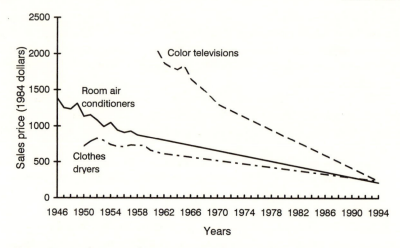

Figure 27-2. Sale Prices of Room Air Conditioners, Clothes Dryers, and Color
Television Sets

of congestion are less than the positive effects of larger population—including
better communications and more competition—on the standard of living in
larger cities.

Quantity and Quality of Education

A reduction in the quality or quantity of education that children receive was
long thought to be a negative effect of population growth. Human capital as
well as physical capital is crucial in the productivity of an economy. And
people might not wish to provide (or authorities might not demand) enough
additional tax revenues to maintain an equivalent level of schooling in the face
of population growth. If so, a larger population, with its larger proportion of
children, might lead to less education on the average, and thus less increase in
the stock of knowledge, than a smaller population.

The conventional theory of population growth's effect upon the amount of
education per child is straightforward Malthus (first edition): A fixed educational budget of money and resources divided among more students implies
less education per student. But as we know from a host of evidence, people
and institutions often respond to population growth by altering the apparently fixed conditions. In agricultural countries, for example, having more
children causes parents to increase their labor on the land. And in industrial
countries, when there are additional profitable opportunities for investment,
people will shift some resources from consumption to investment; children's
education constitutes such an opportunity. Therefore, we must allow for responses contrary to the simple Malthusian pie-sharing theory.

There is no way of knowing from theory alone which of the two effects—dilution of resources or increase of work—will dominate. Therefore we must turn to empirical data. A comparison between rates of population growth in LDCs and the amounts of education given to children shows that an increase in the fertility reduces educational expenditures per child and secondary enrollment, but not primary or post-secondary enrollment.[6] Perhaps the most meaningful result is that the negative effect is nowhere near as great as the simple Malthusian theory would suggest, and in general the effect does not seem to be large if it exists at all.

Many people have assumed that a larger family implies less education per child because of the supposed trade-off between expenditures on additional children versus more education for fewer children. And there is some research supporting that theory.[7] But it is very difficult to ensure that the research is not confounded by underlying causes that predispose to *both* more children and less education. And one study in Kenya has found the hypothesized effect to be absent; indeed, in the very largest families, the youngest children receive larger amounts of education than in less-large families—overall, a very complex pattern.[8] Yet in any case the effects are so small that it is safe to assert that allowing parents to have as many children as they desire will not drag down economic development by reducing the educational level.

This chapter has discussed children as if they are a homogeneous lot, making equal contributions to society. The reader may wonder, however, whether some classes of children, particularly the poor, may be a drain upon the economy even if most children make a positive contribution. There seems to be no evidence for this view, however.[9]

Summary

In addition to the acceleration of progress in knowledge-creation and technology, discussed in the previous chapter, a larger population also achieves economies of scope. A larger population implies a larger total demand for goods; with larger demand and higher production come division of labor and specialization, larger plants, larger industries, more learning by doing, and other related economies of scale. Congestion is a temporary cost of this greater efficiency, but it does not seem to present an ongoing difficulty in the context of production.

Population growth may (or may not) reduce the amount of education that children receive; even if it does, the effect is not nearly as great as simple Malthusian reasoning suggests, and not great enough to have much effect on an economy.

Babies don't create knowledge and improve productivity while still in their cradles, of course. And though the family bears most of the cost, society at large must also contribute to bring the baby to productive adulthood. This means that if you do not look as far as the next twenty-five years, the knowledge that will be created by someone else's baby born today does not interest you, and that baby is therefore a poor social investment for your taxes. But if you feel some interest in and obligation to the longer-run future, perhaps because you yourself are today enjoying the fruits of educational expenses that others paid twenty-five or fifty or one hundred years ago, then you will view the knowledge that will be produced by today's children as a great benefit. In chapter 26 we shall see just how great the benefit is, and how it overwhelms the social cost of the additional children.

28

Population Growth, Natural Resources, and Future Generations

How will the supplies of natural resources be affected by different rates of population growth? Part One discussed the supply of natural resources without reference to population growth. Now we investigate the effects of different rates of population growth, concentrating in this chapter on mineral resources for simplicity.

Let's go back to the Crusoe story in chapter 3 and ask: How are the situations different if both Alpha and Gamma Crusoe are on the island, compared to Alpha being alone? We saw that in the short run, the cost of copper to Alpha will probably be higher if Gamma is there too, unless or until one of them discovers an improved production method (perhaps a method that requires two workers) or a product that can substitute for copper. And Alpha's offspring, Beta, also probably would be better off if Gamma had never shown up. But we of later generations are almost surely better off if Gamma does appear on the scene and hence (a) increases the population size, (b) increases the demand for copper, (c) increases the cost of getting it, and then (d) invents improved methods of getting it and using it, and discovers substitute products.

A larger population due to Gamma and other persons influences later costs in two beneficial ways. First, the increased demand for copper leads to increased pressure for new discoveries. Second, and perhaps even more important, a larger population implies more people to think and imagine, be ingenious, and finally make these discoveries.

The Family Analogy

The analogy of the family is sometimes (though not always) a satisfactory intuitive shortcut toward understanding the effects of population growth. For example, if a family decides to have an additional child, there is less income available to be spent on each of the original family members, as it is with a country as a whole. The family may respond to the additional "need" with the parents working more hours for additional pay, and so it is with a nation. The family may choose to save less, in order to pay for the additional expenses, or to save more in order to pay for later expenses such as education; so it is for a nation as a whole. The additional child has no immediate economic advantages to the family, but later it may contribute to the parents and other relatives; so it is for society as a whole. And like a nation, the family must balance off the immediate noneconomic psychic benefits plus the later economic benefits against the immediate cost of the child. The main way that the family analogy diverges from the situation of a nation as a whole is that an additional person in the nation contributes to the stock of knowledge and to the scale of the market for the society as a whole, which benefits the entire economy, whereas an individual family is not likely to benefit much from its own discoveries.

The family model goes wrong, however, when it directs attention away from the possibility of creating new resources. If one thinks of a family on a desert island with a limited supply of pencils and paper, then more people on the island will lead to a pencil-and-paper scarcity sooner than otherwise. But for a society as a whole, there is practically no resource that is not either growable (such as trees for paper) or replaceable (except energy). And the supply of energy should present no problems, as discussed in chapters 11–13 and below.

If the family starts with a given plot of land and an additional child is born, it would seem as if the result would be less land per child to be inherited. But the family can increase its "effective" land by irrigation and multiple cropping and even hydroponics, and some families respond by opening up whole new tracts of previously uncultivated land. Hence an additional child need not increase the scarcity of land and other natural resources, as appears to be inevitable when one looks at the Earth as a closed resource system; instead, there is an increase in total resources.

But, you ask, how long can this go on? Surely not forever? In fact there is no logical or physical reason why the process cannot indeed go on forever. Let's return to copper as an example. Given substitute materials, development of improved methods of extraction, and discoveries of new lodes in the United States and in other countries and in the sea and perhaps on other planets, there is no *logical* reason why additional people should not increase the availability of copper or copper equivalents indefinitely.

To make the logical case more binding, the possibility of recycling copper at a faster rate due to population growth also improves the supply of the services we now get from it. To illustrate, consider a copper jug that one rubs to obtain the services of a genie. If only the single jug exists, and there are two families at opposite ends of the Earth, each of them can obtain the genie very infrequently. But if the Earth is populated densely, the jug can be passed rapidly from hand to hand, and all families might then have a chance to obtain the recycled jug and its genie more often than with a less dense population. So it could be with copper pots, or whatever. The apparent reason that this process cannot continue—the seeming finitude of copper in the solid earth—is invalid, as we have seen in chapter 3.

Of course, it is logically possible that the cost of the services we get now from copper and other minerals will be relatively higher in the future than now if there are more people in the future. But all past history suggests that the better guess is that cost and price will fall, just as scarcity historically has diminished along with the increase in population. Either way, however, the concept of mineral resources as "finite" is unnecessary, confusing, and misleading. And the notion of our planet as "spaceship earth," launched with a countable amount of each resource and hence having less minerals per passenger as the number of passengers is greater, is dramatic but irrelevant.

To repeat, we cannot know *for certain* whether the cost of the services we get from copper and other minerals will be cheaper in either year $t + 50$ or year $t + 500$ if population becomes 1 thillion rather than 2 thillion in year t. The historical data, however, show that the costs of minerals have declined faster in recent centuries, when population was larger, than in earlier centuries. This is not conclusive evidence that a bigger population implies lower costs. And higher income and a larger base of existing knowledge contribute to the cost-reduction process. But there is much *less* evidence—in fact, none at all—that a higher population in year t means a higher cost and greater scarcity of minerals in year $t + 50$ or $t + 500$.

Do you still doubt that the cost of mineral resources will be lower in the future than now? Do you still doubt that higher population growth now will eventually mean lower mineral costs? If so, I suggest as a mental exercise that you ask yourself: Would we be better off if people in the past had used less copper or coal? How great would our technological capacities to extract, process, and use these materials now be if we were just discovering these materials today?[1]

Jokes don't always go over well in serious books. But a joke that I have long been fond of seems appropriate here. Seventy-year-old Zeke's girlfriend has just left him after thirty years, and Zeke is in despair. His friends try hard to console him, and they especially point out again and again that in time he'll get over it, and might well meet another woman. Finally Zeke turns his tear-stained face to them and says, "But you don't understand. What am I going to do *tonight*?"

Similarly, you may well ask about the near-term effect of population growth on resources, after all this talk about the long run. There is more comfort for you than for Zeke, however. True, within a very short time there is little chance for the natural-resource supply to accommodate to a sudden increase in demand. But population growth is a very slow-acting phenomenon, not changing radically in any short period. And it is not until many years after the birth of a child that the additional person uses much natural resources. For both these reasons, modern industry has plenty of time to respond to changes in actual demand, and we need not fear short-run price run-ups due to increased population growth. This analysis jibes with the continued long-run decrease in the prices of all raw materials, as discussed in chapters 1–3.

A Model of the Increase in Natural Resources

Chapters 1–11 showed that all natural resources—minerals, food, and energy—have become less rather than more scarce throughout human history. But it is counterintuitive, against all common sense, for more people to result in more rather than less natural resources. So here is the theory again: More people, and increased income, cause problems of increased scarcity of resources in the short run. Heightened scarcity causes prices to rise. The higher prices present opportunity, and prompt inventors and entrepreneurs to search for solutions. Many fail, at cost to themselves. But in a free society, solutions are eventually found. And in the long run the new developments leave us *better off than if the problems had not arisen*. That is, prices end up lower than before the increased scarcity occurred.

The sequence by which the stock of new resources is increased was illustrated in a historical account, using the example of energy in England, in chapter 11. The reason for believing that this process will occur even with respect to resources for which we do not have historical data is discussed in chapter 4, "The Grand Theory." It may also help you understand the process by formalizing it in the form of a graph, showing the channels through which population influences the outcome.[2]

The "Energy Crisis" and Population Policy

It is standard wisdom that population growth worsens the energy situation. Here is the typical view of a predecessor agency of the U.S. Department of Energy, in a brochure written for the public at large.

> In other parts of the world, particularly in the developing areas, populations are growing rapidly and each new baby further strains already inadequate energy resources. Thus, if developing areas are to grow economically, it seems clear that they must first deal with the population problem. But the rich nations, too, must control population growth. If not, there simply will not be enough energy to go around, unless per capita energy consumption is held steady or reduced—and that seems unlikely. . . .
>
> We must learn to conserve energy and use it more wisely or we're going to be in serious trouble.[3]

The prevalence of this unsound thinking demands that we inquire into the effects of population upon the supply of energy. We want to know: What will be the effect of more or fewer people upon the future scarcity and prices of energy?

This much we can say with some certainty: (1) With respect to the short-run future—within say thirty years—this year's population growth rate can have almost no effect on the demand for energy or on its supply. (2) In the intermediate run, energy demand is likely to be proportional to population, all else equal; hence additional people require additional energy. (3) For the longer run, whether additional population will increase scarcity, reduce scarcity, or have no effect on scarcity is theoretically indeterminate. The outcome will depend on the net effect of increased demand on the current supplies of energy as of a given moment, together with increases in potential supplies through discoveries and technological advances that will be induced by the increase in demand. In the past, increased demand for energy has been associated with reduced scarcity and cost. There is no statistical reason to doubt the continuation of this trend. More particularly, there seems to be no reason to believe that we are now at a turning point in energy history, and no such turning point is visible in the future. This implies a trend toward lower energy prices and increased supplies.

It is important to recognize that in the context of population policy, who is "right" about the present state of energy supplies really does not matter. Yes, we will care in the years 2000 and 2010 whether there will be large or small supplies of oil and gas and coal at prices relatively high or low compared to now, and even more so if government intervention in the market worsens the situation (as it usually does) and forces us to wait in line at the service station. And it matters to the State Department and the Department of Defense whether our national policies about energy pricing and development lead to large or small proportions of our energy supply being imported from abroad. But from the standpoint of our national standard of living it will matter very little even if energy prices are at the highest end of the range of possibilities as a result of relatively unfruitful technological progress and of maximum increases in demand due to maximum rises in GNP and population. At a very unlikely high price of energy equivalent to, say, $50 per barrel of oil (1992 dollars) there should be enough energy from coal, shale oil, solar power, natural gas, and fossil oil plus oil from biomass—buttressed by the virtually inexhaustible supply of nuclear power—to last so many hundreds or thousands of years into the future, or millions if we include nuclear energy, that it simply does not matter enough to estimate how many hundreds or millions of years. And even if energy would sell at such a most-unlikely high price, rather than the actual 1993 oil price of (say) $15 per barrel, the difference in our standard of living would hardly be noticeable.

From this we may conclude that whatever impact population growth might have upon the energy situation—negative effects through increased demand, positive effects through new discoveries, with a net effect that may be positive or negative—the long-run effect of population growth on the standard of living through its effect on energy costs is quite unimportant. And refined calculations of its magnitude are of no interest in this context.

Are We Running a Ponzi Scheme on Future Generations?

Several writers—among whom the first may have been the Nobel-prize-winning economist Paul Samuelson (in 1975)—have said that population growth constitutes a pyramid game or "Ponzi scheme." Here is how one letter-writer put it:

> Julian Simon's solution for our economic woes is a pyramid scheme for which our children will pay with a degraded environment and a worsened quality of life. Shame on *American Demographics* for touting such stuff.
>   —Barbara Willin, Summerville, South Carolina[4]

A Ponzi scheme is a fraud in which each early buyer is sold a franchise for recruiting several additional buyers, each of whom receives a franchise for recruiting additional buyers, and so on. Each person who succeeds in recruiting his/her full quota makes money. But eventually there are no more buyers to be found because the market is saturated. The scheme collapses, and the later franchise buyers lose their money. The scheme is named after Charles Ponzi, who perfected a similar scheme in the securities market in the 1920s.

But population growth does not constitute a Ponzi scheme: there is no reason to expect resources to run out. Instead, as Part One of this book demonstrates (on the basis of the history of long-run price declines in all natural resources, plus theory that fits the data), resources may be expected to become more available rather than more scarce. Hence there is no reason to think that consumption in the present is at the expense of future consumers, or that more consumers now imply less for consumers in the future. Rather, it is reasonable to expect that more consumption now implies *more* resources in the future because of induced discoveries of new ways to supply resources, which eventually leave resources cheaper and more available than if there were less pressure on resources in the present.

There is a second important difference between a Ponzi scheme and this book's view of population and resources. As the Ponzi scheme begins to peter out, the price of franchises falls as sellers find it more difficult to induce more buyers to purchase, and the system begins to fall apart. But if a resource becomes in shorter supply in any period, price *rises* in a fashion that reduces usage (and presumably reduces population growth), and hence it constitutes a self-adjusting rather than a self-destructing system.

Of course this view of population and resources runs against all "common sense"—that is, against conventional belief. But science is only interesting when it gives us knowledge that is not arrived at by common sense alone.

Natural Resources and the Risk of Running Out

You might wonder: Even if the prospect of running out of energy and minerals is small, is it safe to depend on the continuation of technical progress? Can we be sure that technological progress will continue to forestall growing scarcity and even increase the availability of natural resources? Would it not be prudent to avoid even a small possibility of a major scarcity disaster? Would it not be less risky to curb population growth to avoid the mere possibility of natural-resource scarcities even if the chances really are good that higher population will lead to lower costs? A reasonable person may be "risk averse."

The matter of risk aversion was considered at length in the discussion of nuclear energy in chapter 13; it will also be considered in the context of population and pollution in chapter 30, where risk is more crucial to the argument and to policy decisions. The reader interested in this topic should turn to those discussions. Risk aversion is not, however, very relevant for natural resources, for several reasons. First, the consequences of a growing shortage of any mineral—that is, of a rise in relative price—are not dangerous to life or even to the standard of living, as noted above with respect to energy. Second, a relative scarcity of one material engenders the substitution of other materials—say, aluminum for steel—and hence mitigates the scarcity. Third, a scarcity of any mineral would manifest itself only very slowly, giving plenty of opportunity to alter social and economic policies appropriately. Fourth, just as greater affluence and larger population contribute to the demand for more natural resources, they also contribute to our capacity to alleviate shortages and broaden our technological and economic capacity, which makes any particular material ever less crucial. Fifth and perhaps most important, we already have technology in hand—nuclear fission—to supply our energy needs at constant or declining cost forever.

Even so, let's next say a word about the appropriate level of confidence that progress will continue in the future.

Can We Be Sure Technology Will Advance?

Some ask: can we know that there will be discoveries of new materials and of productivity-enhancing techniques in the future? Behind the question lies the implicit belief that the production of new technology does not follow predictable patterns of the same sort as the patterns of production of other products such as cheese and opera. But there seems to me no warrant for belief in such a difference, either in logic or in empirical experience. When we add more capital and labor, we get more cheese; we have no logical assurance of this, but such has been our experience, and therefore we are prepared to rely upon it. The same is true concerning knowledge about how to increase the yield of grain, cows, milk, and cheese from given amounts of capital and labor. If you pay engineers to find ways to solve a general enough problem—for example, how to milk cows faster, or with less labor—the engineers predictably will do so. There may well be diminishing returns to additional inventive effort spent on the same problem, just as there are diminishing returns to the use of fertilizer and labor on a given farm in a given year. But as entirely new forms of technology arise and are brought to bear on the old problems, the old diminishing-returns functions then no longer apply.

The willingness of businesses to pay engineers and other inventors to look for new discoveries attests to the predictability of returns to inventive effort. To obtain a more intimate feeling for the process, one may ask a scientist or engineer whether she expects her current research project to produce results with greater probability than if she simply sat in the middle of the forest reading a detective novel; the trained effort the engineer applies has a much greater likelihood of producing useful information—and indeed, the very information that is expected in advance—than does untrained noneffort. This is as predictable in the aggregate as the fact that cows will produce milk, and that machines and workers will turn the milk into cheese. Therefore, to depend upon the fact that technical developments will continue to occur in the future—if we continue to devote human and other resources to research—is as reasonable as it is to depend upon any other production process in our economy or civilization. One cannot *prove* logically that technical development will continue in the future. But neither can one so prove that capital and labor and milk will continue to produce cheese, or that the sun will come up tomorrow.

As I see it, the only likely limit upon the production of new knowledge about resources is the occurrence of new problems; without unsolved problems there will be no solutions. But here we have a built-in insurance policy: if our ultimate interest is resource availability, and if availability should diminish, that automatically supplies an unsolved problem, which then leads to the production of new knowledge, not necessarily immediately or without short-run disruption, but in the long run.

I'm not saying that all problems are soluble in the forms in which they are presented. I do not claim that biologists will make us immortal in our lifetime, or even that the length of human life will be doubled or tripled in the future. On the other hand, one need not rule out that biogenetics can create an animal with most of our traits and a much longer life. But such is not the sort of knowledge we are interested in here. Rather, we are interested in knowledge of the material inputs to our economic civilization.

A sophisticated version of this argument is that the cost of additional knowledge may rise in the future. Some writers point to the large teams and large sums now involved in natural-science endeavors. Let us notice, however, how much cheaper it is to make many discoveries now than it was in the past because of the existing base of knowledge and the whole information infrastructure. Simon Kuznets could advance further with his research on GNP estimates than could William Petty. And a run-of-the-mill graduate student can now do some things that Petty could not do. Additionally, a given discovery is more valuable now than it was then; GNP measurement has more economic impact now than in Petty's day. I have calculated that the net present value of the invention of agriculture in social terms at the time of discovery was less than the net present value now of something even as trivial as computer games, because of the small population and income then (discounted even at 2 percent per year)[5] in gross social product from the transition to nuclear fission. And agriculture was the only big discovery for thousands of years, whereas the transistor and nuclear power and lots more inventions occurred within just a few recent decades.

Summary: The Ultimate Resource—Is the Human Imagination in a Free Society

There is no persuasive reason to believe that the relatively larger use of natural resources that would occur with a larger population would have any special deleterious effects upon the economy in the future. For the foreseeable future, even if the extrapolation of past trends is badly in error, the cost of energy is not an important consideration in evaluating the impact of population growth. Other natural resources may be treated in a manner just like any other physical capital when considering the economic effect of different rates of population growth. Depletion of mineral resources is not a special danger for the long run or the short run. Rather, the availability of mineral resources, as measured by their prices, may be expected to increase—that is, costs may be expected to decrease—despite all notions about "finiteness."

Sound appraisal of the impact of additional people upon the "scarcity" (cost) of a natural resource must take into account the feedback from increased demand to the discovery of new deposits, new ways of extracting the resource, and new substitutes for the resource. And we must take into account the relationship between demand now and supply in various future years, rather than considering only the effect on supply now of greater or lesser demand now. And the more people there are, the more minds that are working to discover new sources and increase productivity, with raw materials as with all other goods.

This point of view is not limited to economists. A technologist writing on minerals put it this way: "In effect, technology keeps creating new resources."[6] The major constraint upon the human capacity to enjoy unlimited minerals, energy, and other raw materials at acceptable prices is knowledge. And the source of knowledge is the human mind. Ultimately, then, the key constraint is human imagination acting together with educated skills. This is why an increase of human beings, along with causing an additional consumption of resources, constitutes a crucial addition to the stock of natural resources.

We must remember, however, that human imagination can flourish only if the economic system gives individuals the freedom to exercise their talents and to take advantage of opportunities. So another crucial element in the economics of resources and population is the extent to which the political-legal-economic system provides personal freedom from government coercion. Skilled persons require an appropriate framework that provides incentives for working hard and taking risks, enabling their talents to flower and come to fruition. The key elements of such a framework are economic liberty, respect for property, and fair and sensible rules of the market that are enforced equally for all.

We—humanity—should be throwing ourselves the party to outdo all parties, a combination graduation-wedding-birthday-all-rites-of passage party, to mark our emergence from a death-dominated world of raw-material scarcity. Sing, dance, be merry—and work. But instead we see gloomy faces. They are spoilsports, and they have bad effects.

The spoilsports accuse our generations of *having* a party—at the expense of generations to come. But it is those who use the government to their own advantage who are having a party at the expense of others—the bureaucrats, the grants-grabbers, the subsidy-looters. Don't let them spoil our merry day.

Afternote _____

From the Beach

ONE MERELY needs to read the daily newspaper with open eyes to see evidence that the benefits of natural resources are becoming more available daily, and that the cause is additional people. (If I did not severely limit the number of such items, this book would run a thousand pages—and would never get done.) Consider this one, for example:

An ocean is as fundamental a natural resource as there is. One of the ways that people enjoy the ocean is by riding its surf—and even the most puristic of environmentalists have not yet been heard to complain about the destruction of the ocean by surfing.

Yet the edges of oceans are scarce (though much of humanity takes care to live near oceans and rivers). And access to surfing therefore is expensive in time and money, and hence rather limited.

The future looks bright for surfers, however. A surfer-entrepreneur has invented an artificial surf machine for amusement parks, no matter how far from the ocean.[7]

It should be noted that a human brain was necessary to invent the Flow Rider. If inventor Thomas Lochtefeld's parents had opted not to bring him into the world, it might have been many years, even decades or centuries, before someone made life sweeter for surfing enthusiasts.

Afternote

On the Economics of Chelm
(Pronounced "Khelm")

THOUGH imagination is the key element in the speed of the advance of civilization, we can even get along reasonably well without more of the technical knowledge it produces and not sink into misery. We now have in our hands—really, in our libraries—the technology to feed, clothe, and supply energy to an ever-growing population for the next seven billion years. The amazing part is that most of the specific techniques within this body of knowledge were developed within the past hundred years or so, though these recent discoveries rest on knowledge that had accumulated for millennia, of course.

Indeed, the last necessary additions to this body of knowledge—nuclear fission and space travel and rapid computation—occurred decades ago. Even if no new knowledge were ever invented after those past advances, we would be able to go on increasing our numbers forever, while improving our standard of living and our control over our environment. The discovery of genetic manipulation certainly enhances our powers greatly, but even without it we could have continued our progress forever.

The imagination required for the satisfactory working of the legal-political-economic system may be more crucial in the long run. Unfortunately, though the fundamental ideas have been known for centuries—since Mandeville, Hume, and Smith—most laypersons and even many renowned economists do not understand the nature of the spontaneously cooperating self-organizing social system. Too many people think of society as a zero sum game. Sometimes I think that the only way to get the point across is satire. So consider this excerpt from I. B. Singer's little book about *The Fools of Chelm*:

> The first Chelmites . . . walked around naked and barefoot, lived in caves, and hunted animals with axes and spears made of stone. They often starved and were sick. But since the word "crisis" did not exist yet, there were no crises and no one tried to solve them.
>
> After many, many years the Chelmites became civilized. They learned to read and write, and such words as "problem" and "crisis" were created. The moment the word "crisis" appeared in the language, the people realized there was a crisis in Chelm. They saw that things were not good in their town. . . .
>
> One day Gronam [the first sage of Chelm, as well as its first ruler] ordered Shlemiel to summon the sages to a council.

When they assembled, Gronam said, "My sages, there is a crisis in Chelm. Most of our citizens haven't enough bread to eat, they are dressed in rags, and many of them are suffering from coughs and sniffles. How can we solve this crisis?"

The sages thought for seven days and seven nights, as was their custom. . . .

"What do you suggest, Zeinvel Ninny?" asked Gronam Ox.

"My advice," Zeinvel Ninny said, "is that there should be two fast days each week, namely Monday and Thursday. In this way we will save a lot of bread and there will no longer be a bread shortage."

"That would solve the bread problem, but what about the scarcity of clothing and shoes?" Gronam Ox asked. . . .

"My advice," said Treitel Fool, "is that we put high taxes on shoes, boots, caftans, pants, vests, skirts, petticoats, and all other articles of clothing. The poor will not be able to afford any clothes. This will leave more than enough for the rich. Why worry about the poor?"

"Bad advice!" exclaimed Sender Donkey.

"Why is this bad advice?" asked Gronam Ox.

"It is bad because the poor are the ones who work in the fields and shops. If they are ragged and unshod, they will always suffer from colds, coughs, and sniffles and thus be unable to work. They will not be able to produce enough bread and clothes even for the rich."

"And what do you suggest, Sender Donkey?"

"I suggest," Sender Donkey replied, "that at night, when the rich are asleep, the poor should break into their houses and take their boots, slippers, caftans, dresses, and whatever else they possess. The poor will then be properly dressed and they will be able to work in the fields and shops without catching cold. Why worry about the rich?"

"All wrong," announced Shmendrick Numskull.

"Why is it all wrong?" Gronam asked.

"Because for each rich man in Chelm there are some hundred paupers," said Shmendrick Numskull. "There will not be enough clothes to go around. Besides, the rich are all pot-bellied and the poor are skinny, so the rich people's clothes won't fit."

"What is your solution, Shmendrick Numskull?" asked Gronam Ox.

"I say that clothes should be abolished altogether. The great historians of Chelm tell us that in ancient times our ancestors went about naked and dwelt in caves. They lived by hunting. Let's do the same, and all our problems will be solved."[8]*

---

* The Jewish-caricature drawings by Uri Shulevitz that accompany Singer's text are uproariously funny, but in this day and age even a Jew might be attacked as anti-Jewish if he reproduces them.

29

Population Growth and Land

CHAPTER 8 examined whether farmland is (a) deteriorating in the world as a whole, and (b) being paved over in the United States at a rate that is very high relative to historical standards. On balance, neither is true. And chapter 9 discussed the "vanishing farmland" scam. Chapter 6 examined the long-run possibilities for food production, and found that potential supply is immense and expanding because of technology which already exists, making land become progressively less important. Now we continue those discussions by focusing on whether population growth will squeeze humanity toward the limits of food production because of the limited supply of land. We find that land will continue to be an ever-diminishing constraint even with a growing population.

It is "common sense" that population growth induces immiseration due to increased pressure on the land. Simple arithmetic shows that more people imply smaller farms per farmer, and hence a harder struggle to produce enough to eat, until each of us is nightmarishly scratching out three skimpy meals from eighteen hours' work a day on a plot the size of a window box. "More people, less land," in the words of one population-control organization.* The historical tendency over centuries past toward smaller farms is seen in figure 29-1.

Along with this specter hovers another: additional people causing land to be used up and ruined, especially in arid areas. The semi-governmental *Smithsonian* magazine editorializes that, in the desert, "traditional, more primitive agricultural techniques using natural ecological cycles are all that will work . . . and *that means small populations.*"[1] The head of the Population/Food Fund, Charles M. Cargille, M.D., writes that "overpopulation contributes to . . . deforestation and agricultural practices damaging to soil fertility."[2] And according to the *Christian Science Monitor,* "The will may be needed more to control population than to deal with the more obvious aspects of desertification."[3]

Even as knowledgeable a scholar as Bert Hoselitz—the founder of the important journal *Economic Development and Cultural Change*—in the mid-1950s wrote as follows:

> Since rates of population increase show a tendency to remain high in most Asian countries, it is likely that great pressures for the extension of the agricultural area will

---

* Then called Population/Environment Balance.

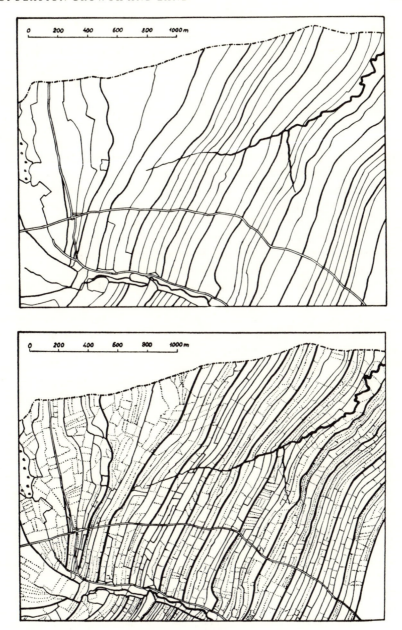

Figure 29-1. A Polish Village's Farm Boundaries

remain. . . . Hence, we have little reason to expect that Asian countries can hope to see within the next decades a decline in the absolute number of persons dependent upon agriculture for their livelihood . . . agricultural population pressure is likely to be greater in future years.[4]

Yet the long sweep of history until the present reveals that population growth has not led to these apparently logical consequences for agriculture, as we saw in chapter 5. Asia is thriving, contrary to all the dire forecasts of a few decades ago. And amazingly, since the first edition of the book we find some African leaders concluding from the comparative economic performances of Asia and Africa that land is not a problem at all—perhaps just the opposite. Ugandan President Yoweri Museveni in 1992 said that "people from East Asian countries with scarce resources and large populations 'may tend to be more disciplined than people who take life for granted.' . . . Some Africans 'have so much land that they don't know what to do with it.'"[5] (This comment must shock the U.S. State Department representatives in Africa who exert heavy diplomatic pressure on African governments to reduce the rate of population growth for the ostensible purpose of preventing the person/land ratio from falling.) Unfortunately, the reasons for Africa's lack of progress are not so simple. Reducing the quantity of land per person is neither necessary nor sufficient to produce a high standard of living—witness land-rich Australia. Africa's problems clearly stem from lack of economic freedom and a low starting level of education rather than lack of land. Both countries' experiences call into question the "common-sense" belief that population growth will inevitably cause bad effects by reducing the land supply.

So: The world eats as well or better now than in earlier centuries, even in present-day poor countries, even though there are more people per unit of land. How can we explain this affront to common sense?

Here is one part of the explanation: Though more land per person was available in the past than at present, people did not farm all the land available to them, for two good reasons. (1) People were physically unable to farm larger areas than they actually farmed. Studies show that the amount of land peasant farmers can handle without modern machinery is quite limited by the availability of human strength and time.[6] (2) More important but even less understood, farmers in the past had little motive for farming more land. In the absence of markets, farmers grow only as much as they expect to eat, as was discussed at length in chapter 4.

Ask yourself, please: Why *would* a subsistence farmer grow more than his family can eat? Does an urban housewife buy so many vegetables in the weekly shopping trip that they spoil? Malthus well understood this "natural want of will on the part of mankind to make efforts for the increase of food beyond what they could possibly consume."[7] It is no more a miracle that output increases when population increases than it is a miracle that you, the reader, manage to have enough vegetables to last the week even when guests are staying with you.

Reduction in the amount of land available to the farmer causes little hardship if previously he was not farming all the land that was available (though he may have to change his farming practices so as to cultivate the same land more intensively). The other side of the coin is that when farmers need more land they make more land, as we have seen in chapter 8. The notion of a fixed supply of farmland is as misleading as is the notion of a fixed supply of copper or energy. That is, people create land—agricultural land—by investing their sweat, blood, money, and ingenuity in it.[8]

But what will happen to the supply of land as income rises and people demand more food luxuries such as meat, which requires large quantities of grain as feed? Or to sharpen the question, how about the effect of a rise in income combined with an increase in population?

If there were to be increased "pressure" on the land, we would expect the existing land to be worked more intensively, which would require additional labor. Therefore we would expect to see a rising proportion of the labor force in agriculture. In figure 29-2 we see that just the opposite has occurred in the United States, as it has in all countries—including the poor ones; the proportion of people working in agriculture has continually declined, and may well decline forever (see chapter 6).

A decline in the *proportion* of people working in agriculture would be enough to sustain progress. But the data give us yet another picture that is so astounding that it seems weird: The absolute number of acres each farmer cultivates eventually *rises* when income becomes high, *despite* increases in population. When we look at data for the United States, Great Britain, and other more-developed countries given in figure 29-3, we see that the absolute number of farm workers is going down, and therefore the absolute amount of land per farm worker is going up, despite the fact that the total population is going up, reversing the earlier trend seen in figure 29-1.

Please re-read the preceding sentence carefully. It does not say that the *proportion* of the population working in agriculture is going down in the richer countries. Rather, it says something much stronger. The *absolute* number of farm workers is going down, and consequently the absolute amount of land per farm worker is going up in these countries. This fact makes it very clear that the combined increases of income and population do not increase "pressure" on the land, in contrast to popular belief and opposite to the state of affairs in poor countries that have not yet been able to adopt modern farming methods.

The extrapolation of this trend for the future is extraordinarily optimistic: As the poor countries get richer, and as their rate of population growth falls, they will reach a point at which the number of people needed to work in agriculture to feed the rest of the population will begin to fall—even though

Percent

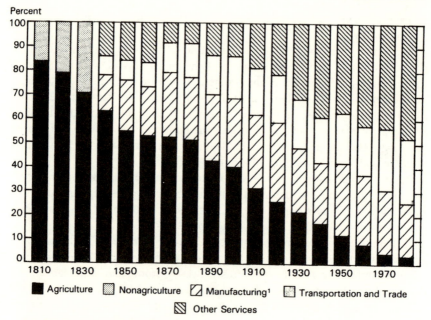

Figure 29-2. Labor Force Shares by Industry

the population gets bigger and richer. So much for a long-run crisis in agricultural land caused by population growth!

Let us push this idea even further, in order to see how a simple-minded extension of trends can lead to absurd conclusions. A continuation of the present trend in the United States, carried to the same absurdity as the nightmare described earlier, would eventually have just one person farming all the land in the United States and feeding everyone else.

Where will this benign trend stop? No one knows. But as long as agriculture is pointed in this economically desirable direction, we need not be concerned about how far the trend will go—especially as there apparently are no technological or environmental forces to stop it.

While countries are still poor they cannot embark on a course of mechanization sufficiently intense to increase total output and at the same time reduce the total number of workers in agriculture. But at least the *proportion* of workers in agriculture falls as they modernize, as is already happening in almost every developing country despite population growth. And eventually the *total* number of farm workers is likely to start falling, too. This is not happening yet, but the poorer countries can expect eventually to experience the same trend that was at work in the past in the now-rich countries.

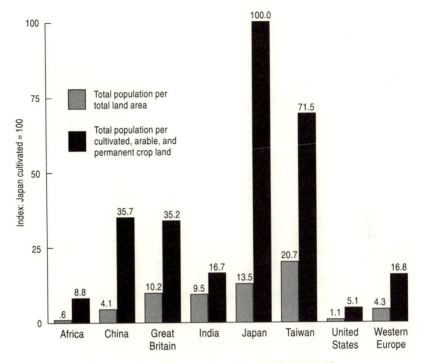

Figure 29-3. Population Densities for Selected Areas of the World

A quick bit of economic education: Upon viewing the decline in the agricultural labor force, some quibbler will say, "But what about all the jobs in agriculture that are lost?" Job "destruction," as Richard B. McKenzie puts it, is a confusing label for the very essence of economic progress—making a given amount of goods with fewer people. This not only enables us to have more goods, but it makes the labor of life easier and more enjoyable. If seven million jobs had not been "lost" in American agriculture since the 1930s—a decline from ten million to three million farmers, while population doubled—scores of millions of Americans would still be eking out short, painful, and poor lives in subsistence farming by following a mule and farming with hand implements, taking the kids out of school most of every year to help get the crops in. Nostalgia for that sort of life is never found among those who have experienced it. (For an extraordinary account of this rural poverty, see William Owens's, autobiography).

Before we consider historical examples, it is useful to look at figure 29-4 and note that neither population density per unit of arable land, or per unit of total land, provides a compelling explanation of whether a country is rich or poor.

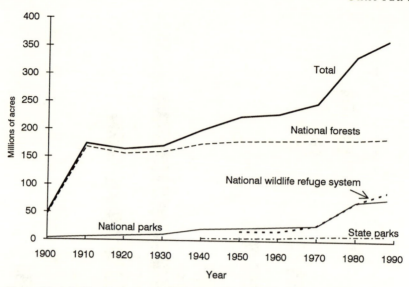

Figure 29-4. Public Recreation Lands in the United States, 1900–1990

Historical Examples

The increase in agricultural output as population rises (with or without an accompanying rise in income) has in most countries been accomplished largely by increases in the amount of land that has been farmed. This accounts for the land statistics that we saw in chapter 8. As population increases, people build more arable land in response to the increased demand for food. Let's consider some examples.

Ireland. In the late eighteenth century and the first half of the nineteenth century in Ireland—a period of very rapid population growth—peasants invested a large amount of labor in new lands, even though they did not own the land.

> Every new holding marked out in mountain or bog made possible the creation of a new family. . . . The state, for all the advice of government committees and private investigators, played no significant part in works of drainage and clearance until the time of the Famine. The landlords, with outstanding exceptions, were hardly more active. The main agent of reclamation was the peasant himself. In spite of the immense discouragement of tenurial relationships which increased rent in proportion, or more than in proportion, to the increase in the value of his holding, he steadily added an acre or two a year to his cultivated area or his sons established themselves on land hitherto unused. The peasant and his children were driven to such arduous and unrewarding work by the two forces which give their distinctive character to

many of the institutions of the Irish countryside, the pressure of population and the landlords' demand for ever increasing rents.[9]

Evidence for the rapidity of Irish land expansion is clear: Over the decade 1841–1851 the amount of cultivated land increased by 10 percent, though even in the previous decade—when population growth was at its fastest before the famine that started in 1845—population increased only at a decadal rate of 5.3 percent, from 7.8 million to 8.2 million.[10] This suggests that rural investment was enough to account for all—plus some more—of the increase in food required by the population growth during those years.

China. From 1400 to 1957 the cultivated acreage in China expanded four-fold-plus, from 25 million hectares to 112 million hectares.[11] This increase in cultivated land accounted for more than half the increase in grain output that sustained the living standard of the eightfold-plus increase in population over the same period, and investment in water-control systems and terracing accounted for much of the rest of the increase in output. "Only a small share of the rise in yields can be explained by improvements in the 'traditional' technology."[12] In this context, where the "rural technology in China was nearly stagnant after 1400,"[13] growth in output had to be accomplished either with increases in capital (including land) or in labor per person, and it is clear that additional investment was very largely, if not almost completely, responsible for the growth. Furthermore, this capital formation seems to have been caused by population growth.

Europe. Wilhelm Abel documented the close relationship between population, food prices, and land reclamation in Europe from the Middle Ages onward, and Slicher van Bath did the same for the period from 1500 to 1900.[14] When population grew at a fast rate, food prices were high, and land creation increased. Population grew very rapidly starting around 1000 (see fig. 22-4). Abel tells us that prices then rose, and "land reclamation was at its peak" starting "in the middle of the eleventh century and its end in the mid-fourteenth century,"[15] the time of the Black Death and depopulation. Even marshes were cultivated during the boom period. "The first great dykes in the Netherlands were probably constructed about A.D. 1000."[16]

Slicher reports that "the higher cereal prices after 1756 stimulated agricultural development. . . . Around Poitiers the area of reclaimed land was usually either 30 or 35 ares [sic] or about 2 hectares. In the former case the reclamation was the work of a day-labourer for a whole winter, in the latter that of a farmer with a team of oxen."[17]

Other countries. Data for Japan show that arable land increased steadily from 1877 until World War II, even though the number of agricultural workers was decreasing steadily.[18] The amounts of livestock, trees, and equipment also rose at rapid rates. These increases in agricultural capital were in response to the rapid increase in Japanese population together with the increase in the level of income in Japan.

In Burma, the amount of land in cultivation rose at an astonishing rate starting in the middle of the nineteenth century. The cultivated area was fifteen times as great in 1922–1923 as in 1852–1853.[19] Over the same period population increased by a factor of almost five.[20] In addition to the increase in population, the opening of the Suez Canal (1869) enabled Burma to sell its rice to Europe. Both these forces gave Burmese farmers an incentive to reclaim land, and they did so with extraordinary rapidity until World War II, when millions of acres were again overrun by jungle.

The foregoing examples show that in the poorer agricultural countries the creation of new land has been the source of most of the long-run increase in agricultural output which has kept up with population growth. But what will happen when there is no more "wasteland" to be converted into agricultural land? Not to worry; we can be quite sure this will never happen. As the available land for crops becomes more and more costly to transform into cropland, farmers will instead crop their existing land more intensively; this practice becomes more profitable than dipping into the pool of undeveloped land, because the unused land is relatively inefficient. The enormous possibilities in this direction are described in chapter 4.

Evidence for this process is found in the international statistics showing that, when population density is higher, the proportion of land irrigated is higher too.[21] This process may be seen particularly clearly in Taiwan and India, where, after farmers exploited a large proportion (but by no means all) of the unused land, irrigation began in earnest.

Let's look more closely at India, because so many good-hearted Westerners have worried about it. The total area of all cultivated land increased about 20 percent from 1951 to 1971.[22] Even more impressive is the 25 percent increase in irrigated land from 1949–1950 to 1960–1961,[23] and then another 27 percent increase from 1961–1965 to 1975.[24] Nor has India reached a high population density even now. Japan and Taiwan are about five times as densely populated, as seen in figure 29-3.

And the yield of rice per hectare is almost four times as great in Japan as in India; vastly more fertilizer is used in Japan, and three times as large a proportion of the agricultural land is irrigated (55 percent versus 17 percent).[25]

Excellent data from Taiwan show how land creation and improvement responded to population growth. During the period from 1900 to 1930 much new land was developed, along with an increase in the amount of irrigated land. Then, from 1930 to 1960, when there was less new land left to develop, more land was irrigated. At the same time, the effective crop area was increased by multiple cropping, and the use of fertilizers allowed total productivity to continue rising at a very rapid rate. This continues the sequence that begins in more "primitive" and sparsely populated areas where the pattern of farming still is to farm a patch for a year or two, then leave it fallow for several years to regain its natural fertility while other patches are farmed (a process I could still see in India in the early 1970s). There the response to population growth is to shorten the fallow period and to improve land fertility with labor-intensive methods.[26]

How much capacity still exists for enhancing land through irrigation, new seeds, fertilizer, and new farming methods? In chapter 6 we saw that the capacity is vast, much much greater than would be required to handle any presently imaginable population growth. The use of traditional farmland is no longer the only way to produce food. And of course our capacity to feed ourselves is not limited to what we now know how to do; it will certainly increase greatly as we make new technological discoveries. No matter how the increase in capacity occurs, however, the key element in developing and harnessing the capacity to replace land with technology is the pressure of an increased demand for food—which arises from an increased world income, population growth, and improved markets so that farm produce can be bought and sold without the prohibitive transportation costs still found in most very poor countries.

But what about "ultimately"? People worry that the process "cannot go on forever."

The earlier chapters on natural resources and energy argue that it makes sense to discuss the future that we can presently foresee—twenty years, one hundred years, even five hundred years from now. To give much weight to an even more distant time—so far in the future that we do not even give it a date except that it is a figure with several zeros in it—is not sensible decision making. Furthermore, there is strong reason to believe that "ultimately"—whatever that term means—natural resources will be less scarce rather than more scarce. And there is no reason to think that land is different in this respect.

Effects of Population Growth on Land Available for Recreation and Enjoyment

The availability of recreational land and wilderness is another facet of the land supply that concerns us. People worry that population growth and an increasing use of land for cities, roads, and agriculture will reduce the amount of recreational land.

It would seem obvious that a larger number of people *must* imply less recreational land and the disappearance of wilderness. But like many intuitively "obvious" statements about resources, this one is not correct.

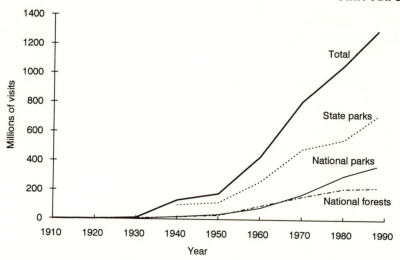

Figure 29-5. Recreational Use of U.S. Public Land System, 1910–1988

The facts: Recreational and wilderness land area has been growing by leaps and bounds during the period for which data are available. Land dedicated to wildlife areas, national and state parks, and recreational uses has risen from 3.3 million acres in 1900 (plus another 46.5 million acres in the national forest system) to 10.6 million acres (plus 160 million) in 1930, 49 million acres (plus 181 million) in 1960, to 176 million acres (plus 186 million in forests) in 1990 (see fig. 29-5).

More important than the area of land given over to recreation is the accessibility of recreational land and wilderness to the potential user. Because of the better means of transportation, the increased level of income, and the larger number of vacation and weekend days off—to which population growth has contributed over the centuries—the average person in a well-off country now has far greater access to many more types of recreational land than in any earlier time. The average American is now richer in ability to enjoy resort areas, recreational areas, and the wildest of wilderness than was a king 200 or 100 years ago.

To put it in economists' terms, the cost of a day in the wilderness has steadily gone down, and the time and money available to enjoy it has gone up, owing in part to population growth. And there is no reason to expect a change in this trend in the future. (On the other hand, the *value* of a day in the wilderness may have decreased as the number of people sharing it has gone up. This tempers somewhat the generally positive conclusion reached above, but not enough to invalidate it.)

The benefits to the individual American can be seen in the rapidly increasing numbers of visits to principal recreation areas. Of course, one may look upon the increased numbers of visits as an indication that the wilderness is not so isolated anymore, and hence that it is less desirable—the point of view of an eighteenth-century prince who wished to enjoy the entire forest all alone and could afford to do so. That imperial attitude differs from the democratic assumption that more people sharing in the enjoyment of something is a good thing even if the experience is not perfect for any one of them.

This section on recreational land has regrettably been limited to the United States because I have not been able to assemble data for other parts of the world. And the complexities of the analysis also would be greater if we were to try to make economic and ethical sense of the conflict between, on the one hand, recreational land in foreign countries, and, on the other hand, agricultural land devoted to larger and smaller rates of population growth in those countries. It is worth pointing out, however, that despite its very high population density, even China has for some time been engaged in an extensive effort to restore the forests that earlier had been cut down to push agriculture higher up the mountain slopes.[27] The purpose of the Chinese reforestation is mainly to preserve the land from erosion. But the outcome will also be a boon for recreation. So high population density is seen to be consistent with increasing forest areas even in China.

More generally, after centuries of decline, the volume of trees is increasing not only in China and the United States, and the total area of the world under forests shows no signs of decline over the decades, as figure 10-7 shows. Of course, the global trend includes regions of decline as well as of growth. Tropical rainforests are being reduced, for example, though nowhere near so fast as the public thinks.[28]

Given that agricultural productivity per acre in presently developed countries is increasing faster than population growth (as well as faster than the growth in total crop production) and given that we can expect all countries to eventually reach this productivity level and go far beyond, it follows that the total amount of land used for crops in poor countries will eventually decline, as it has been declining in the United States. (This decline has been occurring even as U.S. exports of grain have been increasing over the decades, and therefore the trend of less land feeding more people holds even more strongly if we consider only domestic U.S. food consumption.) This suggests that in the future there will be a larger amount of land available for recreation because less land will be used for crops.

For those interested in investment tips: The foregoing implies that, in comparison with recreational land, agricultural land may not be a good investment for the very long run. This contrasts with a perception that has existed since the beginning of agricultural history, to wit, that flat land accessible to markets is more desirable than hard-to-reach hilly or mountainous land—that Illinois land is more valuable than Tennessee land, say. The land of the Canaanites was said to be desirable in the Bible because it was "spacious," and good for agriculture. But in the future, land will be desirable because it is beautiful and interesting for recreation. (Don't rush out today and sink the family fortune into hilly land, however. The long run I am talking about may be one hundred or more years into the future.)

Are these statements that agricultural land is becoming less scarce, and recreational land more available, just science fiction? It seems to me that a fair-minded person who examines agricultural history must conclude that the facts are more consistent with the view that a greater demand for food leads eventually to a higher output per person than with the common view that it leads to a lower output per person. The simple Malthusian speculation about population growth leading to diminishing returns is fiction; the induced increase in productivity is the scientific fact.

Do additional people increase the scarcity of land? In the short run, before adjustments are made—of course they do. It is true with land just as with all resources. The instantaneous effect of adding people to a fixed stock of land is less land to go around. But—and this is a main theme of this book—after some time, adjustments are made; new resources (new lands in this case) are created to augment the original stock. And in the longer run the additional people provide the impetus and the knowledge that leave us better off than we were when we started. (The theory is discussed at greater length in chapter 4.) How you weigh the short-run costs against the intermediate-run and longer-run benefits is a matter of values, of course.

The Future Benefits of "Blight"

One expects that people's constructive activities will constitute some saving for later years—harbors, buildings, and land clearing. But as discussed earlier in chapter 16, a case can also be made that even activities that are not intentionally constructive tend to leave a positive legacy to subsequent generations. That is, even the unintended aspects of people's use of land (and of other raw materials) tend to be profitable for those who come afterward. These examples were given: (1) The "borrow pits" by the sides of roadways, by-products of taking material elsewhere. One may first think of the pits as a despoliation of nature, an ugly scar on the land. But it turns out that borrow pits are useful for fishing lakes and reservoirs. (2) Garbage dumps. Later generations may find dumps profitable sources of recyclable materials. (3) Pumped-out oil wells. The empty hole is likely to have value to subsequent generations, as storage for oil or other fluids, or for some as-yet-unknown purposes.

Conclusion

Is the stock of agricultural land being depleted? Just the opposite: The world's total stock of agricultural land is increasing. Will farmers be farming ever-smaller plots of land as population and income grow? Just the opposite: Despite population growth, increased productivity leads to larger farms per farmer. Does population growth in the United States mean that too much good agricultural and recreational land is being paved over, at the expense of agriculture and recreation? Flatly no: The amount of recreational land is increasing at a rapid clip, and new agricultural land is being made as some older land goes out of cultivation, leaving a very satisfactory net result for our agricultural future.

Afternote _____

Population, Land, and War

THE TRADITIONAL economic motive for war—acquiring farm land—is fast disappearing, as an indirect result of population growth. For economically advanced nations, it does not pay to make war to get another nation's agricultural territory. A sensible citizenry would not even accept a slice of another country as a gift. For example, the United States would get little additional economic benefit from Canada by "owning" it.

Adolf Hitler assaulted Europe with perhaps the worst catastrophe in history since the Black Death because, he said, the German "people" needed more "living room." The biblical Hebrews attacked the Canaanites to obtain a homeland. The settlers of the Americas warred on the Indians for cropland and ranchland. The United States fought with Mexico and Canada to expand its area. Blacks and whites battled for the land of Rhodesia. "Zimbabwe's war wasn't just about voting rights and black men in parliament. The war was all about land," said Moven Mahachi, Zimbabwe's minister for land resettlement.[29]

This idea that population growth breeds war has been used to justify national policies to "control the birth rate," as Margaret Sanger did with respect to Germany, Italy, and Japan prior to World War II. She labeled "overpopulation as a cause of war," and cited John Maynard Keynes as authority. "[I]nternational peace could in no way be made secure until measures had been put into effect to deal with explosive populations."[30] A typical recent statement is ". . . the closer man approaches the limits of ultimate density or 'carrying capacity,' the more probable is nuclear warfare."[31]

But the idea about land and territoriality and population that Hitler held—the idea that has prevailed since the beginning of recorded history—does not apply in a modern world. Additional territory nowadays generally has no value to a nation. And to top it all off, oft-denounced population growth is the underlying cause of this happy situation.

This does not mean that wars have ended. Nations start wars for many reasons. David S. Kleinman argues cogently that if ever a population change might have altered the propensity for war, it should have been the Black Death, by increasing the availability of land—but warring continued unabated.[32] Quincy Wright concluded that economic issues have not been the main cause of war, or even the dominant cause.

> In sum, studies of both the direct and indirect influence of economic factors on the causation of war indicate that they have been much less important than political

ambitions, ideological convictions, technological change, legal claims, irrational psychological complexes, ignorance, and unwillingness to maintain conditions of peace in a changing world.[33]

But it seems inarguable that the desire for more agricultural land has been a major motive for wars in the past.

Ask yourself: Why would a country want a larger land area? And how might it help a nation's material standard of living to increase its land area?

Imagine the United States suddenly owning a chunk of empty land now in Mexico or Canada. The area of U.S. agricultural land already is huge. Yet only about two million people—2 percent of the U.S. labor force—work on farms. Even a *doubling* of the size of the United States would put dirt under the feet of only another two million people. And people in agriculture do not derive higher than average incomes from farming. Therefore, newly made farmers would not gain much by an increase in U.S. agricultural land.

Put it differently. Say a foreign buyer makes a fair offer for all U.S. cropland. The offer would be less than a tenth of *one year's* national income. The market value of U.S. cropland is about what we spend in two years for recreation plus one year's expenditure on tobacco (without even including expenditures on liquor). Clearly, then, all the cropland in the United States would not be worth even a minor skirmish.

Agricultural exports and the balance of payments don't change the picture. Japan has a whopping trade surplus without exporting much food.

Nor is annexing a piece of Canada or Mexico with people on it beneficial. U.S. citizens would not increase their wealth if the Mexican and Canadian owners were to stay where they are and continue to take whatever "rents" the land provides.

Kings in the past have thought to conquer territory in order to "farm" the taxes. But a modern nation cannot rip off some of its residents for the benefit of others.

Nor would more territory make urban people feel less crowded. One's sense of crowding does not depend upon the total land area of the country, or even the land area per person. The most important factor is the size of a person's home in square feet of floor space. Let's hypothetically give each person two rooms measuring 15 feet by 15 feet—a spacious luxury apartment with many times more space than Abraham Lincoln had in the log cabin in which he grew up. If high-rise housing with that much space were built to the height of the Sears Building in Chicago, or the World Trade Center's Twin Towers in New York, or even the Empire State Building, 155 million people could live on Manhattan Island, while more than a billion could live within the land area of New York City.

Still another nonreason for wanting to conquer another nation nowadays is acquisition of its stock of assets. Perhaps in prehistoric times it made some sense for a nomad tribe to attack and expel the inhabitants of a "city" in order to take over its dwellings and utensils. But nowadays if the conquering country is as rich as the conquered, it already has a stock of assets with which its population works. Exchanging all the old stock—or even part of it—for a new and strange stock of assets is not likely to increase the output of its citizens.

The notion of a poor population taking over the developed world, as dramatized in Jean Raspail's *Camp of the Saints*, is even less plausible. The uneducated poor demonstrably have no capacity to operate the instruments of a modern society, or else they would not be poor. A "horde" of them moving into and taking over a rich country would soon find herdsmen sheltering themselves and their flocks in computer factories. As someone once remarked, if Indians and Americans exchanged countries, in a few decades the United States would look like India now, and India like the United States. (On the other hand, if Indian newborns and American newborns exchanged educational upbringings at birth, the countries also would exchange appearances very rapidly.)

The process by which we come to this astonishing state of affairs is even more astonishing. A spurt of population growth, or of income, inevitably puts short-run pressure on resources such as agricultural land. The impending shortages, and the concomitant increase in prices of the resources, cause a search for ways to mitigate the shortages. Eventually some individuals or organizations succeed in finding new solutions to the resource problems. The discoveries eventually cause humanity to enjoy greater availability of resources than if population growth and pressure on resources had never occurred.

30

Are People an Environmental Pollution?

> Most environmental, economic and social problems . . . arise from this driving force: too many people using too many resources at too fast a rate.
> (*Blue Planet Group, Ottawa, Canada, September 1991*)

HUMAN BEINGS get a bad name from some writers on environmental matters. You and I and our neighbors are accused of polluting this world and making it a worse place to live. We are charged with being emitters of such poisonous substances as lead, sulfur dioxide, and carbon monoxide; we are indicted as producers of noise, garbage, and congestion. More people, more pollution, says the bill. Even more ugly, you and I and our neighbors, together with our children, have been referred to as "people pollution" and the "population plague." That is, our very existence is the core of the problem, in their view.

Indeed, the effect of population growth upon the environment has come to be the focus of the antinatalist environmental movement. This is the most recent scare in a sequence in which the antinatalists successively have pointed to purported ill effects on agriculture, natural resources, and education, and then each of these scares in turn was found to be without foundation.

It has come to seem as if one must be against population growth if one is to be for pollution control. And pollution control in itself appeals to everyone, for good reason. A full-length *New York Times Magazine* piece on pollution ended, "The long-term relief is perfectly obvious: Fewer 'capita.'"[1] And the messages in figure 30-1 appeared as a full-page advertisements in leading newspapers. So let us inquire how various rates of population growth would affect the amount of pollution.

The sober question we wish to answer here is: What is the effect of human population size and growth upon pollution levels? The general answer this chapter offers is that, although there may be some short-run increase in pollution due to population increases, the additional pollution is relatively small. And in the long run, pollution is likely to be significantly *less* due to population growth.

We shall also analyze how prudent risk-avoidance fits with our conclusions about population growth's effect on pollution. Though values enter strongly into any such analysis, we shall see that, on the basis of most commonly held values, the desire to avoid risk to humanity from a pollution catastrophe does not lead to the conclusion that population growth should be limited by social policy.

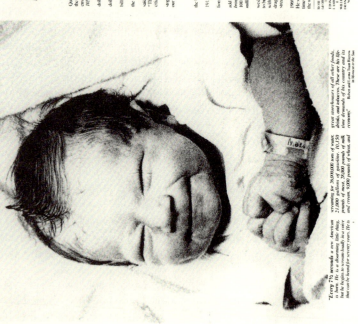

Figure 30-1a. Propaganda on Pollution and Population Growth ("We can't lick the pollution problem without considering this little fellow")

Figure 30-1b. More Propaganda ("Have you ever been mugged? . . .")

Before we begin on the serious work, we should note that most discussion of these matters goes no further than this sort of commonsensical—but wrong—thinking: Given that there are a thousand times as many people on Earth now as there were ten thousand years ago, the volume of waste animal bones that are now produced each year as the result of eating game should be a thousand times as large as the volume then, and the mounds should be much higher in the more populated places than elsewhere. But lo and behold, we do not see huge mounds of bones taking over the planet, as such an analysis would lead us to expect. And we do not find that the most densely populated rich countries—say, Holland, Great Britain, and Japan—are dirtier than (say) less densely populated rich countries such as the United States and Australia, or than sparsely populated poor countries in (say) Africa. We must consider why not.

Income, Growth, Population, and Pollution

The more developed an economy, and the more people it has, the more pollutants it produces; this story has been well told by Barry Commoner, and it is still the main line of conventional thinking on the subject.[2] The total amounts of most kinds of pollutants depend upon the total scale of industry, and this scale may be roughly gauged by a country's GNP (except that beyond some per capita income, the proportion of industrial products in the GNP begins to decline as the proportion of services increases). A less-known story is that along with higher income and its consequent greater supply of pollutants comes a greater demand for cleanup, plus an increased capacity to pay for it and greater technical ability to execute the cleanup; this reduction in pollution as a result of increased income has been documented for the 1970s and 1980s for Europe (see chapter 15, footnote 6). As we saw in chapter 9, the technology for cleaning up already exists in just about every case, and waits only for our will to expend the time and money to put it to work.

For many years governments did not control the flow of industrial pollutants very well. But in recent years there has come a change in the rules of the game in the Western countries due to a combination of rising incomes and consciousness raising by environmentalists. And this has caused the favorable trends in air and water quality that we saw in chapter 9.

If you have any doubt that increases in income are associated with a decrease in pollution, examine the levels of street cleanliness in the richer versus the poorer countries of the world, the mortality rates of richer versus poorer countries, and the mortality rates (or cleanliness of streets) among richer versus poorer people within particular countries.[3]

If increased income makes for less pollution, what is the effect of population growth? You might think that adding people necessarily induces more pollution. Yet in Australia's affluent cities, for example, there is much pollution despite the country's low population. And analyses find only a slight short-run relationship between population growth and pollution.[4] In the long run, however, the total pollution output will be more or less proportional to the labor force (and hence, to population) for a given level of technology, all else being equal as you might expect.

It is not sound, though, to assume that all else is equal. When pollution increases, political forces arise to fight it; this is the force that warred against smoke pollution in Great Britain at the local level beginning centuries ago, and that has had success since the nineteenth century (see chapter 9). Once this process begins, the result may well be less pollution than earlier—or, of course, nothing may happen for a while except an even worse level of pollution.

Also as a result of a higher population, and of the higher income that occurs after a while, new techniques emerge to handle the temporarily worse problems of pollution. And eventually there results a cleaner world than before population and income grew.

Regarding any particular period in the near future, especially in poor countries, the overall outcome simply cannot be known in advance; neither economic logic nor political history can predict with confidence whether the intermediate-run result of the larger population and of the initially higher pollution will be a situation better or worse than if the population had not grown so large. Yet we must keep in mind the empirical fact that over the longest sweep of human history, while population has grown enormously, total pollution—as measured by life expectancy, and by the rate of deaths due to socially transmitted and socially caused diseases such as cholera and smog-caused emphysema—has fallen markedly. We do not live amongst ever-more-huge garbage dumps infested by rats, as in earlier times.

The outcome of more people also depends very heavily on the kind of economic-political system in the given country. As discussed in chapter 9, Eastern European Communist countries suffered much worse damage from pollution than did Western free-enterprise countries, in considerable part because socialism rewards managers for using a high ratio of inputs to outputs, whereas a market system rewards managers for economizing on inputs.

The latest environmental justification for slowing or halting population growth is supposed global warming (see chapter 18 on global warming and the greenhouse effect). A World Bank paper on the subject concludes, "The global negative externality represented by rapid population growth in developing countries provides a strong, new rationale for developed countries, in their own interests, to finance programs that would reduce population growth in developing countries."[5] That is, the old rationales for World Bank population-control programs—economic growth, resource conservation, and the like—having been discredited, a new "rationale" has been developed on the basis of speculative assumptions about global warming's economic effects derived from controversial climatalogical science.

But isn't it obvious, the environmentalists argue, that additional people and additional economic growth will cause us to use more energy and hence emit more greenhouse gases? Therefore, even if we can't be sure of the greenhouse effect, wouldn't it be prudent to cut back on growth? It does make sense that during the next half-century or century there will be increased energy use as a result of more people as well as increased consumption per person. Some forecasts project that the former component will be larger, some the latter.[6] But contrary to the implications of many such writings on the subject, these events need not be seen as malign. Shifts to nuclear fission and to other new sources of energy may result in reduced total emissions even as total energy use goes up—as was the case in the United Kingdom and the United States over the years.

Aesthetics, Pollution, and Population Growth

Because aesthetics are a matter of taste, it is not sensible to dispute about them. For those to whom being alone in a virgin forest is the ideal, other visitors constitute "people pollution"; for those with different tastes, seeing lots of people at play is the best sight of all.

Of those who praise a reduction of population in the name of making the world more beautiful, I ask these questions: (1) Have you not seen much beauty on this Earth that comes from the hands of humans—gardens, statues, skyscrapers, graceful bridges? (2) The population of Athens was only six thousand persons in 1823. Do you suppose that Athens was more beautiful (a) in 1823, or (b) two millennia earlier when it was more crowded? (3) If the world's population now were only a hundredth of what it actually is, would there be a transportation system to get you to Yosemite, the Grand Canyon, the Antarctic, Kenya's wildlife preserves, or Lake Victoria?

We hear calls that humankind should live in equilibrium with nature. The last time we were in equilibrium is when our numbers were small and not growing—nomad tribes. Then we did not change the environment much from century to century. But growth in numbers, civilization, and alteration of the environment went together. Humans ceased to be like other animals, and began to *make*. Equilibrium then necessarily was left behind. Creating is not consistent with equilibrium.

Overall, human creation is greater than human destruction, in the sense that our environment is becoming progressively more hospitable to humankind—a basic theme of this book. The movement away from equilibrium is a movement toward safety and sustenance. This progress carries with it some undesirable features for a while, but eventually we get around to fixing them.

The doomsayers believe we are in a period of greater destruction than creation—that is, headed toward a reduction in the safety and hospitableness of our environment. They speak about the planet being in a worsening "crisis." But if this were true, it would be a complete break with all past trends. Of course this is logically possible. But it is helpful to remember that there have always been plausible-sounding theories of approaching doom, always statements that this moment is different than any that has gone before; the making and believing of such ideas seems to be psychologically irresistible for many. But to succumb to such unfounded beliefs is to court disaster—as groups that have sold all their belongings and gone to mountain tops to await the end of the world have found out.

Pollution, Population, and Risk of Catastrophe

A safety-minded person might say, "With regard to pollutant X, perhaps the additional risk that is induced by a larger population is a small one. But would it not be prudent to avoid even this small possibility?" This question is related to the issue of risk aversion discussed in the section on nuclear energy in chapter 13. To state the problem in its most frightening form: In an advanced technological society there is always the possibility that a totally new form of pollution will emerge and finish us all before we can do anything about it.

Though the incidence of general catastrophes to the human race has decreased from the time of the Black Death onward, and though I'd bet that it is not so, the risk *may* have begun to increase in recent decades—from atomic bombs or from some unknown but powerful pollution. But the present risk of catastrophe will only be known in the future, with hindsight. The arguments in Part One about nonfinite natural resources cannot refute the possibility of some explosive unknown disaster. Indeed, there is no logical answer to this threat except to note that life with perfect security is not possible—and probably would not be meaningful.

It might make sense to control population growth if the issue were simply the increased risk of catastrophe due to population growth, and if only the *number of deaths* mattered, rather than the number of healthy lives lived. A flaw in this line of reasoning is revealed, however, by pushing it to its absurd endpoint: One may reduce the risk of pollution catastrophe to zero by reducing to zero the number of persons who are alive. And this policy obviously is unacceptable to all except a few. Therefore we must dig deeper to learn how pollution ought to influence our views about population size and growth.

The argument that population growth is a bad thing because it may bring about new and possibly catastrophic forms of pollution is a special case of a more general argument: Avoid any change because it may bring about some devastating destruction by a power as yet unknown. There is an irrefutable logic in this argument. In its own terms, adding a few not-too-unreasonable assumptions, it cannot be proven wrong, as follows: Assume that any alteration in industrial technique may have some unexpected ill effects. Assume also that the system is acceptably safe right now. Additional people increase the need for change, and this makes a prima facie case against population growth. And the same argument can be applied to economic growth: Economic growth brings about change, which can bring dangers. (See comments by Ehrlich and Lovins in chapter 13.) Hence economic growth is to be avoided.

Of course, this sit-tight, leave-well-enough-alone posture is possible for us 1990s humans only because economic and population growth in the past produced the changes that brought many of us to the "well enough" state that might now be "left alone."[7] That is, the high life expectancy and high living standard of middle-class people in developed countries could not have come about if people in the past had not produced the changes that got the most fortunate of us here—and if they had not suffered from some changes in doing so. We now are living off our inheritance from past generations the way some children live off the inheritance of parents who worked hard and saved.

There is nothing logically wrong with living off an inheritance without in turn increasing the heritage of knowledge and high living standards that will be left to subsequent generations. But you should at least be clear that this is what you are doing if you opt for "zero growth"—if zero growth really were possible. (In fact, upon close examination, the concept of zero economic growth, unlike zero population growth, turns out to be either so vague as to be undefinable, or just plain nonsense. Furthermore, a no-growth policy provides benefits to the well-off that are withheld from the poor.)[8]

Proponents of zero growth argue that future generations will benefit from fewer changes now. That cannot be ruled out logically. But the historical evidence quite clearly runs the other way: If our ancestors had, at any time in the past, opted for zero population growth or for a frozen economic system, we would certainly be less well-off than we now are. Hence it seems reasonable to project the same trend into the future. Most specifically, a larger economic capability and a larger population of knowledge creators has put into our hands a wider variety of more powerful tools for preventing and controlling threats to our lives and environment—especially communicable diseases and hunger—than society could have bequeathed to us if its size had been frozen at any time in the past.

Furthermore, additional people can also improve the chances of reducing pollution even in their own generation, because additional people create new *solutions* for problems, as well as creating new problems. Let's consider a poor-country example: Higher population density may increase the chance of communicable disease. But higher population density also is the only force that really gets rid of malaria, as we shall see in the next chapter, because the swamps that breed malaria-carrying mosquitoes do not co-exist with settled fields and habitation. And of course, if population growth had never occurred, there would not likely have been the growth of civilization and science that led to the existing armamentarium of pharmaceutical weapons against malaria and improved methods of fighting mosquitoes.

On balance, then, we must put onto the scales not only the increased chance of a pollution catastrophe induced by more people; we must also weigh the benefits of the new knowledge the additional people create to control pollutants and their ill consequences. So it is not at all clear whether the chance of catastrophe (involving ten thousand or one million people) is greater with a world population of six trillion or six billion, or with a growth rate of 2 percent or 1 percent yearly.

Concerning the *indirect* environmental effects of economic and population growth: It would be an error to assume that all (or even most) of such effects are negative. Happy accidents sometimes arise due to growth. If genetic changes occur (they occur naturally, or we would not be here at all), some of the mutants will be "undesirable," but others will be desirable. And some environmental changes also affect species for the good, as this example shows:

Seafood Industry Finds Fish Thrive in Water Discharged by Power Companies

The water, used as a coolant in generating plants, is about 20 degrees warmer when it leaves a plant than when it entered. Cultivating catfish, oysters, shrimp, trout and other marine life in this warm water often cuts in half the length of time it takes them to mature. Cultured Catfish Co. of Colorado City, Texas, says its catfish grow to 1½ pounds in three to four months in the warm water flowing from a Texas Electric Service plant. It usually takes catfish, considered a delicacy in some parts of the U.S., 18 months to grow that big in a natural pond.[9]

Another example of positive indirect effects are the extraordinary habitats provided for animal and vegetable sea life—especially coral, and tropical fish—provided by oil rigs in the Gulf of Mexico and in the Pacific off the California Coast described in chapter 12.

Still—there is our (probably) natural aversion to risk and uncertainty. Even so, we should keep in mind that risk and uncertainty are not all in one direction, and that the major social and cultural changes that would be needed to prevent growth are also fraught with uncertainty, and possible catastrophe. For example, what would be the social and political implications of freezing the present pattern of income distribution among the poor and the rich due to reduced economic growth? What would be the effects on work incentive if people were told that they could not increase their incomes or have more children? What would be the psychological implications of a stationary economy and society? And which legal sanctions would be imposed to enforce these decisions? Certainly none of these matters is of small importance compared with the likely dangers from catastrophic pollution. Hence there is no prima facie case for ceasing economic or population growth due to fear of pollution.

Summary

More people mean higher total output, and this implies more pollution in the short run, all else being equal. But more people need not imply more pollution in the long run, and they may well imply less pollution; this has been the trend in human history as indicated by the most important general index of pollution—increasing life expectancy. Additional people have created new ways of reducing pollution, and contributed additional resources with which to fight pollution. There is strong reason to expect a similar benign course of events to continue in the future.

31

Are Humans Causing Species Holocaust?

SPECIES EXTINCTION is a key issue for the environmental movement.* It is the subject of magazine stories with titles like "Playing Dice with Megadeath," whose subtitle is "The odds are good that we will exterminate half the world's species within the next century."[1] Species "loss" also is the focal point of fund-raising for the environmental organizations. Congress is petitioned time and again for large sums of public money to be used directly and indirectly for programs to protect species and for "debt for Nature" swaps. And species preservation was the subject of major dispute among the nations at the "Rio Summit" in June 1992.

The World Wildlife Fund's fund-raising letter frames the issue as follows: "Without firing a shot, we may kill one-fifth of all species of life on this planet in the next 10 years."

The mass media repeat and amplify this warning. The *Washington Post* quotes a top Smithsonian official, Thomas Lovejoy, saying that "A potential biological transformation of the planet unequaled perhaps since the disappearance of the dinosaur" is about to occur. And the *Post* quotes Edward O. Wilson on this being "the folly our descendants are least likely to forgive us."

The conservationists bludgeon the federal government for money and action based on their apocalyptic claims. In a fund-raising pitch from the World Wildlife Fund, president Russell E. Train describes in detail how the organization rallied support for reauthorization of the Endangered Species Act. The key element was informing Congress that "some scientists believe that up to 1 million species of life will become extinct by the end of this century" unless governments "do something" about it.

"When we talk about the loss of 1 million species," Train says in his letter, "we are talking about a global loss with consequences that science can scarcely begin to predict. . . . The future of the world could be altered drastically if we allow a million species to disappear by the year 2000."

The recommendations that leading biologists and ecologists base upon these nonfacts (as we shall soon show them to be) are very far-reaching.

---

* For a fuller discussion of this topic, see Simon and Wildavsky 1995. I appreciate Aaron Wildavsky's collaboration on this topic.

Edward O. Wilson and Paul Ehrlich actually ask that governments act "to reduce the scale of human activities." More specifically, they want us "to cease 'developing' any more relatively undisturbed land" because "Every new shopping center built in the California chaparral . . . every swamp converted into a rice paddy or shrimp farm means less biodiversity."[2] *Science* magazine applauds these calls for major governmental policy changes. These proposals—slamming the brakes on progress—are what many ecologists hope to impose on the nations of the world. This is no small matter.

The issue first came to scientific prominence in 1979 with Norman Myers's book *The Sinking Ark*. It then was brought to an international public and onto the U.S. policy agenda by the 1980 *Global 2000 Report to the President*. These still are the canonical texts.

Unlike the story in chapter 9 about the loss of farmland scare, where the crisis has vanished instead of the farmland, the scare about extinction of species was not quickly extinguished when its statistical basis was shown not to exist in the early 1980s, but instead continued bigger than ever.

The *Global 2000* forecast extraordinary losses of species between 1980 and 2000. "Extinctions of plant and animal species will increase dramatically. Hundreds of thousands of species—perhaps as many as 20 percent of all species on earth—will be irretrievably lost as their habitats vanish, especially in tropical forests," it said.[3]

Yet the data on the observed rates of species extinction are wildly at variance with common belief, and do not provide support for the various policies suggested to deal with the purported dangers. Furthermore, recent scientific and technical advances—especially seed banks and genetic engineering, and perhaps electronic mass-testing of new drugs—have rendered much less crucial the maintenance of a particular species of plant life in its natural habitat than would have been the case in earlier years.

The key questions are: What is the history of species extinction until now? What are the most reasonable forecasts of future extinction? What will be the results of extinctions (including any new species that come to occupy the niches of those extinguished) on species diversity? What will be the economic and noneconomic impacts of the expected course of species diversity?

Society properly is concerned about possible dangers to species. Individual species, and perhaps all species taken together, constitute a valuable endowment, and we should guard their survival just as we guard our other physical and social assets. But we should strive for as clear and unbiased an understanding as possible in order to make the best possible judgments about how much time and money to spend in guarding them, in a world in which this valuable activity must compete with other valuable activities, including the guarding of valuable aspects of civilization and of human life.

Species Loss Estimates

The basic forecast for loss of species comes from Lovejoy:

> What then is a reasonable estimate of global extinctions by 2000? In the low deforestation case, approximately 15 percent of the planet's species can be expected to be lost. In the high deforestation case, perhaps as much as 20 percent will be lost. This means that of the 3–10 million species now present on the earth, at least 500,000–600,000 will be extinguished during the next two decades.[4]

That statement summarizes a table of Lovejoy's which shows an estimated range of between 437,000 and 1,875,000 extinctions out of a present estimated total of 3–10 million species.

The basis of any useful projection must be some body of experience collected under conditions that encompass the expected conditions, or that can reasonably be extrapolated to the expected conditions. But none of Lovejoy's references contain any scientifically impressive body of experience. The only published source given for his key table[5] is Myers's *The Sinking Ark*.

The Sinking Ark

Myers's 1979 summary may be taken as the basic source:

> As a primitive hunter, man probably proved himself capable of eliminating species, albeit as a relatively rare occurrence. From the year A.D. 1600, however, he became able, through advancing technology, to over-hunt animals to extinction in just a few years, and to disrupt extensive environments just as rapidly. Between the years 1600 and 1900, man eliminated around seventy-five known species, almost all of them mammals and birds—virtually nothing has been established about how many reptiles, amphibians, fishes, invertebrates and plants disappeared. Since 1900 man has eliminated around another seventy-five known species—again, almost all of them mammals and birds, with hardly anything known about how many other creatures have faded from the scene. The rate from the year 1600 to 1900, roughly one species every 4 years, and the rate during most of the present century, about one species per year, are to be compared with a rate of possibly one per 1000 years during the "great dying" of the dinosaurs.
>
> Since 1960, however, when growth in human numbers and human aspirations began to exert greater impact on natural environments, vast territories in several major regions of the world have become so modified as to be cleared of much of their main wildlife. The result is that the extinction rate has certainly soared, though the details mostly remain undocumented. In 1974 a gathering of scientists concerned

with the problem hazarded a guess that the overall extinction rate among all species, whether known to science or not, could now have reached 100 species per year. [Here Myers refers to *Science* 1974, pp. 646–47.]

Yet even this figure seems low. A single ecological zone, the tropical moist forests, is believed to contain between 2 and 5 million species. If present patterns of exploitations persist in tropical moist forests, much virgin forest is likely to have disappeared by the end of the century, and much of the remainder will have been severely degraded. This will cause huge numbers of species to be wiped out. . . .

Let us suppose that, as a consequence of this man-handling of natural environments, the final one-quarter of this century witnesses the elimination of 1 million species—a far from unlikely prospect. This would work out, during the course of 25 years, at an average extinction rate of 40,000 species per year, or rather over 100 species per day. The greatest exploitation pressures will not be directed at tropical forests and other species-rich biomes until towards the end of the period. That is to say, the 1990s could see many more species accounted for than the previous several decades. But already the disruptive processes are well underway, and it is not unrealistic to suppose that, right now, at least one species is disappearing each day. By the late 1980s we could be facing a situation where one species becomes extinct each hour.[6]

We may extract these key points from the above summary quotation: (1) The estimated extinction rate of known species is about *one every four years* between the years 1600 and 1900. (2) The estimated rate is about *one a year* from 1900 to the present. No sources are given by Myers for these two estimates. (3) Some scientists (in Myers's words) have "hazarded a guess" that the extinction rate "could now have reached" 100 species per year. That is, the estimate is simply conjecture and is not even a point estimate but rather an upper bound. The source given for the "some scientists" statement is not a scholarly article by an expert but a staff-written news report.[7] It should be noted, however, that the subject of this guess is different than the subject of the estimates in (1) and (2), because the former includes mainly or exclusively birds and mammals whereas the latter includes all species. While this difference implies that (1) and (2) may be too low a basis for estimating the present extinction rate of all species, it also implies that there is even less statistical basis for estimating extinction rates among lesser known species than there is for birds and mammals. (4) This guessed upper limit in (3) of 100 species per year is then increased and used by Myers, and then by Lovejoy, as the basis for the "projections" quoted above. In the *Global 2000 Report* the language has become "are likely to lead" to the extinction of between 14 percent and 20 percent of all species before the year 2000.[8] So an upper limit for the present that is pure guesswork has become the basis of a forecast for the future which has been published in newspapers to be read by tens or hundreds of millions of people and understood as a scientific statement.

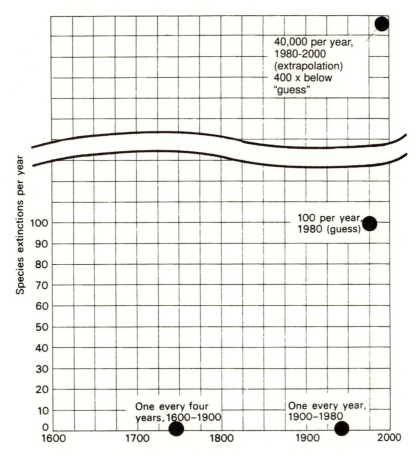

Figure 31-1. Meyers-Lovejoy Estimates of Species Extinction and Their Extrapolations to the Year 2000

The two historical rates stated by Myers, together with the yearly rates implied by Lovejoy's estimates, are plotted together in figure 31-1. It is clear that without explicitly bringing into consideration some additional force, one could extrapolate almost any rate one chooses for the year 2000, and the Lovejoy extrapolation would have no better claim to belief than a rate that is, say, one-hundredth as large. Looking at the two historical points alone, many forecasters would be likely to project a rate much closer to the past than to Lovejoy's, on the basis of the common wisdom that in the absence of additional information, the best first approximation for a variable tomorrow is its value today, and the best second approximation is that the variable will change at the same rate in the future that it has in the past. The uncertainty about the definition of species only adds to the confusion.

Projected change in the amount of tropical forests implicitly underlies the difference between past and projected species-loss rates in Lovejoy's diagram. But to connect this element logically, there must be systematic evidence relating an amount of tropical forest removed to a rate of species reduction. Against the theory, Ariel Lugo details the situation in Puerto Rico, where "human activity reduced the area of primary forests by 99%, but, because of coffee shade and secondary forests, forest cover was never below 10 to 15%. This massive forest conversion did not lead to a correspondingly massive species extinction, certainly nowhere near the 50% alluded to by Myers."[9]

All this implies that there is no basis to prefer as an estimate (a) Lovejoy's huge projected rates of extinction, rather than (b) very modest rates continuing about the same as in the past. And on this estimate depends the decision to implement or not to implement large-scale national policies. (I repeat, I do not suggest that no protection policies should be undertaken. Rather, I suggest that other sorts of data to estimate extinction rates are needed as the basis for policy decisions.)

During the 1980s there was increasing recognition that the rate of species loss really is not known. As of 1989 Myers wrote, "Regrettably we have no way of knowing the actual current rate of extinction in tropical forests, nor can we even make an accurate guess."[10] And Paul Colinvaux refers to the extinctions as "incalculable."[11] One would think that this absence of knowledge would make anyone leery about estimating future extinctions.

Nevertheless, Myers continues, "We can make substantive assessments by looking at species numbers before deforestation and then applying the analytical techniques of biogeography. . . . According to the theory of island biogeography, we can realistically reckon that when a habitat has lost 90% of its extent, it has lost half of its species."[12] This is mere speculation, however. And as noted above, Lugo found disconfirming evidence in Puerto Rico. Yet the conservationists go right on pressing for expensive policies on the unproven assumption that the number of species being extinguished is huge.

It is hard to grasp the abstraction of all species taken together, so some data on birds may be useful in fixing one's thoughts. Although we cannot know which then-unknown species were made extinct, there is some information on bird species, which have long been rather well known. In 1600 there were estimated to be 8,184 species of birds in the world. As of the 1960s, ninety-four of them were thought to be extinct, only six of which had ever lived in North America either exclusively or on that continent and elsewhere, and not all in the United States. And as of the 1960s there were estimated to be four hundred species in the world that did not exist in 1600—a net gain of about three hundred species during the period of vast population growth and settlement of land.[13]

Easterbrook (1995, p. 82) obtained data from the National Audubon Society on trends since 1966 in the numbers of birds of the species Rachel Carson saw as going extinct: "Scorecard: of 40 birds Carson said might by now be extinct or nearly so, 19 have stable populations, 14 have increasing populations, and seven are declining."

The species that are supposedly little known but at great risk of extinction are insects. But recent research on fossils has shown "low rates of extinction" for insects over millions of years, which implies that insects are very resistant to extinction.[14] This squares with recent experience of how hard it is to extinguish an insect such as the mosquito or the Mediterranean fruit fly ("medfly") in California.

Starting in the early 1980s, I published the above critical analysis of the standard extinction estimates. For several years these criticisms produced no response at all. But then in response to questions that I and others raised, the "official" IUCN (the World Conservation Union) commissioned a book edited by Whitmore and Sayer to inquire into the extent of extinctions.[15] The results of that project must be considered amazing.

All the authors—the very conservation biologists who have been most alarmed by the threat of species die-offs—continue to be concerned about the rate of extinction. Nevertheless, they confirm the central assertion; all agree that the rate of *known* extinctions has been and continues to be very low. I will tax your patience with lengthy quotations (with emphasis supplied) documenting the consensus that there is no evidence of massive or increasing rates of species extinction, because this testimony from the conservation biologists themselves is especially convincing; furthermore, if only shorter quotes were presented, the skeptical reader might worry that the quotes were taken out of context. (Even so, the skeptic may want to check the original texts to see that the quotations fairly represent the gist of the the authors' arguments.)

On the subject of the estimated rates:

[Sixty] birds and mammals are known to have become extinct between 1900 and 1950.[16]

It is a commonplace that forests of the eastern United States were reduced over two centuries to fragments totalling 1–2% of their original extent, and that during this destruction, only three forest birds went extinct—the Carolina parakeet (Conuropsis carolinensis), the ivory-billed woodpecker (Campephilus principalis principalis), and the passenger pigeon (Ectopistes migratorius). Although deforestation certainly contributed to the decline of all three species, it was probably not critical for the pigeon or the parakeet (Greenway, 1967). *Why, then, would one predict massive extinction from similar destruction of tropical forest?*[17]

IUCN, together with the World Conservation Monitoring Centre, has amassed large volumes of data from specialists around the world relating to species decline, and it would seem sensible to compare these more empirical data with the global extinction estimates. In fact, these and other data indicate that *the number of recorded extinctions for both plants and animals is very small. . . .*[18]

Known extinction rates are very low. Reasonably good data exist only for mammals and birds, and the current rate of extinction is about one species per year (Reid and Miller, 1989). If other taxa were to exhibit the same liability to extinction as mammals and birds (as some authors suggest, although others would dispute this), then, if the total number of species in the world is, say, 30 million, the annual rate of extinction would be some 2300 species per year. This is a very significant and disturbing number, but it is much less than most estimates given over the last decade.[19]

[I]f we assume that today's tropical forests occupy only about 80% of the area they did in the 1830s, *it must be assumed that during this contraction, very large numbers of species have been lost in some areas. Yet surprisingly there is no clear-cut evidence for this.* . . . Despite extensive enquiries we have been unable to obtain conclusive evidence to support the suggestion that massive extinctions have taken place in recent times as Myers and others have suggested. On the contrary, work on projects such as Flora Meso-Americana has, at least in some cases, revealed an increase in abundance in many species (Blackmore, pers. comm. 1991). An exceptional and much quoted situation is described by Gentry (1986) who reports the quite dramatic level of evolution in situ in the Centinela ridge in the foothills of the Ecuadorian Andes where he found that at least 38 and probably as many as 90 species (10% of the total flora of the ridge) were endemic to the "unprepossessing ridge." However, the last patches of forest were cleared subsequent to his last visit and "its prospective 90 new species have already passed into botanical history," or so it was assumed. Subsequently, Dodson and Gentry (1991) modified this to say that an undetermined number of species at Centinela are apparently extinct, following brief visits to other areas such as Lita where *up to 11 of the species previously considered extinct were refound,* and at Poza Honda near La Mana where six were rediscovered.[20]

[A]ctual extinctions remain low . . . As Greuter (1991) aptly comments, "*Many endangered species appear to have either an almost miraculous capacity for survival,* or a guardian angel is watching over their destiny! This means that it is not too late to attempt to protect the Mediterranean flora as a whole, while still identifying appropriate priorities with regard to the goals and means of conservation."[21]

[T]he group of zoologists could not find a single known animal species which could be properly declared as extinct, in spite of the massive reduction in area and fragmentation of their habitats in the past decades and centuries of intensive human activity. A second list of over 120 lesser-known animal species, some of which may later be included as threatened, show no species considered extinct; and the older Brazilian list of threatened plants, presently under revision, also indicated no species as extinct (Cavalcanti, 1981).[22]

Closer examination of the existing data on both well-and little-known groups, however, *supports the affirmation that little or no species extinction has yet occurred* (though some may be in very fragile persistence) in the Atlantic forests. Indeed, an appreciable number of species considered extinct 20 years ago, including several birds and six butterflies, have been rediscovered more recently.[23]

And here are some comments from that volume on the lack of any solid basis for estimation:

How large is the loss of species likely to be? *Although the loss of species may rank among the most significant environmental problems of our time, relatively few attempts have been made to rigorously assess its likely magnitude.*[24]

It is impossible to estimate even approximately how many unrecorded species may have become extinct.[25]

While better knowledge of extinction rates can clearly improve the design of public policies, it is equally apparent that *estimates of global extinction rates are fraught with imprecision. We do not yet know how many species exist, even to within an order of magnitude.*[26]

[T]he literature addressing this phenomenon is relatively small. . . . Efforts to clarify the magnitude of the extinction crisis and the steps that can be taken to defuse the crisis could considerably expand the financial and political support for actions to confront what is indisputably the most serious issue that the field of ecology faces, and arguably the most serious issue faced by humankind today.[27]

The best tool available to estimate species extinction rates is the use of species-area curves. . . . This approach has formed the basis for almost all current estimates of species extinction rates.[28]

There are many reasons why recorded extinctions do not match the predictions and extrapolations that are frequently published. . . .[29]

This specific observation from the Foreword to that volume is illuminating:

The coastal forests of Brazil have been reduced in area as severely as any tropical forest type in the world. According to calculation, this should have led to considerable species loss. Yet no known species of its old, largely endemic, fauna can be regarded as extinct. (Martin W. Holdgate, "Foreword," in Whitmore and Sayer, p. xvii)

The Risks from Species Loss

Many biologists agree that the extinction numbers are quite uncertain. But they go on to say the numbers do not matter scientifically. The policy implications would be the same, they say, even if the numbers were different even by several orders of magnitude. But if so, why mention any numbers at all? The answer, quite clearly, is that these numbers do matter in one important way: they have the power to frighten the public in a fashion that smaller numbers would not. I find no scientific justification for such use of numbers.

One window on the risks we run from species loss is to look backwards and wonder: What kinds of species may have been extinguished when the settlers clear-cut the Middle West of the United States? Could we be much the poorer now for their loss? Obviously we do not know the answers. But it seems hard to even *imagine* that we would be enormously better off with the persistence of *any hypothetical* species. This casts some doubt on the economic value of species that might be lost elsewhere.

Ecologists draw far-reaching conclusions and call for strong actions based on their beliefs about the rate of species extinction. One "plan to protect North American biodiversity calls for nothing less than resetting the entire continent."

> [T]he project calls for a network of wilderness reserves, human buffer zones, and wildlife corridors stretching across huge tracts of land—hundreds of millions of acres, as much as half of the continent . . . the long-term goal of the Wildlands Project is nothing less than a transformation of America from a place where 4.7% of the land is wilderness to an archipelago of human-inhabited islands surrounded by natural areas. . . . The science is pointing in this direction largely because of a growing conviction among conservation biologists and other scientists that native species, especially big carnivores such as wolves, grizzly bears, and mountain lions, need enormous amounts of space to survive. Giving animals that space can be viewed as the logical extension of laws such as the Endangered Species Act, which mandates that biodiversity must be saved no matter what the cost.[30]

The framers of the plan want to remove roads, because they "expose animals to the hazards of traffic" and "act as funnels for exotic plants."[31] A justification of the plan is to "prevent a mass extinction event." The boosters of this plan are not "extremists"; rather, a person such as Edward Wilson calls himself an "enthusiastic supporter."

The biologists want us to write a blank check, as society would never do for anything else. Nobody would go to Congress and ask for money to give food to hungry children, or put guard rails on highways, without any idea about how many people are at risk. The biologists justify behaving differently in this case on the grounds that we who are nonbiologists cannot understand these matters.

Some have said: But was not Rachel Carson's *Silent Spring* an important force for good even though it exaggerated? Maybe so. But the accounts are not yet closed on the indirect and long-run consequences of ill-founded concerns about environmental dangers. And it seems to me that, without some very special justification, there is a strong presumption in favor of stating the facts as best we know them, especially in a scientific context, rather than in any manipulation of the data no matter how well intended.

Still, the question exists: How should decisions be made, and sound policies formulated, with respect to the danger of species extinction? I do not offer a comprehensive answer. It is clear that we cannot simply save all species at any cost, any more than we can save all human lives at any cost. Certainly we must make some informed estimates about the present and future social value of species that might be lost, just as we must estimate the value of human life in order to choose rational policies about public health care services, such as hospitals and surgery. And just as with human life, valuing species relative to other social goods will not be easy, especially because we must put values on some species that we do not even know about. But the job must be done somehow.

We must also try to get more reliable information about the number of species that might be lost with various forest changes. This is a very tough task, too.

Lastly, any policy analysis concerning species loss must explicitly evaluate the total cost of protective actions—for example, the cost of not logging or not building roads in an area. And such a total cost estimate must include the long-run indirect costs of reduction in economic growth to a community's education and general advancement.

Maintaining the Amazon and other areas in a state of stability might even have counterproductive results for species diversity, according to a recent body of research. Natural disturbances, as long as they are not catastrophic, may lead to environmental disturbance and to consequent isolation of species that may "facilitate ever-increasing divergence," as Colinvaux tells us. Colinvaux goes on to suggest that "the highest species richness will be found not where the climate is stable but rather where environmental disturbance is frequent but not excessive."[32] This is another subtle issue which must be taken into account.

Knowing the Unknowable

The argument that even though we do not know how many species are being extinguished, we should take steps to protect them, is logically indistinguishable from the argument that although we do not know at what rate the angels dancing on the head of a pin are dying off, we should undertake vast programs to preserve them. And it smacks of the condemnation to death of witches in Salem on the basis of "spectral evidence" by "afflicted" young girls, charges that the accused could not rebut with any conceivable material evidence. (Indeed, the entire story of Salem is sharply reminiscent of various antiscientific warnings of environmental apocalypse heard today, as Starkey, the author of an excellent book on the witch scare, noticed many decades ago.[33] Indeed, the Salem witch incident was inflamed, Starkey notes, by a then-current best-seller, Michael Wigglesworth's *Day of Doom*. Verily, there is nothing new under the sun with respect to human nature and the vagaries of our mentalities.*)

* (Actually, I believe that it is possible to estimate the amount of extinction with a sound

Perhaps a more apt analogy is to child abuse or racial discrimination. We know that people exist who might be abused, and that some abuse exists. But in the absence of solid information, it would be folly—and considered entirely unscientific—to say how much.

If something is unknowable at present but *knowable in principle*, then the appropriate thing is to find out. This does not necessarily mean finding out by direct observation only. A solid chain of empirical evidence can lead to a reasonable conclusion. But there must be some reasonable chain of evidence and reasoning.

If something is *unknowable in principle*, at least with contemporary techniques, then there is no warrant for any public actions whatsoever. To assert otherwise is to open the door to public actions and expenditures on behalf of anyone who can generate an exciting and frightening hypothetical scenario.

An interesting aspect of the species-preservation issue is that people who refer to themselves as scientists—for example Paul Ehrlich—and who even denounce others for their apparent lack of scientific knowledge (as Ehrlich frequently does; see the Epilogue), themselves actively and proudly engage in such nonscientific argumentation.

Discussing Matters with the Conservationists

In articles in the mid-1980s in the well-known *New Scientist* magazine, in newspapers, in book form, and at conferences, Aaron Wildavsky and I documented the complete absence of evidence for the claim that species extinction is going up rapidly, or even going up at all. No one has disputed our documentation. Nor has anyone adduced any new evidence since then that would demonstrate rapid species extinction. Instead, the biologists who are shouting up the species extinction scam simply ignore the data that falsify their claims of impending doom.

Why is there such an enormous gulf in what you hear from the conservationists and what you are reading here? And why is there no interchange between them and their critics? Let's consider some of the possible reasons.

1. In the case of species extinction, as with many other public issues, there is a tendency to focus only upon the bad effects, and to exclude from consideration possible good effects of human activities. For example, Lugo notes that "because humans have facilitated immigration [of species] and created new environments, exotic species have successfully become established in the Caribbean islands. This has resulted in a general increase in the total inventories

---

sampling scheme that estimates the amount of species found by the sample in two areas when it is known with a census that the species exist in both places. I'd be happy to work on such a scheme if it were to be adopted.)

of bird and tree species."[34] In tropical Puerto Rico where "human activity reduced the area of primary forests by 99%," as great a reduction as could be imagined, "seven bird species . . . became extinct after 500 years of human pressure . . . and . . . exotic [newly resident] species enlarged the species pool. More land birds have been present on the Island in the 1980s (97 species) than were present in pre-Colombian time (60 species)."[35]

Perhaps conservation biologists make mention of the extinctions but not of the newly resident species because, as Lugo notes, "there is a clear aversion to exotic [newly resident] species by preservationists and biologists (in cases such as predatory mammals and pests, with good reason!)."[36] This aversion to transplanted species may derive from the belief that humankind is somehow artificial and not "natural." Consider the language of Myers, who has played as important a role as any person in raising the alarm about species extinction: "[W]hereas past extinctions have occurred by virtue of natural processes, today the virtually exclusive cause is man."[37]

One should distinguish, of course, between the extinction of an indigenous species found nowhere else, and its replacement with a species found elsewhere. But it should be noted that new arrivals from elsewhere often mutate into entire new species. Furthermore, species thought to be lost in one place often pop up years or decades later in the same or another place—even relatively vulnerable species such as the Allocebus lemur of Madagascar where much of the rain forest has been cut; the lemur had not been seen since 1964, but a primalogist went out to find one and did.[38] Another example: The *capitate milkvitch* flower was found near the city of Afula in Israel in 1993 after not having been seen since 1942.[39]

2. It is difficult to have a sensible and civilized argument with biologists on species extinction. One reason is that they require an almost religious test of fealty, and of credentials—whether one is a biologist—before they will consider a person's testimony as relevant. Jared Diamond says: "Our current concern with extinction is sometimes 'pooh-poohed' by nonbiologists with the one-liner "Extinction is the natural fate of species."[40] In my view, the understanding of data is not the private province of any discipline, and the background of the analyst should not be a test of the validity of the analysis. As long as being a biologist is a criterion for entering the debate, the issue cannot be said to be debated rationally.

Another difficulty is that conservation biologists' goals with respect to species diversity are not easy to understand. Sometimes they emphasize the supposed economic benefits of species diversity. For example, in its widely distributed 1990 fund-raising letter (four letters received by my household alone) The World Wildlife Fund asks, "Why should you care about the fate of these forests thousands of miles away?" and answers, "Because not only do they provide food and shelter to at least half the world's species of wildlife, these tropical forests are also the world's largest 'pharmaceutical factory'—the sole source of lifesaving medicines like quinine, man's most potent weapon against malaria. Hundreds of thousands of people owe their lives today to these precious plants, shrubs, and trees. What would we do without them?" Diamond answers similarly: "We need them to produce the oxygen we breathe, absorb the carbon dioxide we exhale, decompose our sewage, provide our food, and maintain the fertility of our soil."[41]

But other biologists—James Quinn and Alan Hastings, for example—say that "maximizing total species diversity is rarely if ever the principal objective of conservation strategies. Other aesthetic, resource preservation, and recreational values are often more important."[42] And Lovejoy says, most inclusively:

> What I'm talking about is rather the elusive goal of defining the minimum size [of habitat] needed to maintain the characteristic diversity of an ecosystem over time. In other words, I think the goals of conservation aren't simply to protect the full array of plant and animal species on the planet, but rather also to protect them in their natural associations so that the relationships between species are preserved and the evolutionary and ecological processes are protected.[43]

This vagueness of goals makes it very difficult to compare the worth of a species-saving activity against another value. What are the relative worths of maintaining the habitat on Mount Graham, Arizona, for about 150 red squirrels who could be kept alive as a species elsewhere, versus using twenty-four acres for an observatory that would be at the forefront of astronomical science?[44] There is much less basis here for a reasoned judgment in terms of costs and benefits than there is even with such thorny issues as electricity from nuclear power versus from coal, or decisions about supporting additional research on cancer versus using the funds for higher Social Security payments, or for defense, or even for lowering taxes.

Policy making is also made difficult by conservationists asserting on the one hand that the purpose of conserving is that it is good for human existence, and on the other hand that human existence must be limited or reduced because it is bad for other species. "There are many realistic ways we can avoid extinctions, such as by preserving natural habitats and limiting human population growth"[45] is a typical statement of that sort—by the same biologist who urges that humans should preserve the species because humans need them for existence!

3. Still another difficulty in conducting reasoned discussion of the subject with biologists is their attitude toward economists, whose trade it is to assess the costs and benefits of proposed public programs. As one of the most noted of conservation biologists, Peter Raven, asserts, "Perhaps the most serious single academic problem in the world is the training of economists."[46] Raven and other biologists believe that the fundamental structure of economic thought is perverted because it leads to unsound social choices by omitting ecological

propositions the biologists consider crucial. But the conservationists do not render those supposedly omitted matters into a form that a calculus of choice can deal with. Herein lies a major intellectual problem for the issue at hand.

4. Many biologists consider the interests of humans and of other species to be opposed. This leads to humankind being seen in a rather ugly light. "[O]ur species has a knack for exterminating others, and we're become better killers all the time" says one of them.[47] A recent article by another is entitled "Extinction on Islands: Man as a Catastrophe."[48]

5. It is quite clear that species are seen by many as having value quite apart from any role they play in human life, a value that is seen as competitive with the value of human life. Great Britain's Prince Philip, now president of the World Wildlife Fund for Nature International, says, "The need for someone to stand up and speak for the earth with wisdom and insight is urgent."[49] And Raven writes, "Although human beings are biologically only one of the millions of species that exist on Earth, we control a highly disproportionate share of the world's resources."[50] This suggests that it is unfair that we "control" more resources than do eagles, mosquitoes, and the AIDS virus.

There is further discussion of the role of values in debate about species in chapter 38 on values.

These beliefs lead to policy recommendations toward the human race which hinge upon a particular set of values about the worth of humans versus the worth of other species, values which our civilization has traditionally not espoused.

6. Yet one more difficulty is that the conservation biologists have the disconcerting propensity to offer metaphors rather than data in discussions of these matters. For example, in response to the fact that some extinctions are unknown, as indeed the species themselves are unknown, one ecologist (Thomas Lovejoy) supposedly likened species extinction to a library being burned before the books had even been cataloged, and therefore there may still be loss even though we don't know what it is. But such a metaphor can be entirely misleading. The example may hold for the library in Alexandria that burned two thousand years ago; there were irreparable losses because we have never found other copies of the books. But a better analogy for species extinction may be a newsstand burning down when we have every reason to believe that there are other copies of the publications on the stand in many other places. Obviously the only way to distinguish which is the appropriate analogy is by empirical study.

7. One of the arguments for preserving all existing species—and therefore for preserving tropical and other wild habitat—is that we do not know what valuable biological properties might be lost, and something that might be lost "could come in handy sometime." This argument reminds me of my father saving every old piece of string from packages, and every piece of junk he

found on the street, because "it could come in handy sometime." I still have coffee cans taking up shelf space in my basement full of the used bent nails that he extracted, straightened (more or less), and saved until he died.

But the truth is that most of this stuff saved indiscriminately does *not* come in handy. And it takes up valuable space, and costs valuable energy to haul it from one house to another. With the same amount of effort, my father could have built something useful. And with the same space and time cost, I could have done something better.

The argument for saving all habitat in order to save all possible species that might be lost is even weaker than the argument for my father's savings. He at least knew what the pieces of string were, whereas we are being asked to save things whose identity and nature—or even existence, in many cases—or possible usefulness we do not know. And in some cases we are asked to save things that are so trivially different from others that their values can only be aesthetic—for example the "three most endangered species of birds in North America," according to E. O. Wilson: Bachman's warbler, Kirtland's warbler, and the Red-cockaded woodpecker.[51] Would anyone contend that the germ-plasm in these birds is sufficiently different than that in other warblers and woodpeckers—or even birds at large—that losing them would have ill material consequences for humanity in the future?

The problem in thinking well, here as always, is that there are trade-offs between what may be "extinguished" and what we may otherwise create and use. Only by explicitly confronting those trade-offs can we act sensibly.

8. Ecologists are growing to recognize that their own interests are best served by not simply say "No" to the human use of space and other species. Examples include the flourishing of elephants under a market system (see chapter 20), and of fish habitat in British privately owned streams. Another example is alligators: Whereas in the 1970s they were listed as an endangered species, the ecologists now ask people to buy goods made with alligator skins so as to promote the farming of alligators in Florida, both for the sake of the alligator species and as a way of maintaining wetland habitats. The large increase in the quantity of alligators (and a fall in demand) can be seen in the drop of prices from $60 a foot for wild-raised and $180 a foot for farm-raised alligator skins (a difference that is interesting in itself) in the late 1980s, to $20 and $75 a foot respectively in 1993.[52]

Conclusion

There is now no prima facie case for any expensive species-safeguarding policy without more extensive analysis than has been done heretofore. The existing data on the observed rates of species extinction are almost ludicrously out of whack with the doomsters' claims of rapid disappearance, and they do not support the various extensive and expensive programs they call for. Furthermore, recent scientific and technical advances—especially seed banks and genetic engineering—have diminished the economic importance of maintaining species in their natural habitat. But the question deserves deeper thought, and more careful and wide-ranging analysis, than it has been given until now.

I do not suggest we ignore potential extinctions. Rather, I want us to be as clear as possible about the extent of the risks. We should separate the available facts from the guesswork and the purposeful misstatements, in order to improve the public decision-making process. And we should take into account—but in a reasoned fashion—the noneconomic worth of species, in light of the value we place on undisturbed nature and other aspects of life on Earth. It is important that we think as clearly as we can about this problem that is indeed difficult to think about sensibly. I hope that decision makers will think sensibly and coolly about the matter of species before embarking on the sort of resettlement program described above, or on a "crash program" to map diversity[53] which would "absorb the careers of 25,000 biologists" according to Wilson[54] and cost billions of dollars that could be used for other scientific and social purposes, or even just for poor and not-poor individuals' personal benefits.

Afternote

On the Philosophy of Species

DEEP philosophical questions are involved in discussions of the values of species and policies toward their preservation. There is a large literature on the subject, far beyond the scope of this book, and I shall mention just a few issues of particular interest.

1. The supposed "rights" of "other species" is a most puzzling concept. With increasing frequency we see proposals to make allowance for the supposed needs of other species. The justification is *not* that it is useful or pleasing for us humans that animals live in pristine wilderness but, rather, the supposed "rights" of those other species.

I'm not talking here about the kinds of cruelty to animals which seems almost innately revolting to human beings—harshly beating dogs or beasts of burden, pulling the wings off insects, closely crowding animals raised for food, killing wild animals and then using just one small part such as their ivory. Rather, I'm talking about such proposals as the one to destroy the electricity-producing dams on the Elwha River in Washington State to enable wild salmon—as distinguished from hatchery-raised salmon—to live in the river as they did eighty years earlier than the time of writing (1993); the criterion is "fish needs" rather than human needs.[55] Another example is a scientific project that makes a loud underwater sound—comparable to a jet engine—intermittently (an hour on and an hour off) for ten days that can be heard in oceans far away as part of a study of global warming. This study was accused, in connection with the Marine Mammal Protection Act, of "harassment" of marine mammals.[56] (One wonders whether those who worry about this project worry about the effects of storm sounds at sea—incomparably louder than any jet engine—on sea life.) Still another example is the accusation by "animal-rights activists" that inserting genes into cows so that they will produce medicinal products as part of the milk that they give is an "exploitation" of livestock.[57]

It would take a legal scholar to make a proper analysis of the concept of rights in this connection. The most I can do is to suggest some of the questions that must be answered.

The idea of rights is one that a group defines for itself, and/or fights for. True rights cannot be assigned by others. When rights are assigned, the system is dictatorship, and the rights continue to exist just so long as the dictator bestows them. Self-defined rights, on the other hand, involve such matters as laws, a constitution, courts, and the like. The notion of self-defined rights obviously is nonsensical for species other than humans, and calls into question the idea of rights for them.

As to the bestowing of rights, there does not exist a philosophy of dictatorship, so far as I know. How should a dictator, or even a group such as a nation, decide the relative rights of various species? We do so, of course, when we decide what to keep in zoos and parks, and what to exterminate. But we do this on the basis of our policies, not their rights.

Yet there are serious proposals being offered about "restoring and "giving back" the land to the other species, as mentioned earlier in this chapter. The underlying philosophy needs a clear legal and philosophical basis, and not just emotional expression.

2. A curious question concerns the relative strength of our attachment to various species. The following makes sense to me, though I have not found it in animal-rights writings. I can understand making some distinctions among species on an analogous basis to the "natural" distinctions we make among people in our private relationships and loyalties (as discussed so well by Adam Smith in his early philosophical work); we feel closer to closer kin, and hence it makes sense that we feel closer to gorillas than to mice or caterpillars. Similarly, few religious writings urge us to feel close to people who threaten our well-being; the analogy to animals is clear.

Perhaps whatever "duty" we have runs along the above lines. Charity should begin at home, with respect to persons and also with respect to species, according to my feelings. But others feel otherwise—as does the Earth First! group that demonstrated at the Lincoln Monument in Washington call for "Equal Rights for All Species: Save the Rain Forest."[58]

3. Philosophical discussions of species often ignore the inescapable fact that one cannot have one's cake and eat it, too. Reading a wonderful naturalist adventure such as Farley Mowat's *Never Cry Wolf*, I share his excitement and wonder at learning about the wolves in a vast country that contains only a few hundred Eskimos, many caribou and mice and birds, a few thousand wolves, and less obvious species. One feels: This could not happen if "civilization" had occupied the territory, which would be a loss.

The feeling for wilderness solitude was documented in a survey of campers among whom "86 percent . . . objected to having another party camped within sight or sound, while 65 percent said: 'It's best if you meet no one.'"[59]

Yet when a rich person buys a great painting and withdraws it from the public, keeping it for only his/her viewing, we feel that that, too, is a loss. In this latter case, the painting is at least private property, whereas publicly owned areas are no one's personal domain by ordinary law.

The simple problem is the same in both cases, however: Having the property to oneself undisturbed is incompatible with many people enjoying it. Recognition of this simple point must be antecedent to sensible discussion of the matter.

4. The entire issue raises most peculiar questions. Whereas a human violently attacking another living thing is considered odious by many, another animal doing the same thing is merely a fascination to them; this can be seen in the flourishing television channels showing wildlife scenes. And—will there be police to enforce the rights of fish against bears, and baby seals against whales?

A Greater Population Does Not Damage Health or Psychological and Social Well-Being

> [T]he closer man approaches the limits of ultimate density or "carrying capacity," the more probable is nuclear warfare.
> *(Reid and Lyon 1972, preface)*

MOST OF THIS BOOK studies material matters usually considered to be in the domain of economics—the standard of living, natural resources, and even the environment. This chapter now goes beyond ordinary economics to discuss health and related issues in connection with population size and growth, mainly because some readers feel that the subject is incomplete without such discussion.

In earlier centuries high population density often affected health adversely. For example, during the industrial revolution, the death rate was generally higher in cities than in the country because of poor sanitation and contagious diseases. But though many people still believe that the sparsely populated countryside is healthier than the city, there seems no evidence that nowadays higher population density is unhealthy; if anything, the opposite is true. We'll tackle the issue of physical health first; the effects of population density on psychological and social well-being will occupy the second part of the chapter, along with a brief discussion of war.

Population Density and Physical Health

Feeling and being healthy is as valuable as anything else an economy can provide. Moreover, health is a central issue in the functioning of the economy—healthy people work harder and better than sick people, and prevalent illness hinders economic development in many poor countries.

Life expectancy is the key measure of a country's health situation, as discussed in chapter 15. There it was shown that population density and growth have no apparent negative effects on life expectancy; rather, the effects may be positive.

In earlier times, living in areas of high population density—cities—undoubtedly reduced one's life expectancy. In the seventeenth century, when

William Petty wrote about London, the death rate was so much higher in urban than in rural areas (and probably the birthrate was so much lower) that cities like London depended on migration from the country to maintain their populations. In 1841, the life expectancy for males was thirty-five years in London but forty years in the rest of Great Britain.[1] And life expectancy in the United States was still much lower in urban places than in rural areas from 1900 until 1940 for white males: 44.0 versus 54.0 (1900); 47.3 versus 55.1 (1910); 56.7 versus 62.1 (1930); and 61.6 versus 64.1 (1939).[2]

In more recent times in developed nations, however, as communicable diseases have been controlled with sanitation and other public health measures, this disadvantage of population density has disappeared. For example, by 1950–1952 life expectancy in London had reached 67.3 years compared with 66.4 years in the rest of Great Britain.[3]

In most developing countries for which there are data, the death rate is lower in cities than in rural areas, though there are exceptions.[4]

As of 1959–1961 in the United States, the death rate was slightly higher for large cities but lower for small cities, compared to nonmetropolitan counties,[5] but the high inner-city death rate that explains this pattern is surely due to factors other than epidemic disease, unlike earlier times.

More generally, the historical picture in the West during the past half millennium, and in most countries in the world during the past few decades, has shown concurrent growth in all three key factors—population density, income, and life expectancy. This suggests that increased density and increased income—either individually or in combination—benefit people's life expectancy and health, as well as vice versa.

Consider this example of the health in the "good old days" in one of the wealthiest and most civilized places in the ancient world—Metaponto, a Greek colony in the south of Italy.

> In overwhelming numbers, the people had been malnourished, disease-ridden and injury-laden.
>
> Six out of every 10 had decayed teeth. . . . More than three-quarters had tooth enamel malformed in a way known to be caused by serious disease or severe malnutrition . . . 56 percent showed signs of signficant disease or injury . . .
>
> The skeletons also revealed a large number of broken bones that had not been set and had healed in [a] distorted way.

These findings surprised the anthrologist who supervised the work. "You read the liteature of classical Greece and you get the picture of a wonderful society. . . . But what we see now is that things were pretty awful."[6]

Why is health better where there is higher population density? Let's make a negative point first. There is nowadays no reason why population density should worsen health now that the important infectious environmental diseases, excepting malaria, have been conquered. And malaria—which many medical historians consider to have been the most important of mankind's diseases—flourishes where population is sparse and where large tracts of moist land are therefore left uncultivated. In these areas increased population density removes the mosquitoes' breeding grounds.[7]

The Case of Malaria

As Pierre Gourou put it:

> Malaria is the most widespread of tropical diseases. . . . It attacks (or did until recently) something like one-third of the human race, but in practice all the inhabitants of the hot, wet belt may be considered to be more or less infected. Malaria weakens those whom it attacks, for the bouts of fever sap their physical strength and make them unfit for sustained effort. Hence agriculture does not receive all the care it needs, and the food supply is thereby affected. In this way a vicious circle is formed. Weakened by insufficient nourishment, the [infected person's] system offers small resistance to infection and cannot provide the effort required to produce an adequate supply of food. The malarial patient knows quite well that a bout of fever may be the unpleasant reward for hard work. . . .
>
> Undoubtedly, malaria is largely responsible for the poor health, small numbers, and absence of enthusiasm for work of tropical peoples. . . .
>
> In the pre-scientific age, men kept the most serious infectious diseases in check by organizing the total occupation of the land, thus eliminating the breeding places of the mosquito. Such occupation demanded a high density of population and a complete control of land use, and hence the interdependence of a highly organized agricultural system (itself a function of soil quality, reliable climate and a certain degree of technical competence), a dense population and an advanced political organization. . . . It is also difficult to improve sanitation and health in sparsely peopled areas; anti-malarial campaigns stand but small chance of lasting success, whilst the tsetse fly finds such areas very much to its liking, for it is impossible for a population of ten or a dozen persons to the square mile to keep down the vegetation to a level unfavorable to this insect. Health services are difficult to maintain, and doctors and hospitals are inevitably far removed from patients whilst education is almost impossible.[8]

The data in table 32-1 support Gourou's argument, showing that a low population is associated with a high incidence of malaria on Ceylon. Of course one might wonder whether population is low in malarial areas because people simply chose to move away from malaria. But the history of Ceylon suggests otherwise.[9]

> The ancient civilization of Ceylon had centered in the area with hyperendemic malaria. The ruins of 10,000 dams testify to the level and magnitude of this civilization in successive stages of history. Decay of the ancient order was associated with collapse of the irrigation systems, emergence of conditions that favored transmission of malaria, and retreat of the Singhalese to the nonmalarious area of the island.[10]

462   CHAPTER 32

TABLE 32-1

Population, Area, and Population Density of Districts of Ceylon (Sri Lanka) Grouped by the
Endemicity of Malaria in the Districts.

Endemicity of Malaria	Spleen Rates[a] (%)	Population[a]		Area		Population Density per Square Mile
		Number	(%)	Square Miles	(%)	
Not endemic	(0–9)	4,142,889	(62)	5,113	(20)	810
Moderately endemic	(10–24)	1,207,569	(18)	5,271	(21)	229
Highly endemic	(25–49)	994,495	(15)	8,460	(33)	118
Hyperendemic	(50–74)	312,466	(5)	6,489	(26)	48

Source: Frederiksen 1968, in Heer 1968, p. 70.
[a] Average of surveys in 1939 and 1941.   [b] 1946 census.

Likewise, some historians have suggested that the decline of the Roman Empire was in large part due to the spread of malaria after political upheaval and decreased population density interfered with the maintenance of the drainage system.[11]

Looking now to examples of improvement rather than retrogression, the history of England was heavily affected by the decline of malaria induced by population growth. In London, "Westminster was paved in 1762 and the City in 1766 . . . and the marshes near London were drained about the same time." In 1781 a writer observed that "very few die now of Ague [malaria] in London."[12]

The history of the United States also reveals the interplay between malaria, population, and economic development:

[A] a mighty influence buoying up wages paid to the men building canals during the 1820's and 1830's was the danger of yellow fever and malaria. Built through marsh and swamps (in many instances) to reduce construction problems, the canals were known as killers. . . . As the country was settled, the marshy land where malaria was bred was filled in. Buildings covered the waste spaces where [disease carriers] could survive.[13]

Because of DDT and other synthetic pesticides, medical technologists thought for a time that population density was no longer necessary to prevent malaria. Malaria was considered beaten. But throughout the world, the disease has rebounded.[14] India went from 75 million sufferers in 1953 to fifty thousand cases and "total control" in 1968, but in the 1971 epidemic there were 1.3 million reported cases, rising to 5.8 million cases reported in 1976,[15] or by another estimate, "the number of cases reached at least 30 million and perhaps 50 million." As the use of DDT went down, "endemic malaria returned to India like the turnaround of a tide."[16] Also, "Sri Lanka . . . reduced malaria from about three million cases after World War II to just 29 in 1964." But then

DDT was banned. And due to the evolution of pesticide-resistant strains of carrier insects and the concomitant damage to the insects' natural predators, pesticides soon lose their effectiveness. The disease has returned in force; by 1970 Sri Lanka may have had a million cases of malaria per year.*

Barry Commoner gives another example:

> In Guatemala, some twelve years after the start of a malaria "eradication program" based on intensive use of insecticides, the malarial mosquitoes have become resistant and the incidence of the disease is higher than it was before the campaign. The levels of DDT in the milk of Guatemala women are by far the highest reported anywhere in the world thus far.[17]

Other public health experts also are grim about the prospects of fighting malaria with chemicals.

> Asked whether we are winning or losing the battle against tropical diseases, some experts, among them Dr. B. H. Kean of Cornell University Medical College, answer promptly that we are losing. He notes that malaria, for example, seemed almost conquered in the decade or so after World War II. But since then mosquitoes have become resistant to pesticides, and the malaria parasite has learned to cope with some of the more widely used drugs.[18]

Today again the only sure weapon against malaria seems to be increased population density.

Some Other Health Examples

Not only is the infectious-disease drawback of population density a thing of the past, but higher density also has many positive effects on health even aside from control of insects that carry malaria, sleeping sickness (the tsetse fly in Africa), and other diseases. For example, cities in the modern world have safer water supplies than do rural areas. Medical care is better in cities, and medical help arrives quicker or is easier to reach where there is a good transport system, itself the result of population density (see chapter 25).

We must also remember the additional knowledge, created by more people, that contributes to health. *Item:* Modern emergency medical systems in the United States are saving lives after auto accidents and in other emergencies. The population-induced road network of the United States is a key to the success of such systems. A country with a much sparser population would find such emergency service much more expensive. And last, it takes imagination and skill—human minds and hands—to invent and develop such medical systems. *Item:* Electrical wiring is now safer than it used to be. Many old houses have been rewired more safely since wiring ideas were developed by

* *Washington Post*, February 14, 1994, p. A3.

"additional" people—that is, by people who may not have been born if population growth were lower. And new houses are built, with safer wiring, because population growth (together with increased income) creates new demand for houses. (In Ireland, where population has not grown much in the
past century, one seldom saw a new building at the time of the first edition of
this book. I shudder at the electrical monstrosities that must lie within some
of the larger older buildings.)

The Psychological and Sociological Effects of Crowding

Many believe that high population density has bad psychological and sociological effects. This is mere supposition. High population density has indeed
been shown to harm animals. But it has not been shown to harm humans.
Rather, it is too much *isolation* that harms humans. The belief that crowding
harms people is supported only by analogies to animals, analogies that are
patently misplaced.

For hundreds of years biologists have observed that, when animals are confined to a given area with given resources, "unhappy" events occur. An increased death rate was noted by such observers as Benjamin Franklin. Modern
students such as Konrad Lorenz and John B. Calhoun have focused on "anti-
social" and "pathological" behavior in fish, geese, and Norwegian rats. For
example, the title of Calhoun's famous article is "Population Density and Social Pathology." These biologists simply assumed that the same processes necessarily occur with humans.

The earliest—and still most crushing—rebuttal is that given to Benjamin
Franklin by, of all people, Malthus himself after he learned some facts and
wised up subsequent to publishing his first edition. (This episode is described
in chapter 24.)

Biologist Julian Huxley explains how we go wrong in reasoning from animals to people.

> We begin by minimizing the difference between animals and ourselves by uncon-
> sciously projecting our own qualities into them: this is the way of children and of
> primitive peoples. Though early scientific thinkers, like Descartes, tried to make the
> difference absolute, later applications of the method of scientific analysis to man
> have, until quite recently, tended to reduce it again. This is partly because we have
> often been guilty of the fallacy of mistaking origins for explanations—what we may
> call the "nothing but" fallacy: if sexual impulse is at the base of love, then love is to
> be regarded as nothing but sex; if it can be shown that man originated from an
> animal, then in all essentials he is nothing but an animal. This, I repeat, is a danger-
> ous fallacy.
>
> We have tended to misunderstand the nature of the difference between ourselves
> and animals. . . . The critical point in the evolution of man—the change of state

when wholly new properties emerged in evolving life—was when he acquired the use of verbal concepts and could organize his experience in a common pool. It was this which made human life different from that of all other organisms.[19]

And thus human organization is different from animal organization, especially in people's capacity to create new modes of organization.

Here is a similar critique of Lorenz's analogies:

[Lorenz has a] regrettable tendency to describe animal behavior in human terms—"married love" in monogamous geese, for example. This cannot be dismissed as harmless anthropomorphism in the service of popularization, for it promotes the very misuse of analogy that lies at the heart of Lorenz's problems. A curious twist of logic to be sure—impose a human concept by dubious metaphor upon an animal, then re-derive it for humans as obviously "natural." Thus, a drake that tried to copulate with Lorenz's boot is a fetishist by "exact analogy," and a mob of geese frightening off a coati-mundi play the same role as a human picket line.[20]

So much for evidence from the animals. Despite common presumption, the sociological data show that human population density—as measured by the number of people per unit of land area, which is relevant to the issue of population growth on Earth—has no general ill effects on such measures of welfare as longevity, crime rates, mental illness rates, and recreational facilities.[21]

After it became apparent that the concentration of people into cities is not necessarily connected to pathology, those who worry about these matters turned to crowding at home and work. Here the results are mixed about whether people are affected by crowding as animals are. One study of "the effect of household and neighborhood crowding on the relations between urban family members" showed that "crowding is found to have little or no effect,"[22] while Omer R. Galle and co-workers found that a larger number of people per room in Chicago accompanied increased mortality, use of public assistance, juvenile delinquency, and admission to mental hospitals.[23] But density and crowding are not necessarily found together.[24] Slums at urban fringes often have low density, and "these areas have more pathology than high-density slums."[25] The likeliest explanation of the pathology that Galle and associates found is simply poverty.

The most ambitious experimental tests, conducted by psychologist Jonathan Freedman (once an associate of Paul Ehrlich and a believer that density is pathological), led to the conclusions that

[I]ntuitions, speculations, political and philosophical theory appear to be wrong in this respect. . . . People who live under crowded conditions do not suffer from being crowded. Other things being equal, they are no worse off than other people. . . . It took me and other psychologists working in this area many years to be convinced, but eventually the weight of the evidence overcame our doubts and preconceptions.[26]

In any case, the amount of *crowding* (lack of personal space) has been going down in the United States as income has risen, and along with an increase in total population and density in metropolitan areas. The percentage of households living in "crowded conditions" (more than one person per room) has been: *1900*, over 50 percent; *1940*, 20 percent; *1950*, 16 percent; *1960*, 12 percent; *1970*, 8 percent.[27] (Given that this decline has occurred even as population has been rising, would those who worry about crowding offer population growth as a salutary prescription? Relax, I'm just teasing.)

Once I had a conversation with a woman who was frantically worried about the ill effects of crowding—as we sat haunch to haunch in a football stadium packed with seventy-five thousand people! She saw no humor in my pointing out that she seemed to be enjoying herself tolerably well under the circumstances.

Population Growth and Intelligence

In the first half of the twentieth century, many people worried about a decline in human intelligence due to the assumed pattern of differential fertility. The chain of logic went as follows: (1) Poorer families have lower intelligence than richer families. (2) Intelligence is inherited by children from their parents. (3) Poorer families have more children than richer families. (4) The average level of intelligence must fall. This line of argument was again stated by psychologist Richard Herrnstein.[28]

Highly competent and respected statisticians and psychologists even estimated the extent of the decline that was supposedly occurring.

> Cattell estimated that the average I.Q. is declining at the rate of 3 points per generation. Fraser Roberts reported that based upon his studies of the child population of Bath, England, the fall in average I.Q. was about 1½ points per generation. In the United States, Lentz calculated that in the urban population the decline in the median score from one generation to another was as much as 4 to 5 points. Lorimer and Osborn concluded that the average decline in the median I.Q. score was 0.9 of a point per generation.
>
> It should be remembered that these calculations are theoretical and are based upon observations on a single generation. No one has yet reported investigations of I.Q. scores in successive generations which support these claims.[29]

This idea is then extended by some to assess social policies. For example, consider the following remark in the context of discussion of "the Jukes-Kallikaks 'bad heredity' concept": "Can it be that our humanitarian welfare programs have already selectively emphasized high and irresponsible rates of reproduction to produce a socially relatively unadaptable human strain?"[30]

Otis Dudley Duncan criticized this body of thought on both theoretical and empirical grounds.[31] His most telling points are (a) the existing studies of I.Q. change over time did not reveal a decline but rather an increase (though Duncan did not interpret the apparent increase as being meaningful); and (b) applying the same logic to data on differential height (which in contrast to intelligence, is incontrovertibly correlated genetically between parents and children) would lead one to expect a decline in heights from generation to generation, which has not been observed. (It is also relevant that persons with severely limited mental capacities have low life expectancies and few offspring.)

A point which has gotten little or no mention: It is reasonable to assume that a given individual's intelligence (whatever that means), or any aspect of it, is affected by the individual's genes *without assuming* that there is a strong correlation between the intelligence of parents and children due to genetic factors. It is quite possible that any aspect of intelligence depends upon the combination of a large number of genes which may agglomerate in a random fashion. While the individual genes are inherited from the parents, the outcome need not be. This is certainly the case among such conditions as mongoloidism; the mongoloids do not reproduce themselves, and yet they continue to appear in each generation, perhaps at a constant rate. And if homosexuality is affected by genetic makeup, the same would be true of that condition.

My layman's assessment: Lack of empirical support, and the existence of a powerful critique, seem to me to overwhelm the proposition that intelligence declines due to a high birthrate among the poor. Yet the apparently plausible belief continues to reappear in each generation.

As to the effect of family size on children's intelligence, the evidence is so mixed that it defies summary.[32] Whatever I.Q. differences exist among children in families with one, two, or three children are small by any meaningful measure.[33] Other reviews offer conflicting points of view. There is little doubt that, on average, children with *no* brothers or sisters do *worse* than children with one or two siblings. On balance there is little reason to believe that, all else equal, a larger family lessens a child's intelligence or chances in life. And the long-run trend is toward smaller families anyway, as populations grow and countries develop—so all else is *not* equal.

Population Density and War

War between and within nations is perhaps the most grisly outcome that population density or growth is said to threaten. Expanding on the chapter's headnote, the common view is as follows: "At the present rate of world population increase, overpopulation may become *the* major cause of social and political instability. Indeed, the closer man approaches the limits of ultimate density or 'carrying capacity,' the more probable is nuclear warfare.[34] This popular view is espoused by the U.S. State Department, AID and CIA, and has been the justification for population control programs abroad. The simple fact, however, is that there is zero evidence connecting population density with the propensity to engage in war, or even fist fights.

A booklength cross-national statistically intensive multivariable study by Douglas A. Hibbs, Jr., found that "other factors held constant, the rate of population growth does not influence magnitudes of mass political violence within nations."[35] And in a study of six measures of political instability in Latin America between 1968 and 1977, Alfred G. Cuhsan found "no reason to believe that either population growth or density is a cause of political instability."[36]

Nazli Choucri concluded that what she calls "demographic" factors sometimes lead to conflict.[37] But the key demographic factor in her analysis is the *relative* rate of increase in ethnic groups, rather than increase in population size or population density per se. This can be seen most clearly by listing the wars that she considers "archetypical cases" of "population dynamics and local conflict": the Algerian War of Independence, 1954–1962; the Nigerian civil war; the two wars involving Indonesia; the conflicts in Ceylon and El Salvador–Honduras; and the Arab-Israeli series of wars. None of these seem, to my layman's eye, to be conflicts undertaken to obtain more land or mineral resources so as to increase the standard of living of the group initiating the conflict. To show that population growth causes conflict, one would need to show that two neighboring countries or groups, both of whom are growing rapidly, are more likely to come into conflict than two neighboring countries or groups neither of whom are growing rapidly. This Choucri has not shown. In Choucri's way of looking at the matter, conflict could as easily be caused by one country or group *reducing* its growth rate relative to another country or group, as by one *increasing* its relative growth rate. And in fact many have argued that it was just so in the case of France and Germany—that France's low birthrate induced the French-German wars.

Furthermore, as we saw in the afternote to chapter 29, the traditional economic motive for war—acquiring farmland—is fast disappearing. For economically advanced nations, it doesn't pay to make war to get another nation's agricultural territory. And a sensible citizenry wouldn't even take a slice of another country as a gift.

What, Then, Determines Health?

If population density and growth are not the determinants of health in the short run, what does determine how sick or healthy we are? By now the answer has become clear. A community's health depends upon (a) how much

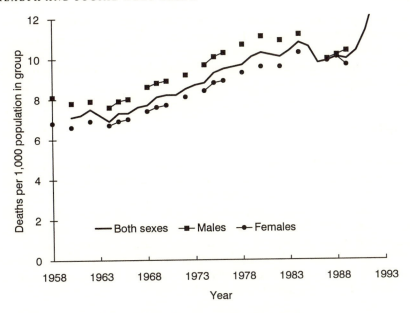

Figure 32-1. Crude Death Rates, by Sex, USSR, 1958–1993

scientific knowledge has already been discovered, which is much the same as asking which year we are talking about; and (b) how economically advanced the community is.

We also know more now about what causes modern populations to become *less* healthy: bad government, for example. One channel through which bad government harms people is through pollution. It now is clear that the recently Socialist countries in Eastern Europe have very high levels of pollution, both because socialism made them poor and because socialism predisposes to pollution over and above the income effect by emphasizing production at any cost. Data on life expectancy in chapter 11 showed that low income and Socialism also predispose to high mortality rates, and that some mortality rates have even been rising in the recently Socialist countries, especially in the working ages for males (see also fig. 32-1 for the old Soviet Union). The morbidity for all causes except cancers (which one generally suffers from only after living to an old age) and auto accidents (which require that the society have many vehicles) are higher in recently Socialist countries, and the unfavorable ratio for socialist versus non-Socialist countries is increasing. Even infant mortality rose in the Soviet Union from the 1970s (though not in the rest of Eastern Europe),[38] in contrast to experience everywhere else in the world. The high rates of alcohol and cigarette consumption in Eastern Europe are interesting in this connection, though subject to several interpretations.

Because factors other than population density and growth explain much of the variation in health, now as in the past, the argument that higher population density does *not* damage health is strengthened.

In the very long run, then, population growth leads to better health because it leads to more discovery of new scientific knowledge (see chapter 26) and to economic advancement.

Conclusions

Regarding the purported ill effects of population density, the charges are many and imaginative. The chapter covered the main ones that people have written about, though there are many other ill effects of population density that one may concoct. The overall verdict must be "Innocent." And this is not for lack of evidence. As the most recent extensive review sums up, "It is reasonable to conclude that the density-pathology hypothesis fails to be confirmed within urban areas. When social structural differences among neighborhoods are considered (held constant) population density appears to make a trivial difference in predicting pathology rates."[39]

33

The Big Economic Picture: Population Growth and Living Standards in MDCs

No one today can deny that the United States has the grossest national production in the world.
 (Paul Ehrlich, quoted in Goodall 1975)

We've already had too much economic growth in the United States.
Economic growth in rich countries like ours is the disease, not the cure.
 (Paul Ehrlich, quoted in Ray 1990)

The most interesting thing to observe is the complete lack of imagination which [the] vision [of Malthus, Mill, and Ricardo] reveals. Those writers lived at the threshold of the most spectacular economic developments ever witnessed. Vast possibilities matured into realities under their very eyes. Nevertheless, they saw nothing but cramped economies, struggling with ever-decreasing success for their daily bread. They were convinced that technological improvement and increase in capital would in the end fail to counteract the fateful law of decreasing returns. James Mill, in his *Elements*, even offered a "proof" for this. In other words, they were all stagnationists. Or, to use their own term, they all expected, for the future, the advent of a stationary state. . . .
 (Joseph A. Schumpeter, History of Economic Analysis, *1954)*

THE MALTHUSIAN THEORY of population growth—accepted until the 1980s by most economists, and by the public accepted still—says one thing. The data say something else entirely. This chapter discusses the theory, presents the facts, and then reconciles fact and expanded theory for the more-developed countries (MDCs). Chapter 34 does the same for the less-developed countries (LDCs). This chapter and the next are tougher reading than most of the others, but I hope you will bear with them. (Read them when your mind is fresh, perhaps.)

The Theory of Population and Income

Classical economic theory apparently shows irrefutably that population growth must reduce the standard of living. The heart of all economic theory of population from Malthus* to *The Limits to Growth* can be stated in a single sentence: The more people using a stock of resources, the lower the income per person, all else equal. This proposition derives from the "law" of diminishing returns: Two people cannot use the same tool at the same time, or farm the same piece of land, without reducing the output per worker. A related idea is that two people cannot nourish themselves as well as one person from a given stock of food. And when one considers the age distribution resulting from a higher birthrate, the effect is reinforced by a larger proportion of children, and thus a lower proportion of workers, in the larger population. Let us spell out these Malthusian ideas.

The Consumption Effect

Simply adding more people to a population affects consumption directly. If there is only one pie, the pieces will be smaller if it is divided among more eaters. The experience of hippies in San Francisco in 1967 illustrates this problem amusingly.

> Most hippies take the question of survival for granted, but it's becoming increasingly obvious as the neighborhood fills with penniless heads, that there is simply not enough food and lodging to go around. A partial solution may come from a group called the "Diggers," who have been called the "worker-priests" of the hippy movement and the "invisible government" of the Hashbury. The Diggers are young and aggressively pragmatic; they have set up free lodging centers, free soup kitchens and free clothing distribution centers. They comb the neighborhood soliciting donations of everything from money to stale bread to camping equipment.
>
> For a while, the Diggers were able to serve three meals, however meager, each afternoon in Golden Gate Park. But as the word got around, more and more hippies showed up to eat, and the Diggers were forced to roam far afield to get food. Occasionally there were problems, as when Digger Chieftain Emmett Grogan, 23, called a local butcher a "Fascist pig and a coward" when he refused to donate meat scraps. The butcher whacked Grogan with the flat side of his meat cleaver.[1]

This consumption effect occurs most sharply within a family. When there are more children, each one gets a smaller part of the family's earnings, if earnings remain the same. We see the effect in Thomas Hardy's *Mayor of Casterbridge*.

---

* The ideas expressed by Malthus, and commonly attributed to him, may individually be found in other earlier writers, but this is not the place for an excursion in the history of economic thought. Schumpeter (1954, pp. 250–60) superbly provides this material.

[Mr. Longways]: True; your mother was a very good woman—I can mind her. She were rewarded by the Agricultural Society for having begot the greatest number of healthy children without parish assistance, and other virtuous marvels.

[Mrs. Cuxsom]: 'Twas that that kept us so low upon ground—that great hungry family.

[Mr. Longways]: 'Ay. Where the pigs be many the wash runs thin.[2]

The Production Effect

Adding people also affects consumption indirectly, through the effect on production per worker. Consider a country that at a given time possesses a given amount of land and a given quantity of factories and other industrial capital. If the country comes to have a larger labor force, production per worker will be lower because each worker comes to have, on the average, less land or tools to work with. Hence, average production per worker will be lower with a larger labor force and fixed capital. This is the classical argument of diminishing returns.

The Public Facilities Effect

If a given population is instantly enlarged by, say, 10 percent in all age groups, there will be 10 percent more people wanting to use the village well or the city hospital or the public beach. An increase in the demand for such freely provided public services inevitably results in an increase in the number of people who are denied service, a decrease in the amount of service per person, or an additional expenditure by the government to increase the amount of public facilities. If the 10 percent population increase also results in a 10 percent increase in the number of people working, and if the productivity of the added people is as great, on the average, as that of the original population, then the added population will have no effect on per capita income. But such a compensating increase in production is not likely. If more children are born, the demand for public facilities—especially schools—will occur before the children grow up, find work, and become productive; and even immigrating adults use at least the customhouse before starting work. And after the additional children join the labor force, they are likely to lower the average worker's productivity at first because of the "law" of diminishing returns discussed earlier, and hence the added workers will not be able to contribute as much in taxes to support public facilities as the average person formerly did. These effects were discussed in chapter 25 (as were the data that called into question these theoretical propositions).

As a result of the increased demand, the average level of public services received is likely to be lower; the average person will receive less education and less health care than if the population remains fixed. And some tax moneys that might have gone into harbors or communication systems may go instead to the education and health care of the added people.

In classical theory, then, sheer numbers of people depress per capita income in two ways: More consumers divide any given amount of output; and each worker produces less because there is less capital, private and public, per worker.

Age-Distribution Effects

As we saw in chapter 23, a faster-growing population implies a larger proportion of children, which means that a larger proportion of the population is too young to work. The smaller proportion of workers must mean a smaller output per capita, all else equal. Therefore, the effect of sheer numbers of people, and the age distribution that occurs in the process of getting to the higher numbers, both work in the same direction, causing a smaller per capita product.

When one also takes women's labor into account, the effect of having a higher proportion of children is even greater. The more children that are born per woman, the less chance she has to work outside the home. For example, in the 1920s and 1930s, when most Israeli kibbutzim were near bare subsistence, strong pressure was often brought upon couples not to have more than two children, in order to enable women to do more "productive" work.[3] And the same is true in China now. (But in the United States, at least, this effect is not as great as one might expect. Calculations show that each baby after the first keeps an average woman out of the labor force for only about half a year.)[4]

There is a counterbalancing effect from the father's work. A wide variety of studies show that an additional child causes fathers to work additional hours, the equivalent of two to six extra weeks of work a year. In the long run this yearly 4 to 10 percent increase in work for an additional child may fully (or more than fully) balance the temporary loss of labor-force time by the mother. (One might say that an additional child "forces" a father to work, which might be called a "bad" outcome. But if he chooses to have the additional child at the cost of working more, it is reasonable to say that he prefers that alternative of having more children and more work to fewer children and less work. This is quite the same as working more hours to have a nicer home or to pay for additional education. Who is to say which choice is "bad" or wrong?)

Age distribution affects income distribution, too. In the discussion of Social Security and saving in chapter 23, we saw that a larger proportion of younger persons implies that more earners will one day support each retired person, which means a better pension for each retired person and a smaller burden on each working-age person.

Other Theoretical Effects

The dilution of capital through reduced saving, and through reduced education per person, are other elements of the standard economic theory of population growth (though chapters 25 and 27 show them to be far smaller drawbacks than commonly thought, and perhaps no drawback at all). The only positive theoretical effect is that of larger markets and larger-scale production, known to economists as "economies of scale" or of "scope," which chapter 27 discussed.

The Evidence versus the Malthusian Theory

The Malthusian supply-side effect of diminishing output from additional workers, and the demand-side effect of less to go around among a larger number of consumers, until the 1980s dominated the conventional economic theory of population growth. And the implication is clear: Additional people must reduce the standard of living, all else equal.

But a very solid body of evidence does not confirm that body of theory. The data suggest that population growth almost certainly does not hinder—and perhaps aids—economic growth. One piece of historical evidence is the concurrent explosion of both population and economic development in Europe from 1650 onward—a positive rather than negative association. Other benign evidence is found in the rates of population growth and output per capita as compared in figure 33-1, which includes contemporary MDCs for which data is available for the past century. No strong relationship appears. Such studies can go wrong unless they are done with competence. Therefore, it is relevant that the first such study was done by Simon Kuznets, who won a Nobel prize for his work with economic data, and who is widely regarded as the greatest economic-demographic historian of the last few centuries.

Studies of the more-recent rates of population growth and economic growth are another source of evidence. Many comparisons have by now been made among various countries (MDCs and LDCs) by almost a score of skilled researchers, using a variety of methods, and there is agreement among them that population growth does not hinder economic growth.[5] These overlapping empirical studies do not show that fast population growth *increases* per capita income. But they certainly imply that population growth does not *decrease* economic growth.[6]

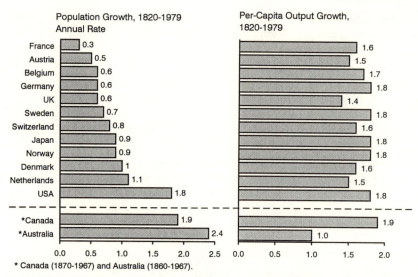

Figure 33-1. The Historical Nonrelationship between Population Growth and the Growth of Living Standards, 1820–1979

To bolster these aggregate data on the overall relationship between population growth and economic growth, there have also been many studies of the relevant elements of the economy—education, savings, investment, and the like. These studies amplify and strengthen the conclusion drawn from the aggregate data that population growth is not a drag on development.[7]

These data, which contradict the simple Malthusian theory, have naturally evoked explanations. One such explanation is that population growth is a "challenge" that evokes the "response" of increased efforts from individuals and societies. There certainly is evidence that people make special efforts when they perceive a special need; this is seen in the second jobs, more hours of work, and other adjustments people make when they have relatively many children. (I summarize much of this evidence in my 1986 book on effort.)

Another reason why population growth does not retard economic growth is that a high proportion of youths in the labor force has advantages: (1) A younger worker produces relatively more than she or he consumes, in contrast to an older worker, largely because of increases in pay with seniority whether or not there is increased productivity with seniority. (2) Each generation enters the labor force with more education than the previous generation; hence a larger proportion of youth implies an increase in the average education of the labor force, all else being equal. (3) Younger workers save a larger proportion of their income than do older workers.

Furthermore, population growth creates additional opportunities and facilitates adaptive changes in the economic and social structures of MDCs, in several ways: (1) A necessary reduction in the size of an organization or work force is always painful. But when the population and the economy are growing, a facility or work force that needs reduction can be reduced in *relative* size by leaving it the same *absolute* size, which is less painful. (2) Cessation of population growth makes it more difficult to staff new departments to adjust to changing conditions. In universities, for example, when there is an overall growth in enrollments, new fields can be staffed by new faculty without cutting back on existing faculty; when there is no overall growth, new fields cannot be staffed without fighting the entrenched faculty, who do not wish to give up the positions they hold.[8] (3) Cessation of growth also means that there are fewer new appointments to be made overall. In American and European universities since the 1970s this lack of growth has struck particularly hard at the numbers of young professors who can be appointed, which has been demoralizing to aspirants for the Ph.D. And it has caused screams of anguish from senior professors who can no longer easily obtain offers elsewhere, which they can use as levers to get their salaries raised. (4) Where new occupational needs arise, they can be filled more easily if there are more youths who might learn these occupations. Hence, population growth facilitates adjustments in the sizes of industries and in occupational structure. (5) When the total economy is growing relatively fast, savings can more easily be found for new investments without having to shift investment out of old capital. This is the physical counterpart to the human-capital phenomena discussed in points (1) and (2) above. (6) Investment is less risky when population is growing more rapidly. If housing is overbuilt or excess capacity is created in an industry, a growing population will take up the slack and remedy the error, whereas without population growth there is no source of remedy for the miscalculation. Hence a growing population makes expansion investment and new entrepreneurial ventures more attractive by reducing risk—as well as by increasing total demand, of course.

A faster-growing population also increases the internal mobility of the labor force. The greater mobility follows from a larger number of job opportunities and a larger number of people in the young age groups, who tend to be more mobile. Internal mobility greatly enhances the efficient allocation of resources—that is, the best matching of people to jobs. As Kuznets wrote, "We cannot exaggerate the importance of internal mobility and of the underlying conditions . . . in the modern economy to allocate and channel human resources."[9] But when population growth is declining, the economy can get stuck with a hard-to-adjust oversupply of people in various occupations.

A More Realistic Model for MDCs

We have seen that population size and growth have a variety of economic effects, some negative and others positive. Economists worth their keep must take account of the size and importance of the relevant forces. Furthermore, if several influences operate concurrently, we must concern ourselves with the overall effect rather than with only a single effect of any one variable at a time. In such a case we can obtain a satisfactory overall assessment only by constructing an integrated model of the economy, and then comparing the incomes produced under various conditions of population growth.

When building such a dynamic model, we must compromise between the greater complexity of a more realistic model and the greater distortion of a more abstract one. Furthermore, different models are required for countries with different economic and demographic conditions. More specifically, we must have separate models for MDCs and LDCs. The model that follows is for MDCs;[10] a model for LDCs is presented in the next chapter.

Whether mathematical or verbal, simple or complex, computerized or not, earlier models of the effect of additional people on the standard of living in MDCs—including those from Malthus to *The Limits to Growth*—share the common root of first-edition Malthus: Adding people who must work and live with the original fixed supply of land and capital implies less income for each person.

If, however, we add to the simple Malthusian model another fundamental fact of economic growth—the increase in productivity due to additional people's inventive and adaptive capacities—we arrive at a very different result. The analysis whose results are presented below does just that. This model is outlined in figure 33-2, where the elements of the usual neo-Malthusian model for MDCs are shown in solid lines and where the novel knowledge-creation elements are shown in dotted lines. That is, this model embodies not only the standard capital-dilution effects but also the contribution of additional people to technological advance through the creation of knowledge and through economies of larger scale. The latter elements have been omitted from population models in the past, but they are crucial to a balanced understanding of the problem.

Three factors may be seen as acting upon the creation of new technological knowledge: (1) the total number of persons in the labor force (or in research and development), who may produce valuable improvements; (2) the total production in a year—the gross national income—with which improvements may be financed; and (3) the per capita income level, which influences the average amount of education a worker receives and hence affects the individual's capacities to make technological discoveries.

The time horizon is roughly 50 to 150 years, short enough to rule out major changes in the natural resources situation. But it is sufficiently long so that the delayed effects of knowledge are able to play their role.*

---

* My 1986 technical book also explores the very long run ideas called "growth theory" and introduces endogenous growth theory. The interested scholar may also examine Nerlove and Raut (1994). Though hardly relevant for policy decisions, that analysis controverts earlier growth theory that concluded that population growth is detrimental in the very long run.

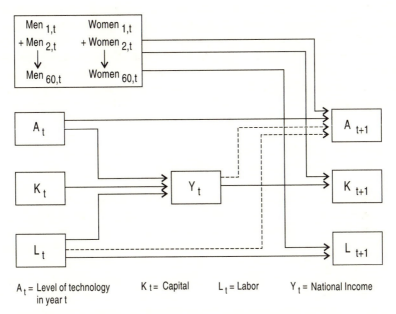

A$_t$ = Level of technology K$_t$ = Capital   L$_t$ = Labor   Y$_t$ = National Income
in year t

Figure 33-2. Model of Population Growth and Economic Growth

Though the model refers to the United States, it is more appropriate to think of this analysis as applying to the developed world as a whole, because the MDCs are scientifically and technologically interdependent. This wider point of view skirts the possibility that one country might ride on the coattails of technological advance created by other countries (which cannot be done well anyway).

You may feel uneasy with the lack of precision in the analysis of how population size and growth affect the creation of new technological knowledge, as discussed in chapter 26. But to simply leave out the effect altogether is to implicitly (and unreasonably) estimate that the effect is zero (which is what the earlier models do). Certainly the effect of population size on knowledge is greater than zero. Where else but from people's minds, past and present, can advances in knowledge come from? Physical capital alone cannot generate ideas—perhaps in the future computers might—though physical capital does enhance "learning by doing."

To put it differently, additional workers certainly are not the only cause of increased productivity. But over any period longer than the business cycle, the size of the labor force is a major influence upon total output. And if we hold constant the stock of physical capital and the original level of technological practice, then population size is the only remaining influence upon total output. Hence, the appropriate argument is about *how* to estimate this factor, and which estimates to use, rather than whether to include it at all.

This model does not treat human beings only as "human capital," a commodity essentially plastic and inert like physical capital. Rather, it treats people *as people*—responding to their economic needs with physical and mental efforts, and the creative spark. Imagination and creativity are not concepts commonly included in economic models, nor are they ever above the surface even here. But let us recognize their importance unselfconsciously, and be willing to give them their due.

The Model's Projections

Streams of income per worker were compared for a wide variety of population-growth structures, including both one-time increases in population size and different rates of population growth such as zero, 1 percent, and 2 percent yearly. And the comparisons were made under a variety of economic assumptions about savings rates, and about the ways that additional people and various income levels affect changes in productivity. The most important result is that, under every set of conditions, demographic structures with more rapid population growth come to have higher per-worker income than less rapid population-growth structures within thirty to eighty years after the birth of the additional child. Most often this happens after about thirty-five years—that is, about fifteen years after the additional person enters the labor force (see fig. 33-3).

It is true that thirty to eighty years is a long way off, and therefore may seem less important than the shorter run. But we should remember that our long run will be someone else's short run, just as our short run was someone else's long run. Some measure of unselfishness should impel us to keep this in mind as we make our decisions about population policy. And it may help to know that the short-run cost differences between the various demographic structures are small by any absolute measure, and also small relative to other variables that are subject to governmental policies.

For purposes of population policy, however, we can reduce the comparisons of the different population-growth structures to a simple form—the trade-off between present and future consumption. This simple trade-off applies to population change just as to such long-lived social projects as dams and environmental changes. That is, a key issue in any overall judgment about population growth is the relative importance we attach to consuming something now versus saving and investing part of it so as to consume even more later on—a major theme of the book.

The effect of additional children upon the standard of living (putting aside the pleasure that children give to their parents) is undoubtedly negative in the short run. In the years while children consume but do not produce, additional children mean less food and less education for each person, or additional effort on the part of the parental generation to fulfill the needs of the addi-

output per worker

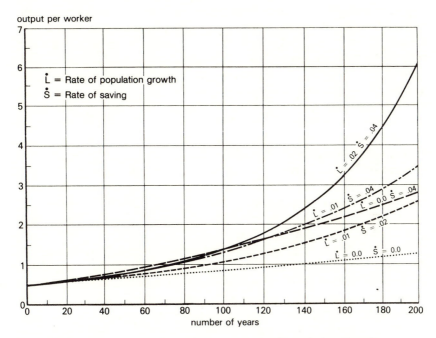

Figure 33-3. Output per Worker with Various Rates of Population Growth

tional children. During this early period, then, children are an investment; their effect upon the standard of living is negative. And if attention is confined to this early period, then additional children count as a negative economic force.

But if, on the other hand, we give weight to the more distant future, then the overall effect of the additional children may be positive. The positive effects will last much longer then the negative effects—indefinitely, in fact—and hence can outweigh the short-run effects even though it is natural to care less about a given period of time in the far future than about an equal period beginning now.

The device used by economists to summarize this stream of future effects is the "discount rate." A low discount rate indicates that one gives relatively more weight to the future than does a high discount rate, though a future benefit or cost always gets *somewhat* less weight than a present benefit or cost. The futurity discount is very similar in concept to an interest rate, and the choice of appropriate discount rate is similar to the decision about the rate of interest one would be willing to accept in borrowing or lending money. If, for example, we set a discount rate of 5 percent per year we mean that, for every year longer we have to wait for a payoff, we require the payoff to be at least 5 percent more than the amount we invested the year before, or else we would not make the investment. If we invest $1.00 now, we would require $1.05 a year from now. If investing does not look that promising, we would rather spend our dollar now than forgo a dollar's worth of consumption until later. If we expect more than $1.05 back, the deal seems worthwhile if the appropriate discount rate is 5 percent.

The model finds that even up to substantial rates of discount—at least 5 percent, to be contrasted with the real inflation-adjusted discount rate of 2–3 percent that seems to prevail in Western society over the long run—faster population growth has a higher "present value" than slower population growth. That is, social investment in population growth would be far more profitable than marginal social investments of other kinds. This finding may be contrasted with the standard conclusion that a lower rate of population growth is better at all rates of discount.

You might check the conclusions drawn from this model with your intuition about whether all the people in the United States would be better off today if there had been half as many people in 1800 or 1850 or 1900 or 1950 as there actually were. It is plain that our ancestors bestowed benefits upon us through the knowledge they created and the economies of scale they left us, and if there had been fewer of those ancestors the legacy would have been smaller. It is worth keeping this in mind when speculating about whether life today and in the future would be better if there were fewer people alive *today*.

Population models such as the one presented here were not accepted before the 1980s because of the preeminence of physical capital in the thinking of economists then. But there has been recognition in recent years of the fundamental importance of knowledge, education, and the quality of the labor force in the productive process.[11] The empirical studies that show the absence of a negative effect of population growth on economic development also have affected the thinking of economists. As a result, the sort of model described here—allowing for the contribution of additional people to technology and human capital—is much more congenial to economists than at the time of the first edition of this book.

Despite the prevailing attitude against population growth, there *never* has been any scientifically valid evidence that population growth has a negative effect on the standard of living. The President's Commission on Population Growth and the American Future of the early 1970s sought hard to find such evidence. The Commission's creators clearly hoped and expected that it would bring in a report that called strongly for fertility reduction. Indeed, as then-President Nixon put it in a message to Congress, "Population growth is a world problem which no country can ignore."[12] But despite its antinatalist origin, the worst the Commission could say was, "We have looked for and have not found any convincing economic argument for continued national population growth."[13]

It is also interesting to note the changes in views of the economists on that Commission. Allen Kelley was responsible for the central review paper on economic aspects of population change, and Richard Easterlin had the task of evaluating Kelley's study. This was the evolution of their views, as described by Easterlin:

> It is instructive, I think, to note Kelley's own statement on the change in his views as a result of this research. Whereas he started out in the expectation that an anti-natal government policy was justifiable on economic and ecological grounds, he ended up in a much more neutral position. In this respect, Kelley's experience is representative, I think, of that of many of us who have tried to look into the arguments and evidence about the "population problem."[14]

Many people in the United States and Europe—school administrators, university teachers, Social Security planners, and publishing houses, for example—have by now seen the face of zero population growth, and many have not liked what they have seen. Slower population growth and diminished demand have not brought the expected benefits, especially in education. By 1980, the lower schools were suffering from diminished enrollment. Instead of school systems feeling flush with resources in times of declining enrollments, a newspaper story headlined "Empty-Desk Blues"[15] told of increasing budget problems in the schools despite the declining demand. And at the time of writing in 1992, the universities are complaining of "shrinking classes" and diminished pools of talent—even so few students that they must close. "Indicators of serious trouble," complained a newspaper that for long has asked for lower population growth (the editorial even complains that the situation is making students "jumpier" than before!).[16] Low population growth brings a cut in real salaries for many, and a lack of the excitement that growth usually brings for all. In the 1960s Singapore gave people financial incentives to have fewer children. But after observing the results, Singapore turned completely around in the 1980s and gave incentives (though only to the middle class) to have *more* children. There are other reasons, too, for budget problems in schools. School systems in the United States face both rising costs and voter opposition to higher tax rates. Nevertheless, it is illogical and ironic that less demographic pressure should be associated with worsened budget squeezes in the schools. In contrast, when enrollments grow, communities somehow have found the way to support education well; witness the unprecedented and huge influx of ex-servicemen into United States colleges after World War II.

Adam Smith had it right: "The progressive state is in reality the cheerful and the hearty state to all the different orders of the society. The stationary is dull; the declining melancholy."

At the Cost of the Poorer Countries?

Does the increase in the MDC standard of living as a result of population growth come at the expense of the poorer countries? Many assert that a country is "overpopulated" if it is not self-sufficient in food and other raw materials, and then leap to the judgment that poor countries are thereby being exploited. Consider these paragraphs, for example, by Paul Ehrlich.

> Few Europeans seem to realize that they must draw heavily on the rest of the world for the resources necessary to maintain their affluence. Few also seem to realize that, with a few exceptions, European nations could not feed themselves without importing food (or fertilizer, or the petroleum to run farm machinery, etc.). . . .
>
> Even an island nation like Great Britain seems relatively oblivious to her extreme degree of overpopulation. . . . The fact of Great Britain's almost total dependence on the rest of the world is only dimly perceived, and the continuance of today's world trade system is simply taken for granted.[17]

But Ehrlich himself (in his sort of rhetoric) "fails to realize" that exchange is a fundamental and necessary element of human civilization, and that it is quite misleading to think of one trade partner "supporting" another. Saudi Arabia no more "supports" the Netherlands by exporting oil than the Netherlands "supports" Saudi Arabia by exporting electronic goods. If you are a white-collar worker, you support a farmer with what you produce just as much as the farmer supports you. To divide the exchange in half and call one direction "supportive" and the other "exploitive" can only be misleading. Any attempt to make each of us self-sufficient pushes us back toward the short, sickly, hungry, impoverished life of subsistence agriculture.

Yet another misleading idea underlies the belief that the so-called dependence of densely settled on sparsely settled areas is a sign of overpopulation. This view implicitly assumes that national borders are the only ones that matter. If one is thinking of war, that certainly is true. But in the peacetime that I assume we are discussing, Chicago is at least as "dependent" on downstate Illinois for soybeans as is Tokyo, yet no one thinks that Chicago is overpopulated because it is not self-sufficient in soybeans. To make the sort of distinction Erhlich makes between the United States and Japan—to call the latter "overpopulated" because it gets its soybeans from abroad—is an archaic nationalistic theory of economics called "mercantilism," a theory that was demolished by Adam Smith in 1776. The more general charge that MDCs "exploit" the LDCs and "rape" them of the resources that they should be saving for their own use was dispatched in chapter 28.

Summary

The earlier and still-popular models of population growth's effects in MDCs—all founded on the Malthusian idea of diminishing returns—are directly contradicted by the empirical data. These models say that adding more people causes a lower standard of living; the data show no such thing. This chapter describes a theoretical population model that is more consistent with the facts.

The increases in productivity that result from the larger scale of industry, and from the additional knowledge contributed by additional people, are here added to a simple economic model of a more-developed country. The model works with a range of assumptions that I trust are realistic. The results indicate that developed countries with faster rates of population growth initially fall behind in per capita income, but only very slightly. Later they do better than those with lower rates of population growth, usually in thirty to eighty years. That is, for the first thirty to eighty years after the birth of an additional child—thrity-five years is perhaps the most common period in the models— per capita income is very slightly lower because of the additional child. But after that period, per capita income is higher with the additional child, and the advantage of the faster population growth comes to be very considerable. Thus, though an increment of population initially has a small negative effect upon economic welfare, after a few decades the effect becomes positive, and large.

Most telling of all (but hard to tell nontechnically), computations that combine the longer-term and the shorter-term population effects in a standard present-value framework of investment analysis indicate that even at costs of capital that are quite high relative to the social cost of capital, faster population growth has a higher present value than does slower population growth in almost all model variations. That is, higher population growth in MDCs is an attractive social investment as compared with other social-investment possibilities.

To achieve a reasonable understanding of the effects of population growth, we must extend our horizon beyond the near-term years and weigh together the effects of the long run and the short run. When this is done, population growth in the MDC world is seen to be beneficial, rather than being the burden it appears to be in earlier Malthusian models which have only a short-run perspective.

Afternote 1 _____

William Shakespeare, Procreation, and the Economics of Development

IN THE SPAN of fourteen lines and however long it took to write them, William Shakespeare arrived at the heart of the demographic-economic vision for which moderns such as I have had to struggle long and hard, and which is embodied in this chapter. Of course it may be romantic, contrary to fact, and even counterproductive to think that Shakespeare arrived at this vision in a blinding flash. Perhaps he, too, struggled for it through many years before he compressed it into a few rhymes. But without doubt he got there without the help of the great predecessors who built the steps and lighted the way for us moderns, and without the data collected over two centuries that now provide the substrate for the idea.

Of course Shakespeare's Sonnet 1 does not comprise a theory of the human enterprise's demographic-economic development. Yet the sonnet takes up themes and expresses a vision uncannily parallel to the present theory of that subject. My aim here is to use the sonnet to illuminate that theory—to see the theory more clearly and show it to be more persuasive than it might otherwise appear.

The "good" that Shakespeare wishes to advance is poetic truth, indistinguishable from beauty. This is the parallel to the natural resources and standard of living which are the subject of contemporary study of economic development. More about this shortly.

Let us examine Sonnet 1. (That number may be more than a coincidence, just as it is not a coincidence that Genesis comes at the beginning of the Bible.)

Sonnet 1

From fairest creatures we desire increase,
That thereby beauty's rose might never die,
But as the riper should by time decease,
His tender heir might bear his memory;
But thou, contracted to thine own bright eyes,
Feed'st thy light's flame with self-substantial fuel,
Making a famine where abundance lies,
Thyself thy foe, to thy sweet self too cruel.
Thou that art now the world's fresh ornament
And only herald to the gaudy spring,
Within thine own bud buriest thy content

And, tender churl, mak'st waste in niggarding.
Pity the world, or else this glutton be,
To eat the world's due, by the grave and thee.

Shakespeare begins by assuming that "From fairest creatures we desire increase"—that is, that there should be more of such creatures. By "creatures" Shakespeare means people, our human species. That Shakespeare has such a demographic-like process in mind is clear from his third and fourth lines—death preceded by birth and renewal. And we may suppose that Shakespeare is interested in the human race as a whole, not only in its most beautiful specimens. In *The Tempest* (V.i.181), we read "How beauteous mankind is!"

If Shakespeare is indeed talking about people as if humans have a place different than other creatures in the scheme of things, the sonnet immediately takes its leave of those in our society today who believe that "other species have rights, too" (see chapter 38). These persons assert that when there is a conflict or trade-off between the increase of people and the increase of other species, the former must be constrained for the sake of the latter. These thoughts do not square with Shakespeare's ordering of the species.

The sonnet's first line suggests that Shakespeare desires increase in the number of fair creatures for their own sake, just as many people look with satisfaction upon a populous, prosperous community. This sets him apart from many people in our age, for whom the increase of the human population is not a value in itself.

I do not suggest that Shakespeare was calling for an indiscriminate increase in people. Indeed, he mentions only the fairest, which we might interpret as the most talented. But perhaps if asked, Shakespeare would have agreed that talent is spread widely, and that most people create a bit more than they use or destroy. And perhaps he would also have agreed that because it is difficult to predict where the bud of talent may sprout—he himself being a most powerful example—the best way to increase the number of the fair is to increase the total number of people.

In his second line, Shakespeare gives us yet another reason for desiring increase: survival of humankind. Many persons today consider this idea "primitive" and logically unwarranted. Rather, the stabilization and zero growth of the population is seen as a value.

Even for many among those who care about survival of humankind, survival of the race as a whole is subordinate to increase of their own ethnic or religious subgroup. And this preference is often sentimental rather than a matter of seeking larger numbers to help them prevail in political conflict. In contrast, Shakespeare's only special pleading is in favor of people who are "beautiful" and creative.

Let us turn now to Shakespeare's description of the mechanism of the advance of civilization, the most remarkable aspect of this sonnet. For Shakespeare, progress rather than just stability is within our powers and possibilities; this is implicit when he writes of increase and abundance rather than merely maintenance and subsistence. Here is no pinched and dismal Malthusian vision of humanity's place on the globe, but rather an expansive and optimistic outlook of human dominion.

But then Shakespeare warns that we humans may forgo our opportunities by narcissistic preoccupation with our own luxurious living—by taking from the common pot of humanity without putting back into it. "[C]ontracted to thine own bright eyes," Shakespeare tells us, humanity can make "a famine where abundance lies" by feeding our own "light's flame with self-substantial fuel." That is, we can fail to employ our capital, the true nature of which is the human drive to create and improve and advance. Instead, humanity may devote its energies to consumption and self-satisfaction, thereby burying within one's "own bud" our "content." I was taken aback by the combination of beauty and understanding of life with which these few lines are suffused. The lines surpass in *both* respects other writings on the subject, scientific and artistic.

Here we must pause to discuss the nature of the "good" that might either be created in "abundance," or be made so scarce as to cause a "famine." Shakespeare certainly did not envision a process of economic development such as engages contemporary analysis of the subject, wherein we wish to increase the supply of consumer and investment goods, as well as natural resources, in order to live longer and better. Rather, Shakespeare cared about the world's stock of poetic truths such as he struggled to give us. And poetic truth is of course interrelated with—perhaps is identical to—the aesthetic aspect of life which Shakespeare calls "beauty," and which may be physical or artistic or spiritual. G. Wilson Knight argues forcefully that in the sonnets there is an interpenetration of the ideas of time (both past and future), material beauty, poetry, immortality, truth, nature, and art.[18] A key idea is that the immortal "substance" of poetic beauty is "distilled" from the mere "show" of human beauty, "A liquid prisoner pent in walls of glass" (Sonnets 5, 6). This transmutation of physical beauty into poetic truth provides the best of reasons for Shakespeare to write poems about a particular beautiful young man. And indeed, Knight writes that "The poet knows well that his poetry is more than his ordinary self. It is 'the very part was consecrate to thee,' his own 'spirit,' 'the better part of me,' to be contrasted with the element of 'earth' which is 'the dregs of life,' bound for death ([Sonnet] 74). This 'better part' . . . is a refined state of being, like the refinement of distilled essences."[19]

From an economic point of view, the good that we may call truth-and-beauty is conceptually no different than raw materials such as grain, or processed goods such as services and manufactured products. As information and knowledge constitute an ever-larger part of our economy with every passing year, and tangible goods (especially natural-resource materials, including energy) become an ever-smaller share of inputs, there should be less and less difficulty in agreeing that truth-and-beauty—call it art, if you like—is a good which may be construed theoretically in ways similar to the ways we construe other economic goods. A key respect in which truth-and-beauty is like knowledge, and thereby like the supply of natural resources that flows from knowledge, is that our stocks of both sorts of intellectual goods are not depleted by use, but instead continue forever to enhance human life.

Then Shakespeare proceeds to tell us that we may waste our chances, not only by gluttony and self-devotion, but also by attending to conservation rather than creation. He tells us that a society "mak'st waste by niggarding." This is a striking vision of the nature of civilization. It may be seen as parallel to the following sequence: Increase in population size, and rise in the standard of living, force upon us new problems. These emerging problems lead to the search for solutions (though great developments may also arise in a more spontaneous fashion). And the solutions arrived at leave us better-off materially, and perhaps with more efficient social organizations, than if the problems had never arisen in the first place. (Hence we need our problems because eventually we benefit from them.)

The resonance of the sonnet suggests that Shakespeare would have been sympathetic to this process. He would have felt at home, I think, with the notion that humanity not only needs to have problems solved, but also needs to impose bigger and better problems upon ourselves as a challenge to our creative powers—for the benefit of the human spirit as well as for the eventual benefit of our descendants.

So I say with Shakespeare, "Pity the world, or else this glutton be, to eat the world's due, by the grave and thee."

It is interesting to contrast Shakespeare's view of the course of civilization and productive economy with that of Bernard Mandeville, who lived not much later. Mandeville also expressed himself in rhyme but he clearly was a social scientist by inspiration rather than a poet. (See the lengthy prose notes following the short rhyming pages of *The Fable of the Bees*.) Mandeville saw improvement and advance as inevitable, brought about by the same selfish qualities that Shakespeare lamented, qualities which Mandeville might also not have admired or enjoyed but nevertheless saw as a constant element in human nature. And Shakespeare referred (*King Henry V*, I.ii) to the same mysterious phenomenon of social organization and spontaneous cooperation among insects that Mandeville described in *The Fable of the Bees*; it may already have been a common insight in English culture by them. It is pleasant to imagine a meeting of the two men, each describing his vision and with the other instantly seeing the point and joining the other's vision to his own in a grand amalgamation.

Afternote 2 _____

How Immigrants Affect Our Standard of Living

IMMIGRATION, illegal and legal, has touched a sore spot in American public opinion for 150 years and more. The reasons opponents of immigration give are mostly economic—jobs, welfare, and housing. But in fact, American citizens can do well while doing good by admitting refugees. Rather than being a matter of charity, we can expect our incomes to be higher rather than lower in future years if we admit more Cubans, Haitians, Indo-Chinese, Mexicans, Italians, Filipinos, and other ethnic immigrants.

The first edition discussed the economic effects of immigration, but since then I have written an entire book on this subject, and it no longer makes sense to tackle the subject here in brief.[20] Instead, here is a thumbnail summary:

Immigrants pay much more in taxes than the cost of the welfare services and schooling that they use. In fact, the average immigrant family uses *less* welfare services and pays *more* taxes than the average native family! This is because immigrants are not old, tired, and without skills. Rather, they are on average in the early prime of their work lives. And they are about as well educated as the native labor force, with a much larger proportion of professional and technical persons such as doctors and engineers.

Immigrants directly raise productivity with the new scientific and technical ideas that they invent. They also improve productivity indirectly by way of their earnings, which when spent increase the overall volume of goods and services produced, which in turn causes industries throughout the economy to learn how to produce more efficiently.

Immigrants have no observable negative effect upon unemployment, many recent studies agree. This is mainly because they not only take jobs, but with their earnings which they then spend, they make as many jobs as they take. Furthermore, they make additional new jobs with the new businesses that they open.

Immigration promotes progress toward all of the United States national goals at once—a stronger economy, heightened productivity, increased international competitiveness, better international relations.

34

The Big Picture II: LDCs

> If population be connected with national wealth, liberty and personal security is the great foundation of both. . . .The statesman in this, as in the case of population itself, can do little more than avoid doing mischief.
>
> (*Ferguson 1995*)

IN TIME, the countries we now refer to as less-developed will fall into the category of more-developed countries discussed in chapter 33. But for now, their situations are still sufficiently different to warrant separate discussion, though it should be noted that the basic economic principles apply equally in all cases.*

During several decades starting in the 1960s, economic models of the effect of population growth upon the standard of living in less-developed countries (LDCs) have had great influence on governmental policies, as well as on the thinking of social scientists and the public. Phyllis Piotrow's historical account attributes enormous impact to Ansley J. Coale and Edgar M. Hoover's book of 1958 which concluded that population growth hampers LDC economic growth: "The Coale-Hoover thesis eventually provided the justification for birth control as a part of U.S. foreign aid policy."[1] The highest-ranking State Department official involved in population matters, immediately after his appointment in 1966, prepared an extensive position paper:

> Adopting completely the Coale-Hoover thesis . . . [Philander] Claxton [Jr.] argued that the U.S. government must move from reaction and response to initiation and persuasion. . . . By the time the paper reached the Secretary of State's desk, it had already achieved part of its purpose. All the appropriate State Department and Aid bureaus had reviewed, revised, commented, added to, and finally cleared the document. The rest of its purpose was accomplished when [Secretary of State Dean] Rusk agreed to every single one of Claxton's ten recommendations.[2]

This U.S. policy, based on a now-falsified model, continues to the time of writing. The foreign activities that are part of it expend more funds than ever in activities as shady as ever that may again draw other countries' hostility to the United States, as happened in India and elsewhere. More about these

---

* Some members of the economics profession for decades after World War II thought that different economic principles applied to economic development, but that view is now happily passé.

political aspects was said in the first edition, but the subject is now so extensive that it must be left for part of a subsequent book.

Since the first edition, U.S. policy has become more complex, however. At
the 1984 UN World Population Conference, the United States declared that
the effect of population growth is "neutral." The material presented in this
book, and in its 1977 technical predecessor, played some role in this turnabout—to what extent it would be hard to say, given that I played no role in
person, contrary to what population "activists" have flattered me with. But the
politics of the matter since then have been turbulent, with the population-
control movement still being exceedingly dominant in the Congress, and U.S.
AID continuing its foreign activities much as before.

This history makes clear the importance of having a sound economic-
demographic model for LDCs, which in turn requires sound empirical research and sound theory. Progress has been aided by the landmark 1986 Report of the National Research Council of the National Academy of Sciences,
which repudiated the Coale-Hoover view, and arrived at a point not far from
what is discussed here, as mentioned in the Introduction.

The Conventional Theoretical Models

The long-accepted population model of Coale and Hoover has two main elements: (1) an increase in the number of consumers, and (2) a decrease in
saving due to population growth (a proposition whose validity was discussed
in chapter 25, with ambiguous results). Their well-known conclusion is that,
whereas in India with continued high fertility, income per consumer during
1956–1986 could be expected to rise from an index of 100 to 138, with declining fertility it could be expected to rise from 100 to 195—that is, India
could expect some two and a half times as fast economic growth with low
fertility as with high fertility.

It is crucial to notice that the main Coale-Hoover model simply *assumed*
that the total national product in an LDC would not be increased by population growth for the first thirty years, either by a larger labor force or by additional productive efforts. Therefore, their model boils down to the ratio of
output divided by consumers; an increase in the number of consumers decreases the per capita consumption, by simple arithmetic. In their words, "The
inauspicious showing of the high-fertility case in terms of improvement in
levels of living is traceable entirely to the accelerated growth in the number of
consumers that high fertility produces."[3] To repeat: The main mechanism producing the Coale-Hoover result is simply an increase in the denominator of
the output/consumer ratio, where output is the same *by assumption* for the first
thirty years for all rates of population growth.

Subsequent LDC models (including a variant by Coale and Hoover) took into account that a faster-growing population produces a larger labor force, which in turn implies a larger total output. But this modification still implies Malthusian capital dilution, and while slightly altering the main Coale-Hoover result, such a model still necessarily indicates that a faster-growing population leads to a lower output per worker and lower per capita income.

In sum, the conventional theory suggests that a larger population retards the growth of output per worker in LDCs. The overwhelming element in the conventional theory is the Malthusian concept of diminishing returns to labor, operating with the assumption that the stock of capital (including land) does not increase in the same proportion as labor.

Another important theoretical element is the dependency effect, which suggests that saving is more difficult for households where there are more children, and that higher fertility causes social investment funds to be diverted away from industrial production. Combined in simulation models, these conventional elements imply that relatively high fertility and population growth diminish the output per worker (and even more the income per consumer, because the proportion of consumers to workers is higher when the birthrate is higher).

Again—The Data Contradict the Popular Models

But the empirical studies data do not support this a priori reasoning. The data do not show that a higher rate of population growth decreases the rate of economic growth, for either LDCs or MDCs. These data include the long-run historical data shown in figure 33-1. Also relevant are cross-sectional studies that relate the rate of population growth to the growth rate of per capita income in various LDCs; no correlation between the two variables is found.[4]

Another sort of study plots the growth rate of per capita income as a function of population *density*. Roy Gobin and I found that density has a *positive* effect on the rate of economic growth, as seen in figure 34-1.[5] And a study by J. Dirck Stryker found that among the French-speaking African countries, lower population density is associated with lower economic growth—that is, higher population density implies a higher standard of living.[6] And Kelley and Schmidt (1994) have massively confirmed the Simon-Gobin finding.

Check for yourself: Fly over Hong Kong—just a few decades ago a place seemingly without prospects because of insoluble resource problems—and you will marvel at the astounding collection of modern high-rise apartments and office buildings. Take a ride on its excellent smooth-flowing highways for an hour or two, and you will realize that a very dense concentration of human beings does not prevent comfortable existence and exciting economic expansion—as long as the economic system gives individuals the freedom to exercise their talents and to take advantage of opportunities. And the experience

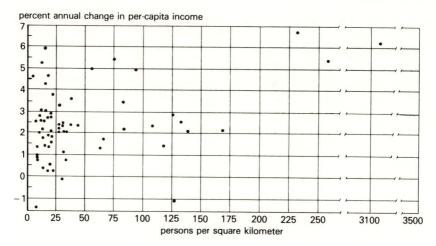

Figure 34-1. Economic Growth Rates Related to Population Density in LDCs

of Singapore demonstrates that Hong Kong is not unique. Two such examples do not prove the case, of course. But these dramatic illustrations are backed by the evidence from the aggregate sample of countries, and hence do not mislead us.

Hong Kong is a special thrill for me because I first saw it in 1955 when I went ashore from a U.S. Navy destroyer. At the time I felt great pity for the thousands who slept every night on the sidewalks or on small boats. It then seemed clear to me, as it must have to almost any observer, that it would be impossible for Hong Kong to surmount its problems—huge masses of impoverished people without jobs, total lack of exploitable natural resources, more refugees pouring across the border each day. But upon returning in 1983, I saw bustling crowds of healthy, vital people full of hope and energy. No cause for pity now.

The most important benefit of population size and growth is the increase it brings to the stock of useful knowledge. Minds matter economically as much as, or more than, hands or mouths. Progress is limited largely by the availability of trained workers.

The Role of the Political-Economic System

A crucial element in the economics of resources and population is the extent to which the political-social-economic system provides personal freedom from government coercion. For an economy to grow, individuals require a social and economic framework that provides incentives for working hard and taking risks, enabling their talents to flower and come to fruition. The key elements of such a framework are economic liberty, respect for property, and fair and sensible rules of the market that are enforced equally for all.

To illuminate the importance of the system as a crucial condition for whether additional people quickly become a benefit, it is useful to mention two extreme situations when additional people have been a negative force—sometimes reducing the standard of living all the way to misery and subsistence—rather than a force for growth, simply because of a lack of economic freedom:

1. A shipful of illiterate African slaves coming toward the United States. Additional slaves on the ship would only contribute toward faster death aboard, because freedom was totally absent.

2. A German prisoner-of-war camp for British soldiers in World War II. Despite the large stock of technology among the inmates in such a situation, and despite modern values and free-enterprise culture, the outside authority structure was strong enough to prevent any real growth. Additional inmates would not produce faster growth, only more crowding. If conditions got bad enough, the additional misery might lead to an explosion, and conceivably toward the "growth" of an escape. But chances of the latter were small.

Technology is not enough to distinguish the above two cases from that of, say, Hong Kong, where the addition of so many people after World War II almost surely did have a positive effect upon growth, as in Singapore. Values and culture also are not enough to distinguish. Only the social system, including the low taxation of Hong Kong, can distinguish the cases. China is much more like a prison than is Hong Kong because it suppresses mobility and opportunity. And if one takes the political-economic structure of China as given, the Chinese may be right that slower population growth means a higher standard of living in the present generation.*

Powerful evidence that the world's problem is not too many people, but lack of political and economic freedom, comes from pairs of countries that have the same culture and history, and had much the same standard of living when they split apart after World War II—East and West Germany, North and South Korea, Taiwan and China. In each case the centrally planned economy began with less population "pressure," as measured by density per square kilometer, than did the market-directed economy. And the Communist and non-Communist countries also started with much the same birthrates. But the market-directed economies have performed much better economically than the centrally planned economies (see table 34-1). This powerful explanation

---

* Of course exceptional individual events can occur in unpromising circumstances. A little town in Illinois can produce several gold medalists in speed skating because of one person's vision. Occasional great minds may come out of backward villages in Serbia (Michael Pupin) and Lebanon (Philip Hitti), simply because of inexplicable accidents such as a broken arm that keeps a child from returning to his/her village (see their autobiographies).

TABLE 34-1a

Population and Density and Growth, Selected Countries 1950–1983

	East Germany	West Germany	North Korea	South Korea	China	Tai-wan	Hong Kong	Singa-pore	USSR	USA	India	Japan
Population per Sq. km., 1950	171	201	76	212	57	212	2236	1759	8	16	110	224
% Change in Pop., 1950	1.2	1.1	−7.8	0.1	1.9	3.3	−10.4	4.4	1.7	1.7	1.7	1.6
% Change in Pop., 1955	−1.3	1.2	3.5	2.2	2.4	3.5	4.9	4.9	1.8	1.8	1.9	1.0
% Change in Pop., 1960	−0.7	1.3	3.0	3.3	1.8	3.1	3.0	3.3	1.8	1.7	2.0	0.9
% Change in Pop., 1970	−0.1	1.0	3.0	2.4	2.4	2.2	2.2	1.7	1.0	1.1	2.2	1.3
% Change in Pop.,			2.1–	1.4–	1.3–				0.7–	2.1–		
1983	−0.3	0.2	2.6	1.6	1.6	1.8	1.5	1.2	0.9	0.9	2.2	0.6

Sources: Population per square km.: United Nations Educational, Scientific, and Cultural Organization, *UNESCO Yearbook* (1963, pp. 12–21). Percentage change in population: U.S. Department of Commerce, *World Population* (1978); United Nations, Report on *World Population* (1984).

TABLE 34-1b

Real Income per Capita, Selected Countries, 1950–1982

	East Germany	West Germany	North Korea	South Korea	China	Tai-wan	Hong Kong	Singa-pore	USSR	USA	India	Japan
Real GDP per capita, 1950[a]	1480	1888	n.a.	n.a.	300	508	n.a.	n.a.	1373	4550	333	810
Real GDP per capita, 1960	3006	3711	n.a.	631	505	733	919	1054	2084	5195	428	1674
Real GDP per capita, 1970	4100	5356	n.a.	1112	711	1298	2005	2012	3142	6629	450	4215
Real GDP per capita, 1980	5532	6967	n.a.	2007	1135	2522	3973	3948	3943	8089	498	5996
Real GNP per capita, 1950[b]	Same as W. Germ.	2943	Same as S. Korea	193	n.a.	417	1053	n.a.	n.a.	7447	217	649
Real GNP per capita, 1960	n.a.	3959	n.a.	473	n.a.	429	979	1330	n.a.	8573	220	1403
Real GNP per capita, 1970	6584	6839	556	615	556	868	1807	2065	4670	10769	219	4380
Real GNP per capita, 1982	9914	11032	817	1611	630	2579	5064	5600	5991	12482	235	9774

Sources: Real GDP per capita: Summers and Heston (1984). Real GNP per capita: International Bank for Reconstruction and Development (IBRD), *World Tables* (1980). GNP deflator: Council of Economic Advisors (1986, Table B-3).

[a] Figures for real gross domestic product (GDP) per capita are based on 1975 international prices.

[b] Figures for real gross national product (GNP) per capita are based on 1981 constant U.S. dollars.

TABLE 34-1c

Life Expectancy and Infant Mortality, Selected Countries, 1960–1982

	East Germany	West Germany	North Korea	South Korea	China	Taiwan	Hong Kong	Singapore	USSR	USA	India	Japan
Life Expectancy at Birth, 1960	68	69	54	54	53	65	65	64	68	70	43	68
Life Expectancy at Birth, 1982	73	74	65	68	67	73	76	73	69	75	55	77
Infant Mortality, 1960	39	34	78	78	165	32	37	35	33	26	165	30
Infant Mortality, 1982	12	12	32	32	67	18	10	11	28	11	94	7

Source: IBRD, *World Development Report* (1985, pp. 260–61).

TABLE 34-1d

Industrialization and Urbanization, Selected Countries, 1960–1982

	East Germany	West Germany	North Korea	South Korea	China	Taiwan	Hong Kong	Singapore	USSR	USA	India	Japan
% Labor Force in Agric., 1960	18	14	62	66	n.a.	n.a.	8	8	42	7	74	33
% Labor Force in Agric., 1980	10	4	49	34	69	37 (1978)	3	2	14	2	71	12
% Urbanized, 1960	72	77	40	28	18	58	89	100	49	70	18	63
% Urbanized, 1982	77	85	63	61	21	70 (1980)	91	100	63	78	24	78

Sources: Labor force in agriculture: IBRD, *World Development Report* (1985, pp. 258–59). Urban population: IBRD, *World Development Report* (1985, pp. 260–61).

TABLE 34-1e

Education and Consumption, Selected Countries, Various Years

	East Germany	West Germany	North Korea	South Korea	China	Tai-wan	Hong Kong	Singapore	USSR	USA	India	Japan
Higher Education Enrollment, 1960	16	6	n.a.	5	n.a.	n.a.	4	6	11	32	3	10
Higher Education Enrollment, 1980	30	30	n.a.	22	1	n.a.	12	10	21	56	9	31
Newsprint per Person, 1950–54	3.5	5.1	n.a.	0.6	n.a.	0.9	4.3	n.a.	1.2	35.0	0.2	3.3
Newsprint per Person, 1982	9.6	21.5	0.1	5.8	1.2	n.a.	16.4	32.1	4.5	44.1	0.4	24.0
Telephones per 100 Pop.,1983	20.6	57.1	n.a.	14.9	0.5	25.8	38.2	36.7	9.8	76.0	0.5	52.0
Autos per 100 Pop., 1960	0.9	8.2	n.a.	0.1	.005	0.1	1.0	4.2	0.3	34.4	0.1	0.5
Autos per 100 Pop., 1970	6.7	24.1	n.a.	0.2	.018	n.a.	2.8	7.2	0.7	43.9	0.1	8.5
Autos per 100 Pop., 1984	18.9	41.3	n.a.	1.1	.010	3.1	4.6	9.3	3.9	55.5	0.2	22.8

Sources: Higher education: IBRD, *World Development Report* (1985, pp. 266–67). Newsprint: *UNESCO Yearbook* (1963, pp. 400–409). Telephones: U.S. Department of Commerce, *Statistical Abstract* (1986, p. 845). Automobiles: Motor Vehicle Manufacturers Association of the U.S. Inc., *World Motor Vehicle Data* (various years).

of economic development cuts the ground from under population growth as a likely explanation.

A bus trip across the Karelian peninsula—seeing first the part now in Finland, and then the part that was in Finland until 1940 but afterwards was in the Soviet Union and now is in Russia—reveals differences like night and day at the border. And table 34-2 shows dramatically different 1990s living standards in two towns on opposite sides of the (then) Czechoslovakia-Austria border, and in East and West Germany, which had similar standards of living before World War II, but vastly different situations now.

Or consider Mauritius. In the 1960s, James Meade, the Nobel-prize-winning British economist—but also a believer in eugenics, who embodied in his work the idea that a human life could be so poor materially that it was better not lived; see chapter 23—offered Mauritius as his example of a densely crowded country whose rapid birthrate was ruining its chances of economic development. He foresaw terrible unemployment, and Mauritius did suffer

TABLE 34-2
Living Standards East and West, Late 1980s

To Buy . . . the Average Factory Employee Must Work . . .

	1988	
	Czechoslovakia *(Cesky Krumlov)*	*Austria* *(Freistadt)*
One pound steak	2.5 hours	1 hour
Shoes	22 hours	11 hours
One month's rent	25 hours	41 hours
Color televison	565 hours	109 hours
Compact car	4,130 hours	2,054 hours
Three-bedroom house	43,487 hours	20,547 hours

The Two Germanys, 1987
Working Hours Needed to Buy Various Goods

	West	*East*
Car	607	3,807
Refrigerator	40	293
Man's suit	13	67
Percentage of Housing Facilities with		
Central heating	70%	36%
Indoor toilet	95%	60%
Bath/shower	92%	68%

Sources: Washintion Post, September 18, 1988, p. A25. Wall Street Journal, September 4, 1987, p. 1.

this blight for many years. But in the early 1980s Mauritius radically changed its economic-political framework, allowing free enterprise a chance to flourish. By 1988 one could read that "Offshore Jobs Dynamo Offers Model for Africa. . . . The government here says that unemployment, which ran at 23 percent six years ago, no longer exists."[7] This is as close to an economic miracle as this world is likely to see. The change over those few years had nothing to do with changes in Mauritius' birthrate, nor was there a reduction in the high population density. Economic freedom was the only new element.

Some readers (though fewer than at the time of the first edition) may not know how well the poorer countries have been progressing. Contrary to common belief, per capita income in LDCs has been growing as fast as or faster than in the MDCs, despite the fact that population growth in LDCs has been much faster than in MDCs. This is prima facie evidence that population growth does not have a negative effect on economic growth. Indeed, the fact that countries with high densities have higher income *levels* on average implies that they must on average have had higher *growth* throughout the past than countries with lower population densities.

Aggregate statistics sometimes lack conviction because they are abstract. To give the data more realism, let us consider the change in a typical Indonesian village between 1953 and 1985 when Nathan Keyfitz studied it:

> [In 1985 the villagers] typically wear shoes, have houses of brick and plaster, and send their children to the elementary school in the village. Some have electric lights and a television set, own a motorcycle, and hope their children will go to the second-ary school a few kilometers away. Thirty-one years earlier shoes were rare, houses were almost all of thatch and bamboo with earth floors; lighting was at best with kerosene, and even that was something of a luxury; there was no primary school.[8]

Keyfitz calculated that per person income rose about 3 percent per year, a very respectable rate by any measure. People's diets had improved. The poor-est class improved itself considerably—the daily wage in terms of kilos of rice doubling.[9]

The poor also improved in dignity and independence, Keyfitz reports. Con-cerning the responsibility of each citizen to "spend one night per week on guard duty. . . . In our earlier visit we found that the landowner could order one of his gedok [subservient client-dependents] to take his place; today that is more difficult. The patron cannot even send one of his gedok on a daytime errand in the matter-of-fact way that was once acceptable. At one time the village headman's land was cultivated for him by village laborers acting with-out pay; now the headman has to pay them the going wage." One cause may be that "much easier travel, by which nearly everyone has a chance to observe the freedom of nearby towns, not to mention larger cities . . . makes them intolerant of unnecessary bondage at home."[10]

One of the most arduous and omnipresent tasks of women in 1953 was pounding rice to hull it. In 1985 the job was done with mechanical rice dryers and hullers, operated as businesses.

Population grew substantially, from 2,400 to 3,894,[11] so income grew de-spite population growth (or because of it), the opposite of what Malthusian Coale-Hoover type theory would expect.

Keyfitz and his colleagues assumed in advance that in 1985 "unemploy-ment would be the great problem of the village," because of population growth. But they found that this was not so. Better-off people were using their additional income to hire others, who had now become specialized workmen, to build houses professionally instead of do-it-yourself productions; schools and mosques were being built, too. The researchers also found, contrary to their expectations, that the proportion of the crop going to labor had risen and the proportion going to the landowner had fallen,[12] the opposite of what sim-ple Ricardian theory of increased population would predict; increased pro-ductivity of the land is the explanation.

Keyfitz's systematic account of the East Javanese village squares with the vivid anecdotal descriptions by Richard Critchfield, who over a quarter century visited villages in poor countries, and then revisited some (1981). The universal improvement that he found came as a surprise to him.

My personal experiences agree. In almost all the non-European countries I visited from the beginning of the 1970s to the present—Israel, India, Iran, China, the Soviet Union, Thailand, Hong Kong (yes, there is agriculture in Hong Kong), Philippines, Colombia, Costa Rica, Chile, and others—I have made it my business to visit agricultural villages, and to ask (through translators, of course) villagers about their farming practices at present and in the past, about their possessions and consumption present and past, and about the number and the education of their children. (Only in the Soviet Union was it not possible for me to find out what was what, despite the bluntest possible inquiries.) Improvement could be seen everywhere, in all respects—tractors, roads to the market, motorbikes, electric pumps for wells, schools where there were none before, and children gone on to university in the city.

A Model That Reconciles Theory and Evidence for LDCs

When the theory and the data do not jibe, either (or both) may be at fault. The available raw data have been re-examined several times, always with the same anti-Malthusian result. Let us therefore turn to a re-examination of the theory.

The model whose results are presented below includes the standard economic elements of the well-known earlier models, plus the main additional effects discussed in earlier chapters but left out of earlier models. These newly added elements include, among others: (1) the positive effect of increased demand (due to a larger population) upon business and agricultural investment; (2) the propensity of people to devote more hours to work and fewer hours to leisure when family size increases; (3) the shift in labor from agriculture to industry as economic development proceeds; and (4) economies of scale in the use of social infrastructure and other sources. All of these elements are well documented.

Further, if we are to understand the effect of population growth upon income and the standard of living, we must know the effect of income on population size and growth. All else being equal, income raises fertility and reduces mortality. But other factors do not remain the same while income changes, except in the very short run. In the long run, an increase in income in a poor country with a high fertility rate reduces the fertility rate. (This is the demographic transition described in chapter 23, which results from income-induced changes in mortality, urbanization, the higher costs of rearing children, and so on.) And after some point, mortality no longer falls significantly with additional income. Hence the long-run effect of an increase in income is a decrease in the rate of population growth. These effects also must be added to a realistic simulation.

When these important economic elements are included, rather than excluded as they are from earlier economic-demographic models of LDCs of the Coale-Hoover variety, and when reasonable assumptions are made about the various dimensions of the LDC economy, the results are very different than those from past models. The simulation indicates that moderate population growth produces considerably better economic performance in the long run (120 to 180 years) than does slower-growing population, though in the shorter run (up to sixty years) the slower-growing population performs slightly better. A declining population does very badly in the long run. And in the experiments with the "best" estimates of the parameters for a representative Asian LDC (the "base run"), moderate population growth has better long-run performance than either fast population growth (doubling over thirty-five years or less) or slow population growth.

Experiments with one variable at a time reveal that the difference between these results and the opposite results generated by previous models is produced, not by any single variable, but by the combination of the novel elements—the leisure-versus-work decision with extra children in the family, economies of scale, the investment function, and depreciation; no single factor is predominant. And over the range of positive population growth, different parameters lead to different positive rates of population growth as "optimum." This means that no simple qualitative theory of population growth of the classical Malthusian sort can be very helpful, and a more complex, quantitatively based theory such as this one is necessary.

For the interested technical readers, a fuller statement of the findings follows. Others may skip ahead.[13]

1. Using those parameters that seem most descriptive of LDCs today, the model suggests that very high birthrates and very low birthrates both result in lower long-run per-worker outputs (hereafter referred to as "economic performance") than do birthrates in between. It will surprise few that very high birthrates are not best. But the outcome that moderate birthrates produce higher income in the long run than do low birthrates runs very much against the conventional wisdom. The same result appears with quite different levels of the various parameters. The moderate-fertility populations also enjoy more leisure in the long run than do the low-fertility and high-fertility populations.

2. In a variety of conditions, over quite a wide range of moderate to high birthrates, the effect of fertility upon income is not spectacularly large— seldom as much as 25 percent, even after 180 years (though the difference in results produced by low and moderate birthrates is great). This is quite surprising at first thought. But it is what Kuznets anticipated:

> [G]iven the political and social contest, it does not follow that the high birth rates in the underdeveloped countries, per se, are a major cause of the low per capita income;

nor does it follow that a reduction of these birth rates, without a change in the political and social context (if this is possible), will raise per capita product or accelerate its rate of growth. We stress the point that *the source of the association between demographic patterns and per capita product is a common set of political and social institutions and other factors behind both* to indicate that any direct causal relations between the demographic movements and economic growth may be quite limited; and that we cannot easily interpret the association for policy purposes as assurance that a modification of one of the variables would necessarily change the other and in the directions indicated by the association.[14]

The results of my model suggest a population "trap"—but a benevolent one very different from the Malthusian trap: If population growth declines too fast as a result of increasing income, total output fails to rise enough to stimulate investment; depreciation is then greater than investment, and income falls. In the model, this results in a return to higher fertility and then another cycle. Hence the ill results follow from population decline in this model, rather than from population increase as in the Malthusian trap.

3. The advantage of moderate birthrates over low birthrates generally appears only after quite a while—say, seventy-five to one hundred years. This is another reason why the results found here differ from those of the Coale-Hoover and similar models in which the time horizon is only twenty-five to thirty years (fifty-five years in the Coale-Hoover minor extension), whereas the time horizon here is 180 years (or longer in some cases). This points up the grave danger of using short-horizon models in the study of population growth. Population effects take a long time to begin and a much longer time to accumulate.

4. Perhaps the most important result of this simulation is that it shows that there are some reasonable sets of conditions under which fairly high fertility has better economic performance at some times than does low fertility, but there are also other reasonable sets of conditions under which the opposite is true. There are even sets of conditions well within the bounds of possibility under which extremely high fertility offers the highest income per capita and output per worker in the long run. That is, the results depend upon the choice of parameters within ranges that seem quite acceptable. This implies that any model of population that concludes that any one fertility structure is unconditionally better or worse than another must be wrong, either because that model's construction is too simple or for some other reasons. The sole exception to this generalization is fertility below replacement. Such a low-fertility structure does poorly under every set of conditions simulated here, largely because a reasonable increase in total demand is necessary to produce enough investment to overcome the drag of depreciation.

In sum, the differences between the results produced by this method and the results obtained by Coale and Hoover are due to the inclusion in this model of several factors omitted from the Coale-Hoover model: (a) the capacity of people to vary their work input in response to their varying income aspirations and family-size needs; (b) an economies-of-scale social-capital factor; (c) an industrial investment function (and an industrial technology function) that is responsive to differences in demand (output); and (d) an agricultural savings function that is responsive to the agricultural capital/output ratio. These factors together, at reasonable parameter settings, are enough to offset the capital-dilution diminishing-returns effect as well as the effect of dependency on saving found in the Coale-Hoover model. The difference in overall conclusions between this model and others, however, is also due to the much longer time horizon used in this model.

One's judgment about the overall effect of an additional child depends upon the discount rate chosen for weighing the costs and benefits in immediate periods together with periods further into the future, as was discussed in the context of the MDC model in chapter 33. If we give little or no weight to society's welfare in the far future, but rather pay attention only to the present and the near future, then additional children clearly are a burden. But if we weigh the welfare of future generations almost as heavily as the welfare of present generations, then additional children now are on balance a positive economic force. In between, there is some discount rate that, depending upon the circumstances of each country, marks the point at which additional children now are at the borderline of having a negative or positive effect. The choice of that discount rate is ultimately a matter of personal values, which we shall take up in chapter 38.

In brief, whether we assess the effect of additional children now as being negative or positive depends largely upon our time perspective. And given the economic analysis developed here, anyone who takes a long-range view—that is, gives considerable weight to the welfare of future generations—should prefer a growing population to a stationary or declining population.

Some Objections Considered

This and the previous chapter have reached conclusions contrary to prevailing popular opinion as well as to most of the professional literature since before Malthus (though professional opinion has shifted in the 1980s). Therefore, it may be useful to consider some of the objections to these conclusions. Of course, the full text of this book and my 1977, 1987, and 1992 books, including both the analysis and the empirical data, constitute the basic rebuttal to these objections. The following paragraphs take up the objections in a lighter and more casual fashion.

Objection 1. But population growth must stop at *some* point. There is *some* population size at which the world's resources must run out, *some* moment at which there will be "standing room only."

When someone questions the need to immediately check population growth in the United States or in the world, the standard response ever since Malthus has been a series of calculations showing how, after population doubles a number of times, there will be standing room only—a solid mass of human bodies on the Earth or in the United States This apparently shows that population growth ought to stop sometime—well before "standing room only," of course. But even if we stipulate that population growth must *sometime* stop, by what reasoning do people get from "sometime" to "now"? At least two aspects of such reasoning can be identified.

First, the stop-now argument assumes that if humans behave in a certain way now they will inevitably continue to behave the same way in the future. But one need not assume that if people decide to have more children now, their descendants will continue to have them at the same rate indefinitely. By analogy, because you decide to have another beer today, you must automatically drink yourself to death. But if you are like most people, you will stop after you recognize a reasonable limit. Yet many seem to have a "drunkard" model of fertility and society: if you take one drink, you're down the road to hell.

Another line of reasoning that leads people away from the reasonable conclusion that humankind will respond adaptively to population growth derives from the mathematics of exponential growth, the "geometric increase" of Malthus. The usual argument that population will "explode" to a doomsday point is based on the crudest sort of curve fitting, a kind of hypnotism by mathematics. Starkly, the argument is that population will grow exponentially in the future because it has always grown so in the past. This proposition is not even true historically, as we saw in chapter 22; population has remained stationary or gotten smaller in large parts of the world for long periods of time (for example, in Europe after the Roman Empire, and among aborigine tribes in Australia). And many other sorts of trends have been reversed in the past before being forced to stop by physical limits (the length of women's skirts, and the spread of Christianity and Islam).

If you are attracted to the sort of curve fitting that underlies most arguments about the need to control population growth, you might do well to consider other long trends that we have discussed earlier. For example, the proportion of people who die each year from famine from natural causes has surely been decreasing for at least a century since the beginning of mankind, and even the *absolute* number of people who die of famine has been decreasing despite the large increases in total population (see chapter 5). An even more reliable and important statistical trend is the steady increase in life expectancy over recorded history. Why not focus on these documented trends rather than on the hypothetical total-population trend?

An absurd counterspeculation is instructive. The exponential increase of university buildings in the past decades, and perhaps in the past one hundred years, has been much faster than the rate of population growth. Simple-minded curve fitting will show that the space occupied by university buildings will overtake and pass the amount of space in which people stand long before there is "standing room only." This apparently makes university growth the juggernaut to worry about, not population growth!

Some will reply that the analogy is not relevant because universities are built by reasonable people who will stop when there are enough buildings, whereas children are produced by people who are acting only out of passion and are not subject to the control of reason. This latter assertion is, however, empirically false, as we saw in chapter 24. Every tribe known to anthropologists, no matter how "primitive," has some effective social scheme for controlling the birthrate. Children are born for the most part because people choose to have them.

Even the proposition that population growth must stop *sometime* may not be very meaningful (see chapter 3 on "finitude"). The length of time required to reach any absolute physical limits of space or energy is far into the future (if ever), and many unforeseeable things could happen between now and then that could change those apparent limits.

Objection 2. But do we have a right to live high on the hog—consume all we want, have as large families as we want—and let later generations suffer?

The facts suggest that the opposite assumption is the more appropriate: If population growth is higher in a given generation, later generations benefit rather than suffer. During the industrial revolution in England the standard of living might (or might not) have been higher for a while if population had not grown so quickly. But we today clearly benefit from that high population growth rate and the consequent high economic growth of that period, just as the LDC model suggests.

Objection 3. Your models emphasize the long-run positive effects of population growth. But as Keynes said, in the long run we're all dead.

I've addressed Keynes's clever-but-silly wisecrack in chapter 12. It's true that you and I will die. But in the long run others will be alive, and those people matter—just as the future of the "planet" properly matters to ecologists and others. And as emphasized earlier, one's overall judgment about population growth depends upon one's discount rate—how you weigh the immediate and the future effects against each other.

Summary

History since the industrial revolution does not support the simple Malthusian model or the Coale-Hoover extension. No negative relationship between population growth and economic growth is revealed in anecdotal history, in time-series studies over the past 100 years, or in contemporary cross-sections.

Rather, the data suggest that there is no simple relationship at all, for either less-developed-countries (LDCs) or for more-developed-countries (MDCs) (as discussed in the previous chapter).

For MDCs, the most general and most appealing explanation of this discrepancy between theory and evidence is the nexus of economies of scale, the creation and adaptation of new knowledge by additional people, and the creation of new resources from new knowledge. Therefore the MDC model in chapter 33 incorporates this fundamental influence on economic progress that has previously been left out of population models. And that model—more complete than Malthusian and neo-Malthusian models such as *The Limits to Growth*—indicates that, after a few years during which a representative additional child has a net negative effect, the net effect upon per capita income comes to be positive. And these positive long-run effects are large compared with the added costs to the community until the child reaches full productivity. A present-value weighing of the short and long run at reasonable costs of capital reveals that the on-balance effect of additional persons is positive, an attractive "investment" compared to other social investments.

In LDCs the explanation is somewhat different, but the outcome is similar. Additional children influence the LDC economy by inducing people to work longer hours and invest more, as well as by causing an improvement in the social infrastructure, such as better roads and communication systems. Additional population also induces economies of scale in other ways. The upshot is that, although additional children cause additional costs in the short run, a moderate rate of population growth in LDCs is more likely to lead to a higher standard of living in the long run than either zero population growth or a high rate of population growth.

Afternote _____

The Limits to Growth, Global 2000, and Their Relatives

THE *Limits to Growth* simulation of 1972, in which people breed to the exhaustion of natural resources, is so devoid of meaning that it is not worth detailed discussion or criticism. Yet it is taken seriously by many people to this day, and it is therefore a fascinating example of how scientific work can be outrageously bad and yet be very influential.

The *Limits to Growth* was immediately blasted as foolishness or fraud by almost every economist who read it closely and reviewed it in print, for its silly methods as well as for disclosing so little of what the authors did, which makes close inspection impossible. To use the book authors' sort of language, the whole *Limits to Growth* caper was public-relations hype, kicked off with a press conference organized by Charles Kytle Associates (a public relations firm) and financed by the Xerox Corporation; this entire story, along with devastating commentary, was told in detail in *Science* the week following the book's appearance in 1972. (The public relations campaign may not be a bad thing in itself, but it certainly shows the manner the authors and the sponsoring Club of Rome intended to have their material make its way in the world of ideas.)

One strong reason not to put stock in the *Limits to Growth* predictions is that the model was quickly shown to produce *rosy* forecasts with only minor and realistic changes in the assumptions.[15] The most compelling criticism of the *Limits to Growth* simulation, however, was made by the sponsoring Club of Rome itself. Just four years after the foofaraw created by the book's publication and huge circulation—an incredible four million copies were sold—the Club of Rome "reversed its position" and "came out for more growth." But this about-face has gotten relatively little attention, even though it was written up in such places as *Time* and the *New York Times*.[16] And so the original message is the one that remains with many people.

The explanation of this reversal, as reported in *Time*, is a masterpiece of face-saving double-talk.

> The Club's founder, Italian industrialist Aurelio Peccei, says that *Limits* was intended to jolt people from the comfortable idea that present growth trends could continue indefinitely. That done, he says, the Club could then seek ways to close the widening gap between rich and poor nations—inequities that, if they continue, could all too

easily lead to famine, pollution and war. The Club's startling shift, Peccei says, is thus not so much a turnabout as part of an evolving strategy.[17]

In other words, the Club of Rome sponsored and disseminated untruths in an attempt to scare us. Having scared many people with these lies, the club can now tell people the *real* truth. (I have been waiting in vain since the first edition for them to sue me for libel in that previous sentence.)

But it is possible that the Club of Rome did not really practice the deceitful strategy that it now says it did. Maybe the members simply realized that the 1972 *Limits to Growth* study was scientifically worthless. If so, the Club of Rome then lied about what it originally did, in order to save face. From the outside, we have no way of knowing which of these ugly possibilities is the "truth."

Is my summary of the reported facts not fair? Perhaps I should use quieter language, because I know that some will find the use of words like "lie" sufficient reason to reject what I am saying. But I have no public relations firm to magnify my message a millionfold in the media, nor do I have a message that people are waiting breathlessly to hear. So I must use strong language to get this point across. And—is there really anything wrong with calling a documented and self-confessed lie a lie?

Surely this is one of the more curious scientific episodes of recent years. *The Limits to Growth* authors have not recanted, to my knowledge, even though their sponsors have. But neither did the authors confront and contradict their sponsors when the sponsors recanted. The whole matter seems to have passed with little notice, and *The Limits to Growth* continues to be cited in the popular press as authoritative. If the shoe were on the other foot, I would surely hear plenty from such organizations as Zero Population Growth and the Environmental Fund.

The *Global 2000 Report to the President* of 1980, done for President Jimmy Carter in conjunction with the Council on Environmental Quality and the Department of State, was a later incarnation of material similar to *The Limits to Growth*, done by many of the same people. It differs in that it was an "official" document with all the influence that such status automatically confers. Like *Limits to Growth*, the conclusions of *Global 2000* are almost wholly without merit largely because of the absence of the long-run trend data that show that resources are becoming more rather than less available, and that our air and water have been getting cleaner rather than dirtier. Even the authors of the *Global 2000 Report* agree that such trends are the proper basis for such a study, but they nevertheless relied upon the same old discredited Malthusian theorizing that has led one after another of these studies to make forecasts that were soon falsified by events—as was the case with *Limits to Growth* and *Global 2000*. Yet this study, too, was heavily ballyhooed, and became the basis for many policy decisions. *The Resourceful Earth*, which Herman Kahn and I edited in 1984, presents solid scholarly material on most of the questions addressed by *Global 2000*, having much in common with the material in this book.

In 1992 there appeared a sequel, *Beyond the Limits*, by the group that produced *Limits to Growth*. The main message was still very dour, but this time the authors built themselves an intellectual escape hatch. They say they may seem to have been wrong, but their ideas were really correct. They simply erred on the date for disaster. (Imagine your reaction if a weather forecaster asked not to be marked wrong because the snowstorm that he or she forecast for tomorrow was simply misdated by four months.) This is in the tradition of Malthus, who changed almost everything in his second edition except the conclusions that made him famous. The *Limits* authors now suggest we have a choice. If we change our ways, we can avoid collapse. But "if present trends remain unchanged, we face the virtually certain prospect of global economic collapse in the next century."

Part Three _____

BEYOND THE DATA

I know that it is a hopeless undertaking to debate about fundamental value judgments. For instance, if someone approves, as a goal, the extirpation of the human race from the earth, one cannot refute such a viewpoint on rational grounds.

(*Albert Einstein*, Ideas and Opinions, *1954*)

The liberal reward of labour, therefore, as it is the effect of increasing wealth, so it is the cause of increasing population. To complain of it, is to lament over the necessary effect and cause of the greatest public prosperity . . . it is in the progressive state, while the society is advancing to the further acquisition . . . of riches, that the condition of the labouring poor, of the great body of people, seems to be the happiest and the most comfortable. It is hard in the stationary, and miserable in the declining state. The progressive state is in reality the cheerful and the hearty state to all the different orders of the society. The stationary is dull; the declining melancholy.

(*Adam Smith*, The Wealth of Nations, *1776*)

"How much do babies cost?" said he
The other night upon my knee.
"For babies people have to pay
A heavy price from day to day—
There is no way to get one cheap.
Why, sometimes when they're fast asleep
You have to get up in the night
And go and see if they're all right.
But what they cost in constant care
And worry, does not half compare
With what they bring of joy and bliss—
You'd pay much more for just a kiss."

(*"What a Baby Costs,"* in Collected Verse of Edgar A. Guest, *1946*)

35

How the Comparisons People Make Affect Their Beliefs about Whether Things Are Getting Better or Worse

MY MOTHER was born in 1900. One of her brothers died of diphtheria in infancy, with the doctors helpless. In 1937, her only son was saved from death at age five by the first new wonder drug, sulfanilamide. In her eighties she knew that her friends had mostly lived extraordinarily long lives, mostly in good health. She was grateful for the new miracles of medical science, and she appreciated the convenience and comfort provided by such modern inventions as the telephone, central heating with gas, and airplanes.

Yet Mother insisted that life was worse in the 1980s than when she was young. When I pressed her why she thought so, she said, "The headlines in the newspaper are all bad."

When I say to her that pollution is decreasing in the United States, my wonderful Aunt Ruth, now in her eighties, responds, "But the pollution in the bay [near her home in Queens, New York] is much worse than when we moved here." When I remind her of the pollution in the water that killed children with typhoid and diphtheria when she was young, she sighs, "I guess you're right," but I don't think I have changed her outlook much.

When I say to my wonderful Aunt Anna, also in her eighties, that everything material is better now than when she was young, she answers, "But you read in the papers about so much wrong-doing." Reminding her of the horrors of two world wars—when paradoxically there often was good news in the papers—and mentioning the frauds of the 1920s, brings her to nod agreement, but that's only because she loves her nephew, I think.

How could these people of generally good judgment and usually cheerful nature hold beliefs so contrary to the facts, on the basis of such flimsy and ephemeral evidence? The only plausible answer is—as I wrote in the Introduction—that none of us can carefully inspect the evidence for most of the beliefs that we hold, and out of convenience we simply adopt the most easily available ideas. This is not an intellectual scandal; when a *Newsweek* story can be headed "More Bad News for the Planet" (March 28, 1988, p. 63) in a year and a decade of almost unbroken good news for the planet and the human enterprise, who can blame casual readers from sharing that point of view? It is another matter, however, when people insist on holding onto these ideas even when they are provided more reliable information, just because the beliefs have become so ingrained.

As another *Newsweek* column (Robert J. Samuelson, April 4, 1988, p. 51) noted, "Looking for Bad News? The better the economy does, the more we worry that its good behavior won't continue." He observed that economists are "expressing their doubts spotting a lot of potential problems, but their analyses aren't especially focused. They reflect a general anxiety about the future as much as a clear picture of what lies ahead. It's a bewildering game; everyone keeps getting good news and looking for the bad." In the midst of a spate of excellent economic news and a better state of the economy than in many years, those economists, like others, seem to seek ways to characterize the situation as frightening or worsening even when the signs point the other way.

This book is full of strong evidence—the bet offered in the Introduction dramatizes the facts—that the overall trend is toward things getting better rather than worse. Why, then, do people have a negative perception despite the positive trend?

Surely an important cause of the belief that things are going poorly, and that the future outlook is gloomy, is the type of comparisons that a person makes. The effect of looking at short-run and inter-group comparisons rather than long-run absolute comparisons was mentioned in the discussion of black and white infant mortality in chapter 22. Full discussion of the subject of comparisons fills another book (Simon 1993); I can only touch on the subject here.

Wise people have written for thousands of years that whether a person feels happy or sad depends in considerable part on the benchmark against which you compare what you believe to be your current state of affairs. So important is this element in our mood that it is the key element in psychological depression. The choice of benchmark for comparison is seldom forced on us by the world, but rather is mainly within our control.

The development of the personal computer and people's feelings about it illustrates the point. People commonly are delighted with their first computer because they see immediately how much it eases their work. But we quickly take the computer for granted, and even become dissatisfied that it does not work even faster. A delay of a few seconds becomes irksome, even as the computer is saving hours or days compared to the pre-computer situation. The old programs feel "clunky." The result is a continual desire for faster and faster computers, bigger and bigger hard drives, more and more worksaving utilities, and ever-fancier refinements on the programs. Because of this trend of rising expectations and rising desires, many people wind up no happier in their work than before they had computers.

Another example: An obstetrician in Washington, D.C. announced in 1990 that he was quitting the practice of obstetrics because for the second time a prospective mother had asked of him the impossible—that he guarantee her a perfect baby. In years past, when life in general and childbearing in particular were so much more risky than now, no woman would have even thought of such a request. But now women expect and demand complete safety and flawless offspring. This shows how quickly we take for granted an improvement in our lives, and compare other states of affairs to the new and improved state rather than to how it used to be. And if our prospects are not better than the newly improved state, we grouse. This psychological mechanism of rising expectations explains much about people's thinking about population, resources, and the environment.

The public demands an ever-increasing purity of air and water. In itself that certainly is a good thing. But when the public judges that our air and water now are "dirty" and "polluted," this makes no sense if one remembers the terrible pollutions that were banished in the past century or so—the typhoid fever that polluted even the Hudson River at New York, the smallpox that humanity has finally pursued to the ends of the Earth and apparently eradicated, the dysentery and cholera that distressed and killed people all over the world as it still does in Asia and Africa, the plagues and other epidemics that harm us much less than in generations past, or not at all. Not only are we in the rich countries free of malaria (largely due to our intensive occupation of the land; see chapter 32), but even the mosquitoes that only cause itches with their bites are now so few in many affluent urban areas that people no longer need window screens for their homes, and can have garden parties at dusk.

It is a proof of our extraordinary success in healing the Earth that the horrors of the past which were transmitted by filthy air and water are no longer even thought of as pollutions.

Now that we have largely overcome humanity's historic enemies—wild animals, hunger, epidemic disease, heat and cold—we worry about a large new class of phenomena in the environment and in society. This saying expresses this idea: No food, one problem; plenty of food, many problems.

Apparently it is built into our mental systems that no matter how good things become, our aspiration level ratchets up so that our anxiety level declines hardly at all, and we focus on ever-smaller actual dangers. Parents manage to worry about their kids' health and safety even though the mortality of children is spectacularly lower than in prior decades and centuries. And orthodox Jews and Muslims in the United States continue to worry about whether their food is ritually pure even though the protections against ritual contamination are remarkably better than in the past.

Once upon a time orthodox Jews said that "A Jew eats a small pig every year without knowing it." Nowadays, with plastic wrapping at the manufacturer, and the microscopic examination techniques of modern science, the level of purity is much higher than in the past. But the level of concern does not abate.

We cause ourselves lots of grief by the comparisons we make. We fail to enjoy our good fortune. In a very poor largely Hispanic town of New Mexico, this sign was in front of a ramshackle church: "The proper attitude is gratitude." Yet the more we really have to be grateful for, it seems, the less grateful and the more dissatisfied we become—the phenomenon noted by the philosophers of all ages. Instead of gratitude, our attitude is "What have you done for me lately?" Still one more saying from a football coach's wall: "Attitude is a matter of choice."

This mental quirk has consequences beyond keeping us from enjoying our improved life as much as we might. It also leads to the call for government to "fix" the supposedly bad conditions. And these calls for more government, predicated on the assertion that things have been getting worse when in fact they have been getting better, are likely to lead to fixing what ain't broke, and causing trouble thereby.

One of the problems in understanding modern life are the implicit comparisons to the past (often a nonexistent past) that people often make. We imagine Africa as people swinging from the trees like Tarzan, pre-Columbus North America as native Americans sitting around campfires and growing up to tall strong adulthood on plentiful organically grown pesticide-free food, never suffering the difficulties of adolescence; the U.S. Middle West as a fertile area where people needed to do no more than throw seeds upon the ground for there to be bountiful harvests; Europeans spending most of their time dancing around the Maypole and only rarely having to pull a forelock in respect to some authority; almost no one dying before old age, death being sudden and painless; and microorganism diseases such as tuberculosis and plague being mere romantic interludes suffered by a few artists.

But these faulty comparisons are not inevitable. You can train yourself to reflect on the comparison between what you have and what you had in the past, rather than on between what you have and what you might have, or what others have. I get enormous pleasure from having an alarm clock with a snooze bar so that I can be awakened, hit the bar, and grab another nine minutes of lovely sleep. I keep in mind how it was to work without a computer and a copy machine. And I remember how Oliver Wendell Holmes carried in a satchel the manuscript of his first book with him to every social engagement, for fear of losing it in a fire while he was away. Nor was this an imagined fear; at least one author lost forever the only copy of his novel on the New York subway. Copy machines and electronic copy relieve authors of this nightmare.

If one does not reflect on comparisons with how things used to be, and instead one focuses on some particular phenomenon which has temporarily gotten worse, or spends one's time thinking about politics or relative poverty where there are *by definition* as many losers as winners and where some sordidness is an inevitable outcome of our human nature, then one will fail to see all the long-term good news about the material conditions of life.

Another problem with our comparisons: Consider the data in various countries in various years asking people how happy they are. The distribution of poll results in any year is relatively independent of how rich the country is, or compared to itself in other years, or compared to other countries (though there is some slight positive association with income). Apparently individuals' benchmarks move in such a fashion that people stay in much the same relationship to their personal benchmarks. As to why there is a distribution among individuals, one might just as well put it down to genetic and/or early influences as to anything else.

Some Reflections on Jogging through San Francisco

Jogging and walking through the beautiful streets and extraordinary modern buildings of downtown San Francisco, I thought: Instead of standing in the present and making comparisons backwards, let us place ourselves at various moments in the past and look forward, asking at each point: What is it that at this moment I most want for humanity and civilization?

Our early wants were material. The first great want surely was defense against wild beasts. Not only have we learned how to protect ourselves against big lions and bears, but we have also succeeded in conquering most of the small things—mosquitoes, microbes, and soon even viruses.

Thousands of years ago we also wanted a steady supply of food. Progress was slow and irregular, but now we have succeeded beyond our wildest dreams.

We have wanted cheap energy to heat and fuel our lives. That problem is solved forever with nuclear power.

We have wanted metals and spices, and people foraged and traded for them all through the world in ancient times. Nowadays, abundant quantities of them cost only insignificantly small parts of our total expenditures.

The human mind fulfilled these wants, as Prometheus bragged (see p. 592).

More than anything else, we have wanted to forestall bad health and early death, particularly for our children. In the past couple of centuries we have spectacularly succeeded in our fight against untimely mortality. Only quantitatively small parts of the job remain yet to be done.

Starting a few hundred years ago during the industrial revolution, reformers most wanted liberation from back-breaking and mind-stultifying work in factories. Machines and robots now do that work for us, as they have also liberated women from heavy and repetitive chores in the home.

We have wanted such great wars as the U.S. Civil War, World War I, and World War II to cease, and for our world to be at peace. The world is now safe from mass war to an almost unprecedented degree. We have wanted our fear of war reduced, and in the past few years we have received that gift, too.

Is this assessment balanced? What about the supposed ills and evils of today that were not foreseen in the earlier times—the supposed breakup of the family, increasing numbers of homeless people on city streets, automobile and airplane deaths, nuclear fear in children, and other contemporary pathology (actual or mythical)? Here we must come to grips with the central premise of economic thought—that what the individual chooses is called "better." We can try to imagine whether people in those earlier times would prefer to have had the troubles which they wished to end, and which we have ended, versus the supposed new troubles of today. My guess is that when faced with wild beasts and decimated by plague, and given an imagined choice, earlier people would have chosen life in the twentieth century with its attendant new worries in preference to their problems.

Furthermore, in our times one almost always has a choice between living with and without any particular pathology. If one does not like the supposed high urban crime rate, one may live in a small town and be free of urban problems—yet still be safe from the evils of earlier times that we have gotten rid of. As to the supposed new threats of destruction such as nuclear war, it seems to me that a fair and rational assessment must be in terms of their demonstrated destruction up till now; the number of people killed by nuclear warfare until now is minuscule compared to other destroyers. Of course this is not a fair way to look at the overall risk. But neither would be the kind of scary scenario cooked up by some anti-nuclear war protesters.

Footnote: Nowadays in San Francisco one sees pedi-cabs carrying tourists and powered by healthy, well-muscled college boys. These pedi-cabs are almost a parody of the pedi-cabs that one saw in China years ago and can still see in India, ridden by bone-thin family heads eking out a bare living as long as health holds. The San Francisco pedi-cabs dramatize how our world has changed. Pedi-cab work nowadays can be done as an amusing and lucrative summer job. Can one doubt that this change, getting rid of back-breaking, life-destroying labor, is for the better?

Low-calorie cheese also shows how much we have achieved in things that people wanted in the past—to eat more rather than fewer calories. And the cheese can be eaten solely for its taste value; ignoring and even trying to get rid of calories.

36

The Rhetoric of Population Control: Does the End Justify the Means?

The ranking black lawmaker in the Illinois House and the Republican sponsor of a bill which would offer poor persons a chance for a free sterilization with a $100 bonus thrown in . . . squared off and traded verbal blasts Wednesday in the House Human Resources Committee where Rep. Webber Borchers was presenting his free vasectomy bill.

Though observers said Borchers may have won the battle of insults, Rep. Corneal Davis, an aging and rotund black preacher who has spent 30 of his 70-some years in the House, relished the satisfaction of having the bill defeated. . . .

Davis set the tone for the hearing on the bill soon after the committee sat down.

"Where is Borchers?" the Democratic assistant minority leader said, waving an arm at the ceiling. "He ought to take his bill and go back to Nazi Germany."

Thirty minutes later Borchers, a Decatur landowner who boasts of his ultraconservatism, arrived to explain his bill.

"This bill would allow persons who have an income of $3,000 or less to get a free vasectomy and a $100 bonus . . . ," Borchers began.

But Davis had sprung to his feet.

"Are you sincere about this?" the Chicago Democrat asked sarcastically.

"Sit down," Borchers yelled back.

"I am a preacher and I didn't want to lose my cool with you," Davis said.

"Why don't you listen? Sit down," Borchers said as both men's words began to get lost in the uproar.

Rep. Louis Capuzi, R-Chicago, chairman of the Human Resources Committee, pounded the gavel but it took several minutes for the two men to become silent.

Davis sat down and Borchers continued speaking.

"This bill was suggested to me by a black woman in Chicago," Borchers said.

Davis's eyes flared with rage but he remained silent. Borchers said the bill was similar to one passed in Tennessee. He estimated that more than 19,000 children are born to families receiving public aid each year and that the state would stand to save $20 million in welfare payments under the voluntary sterilization plan.[1]

THE DAVIS-BORCHERS interchange illustrates the subject of this chapter, the passions and the rhetoric found in discussions of resources and population. The next chapter examines how such rhetoric becomes established as "common knowledge," and explores some of the reasoning that underlies common doomsday beliefs about population.

Inflammatory Terminology and Persuasion by Epithet

Fear of population growth has been inflamed by extravagant language. Examples are the terms "population explosion," "people pollution," and "population bomb." These terms are not just the catchwords of popular wordsmiths, whose rhetoric one is accustomed to discount. Rather, they have been coined and circulated by distinguished scientists and professors. One example comes from demographer Kingsley Davis, who began a recent article in a professional journal, "In subsequent history the Twentieth Century may be called either the century of world wars or the century of the population plague."[2] (Margaret Sanger also wrote of China that "the incessant fertility of her millions spread like a plague.")[3] Davis also has said that "Over-reproduction—that is, the bearing of more than four children—is a worse crime than most and should be outlawed."[4] Or biologist Paul Ehrlich: "We can no longer afford merely to treat the symptoms of the cancer of population growth; the cancer itself must be cut out."[5] And it was in his Nobel Peace Prize speech, of all places, that agronomist Norman Borlaug spoke of "the population monster" and the "population octopus."

Writers vie with each other to find the ugliest possible characterization of human beings. From a Greenpeace leader, "[O]ur species [is] the AIDS of the Earth: we are rapidly eroding the immune system of the Earth."[6] Other niceties were quoted in chapter 22.

Such language is loaded, pejorative, and unscientific. It also reveals something about the feelings and attitudes of contemporary antinatalist writers. Psychiatrist Frederick Wertham pointed out that many of these terms have overtones of violence, for example, "bomb" and "explosion," and many show contempt for other human beings, such as "people pollution." Referring to expressions such as "these days of the population explosion and the hydrogen bomb" and "both nuclear weapons and population growth endanger mankind," he wrote, "The atomic bomb is the symbol, the incarnation, of modern mass violence. Are we justified in even speaking in the same vein of violent death and birthrate? And is it not a perverse idea to view population destruction and population growth as twin evils?"[7]

There is no campaign of counter-epithets to allay the fear of population growth, perhaps because of a Gresham's law of language: Ugly words drive out sweet ones. Reasoning by epithet may well be part of the cause of the fear of population growth in the United States.

Not only epithets but also value-smuggling neologisms have been used against fertility. The term "childfree" is a neologism coined by NON—the National Organization for Non-Parents—as a replacement for "childless." Their intention is to substitute a positive word, "free," for a negative word, "less." This neologism is an interesting example of skillful propaganda.

Whereas the term "less" is only slightly pejorative—you can have less of something good (love) *or* of something bad (acne)—the term "free" *always* seems
better than "unfree," and one can only be free of something bad. If not having
children makes you "free," then this clearly implies that children are bad. In
a similar vein, you now hear people speak with pain of "wetlands lost," a
phenomenon earlier referred to with pleasure as "swamps drained."

Phony Arguments, Crude and Subtle

Some of the antinatalist propaganda is subtle. While seeming to be only
straightforward birth-control information, in reality it is an appeal to have
fewer children. Planned Parenthood was responsible for such a campaign on
television and radio. The campaign was produced by the Advertising Council
as a "public service" and shown on television during time given free by the
broadcasters as part of their quid pro quo to the public in return for their
licenses; that is, it was indirectly paid for by taxpayers. The following is drawn
from a letter written in complaint to the Advertising Council decision makers—the only letter they said that they had ever received.

> You may have seen an advertising campaign staged by Planned Parenthood that ran
> on radio, television, and in many national magazines. There were a number of spe-
> cific ads in the campaign including one that was headlined "How Many Children
> Should You Have? Three? Two? One?"; another that adduced "Ten Reasons for Not
> Having Children" and, finally, the most offensive one was called the "Family Game":
> the game was staged on a great monopoly board and every time the dice of life were
> thrown and a child was born—rather like going to jail without passing "go"—the
> background audio announced the disasters that came in the wake of children—
> "there goes the vacation," or "there goes the family room. . . ."
>
> One of the ads enjoins young people to "enjoy your freedom" before, by having
> children, you let some of that freedom go. Such a theme . . . continues the view that
> the contribution children make to persons and to society is a purely negative one. In
> this view children are a loss: they take space, constrict freedom, use income that can
> be invested in vacations, family rooms, and automobiles. We find no consideration
> here of how children enhance freedom, and of how the advantages of freedom itself
> are realized when shared rather than prized as a purely personal possession. Finally,
> one of the ads encapsulates the spirit of the entire campaign: "How many children
> should a couple have? Three? Two? One? None?" Such an ad belies the claim that the
> advertising avoids the designation of any specific number of children as "preferred."
> Why not 12? 11? 10? or six? five? four? In the same ad, in order to lead audience
> thinking, it is noted that the decision to have children "could depend on their con-
> cern for the effect population growth can have on society." The direction of the effect
> on society is implied, but nowhere is the effect analyzed, or even clearly stated.

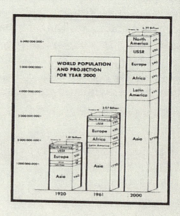

Figure 36-1. Advertisement by the Campaign to Check the Population Explosion

In summary, the ads not only teach family planning but recommend population control. Moreover, they do this by defining the range of acceptable family size as between zero and three, by placing children as negative objects alongside the positive goods supplied by industry, by equating the bringing up of children with merely equipping them with these same goods, by viewing children as an essential constriction of human freedom, and by suppressing a view of life and children that might lead people to think that having more children is a positive and rewarding act. There are values, not just techniques embodied in those ads.[8]

Not all antinatality rhetoric is that subtle. Some is crude name calling, especially the attacks on the Catholic church and on people with Catholic connections. An example is the bold black headline on the full-page ad that was run in national magazines: "Pope denounces birth control as millions starve" (fig. 36-1). Another example is the dismissal of opposing views by referring to the happenstance that the opponent is Catholic. Consider, for example, the religion-baiting of Colin Clark—a world-respected economist who presented data showing the positive effects of population growth—by sociologists Lincoln and Alice Day: "Colin Clark, an internationally known Roman Catholic economist and leading advocate of unchecked population growth . . ." (Lincoln Day also likened me to a "defrocked priest.") And Jack Parsons writes, "Colin Clark, the distinguished Roman Catholic apologist . . . refrains from discussing optimization of population at all . . . an extraordinary omission." Gunnar Myrdal is not a Catholic and is a Nobel prize winner, and yet *he* called the concept of an optimum population level "one of the most sterile ideas that ever grew out of our science." But Parsons feels free to attribute religious motives to Clark's choice of technical concepts and vocabulary when Clark does not mention this "optimization" concept. And in the widely read text of Paul Ehrlich and others, *Population, Resources, and Environment*, we find a reference to Clark as an "elderly Catholic economist," an innovation in the name calling by referring to Clark's age as well as to his religion.[9]

As a firsthand example in the same vein, my own views—which had already become those of this book—were described by Paul Silverman, a biologist, before a packed auditorium on the first and greatest Earth Day, in 1970, as "inspired by Professor Simon's contact with the Bible. . . . Indeed, a new religious doctrine has been enunciated in which murder and abstinence from sex are not distinguishable."[10]

Grabbing Virtue, Daubing with Sin

A rhetorical device of the antinatalists (as of all rhetoricians, I suppose) is to attribute to themselves the most virtuous and humanitarian of motives, while attributing to their opponents motives that are self-serving or worse. Biologist

Silverman again: ". . . people such as Paul Ehrlich and Alan Guttmacher and presumably myself . . . out of our great concern for the future of the world and the threat to the quality of life . . . have urged that voluntary means be adopted for bringing about restraints on the overburdening of our environment by overpopulation. . . . We must, we can, and we will achieve a fine and beautiful world for ourselves and our children to inherit. . . . We can realize a new quality of life, free from avarice which characterizes our current society."[11] (A few minutes before, the same speaker had said, "If voluntary restraints on population growth are not forthcoming, we will be faced with a need to consider coercive measures"—similar to Ehrlich's "by compulsion if voluntary methods fail.") (See my 1991 book, selection 58, for more discussion of how the population-control organizations assume the moral high ground and deny it to others.)

Why Is Population Rhetoric So Appealing?

Let us consider some of the reasons that antinatality rhetoric has won the minds of so many people. (For more extended discussion, see my 1991 book, selection 52.)

Short-Run Costs Are Inevitable, whereas Long-Run Benefits Are Hard to Foresee

In the very short run, the effects of increased births are negative, on the average. If your neighbor has another child your school taxes will go up, and there will be more noise in your neighborhood. And when the additional child first goes to work, per-worker income will be lower than otherwise, at least for a short while.

It is more difficult to comprehend the possible long-run benefits. Increased population can stimulate increases in knowledge, pressures for beneficial changes, a youthful spirit, and the "economies of scale" discussed earlier. That last element means that more people constitute bigger markets, which can often be served by more efficient production facilities. And increased population density can make economical the building of transportation, communication, educational systems, and other kinds of "infrastructure" that are uneconomical for a less-dense population. But the connection between population growth and these beneficial changes is indirect and inobvious, and hence these possible benefits do not strike people's minds with the same force as do the short-run disadvantages.

The increase in knowledge created by more people is especially difficult to grasp and easy to overlook. Writers about population growth mention a greater number of mouths coming into the world, and even more pairs of hands, but they never mention more brains arriving. This emphasis on physical consumption and production may be responsible for much unsound thinking and fear about population growth.

Even if there are long-run benefits, the benefits are less immediate than are the short-run costs of population growth. Additional public medical care is needed even before the birth of an additional child. But if the child grows up to discover a theory that will lead to a large body of scientific literature, the economic or social benefits may not be felt for a hundred years. All of us tend to put less weight on events in the future compared with those in the present, just as a dollar that you will receive twenty years from now is worth less to you than is a dollar in your hand now.

The above paragraphs do not imply that, on balance, the effect of increased population will surely be positive in any longer-run period. The fact is that we do not know for sure what the effects will be, on balance, in fifty or one hundred or two hundred years. Rather, I am arguing that the positive effects tend to be overlooked, causing people to think—without sound basis—that the long-run effects of population growth *surely* are negative, when in fact a good argument can be made that the net effect *may* be positive.

Intellectual Subtlety of Adjustment Mechanisms

In order to grasp that there can be long-run benefits from additional people, one must understand the nature of a spontaneously ordered system of voluntary cooperation, as described by Mandeville, Hume, Smith, and their successors (see page 410). But this is a very subtle idea, and therefore few people understand its operation intuitively, and believe explanations based on it.

Not understanding the process of a spontaneously ordered economy goes hand-in-hand with not understanding the creation of resources and wealth. And when a person does not understand the creation of resources and wealth, the only intellectual alternative is to believe that increasing wealth must be at the cost of someone else. This belief that our good fortune must be an exploitation of others may be the taproot of false prophecy about doom that our evil ways must bring upon us. (See below on the prophetic impulse.)

Apparent Consensus of Expert Judgment

Antinatalists convey the impression that *all the experts* agree that population is growing too fast in the United States and that it is simply a *fact* that population is growing too fast. An example from Lester Brown: "There are few if any informed people who any longer deny the need to stabilize world population."

Other examples come from Paul Ehrlich, "Everyone agrees that at least half of the people of the world are undernourished (have too little food) or malnourished (have serious imbalances in their diet)." And, "I have yet to meet anyone familiar with the situation who thinks India will be self-sufficient in food by 1971, if ever." And from a *Newsweek* columnist and former high State Department official: "Informed men in every nation now know that, next to population growth and avoidance of nuclear war, the despoiling of nature is the biggest world problem of the next 30 years."[12]

These "everyone agrees" statements are just plain wrong. Many eminent experts did not agree with them when they were made (and now the consensus disagrees with them, as discussed in chapter 34). But such assertions that "everyone agrees" may well be effective in manipulating public opinion. Which nonspecialist is ready to pit his or her own opinion against that of all the "informed people"?

Population as a Cause of Pollution

Fear of population growth is surely heightened by the linking of population and pollution issues. It has come to seem that if one is for pollution control then one must be against population growth. And pollution control in itself appeals to everyone, for very substantial reasons.

To understand why the link-up of population control and pollution control has occurred with such force, we must understand the nature of the rhetoric on both sides of the argument. One can directly demonstrate that more people increase the flow of a pollutant—for example, more cars obviously make more emissions. The argument that more people may reduce pollution is less direct and not so obvious. For example, as more people create a worse auto-emission pollution problem, forces of reaction arise that may eventually make the situation better than ever before.

Furthermore, the ill effects of people and pollution can be understood deductively. More people surely create more litter. But whether the endpoint after a sequence of social steps will be an even cleaner environment can only be shown by an empirical survey of experiences in various places: Are city streets in the United States cleaner now than they were one hundred years ago? Such empirical arguments are usually less compelling to the imagination than are the simplistic deductive arguments.

Population, Natural Resources, and Common Sense

With respect to natural resources, the population-control argument apparently makes perfect "common sense." If there are more people, natural resources will inevitably get used up and become more scarce. And the idealistic, generous side of young people responds to the fear that future generations will be disadvantaged by a heavy use of resources in this generation.

Perhaps such a doomsday view of natural resources is partly accounted for by the ease of demonstrating that more people will cause some particular negative effects—for example, if there are more Americans there will be less wilderness. The logic of the rebuttal must be global and much more encompassing than the logic of the charge. To show that the loss of wilderness to be enjoyed in solitude is not an argument against more people, one must show that an increase in people may ultimately lead to a general expansion of the "unspoiled" space available to each person—through easier transportation to the wilderness, high-rise buildings, trips to the moon, plus many other partial responses that would not now be possible if population had been stationary 100 years ago. It is obviously harder to show how good is the sum effect of these population-caused improvements than it is to show how bad is the partial effect of a decrease in this or that wilderness area that one may enjoy in solitude. Hence the result is a belief in the ill effects of population growth.

Judgments about People's Rationality

At the bottom of people's concern about population growth often lies the belief that other people will not act rationally in the face of environmental and resource needs. Arguments about the need to stop population growth now often contain the implicit premise that individuals and societies cannot be trusted to make rational, timely decisions about fertility rates. This is the drunkard model of fertility behavior refuted in chapter 24.

One of the themes that runs through much of the population movement is that the experts and the population enthusiasts understand population economics better than other persons do. As John D. Rockefeller III put it, "The average citizen doesn't appreciate the social and economic implications of population growth."[13]

It is not obvious why a politician or businessman—even though a very rich one—should have a clearer understanding of the costs of bearing children than "an average citizen." But Rockefeller has much power to convert his opinion into national action.

Forces Amplifying the Rhetoric

Media Exposure

Antinatality views get enormously more exposure than pro-natality or neutralist views. Paul Ehrlich has repeatedly been on the Johnny Carson show for an unprecedented hour; no one who holds contrary views gets such media expo-sure. This is also clear from a casual analysis of the titles of articles listed in the *Reader's Guide to Periodical Literature*.

Money

The leaders of population agencies that have vast sums of money at their disposal—UNFPA and USAID—take as their goal the reduction of population growth in the poorer countries. Scientists who work in population studies and who have a reasonable degree of career prudence are not likely to go out of their way to offend such powerful potential patrons. Individuals and organiza-tions hitch all kinds of research projects to this money-star. Furthermore, various agencies such as UNFAO realize that their own budgets will be larger if the public and government officials believe that there are fearsome impend-ing dangers from population growth, environmental disaster, and starvation. Therefore, their publicity organs play up these threats.

Standards of Proof and of Rhetoric

The standard of proof demanded of those who oppose the popular view is much much more exacting than is the standard of proof demanded of those who share the popular view.[14] One example: Decades ago the scientific proce-dure of the *Limits to Growth* study was condemned by every economist who reviewed it, to my knowledge. Yet its findings are still acclaimed and retailed by the "population community." But if I say that the world food situation has been improving year by year, you will either say "Prove it," or "I won't believe it." Or consider an advertisement run in national newspapers (fig. 36-2). No one asks for proof of the statements in that advertisement.

Furthermore, anti-doomsday people are in a double bind rhetorically. The doomsdayers speak in excited, angry, high-pitched voices, using language such as *Famine 1975!* They say that such tactics are acceptable because "we are faced with a crisis . . . the seriousness of which cannot be exaggerated."[15] The fears they inspire generate lots of support money from the UN, AID, and pop-ular fund-raising campaigns in full-page advertisements.

Many anti-doomsday people, on the other hand, speak in quiet voices—as reassurance usually sounds. They tend to be careful people. And they are totally ignored. The great geologist Kirtley F. Mather wrote a book called *Enough and To Spare* in 1944 that reassured the public that resources would be plentiful; it was withdrawn from the University of Illinois library just twice—in 1945 and 1952—prior to my 1977 withdrawal. But there are literally arm-fuls of books such as Fairfield Osborn's 1953 *Limits of the Earth* that have been

THE WALL STREET JOURNAL, THURSDAY, JAN. 13, 1977

Let's Tell It Like It Is

DEPEND ON US FOR MORE ~~FOOD~~ Hunger

Increased famine in the developing world in Asia, Africa and Latin America is inevitable because:

1. Food production cannot keep pace with runaway growth in population, and
2. Population growth in those areas is out of control. It cannot, and will not, be stopped in the foreseeable future, using conventional methods now being practiced or contemplated by our foreign aid establishment.

Last year, The Environmental Fund sponsored an advertisement ("The Real Crisis Behind the Food Crisis") which elaborated on the above statement. Its publication stimulated a surprising 23,000 replies (all but 13 in agreement with the analysis). Many asked, "What can we do about it?"

Indeed, how can Americans ameliorate the impending tragedy?

First, we must understand that we are being misled into believing that the United States has no problem with excessive population growth.

Second, we are being misled into thinking that many poor nations of Asia, Africa and Latin America are successfully coping with their runaway population growth.

Both assumptions are wrong.

The United States has a serious population problem; the vast majority of the hungry nations have an even more serious one. Yet nearly all nations, the United States included, lack any sort of population stabilization program. Most do not want one.

Unless people lower the birth rate (or nature raises the death rate) the world's population will quadruple during the lifetime of many of us now reading this page.

This insupportable growth is not the result of an increase in the birth rate. It is the result of a precipitous drop in the death rate, with no accompanying drop in the birth rate. It takes no special foresight to see that birth rates must come down, or death rates will climb to what used to be considered "normal".

The U.S. Department of Agriculture has announced that the world can no longer rely on U.S. food aid gifts or concessional sales to fill the world food gap.

This unusually candid declaration from the USDA provoked an immediate and vigorous response from various groups, organizations and individuals. Some, recognizing the wastes of an affluent society, declared that the problem was not limited capacity, but a reluctance to distribute resources fairly. Others declared that it was a moral imperative for us to become the "breadbasket of the world" today, and that the future would take care of itself. Still others are lobbying in Washington to establish food aid as "the cornerstone of our foreign policy", i.e., charity-by-law. Even granting the consent of the taxpayers and the good intentions of the lobbyists, this course of action is a prescription for disaster.

THE ADVERSE EFFECTS OF FOOD AID

Consider what food aid does.

Each piece of land has a specific carrying capacity. That capacity can be altered by fertilizer, improved management, and superior crop varieties. But there are still definite limits to how many people a given unit of land can support. Food aid violates the carrying capacity principle by artificially allowing more people to live on the land than can live from it.

Today, in order to provide large amounts of food aid, the donor country must overcultivate its own land, farming marginal acres, destroying the topsoil, and reducing its future ability to produce. When a 10,000 ton freighter loaded to the scuppers with U.S. wheat sails forth, it carries with it 200 tons of nitrogen, 41 tons of phosphorus, and 50 tons of potassium – all lost forever from the fertility of our soils.

THE INVERTED ETHICS OF FOOD AID

Food aid also enables the donor to postpone facing the grim reality which no one wants to face, which is: unless population growth is stabilized, the inescapable result of saving lives today will be an even greater number of lives lost tomorrow.

Those who ask the United States to increase its foreign aid commitment so that more food may be sent to the hungry overseas, simply misunderstand the problem: there are now too many people for the carrying capacity of the land. This year, the world's population will add 93 million people; next year, 95 million. Within eight years, 800 million people will be added to the world.

Nearly all of the 123 countries of Asia, Africa and Latin America – whether or not they have "benefited" from the U.S. foreign aid program – now have more poor, more illiterate, more hungry people than they had when this program began. Yet today, the U.S. development establishment allows recipient nations to count on food shipments from this country or to depend on the empty promise that those shipments will continue tomorrow – no matter how large populations grow.

This is a cruel deception.

By means of promises, declarations and resolutions, the United States is assuming a role it cannot play, and responsibilities it cannot carry out. This perception of the United States as a limitless cornucopia is a dangerous delusion to all concerned. It is dangerous to Americans because it isn't true, and, like all evasions of reality, it eventually leads to disillusionment and despair.

But it is an even more dangerous disservice to the leaders of the crowded and hungry nations. Belief in these promises enables them also to evade reality, to evade the hard decisions that must be made if their mushrooming populations are to be matched by their own resources.

WHAT AMERICA CAN DO AT HOME AND ABROAD

In order to help anyone at all – at home or abroad – Americans must learn to distinguish fact (the carrying capacity of the land) from fancy ("We can feed the world, if we really want to"). We must learn to distinguish pride in our achievements from the vanity of our ambitions. America cannot control the world, but perhaps we can influence policy. We can do it better and more honestly if the United States first puts its own house in order – which means facing the American population problem (our own growth rate will double our population in 47 years).

To put our own house in order, the United States should:

A. Enact a national population stabilization program
B. Encourage smaller families
C. Stop illegal immigration, which now doubles our annual growth rate
D. Balance legal immigration with emigration

All of these are necessary steps for our own benefit; in addition, they will also enable us to face our overpopulated neighbors with a clearer conscience and increased credibility.

Obviously, our most direct opportunity to deal with the population problem abroad is in the area of foreign policy, and there we should:

E. Stop any U.S. foreign aid program which encourages population growth

One way of doing this would be for the Congress to enact a Resolution along these lines:

WHEREAS we are aware, and are rightly fearful, of the ominous consequences of the growing world food/population crisis; and

WHEREAS the consequence of continued population growth will be increased human misery; and

WHEREAS increasing food production and/or availability, which lowers the death rate without influencing the birth rate, accelerates population growth; and

WHEREAS agricultural production cannot keep pace with a world population growth rate that would double our numbers every twenty-five years;

NOW THEREFORE BE IT RESOLVED that it is the sense of Congress that a moratorium be declared on all U.S. food aid and technical assistance to any country if:

1. its population growth rate is above the world average, **unless**
2. it officially acknowledges that its national birth rate must be lowered and unless it adopts stringent measures to control population growth, which measures must be judged adequate by the United States as the donor nation.

What would be the value of such a moratorium?

It might awaken the leadership of the developing countries to the urgency of their population problem. For the United States, through this Resolution, to say it cannot endorse the unrestricted use of its assistance funds, because to do so will increase the sum of human suffering, would be a total reversal of what the world has been hearing for the past quarter of a century.

Why haven't the leaders of the developing world taken the necessary steps to check their population growth rates? Why are countries with the fastest-growing populations often the least willing to acknowledge the existence of a problem?

One answer is the optimism generated by the American scientific community and development establishment. Year after year, since we initiated the foreign aid crusade, the leadership of the hungry nations has heard that the agricultural profession can solve the food problem if given enough support. It cannot.

A moratorium would not eliminate all foreign assistance. Our government should continue not only to help, but to expand its assistance to those few developing countries with population growth rates lower than the world average. But it should **concentrate its assistance on those countries which clearly show through active practices, a determination to decelerate their rate of population growth.** The moratorium would affect only these nations which will not do so.

Many will feel that such a moratorium is morally wrong.

Those who feel this way must weigh the morality of the moratorium against the morality of any action which contributes to overpopulation. Overpopulation today makes it impossible for half of those within the hungry nations to have the diet necessary to protect them against debilitating diseases that bring early death. Overpopulation makes whole nations dependent upon the vagaries of the weather to prevent famine in their lands. Overpopulation leads to more suffering and more deaths, to war, and to chaos.

None of this is new, **but the number of people involved is new.**

Who, then, are the moral – those who advocate steps that will decelerate population growth, or those who advocate steps that will encourage population growth?

A moratorium on assistance will not abandon the developing world of Asia, Africa and Latin America to a future without resources. We sometimes forget that the world consists of independent nations that possess convictions of their own and the ability to order their priorities on how to spend their money. Every year they spend, for instance, $28 billion on armaments. We may not think this makes much sense, but it is their decision.

Might not declaring a moratorium on assistance be the alarm signal that would alert the leadership of such countries to the necessity for different decisions?

For too long, we have tried to solve the food crisis without trying to solve the problem which causes it. Confusing the effect with the cause, we have been told to tighten our belts, and "asceticize" our diets, so that more food could be shipped to the world's hungry. None of the variations on this theme deal with the cause of the crisis: runaway population growth.

Whether your most urgent concern is peace, freedom, the food supply, civil liberties, the environment or social justice, it's a lost cause unless the population of the world is stabilized. We share these concerns, and all are compelling reasons why population stabilization is essential.

If you have a better solution, tell us. Tell us how you would solve the problem.

The Environmental Fund does not solicit contributions or memberships. However, we would welcome your comments and if you would like to be on our mailing list, please let us know.

Mr. Justin Blackwelder, President
THE ENVIRONMENTAL FUND, INC.
1302 18th Street, N.W.
Washington, D.C. 20036

Name ______________________________

____

Address ______________________________

______________________ Zip Code __________

Comments: ______________________________

____

____

____

THE ENVIRONMENTAL FUND

1302 EIGHTEENTH STREET, N.W. • WASHINGTON, D.C. 20036 • 202-293-2548

Directors: JUSTIN BLACKWELDER • EMERSON FOOTE • GARRETT HARDIN • WILLIAM C. PADDOCK • BURNS W. ROPER • ADOLPH W. SCHMIDT

Figure 36-2. Advertisement by The Environmental Fund

read vastly more frequently. Even a book published by a vanity press and written by a retired army colonel who has Malthus's first name as "Richard" and who believes that *Overpopulation* (the title of the book) is a plot of the "Kremlin gangsters" had been withdrawn ten times between 1971 and 1980 (when I checked), and untold more times between its 1958 publication and 1971, when the charge slip was changed.[16]

Finally—The Piper

Many of those in favor of population control are frank to admit the use of emotional language, exaggerated arguments, and political manipulation (see the next chapter on the issue of truth). They defend these practices by saying that the situation is very serious.

Would the environment have gotten cleaner without the exaggerated and untrue scary statements made by the doomsayers starting in the late 1960s? Perhaps they helped speed the cleanup of our air and water—perhaps. But without false alarms, Great Britain started on its cleanup earlier than did the United States, and went further, faster. And even granting some credit to the doomsayers, were the benefits worth the costs? Billions of dollars were wasted preparing the airplane industry for $3-per-gallon gasoline, and tens of billions wasted worldwide on raw materials purchased in fear that metal prices would soar.

Much more expensive was the loss of public morale and the spirit of adventurous enterprise due to false environmental scares. And most costly, in my view, has been the inevitable loss of trust in science and in our basic institutions as people realized that they had been systematically fooled.

Exaggeration and untruth run up debts with the piper, who eventually gets paid. Philip Handler, president of the National Academy of Sciences, was a strong supporter of environmental and population control programs. But even he worried about the piper.

> It is imperative that we recognize that we know little and badly require scientific understanding of the nature and magnitude of our actual environmental difficulties. The current wave of public concern has been aroused in large measure by scientists who have occasionally exaggerated the all-too-genuine deterioration of the environment or have overenthusiastically made demands which, unnecessarily, exceed realistically realizable—or even desirable—expectations. . . .
>
> The nations of the world may yet pay a dreadful price for the public behavior of scientists who depart from . . . fact to indulge . . . in hyperbole.[17]

As far back as 1972, John Maddox, the long-time editor of *Nature*, warned that

[T]here is a danger that much of this gloomy foreboding about the immediate future will accomplish the opposite of what its authors intend. Instead of alerting people to important problems, it may seriously undermine the capacity of the human race to look out for its survival. The doomsday syndrome [the name of his book] may in itself be as much a hazard as any of the conundrums which society has created for itself.[18]

This may already have come to pass. In 1992 Theodore Roszak refers to himself as one of "those of us who presume to act as the planet's guardians" and who agrees that "the important thing is to spread the alarm" because "there is no question in my mind that these problems are as serious as environmentalists contend." He finds himself taken aback by physician Helen Caldicott's warning that "every time you turn on an electric light you are making another brainless baby" because nuclear power is the cause of anencephalic births along the Mexican border. "Despite my reservations, I do my best to go along with what Dr. Caldicott has to say—even though I suspect . . . that there is no connection between light bulbs and brainless babies." But he worries that "a fanatical antienvironmental backlash [is] now under way" because of the exaggerations and falsehoods.[19]

Were it occurring, a fanatical backlash would not be a good thing; fanaticism of any kind will be destructive in these matters, where cool scientific consideration of the evidence is so desperately needed to assess dangers of all kinds. But this is what Handler and Maddox warned of—the piper that will finally be paid for untruths about population, resources, and environment.

This raises the question: To what extent is the current public belief that the U.S. economy and society are on the skids related to false doomsday fears that we are running out of minerals, food, and energy? And to the unfounded belief that the United States is an unfair plunderer of the world's resources, a supposed "exploitation" that people believe must bring grave consequences for the United States?

And when we count the costs of the doomsayers' excesses we must remember the tragedy of the human lives not lived because countries such as China and Indonesia prevent births in the name of the now-discredited doctrine that population growth slows economic development. It will fall to the future historian to balance the questionable benefits against those undeniable costs.

More on this subject in the next chapter.

Afternote 1 _____

A Rhetorical Analogy

AN ANALOGY helps explain the power inherent in the antigrowth rhetoric. Think how much easier it is to argue that the automobile is detrimental to life and health than that the auto is beneficial. To dramatize how dangerous cars are for people, you need only the number of people killed and maimed, plus a few gory pictures of smashups. That's strong stuff. But to argue that the auto is beneficial to health you need to show a lot of relatively small, indirect benefits—the ability to get to a doctor or hospital by car when it could not be done otherwise; the therapeutic results of being able to take a trip into the countryside; the improved transportation know-how that eventually saves lives (the emergency health systems discussed in chapter 18 are an example); and so on. My point here is not to prove that cars are, in fact, beneficial on balance, but only to illustrate how much easier it is rhetorically to show their maleficence than their beneficence. Just so it is with arguments about population growth.

Afternote 2

Planned Parenthood's Rhetoric

JUST A FEW examples of Planned Parenthood/World Population's rhetoric are given here. But PP/WP is a very large and important organization, and many people still identify it only with its older aims and find it hard to believe that it engages in the practices that it does.

Consider one of its mailings. The only message in the "donor's card" is, "Yes, I will help contain runaway population growth by supporting the crucial work of Planned Parenthood," plus this assertion by Robert McNamara: "Excessive population growth is the greatest single obstacle to the economic and social advancement of most societies in the developing world."[20] Some of the statements in the fund-raising letter are:

> Thai women and millions of other women like them in India, China, Africa and throughout the developing nations control our destiny. *Their decisions—decisions of hundreds of millions of young women—about their family's size—control your future more surely, more relentlessly than the oil crisis or the nuclear arms race.*
>
>   ... [U]nless population growth is harnessed and slowed to meet the limited resources and human services of these nations, development of nations will be shattered. Chaos, mass famine and war will continue to increase. We will be affected for better or worse.
>
> The great tinderbox for revolution and international anarchy is rising expectations of the world's masses coupled with unrestrained population growth. *Starvation, revolution and violent repression will fill our headlines unless human fertility is reduced to meet the finite limits of available resources and services. International Assistance.* In developing countries of the world, the population "time bomb" ticks on, putting ever-increasing strains on the scarce resources of our planet, locking large areas of the globe into self-perpetuating poverty and setting the stage for famine and war.[21]

A fund-raising letter by Margaret Mead is shown in figure 36-3. When I included this in the first edition, suggesting as I do that she made a scad of wild assertions for which she had no evidence, and for which there is counter-evidence, friends regretted that I would take on such a wonderful woman and scientist. Since then it has become clear beyond a doubt that her most important "scientific" work was based entirely upon a hoax. Such a high degree of foolability then is consistent with being similarly fooled later on by the false claims about the effects of population growth by the population-control establishment on whose behalf she wrote.

MARGARET MEAD
515 MADISON AVENUE
NEW YORK, N. Y. 10022

Dear Friend:

Within today's crowded world there is a tremendous increase in suffering
and brutality. Growing numbers of children are beaten or neglected. In New
York City child abuse cases have risen 30% and similar increases are reported
throughout this country and in other parts of the world. Children are the main
victims of overpopulation. Due to the population explosion 500 million of them
are chronically hungry -- living in misery and degradation. It is their generation and those still unborn who will pay the frightful penalties for our un-
bridled growth and for our reckless abuse of the environment.

Each day world population is increased by 190,000 and our earth is scarred
by our efforts to provide for them. Mass famines have been temporarily averted
but 12,000 a day still die of starvation. Irreplaceable resources are being
wantonly depleted and in some countries water is sold by the glass. Our land,
air and water are so toxic with chemicals and wastes that the Secretary General
of the United Nations has warned that "if current trends continue, the future
of life on earth could be endangered." This is not the world we want to bequeath
to our children.

In America, our population is expected to climb to nearly 300 million by
the end of the century and three out of four of us will be living in extremely
congested cities. We are beginning to feel the congestion now -- in our crowded
schools and clogged highways; in the destruction of our environment; in the
erosion of the quality of life.

One of the grimmest aspects of the population explosion is the poverty it
perpetuates and intensifies. In America 14,400 are hungry and 39 million
are classified poor or near-poor. Half of our impoverished children come from
families of five or more. Stunted by hunger, lacking in schooling and skills,
they rarely break free from poverty's grip. What is true for these deprived
Americans is tragically also true in many other nations.

Planned Parenthood/World Population is the only private organization through
which you as an individual can work to curb population growth abroad in 101 countries and in our own. PP/WP programs of direct service, technical assistance,
public education, research and training are cutting birth rates in selected areas
around the globe. Most national family planning programs in other countries began as PP activities and are carried on with our continuing help. And 650 U.S.
clinics run by Affiliates provide contraceptive help to almost half a million.

War, famine and plague are both unthinkable solutions and untenable ones.
In World War II twenty-two million died: it takes less than four months to add
that number to the world's population. Birth control is the only humane and
rational answer to our population dilemma. PP/WP programs here and abroad will
cost $40 million in 1971. Please send your tax-deductible gift today to help
assure a worthwhile life for future generations.

Sincerely,

P.S. If you have already contributed to your local PP/WP Affiliate, please share
this appeal with a friend. We are grateful for your interest and support.

Figure 36-3. Fund-raising letter from Margaret Mead for Planned Parenthood

Letters by other celebrities mention famine, drought, flood, "the crush of visitors [that] forced the National Park Service to close one entrance to Yosemite National Park last summer," packed campgrounds, despoliation of fragile ecology, cars and trucks clogging expressways, people dying in the streets of starvation, and the following:

In India entire families commit suicide to escape a lingering death from starvation. In Bangladesh famished infants are thrown into rivers to drown. Hungry hordes of abandoned children roam the cities of Latin America looting, terrorizing and scavenging for food. By conservative estimates 400 million people—a tenth of humanity—live on the ragged edge of starvation, 12,000 a day die of hunger as food-short nations sink deeper into crisis and anguish. Regional crop failures this year will almost certainly mean mass famine. For 10 to 30 million, the Malthusian nightmare may become reality. . . .

A family of thirteen is found living in a basement flooded with water and smelling of sewer gas. The children are cold and hungry. This is "the other America"—a land of limited opportunity, of corrosive poverty. Sixty percent of our poor live in urban centers, in enclaves of misery stretched like scars across the nation.

Last spring eleven mayors met to warn of the collapse of U.S. cities, rapidly becoming "repositories for the poor." In Boston one in five gets public assistance; in N.Y.C. one in seven; in Los Angeles one in eight. These agonizing statistics underscore today's welfare crisis. Agonizing because for each person getting aid, someone eligible is not; agonizing because welfare benefits guarantee only a life of grinding poverty, physical survival and little else. . . .

On an afternoon in N.Y. not too long ago four boys were playing in the streets when suddenly from a second story window a shot rang out and a 13-year old fell to the ground dead. The man who killed him said he couldn't bear the noise, that he was a night worker and had to get his sleep. In Paris three recent murders were attributed to noise and now studies in England and America suggest it is a cause of serious mental disorder provoking many to acts of violence.

The city dweller is constantly assailed by noise, doubling in volume every 15 years and now approaching levels which can cause permanent damage. Three out of five American men have lost some hearing and growing evidence links noise to heart disease. And still our cities swell until finally 80% of us will live in crowded and festering sinks and pollution will be a personal hazard and affront. We are hastening to what Archibald MacLeish has called "the diminishment of man."

Along with one of the Mead letters came a reprint of Paul Ehrlich's "Eco-Catastrophe," a dramatically frightening doomsday document. It predicted—for the 1970s!—"the end of the ocean," falling agricultural yields, smog disasters for New York and Los Angeles ("nearly 200,000 corpses"), "birth of the Midwestern desert"; and "both worldwide plague and thermonuclear war are made more probable as population growth continues; . . . population control was the only possible salvation suggested."[22]

Perhaps most astonishing is Planned Parenthood's prodigal use of money—
some of it public money—and phony emotional appeals in a twenty-eight-
page supplement in the *New York Times*, sponsored by PPFA together with the
Population Crisis Committee. PP/WP also was a main sponsor of the antinatal
television campaign discussed in this chapter. All these activities make it very
clear that Planned Parenthood's goal is fewer births.

As to the rhetorical tactics used in pursuit of this goal, the arguments used
and the issues raised in connection with population growth—parking problems, famine, crime in the streets, mental disorder, and so on—are simply
wild speculations, many flatly contradicted by the evidence given elsewhere in
this book, for example, with respect to famine. Or worse, they are plain untruths—for example, that population growth increases mental disorder. The
best that can be said of these mindless Planned Parenthood activities is that
they are undertaken by people who are sincerely motivated by a public spirit
but who have never given attention to the facts or thought through to the
consequences, and who simply assume that "everyone knows" that the rhetoric is true. That's the most favorable construction I can give to Planned Parenthood's bumper-sticker campaign:

POPULATION NO PROBLEM? HOW DENSE CAN YOU GET? SUPPORT PLANNED PARENTHOOD

Some Planned Parenthood people say privately that these sorts of appeals
do not reflect a change in Planned Parenthood's mission from the original
"Children by choice—not chance," but are only used because they are effective in fund raising. If that is so, then what is the moral basis of such behavior?
Either PP/WP is getting money under false pretenses, or it is simply altering its
behavior to produce maximum contributions.

37

The Reasoning behind the Rhetoric

I know no time which is lost more thoroughly than that devoted to arguing
on matters of fact with a disputant who has no facts, but only very
strong convictions.

(*James E. Thorold Rogers*, Six Centuries of Work and Wages, *1901*)

THE EDITOR of the world's most important scientific journal, Daniel Koshland, repeats in editorial after editorial that "Increasing population and increasing industrialization pose threats to the environment. . . . The population explosion has to move to top priority." He calls for "programs for effective population control." And he insists that we must undertake "restrictions to our freedoms" such as moving closer to each other in the cities, and driving fewer cars, in order to stop "dooming our ecosystem," "preserve agriculture lands," and avoid "the energy crisis that is bound to come in the not-too-distant future."[1]

All this is written without any supporting data as if there cannot be any question about these propositions—but in stark contradiction to the data and analysis of articles that had appeared earlier in the same journal. The message is that the danger is so great that we should not bother with the ordinary evidential procedures of science.

If such opinions are not scientific, then what is the reasoning behind them? Earlier chapters suggested some explanations for people's doomsday fears about minerals, food, and energy—especially the seductively simple twin notions of a fixed stock of resources and the "law" of diminishing returns. This chapter focuses on explanations for doomsday fears about population growth, though all such fears have much in common. The discussion is truncated because a scant treatment here is better than no treatment at all. The reasoning behind these matters, together with a discussion of the politics, requires an entire book to explain. I hope that such a book is forthcoming soon.

One type of "reasoning" behind scary beliefs about population growth turns out to be circular reasoning, which amounts to no reasoning at all. Bad news feeds on itself. Koshland himself chides others for unnecessary "gloom and doom" because, as he notes correctly, "Some people enjoy gloom. Bad news sells newspapers."[2] (Maybe this means he has changed his mind about population, resources, and the environment, though I have not seen any such statement.)

Rhetoric and Justification

What "Everyone Knows"—The Vicious Circle

It is a truism (not true, of course) that resources are getting more scarce, and that population growth exacerbates the problem. You have read numerous examples of such statements in previous chapters by persons who are supposedly experts. These pessimistic assertions have become so accepted that eminent people in other fields treat them as assumptions in their own work, on an "everyone knows" basis—the way everyone knows that without sunshine the flowers will not grow. Just a few examples of persons publicly decrying population growth—even signing petitions to the president and endorsing full-page advertisements that run in the nation's most-read newspapers—that I have stumbled across in casual reading: Nobel agronomist Norman Borlaug; sociobiologist Edward Wilson; author Isaac Asimov; columnist Jack Anderson; Nobel physicists Murray Gell-Mann and William Shockley; Andrei Sakharov; basketball player Wilt Chamberlain; columnist Ann Landers; her sister, columnist "Dear Abby"; and John D. Rockefeller III. Children's singer Raffi Cavoukian says, "I clearly have heard the urgency of the Earth's cry . . . I really heard it to every cell of my body." The *Hammond World Atlas* says that "the victory over nature, which had balanced population with food supply and space, is bitter, for the population has 'exploded.'" Nobel prize winners such as Linus Pauling and Wassily Leontief even serve on the board of directors of an organization claiming that "environmental degradation, traffic jams, deteriorating infrastructure and homelessness" are evidence for "the primary cause of these problems—overpopulation." And there is a bucket more, including newspaper editorial writers, U.S. senators and representatives. During his campaign for the presidency and then the vice presidency of the United States, Al Gore said that "the Earth's environment must and will become the central organizing principle of the post–Cold War world," told the American Statistical Association of "a dramatic change in the relationship between the human species and the earth," and said that of the causes, "Number one [is] population"; and then the statisticians feted him despite his being as bad an abuser of statistics, when writing about this subject, as any person in public life.[3]

Prominent psychologists and psychiatrists exhibit a high level of worry about population growth—O. H. Mowrer, Albert Bandura: "With growing populations and the spread of life styles emphasizing material consumption, both of which tax finite resources, people will have to learn to cope with new realities of existence"; Gerald Klerman gives "overpopulation, and ecological destruction" as two of the main "adverse global events" that have caused "the emergence of a new age of melancholia."[4] Like so many biologists, these psychologists simply assert, without consulting any data on the subject.

Plain citizens write letters to the newspaper saying things like "[a] world without population curbs . . . would be a sickening, violent, depressing, congested hell, with the complete destruction of the human race, all animals, and the world's natural environment."[5]

The weight of doomsday opinion is indicated by the long list of such books found in any library. In contrast, the few books by Wilfred Beckerman, Herman Kahn, John Maddox, and James Weber were the rare exceptions of opposing voices at the time of the first edition. Happily, this literature has grown by leaps and bounds since then, as may be seen in the starred references at the end of this edition. Yet popular thought has changed little.

So deeply has the notion of a "population explosion" sunk into the popular consciousness that the term appears in *The Living Bible*, a widely read paraphrase of the Old and New Testaments. In this version, the story of Noah begins in this manner: "Noah was 500 years old and had three sons, Shem, Ham, and Japheth. Now a population explosion took place upon the earth" (Genesis 6). And of course the flood followed.

Proof that the "population movement" has succeeded in convincing people that population growth is bad is seen in the discrepancy between people's beliefs about their own local situation and the situation of their nation as a whole. Polls in the United States and in Great Britain find that people do not think that their own neighborhoods—about which they have direct information from their own observations—are overpopulated. But they do say that their country as a whole—which they know mostly from reports in the media—is overpopulated.[6] Similarly, people are much more concerned about population growth in the world than in their own countries; first-hand knowledge dispels such concerns that are created in the far-away abstract by scare stories in the newspaper and on television. The same is true for the environment (see pp. 220). What else can account for people reaching this conclusion other than successful rhetoric and widespread publicity?

Test this for yourself. Ask yourself and your children whether the country is overpopulated, or whether population is growing too fast. Then ask about your block and your neighborhood. There is a curious inconsistency here. You say your house is fine but mine is overpopulated, and I say mine is fine but yours is overpopulated. What would an impartial observer learn from this about the condition of the community of houses?

The media and the pollsters are engaging in what is known in the stock market as a "wash sale"—the media create the opinion, the pollsters measure it, and the media then report the polls as news, and use the results as the basis of policy recommendations based on "public opinion." An integral part of the process is that journalists themselves are victims of this misinformation process, just as are other persons, and then perpetuate the entire cycle in perfectly good faith (along with other motivations).

The most obvious reason that doomsday fears get disproportionate public attention is that bad news is newsworthy, and frightening forecasts cause people to sit up and take notice. But why are frightening forecasts that run counter to the evidence made by the forecasters in the first place? And what explains the related activist movements? Here I shall do no more than present a list of the possibilities.

Certainly Thomas Littlewood is right when he says that "humanitarian and bigot can find room under the same tent."[7] There is also lots of space under the tent for many fellow-traveling motives, both generous and selfish.

Simple World-Saving Humanitarianism

Many people who give time and money to population activities are unmistakably motivated by sincere good will; the donors wish that poor people at home and abroad will have a better life.

Taxation Fears

The haves naturally worry that there will be an increase in the number of have-nots to be supported at public expense, both domestically and internationally. This theme is found in Malthus and is an underlying motive in much population activity. Where the have-nots differ racially from the haves, it is difficult to separate this motive from racism.

Supposed Economic and Political National Self-Interest

The pull-up-the-ladder "lifeboat ethics" of Garrett Hardin—we are fighting for places in a small lifeboat that is the Earth, and so "every life saved this year in a poor country diminishes the quality of life for subsequent generations"—is a dramatic elaboration of the self-interest motive.[8]

Fear of Anti-Western Ideologies

The belief that communism and, more recently, various anti-Western political movements, would win out in the poor countries has caused some people in rich countries to want to reduce population growth in the poor countries.

In the cold war between the Communist bloc and the free world, in every area where the Red penetration is most successful—the Middle East, Indonesia, Japan, Guatemala, British Guiana and North Africa—population pressure is severe and increasing . . . one of the most potent factors in the success of the Reds in their campaign for world domination. . . .[9]

Dislike of Business

Some people dislike business because of its self-interest profit motive. And they attribute to business people a desire for the larger markets population growth brings. In reaction, they favor population reduction.

Others, Thomas Mayer suggests, charge business with polluting and wasting resources because they want to transfer control of economic activity to the government. He further suggests that this desire is a sequel to the attempt to shift control to government "experts" on the grounds of greater efficiency, an argument now wholly discredited.[10]

Belief in the Superiority of "Natural" Processes

Some people feel that the use of resources by humans is a disturbance of the natural ecological order, and that each such disturbance is likely to be damaging in the long run. For some, this reflects an assumption that natural systems are so complex that human interference—even just increased numbers—is bound to result in unexpected destruction. For others, a mystical or religious faith underlies this belief.

Religious Antagonisms

Religious groups worry that other groups' higher birthrates will make them more powerful. In the past, for example, U.S. Protestants have feared population growth by U.S. Catholics, and Hindus in India fear the higher birthrates of Muslims.

Racism

Bolstering anecdotal evidence that racism has been a key motivation in domestic and international population activities are data showing that the opening of state-supported birth-control clinics is closely related to the concentrations of poor black people in various states.[11] As of 1965, 79 percent of the new state-supported clinics in the United States were in the ten states of Alabama,

Arkansas, Florida, Georgia, Kentucky, Mississippi, North Carolina, South Carolina, Tennessee, and Virginia, which had only 19 percent of U.S. population. Analysis that holds per capita income constant shows that the proportion of blacks in a local population was closely related to the density of family-planning clinics.[12] It seems reasonable to conclude that southern society's birth-control policies were motivated, at least in part, by the desire to reduce the fertility of blacks. The motivation may be racial antagonism, or it may be that southern whites believe that blacks make welfare demands upon the state in excess of their contributions, or both together.[13]

The Belief of the Better Educated That They Know What Is Best for the Less Educated

Many unselfish well-off persons think they know better than do poor people what is good for the poor and for the world. Most of us secretly believe that we know how some others should live their lives better than they themselves know. But this belief matters only when it is hitched up with arrogance and the willingness to compel others to do what we think they ought to do.

Lack of Historical Perspective

Absence of a sense of history clearly is an important cause of doomsday fears. A bad reversal in some positive trend line—say, the 1973 oil price rise, or the bad harvests in the early 1970s—leads people to chart just a few years' experience prior to the bad turn of events, and then to extrapolate a negative future trend. If one draws long-run historical graphs instead—the sort shown in earlier chapters on mineral resources, food, and energy—the bad turn of events usually can be seen as only a blip on the line, and the overall trend may be seen to be positive rather than negative.

The doomsayers avoid confronting historical experience by saying that their interest is the future rather than past. But neglect of the past is utterly unscientific. To be valid, science must be based on experience; all sound theories ultimately derive from experience and must be tested against it. The doomsayers' Malthusian theory fails every confrontation with the data.

The Prophetic Impulse

Prophetic reasoning is nicely illustrated by a book about U.S. water policy in the West, *Cadillac Desert*, by Marc Reisner.[14] Reisner appreciates the economic benefits that great water projects bring, and he admires the imagination and efforts of the people who built them. And he does a fine job of exposing counterproductive schemes that subsidize water to farmers at the cost of high bills to taxpayers, shortage of water to consumers, and unnecessary destruction of some lovely parts of nature. But he does not seem to understand the process of the development of knowledge in response to perceived problems, which leads to the creation of new resources and wealth, which expands the base for civilization and population. Therefore he believes that eventually there will be retribution. He quotes with approval:

> The forces involved . . . are comparable to those met by a boy who builds a castle on the sandy ocean beach, next to the water, at low tide. . . . [I]t is not pessimism, merely an objective evaluation, to predict the destruction of the castle.[15]

And Reisner entitles his last chapter, "A Civilization, If You Can Keep It." The book is full of phrases about "insidious forces" salting up the land, claims that "now the desert is encroaching on the islands of green," comments about "infrastructure in varying stages of collapse," "water development that, though amazingly fruitful in the short run, leaves everyone and everything more vulnerable in the end," "the big main-stem reservoirs, which will end up being choked by silt." "The cost of all this . . . was a vandalization of both our natural heritage and our economic future, and the reckoning has not even begun," "a monstrous travesty against nature," "a precarious foothold against the forces of nature." He is sure that "somewhere down the line our descendants are going to inherit a bill for all this vaunted success," and "they may find themselves wishing that we had left things pretty much as they were"; though if "we" had, there would be no basis for the lives of "they." . . . He writes that "Like so many great and extravagant achievements, from the fountains of Rome to the federal deficit, the immense national dam-construction program that allowed civilization to flourish in the deserts of the West contains the seeds of disintegration." He expects us to share "the hoary [sic] fate of almost every irrigated civilization."[16]

In brief, the Empire of Nature must strike back. Construction now means destruction later, because construction means *using up resources*, in his view, rather than *building up resources*. We must pay the piper's price sometime, because we've overdrawn our account with nature, in this view. The only sound course is to mend our evil ways, to pull in our horns and live ascetically.

Such has been the voice of prophecy in all times.

Fitness of the Human Race

Improvement of the human race—or of the genetic quality of one's own countrymen—has in the past been one of the important motives of population activists, especially with respect to immigration and sterilization policies.

Indeed, eugenics—which should not be confused with the scientific discipline of genetics—was one of the main themes of Margaret Sanger, the same woman whom I honor for her work in helping people have "Children by Choice—Not Chance."[17] "More children from the fit, less from the unfit—that is the chief issue of birth control," she wrote.[18] She said that she "sought first to stop the multiplication of the unfit. This appeared the most important and greatest step towards race betterment."[19] She also lamented that the United States had not enacted immigration laws before 1907 to bar those with "mental, physical, communicable, or loathsome disease, and also illiterate paupers, prostitutes, criminals, and the feebleminded. Had these precautions been taken earlier our institutions would not now be crowded with moronic mothers, daughters, and grand-daughters—three generations at a time, all of whom have to be supported by tax-payers who shut their eyes to this condition, admittedly detrimental to the blood stream of the race."[20] Belief in eugenics also was the intellectual foundation of Nazi murder policies, of course, as black a page as there is in human history.

The roots of the eugenics motive are some compound of unproven genetic ideas about intelligence and physical health, unselfish devotion to mankind, and narrow in-group preferences. (See the next chapter.)

The proponents of eugenics have been sufficiently successful in politicking over the decades so that tax moneys are being used to involuntarily sterilize poor people (often black) without medical justification. As a result of the eugenics movement, which has been an intertwined partner with the population-control movement for decades, there are laws now on the books of thirty states providing for the involuntary sterilization of the mentally defective.[21]

In famous exemplary cases, a perfectly normal young black woman was sterilized under the guise of being given a birth-control shot,[22] and a childless married woman who went to have a small uterine tumor removed was sterilized without her knowledge or consent.[23] At just one institution in Virginia—the Lynchburg Training School and Hospital—four thousand "patients" were sterilized between 1922 and 1972 as "misfits" in order to avoid "racial degeneracy." The superintendent of the Lynchburg institution was a eugenics enthusiast who aimed to produce genetic purity.[24] The law sanctioning this practice was upheld by the U.S. Supreme Court, though changed since then. And in 1976, a North Carolina law was upheld in state and federal courts that permitted the sterilization of "mentally retarded" or "mentally ill" persons. Sterilization could be authorized if "because of a physical, mental, or nervous disease or deficiency which is not likely to materially improve, the person would probably be unable to care for a child or children or, because the person would be likely, unless sterilized, to procreate a child or children which probably would have serious physical, mental or nervous deficiencies." Furthermore, certain health officers were given the "duty" of starting the process if

(1) . . . sterilization is in the best interest of the mental, moral or physical improvement of the retarded person,

(2) . . . sterilization is in the best interest of the public at large,

(3) . . . [the retarded person] would be likely, unless sterilized, to procreate a child or children who would have a tendency to serious physical, mental, or nervous disease or deficiency or; because of a physical, mental or nervous disease or deficiency, which is not likely to materially improve, the person would be unable to care for a child or children.

The U.S. Federal District Court said that "evidence that is clear, strong, and convincing that the subject is likely to engage in sexual activity without using contraceptive devices and that either a defective child is likely to be born or a child born that cannot be cared for by its parent" is grounds for sterilization. Perhaps most frightening, the Supreme Court of North Carolina stated that the state may sterilize because "the people of North Carolina also have a right to prevent the procreation of children who will become a burden to the State." In other words, if you do poorly on an IQ test, or if a physician says that you are mentally ill—both of which could happen to most of us under certain circumstances, as happened to many antigovernment activists in the USSR— then you could be forcibly sterilized.[25]

A typical eugenics impulse: The California firm of Robert Klark Graham obtained the sperm of five Nobel laureates, the first volunteer being Nobelist William Shockley, who has argued that whites are inherently smarter than blacks.[26] Graham hopes to improve the intelligence of Americans by disseminating this sperm.

Eugenics thinking is much involved with particular values, as discussed in the next chapter.

Conclusion

Though an important motivation of many people working against population growth surely is the simple good-will desire to help poor people get ahead, now and in the future,[27] not absent from this movement are the beliefs that (a) poor people, and especially poor non-white, non-Anglo-Saxon, non-Protestants, are inherently inferior; and (b) the present and future well-being of all U.S. taxpayers will be best served by reducing the birthrate among these peoples and immigration of them. These ideas are not only dangerous but are scientifically unfounded. And these beliefs have led to shocking prescriptions: Do not lower the death rate of poor people, and get the poor not to reproduce, even if the means used are economic pressure or physical coercion. We even hear something like this from the editor of the most important scientific journal in the world: "To feed starving populations is desirable, but if new crops help add a billion people to a crowded globe, is that necessarily good?"[28]

Having government exert pressure—domestically with sterilization laws and policies, and internationally by tying food aid to fertility reduction—would be questionable at best even if the scientific propositions upon which these policies are founded were objectively supported. But these policies are *not* scientifically warranted. Even less noble, some part of the motivation in population campaigns is pure selfishness, the desire to keep for ourselves what we can, against the supposed (but nonexistent) drains of our resources by the children of the poor and nonwhites, and by the "yellow [and brown] peril" of immigration. This is the witch's brew at its nastiest.

38

Ultimately—What Are Your Values?

Human happiness, and certainly human fecundity, are not as important as a wild and healthy planet. I know social scientists who remind me that people are part of nature, but it isn't true. Somewhere along the line—at about a billion years ago, maybe half that—we quit the contract and became a cancer. We have become a plague upon ourselves and upon the Earth. It is cosmically unlikely that the developed world will choose to end its orgy of fossil-energy consumption, and the Third World its suicidal consumption of landscape. Until such time as Homo sapiens should decide to rejoin nature, some of us can only hope for the right virus to come along.
　(David M. Graber, National Park Service research biologist)[1]

The market for cat food in the U.S. "is two-and-a-half to three times the size" of the baby food market, says Anthony J. F. O'Reilly, president of H. J. Heinz Co., a major producer of both products. "That will tell you something about our changing tastes," the executive cracks.
　(Wall Street Journal, *January 31, 1980*)

If we didn't have birthdays, you wouldn't be you.
If you'd never been born, well then what would you do?
If you'd never been born, well then what would you be?
You might be a fish! Or a toad in a tree!
You might be a doorknob! Or three baked potatoes!
You might be a bag full of hard green tomatoes.
Or worse than all that . . . Why, you might be a WASN'T!
A Wasn't has no fun at all. No, he doesn't.
A Wasn't just isn't. He just isn't present.
But you . . . You ARE YOU! And, now isn't that pleasant!

Then, out of the water! Sing loud while you dry!
Sing loud, "I am lucky!" Sing loud, "I am I!"

If you'd never been born, then you might be an ISN'T!
An Isn't has no fun at all. No he disn't.
He never has birthdays, and that isn't pleasant.
You have to be born, or you don't get a present.
　(Dr. Seuss, Happy Birthday to You!, 1959)[2]

A SMALL NUMBER of academics—many of them biologists, and almost none of them economists—have convinced a great many politicians and laymen that rational population policies with respect to fertility, mortality, and immigration can be deduced directly from actual or supposed facts about population and economic growth. The persuaded politicians believe it is "scientific truth" that countries should reduce their population growth. And the persuading academics want the politicians and the public to believe that such judgmental propositions really are "scientific." For example, the front page of the canon book of the population-control movement in the United States, *The Population Bomb*, says, "Paul Ehrlich, a qualified scientist, clearly describes the dimensions of the crisis . . . over-population is now the dominant problem . . . population control or race to oblivion?"

But it is scientifically wrong—outrageously wrong—to say that "science shows" there is overpopulation (or underpopulation) in any given place at any given time. Science can only reveal the likely *effects* of various population levels and policies. Whether population is now too large or too small, or is growing too fast or too slowly, cannot be decided on scientific grounds alone. Such judgments depend upon our values, a matter on which science does not bear.

Whether you think that it is better for a country to have a population of, say, fifty million human beings at a $4,000 per capita yearly income, or one hundred million at $3,000, is strictly a matter of what you consider important. And further, please keep in mind that if the empirical studies and my theoretical analysis are correct, the world can have *both* a larger population and *higher* per capita income. This is as true for less-developed as for more-developed countries. But the judgment about whether this is good news or bad news, and whether population is growing too fast or too slowly, or is now too large or too small, depends on values. This is reason enough to say that science does not show that there is overpopulation or underpopulation anywhere.

Because of the belief that population policies can be deduced from scientific studies alone, particular values enter implicitly into policy decisions, without explicit discussion of whether the values really are those that the decision makers and the community desire to have implemented. For a leading example, because almost all economic analyses of "optimum" rates of economic growth take per capita income as the criterion, this criterion implicitly becomes the community goal and the guideline for policy makers. In some cases values are smuggled in consciously, though without discussion; in other cases the values enter without any conscious recognition.

This chapter presents a list of some important values related to population policy. Some of these values are discussed in more detail in the next chapter, where I express some of my own views. A discussion of the rhetoric of the antipopulation movement that appeared in chapter 22 of the first edition is related to the subject of this chapter; a central element is the claim to being compassionate, and the charge that those who do not wish to spend taxpayers' money for various welfare purposes lack compassion, with the implicit assumption that people's welfare is best advanced by government action rather than through voluntary spontaneously cooperating systems. Discussion of various related religious values may be found in my 1990 book.

Some Values Relevant to Population Policy

The Rate of Discounting for Futurity

The relative importance given to the nearer term versus the further future affects investment decisions. It enters into every weighing of the costs and benefits of resource use and population growth. This was discussed in chapter 19.

The proposition that we should focus on the short run, and not pay attention to the benefits of more people that accrue in the long run because "in the long run we're all dead"—Keynes's famous foolish phrase discussed in chapter 12—has a curious similarity to the thinking of young children. For children there really is a free lunch—consuming without having to work to pay for the goods—for twenty years. And children are not predisposed to invest and save for the future—every parent knows how hard it is to induce children to study now in order to have the benefits of education in adulthood, and to know the virtues of saving money. But the activity that children find least natural—hard work—becomes emotionally necessary to most of us later on in the life cycle. The need to work, and to create, may be seen most purely in gardening, where the work is almost its only reward. It is as if we need to cultivate and produce in order to give back what we have earlier taken in during our lives. The psychological explanation here is mere speculation, of course, but the need to work even when the product of that work makes no material difference to the worker is as much a plain undeniable fact as is the need of children to play. The attitude that we should consume without attending to what we leave behind, and without considering how many and which persons we will leave behind, is analogous to the childhood stage of the life cycle.

There is a curious contradiction in the thinking of the population control-environmentalist movement with respect to the future. On the one hand, they say they want to "save the planet" for our children and grandchildren. On the other hand, they want to reduce as much as possible the number of children and grandchildren for whom the planet is to be "saved."

Altruism versus Selfishness

Our willingness to share our worldly goods—either directly or (more commonly) indirectly through taxation—affects a variety of population-related policies, as has been discussed vehemently at least since Malthus. Should additional children or immigrants be welcomed into a community if there will be an immediate burden upon others (though benefit later on)? Should the poor be supported by welfare rather than left to die? Each of us has some willingness to contribute to others, but that willingness differs from person to person, and from moment to moment. In discussion, this factor usually gets tangled up with the matter of whether the transfers are a sacrifice contribution or an investment. This value will be discussed at length in the next chapter.

Racism

In our private behavior we tend to favor our kin, our co-religionists, those who come from the same place, and those of similar race. This partiality is largely beneficial; charity begins at home has much to commend it as a principle of human action. But allowing such tastes to affect *public policy* with respect to immigration, welfare, and birth-control campaigns is another matter; certainly these tastes often do influence public policy, especially with respect to race.

Space, Privacy, and Isolation

This is the Daniel Boone/Sierra Club value. How much of your isolation in the forest are you prepared to give up so that others may also enjoy the experience?

The Right of Inheritance

Should only the blood descendants of the builders of a country be allowed to enjoy its fruits, or should others be allowed to come in and enjoy them, too? This issue is at the heart of immigration policy in the United States, Australia, Israel, Great Britain, and every other country in which the standard of living is higher than in the country of some potential immigrants. The issue also arises domestically. For example: Are native Americans or blacks morally entitled to partake of the benefits of social investments made by whites in past years? Do whites have a responsibility to repay African-Americans for the profits made by exploiting slave labor in previous centuries?

The Inherent Value of Human Life

Can some people's lives be so poor in standard of living that they would have been better off had they never been born? "Humane Society and health officials say that feral cats lead miserable, disease-ridden lives and that killing them is more humane than leaving them on the streets."[3] Many have values about poor people exactly similar to these values about cats, but since Nazi times the view is applied publicly only to the unborn rather than to people already born.

A contrasting value is that no life is so poor in goods that it does not have value. Still others believe that only the individual should be allowed to decide whether his or her own life is worth living. Surprisingly to me, the issue of these conflicting values which are crucial (though usually only implicit) in deliberations about population policy, is rarely the subject of explicit discussion. At least one economist developed a model in which he made explicit the assumption that some people's lives have "negative utility"—a truly amazing piece of economic analysis, to my mind.[4] But this technically elegant essay raised no furor of backlash in the literature.

The Acceptability of Various Methods of Preventing Life

To some people, abortion or contraception or infanticide are acceptable; for others, any of these may be unacceptable.

A Value for Numbers of People

Both the Bible, which urges people to be fruitful and multiply, and the utilitarian philosophy of "the greatest good for the greatest number" lead to a value for more people. This value may be held by those who do not believe in a personal God as well as those who do. Many people of all theological beliefs do not share this value. (It would be unsound for the reader to infer from anything written in this book that I hold any particular theological belief, though several have ventured to do so in print.)

Animals and Plants versus People

According to the Bible, "And God said, Let us make man in our image, after our likeness, and let them have dominion over the fish of the sea, and over the fowl of the air, and over the cattle, and over all the earth. . . . Be fertile and increase, fill the earth and master it and rule the fish of the sea, the birds of the sky, and all the living things that creep on earth" (Genesis 1:26–28). (This does not imply that humans should treat the world about them with lack of care: "[R]eplenish the earth," says Genesis 1:28.)

In sharp contrast is the view of some environmentalists. Consider, for example, the "Greenpeace Philosophy" of the whale-protecting group: "Ecology teaches us that humankind is not the center of life on the planet. Ecology has taught us that the whole earth is part of our 'body' and that we must learn to respect it as we respect life—the whales, the seals, the forests, the seas. The tremendous beauty of ecological thought is that it shows us a pathway back to an understanding and apprecia tion of life itself—an understanding and appreciation that is imperative to that very way of life."[5]

Many of the environmentalist views are held and expressed with quasi-religious fervor, as others have noted.[6]

A sharp shift in values has occurred over the decades:

> Thus the nineteenth-century child was taught that nature is animated with man's purposes. God designed nature for man's physical needs and spiritual training. Scientific understanding of nature will reveal the greater glory of God, and the practical application of such knowledge should be encouraged as part of the use God meant man to make of nature. Besides serving the material needs of man, nature is a source of man's health, strength, and virtue. He departs at his peril from a life close to nature. At a time when America was becoming increasingly industrial and urban, agrarian values which had been a natural growth in earlier America became articles of fervent faith in American nationalism. The American character had been formed in virtue because it developed in a rural environment, and it must remain the same despite vast environmental change. The existence of a bounteous and fruitful frontier in America, with its promise not only of future prosperity but of continued virtue, offers proof that God has singled out the United States above other nations for His fostering care. The superiority of nature to man-made things confers superiority on the American over older civilizations. That Uncle Sam sooner or later will have to become a city dweller is not envisaged by these textbook writers, although their almost fanatical advocacy of rural values would seem to suggest an unconscious fear that this might be so.[7]

This shift in values can be seen neatly in the wonderful book *Birds of America*, published in 1917.[8] The descriptions of many birds include evaluations of their effects on humanity in general and on farmers in particular; a bird that helps agriculture was more highly valued than a bird which harms it. Nowadays naturalists often evaluate humankind for our effect upon the birds rather than vice versa.

The shift in values can also be seen in the 1990s call for the return of wolves to Yellowstone National Park about seventy years after Congress passed a law to eradicate them because of their danger to cattle and humans.[9]

Individual Freedom versus Community Coercion

Another important value in debates about population. The willingness to coerce others to attain one's ends with respect to conservation, the environment, and population growth is illustrated at many places in this book.

Eugenics

The beliefs that the human race (a) can, and (b) should, be improved by selective breeding was rife in the 1920s and 1930s. Along with these beliefs has gone the belief in the benefit of race-selective immigration policies. These beliefs bulked large in the thinking of Margaret Sanger when she began the organizational activities that led to Planned Parenthood.[10] Earlier on, eugenics and the Eugenics Society of London had been one of the main channels of thought that led to the founding of the Population Investigation Committee in Great Britain, as important a population research center as any in the world. J. M. Keynes began as a strong supporter of eugenics, which went hand-in-hand with his then-Malthusian economic outlook. When he later invented Keynesian economics, which saw benefit in a larger market, he flip-flopped and favored larger populations for a while. He later flip-flopped again, and again came to worry about population growth. But all this time he remained a strong supporter of eugenics, serving as a director of the Society from 1937 to 1944, and being the vice president in 1937.[11] So the connection between Malthusianism and population control is close historically.

Some of the main population institutions in the United States, too, arose out of interest in eugenics—for example, the Population Reference Bureau and Planned Parenthood.[12] Since Hitler's demise this idea has dropped out of public statements, and I do not assert that present officials of these groups are eugenicists (though I would like to hear them deny it publicly). But their original aim of population control in the poor countries and among poor persons continues unchanged. And the association between the ideas of eugenics and population control are joined together in the writings of such persons as Garrett Hardin.[13]

The concept of lives that are "not worth living"—used in the title of a book in 1920 by two German professors, one of law and one of medicine[14]—is central to eugenics, and was also central to Nazi ideology; by 1941, seventy thousand patients had been killed by physicians in German hospitals.[15] It reappears in many apparently benign guises—even abstract economic analysis by a Nobel-prize-winning economist.[16] And economist James Meade was a member of the Eugenics Society from the 1930s to the 1970s, and was treasurer in the 1960s. (He also analyzed the situation of the island of Mauritius and concluded that population growth was its bane. As was discussed in chapter 34, in the 1980s Mauritius went from large unemployment to labor "shortage" in a handful of years by changing to a free-enterprise system.)

The eugenics view was widely rejected with horror during and after the Hitler period. But it is again with us. R. J. Herrnstein entitles an article "IQ and Falling Birth Rates," and asserts that "the average intelligence of the population will decline across generations to the extent that reproduction shifts toward the lower end of the [income] scale,"[17] and he quotes with approval that "Vining tentatively infers the equivalent of a four-to-five point drop in IQ over the five or six generations spanning the demographic transition in the United States"—that is, Americans supposedly have gotten less intelligent over time. Herrnstein therefore favors policies encouraging fertility among high-income, high-education groups and discouraging population growth among others.

As discussed in chapter 32, the evidence persuades me that one cannot improve the level of human intelligence by selective breeding as Herrnstein suggests, and hence eugenics policies have little or no rationale—and they would be unacceptable to me even if there were evidence in their favor.

The Value of Progress

Of all the values that I have long held without examining it, the value for progress—along with the value of human life, no matter whose it is—is perhaps the most important. Perhaps my unthinking acceptance of this value is at least partly a result of my being an American; the value has been associated with both political parties, in early as well as in present times. Thomas Jefferson wrote:

> [W]e are bound with peculiar gratitude . . . that [we are] permitted quietly to cultivate the earth and to practice and improve those arts which tend to increase our comforts . . . to direct the energies of our nation to the multiplication of the human race, and not to its destruction.[18]

A very different sort of political thinker wrote something quite similar:

> The settlement of this great and generous land and the development of its resources created a diverse and expansive American republic of hope, opportunity, experimentation, mobility, and personal freedom.[19]

It came as a surprise to me that many others do not as a matter of course consider it desirable that people should have greater access to educational and economic opportunity, better health, and the material goods that constitute the standard of living. Perhaps it is not surprising that the Duke of Wellington commented on the first railroad in Great Britain that it would "enable the lower orders to go uselessly wandering about the country."[20] And the present Duke of Wellington inveighs against the birth of additional people who might share the pleasures of life in England and on the planet with him. But there are also many who are not members of the "nobility" who associate negative spiritual and metaphysical values with various aspects of progress. For example, when "progress" in painkilling drugs is mentioned, they mention drug abuse in return. And their views are in no manner inherently illogical or foolish, though they may be unpalatable to others.

Values Masquerading as Rights or Other Entitlements

The concept of rights—apart from any specific body of secular law—has become used widely in discussion of subjects related to people and other species (a subject introduced in chapter 10). Such rights are often asserted without explicit justification as if they are undeniable. A typical example is a letter to the editor following a (facetious) article about a man's battle with moles in his lawn:

> What makes him think that he owns the world and has more right to inhabit it than moles? Were your readers supposed to chuckle over his escapades of trying to poison, gas and shish kebab a helpless animal? Who really cares what Mr. Sautter's lawn looks like?[21]

Or this from the Indian ambassador to the United States:

> The view that the human race is endowed with the divine right to ruthlessly exploit planetary resources for its own short term benefit is no longer valid and must be decisively rejected . . . we must shed the quaint belief that ours is a race in some special way entitled to exploit this planet infinitum for its own selfish purpose.[22]

There is further discussion of values concerning various species in chapter 31 on species.

The likening of the human species to cancer and other virulent diseases has long been a common piece of rhetoric (see first edition, pages). Now AIDS has become a favorite analogy to people. "We, the human species, have become a viral epidemic to the earth . . . the AIDS of the earth."[23] And "if radical environmentalists were to invent a disease to bring human populations back to sanity, it would probably be something like AIDS."[24] Author William Vollmann is quoted in *Publishers Weekly*: "[T]he biggest hope that we have right now is the AIDS epidemic. Maybe the best thing that could happen would be if it were to wipe out half or two-thirds of the people in the world."[25] *The Economist* wrote in an editorial: "The extinction of the human species may not only be inevitable, but a good thing."[26] And another by the eminent biologist E. O. Wilson: "The sin our descendants are least likely to forgive us is the loss of biological diversity."[27]

There is an interesting contradiction here, as Robert Nelson pointed out.[28] On the one hand, *Homo sapiens* is said to be no different than other species; on the other hand, it is the only species whom the environmentalists ask to protect *other* species. They attribute to us a special duty, but not a special privilege.

Conclusion

My aim here is not to discuss the above values, but simply to point out that they operate importantly in discussion of these matters. Their universal validities are usually taken for granted by those who assert them, though to others they may seem to be simply odd preferences which may be atypical, unhallowed by tradition, quite arguable, and perhaps no more than one person's tastes. (The status of other values discussed in this chapter may be the same as far as arguability goes.)

The Key Values

> If the less stringent curbs on procreation fail, someday perhaps childbearing will be deemed a punishable crime against society unless the parents hold a government license. Or perhaps all potential parents will be required to use contraceptive chemicals, the governments issuing antidotes to citizens chosen for childbearing.
> *(Stewart M. Ogilvy, Honorary President of Friends of the Earth)*[1]

> Just as we have laws compelling death control, so we must have laws requiring birth control—the purpose being to ensure a zero rate of population increase. We must come to see that it is the duty of government to protect women against pregnancy as it protects them against job discrimination and smallpox, and for the same reason—the public good. No longer can we tolerate the doctrinaire position that the number of children a couple has is a strictly private decision carrying no social consequences.
> *(Dr. Edward Chasteen)*[2]

THE PRECEDING CHAPTER listed values that come into play whenever population issues are discussed—even in scientific discourse. Now let's consider some of these values at greater length—hopefully, not too-great length—because the issues raised in various chapters come together here at the end. Ultimately, every belief about resources, the environment, and population comes down to values. And policies are choices (well informed, we hope) based on some ranking of these values, though not always expressed or admitted by the policy makers.

Altruism versus Selfishness

The issue of altruism underlies several of the specific issues below, and appears at various other places in the book. Hence, we need to consider the general value for putting a bit of our energy and resources into the community pot for others to have in the future, as well as taking out of the community pot for our own use the resources that our ancestors sacrificed to bestow upon us.

This matter came up earlier in discussions of Keynes's phrase "In the long run we are all dead," which implies that we should focus upon only what is good *for us and our own generation*, rather than consider *future generations* as well (see chapter 12 and below).

Quite analogous is another issue: Should we address ourselves only to the demographic welfare of our particular countries or ethnic or religious groups, or should we take the cosmopolitan view that all human beings' welfare matters to us? Those who have a strong value for the strength and persistence of their own group often believe that it is *relative* strength that matters, and therefore they prefer that other groups not grow or even decline in size, along with the increase in their own group. Obviously this value affects one's views of various population policies.

The lives of people of other countries, ethnicities, and religions matter to me, irrespective of the fates of the groups to which I belong. I take pride and pleasure in the human race as a whole as well as in my own groups.

Misunderstanding is common about the connection between particular economic-political philosophies and altruistic values and activity. The free-market ideology in no way precludes a group from redistributing to other groups in the present or future as generously as it chooses; Milton Friedman makes this point again and again. This school of thought argues that redistribution in *money* is more efficient than redistribution in *goods*, but there is no limit except community values and wealth on how much a community should redistribute from the richer to the poorer. Conversely, there is nothing in Socialist doctrine that makes it incumbent upon one country or group to give from its wealth to those who are poorer.

The Malthusian objection to redistribution as restated forcefully in our times by Garrett Hardin—that supporting the poor is a bad policy because it keeps more of them alive to the detriment of all—has no role in the intellectual framework of this book. Both the data and the theory set forth here imply that additional poor persons in this generation do *not* make others poorer in this and future generations; the supposed depletion of resources upon which the Malthus-Hardin argument hinges is simply wrong. Hence the rest of their argument falls to the ground.

More about this issue under the heading "The Born and the Unborn" below.

The Value of a Poor Person's Life

Some have written that the lives of the very poor are so miserable that an economic policy does them a service if it discourages their births. This assumption obviously depends entirely upon one's values and view of the world.

The belief that very poor people's lives are not worth living comes out clearly when Paul Ehrlich writes about India.

> I came to understand the population explosion emotionally one stinking hot night in Delhi. . . . The streets seemed alive with people. People eating, people washing, people sleeping, people visiting, arguing, and screaming. People thrusting their

hands through the taxi window, begging. People defecating and urinating. People clinging to buses. People herding animals. People, people, people.[3]

Ehrlich writes nothing about people laughing, loving, or being tender to their children—all of which one also sees among the poor in India.

Yes, there is misery in India. I, too, have witnessed and winced at it. Intestinal disease is everywhere and blindness is not uncommon. A fourteen-year-old girl catches bricks on a construction job for a dollar a day while her baby, covered with flies and crying, lies on a burlap sack on the ground below the scaffold on which the young mother works. A toothless crone of indeterminate age, with no relatives in the world and no home, begins with a cake of wet cow-dung to lay a floor for a new "dwelling" of sticks and rags, by the side of the road. All this I have seen. And yet these people must think their lives are worth living, or else they would choose to stop living. Because people continue to live, I assume that they value their lives positively. And those lives therefore have value in my scheme of things. Hence I do not believe that the existence of poor people—either in poor countries or, a fortiori in the United States—is a sign of "overpopulation."

The most important scientific magazine in the world headed a news story "Planetary Malignancy," and went on to precis an article likening the "proliferation of human communities" to "a malignant ecopathological process" that is "ultimately ecocidal."[4] Based on the same notion that population growth is a destructive phenomenon—without any mention of the value of life in itself—the recently declassified U.S. National Security Council 1974 basic plan describes continuing covert U.S. population-control programs in Africa that utilize just about every dirty political and media trick to coerce the Africans to have fewer children. These programs run the risk of causing destructive political fallout for the United States, as happened in India in the 1970s when the United States was implicated in coercive sterilization programs. (This subject was discussed at greater length in the first edition, chapters 2 and 23, and will be discussed further in a book I hope follows soon.)

The Born and the Unborn

One hears that "It doesn't make sense to take into account the lives of people who have not yet been born." This comes up in two contexts: (1) with respect to the long-run effects of population growth upon the economy fifty or one hundred or two hundred years in the future; and (2) when someone like me suggests that the level of per capita income in the short run is not the only criterion, and not the end-all and be-all of population economics, but that the sheer number of people alive, enjoying life, may also be relevant.

In reality, most people and all societies act in ways that show concern for people who have not yet been born, whether or not they justify these actions metaphysically. Governments build public works to last beyond the lifetimes of the present generation, explicitly taking future generations into account. And young families take their own unborn children into account when they save money or buy a house with enough space for children. So taking unborn children into account is a basic fact of life, and hence requires no defense when we are considering the long-run as well as the short-run benefits of population growth. Furthermore, many of the people who make this objection are themselves ecologists who properly urge that we should take a long-run view of the planet's welfare. It seems to me that it would be sensible for ecologists to apply the same sort of thinking to economics as they do to biology and the environment.

But let us go further. Some people say that they cannot *feel* a concern for unborn children. Granted. But does this imply that it is foolish or impossible for *others* to feel such a concern? You certainly can feel concern for someone you do not know—and similarly for an unborn person. For example, prospective parents often imagine terrible events in which their unborn children would be injured or killed; this thought can arouse an emotion much stronger than an imagined (or real) scene in which a living person on another continent, of another race and nationality, is injured or killed. It seems to me beyond doubt that at least *some* people feel a sentimental tie to children who are not yet born, and who might not be born.

Given that some people take unborn children into account, it is clear that the importance of unborn children can vary among persons, all the way from zero to high. This is the sort of value about which economics and other science has nothing to say. As an individual, I myself attribute value to unborn children. And since this value gets so little public expression—some people assuming that it does not exist—I will take this opportunity to say a few words about it, even at the risk of seeming preachy.

Holding the standard of living constant, I think it better to have more rather than fewer people. Even if more people implied a somewhat lower long-run income level—which is not the case—I would be in favor of a somewhat lower standard of living per person if more people were alive to enjoy it.

But what does it mean to like the idea of more people? To me it means that I do not mind having more people in the cities I live in, and seeing more children going to school or playing in the park. I would be even more pleased if there were more cities and more people in unsettled areas—or if there were another planet like this one. It means that if faster growth means more crowded parking lots for a while, I prefer having the more people. Others see it differently, as seen in that Planned Parenthood bumper sticker: "Population Growth: How Dense Can You Get?"

I hold this value for more life because it is generally consistent with the rest of my preferences and tastes. It is a value that many other people hold, too, perhaps unconsciously. And others may come to recognize its importance to them as they come to recognize, as I did, that population growth bodes well rather than ill for civilization, in the long run.

Keynes's remark "In the long run we are all dead" came up earlier. Within that clever phrase lies much of the confusion, and much of the conflict over values, that is at the heart of discussions about population growth.

Let us focus first on the word "we." Its definition determines whether Keynes's remark is literally true or literally false. If "we" means those of us who are now having this discussion, the remark is literally true. But if "we" includes our children, and our children's children, and their children, and on and on, then the remark is literally not true, because that chain of being need not ever end.

So which meaning of "we" should we adopt? (If *neither* makes sense, then the remark is obviously meaningless.) This is a matter of values. And here we should note that the basic ecological viewpoint—which I respect greatly— assumes the ongoing "we," as is implicit in ecology's attention to the long run, and indirect effects of contemporary actions. And this "we" is thoroughly in keeping with the viewpoint that we should not consider only the benefits that we ourselves can derive from present-day changes, but we should also con- sider the benefits that we should bestow upon our posterity as our ancestors bestowed benefits upon us.

Unfortunately, however, many persons who call themselves ecologists com- pound confusion by concurrently using both definitions of "we." When some- one like me says that we ought to reckon not just the immediate but also the long-run effects of population growth, these persons parrot Keynes's remark. (You hear it so often it really does sound like a parrot.) But when I or another economist put less weight on the same event a century from now than now, and laugh at worrying about what might happen seven billion years from now, these same persons accuse us of being selfishly myopic.

The only approach to this issue which is not hopelessly inconsistent, and which enables us to make sensible decisions about public and private policies, is to use the concept of discounting future events with an appropriate dis- count factor. This is one of the handful of most basic economic ideas, and its use is crucial here.

What Is to Be Lost?

The following catchy argument, derived from Pascal's Wager, is found in Ehr- lich's *Population Bomb*: If population control is undertaken and is successful in preventing births, but it turns out to be unnecessary, then what is lost?[5] As mentioned in the introduction, Ehrlich and others suggest that nothing is lost. But unlike the case with Pascal's Wager, where the only "loss" is that the wagerer lives a righteous life without "needing" to, one's answer to Ehrlich's question depends upon one's values. If you value additional human lives, and some lives are unnecessarily prevented from being lived, that is an obvious loss. The fact that this is not a loss in Ehrlich's eyes tells us his implicit values. This point of view does not square with the Dr. Seuss extract at the beginning of chapter 38.

The Ehrlich argument boils down to an inverted (or perverted) Golden Rule: Do unto others—prevent their existence—what you are glad no one did to you.

There is an unhappy analog here to the "compassion" shown by special interest groups and legislators when they "generously" manipulate the governmental mechanism to take money from some taxpayers in order to give it to some other persons or activities whom they think deserving. This is charity on the cheap—the sense of doing good without having to sacrifice from your own pocket to pay for it. This is often seen in initiatives labeled as "saving the environment."

The population-control analog is that the Ehrlich doctrine takes away from those who might live them the lives that they might live, and the lives of children from parents who would like to bring them into the world and enjoy them. And Ehrlich et al. recommend this policy without first showing the way by sacrificing their own lives—which I would guess they would claim are too valuable to be sacrificed (and about which I would agree! We need *all* of us). They are giving others' lives away under the justification that it is good for the unborn not to live, and for the rest of humanity that they not live.

Ehrlich et al. sometimes say that they themselves abstain from having children, or limit their number, for the good of others. Maybe this is their intention, or maybe they are claiming as a sacrifice something they would do anyway. If they are really abstaining, it is most regrettable, because their children—like others—would enrich the rest of us, on balance.

The Value of Per Capita Income in the Short Run

Economists have long used the concept of an "optimum population" for a given country, which sounds very scientific. But discussions about optimum population sizes or growth rates must have some criterion of better and worse, and this criterion is usually the short-run per capita income of the present population, including the "quality of life" as income.

No one, however, is prepared to take the short-run income criterion to its logical conclusions: do away with lower-income people. Removing the lower half of the income distribution in any country will raise the average income of the remaining people by simple arithmetic. And logically this should continue to the point at which only one person is left—the richest person at the start. Of course this is absurd, but it is the kind of absurdity that the criterion leads to.

Here is another way to raise per capita income and wealth in the short run, then: Drive the birthrate down to ridiculously low levels, and perhaps to zero births—the particular level depending upon the weight one gives to the future relative to the present. For example, if the future is discounted at, say, 10 percent per year, the value of per-person income would be maximized into the infinite future if people stop having babies completely. This is because it takes a long time before babies begin to produce, though they consume immediately. Hence a baby born today lowers the income of everyone else, on average, by simple arithmetic. So having no babies at all next year would be good for computed per capita income next year. But no one wants to go that far with the average-income criterion, either.

The value that in the past I subscribed to as a criterion for decisions about population growth is one that I think a great many other people also subscribe to, as they will find if they inspect their beliefs closely. In utilitarian terms it is "the greatest good for the greatest number." Under the influence of Hayek's writing, however, I no longer rely on this value because the idea of adding people's happinesses is fraught with difficulties so great that it is unworkable. Instead, I now use what I call the "expanded Pareto optimum"—that is, that if no one is made worse off, and there are more people to enjoy life, that is a preferable state of affairs. And in the long run, population growth is consistent with a larger expanded Pareto optimum.

Other things being equal, a greater number of people is a good thing, according to this value criterion. If forced to choose, I might well prefer to have more people and a lower per capita income in the immediate future. But even if such conditions were to exist, any income decline would be only temporary; in the long run, per capita income will be higher if there are more children (or more immigrants) now. Hence this choice is an unlikely one.

(This leaves aside the issue that any trade-off between fewer people and less income implies government coercion, which I would find odious even if there were an economic argument in its favor—which there is not.)

This criterion seems to be consistent with our other values—our abhorrence of killing, and our desire to prevent disease and early death. Indeed, why should we feel so strongly that murder is bad, and that children in war-torn countries should be saved, and then not want to bring more people into the world? If life is good and worth supporting, why does preventing murder make sense, but not encouraging births? I understand well that a death causes grief to the living—but I am sure that your abhorrence of killing would also extend to the extermination of a whole group at once, under which conditions there would be no one to suffer grief. So, what are the differences between the murder of an adult, the infanticide of another's child, and the coercion of someone else not to have a child? The main difference between murder and forcing someone not to bear children is that murder threatens our *own* persons, and unregulated murder would rip up the fabric of our society—good reasons indeed to be against murder. But we also condemn murder on the moral ground that murder denies life to someone else—and in this respect (and *only* in this respect) it seems to me that there is no difference between murder, abortion, contraception, and abstinence from sex.

I am not *equating* abortion or contraception to murder, and I am *not* branding as immoral all who do not have as many children as are biologically possible. Nor do I want to impose upon you my own values, and these their conclusions. Rather, I just wish us to get clear on the meaning of the moral distinctions we make. Again, lest these words be taken out of context—and they probably will anyhow—I am not equating murder to abortion or contraception. What I *am* saying is that the single similarity among them—acting so that potential human life will not be lived—should make us aware of the full consequences of abortion and contraception.

The Value of Saving versus the Value of Creating

The conflict between the value of saving versus the value of creating is personified by auto mechanic Louis Wichinsky. He worked out a system for his car to burn vegetable oil, and his input is the *used* vegetable oil he gets from the deep-frying operations at his local diner and Burger King.[6]

Curiously, though he is a creative person—witness his invention—he turns the creative energy to saving old oil, rather than to developing better ways to create the new oil that he believes should be obtained from rapeseed. His only contribution to the issue of how to produce the oil is to say some southern states should be "ordered to grow nothing but rapeseed."

This predilection away from building and toward saving—usually through government coercion of other people—is seen in the money-collecting campaigns of "environmental" organizations. Next time someone comes to your door to ask for donations—often in the guise of asking for your signature to a petition—ask some close questions. It is likely that the solicitor will collect for an environmental organization; every stranger who has come to our door for the past eight years has been from an environmental organization. (This excludes the Girl Scouts and the cancer and heart groups, who are neighbors.) Ask if the solicitor is getting paid, and you usually learn that he or she gets a commission of 30 percent or more "off the top," with other chunks going to the persons up the line. Then ask what the organization will use the residual money for, and the answer always is: political activity, and consciousness raising (which often means soliciting more money). Never will the money be used to clean up a playground or to plant trees, and certainly not to build a hospital or a park. The aim is not to *build* and *create*, but only to "protect"—which usually means stopping the progress of others who want to build factories, stores, waste disposal facilities, homes, and resorts.

The Question about Sound Judgment

The organization People for the Ethical Treatment of Animals (PETA) placed a newspaper advertisement in which they compared the meatpacking industry to a notorious mass killer who ate the dead bodies of his victims.[7] The same organization seeks to ban the horse-drawn tourist carriages in Washington, D.C.[8] And animal rights groups have successfully halted research on brain injuries that involve shooting 125 anesthetized cats in the brain each year.[9] What should one make of such ideas? Are the implicit values lopsided?

A key failing of many doomsayers with respect to the environment is a lack of proportion in their judgments, together with a willingness to force those judgments upon others. If homeowner Green is so concerned about his lawn that he does not want to have any children lest his kids trample the grass, one would consider this attitude not illogical but somehow out of proportion—a bit hysterical, perhaps. If, however, Green begins to agitate that *no one else* in the neighborhood should have children because the neighbor children might trample on Green's lawn, or on the lawns of still other homeowners, one would consider Green to be a bit nutty—or perhaps dangerously nutty.

This is akin to doomsayers' behavior with respect to various potential dangers—nuclear power, chemical contamination, and so on. In such cases the doomsayers are literally prepared to throw out the baby with the bath water. (Indeed, the phrase seems made to fit this situation.) They are prepared to sacrifice massive benefits to others to reduce low-probability risks to themselves.

Not only do the doomsayers seem to make evaluations that are out of proportion—the dangers tend to be exaggerated—but they wholly overlook the potential positive long-run effects of the problems induced by the additional people. Maybe kids running over the lawn do not benefit us by causing improvements in lawn-care technology. But more people putting pollutants into the air eventually leads to the search for solutions which eventuates in inventions that in the end leave us better off than if the problem had not arisen. It is this crucial dynamic process that is wholly left out of the doomsayers' thinking on these matters, and it makes their behavior even less appropriate to the situation—and therefore even more hysterical.

With respect to natural resources, the lack of proportion in thought, and the resulting hysteria, apparently result from a wholly incorrect assessment of the trends. The usual historical process again is: (a) more people, (b) more problems, (c) more search for solutions, (d) finding solutions that leave us better off than before we had begun. The evidence for this process is powerful: the observed long-run increase in availability rather than increasing scarcity of natural resources, as shown by the prices.

These apocalyptics are "unbalanced," in the most basic sense. The media contribute to this—while literally paying lip-service to "balance"—by playing up the most dramatic forecasts of doom that they can find a justification for publishing.

One journalist wrote that he prefers that there would be another seven thousand elephants on Earth rather than another billion people.[10] The trade-off here is more than a hundred thousand people for one elephant. Does he really mean that? Is each elephant worth 100,000 people? In what sense? How would this square with other judgments we make in society?

One can think it important that we have elephants in zoos, in game reserves, and other places where we human beings can benefit from them, but not think of elephants' lives as being good in themselves. This is in contrast to the view that elephants' lives are good in themselves, even if they are not part of our human life at all. One cannot logically quarrel with the latter value. But perhaps those concerned about elephants might ask themselves whether their viewpoint is consistent with their abhorrence of the death of a person unnecessarily, or a person's sickness.

For some, non-human nature simply comes before anything human. There is a conflict about water that is used in towns and in Everglades National Park, where the great white heron and the American crocodile use it. The Park superintendent said, "We have urban demands, agricultural needs and the park all competing. When the pie is divided, we want guarantees that the park's slice comes out first."[11]

Where is a sensible balance between yew trees and the lives of cancer patients? About sixty pounds of yew bark—which means the death of about three yew trees—is required to treat a single breast-cancer patient. The National Wildlife Federation and the Sierra Club fought against the Forest Service harvesting the trees for this purpose.[12] Judgment comes into play here in two respects: (1) the specific trade-off between the lives of trees and people that is considered acceptable; and (2) the likelihood that the endpoint will be the extinction of yew trees. The second judgment quickly proved unsound; the synthesis of taxol—the product derived from the yew bark—was quickly developed.[13] Hence the yew is most unlikely to be wiped from the face of the Earth.

Certainly there is *some* reasonable trade-off between human beings and animals (a subject which was introduced earlier in this chapter and in chapter 10). If I am told that a fireman died to save the lives of a zoo, or a forest reserve full of animals, I am saddened but not horrified or outraged, any more that I am if a fireman dies to save a museum full of paintings. The key question is:

what trade-offs will we consider thinkable and reasonable? One fireman for one elephant? or a thousand firemen for one elephant? or one fireman for seven thousand elephants?

Dave Foreman, the founder of the Earth First! group which engages in "ecological sabotage" such as pulling up survey stakes, pouring sand into the crankcases of bulldozers, toppling power line towers, and putting spikes in trees one of which shattered the blades of a timber saw and nearly killed its operator[14]—offers this trade-off: "[A]n individual human life has no more intrinsic [worth] than does an individual Grizzly Bear life."[15] And the slogan of PETA's philosophy is "A rat is a pig is a dog is a boy."[16]

These values affect our daily life. An animal rights group made clear that for public choices the life of a human is of no more value in their scheme of things than the life of a baboon. A baboon liver was transplanted into a person who would otherwise die, and who could not even use a human liver transplant if it were available. The result: "An animal rights group said it will picket the hospital Tuesday to protest the use of animals as organ donors. . . . 'Animals are more than spare parts for humans'" said People for the Ethical Treatment of Animals (PETA).[17] And after the person died, a spokesman for the Fund for Animals said, "Animal rights groups should feel vindicated, though we don't applaud the death of any person."[18]

So even if we agree that there is *some* number of trees or animals that might be traded for a human life, the number matters a lot. Unlike George Bernard Shaw's remark—Now that we have established what you are, madam, it is simply a matter of deciding on the price—the price matters greatly in human-animal trade-offs, and in fact reveals what one's principles are.

The implicit cost of saving a single condor or wild burro may be in the hundreds of thousands of dollars. This may be far more than the cost of saving an additional human life by building better highways, say. Does this valuation by the doomsayers seem in reasonable proportion, given our other values? It seems to rest on the idea of "save the burros (or the snail darter) at any cost." Indeed, in surveys people often say we must save the environment "at any cost." But if the respondents themselves were forced to pay that cost in some way—that is, if their remarks were to be translated into some action that they themselves could control or pay for—it is not likely that they would so whole-heartedly back these statements with action. Yet these poorly constructed survey questions influence policy makers.

People as Destroyers and Creators

"If we have more children, when they grow up there will be more adults who can push the nuclear button and kill civilization," some say.

True. More generally, as one writer reduced the matter to an absurdity: "All human problems can be solved by doing away with human beings."[19] But to have more children grow up is also to have more people who can find ways to avert catastrophe.

When Is Coercion Justified?

Chapters 20 and 21 discussed coercion with respect to conservation and waste disposal. Now the subject is coercion with respect to the number of children people have. Some people advocate forced birth control "if necessary." Again to quote Ehrlich, "We must have population control at home, hopefully through a system of incentives and penalties, but by compulsion if voluntary methods fail."[20] Garrett Hardin is even more explicit in his famous "The Tragedy of the Commons," saying "Freedom to breed is intolerable."[21] He refers to his viewpoint as "lifeboat ethics."

The logic for having the state control the number of children parents may rear has been stated as follows.

> In conditions of scarcity the civil right to have unlimited births simply does not exist. Such a claim [the right to have children] is attention-getting and suspect. It is a favorite argument of minorities in support of their own overproduction of births. The right to have children fits into the network of other rights and duties we share and must dovetail with the rights of others. When all of us must curtail our production of children none of us has an overriding civil right of this kind. The closer we live together and the more of us there are, the fewer civil rights we can exercise before they infringe upon those of another. This adverse relation between dense population and personal freedom is easily documented around the world. It is time for people sincerely interested in civil rights to expose such special pleading, and to intervene when it is leveled against local or national programs.[22]

A briefer statement is that of Kingsley Davis: "It can be argued that over-reproduction—that is, the bearing of more than four children—is a worse crime than most and should be outlawed."[23]

Many Americans have become persuaded of the necessity of such coercion, as these Roper poll results[24] show:

> Q. The population crisis is becoming so severe that people will have to be limited on the number of children they can have.
> A. Agree 47%
>   Disagree 41%

And the astonishing kinds of programs that have been suggested in the "population community" are summarized in table 39-1.

Some countries have enacted into law coercive policies with respect to fertility. In India during the first Indira Gandhi period, in the state of Tamil

TABLE 39-1

Examples of Proposed Measures to Reduce U.S. Fertility, by Universality or Selectivity of Impact

| Universal Impact: Social Constraints | Selective Impact Depending on Socio-Economic Status | | Measures Predicated on Existing Motivation to Prevent Unwanted Pregnancy |
	Economic Deterrents/Incentives	Social Control	
Restructure family:	Modify tax policies:	Compulsory abortion of	Payments to encourage
(a) Postpone or avoid	(a) Substantial marriage	out-of-wedlock	sterilization
marriage	tax	pregnancies	Payments to encourage
(b) Alter image of ideal	(b) Child tax	Compulsory sterilization of	contraception
family size	(c) Tax married more than	all who have 2 children	Payments to encourage
Compulsory education	single	except for a few who	abortion
of children	(d) Remove parents' tax	would be allowed 3	Abortion and sterilization
Encourage increased	exemption	Confine childbearing to	on demand
homosexuality	(e) Additional taxes on	only a limited number	Allow certain contraceptives
Educate for family	parents with more than	of adults	to be distributed non-
limitation	1 or 2 children in	Stock certificate-type	medically
Fertility control agents	school	permits for children	Improve contraceptive
in water supply	Reduce/eliminate paid	Housing policies:	technology
Encourage women to	maternity leave or	(a) Discouragement of	Make contraception truly
work	benefits	private home ownership	available and accessible
	Reduce/eliminate	(b) Stop awarding public	to all
	children's or family	housing based on	Improve maternal health
	allowances	family size	care, with family
	Bonuses for delayed		planning as a core
	marriage and greater		element
	child spacing		
	Pensions for women of 45		
	with less than N children		
	Eliminate welfare payments		
	after the first 2 children		
	Chronic depression		
	Require women to work		
	and provide few child		
	care facilities		
	Limit/eliminate public-		
	financed medical care,		
	scholarships, housing,		
	loans, and subsidies to		
	families with more than		
	N children		

Source: Reproduced from Elliott et al. 1970. Originally, Frederick S. Jaffe, "Activities Relevant to the Study of Population Policy for the U.S.," Memorandum to Bernard Berelson, March 11, 1969.

Nadu, "Convicts . . . who submit to sterilization [could] have their jail term reduced"; and in the state of Uttar Pradesh, "Any government servant whose spouse is alive and who has three or more children must be sterilized within three months, pursuant to a state government order issued under the Defense of Internal Security of India Rules. Those failing to do so will cease to be entitled to any rationed article beyond the basic four units."[25] In the state of Maharashtra, population fifty million, the legislature passed an act requiring compulsory sterilization for all families with three or more children (four or more if the children were all boys or all girls), but this measure did not receive the necessary consent of the president of India. And in other states in India, in Singapore,[26] and perhaps elsewhere, public housing, education, and other public services have been at times conditioned on the number of children a family has. It is this possibility of coercion—by penalty, taxation, physical compulsion, or otherwise—that concerns me most. Singapore has now reversed its course and on eugenics grounds (see page 483) now offers incentives for middle-class persons to have *more* children than they would otherwise choose to bear. (This switch should be sobering to any country that wants to *restrict* births.) But I am against government pressure in either direction, both because I am opposed to such pressure in itself as well as because I do not think that any government knows better than the parents what will be good for the society as a whole.

I hope you share my belief that it is good for people to have the greatest freedom to run their own lives. Such a desire for individual self-determination is entirely consistent with full information about birth control, because information increases ability to have the wanted number of children. It is also consistent with legal abortion (but also consistent with abhorring abortion). And it is consistent with public health and nutrition measures to keep alive all the children that people wish to bring into the world. I am unqualifiedly in favor of all these policies to increase the individual's ability to achieve the family size she or he chooses. The same belief leads me to be against coercing people not to have children. By definition, coercion reduces people's freedom to make their own decisions about their own lives.

Following on the Tiananmen Square massacre of 1989, there was much discussion about human rights in China. But the largest-scale violation of human rights in China—indeed, aside from the killing campaigns and famines in the Soviet Union and China, one of the grossest violations of human rights in history—is the denial to 100 million Chinese couples of the right to have another child. More specifically, at issue is the forcing of IUDs into the wombs of 100 million Chinese women against their will, the compulsory X-rays of these women every three months to ensure that the IUDs have not been removed, and the punishment and sometimes forced abortion of those women who have children anyway. Added in 1993 to this long-standing policy was a proposal for compulsory abortions and sterilizations, as well as a ban against marrying, for people with "hepatitis, venereal disease or mental illness"; also mooted by the Chinese was a policy to kill "congenitally abnormal" children. The province of Gansu already had a program in operation of mandatory sterilization for the "mentally retarded."[27]

There is a puzzle here: Why do we not hear from the feminist movement about this violation of women's rights? Or from Planned Parenthood about this violation of reproductive rights? Or from the African-American organizations about the U.S. actions in Africa to coerce governments to reduce their birthrates? Noninterference with other countries is a nonissue in this context; Planned Parenthood has long been involved in international population-control activities. What's going on here?[28]

In the first edition I wrote: "Though I would vote against any overall U.S. policy that would coerce people not to have children—including taxes on children greater than the social cost of the children—I do accord to a community the right to make such a decision if there is a consensus on the matter." I would not write that now. I have seen more and more evidence of how poorly governmental regulation of private activities turns out—how often the results are just the opposite of what was intended (see chapters 5–7 and 17–18 on agriculture and the environment)—just as Friedrich Hayek and Milton Friedman have long argued. I also have been increasingly impressed by the likelihoods that (a) the so-called cleverest people are wrong about these and other fundamental matters—see the comments in various chapters about how wrong have been the predictions with respect to population and resources of economist John Maynard Keynes, philosopher Bertrand Russell, Nobel-winning mathematical economists Paul Samuelson, Wassily Leontief (member of the board of Population-Environment Balance), Jan Tinbergen, James Meade, and many many others; and (b) the willingness (or eagerness) of such clever people to bend government policy and hence the lives of a country's citizens to the yoke of their ideas, to disastrous ends; the example of the eugenics movement in Great Britain (here I mention Keynes again, Nobel-prize-winning mathematical economist James Meade, the founders of the population research establishment in Great Britain—whom I honor for their many path-breaking scientific discoveries in demography, despite the origin of their interest) and of course the horrible history of the eugenics idea and population control in Nazi Germany. I am not saying that many of the contemporary activities of organizations that began with the wrongest and most dangerous ideas about human nature believed in by their founders such as Margaret Sanger (see her autobiography) should now be considered tainted; I think that the population-control organizations should be examined for what they are now, not for what they were then. But I do believe that there is a continuing dangerous possibility that such organizations get so carried away by their general beliefs in the necessity of population control that they want to impose their ideas through the government apparatus, and I now do not believe that the government ever should have the right to do so, all the more because I have seen how these matters so often proceed on the basis of scientific ignorance and messianic zeal.

The Value for Truth

Perhaps the most important value in discussions of population and environmental policy is the value for truth.

Journalists often inquire into scholars' motivations. Several have asked me, "Why are you saying these things?" They seem doubtful when I answer that my strongest motivation is simply to find and state the truth about these matters. But perhaps this would seem more credible if you know that when I originally got interested in the economics of population I had exactly the opposite belief that I now have—I believed that population growth was, along with war, the greatest of dangers to humanity. It was only after I began to study the subject and found that the data did not support that original belief that my thoughts changed. And I was not disposed to close my eyes to the evidence because it did not square with my original beliefs. Rather, it was my beliefs that had to change, and I felt the need to study the subject more deeply to arrive at a satisfactory body of theory and empirical information. That's how I got into this field—just the opposite of being drawn to the field by beliefs that I now hold. (Does this mean that I claim to be perfectly truthful in all aspects of my life? Of course not; I'm as human as the next person.)

In my view, untruth is the ugliest and most dangerous pollution that humans face today. It is just about the only current pollution that cannot somehow be transformed into a product of value.

The various chapters contain many illustrations of statements so contrary to fact that they are either the product of ignorance or cynical dishonesty— between which it is often difficult to distinguish. Occasionally, however, one comes upon a falsehood so blatant that it seems impossible that it is other than an out-and-out lie. The self-confessed lie of the Club of Rome detailed in chapter 2 is one example. Here is another, authored by the Sierra Club: "Giant lumber companies . . . are deforesting the U.S. at the fastest pace in our history" (fund-raising letter, no date). Compare that statement with the figures in chapter 10 that show an increase rather than a decrease in U.S. timber growth.

Still another example is found in the following statement by Haroun Tazieff, an eminent volcanologist who served as French secretary of state for the prevention of natural and industrial disasters, about his experience with dioxins and PCBs:

> [When] I was . . . a Citizen Lambda [John Doe] I had believed in what was thus universally and imperatively affirmed as incontestable truth: that PCBs, and the dioxins they emit when heated to 300° Celsius, were frightful poisons. One or two

years of this propaganda had led government officials—just as incompetent as I was in matters of polychlorobiphenyls—to make them officially illegal.

A half-dozen years later, I found myself responsible for the prevention of disasters, natural and technological, for the French government. The natural ones I knew quite well, since they are related to my profession. As for technological disasters, it was necessary to inform myself. The very first dossier I asked to have delivered to me—so much had I been convinced of the extreme hazard of PCBs—was the one on the explosion at the chemical plant in Seveso, Italy, in July 1976. The study of this dossier and the inquest I led at the time revealed to me, first of all, that this so-called catastrophe had had not one single victim. (This gives the "Hiroshima of Chemistry," as it had been baptized by an ostensibly serious monthly science magazine, a tinge of anticlimax.)

Second, I learned that dioxins, according to the judgment of all the actual experts consulted (and of the very knowledgeable Academy of Science), are not at all "frightful" and have never, anywhere, killed anyone.

Thus, the matter of presenting the industrial accident at the ICMESA factory in Seveso as an apocalyptic catastrophe was a matter of deliberate disinformation—in less diplomatic language what one calls a lie.[29]

The stories of Love Canal and Agent Orange in Vietnam are quite similar to that of Seveso.

Sometimes public figures are frank about ignoring or manipulating the facts. Ambassador Richard Benedick stated: "A global climate treaty must be implemented even if there is no scientific evidence to back the greenhouse effect."[30] Former Senator Tim Wirth said, "We've got to ride the global warming issue. Even if the theory of global warming is wrong, we will be doing the right thing anyway, in terms of economic policy and environmental policy."[31] Here is another report, about Vice President Albert Gore, Jr.

Lately Gore and the distinguished biologist Paul Ehrlich have ventured into dangerous territory by suggesting that journalists quietly self-censor environmental evidence that is not alarming, because such reports, in Gore's words, "undermine the effort to build a solid base of public support for the difficult actions we must soon take."[32]

The fact that there are *any* such reports in print is amazing, because people try to hide evidence of dishonest tactics. The existence of such public reports is strong evidence that a lot of this is going on. And it suggests that the participants are so convinced of the virtue of their ends that they believe that any means are justified, no matter how indecent.

Here is my own value in this connection (whether or not I manage to live up to it): I believe that one should never shade the truth for effect, no matter how slight the exaggeration or the omission, and no matter how important the issue. And I believe that anyone who desires the label "scientist"—as I do— owes it to readers to present a balanced selection of the available evidence, even when one desires to advocate a particular point of view (which is entirely compatible with being a scientist). Yes, I try to put matters as sharply as possible, both to catch your attention and make my exposition as clear as I can, which leads some critics to label me "extreme" or "exaggerated" or "intemperate." But writing pointedly is very different from manipulation of the evidence to achieve those aims.

I hold this value for its own sake, and also because I believe that tampering with the truth is harmful in the long run—possibly harmful to one's own cause (John Stuart Mill taught excellently in *On Liberty* that people with minority views inevitably lose much more than they gain if they resort to the cheap tricks that people espousing majority views can get away with), and surely harmful to the overall cause of human progress. I do not claim that I live up to this ideal perfectly, only that I hold the value.

Herman Kahn liked to say, "I'm not an optimist, I'm a realist." I aspire to describe the situation as it really is. Based on the trends, the material future looks extremely bright. But that conclusion emerges from the data and from the theory built on those facts, not from a predetermined point of view.

Many do not believe that scientists should simply try to tell it like it is. For example, climatologist Stephen Schneider—who has been the most vigorous academic proponent of the view that the planet is warming due to CO_2 and other emissions, and that governments should intervene in individual's lives to change the course of events—takes this position:

> On the one hand, as scientists we are ethically bound to the scientific method, in effect promising to tell the truth, the whole truth, and nothing but—which means that we must include all the doubts, the caveats, the ifs, ands, and buts. On the other hand, we are not just scientists but human beings as well. And like most people we'd like to see the world a better place, which in this context translates into our working to reduce the risk of potentially disastrous climatic change. *To do this we need to get some broad-based support, to capture the public's imagination. That, of course, entails getting loads of media coverage. So we have to offer up scary scenarios, make simplified, dramatic statements, and make little mention of any doubts we might have.* This 'double ethical bind' we frequently find ourselves in cannot be solved by any formula. *Each of us has to decide what the right balance is between being effective and being honest.* I hope that means being both.[33]

The italics in the quotation above are mine, and indicate the quotation that I had intended to provide here. But Stephen Schneider complained that that quote (which I also used elsewhere) was not "in context." So I am happy to include the entire section.

A curious aspect of Schneider's case is that (as discussed in chapter 18) in the 1970s—a short time before he began to offer up scary scenarios of global warming—he had urged that the planet is cooling, and that steps should be taken to mitigate that effect. So one wonders: Does this sort of person ever stop and ask himself such questions as: Why should anyone believe me now if I was so wrong then? Would it have been a good thing if I had then been more effective in getting the public's attention? What about if I had stretched the truth then as I now advocate doing—would that have been a good thing?

Another example of bending the truth for environmental ends is the supposed Fifth Gospel speech of the nineteenth-century Suquamish Indian Chief Seattle about how "The earth is our mother . . . I have seen a thousand rotting buffaloes . . ." and so on. The speech was written by a scriptwriter for a 1972 film. And though the truth has long since been made known, the environmental groups continue to publicize the speech. A children's book about the speech sold 280,000 copies in six months, and was nominated for an American Booksellers Association Abby Award. (The winner of the award the previous year was a faked autobiography of a white man who claimed to have been raised by Cherokee Indians.)[34]

Still another example: Tom Horton, a Chesapeake Bay Foundation staff member, and Cindy Dunn, a field officer of the Alliance for the Chesapeake Bay, discussed the relationship of publicity to the state of the bay.

> "I think it's safe to say it's declining," says Dunn.
>
> "Changing," says Horton.
>
> Why, then, is it so frequently described as dying?
>
> "To raise money," Horton says, laughing.
>
> "It's hard to get people's attention," says Dunn. "If you said the bay is suffering from eutrophication, you've just glazed over your public[s' eyes]."[35]

Here is how truth was perverted by network television in Somalia:

> In the famine-stricken town of Baidoa, the crew set up an expensive satellite system in the courtyard of the regional hospital, so the well-paid correspondent could broadcast live with scenes of people dying in the background. The crew also wanted to film a surgeon performing an abdominal operation—but asked to place a garbage pail filled with bloody, amputated limbs on the operating table, next to the patient, because it would make a better image.[36]

An unusual view from the inside of the truth-bending process comes from Gene Lyons, a *Newsweek* writer who initiated a story on wildlife in Yellowstone Park, following on a book by Alston Chase[37] that was very critical of the National Park Service. The series of events were, in brief, that "the National Park Service lied—not once, but many times. Most distressing of all, however, was that my editors bought it."[38] And the decision makers "bought it" not because the truth was not brought to their attention but because "they're afraid of it."[39] Nor was that occurrence unusual. The "NPS has been sacrosanct for so long that it has grown unaccustomed to dealing with reporters who do any more than write down what they're told and compose what are known in the trade as 'puff pieces.'"[40] Lyons, a writer with very considerable credentials who quit his job because of this incident of falsification of the truth, concludes as follows: "What my story tells readers . . . is difficult to say. At present the urban-sentimental, wildlife-as-welfare-client view of natural resource issues is the prevailing belief of the national press."[41]

One does not often find documentation of falsification such as Lyons provided, because it is human nature that few of us are willing (and consider themselves able) to throw up a job in defense of the truth.

Here again is the epigraph from chapter 18:

> Perhaps the most disappointing aspect of the [Alaska National Wildlife Refuge pollution] debate is the false information being disseminated by well-meaning zealots who oppose any human activity on the Coastal Plain. Do they believe that their cause is so just that they are above and beyond the truth? (Walter Hickel, former governor of Alaska, 1991)

Caring about getting the facts right—especially the numbers—is a crucial part of commitment to the truth. Consider the species-loss case in chapter 31, and the Kurt Waldheim statement about famine in chapter 5. Still another example is the assertion that "140,000 Mexican women die yearly from illegal abortions," given in the medical magazine *Hippocrates*, which got the number from a book by Alan Riding, a former *New York Times* reporter. The assertion is patently ridiculous, because the total number of deaths from *any* cause of women in the childbearing ages of 15–44 was only about twenty thousand per year in the 1980s. Upon inquiry by another journalist,[42] neither the magazine nor the book author nor prestigious publisher Alfred A. Knopf would correct the error. Some combinations of pride and ideology can be greater than commitment to truth.

Values about Population in Relation to Other Values

There is a tendency among most of us human beings to attribute an entire constellation of values that are not ours to people who differ from us in some particular value. This polarization often is used to make our opponents seem to be devils so as to get others to reject the opponents and the particular value in issue.

Population and political attitudes are an excellent case in point. Those who are for (against) population control and consider themselves to be of the political Right refer to those who are against (for) population control as being on the political Left; those who are for (against) population control and consider themselves to be of the political Left refer to those who are against (for) population control as being on the political Right. Those who do not accept the view of population growth presented in my work have referred to this view both as Leftist and Marxist, and as Rightist and Radical Rightist. Because the

Reagan administration was closer to this view than the previous Carter administration, and closer than the Democratic Congress, Planned Parenthood has spent large sums of money "accusing" those who are against population control of being the "Radical Right."

In fact, views about population growth (and about immigration) span the political spectrum, and all political groups are split on these issues. The only exception is the Libertarians—who vehemently reject both the labels "Liberal" and "Conservative," and are consistently in favor of complete reproductive freedom and against barriers to immigration, both on grounds of their value of free choice. The Austrian economists, and Milton Friedman, share this and many other views with the Libertarians, and reject the label "Conservative" when others apply it to them (see Hayek's essay "Why I Am Not a Conservative"),[43] though they do not consider themselves to be Libertarians in general; if the reader insists on placing me in some niche, the closest niche is that of Hayek and Friedman (who disagree with each other in many important ways), and more generally, the niche of David Hume and Adam Smith. It should be noted here, however, that the nineteenth-century writer who had the soundest understanding and presented the best statement of population economics, taking into account the role of knowledge creation, was Friedrich Engels, and through him, Marx.

Summary

Science alone does not, and cannot, reach conclusions whether any population size is too large or too small, or whether the growth rate is too fast or too slow. Science can sometimes give citizens and policy makers a better understanding of the consequences of one or another decision about population. Sadly, however, scientific work on this subject has too often only misinformed and confused people. Social and personal decisions about childbearing, immigration, and death inevitably hinge upon values as well as upon probable consequences. There is necessarily a moral dimension to these decisions over and beyond whatever insights science may yield.

Conclusion

The Ultimate Resource

No food, one problem. Much food, many problems.
  (*Anonymous*)

The humour of blaming the present, and admiring the past, is strongly rooted in human nature, and has an influence even on persons endued with the profoundest judgment and most extensive learning.
  (*David Hume, "Of the Populousness of Ancient Nations," in 1777/1987*)

RAW MATERIALS and energy are getting less scarce. The world's food supply is improving. Pollution in the developed countries has been decreasing. Population growth has long-term benefits, though added people are a burden in the short run. Most important, fewer people are dying young.

These assertions, publicly stated in 1970 and then in the first edition of this book in 1981, have stood the test of time. The benign trends have continued until this edition. Our species is better off in just about every measurable material way. (The introduction lists others among the more dramatic findings of the book. Each chapter ends with a summary on its particular topic.) And there is stronger reason than ever to believe that these progressive trends will continue indefinitely.

Indeed, the trends toward greater cleanliness and less pollution of our air and water are even sharper than before, and cover a longer historical period and more countries (though the environmental disaster in Eastern Europe has only recently become public knowledge). The increase in availability and the decrease in raw materials scarcity have continued unabated, and have even speeded up. None of the catastrophes in food supply and famine that were forecast by the doomsayers have occurred; rather, the world's people are eating better than ever. The conventional beliefs of the doomsayers have been entirely falsified by events during past decades.

When we widen our scope beyond the physical matters of mortality, natural resources, and the environment covered in this book—to the standard of living, freedom, housing, and the like—we find that all the trends pertaining to economic welfare are heartening, also. Perhaps most exciting, the quantities of education that people obtain all over the world are sharply increasing, which means less tragic waste of human talent and ambition. (The evidence for those matters is found in Simon 1995.)*

---

* Almost no one challenges the facts of these benign trends—and those few who do, refuse to

Many of the trends reported here are in fact commonplace among the scientists who study them. The consensus of agricultural economists has consistently been an optimistic point of view about food supply, and the consensus of natural resource economists has never been gloomy. But the scientific consensus with respect to *population growth* largely changed in the 1980s. The consensus of population economists is now not far from what is written in this book; the profession and I agree that in the first few decades the effect of population growth is neutral. Such institutions as the World Bank and the National Academy of Sciences have recanted their former views that population growth is a crucial obstacle to economic development. (I am still in the minority when I emphasize the long-run benefits, on balance, of more people.)

The central issue is the effects of the number of people upon the standard of living, with special attention to raw materials and the environment. On balance the long-run effects are positive. The mechanism works as follows: Population growth and increase of income expand demand, forcing up prices of natural resources. The increased prices trigger the search for new supplies. Eventually new sources and substitutes are found. These new discoveries leave humanity better off than if the shortages had not occurred.

The vision which underlies and unifies the various topics is that of human beings who create more than they destroy. But even talented and energetic people require an incentive to create better techniques and organizations, and protection for the property that is the fruit of their labors. Therefore, the political-economic structure is the crucial determinant of the speed with which economic development occurs. In the presence of economic liberty and respect for property, population growth causes fewer problems in the short run, and greater benefits in the short run, than where the state controls economic activity.

In evaluating the effects of population growth, it is crucial to distinguish between the long run and the short run. Everyone agrees that in the short run additional people cause problems. When the pilgrims arrived in the United States, real problems arose for the native Americans. ("There goes the neighborhood.") And when some Indians pointed out that there would be benefits in the long run, each of the others said, "Not in my hunting grounds." Babies use diapers and then schools before they become economically productive. Even immigrants need some services before they get to work.

In the short run, all resources are limited—natural resources such as the pulpwood that went into making this book, created resources such as the number of pages Princeton University Press can allow me, and human resources such as the attention you will devote to what I say. In the short run,

---

bet on their assertions, or even on the future continuation of these trends. It is the conclusions drawn from these trends, plus the theoretical explanation of them given in the book, that others disagree with, and even feel cheated by. These conclusions literally "defy belief"—that is, they challenge deeply held convictions, and therein lies the difficulties these ideas face.

a greater use of any resource means pressure on supplies and a higher price in the market, or even rationing. Also in the short run there will always be shortage crises because of weather, war, politics, and population movements. The results that an individual notices are sudden jumps in taxes, inconveniences and disruption, and increases in pollution.

But what about the effects in the longer run? What would life be like now if the native Americans had managed to prevent immigration from Europe and there had been no population growth from then until now? Or if growth had stopped ten thousand years ago on Earth when there were only a million people? Do you think that our standard of living would be as high as it is now if the population had never grown from about four million human beings perhaps ten thousand years ago? I don't think we'd now have electric light or gas heat or autos or penicillin or travel to the moon or our present life expectancy of over seventy years at birth in rich countries, in comparison to the life expectancy of twenty to twenty-five years at birth in earlier eras, if population had not grown to its present numbers.

The longer run is a very different story than the shorter run. The standard of living has risen along with the size of the world's population since the beginning of recorded time. And with increases in income and population have come less severe shortages, lower costs, and an increased availability of resources, including a cleaner environment and greater access to natural recreation areas. And there is no convincing economic reason why these trends toward a better life, and toward lower prices for raw materials (including food and energy), should not continue indefinitely.

Contrary to common rhetoric, there are no meaningful limits to the continuation of this process. (Resolving this paradox entailed considerable explanation in the early chapters.) There is no physical or economic reason why human resourcefulness and enterprise cannot forever continue to respond to impending shortages and existing problems with new expedients that, after an adjustment period, leave us better off than before the problem arose. Adding more people will cause us more such problems, but at the same time there will be more people to solve these problems and leave us with the bonus of lower costs and less scarcity in the long run. The bonus applies to such desirable resources as better health, more wilderness, cheaper energy, and a cleaner environment.

This process runs directly against Malthusian reasoning and against the apparent common sense of the matter, which can be summed up as follows: The supply of any resource is fixed, and greater use means less to go around. The resolution of this paradox is not simple. Fuller understanding begins with the idea that the relevant measure of scarcity is the cost or price of a resource, not any physical measure of its calculated reserves. And the appropriate way for us to think about extracting resources is not in physical units, pounds of copper or acres of farmland, but rather in the services we get from these resources—the electrical transmission capacity of copper, or the food values and gastronomic enjoyment the farmland provides. Following on this is the fact that economic history has not gone as Malthusian reasoning suggests. The prices of all goods, and of the services they provide, have fallen in the long run, by all reasonable measures. And this irrefutable fact must be taken into account as a fundamental datum that can reasonably be projected into the future, rather than as a fortuitous chain of circumstances that cannot continue.

Resources in their raw form are useful and valuable only when found, understood, gathered together, and harnessed for human needs. The basic ingredient in the process, along with the raw elements, is human knowledge. And we develop knowledge about how to use raw elements for our benefit only in response to our needs. This includes knowledge for finding new sources of raw materials such as copper, for growing new resources such as timber, for creating new quantities of capital such as farmland, and for finding new and better ways to satisfy old needs, such as successively using iron and aluminum and plastic in place of clay or copper. Such knowledge has a special property. It yields benefits to people other than the ones who develop it, apply it, and try to capture its benefits for themselves. Taken in the large, an increased need for resources usually leaves us with a permanently greater capacity to get them, because we gain knowledge in the process. And there is no meaningful physical limit—even the commonly mentioned total substance of the Earth—to our capacity to keep growing forever.

There is only one important resource which has shown a trend of increasing scarcity rather than increasing abundance. That resource is the most important of all—*human beings*. There are more people on Earth now than ever before. But if we measure the scarcity of people the same way that we measure the scarcity of other economic goods—by how much we must pay to obtain their services—we see that wages and salaries have been going up all over the world, in poor countries as well as in rich countries. The amount that you must pay to obtain the services of a driver or a cook has risen in India, just as the price of a driver or cook—or economist—has risen in the United States over the decades. This increase in the price of peoples' services is a clear indication that people are becoming more scarce even though there are more of us.

The most dramatic evidence that development of countries does not depend upon their rates of population growth is shown by the economic histories from 1950 onward of the three pairs of countries that began with the same demographic rates as well as the same histories and cultures but were split into two very different political-economic systems: North and South Korea, East and West Germany, Taiwan and China. The countries with controlled economies and unfree societies have performed abysmally compared to their twins. The enormous influence of the political-economic system leaves nothing for population change to explain in these individual countries.

Many who oppose population growth assume that additional people now would not have positive effects in the long run. Or, at least they put a low weight on those future positive effects. And they believe that more people now implies that the air will be dirtier than otherwise ten years in the future (say), and there will be less natural resources available. And they assume that the standard of living would be lower than otherwise.

An interesting aspect of this short-run view is that many who hold it are ecologically minded. One of the great intellectual strengths of ecology is its long view of the consequences of present happenings, and a propensity to search out the indirect and hard-to-see consequences, both of which tendencies it shares with economics. If one raises one's eyes beyond the most immediate future, we see that the negative short-run effects are more than countered. This is seen in the trend evidence of long-run progress. And there is solid theory that fits these facts. That theory again is as follows: More people, and increased income, cause problems in the short run. This increased scarcity of resources causes prices to rise. The higher prices present opportunity, and prompt inventors and entrepreneurs to search for solutions. Many fail, at cost to themselves. But in a free society, solutions are eventually found. And in the long run the new developments leave us better off than if the problems had not arisen. That is, prices end up lower than before the increased scarcity occurred. We have seen many examples of this process, such as the energy transition from burning wood to coal to oil to nuclear power (chapter 11), and in the development of ways to handle wastes so as not only to reduce the scope of the problem but also to convert "bad" waste to economic "goods."

At work is a general process that underlies all the specific findings in the book: humans on average build a bit more than they destroy, and create a bit more than they use up. This process is, as the physicists say, an "invariancy"[1] applying to all metals, all fuels, all foods, and all other measures of human welfare, in almost all countries at almost all times; it can be thought of as a theory of economic history. The crucial evidence for the existence of this process is found in the fact that each generation leaves a bit more true wealth—the resources to create material and nonmaterial goods—than the generation began with. That is, the standard of living of each generation is on average higher than the generation before.

Indeed, it is necessarily so. If humankind did not have a propensity to create more than it uses, the species would have perished a long time ago. This propensity to build may be taken as a fundamental characteristic that is part of our evolution. This is the overarching theory that explains why events turn out in exactly the opposite fashion from what Malthus and his followers foresaw.

Underlying the thinking of most writers who have a point of view different from mine is the concept of fixity or finiteness of resources in the relevant system of discourse. This concept is central in Malthus, of course. But the idea probably has always been a staple of human thinking because so much of our situation must sensibly be regarded as fixed in the short run—the bottles of beer in the refrigerator, our paycheck, the amount of energy parents have to play basketball with their kids. But the thema underlying my thinking about resources (and the thinking of a minority of others) is that the relevant system of discourse has a long enough horizon that it makes sense to treat the system as not fixed, rather than finite in any operational sense. We see the resource system as being as unlimited as the number of thoughts a person might have, or the number of variations that might ultimately be produced by biological evolution. That is, a key difference between the thinking of those who worry about impending doom, and those who see the prospects of a better life for more people in the future, apparently is whether one thinks in closed-system or open-system terms. For example, those who worry that the second law of thermodynamics dooms us to eventual decline necessarily see our world as a closed system with respect to energy and entropy; those who view the relevant universe as unbounded view the second law of thermodynamics as irrelevant to this discussion. I am among those who view the relevant part of the physical and social universe as open for most purposes. Which thema is better for thinking about resources and population is not subject to scientific test. Yet it profoundly affects our thinking. I believe that here lies the root of the key difference in thinking about population and resources.

Why do so many people think of the planet and our presently known resources as a closed system, to which no resources will be added in the future? There are a variety of reasons. (1) Malthusian fixed-resources reasoning is simple and fits the isolated facts of our everyday lives, whereas the expansion of resources is complex and indirect and includes all creative human activity—it cannot be likened to our own larders or wallets. The same concepts, rhetoric, and even wording pop up in one resource and environmental scare after another—with respect to water as to oil,[2] fluoridation of drinking water as with nuclear power,[3] global warming as with acid rain as with the ozone layer.[4] (2) There are always immediate negative effects from an increased pressure on resources, whereas the benefits only come later. It is natural to pay more attention to the present and the near future than to the more distant future. (3) There are often special-interest groups that alert us to impending shortages of particular resources such as timber or clean air. But no one has the same stake in trying to convince us that the long-run prospects for a resource are better than we think. (4) It is easier to get people's attention (and television time and printer's ink) with frightening forecasts than with soothing forecasts. (5) Organizations that form in response to temporary or nonexistent dangers, and develop the capacity to raise funds from public-spirited citizens and governments that are aroused to fight the danger, do not always disband when the danger evaporates or the problem is solved. (6) Ambition and the urge for profit are powerful elements in our successful struggle to satisfy our needs. These motives, and the markets in which they work, often are not pretty, and many people would prefer not to depend on a social system that employs these forces to make us better off. (7) Associating oneself with environmental causes is one of the quickest and easiest ways to get a wide reputation for high-minded concern. It requires no deep thinking and steps on almost no one's toes.

The apparently obvious way to deal with resource problems—have the government control the amounts and prices of what consumers consume and suppliers supply—is inevitably counterproductive in the long run because the controls and the price fixing prevent us from making the cost-efficient adjustments that we would make in response to the increased short-run costs, adjustments that eventually would more than alleviate the problem. Sometimes governments must play a crucial role to avoid short-run disruptions and disaster, and to ensure that no group consumes public goods without paying the real social cost. But the appropriate times for governments to play such roles are far fewer than the times they are called upon to do so by those inclined to turn to authority to tell others what to do, rather than allow each of us to respond with self-interest and imagination.

One of the main themes of this book, which this edition emphasizes even more than the first edition because there is now a greater weight of evidence behind it, is the proper role of government; to set market rules that are as impersonal and as general as possible, allowing individuals to decide for themselves how and what to produce and what to consume, in a manner that infringes as little as possible on the rights of others to do the same, and where each pays the full price to others of the costs to others of one's own activities. Support for this principle appears in chapter after chapter as we view the history and the statistical data on such issues as food production, supply of natural resources, and the like.

It is not only the human mind and the human spirit that are crucial, but also the framework of society. The political-economic organization of a country has the most influence upon its economic progress. In 1742 (first edition), the man whom I regard as the greatest philosopher who ever lived, and one of the greatest economists of all time—David Hume—wrote this: "Multitudes of people, necessity, and liberty, have begotten commerce in Holland."[5] In that one short sentence, Hume summarized everything important about economic progress—*economic liberty*, which comes from a country being "ruled by laws rather than men," allows people to make the most of their individual talents and opportunities; *necessity*—that is, in Holland's case, the lack of great stretches of fertile land on which to grow crops easily, and therefore the necessity of creating new fertile land by fighting the sea for that land; and *multitudes of people*—the human talent to invent new ways of doing things and of organizing an effective society. That is the heart of the story told in this book.

The greatest asset of the United States and of other economically advanced countries is the political and legal and economic organization. Compare how easy it is to do business (for example get inputs from suppliers) in the United States with the way it was in the Soviet Union, and as it will certainly continue to be in Russia for some years after this is written in the 1990s.

But again, people look at the matter in the small rather than in the large, and don't see the long-run benefits of problems. Perhaps our willingness to believe that "clever" people can make sound decisions and render useful advice when in such positions as head of the World Bank or IMF is related to our belief that people can find a pattern even when there is no pattern. We are reluctant to think that we as human beings can do no better than chance in such matters.

Is Our Age Different from Ages That Have Gone Before?

Again and again I have argued the importance of taking a long view backwards so that we can see the continuity of the trends. People err by thinking that their age is different than all that have gone before. Especially this is true when they think about the dangers of their own age.

Having said this, I note that our age is fundamentally different than any other age that has been or that could come, most especially in mortality and life expectation. One can only go once from an expectation of twenty-five to seventy-five years of life at birth.

The change in opportunity is almost as great, and perhaps almost as unrepeatable. One can only progress once from almost no access to secondary and tertiary education to almost universal access to them. And the idea of going beyond does not seem to be something that society bestows or could bestow.

And materially: Sometimes I think that our very last physical needs are being taking care of, to the extent that technology can do so. In my own short lifetime we have gone (even in a rich country) from shoveling coal into the furnace and banking it at night, and winding up a spring alarm clock with a chain at the end to open the furnace in the morning, and then carrying out the ashes to the street in a bucket—ashes which might also be used to harden the mud in the spring on the basketball court—to fully automatic furnaces with fully automatic thermostats and air conditioners, and the like. How much further can we go? Does this all mean that I lack imagination when I cannot see further directions for technology in these respects? You go away from home, pick up the telephone, dial some numbers, and anyone who has called you can be heard on your tape machine. How could communication be improved much from this? How much can frustration be reduced from this? Of course frustration is always a function of expectations. But . . .

What Does the Future Hold?

The years since its publication have been kind to the forecasts of the first edition. Or more importantly, the years have been good for humanity. The benign trends have continued until this edition. Our species is better off in just about every measurable material way. And there is stronger reason than ever to believe that these progressive trends will continue indefinitely.

Based on these trends, the long-run material prospects are so favorable and so certain that (as I mentioned earlier) I am prepared to bet on them, expanding the offer made in the first edition. I'll bet a week's or month's pay that just about any trend pertaining to human welfare will improve rather than get worse (my winnings go to charity).

People alive now are living in the midst of—and from one point of view, just ending—the most extraordinary two centuries in human history—the years both before us and probably after us, too. Humanity will soon have succeeded in the historic battle against early death. Most inhabitants of the rich countries already are reasonably sure of a satisfying diet, decent shelter, and access to sufficient education. What is still to come is to bring these benefits to all on Earth. And that may take half a century or a century.

Some writers worry that unsound ideas will stop progress and bring down civilization. Their slogan is "Ideas have consequences." Yes, ideas matter, and fighting for the truth can make a difference in how fast we make progress. Unlike those writers, however, I do not think that ideas are decisive in the long run. Yes, Marxism and a belief in rational social control turned Eastern Europe backwards and created havoc for seventy-five years and probably much more. Yes, anti-growthers who close their eyes to science can stop nuclear power for a while, and waste billions on unnecessary cleanup campaigns. But I believe that in the long run, in a world of modern global communication and mobility, real material improvements cannot be prevented forever. Nuclear power will have its way because it is just too much better than alternatives for antinuclear zealots to deny it to others forever. Poor women and men want to improve their lot, married couples want to have children, and people want freedom; these tendencies are so deeply and "naturally" ingrained in most human beings that abstract arguments about overpopulation or the virtues of simple living or the subordination of the individual's desires to the state will convince only a small fraction of the most persuadable for more than a short time. As Lincoln said, You can only fool some of the people some of the time. Human nature seeks human betterment on average; there is enough evidence of this in history—perhaps most especially the indisputable evidence that each generation tends to leave more to its descendants than it acquired from its ancestors—so that the proposition can be taken as fact without further corroboration.

Writers and scholars are entitled to think themselves a bit more important than they really are; Adam Smith even advises the wisdom of that. But I think that some of us flatter ourselves *too* much when we think that our ideas—or those of our opponents—are so powerful that they can affect the course of human development more than temporarily (although even temporary effect is important).

Material insufficiency and environmental problems have their benefits, over and beyond the improvements which they evoke. They focus the attention of individuals and communities, and constitute a set of challenges which can bring out the best in people. (The competition from Japan illustrates how we need our problems. The United States and Europe will certainly be much better off in the next few decades because the Japanese came along to make us pull up our socks.) In the absence of such problems, people turn to less pressing material problems, such as ever-less-threatening and ever-more-benign environmental conditions (see chapter 15), and to nonmaterial issues such as intergroup equity, which often bring out the worst rather than the best in people. Material success even leads people to question whether that success indicates human progress or instead causes greater problems; a familiar example is the lament that young people with too much time and money cause trouble for themselves and others. Again: no bread, one problem; plenty of bread, many problems.

As Beisner puts it, we can forecast with certainty that humanity will be richer in the future than now; we cannot forecast with any confidence whether at any given future time humanity will be more or less evil than now.[6] It may be that for at least some time—until the evolution of our knowledge and our society, together with our imaginations, put us onto a new track—the developed world will suffer from a shortage of challenges to bring out the best in people. It may be that, just as additional people are the ultimate resource to resolve human problems, the absence of satisfying challenges may be the ultimate shortage.

I do not say that everything now is fine, of course. Children are still hungry and sick; some people live out lives of physical and intellectual poverty, and lack of opportunity; war or some new pollution may do us all in. What I am saying is that for most of the relevant economic matters I have checked, the trends are positive rather than negative. And I doubt that it does the troubled people of the world any good to say that things are getting worse though they are really getting better. And false prophecies of doom can damage us in many ways.

Is a rosy future guaranteed? Of course not. There always will be temporary shortages and resource problems where there are strife, political blundering, and natural calamities—that is, where there are people. But the natural world allows, and the developed world promotes through the marketplace, responses to human needs and shortages in such manner that one backward step leads to 1.0001 steps forward, or thereabouts. That's enough to keep us headed in a life-sustaining direction.

Which should be our vision? The doomsayers of the population-control movement offer a vision of limits, decreasing resources, a zero-sum game, conservation, deterioration, fear, and conflict, calling for more governmental intervention in markets and family affairs. Or should our vision be that of those who look optimistically upon people as a resource rather than as a burden—a vision of receding limits, increasing resources and possibilities, a game in which everyone can win, creation, building excitement, and the belief that persons and firms, acting spontaneously in the search of their individual welfare, regulated only by rules of a fair game, will produce enough to maintain and increase economic progress and promote liberty?

And what should our mood be? The population restrictionists say we should be sad and worry. I and many others believe that the trends suggest joy and celebration at our newfound capacity to support human life—healthily, and with fast-increasing access to education and opportunity all over the world. I believe that the population restrictionists' hand-wringing view leads to despair and resignation. Our view leads to hope and progress, in the reasonable expectation that the energetic efforts of humankind will prevail in the future, as they have in the past, to increase worldwide our numbers, our health, our wealth, and our opportunities.

So to sum up the summary: In the short run, all resources are limited. An example of such a finite resource is the amount of time and attention that you will devote to what I have written. The longer run, however, is a different story. The standard of living has risen along with the size of the world's population since the beginning of recorded time. There is no convincing economic reason why these trends toward a better life should not continue indefinitely.

The key theoretical idea is this: Increased population and a higher standard of living cause actual and expected shortages, and hence price rises. A higher price represents an opportunity that attracts profit-minded entrepreneurs and socially minded inventors to seek new ways to satisfy the shortages. Some fail, at cost to themselves. A few succeed, and the final result is that we end up *better off* than if the original shortage problems had never arisen. That is, we need our problems, though this does not imply that we should purposely *create* additional problems for ourselves.

Of course progress does not come about automatically. And my message certainly is not one of complacency, though anyone who predicts reduced scarcity of resources has always drawn that label.[7] In this I agree with the doomsayers—that our world needs the best efforts of all humanity to improve our lot. I part company with them in that they expect us to come to a bad end despite the efforts we make, whereas I expect a continuation of successful efforts. And I believe that their message is self-fulfilling, because if you expect your efforts to fail because of inexorable natural limits, then you are likely to feel resigned, and therefore to literally resign. But if you recognize the possibility—in fact the probability—of success, you can tap large reservoirs of energy and enthusiasm.

Adding more people causes problems, but people are also the means to solve these problems. The main fuel to speed our progress is our stock of knowledge, and the brake is our lack of imagination. The ultimate resource is people—skilled, spirited, and hopeful people who will exert their wills and imaginations for their own benefit, and inevitably they will benefit not only themselves but the rest of us as well.

Afternote 1 _____

"Born without a Chance"

Born without a Chance

The Time: Napoleonic in Europe, Jeffersonian in
   America.
The Scene: An outlying border state, sometimes called
   "the dark and bloody ground."
The Exact Date: February 12, 1809.

A squalid village set in wintry mud.
A hub-deep oxcart slowly groans and creaks.
A horseman hails and halts. He shifts his cud
And speaks:

"Well, did you hear? Tom Lincoln's wife today.
The devil's luck for folk as poor as they!
   Poor Tom! poor Nance!
Poor youngun born without a chance!

"A baby in that Godforsaken den,
That worse than cattle pen!
Well, what are they but cattle? Cattle? Tutu!
A critter is beef, hide and tallow, but
Who'd swap one for the critters of that hut?
   White trash! small fry!
Whose only instincts are to multiply!
   They're good at that,
And so, today, God wot! another brat!

"Another squawking, squalling, red-faced good-for-naught
Spilled on the world, heaven only knows for what.
   Better if he were black,
For then he'd have a shirt upon his back,
And something in his belly, as he grows.
More than he's like to have, as I suppose.
   Yet there be those
Who claim 'equality' for this new brat,
   And that damned democrat
Who squats today where Washington once sat,

He'd have it that this Lincoln cub might be
Of even value in the world with you and me!

"Yes, Jefferson, Tom Jefferson, who but he?
Who even hints that black men should be free.
That featherheaded fool would tell you maybe
A president might lie in this new baby!

In this new squawker born without a rag
To hide himself! Good God, it makes me gag!
   This human spawn
Born for the world to wipe its feet upon
   A few more years hence, but now
More helpless than the litter of a sow,
And—Oh, well! send the womenfolks to see to Nance.

"Poor little devil! born without a chance!"
(Edmund Vance Cooke; suggested by Donald Bishop)

Afternote 2

Prometheus Bound

For men at first had eyes but saw to no purpose; they had ears but did not hear. Like the shapes of dreams they dragged through their long lives and handled all things in bewilderment and confusion. They did not know of building houses with bricks to face the sun; they did not know how to work in wood. They lived like swarming ants in holes in the ground, in the sunless caves of the earth. For them there was no secure token by which to tell winter nor the flowering spring nor the summer with its crops; all their doings were indeed without intelligent calculation until I showed them the rising of the stars, and the settings, hard to observe. And further I discovered to them numbering, pre-eminent among subtle devices, and the combining of letters as a means of remembering all things, the Muses' mother, skilled in craft. It was I who first yoked beasts for them in the yokes and made of those beasts the slaves of trace chain and pack saddle that they might be man's substitute in the hardest tasks; and I harnessed to the carriage, so that they loved the rein, horses, the crowning pride of the rich man's luxury. It was I and none other who discovered ships, the sail-driven wagons that the sea buffets. Such were the contrivances that I discovered for men—alas for me! For I myself am without contrivance to rid myself of my present affliction.

Chorus

What you have suffered is indeed terrible. . . .

Prometheus

Hear the rest, and you will marvel even more at the crafts and resources I contrived. Greatest was this: in the former times if a man fell sick he had no defense against the sickness, neither healing food nor drink, nor unguent; but through the lack of drugs men wasted away, until I showed them the blending of mild simples wherewith they drive out all manner of diseases. It was I who arranged all the ways of seercraft, . . . Beneath the earth, man's hidden blessing, copper, iron, silver, and gold—will anyone claim to have discovered these before I did? No one, I am very sure, who wants to speak truly and to the purpose. One brief word will tell the whole story: all arts that mortals have come from Prometheus.

(The Complete Greek Tragedies, *vol. 1*, Aeschylus, *David Grene and Richmond Lattimore, eds. [Chicago: University of Chicago Press, 1959], pp. 327–28)*

Epilogue _____

My Critics and I

[A] violent outcry has been made against the book, exactly answering the
expectation I always had of the justice, the wisdom, the charity, and fair dealing
of those whose good will I despaired of. It has been presented by the Grand Jury
and condemned by thousands who never saw a word of it. It has been preached
against before my Lord Mayor; and an utter refutation of it is daily expected from a
reverend divine, who has called me names in the advertisements and threatened
to answer me in two months time for above five months together. . . . [He] shows
a fine talent for invectives and great sagacity in discovering atheism.
  (*Bernard Mandeville*, Fable of the Bees, *1705*)

In general, opinions contrary to those commonly received can only obtain a hearing
by studied moderation of language, and the most cautious avoidance of unnecessary
offence, from which they hardly ever deviate even in a slight degree without losing
ground: while unmeasured vituperation employed on the side of the prevailing
opinion really does deter people from professing contrary opinions, and from
listening to those who profess them.
  (*John Stuart Mill*, Utilitarianism, Liberty, and Representative Government, *1859*)

'Tis the majority
In this, as all, prevails.
Assent, and you are sane;
Demur,—you're straightway dangerous,
And handled with a chain.
  (*Emily Dickinson, "Much madness is divinest sense"*)

IT SEEMED like a useful and entertaining idea when Jack Repcheck, editor at
Princeton University Press, suggested that a reply to critics of the first edition
be included in this second edition. It would be an opportunity to discuss the
validity of criticisms of central issues, and thereby either strengthen the book's
arguments or tell which arguments were validly criticized and hence abandoned in this edition.

When I came to write this, however, I saw that the situation was not what
we had envisioned. Despite the gratifyingly large amount of attention the book
received, there has been little serious criticism by economists. A large proportion of the attacks have come from biologists, who for many decades and
centuries—back to Benjamin Franklin, as discussed on page 343—have

voiced the strongest fears of population growth.[1] And much of what they write is outside the framework of economics (though the subject of the book is the economics of population), and even outside of ordinary scientific discourse, as will be seen below.

I'll first address the substantive issues, then discuss the personal attacks. Lastly, I'll offer some observations on the nature of the criticism, and on its effects.

One reason for the paucity of serious criticism of the book's theory and factual base is that much of the book's core argument is not at all novel or radical, though it seems so to noneconomists. Indeed, much of what is written here had been settled wisdom before I came along.

Food. The benign trends in food production and consumption have been known to respected agricultural economists—M. K. Bennett and Theodore Schultz perhaps preeminent among the consensus—since the 1950s or the 1960s. From them I learned the central ideas conveyed about agriculture here. Even those who were dubious about agriculture a decade or two ago have now come around to this consensus, perhaps mainly because of the continued accumulation of data which have ever more sharply contradicted the doom-sayers. For example, we now read in the newspaper:

> The World Bank . . . on the eve of a two-day conference on "Overcoming Global Hunger" . . . sought to refute the Malthusian thesis that the world will reach a point where it cannot produce enough food for an expanding population. In fact, said bank Vice President Ismail S[i]rageldin, agricultural prices are "at their lowest levels in history" and world food production "rises faster than the population."[2]

For anyone who has followed the World Bank's utterances since the 1970s, this public statement represents an amazing turnaround.

Evidence of this consensus about the trends can be found even in the most unlikely of places. Lester Brown and his Worldwatch Institute—Brown having been one of the harsh critics of this book—continue to warn of impending food shortages, just as Brown has for decades (see chapters 5–7 and my 1990 book). In 1994 they warn that (according to the newspaper) "After 40 years of record food production gains, output per person has reversed with 'unanticipated abruptness.'"* In other words, they implicitly confess that all the earlier dire warnings by Brown were wrong and the food situation has improved, rather than deteriorated as he had forecast it would—a confirmation of what the consensus of agricultural economists has said for decades. Yet as always in the past, Brown once more reads into an inevitable current irregularity in the trend a change in the long-term pattern. And the press gives it huge play without even consulting the mainstream agricultural economists.

---

* *Los Angeles Times,* January 18, 1994, p. H1.

Natural resources. Similarly, under the influence of Harold Barnett and Chandler Morse's 1967 *Scarcity and Growth* (the great book which was my tutor), many resource economists had long ago moved far toward the position on which this book stands with regard to natural resources. True, I push these ideas further than most, but this is not a theoretical difference; the main novelty here on resource topics is the broad data that I provide, together with the explicit assertions about nonfiniteness which might even be considered implicit in some predecessors' writings.

Pollution. Early in this century A. C. Pigou provided the basic economic theory of environmental pollution that is the backbone of my chapters on that topic. Nothing radical in this book for economists to criticize.

Population growth. With respect to the effects of population growth itself, the economics profession as a whole did not endorse it as I did in the first edition or in my earlier professional work. But for centuries there have been important voices arguing in favor of population growth, including William Petty, David Hume, and Adam Smith. Malthus himself reversed his position in the second edition of his *Essay*. Even economists not persuaded of population growth's advantages have never worried greatly about its consequences because of the economist's emphasis on the remarkable properties of spontaneous economic adjustment to change. So it was not very surprising when during the 1980s there was a shift among professional economists who study the economics of population effects to the position where they now stand, as encapsulated in the 1986 NAS report which is not far from the position of this book, though that fact is not reflected in the popular press. (The few economists who call their work "ecological economics" and take a strong negative position on growth are far from the mainstream of economics.)

Before proceeding to discuss substantive criticisms and negative rhetoric, it should be noted that a fair amount of the huge attention the book received— the reviews in journals, magazines, and newspapers that found their way to me came to an amazing 150, with many more since then in books and in personal correspondence—has been positive. I am grateful for the helpful ideas and positive words. No more will be said about the positive comments here, with the sole exception of two letters from Friedrich Hayek appended to this chapter.

Substantive Issues

Martha Campbell, a political scientist and founder of two population "activist" organizations, collected and published the major substantive criticisms of my work on population. Her aim was to provide a compendium of refutations of my work. To her credit, Campbell stuck to discussable issues and left aside the sorts of nonsubstantive ad hominem attacks to be discussed later. The compendium appeared in *Focus* (vol. 3, no. 1, 1993), a publication of Carrying Capacity Network, an organization dedicated to reducing the rate of population growth.

I'll address all the main issues in Campbell's review so that the reader can be sure that I'm not ducking fundamental criticisms. (It is a shame that I have to resort to devices like this to assure the reader that I'm being honest, but as you will see below, my scientific integrity is regularly called into question by those who dislike the ideas contained here.) I shall take up issues largely in the order in which Campbell gives them; a few that either seem to be confused or trivial will not be mentioned. I will start at her beginning and march down through her list; luckily, Campbell put the most important issues first. This sequential procedure should also work to reassure the reader that I am not avoiding the hard issues and selecting the creampuffs for reply. Furthermore, the fact that I address myself mostly to the critics she marshals should add confidence that I am not hunting-and-picking through the literature for the arguments I can most easily deal with. (This sounds defensive, of course; later you'll see why.)

It is worth noting again that though the main issues the book addresses are economic, only a small proportion of Campbell's criticisms are by academic economists; most are by sociologists and organizational advocates.

Finiteness

The first issue listed is finiteness; indeed, the central focus of substantive criticism is the concept of finiteness. My general reply is presented in the context of the argument itself in chapters 3 and 4. In Campbell's list the issue is mentioned first (raised by Herman Daly and John Cobb) in connection with my merely linguistic illustration of the concept of finiteness in mathematics where it is defined as countability, using the example of a geometric line. I discuss this metaphor and the criticism of it in chapter 3. (I probably should have foregone this excursion into pure logic and avoided misleading some readers.)

Lindsey Grant then attacks what he calls

> a faith in infinite substitutability that Simon probably acquired from the academic economists. The assumption is not based on any systematic rationale, nor is it buttressed by any evidence. . . . Biologists and ecologists have been trying without success to persuade the economists that the assumption is terribly dangerous in a finite world."

I do not say that "infinite substitutability" is possible now or at any future moment. What I do say is that substitutability is *increasing* with the passage of time; there have been more and cheaper substitutes for each raw material with the passage of time.

Finiteness by itself is not testable, except insofar as the fact that no one is able to state the absolute size of the relevant system (our cosmos) demonstrates the absence of finiteness in its dictionary sense. But the relevant evidence we have available—decreasing prices and increasing substitutability—is not what one would expect from a finite system. (Hence the critics are reduced to saying that all the evidence of history is merely "temporary" and must reverse "sometime," which is the sort of statement that is outside the canon of ordinary science.)

There is no doubt that my assertion of nonfiniteness is anti-commonsensical and, indeed, mindboggling; regrettably (and contrary to what Grant and others assert) it is not explicit in standard economics, though it is not incompatible with standard received economics. But the critics simply do not come to grips with the matter that the available data are not consistent with the assumption of finiteness.

In the same section Keyfitz disagrees with other critics and agrees with me that "there seem to be adequate amounts of the nonrenewable resources" (though I would not put it that way). He then argues that the real problem is overuse of *renewable* resources. But presumably this could only be so if the supply of renewable resources is limited by some nonexpandable (finite) resources. If so, it is simply another form of the above discussion of finite resources.

Preston has written that there is no benefit in having additional people in the present period because the only question is whether a given increment of people will live now or some time in the future. "It is surely possible that by having more [people] now we are reducing the numbers who may be alive at future dates—for example, if we have increased the risks of social or environmental disaster" (1982, p. 177). A reasonable interpretation of this is that more people contending for resources in a given period can have bad effects, and that more use in one period means less to be used in later periods. But once again this depends on the assumption of a fixed (finite) quantity of resources, the "common sense" assumption which I hope I have dispatched (or at least called into question) in chapters 3 and 4. This criticism also implicitly assumes that the present value of the contribution of a given person to the creation of knowledge is the same whether the person lives in one period or another, a complex idea which would need some arguing to make plausible.

Nothing I have written is intended to suggest that *during any particular period* there may not be too much use of any resource, renewable or nonrenewable; indeed, I expect temporary overuses (for example, overuse of forest resources in various countries in various centuries) just as I expect boom-and-bust cycles in all other human endeavors. But this is a matter of management and adjustment in dealing with, and riding out, the ups and downs, rather than a matter of ultimate finiteness.

Knowledge and Population

The second issue in Campbell's list is the endogeneity of growth with respect to human numbers. The first-mentioned critic (H. W. Arndt) says: "The notion that technological progress is a function of population because the larger the population the larger the number of inventive minds strains credulity." In *my* view, the notion that increase in knowledge is *not* a function of the number of people seems to strain credulity; after all, where does knowledge come from except from human minds? But credulity is not the test; the conclusion should depend not on what one or another person finds credible, but rather evidence should be the test.

Neither Arndt nor anyone else brings evidence to bear *against* the proposition, while in this book and my other books (see especially Simon 1992), much evidence is presented in the book in support of the proposition that there is a strong connection between population and production of knowledge, holding income level constant.

Here is one more piece of data which I came across after completing the book: According to Derek de Sola Price, each working scientist produces about three technical papers in a lifetime, a number which has remained rather constant over the years.[3] Price also presents many time-series which show that there has been a huge rise in the amount of new knowledge as measured by the number of scientific journals, citations, and the like, during the past four or so centuries as population has risen. This squares with all the other evidence provided in this book.

The critics attack these data by reducing my argument to a vulgar form in which I do not make it—that the amount of new technology produced should be a function of numbers without consideration of other variables such as education. Thomas Merrick says that "few of the technological advances now available to LDC's were developed by LDC's." He even suggests that "many modern technologies in fact exacerbate LDC problems." And Keyfitz says, "Julian Simon thinks it [technology] is driven by population; if that were so the inhabitants of squatter colonies in Mexico City or hungry cattle herders in the Sahel would be very creative." This issue is dealt with in chapter 26 wherein I discuss why China and India do not now produce as much new technology, and are not as rich, as the Western countries. And in the evidence pertaining to the amount of science in various countries that Love and I developed (see page 382), we held constant the per capita income of the various countries as a proxy for educational level; the production of technology then is demonstrably a function of education as well as a function of numbers.

Campbell quotes A. Bartlett as writing that I regard "Mozart and Einstein as mere statistical events. In this simple view, the more births the more Mozarts" (the issue dealt with just above). But Bartlett then continues, "This suggests that we should breed to the maximum biological rate and we should deplore the natural growth limitation processes whose existence he has praised."

Never have I written that we should "breed to the maximum," nor is it implied by the previous statement by Bartlett (which also is a vulgarized form of my argument); this is typical of much of the criticism—implying to me a view I do not hold, and then criticizing it as ludicrous. Furthermore, there are many costs and benefits of there being more or fewer people other than the production of new knowledge, important though that may be.

In the same section Campbell quotes Peter Timmer: "Wise and sensitive policy aimed at solving the short-run problems that Simon ignores is the pressing issue for most of mankind." I do not at all "ignore" short-run effects. But I do insist that long-run effects should be considered also, and the entire range of effects over time should be brought together into a present value calculation; it is the attending *only* to short-run effects that has badly misled so many writers, because the longer-run effects often are the opposite of the short-run effects. Indeed, this is true of all investments; the outgo happens early while the income only occurs later.

Sirageldin and Kantner do not seem to grasp this fundamental aspect of the investment process. Campbell quotes them: "The main thesis . . . is that a moderate rate of population growth, although harmful in the short-run [which Timmer above says that I "ignore"], is beneficial in the long-run . . . [This thesis] is logically inconsistent. If it is true for today, it cannot be true for tomorrow . . . Otherwise, the detrimental short-run effect will persist forever. . . ." This thesis is no more inconsistent than is any other description of the reversing time-path of a successful investment; the early cash flow is negative, but the later cash flow is sufficiently positive to render the investment profitable.

Daly and Cobb simply dismiss the question with a neat dig at this book and this writer: "In sum, all the talk about knowledge and the mind as an ultimate resource [the title of this book] that will offset limits imposed by finitude, entropy, and ecological dependence seems to us to reflect incompetent use of the very organ alleged to have such unlimited powers" (1989, p. 199).

A recent important development in economics has been the theory of endogenous growth. That theory is consistent with the argument I make in this book.[4]

Population and Growth

Campbell first quotes Preston that "Even if we accept Simon's view, it was mortality-driven population growth, not fertility-driven growth." Either I inadvertently slipped somewhere in my writing, or Preston slipped in reading, because I have never held any view other than that it was the drop in mortality in the past two centuries that caused the huge increase in population. Hence it could not have been an increase in fertility that caused the first-ever sustained worldwide increase in living standards that has occurred since perhaps 1750, as Preston suggests I assert. Indeed, another critic—Thomas L. Wayburn—believes that he can "discredit him [Simon] once and for all. We should be suspicious of a scholar who publishes a paper with one serious error in it." The supposed error? My statement—which is what Preston taxes me for *not* making—that "It is this decrease in the death rate that is the cause of there being a larger world population nowadays than in former times".[5]

Attention is paid to fertility in this book simply because fertility control rather than mortality control is the central focus of population policies. Indeed, one of the most poignant graphs in the first edition is the decline in funds devoted by AID to health programs abroad relative to fertility programs.

Ansley Coale suggests (in Campbell) that my argument is defective because "a substantial fraction (perhaps an unchanging fraction) of people of labor force age will still depend on agricultural activities," and he refers to Bangladesh as an example. If indeed the agricultural-sector proportions of poor countries were not declining, economic growth would indeed be hampered. But by now there is solid evidence that even those countries where the matter was long questioned by some economists—such as India—have commenced the process that has appeared everywhere else in the world; for much data, see Sullivan.[6]

Population and Environment

Thomas Stoel is the first mention in this section of Campbell's review: My "argument is fundamentally defective, for increased life expectancy is mainly a function of access to health care (as well as a reflection of public health progress in water filtration, improved sanitation, and better nutrition), not of pollution." But it was the decline in pollution—greatly assisted by better sanitation—that brought about the stunning declines in mortality. The problem is that the word "pollution" has changed its meaning simply because the great killing disease pollutions of the past—cholera, typhoid fever, diphtheria, and the like—have now been conquered in the rich countries; people now think of pollution as the relatively minor dangers (relative to the past) of pesticides and various carcinogens. This shift in meaning is documented in chapter 16. Certainly vaccination and other public-health measures have mattered greatly, as has better nutrition (which is hardly a matter of "public health progress," as Stoel calls it, but rather of *private* progress). But the gains in life expectancy due to conquering the great water and air pollutions of the past are undeniable.

Food

"Three chapters on famine and food supply ignore completely the issue of food self-sufficiency in the developing countries. The fact that almost all developing countries have become net importers of grain is not mentioned" (Sirageldin and Kantner 1982 in Campbell 1993). Even if the "fact" that they refer to were true, it is not relevant to any policy decisions. The aim of self-sufficiency is exactly the sort of fallacy that economics has been most successful in showing to be counterproductive; it is the opposite of the principle of comparative advantage, about which almost all economists agree.

Family Planning

Campbell herself writes that "he [Simon] does not believe that governments should support family planning programs." I do not know how she has inquired into my beliefs on the subject. But my public record is clear: I have written again and again that I believe that helping a couple get the number of children that the couple wants is one of the great works of humanity. And to the extent that governments do just that, I generally support their activities. It is only when they conduct a coercive or propagandistic population-control program under the false label of "family planning" that I do not support the activity; it then is a limitation of peoples' liberties rather than an extension of their capacities.

I am flattered by the stature of some of the people who have denounced me at one time or another. For example, my 1980 *Science* article was sharply criticized by the president of the National Academy of Science, Philip Handler, along with five other notables—Nobel-prize-winner Norman E. Borlaug, director, International Wheat and Maize Improvement Center; Lincoln Gordon, former assistant secretary of state for Inter-American Affairs; Marshall Green, former coordinator of Population Affairs, State Department; Edwin M. Martin, former assistant secretary of state for Economic Affairs; Russell W. Peterson, president, National Audubon Society; they, on the letterhead of the Population Crisis Committee, wrote a long critical letter to *Science* about my work, using as ammunition statements and language that seemed almost cadged from the *Global 2000 Report to the President*. They said (among many other things) that over the next twenty years, "At the present rate, some 40 percent of the world's rain forests may disappear." For fun, I wrote to distinguished biologist Handler asking for the basis of the "40 percent" assertion. He replied in part:

I frankly doubt that there exists anywhere what could fairly be considered what you refer to as a "solid time series" on rain forests. It was for this reason that in our letter to SCIENCE we stated the concept of conversion of moist tropical forest in such equivocal terms, speaking of "some 40%" and that that portion "may" disappear. . . .

I doubt that the "some 40%" used in our letter to SCIENCE could be defended with any appreciable precision; there are some who feel that the current trends virtually assure complete destruction, others who feel that the situation is less catastrophic. What I think we were saying is that conversion rates are rapid and that a very substantial amount of the remaining most forest will be gone in the easily foreseeable future.

A less equivocal term than Handler's "equivocal terms" is "weasel words," meaning "not the plain complete truth." It grieves me that people of such achievements as Handler can stray so far from the precepts of the science they love so well to stretch the truth this way. But somehow my work evokes such responses in otherwise thoughtful and responsible people.

Epithets and Ridicule

The volume of *substantive* negative comment as discussed above has been small compared to the volume of ad hominem attack. (Kind friends have sent me enough examples to fill cardboard boxes.) I shall now relate some of the grosser examples, with several motives: (1) You may be able to infer something about the impact of the work itself from these reactions; as an old lawyer's saying goes: "When you have the law on your side, pound the law. When you have the facts on your side, pound the facts. When you have neither the law nor the facts going for you, pound the table"—or in this case, pound me, and that's a good sign. (2) I hope it induces you to imagine what it would do to you to have so many people respond to your work in this fashion. (3) I can't resist teasing them with their own words. And by publicizing their nastiness and ridicule I may make the ridiculers seem ridiculous. I have no other way of fighting back.

Attacks on Integrity

Other charges against me are often compounded with the charge of dishonesty. For example, in a 1983 commencement address at Knox College, a distinguished botanist took the time to say about my work: "His ignorance of the biological realities would simply be laughable if it did not have such dangerous potential consequences. It seems almost unbelievable in the face of known facts. . . ," that I use an "intellectually dishonest strategy," that it is "immoral to pretend that everything is fine when the facts so clearly tell us otherwise," and that I do this for "short-term political gains" (Raven 1983, p. 7). And there is lots more of such impugning my character and motives.

Consider this letter which a colleague of mine received from Robert May, a distinguished zoologist, former head of the department of zoology at Oxford, and the chief scientific adviser to the British government:

> What Simon and Wildavsky do, in essentials, is take the rates of certified extinctions for vertebrate animals (which extinction rates are themselves certainly an underestimate), since 1600, and treat these numbers as if they applied to all one million or more known animal species, rather than the roughly 40,000 known vertebrate species. They then build on this initial silliness, in a letter whose tone is ill-suited to serious intellectual discourse.
>
> It is very difficult for me to see how any serious and honest person, acting in good faith, could do something so stupid as to take documented extinction figures which pertain essentially to vertebrates and treat them as if they applied to all metazoans. These authors have, I might add, also been very resistant to having this and other factual errors pointed out to them.
>
> Sadly, I conclude that what we are dealing with here is not an honest pursuit of intellectual understanding, but rather with some other agenda (or possibly with stark stupidity, or even both).

In fact, I (with Wildavsky or alone) never have made any estimate of the overall rate of species extinction, as may be ascertained in chapter 31. But even if I had done so in the fashion May described, which would indeed be foolish, would that be a basis for inferring dishonesty? And what is my "agenda"? I represent no organization, and I receive no money in consulting or research grants (which is true of few competent people in the field), a matter that allows me to be a particularly free person.

I wrote the colleague saying that I would quote May's words on the dustjacket of this book, and I sent May a copy of the letter (to tease him, I confess). May then threatened me with lawyers. As I wrote to him[7], "There does seem to be something funny about you wanting to sue me to prevent me from printing the ugly things you say about me."

Thomas Wayburn speculates on the content of an "agenda" such as May alludes to. "People who try to tell us that the earth is big enough to accommodate a much larger population probably have their own hidden agendas. For example, they may want to ensure a cheap, readily available labor supply for themselves or for those they serve, or they might hope that many more dissatisfied people will give them political power faster. Thus, they hope to make things better by making things worse. . . . One such critic is Julian L. Simon."[8]

The Special Case of Paul Ehrlich

For economy of treatment of the matter of attack rhetoric, let's focus on just one critic, Paul Ehrlich, who has directed a great deal of colorful language in my direction (see also his comments in the afternote to chapter 15, and my interchange with him in Simon 1990, selection 43). He is a treasure-trove of snappy quotes (for other of his remarks, please look him up in the index of this book) useful for writers who are critical of me and also for me in this chapter to show how he works; for example, he (with Anne Ehrlich) confer on me the leadership of a "space-age cargo cult."[9]

One of Ehrlich's main devices is attributing some combination of stupidity and scientific ignorance to those with whom he disagrees. In a talk to 200,000 people in person (how many more on television I do not know) on Earth Day 1990,[10] Ehrlich alluded to the title of this book, saying "The ultimate resource—the one thing we'll never run out of is imbeciles," which got a good laugh from the crowd;[11] he frequently uses words like "ignorant," "crazy," "imbecile,"[12] and "moronic."[13] In an essay entitled "Simple Simon Environmental Analysis," which is a commentary on a preceding short essay of mine,[14] the Ehrlichs refer to "a few uninformed people [who] claim that population growth is beneficial," and write, "The connections between economic growth, population growth, and quality of life are much more subtle and complicated than Simon imagines."[15] "Getting economists to understand ecology is like trying to explain a tax form to a cranberry. It's as if Julian Simon were saying that we have a geocentric universe at the same time NASA's saying the earth rotates around the sun. There's no reconciling these views. When you launch a space shuttle you don't trot out the flat-earthers to be commentators. They're outside the bounds of what ought to be discourse in the media. In the field of ecology, Simon is the absolute equivalent of the flat-earthers."[16] (Minor comment: I'm not "in the field of ecology.")

Then others copy Ehrlich's colorful language. The former medical director of International Planned Parenthood Foundation, Malcolm Potts, writes, "Julian Simon—and his fellow flat-earthists—assured Washington decision makers that entrepreneurs and Nobel prize winners would be popping up from the streets of Calcutta propelled by the glorious multiplication of human numbers."[17]

Ehrlich taxes me as follows: "Misdefining the problem, selective use of data, analyses of time series over inappropriate intervals, and determined ignorance of the most basic tenets of science. Indeed, the book contains so many childish errors that it would take work of equal length to detail them" (Paul Ehrlich, with Anne Ehrlich, 1985).

Ehrlich frequently recycles the same remarks: "To explain to one of them the inevitability of no growth in the material sector, or . . . that commodities *must* become expensive would be like trying to explain odd-day-even-day gas distribution to a cranberry."[18] And "The views of . . . Simon are taken seriously by a segment of the public, even though to a scientist they are in the same class as the idea that Jack Frost is responsible for ice-crystal patterns on a cold window."[19] "Simon apparently doesn't know the difference between an old-growth virgin forest (with its critical biodiversity intact) and a tree farm."[20] And when asked "his opinion of Simon, he said, 'that's like asking a nuclear physicist about horoscopes.'"[21]

Ehrlich and I have never debated face to face. He says that he has refused because I am a "fringe character."[22] We have only locked horns directly in two cases, and in both incidents he has been demonstrably wrong. He and his colleagues based their criticism of my 1980 *Science* article (that conveyed some of the findings of this book) on what turned out to be a typographical error in a source. If I had been in their shoes, I would have been chagrined and embarrassed when this was discovered. But Ehrlich replied: "What scientist would phone the author of a standard source [as I did] to make sure there were not typos in a series of numbers showing a general trend with which every analyst in the field is completely familiar?"[23] (That must be one of the most peculiar lines ever written by a member of a profession whose business is the search for scientific truth.) I consider it very significant that Ehrlich has suffered no apparent damage from being so wrong; I know of no mention of the incident in print.

Our other encounter was the bet mentioned on page 35, following on the 1980–1981 interchange in *Social Science Quarterly* (reproduced in my 1990 book). Many people have asked him about its outcome, and a few of the answers have been passed on to me. To a college newspaper: "The bet doesn't mean anything."[24] On BBC television: "It was an excellent bet. We happened to lose it. You can lose making an excellent bet."[25] (Indeed that is quite correct. But one should then be anxious to repeat the bet—which Ehrlich refuses to do.) But on the same program he said, "I debated a long time about whether to take him up on the bet because it was the wrong bet (but compare his remark cited on page 35 about how anxious he and his colleagues were to make the bet, and to make it much larger). On the other hand, it was very hard to explain the right bet to him and finally we decided that if we took the bet we'd shut him up for at least ten years." To a book interviewer: "We knew if we bet on metals there would be a fair chance we'd lose. But we knew at the very least that if we took him on we could keep him quiet for a decade. But the bet was trivial; we could have bet on the state of the atmosphere or on biodiversity loss. . . ."[26] And "The bet doesn't mean anything. Julian Simon is like the guy who jumps off the Empire State Building and says how great things are going so far as he passes the 10th floor. I still think the price of those metals will go up eventually. . . . I have no doubt that sometime in the next century food will be scarce enough that prices are really going to be high even in the United States."[27] But to repeat, of course Ehrlich will not bet again.

Ehrlich (with Stephen Schneider, 1995) has also written that he "once made the mistake of being goaded into making a bet with Simon on a matter of marginal environmental importance [prices of metals]." And he told a reporter that "I got schnookered. . . . Prices of metals really don't have much to do with environmental quality." But in 1980 Ehrlich and his colleagues said they would "accept Simon's astonishing offer before other greedy people jump in." Goaded? And concerning "marginal importance" and "schnookered," check the voluminous writings about the importance of scarcities he predicted for food and other natural resources—scarcities which are best measured by prices, of course (*San Francisco Chronicle* opinion column, May 18, 1995).

Others have attempted to explain the bet away, too. Norman Myers writes: "The Ehrlich group lost the bet, but through unusual circumstances of the 1980s that prompted Simon himself to write. . . . 'I have been lucky that this particular period coincided so nicely with my argument.'"[28] Myers's statement is false; I was *not* "prompted" by "unusual circumstances" to say "I have been lucky." Rather, there always is a certain amount of uncertainty in any wager, and the soundest wager can be lost if one has bad luck; that is all that I meant. In fact, I consider the circumstances in the 1980s not the slightest bit unusual.

(If Mr. Myers himself believes that the circumstances were unusual, why will he not take me up on my offer to repeat the wager—for any period he picks, for any commodities? During a debate with him I repeatedly challenged him to wager on this or any other trend of material welfare. But he merely ignored my offer, just as Ehrlich and others have ignored the offer of another go-round—in the same breath as they try to explain away losing the first time.)

An entire article was devoted to "How Julian Simon Could Win the Bet and Still Be Wrong." The argument is: "Most economists would have bet on Simon from the start . . . but many of them also know that Ehrlich is right. Quality of life did deteriorate worldwide in the ten year interval."[29] (Nobody said that the bet was an index of "quality of life." But in any case, quality of life has *not* deteriorated, as this book shows aplenty.)

One of Ehrlich's devices is to refer to "Julian Simon, a specialist in mail-order marketing,"[30] a device copied with variation by Garrett Hardin as in "marketing expert Julian Simon."[31] I plied that trade for two years ending in 1963 (plus writing a book on the subject that still sells well in the fifth edition, I'm pleased to say). Unfortunately, there are many to whom the idea of private business is incompatible with truth or honor or public service, and Ehrlich clearly is playing to them. He probably also is suggesting that a former businessperson cannot be a sound scholar.

Sometimes Ehrlich combines this device with not mentioning my name, as in "an economist specializing in mail-order marketing."[32] Here he actually writes a falsehood about my specialty at present (and the past thirty years), which he does again in another variation, referring to me without name on television as "a Professor of Mail-Order Marketing";[33] a more litigious person might sue him.

Politicized Criticism

One of the difficulties in having a reasoned discussion with my critics is that many frame their criticisms in political terms.

Attacks from the Far Right and Far Left

Politically tinged attacks come from both sides of the political spectrum. From what I can tell, the politics of some of these people is at the far Left and some at the far Right. They attack me as being (presumably) the opposite of what they themselves are.

I have been attacked by people who call themselves "conservatives" as a Marxist and a Red (especially with respect to immigration), and by still others as a libertarian. An article entitled "Simon Says: Take One Giant Step to Unreality," begins: "The most important thing to know about Julian Simon is that he is motivated by ideology. As a libertarian, his focus is the individual; but not all individuals, just those deemed oppressed by 'society.' . . . Knowing where Simon is coming from helps when trying to make sense of his arguments. The hodge-podge of 'evidence,' the bold but unsupported assertions and his constant mixing of apples and oranges stem from the fact that his research is not aimed at seeking the truth. . . . His research is for propaganda purposes."[34]

Perhaps because those of far-Right persuasion are relatively rare in academia, attacks on me as a "lousy Red" tend to come on scrawled postcards without signature. One such flattered me with a death threat which a neighbor in the Secret Service thought worth having the FBI track down.

Those on the Left dismiss me as motivated by religious or other traditional ideas. Many tar me with the brush of putative association with political conservatism (though I do not subscribe to that doctrine any more than I am a "liberal"). For example, the distinguished demographer Nathan Keyfitz makes it seem that I am of their party when he writes that "the applause that Simon gets from the political right on his other views is more muted on immigration," though he is indeed correct that the Right criticizes me on immigration.[35] And a review of my 1986 book in the main sociological review medium, *Contemporary Sociology* begins:

> Never has a conservative neoclassical economist attempted so rigorous a defense of the weakest points of Marxist population theory.[36]

It was a joy to reply to that, beginning as follows:

> I am anxious to set the record straight on this sentence, lest my family think I've gone round the bound with respect to "conservative," some colleagues take comfort that I have turned "neoclassical," and friends take fright about the Marxism.[37]

The reviewer, Douglas Anderton, responded:

> My characterization of Simon's central arguments as conservative, neoclassical, and consistent with Marxist population theory are all accurate. Simon responds that he does not consider himself personally conservative.

It is easy to make fun of the inaccuracy and illogic of Anderton's reply. For example, the review referred to *me* as "conservative," but when that becomes patently untenable—it would be nigh impossible to say with a straight face that a *person is* conservative when a person refuses such a label—the response shifts to my *argument* as being conservative. And, my argument goes from being a "point of Marxist population theory" to being "consistent with" Marxist thought after I note that it originated with the founding father of classical economic thought two hundred years before Marx. But the key point here is not how far the reviewer reaches to be critical; rather, the key point is the extent to which the reviewer's politics, and his beliefs about what mine are, suffuse his review.

As to the substance of Anderton's review, it boils down to this last sentence in the response: "I am simply suggesting that, in this text, Simon has ignored the basic physical realities of entropy." In other words, a sociologist instructs us that the physics of cosmology—a subject now enlivened by fundamental speculative differences (see chapter 3)—as embodied in that old chestnut entropy, makes nonsense of what I write about population economics. Once again, it all comes back to the assertion that our cosmos and our planetary resources are "finite."

Political attacks of this stripe are reminiscent of the switch in the language applied to Soviet leaders antedating the collapse of the USSR. Before sympathizers found out how murderously cruel the Socialist Stalinist-Marxist regime was, and still looked on it with favor, people who referred to *themselves* with such labels also referred to the USSR as "left-wing" and "progressive" and "liberal." After even the most sympathetic apologist could no longer deny the truth of the brutality, the former apologists began to refer to the Stalinist types still in power as "conservative" and "right-wing," and the anti-Socialist free-market Russians as "liberal." In other words, "right-wing" and "conservative" often are simply pejorative rather than referring to a particular sort of political or economic thought.

Many of the critics from both ends of the political spectrum seem to have in common that they believe in "rational" governmental control of individuals and society. Chinese tracts on population write that just as the production of goods "must" be planned, the production of human capital also must be planned. The zealous Right wing and the zealous Left wing both want the state—and of course, themselves as leaders of the state—to tell people what to do. The wings differ somewhat in what they want to control—whether people's personal or business lives, though they may agree in such matters as wanting authorities to regulate how a person maintains the lawn in front of the house. (I just read of a couple being hauled into court in South Salt Lake City for "failing to maintain their landscape" due to insufficient watering.)[38] It is with respect to governmental control of the acts of individuals that my values diverge most sharply from those of both political wings who criticize this book on political grounds.

This book argues that the reasons both those on the far Left and far Right give for wanting to control individuals' demographic behavior are not valid economically. Many on the far Right want to reduce immigration, and they offer supposed economic reasons for doing so; they attack me because my work suggests that their reasons are not sound. Some among the far Right, and perhaps among the far Left, too, also want other nations to actively control population growth because they wish to prevent an increase in the numbers of people in non-European countries, either for fear of becoming numerically inferior for military reasons (a view which the U.S. Central Intelligence Agency has advanced for decades; see U.S. National Security council 1974) or because of the desire that the proportion of white people will not decline more rapidly than is happening.

Response to the Personal Attacks

One cannot argue with personal attacks. One can, however, attempt to explain them. Concerning the *purpose* of the attacks, I see them as a device for marginalizing, devilizing, and thereby dismissing from consideration people like me so that their ideas should not be taken seriously. As to *explaining* why such passions are aroused, one can learn from the history of the theory of relativity. (More generally, see chapter 37 on the nature of the thinking and the central concepts at work in these discussions—the central cause of the difference in conclusions.)

Bertrand Russell said that "the theory of relativity depends, to a considerable extent, upon getting rid of notions which are useful in ordinary life."[39] And in the Middle Ages, accepting the idea that Earth should be considered round for astronomical purposes required that people get past the everyday idea that the surface of a pond is flat, and that a ball does not roll on a table. Similarly, understanding the economics of natural resources such as energy requires leaving aside the everyday idea that there *must* be a "finite" quantity of them, and therefore that using some must mean there is less left, hence increased scarcity. Just as Russell tells us that with Einstein's work "the old ideas of space and time had to be changed fundamentally,"[40] the everyday concept of the stock of a resource as measured by physical quantity must give way to the economic concept of the stock of a resource as measured by its price. The doomsayers jeer at this anti-commonsensical idea just as Copernicus's and Galileo's opponents jeered at their conception of the cosmos—which makes it rather ironic, incidentally, that Ehrlich et al. choose the epithet "flat-earther" to throw at me. (Relax, I'm not comparing myself to those greats—I'm just suggesting we can learn from their experiences.)

Famous science writer Isaac Asimov expressed the bewilderment of a person who at least faced up to this intellectual predicament, as Ehrlich et al. do not. Asimov read about the resources bet and then wrote:

> Naturally, I was all on the side of the pessimist and judge my surprise when it turned out he had lost the bet; that the prices of the metals had indeed fallen; that grain was cheaper; that oil . . . was cheaper; and so on.
>
> I was thunderstruck. Was it possible, I thought, that something that seemed so obvious to me—that a steadily rising population is deadly—can be wrong?
>
> Yes, it could be. I am frequently wrong.

Asimov permitted himself to be bewildered. "I don't understand this," he wrote. And he says about economics in general: "I cannot understand it, and I cannot believe that anyone else understands it, either. People may say they understand it . . . but I think it is all a fake."[41]

Unlike Asimov, the doomsayers refuse to allow themselves to be bewildered by the facts. Instead, they simply reject the facts and deride anyone who presents the facts. Garrett Hardin writes:

> To really get to the heart of the matter [population growth], we must ignore statistical arguments and opt for the commonsense approach.
>
> As the logician . . . Quine has said, "Science itself is a continuation of common sense. Therefore, this essay will avoid statistics. The opaqueness of statistical arguments makes it easy for analysts to 'get away with murder.'" Though often wonderfully useful, statistics can also serve as a substitute for thought . . . empirical studies . . . can be so selected and arranged as to seem to support faith in perpetual growth, the religion of the most powerful actors in a commercial society . . .
>
> On the one hand, a legion of economists say, "Why worry? An increase in people doesn't matter.". . . On the other hand, a brigade of environmentalists assert that shortages are real and ultimately decisive.[42]

In a debate with Dennis Meadows, every time someone asked him how he squared his Malthusian theory with the data I showed, he answered: "Simon looks at the past; I look at the future." Scientific data, of course, necessarily refer to past.

In an article on the bet, columnist Jessica Mathews said that my views on "finiteness" are "palpable nonsense."[43] The word "palpable" means *felt*. No doubt Mathews *feels* that what I have to say is nonsense; it is indeed not common sense. But feeling is not a scientific argument. And assertions and policy conclusions drawn from feeling—as is often the case in these matters— are likely to mislead us when they run counter to the scientific evidence.

(Typically, Mathews attempts to marginalize me by referring to my ideas as "extreme." She notes that Ehrlich lost the bet, I won, and then she asserts that the truth apparently is somewhere in between these extremes. Because she derided the bet as being on the wrong matters, I wrote to her: "Would you like to bet on any of these matters? If you can propose a measure or measures for worldwide pollution . . . I would probably be happy to wager on that one, also." But she prudently did not respond.)

Why the Vehemence?

From a letter from Margaret Maxey:

> 25 February 1994
>
> I had the dubious fortune this past May to be an invited panelist in Montreal at an international conference on energy. One of the panelists was with the World Bank. In response to a vitriolic comment from the floor about *The Ultimate Resource*, which I had praised in my portion of the panel, the nameless [World Bank representative] opined that "Julian Simon is a criminal!"

Perhaps a third of the 1982 presidential address to the Population Association of America was devoted to attack on my work as an "insult" to the demographic profession. That dignitary (in a later book review) called my 1981 book "filled with incomplete analysis, selective documentation, and false analogies," referred to the "absurdity of Simon's main arguments," and summarized by saying that "it is dismaying and more than a little discouraging after more than three decades of concerted effort to bring sense into the analysis of this vital area of human affairs, that a book so lacking in serious merit should receive such widespread attention. . . . This is not an area for frivolous approaches or one where academics may contend confusedly with no great harm to anyone. It is an area where an effective mobilization of public will and commitment based on understanding of issues is essential."[44]

A World Wildlife Fund official was quoted in the Cox newspapers as saying about me, "The man's a terrorist."[45] And here is Garrett Hardin's innimitable language:

> Simon's conclusions are highly palatable to budget evaders, car salesmen, realtors, advertisers, land speculators, and optimists in general; scientists find them appalling . . . like the fast change artist at a county fair, befuddles the reader with rapid rhetorical interchanges . . . sleight of hand.[46]

When in a taped interchange I asked Hardin why he spoke with such vehemence and used so many ad hominems, he replied that my *Science* article "raised the blood pressure of the scientific community a good twenty points."[47]

A colleague gave a talk about population, resources, and environment to "grassroots lobbyists for U.S. aid programs." He "commented to the chairman . . . just before we went to the podium, 'Really you should have had Julian Simon here, not me.' His response was electric: 'Oh no, not him. We could not afford the cost of all the bodyguards we'd need to keep them [the audience] from tearing him apart.' "[48]

After Garrett Hardin and I debated at the University of Wisconsin in 1989, sociologist William Freudenburg wrote

> [T]o express both admiration and apologies . . . [because he was] appalled at the "hospitality" that all of us, collectively, offered to you and to your ideas.
>
> The admiration . . . partly for the equanimity with which you responded to behaviors that I found to be downright childish. . . . I find it quite ironic that the people who think of themselves as "real" scientists were the ones coming up with excuses for not dealing with data, resorting to *ad hominem* attacks, and generally showing a disdain for scientific methods that I formerly thought would be found only among book-burners.

The Effects of the "Criticism"

The attacks have hampered the dissemination of these ideas, just as intended by the attackers; I regret giving them this satisfaction, but so it is. There were many complaints that *Science* published my first "public" article on the subject. Ehrlich said, "Could the editors have found someone to review Simon's manuscript who had to take off his shoes to count to 20?"[49] This is part of his judgment that views like mine, like those of "flat-earthers," should not be published because they are not within the accepted mainstream view. "The notion that the world is flat is not in the spectrum of ideas that must be included in the news for balance. Few reporters or editors, however, have had the basic education that would provide a similar filtering capacity for statements on environmental issues."[50] Indeed, the then-editor of *Science* said he "want[ed] to censor the paper a bit."[51] And his successor editor at that most important scientific journal in the world withdrew an invitation to me to write an article therein after I told him of the prior incident, which he was not aware of. (The day of the invitation he told me he prided himself on publishing controversial material; the next day, when withdrawing the invitation, he praised my "integrity" in informing him of the previous incident.)[52]

Or consider that the most prestigious population research group in the world—Princeton's Office of Population Research, whose long-time director was a tennis partner of the president of the university—complained to that president that Princeton University Press should not publish my books. The incident is captured on paper in correspondence between my editor at the Press and the Princeton president. In an article about the incident as part of being an editor, Sanford Thatcher wrote that as a result of the books' "direct challenge to some of the academic scholarship emanating from Princeton's own Office of Population Research . . . various of [its] faculty made their displeasure known to the University's administration after the book was published."[53]

Then there is the correspondence between the Mellon Foundation and the august American Association for the Advancement of Science (AAAS), also on paper. A committee of the AAAS sought funds to study the relationship of population, resources, and the environment. Among other potential funding sources, the committee turned to the Andrew W. Mellon Foundation and received a feasibility grant. This is an excerpt from a letter to AAAS discussing further funding, signed by J. Kellum Smith, Jr., vice president and Secretary of that foundation:

> Because the links among population, resources, and environment are so obvious and strong . . . I hope the suggestion of an alternative title [to the original one] does not indicate diffidence, in your group, on the matter of facing up to the malign consequences of rapid population increase. Should such diffidence exist, I would suppose that it might cripple the program and that therefore the exercise might as well be halted forthwith. . . .
>
> I am disconerted by the suggestion that there is a problem in handling "the widely divergent views of the Cornucopians and Malthusians." If by "the Cornucopians" is meant Julian Simon and his few allies, I should think a footnote would be sufficient to dispose of them. . . .
>
> If there is nervousness on the point, it had better be faced up to forthwith. The issue of population increase is central to the proposed program.[54]

For information about such curious episodes as a campaign to have me fired from the University of Illinois for having written this book, see my 1990 book, part 8.

I'll spare you more examples.

Lest the reader be amazed at the human propensity to suppress opposing views, consider the case of as great a philosopher who has lived, David Hume. His *History of the Stewarts* "was . . . unquestionably much the most important work that had recently come from any Scotch pen, yet in a periodical instituted for the very purpose of devoting attention to the productions of Scotch authors [The *Edinburgh Review*], this work of his remained absolutely unnoticed. Why this complete boycott of Hume by his own household? [He was good friends with the staff.] . . . the ignoring of his writings [can be explained by] the intense *odium theologicum* which the name of Hume excited at the moment, and which made it imperative, if the new *Review* was to get justice, that it should be severed from all association with his detested name."[55]

All this ugly opposition has led others to steer clear of me even when they believe that the work is sound and the conclusions correct—and even when they refer to themselves as my friends, and say nice things in private. This has been painful as well as damaging. But if I can feel as if I'm in the same boat with as great a man as David Hume in at least this respect, that's considerable comfort.

Two Letters from Hayek: Excerpts

Lest I leave the impression that the reaction to this book and to the rest of my work on population has been entirely negative, I attach letters from as great an economist as has lived in the twentieth century, Nobel-prize-winning Friedrich Hayek.

URACHSTRASSE 27

D-7800 Freiburg (Breisgau)

March 22, 1981

Dear Professor Simon,

I have never before written a fan letter to a professional colleague, but to discover that you have in your *Economics of Population Growth* provided the empirical evidence for what with me is the result of a life-time of theoretical speculation, is too exciting an experience not to share it with you. The upshot of my theoretical work has been the conclusion that those traditional rules of conduct (esp. of several property) which led to the greatest increases of the numbers of the groups practicing them leads to their displacing the others—not on "Darwinian" principles but because based on the transmission of learned rules—a concept of evolution which is much older than Darwin. I doubt whether welfare economics has really much helped you to the right conclusions. I claim as little as you do that population growth as such is good—only that it is the cause of the selection of the morals which guide our individual action. It follows, of course, that our fear of a population explosion is unjustified so long as the local increases are the result of groups being able to feed larger numbers, but may become a severe embarrassment if we start subsidizing the growth of groups unable to feed themselves.

Sincerely,

F. A. Hayek

SHIMODA TOKYU HOTEL

Shimoda, Nov. 6, 1981

Dear Professor Simon,

. . . I have now at last had time to read [*The Ultimate Resource*] with enthusiastic agreement. So far as practical effect is concerned it ought to be even more important than your theoretical work which I found so exciting because it so strongly supports all the conclusions of the work I have been doing for the last few years. I do not remember whether I explained in my earlier letter that one, perhaps the chief thesis of the book on *The Fatal Conceit*, the *first draft* of which I got on paper during the past summer, is that the basic morals of property and honesty, which created our civilization and the modern numbers of mankind, was the outcome of a process of selective evolution, in the course of which always those practices prevailed, which allowed the groups which adopted them to multiply more rapidly (mostly at their periphery among people who already profited from them without yet having fully adopted them). That was the reason for my enthusiasm for your theoretical work.

Your new book I welcome chiefly for the practical effects I am hoping from it. Though you will be at first much abused, I believe the more intelligent will soon recognize the soundness of your case. And the malicious pleasure of being able to tell most of their fellows what fools they are, should get you the support of the more lively minds about the media. If your publishers want to quote me they are welcome to say that I described it as a first class book of great importance which ought to have great influence on policy.

With best wishes,

Sincerely,

F. A. Hayek

*   *   *

Let's end this Epilogue with a quotation from John Stuart Mill in *On Liberty*:

The worst offence . . . which can be committed by a polemic is to stigmatise those who hold the contrary opinion as bad and immoral men. To calumny of this sort, those who hold any unpopular opinion are peculiarly exposed, because they are in general few and uninfluential, and nobody but themselves feels much interested in seeing justice done them; but this weapon is, from the nature of the case, denied to those who attack a prevailing opinion: they can neither use it with safety to themselves, nor, if they could, would it do anything but recoil on their own cause. In general, opinions contrary to those commonly received can only obtain a hearing by studied moderation of language, and the most cautious avoidance of unnecessary offence, which they hardly ever deviate even in a slight degreee without losing ground: while unmeasured vituperation employed on the side of the prevailing opinion really does deter people from professing contrary opinions, and from listening to those who profess them.[56]

Notes

Preface

1. Donald Bishop, with the help of the Marine historian, was kind enough to exhume the oration in 1993. It was Chaplain Roland B. Gittlesohn, a Navy lieutenant, who said,

> This is perhaps the grimmest, and surely the holiest task we have faced since D-Day. Here before us lie the bodies of comrades and friends. Men who until yesterday or last week laughed with us, joked with us, trained with us. Men who were on the same ships with us, and went over the sides with us, as we prepared to hit the beaches of this island. Men who fought with us and feared with us. Somewhere in this plot of ground there may lie the man who could have discovered the cure for cancer. . . .

2. *Newsweek*, March 30, 1970, p. 87.
3. *Saturday Review*, March 11, 1972, p. 49.
4. *Washington Post*, "From a Report for Negative Population Growth," May 1991.
5. Ehrlich, 1968, p. 198.
6. Stephen R. C. Hicks, "Global Problems Are Too Big for Little Kids," *Wall Street Journal*, April 16, 1991, p. A20.

Introduction
What Are the *Real* Population and Resource Problems?

1. Simon 1989.
2. Barun Mitra suggested this contradiction to me.
3. Critchfield 1981, pp. x, 336.
4. Schumpeter 1954, p. 571.
5. Sidney Homer, *A History of Interest Rates* (New Brunswick, N.J.: Rutgers University Press, 1963).
6. Moses Hadas, ed., *The Complete Works of Tacitus*, trans. from the Latin by Alfred John Church and William Jackson Brodribb (New York: Random House, 1942).
7. Quoted by Lebergott 1984, frontispiece.
8. 1676/1899, pp. 243–44.
9. Flexner 1969, pp. 342–43.
10. Rae 1965, p. 343.
11. Young 1774, p. xi.
12. 1776, Cannan edition 1937, bk. 2, chap. 3, p. 327; quotation courtesy of David Friedman.
13. Young 1774, p. ix.

Chapter 1
The Amazing Theory of Raw-Material Scarcity

1. Ehrlich and Ehrlich 1974, p. 7.
2. This section draws upon Simon 1975a, pp. 267–78.
3. Bauer 1976, p. 63.
4. From Simon 1978a, pp. 390–94.
5. Barnett and Morse 1963, p. 220.
6. *Economic Report of the President* 1991 (Washington, D.C.: GP0), p. 298.
7. Figures for 1987, *U.S. Statistical Abstract* 1990, p. 686.
8. Beisner n.d.
9. Peter Drucker, "A Troubled Japanese Juggernaut," *Wall Street Journal*, November 22, 1977, p. 11.
10. Federal Reserve Bank of Dallas, 1991 Annual Report, p. 8.
11. Ibid.
12. Two technical notes: (1) Inflation and the cost of storage are automatically allowed for in the market prices, so there is no hidden benefit to me from those sources. (2) One could ot make the same sort of wager by dealing in the common stocks of firms that produce the raw materials, because those firms' stock prices are influenced by changes in their production capacities due to technological change. This is in contrast to a tone of copper at fixed market grade, which is physically the same from year to year.
13. Ehrlich 1970, quoted by Dixon 1973.
14. Ehrlich 1981; Ehrlich 1982.
15. See Brown and Field 1978 for an exposition of this point of view.
16. Philip Moeller, October 26, 1988.
17. March 28, 1990, A2.
18. See Barnett and Morse 1963.

Chapter 2
Why Are Material-Technical Resource Forecasts So Often Wrong?

1. Earl Cook 1976, p. 679.
2. This discussion draws on Nordhaus 1974, p. 23.
3. Kuznets, quoted by Rosenberg 1972, p. 6.
4. *Report on the Limits to Growth* 1972, p. 37, as quoted by Weber 1977, p. 62.
5. Cloud, quoted by Weber 1977, p. 62.
6. Kahn et al. 1976, p. 101.
7. Mather 1944, p. 29.
8. Brown, Bonner, and Weir 1963, p. 92.
9. Goeller and Weinberg 1978, p. 4.
10. Ibid., p. 10.
11. McKelvey, quoted by Weber 1977, p. 47.
12. Meadows, Meadows, and Randers 1992, dust jacket.
13. *The Woodlands Forum*, vol. 7, Fall 1990, pp. 6, 7.
14. *Wall Street Journal*, April 1, 1983, p. 13.

15. Slade 1982, p. 136.
16. Brobst 1979, p. 115.

Chapter 3
Can the Supply of Natural Resources—Especially Engergy— Really Be Infinite? Yes!

1. Meadows et al. 1974, p. vii.
2. Gurr 1985, p. 52.
3. Akins 1975, p. 289.
4. U.S., The White House 1972, Signet ed., pp. 2–3.
5. Meadows et al. 1974, p. 265.
6. Russell 1953, p. 99.
7. Keynes 1920, pp. 24, 25, 94.
8. Gosline 1970.
9. Philip Abelson, *Science*, November 11, 1988, p. 837, editorial.
10. U.S., The White House 1952, summary of vol. 1, pp. 12–13; idem, p. 1.
11. Ibid., p. 2.
12. Ibid., p. 1.
13. Fuller 1969, p. 4, quoted by Weber 1977, p. 45.
14. For discussion of operational or working definitions, see a text on research methods, such as Simon and Burstein 1985.
15. Ivan Amato, "New Alchemy: Fooling Mother Nature," *Washington Post*, August 20, 1989, p. B3.
16. *Wall Street Journal*, November 11, 1988, p. B4.
17. *Washington Post*, May 31, 1991, p. D1.
18. *Wall Street Journal*, August 30, 1991, p. B1.
19. *Wall Street Journal*, August 30, 1991, p. B1.
20. *Business Week*, August 19, 1991, p. 110.
21. Sheldon Lambert, quoted in *Newsweek*, June 27, 1977, p. 71.
22. Telephone conversation about June 8, 1994. Tipler goes even further and says that the laws of physics *mandate* perpetual growth, but that goes far beyond anything discussed here—as indeed do *any* laws of physics have little or nothing to do with change within the economic horizon of this book.
23. Dyson 1988, p. vii.

Chapter 4
The Grand Theory

1. Rifkin 1989.
2. Wiener 1950, p. 58.
3. Georgescu-Roegen 1971, 1979; Daly 1973, 1977.
4. Georgescu-Roegen 1979, p. 99.
5. Hawking 1988, p. 150.
6. Ibid., pp. 135–36, his italics.
7. Ibid., p. 129.

8. Penrose 1989, p. 4.
9. Tipler 1992.
10. *Washington Post*, November 23, 1989, p. A20.
11. Daly and Cobb 1989.
12. Hawking 1988, p. 137.
13. Hardin, letter, November 17, 1981.
14. Ehrlich 1981, and in Simon 1990, p. 372.
15. *Science*, vol. 243, 13 January 1989, p. 168.
16. *Science*, vol. 246, 17 November 1989, p. 885.
17. *Harvard Magazine*, reference lost, p. 52.

Chapter 5
Famine 1995? Or 2025? Or 1975?

1. *Washington Post* (*Herald Tribune*), January 2, 1986.
2. Associated Press (hereafter cited as AP), February 12, 1975.
3. Edouard Souma in *Chicago Sun-Times*, November 26, 1976, p. 18.
4. Advertisement of Arno Press, 1977.
5. *Wall Street Journal*, October 30, 1975.
6. Quoted in *Time*, April 1, 1974, p. 40.
7. *Wall Street Journal*, December 13, 1976, editorial page.
8. Ehrlich 1968, p. xi.
9. Fichter 1972, pp. 24–25.
10. Ehrlich 1968, p. xi.
11. *Newsweek*, November 11, 1974, p. 16.
12. Paddock and Paddock 1967, p. 222.
13. Ehrlich in Reid and Lyon 1972, p. 13.
14. Simon 1977.
15. Keynes 1920/1971.
16. Johnson 1974a.
17. Sanderson, in Abelson, 1975, p. 1.
18. Abercrombie and McCormack, 1976, p. 482.
19. Abel 1980, p. 39.
20. Johnson 1974b, p. 17.
21. Johnson 1973, pp. 6–7.
22. Conquest, 1986, pp. 301–303.
23. Ashton, Hill, Piazza, and Zeitz 1984.
24. Aird 1982, p. 268.
25. Eberstadt 1988, p. 144.
26. *Washington Post*, March 16, 1991, A 16.
27. Fichter 1972, p. 25.
28. This section draws heavily upon Clark 1967, p. 124; Bennett 1954; and Poleman 1975.
29. *Newsweek*, September 11, 1972, p. 38.
30. AP, in *Champaign-Urbana News Gazette*, January 10, 1978, p. A-5.
31. Letter from Helen Ware, March 20, 1978.
32. *Arizona Daily Star*, July 10, 1980, p. F-1.

33. *Science*, November 8, 1991, p. 790.

34. *New York Times*, April 29, 1988, quoted in *The Freeman*, September 1988, p. 331.

Chapter 6
What Are the Limits on Food Production?

1. *New York Times*, February 6, 1977, p. 24.

2. *Restaurants and Institutions*, December 11, 1989, p. 762.

3. Bugbee and Salisbury 1988.

4. Field 1988.

5. Godfriaux 1987.

6. For example, Vitousek, P. Ehrlich, and A. Ehrlich 1987.

7. Clark 1967, p. 157.

8. *Tree Topics*, 15 July 1991, quoting Royce Kurtz, "Timber and Treaties," *Forest & Conservation History 35*, April 1991, pp. 56–64.

9. Juskevitch and Guyer 1990.

10. Gasser and Fraley 1989.

11. *Wall Street Journal*, November 1, 1989, p. B4.

12. *Wall Street Journal*, April 13, 1992, p. 1; Bogorad n.d., p. 553.

13. Quoted by Wise 1984, p. 125.

14. Wise, forthcoming.

15. *Forbes*, December 24, 1990, p. 132.

16. William Booth, *Washington Post*, August 22, 1992, p. A8.

17. *Washington Post*, October 21, 1989, p. A3; November 26, 1989, p. H2.

18. Patoski 1992.

19. *Washington Post*, November 26, 1989, p. H2.

20. Field 1988, p. 51.

21. William Booth, *Washington Post*, August 22, 1992, p. A1.

22. Harlan 1976, p. 90.

23. Ibid., p. 89.

24. Ibid., p. 95.

Chapter 7
The Worldwide Food Situation Now

1. Schuettinger and Butler 1979, p. 25.

2. William Bradford, *Of Plymouth Plantation*, edited by Samuel Eliot Morison (New York: Knopf, 1963), reprinted in the *Journal of Political Economy*, vol. 99, August 1991, back cover.

3. Pequet 1990, pp. 59–60.

4. *The Brookings Bulletin* 1976, 13:1.

5. Sanderson, in Abelson 1975, p. 3.

6. *Newsweek*, 14 March, 1977, p. 85.

7. *Wall Street Journal*, July 7, 1977, p. 28.

8. *Wall Street Journal*, October 10, 1977, p. 22.

9. *Newsweek*, August 15, 1988, p. 36.

10. *Washington Post*, September 26, 1989, A3.
11. Werner Fornos, *Population Politics*, Feb./March 1991, 43–51.
12. Zinsmeister 1989, p. 27.
13. *Farm Journal*, May 1990, p. 16.
14. *The Furrow*, Summer 1992, p. 7.
15. Zinsmeister 1989, p. 27.
16. *Washington Post*, July 26, 1992, p. A3.
17. *Washington Post*, October 20, 1992, A3.
18. For example, Gardner 1981; Bovard 1989; Luttrell 1989; Zinsmeister 1989.
19. *Champaign-Urbana News Gazette*, February 27. 1977, pp. 13–14.
20. *Newsweek*, April 11, 1977.
21. *Wall Street Journal*, August 29, 1977, pp. 1, 12.
22. Don Kendall, "Consumer and Farmer Lose Either Way," AP story in *Champaign-Urbana News Gazette*, July 17, 1977, p. 14-A.
23. *Champaign-Urbana News Gazette*, January 17, 1978, p. A-5.
24. *Newsweek*, 30 January, 1978, p. 29.
25. Ehrlich 1968, pp. 40–41.
26. Don Kendall, "U.S. Ag Experts to India Shift," AP story in *Champaign-Urbana News Gazette*, September 9, 1977, p. A-3.
27. *New York Times*, August 28, 1977, p. 11.
28. Kasturi Rangan, "Indian Price Supports Lead to Bigger Grain Crops," *New York Times*, November 28, 1976.
29. Aird 1982, p. 268.
30. *Statistical Yearbook of China* 1983, p. 105.
31. Ibid., p. 13.
32. Watson 1988, p. 15.
33. Eberstadt 1988, p. 144.
34. Ibid., pp. 19, 71.
35. Ogaya and Tsuya 1988, p. 15.
36. UN Demographic Yearbook 1990, p. 179.
37. Brown 1978, pp. 86–90.
38. Ogaya and Tsuya 1988, p. 35.
39. FAO *Production Yearbook* p. 27.
40. *Wall Street Journal*, December 29, 1976, p. 1.
41. *Wall Street Journal*, December 20, 1976.
42. Ibid.
43. Rydenfelt 1984, p. 111.
44. Schuettinger and Butler 1979.

Chapter 8
Are We Losing Ground?

1. Eckholm 1976, p. 9.
2. *New York Times*, April 15, 1976.
3. *New York Times*, August 28, 1977, p. 1.
4. *Newsweek*, 19 September, 1977.

5. Fichter 1972, pp. 36–67.
6. Eckholm, letter of July 15, 1991.
7. *Washington Post*, March 8, 1993, A2.
8. Kumar 1973, p. 112.
9. Ibid., p. 259.
10. Barlowe 1972, p. 46.
11. *Wall Street Journal*, February 24, 1977, p. 1.
12. Eckholm 1976, p. 19.
13. *Washington Post*, July 21, 1991, A18.
14. Schlesinger et al. 1990, p. 1043.
15. *The Furrow*, January 1993, pp. 30, 31.
16. Wagret 1968, p. vi.
17. Ibid., p. 85.
18. Ibid.
19. *Wall Street Journal*, June 28, 1991, p. 3A.
20. Malthus 1803, p. 78.
21. Childe 1950, pp. 138–39.
22. Robert M. Adams 1976, p. 19.
23. U.S. the White House 1967, 1:64.
24. For example, *Science*, 3 April, 1992, p. 28.
25. Epstein 1965, p. 177.
26. University of Illinois, *Student-Staff Directory*, 1976–1977, inside front cover.
27. *Champaign-Urbana News Gazette*, March 6, 1977, p. 1.
28. *Newsweek*, 7 September, 1977, p. 67.
29. *Newsweek*, 20 November, 1974, p. 83.
30. Shoji 1977, p. 62ff.
31. *Chicago Tribune*, February 26, 1978.
32. Roberts 1989, p. 72.

Chapter 9
Two Bogeymen: "Urban Sprawl" and Soil Erosion

1. For more details, see Easterbrook 1986 and Simon 1990.
2. Frey, forthcoming.
3. Ibid.
4. 1974 study, *Our Land and Water Resources*.
5. Dunford 1983, pp. CRS-v and CRS-10.
6. Fischel 1988, p. 202.
7. *Washington Post*, January 28, 1994, A16.
8. *Daily Illini*, March 30, 1977, p. 7.
9. "USDA Says Quality of Cropland on Rise," *Champaign-Urbana News Gazette*, March 5, 1978, p. V-7.
10. Raymond 1984, p. 246.
11. 1992, p. 1.
12. Bills and Heimlich 1984.
13. Swanson and Heady 1984.

Chapter 10
Water, Wood, Wetlands—and What Next?

1. Bisson and El-Baz, no date and references, therein.
2. Wilson and Ramphele 1989.
3. *Washington Post*, February 28, 1992, A3; July 5, 1992, A3.
4. *Washington Post*, April 25, 1990, A3.
5. *Washington Post*, July 11, 1990, A3.
6. Hayward 1991.
7. Howe 1979; Anderson 1995.
8. Leopold 1991, p. 7.
9. Hayward 1991.
10. See Reisner 1986, and quotations of him in chapter 38.
11. In 1850, wood supplied 90 percent of U.S. energy, and 50 percent in 1885. Reference lost.
12. All information in this paragraph is from Sherry H. Olson 1971, p. 2.
13. U.S. Council on Environmental Quality, 1976, p. 315.
14. Adler 1992, p. 19.
15. *Tree Topics*, October 15, 1991.
16. Kauppi, Mielkainen, and Kuusela 1992, p. 70.
17. Ibid. p. 71.
18. Ibid. pp. 70–71.
19. Schulze 1989.
20. U.S. Forest Service 1982, p. 149.
21. *Chemical Week*, February 10, 1988, p.21; see also *Science News*, August 1, 1987, p. 72.
22. *Washington Post*, December 22, 1991, p. A12.
23. *Washington Post*, February 17, 1991, A8.
24. *Washington Post*, April 30, 1991, C4.
25. *Wall Street Journal*, January 9, 1991, A 10.

Chapter 11
When Will We Run Out of Oil? Never!

1. Goeller and Weinberg 1978.
2. Stan Benjamin, "U.S. Energy Use Like Spending the Family Fortune," in *Champaign-Urbana News Gazette*, May 4, 1977, p. 37-C.
3. Jevons 1865, pp. xiv and xvi.
4. Barnett and Morse 1963, p. 181.
5. *Wall Street Journal*, August 22, 1979, p. 6.
6. Kahn et al. 1976, pp. 94–95. Originally from Presidential Energy Program, *Hearings before the Subcommittee on Energy and Power of the Committee on Interstate and Foreign Commerce*, House of Representatives, 1st session on the implications of the president's proposals in the Energy Independence Act of 1975, serial no. 94–20, p. 643 (Washington, D.C.: GPO, February 17, 18, 20, and 21, 1975). DiLorenzo and Bennett 1991, pp. 10–11.
7. Folsom 1988.

8. See Schuettinger and Butler 1979.

9. Madigan 1981, pp. 12, 55, 56.

10. *Daily Illini*, April 4, 1976, p. 7.

11. Hazel Henderson, letter to the editor of the *New York Times*, dated August 16, 1975 (italics added).

12. *Wall Street Journal*, June 4, 1977, p. 18.

13. *Wall Street Journal*, April 27, 1977, p. 22.

14. Ibid.

15. *Wall Street Journal*, September 16, 1977, p. 14.

16. Ibid.

17. Burnett and Ban 1989, p. 306.

18. *Oil Daily*, 4–1–92.

19. *Energy Information Digest*, August 1991, p. 3, quoting from *Science*, June 28, 1991.

20. Kahn et al. 1976, pp. 58, 83.

21. Cohen, in Simon 1995; Rothwell 1992.

22. Edison Electric advertisement, *Wall Street Journal*, September 17, 1992, p. B5.

23. *Science*, December 4, 1992, p. 1574.

Chapter 12
Today's Energy Issues

1. *Advertising Age*, September 24, 1979, p. 48.

2. *Champaign-Urbana News Gazette*, October 16, 1977, p. 2-A.

3. Rafe Pomerance in *Wall Street Journal*, August 20, 1992, A1.

4. Merklein and Hardy 1977, p. 39; *Middle East Information Series* 1974, p. 104.

5. Bernardo Grossling, quoted in the *Wall Street Journal*, September 14, 1977, p. 18; and American Petroleum Institute, *Basic Petroleum Data Book*, January 1992, table 22a.

6. Joseph Barnea, quoted in the *Wall Street Journal*, September 14, 1977, p. 18, from UN Pergamon Press book, suggests that the estimate would rise by a factor of 100.

7. *Wall Street Journal*, May 3, 1977, p. 1.

8. Lynd et al., 1991.

9. *Washington Post*, February 27, 1990, C1.

10. Rose, in Abelson 1974, p. 91.

11. Cohen, in Simon 1995. The calculation is quite dependent on the choice of the assumed cost of capital, especially when the construction period is very long.

12. Brown, Flavin, and Postel 1991, p. 62.

13. Cheyfitz 1944, p. 130.

14. For sound assessments of the subject see Michaels and Lave, both in Simon 1995; for a brief discussion, see chapter 18 on environmental scares.

15. See articles in Abelson 1974.

16. *Wall Street Journal*, August 22, 1979, p. 6.

17. Howard Benedict, "Giant Space Power Plant Urged by Boeing Study," AP story in *Champaign-Urbana News Gazette*, February 9, 1978, p. 1.

18. *Newsweek*, April 17, 1978, p. 101.

19. Daniel J. Jourdan, letter to editor, *Washington Post*, September 8, 1990, A20.

20. *Newsweek*, August 20, 1990, p. 40.

21. NAS reference; see also Bernard Cohen 1984; forthcoming.

22. National Academy of Sciences 1979, pp. 487–88.

23. Bernard L. Cohen 1977.

24. Fred A. Donath, "Deep Storage Could Solve Nuclear Waste Problem," *Champaign-Urbana News Gazette*, May 8, 1977, p. 2-A.

25. Marvin Resnikoff, "Nuclear Wastes—The Myths," *Sierra*, July/August 1980, pp. 30–35.

26. *Washington Post*, January 27, 1990, A3.

27. Shmuel Yaari 1974, p. 4.

28. Shah of Iran, quoted in *Jerusalem Post*, September 27, 1974.

29. Mitchell 1974, table A-3, p. 82.

30. *Near East Report*, August 28, 1974, p. 188.

31. *Newsweek*, March 3, 1975, p. 31; see also *International Economic Report of the President* 1974; Zonis 1976.

32. Barkai 1977, p. 16.

33. *New York Times*, December 25, 1977, p. E-3.

34. *Wall Street Journal*, December 23, 1977, p. 2.

35. Ibid.

36. *Washington Post*, June 25, 1989, p. H7.

37. Charles Krauthammer in *Washington Post*, March 5, 1993, A21.

38. *Wall Street Journal*, July 14, 1978, p. 1.

39. *Wall Street Journal*, August 14, 1978, p. 2.

40. "Possible Misconduct within Energy Unit Is Charged in Study of Oil-Pricing Cases," *Wall Street Journal*, December 11, 1978, p. 10.

41. "Kerr-McGee to Settle U.S. Oil-Price Claims," *Wall Street Journal*, February 9, 1979, p. 4.

42. Margaret Gentry, "Natural Gas Company to Pay $1 Million Fine," *Champaign-Urbana News Gazette*, July 28, 1979, p. 1.

43. Rich Jaroslovsky, "U.S. Is Accusing Nine Major Oil Concerns of $1.1 Billion in Consumer Overcharges," *Wall Street Journal*, November 9, 1979, p. 2.

44. "Mobil Oil Ordered to Pay $500,000 Fine on Criminal Charges Involving Gas Sales," and "Indiana Standard Settles Price Case for $100 Million," *Wall Street Journal*, February 15, 1980, p. 3.

45. "The Price is Wrong—By $716 Million," *Newsweek*, February 25, 1980, p. 60.

46. *Wall Street Journal*, August 13, 1980, p. 27.

47. *Wall Street Journal*, April 13, 1977, p. 24.

48. U.S., the White House 1952, 1:21.

49. For a full day-to-day commentary from this point of view, one need only read the editorials of the *Wall Street Journal* (which, by the way, is no friend of the oil companies' policies).

50. The above paragraph was adapted from Donald Bauder, "Energy Program: Huge Spending," Copley News Service in *Champaign-Urbana News Gazette*, June 16, 1978, p. A-4. Originally from Supran Energy Corp.; also *Budget of the U.S. Government, Fiscal Year 1992*; *Energy Statistics Sourcebook*; *Oil and Gas Journal Energy Database*; phone conversation between Grant Thompson and George Hoffman of the personnel department of DOE.

51. Robert Samuelson, *The Washington Post*, February 27, 1991, A25.

52. Driessen 1987, p. 14.

53. Wells 1962, p. 213.
54. Brown et al. 1991, p. 40.
55. Lewis 1990, pp. 255–56.
56. Daly 1979, p. 77, name of source lost.

Chapter 13
Nuclear Power: Tomorrow's Greatest Energy Opportunity

1. Karl Cohen 1984; Bernard Cohen, forthcoming; Rothwell 1992, finds coal to be perhaps 20 percent cheaper.
2. Bethe 1969, p. 92.
3. See also Bernard Cohen article and book.
4. Taylor 1989; Gray 1989.
5. *Newsweek*, August 13, 1990, p. 65.
6. Larry Thompson, "Scientists Reassess the Long-Term Impact of Radiation," *Washington Post*, August 14, 1990, pp. 12–14.
7. Ibid. *Newsweek* and *Washington Post*.
8. *International Herald Tribune*, October 15, 1992, p. 9.
9. *Journal of the American Medical Association* 1989, p. 2729.
10. Ibid. p. 2728.
11. Ibid.
12. *Science*, "News and Comment," May 31, 1991, p. 1245.
13. "Newsline," *Journal of Nuclear Medicine*, vol. 31, November 1, 1990, 11A.
14. Wing 1991.
15. Sagan 1989; Wolff 1989.
16. Abelson 1991.
17. Hoyle and Hoyle 1980, pp. 59–61.
18. *Access to Energy* 18, July 1991, p. 1.
19. *Wall Street Journal*, June 18, 1992, p. A5.
20. Lovins 1977.
21. *Washington Post*, December 13, 1990, p. E3.

Chapter 14
A Dying Planet? How the Media Have Scared the Public

1. *Washington Post*, April 16, 1989, p. F7.
2. "Blue Planet: Now or Never—A Statement," Blue Planet Group, September 1991, Ottawa, Canada (4-page xerox).
3. April 16, 1990 broadcast.
4. Fichter 1972, pp. 28–35.
5. Adler 1992, p. 27.
6. Metzger and Whittaker 1991; see London 1984 for a devastating analysis of environmental untruth in school texts.
7. Adler 1992.
8. Sherman 1990, p. 226.
9. Environmental Research Associates, *The Environmental Report: The Power of Children*, reported in *Public Opinion*, U.S. Council for Energy Awareness, November 1992.
10. *New York Times*, January 23, 1977, p. 44.

11. Shapiro 1991.
12. MG/AP poll 31, May 11–20, 1990.
13. *New York Times*/CBS, March 30–April 2, 1990.
14. *Wall Steet Journal*, August 2, 1991, A1. For more data, see Dunlap 1991.
15. *The Harris Poll*, April 1, 1990.
16. *Roper Reports 92–1*, p. 25.
17. MG/AP poll 31, May 11–20, 1990.
18. *Fortune*, March 26, 1990, p. 226.
19. MG/AP poll 31, May 11–20, 1990.
20. CBS News Poll, April 16, 1990.
21. Gilbert n.d., pp. 121–22.
22. Richard Harwood, ombudsman, *Washington Post*, May 31, 1992, C6.
23. Bloomgarden 1983, p. 48.
24. 1972, quoted by Dunlap and Scarce 1991, p. 651.
25. Opinion Research Corporation, quoted by Wattenberg 1974, p. 226.
26. *Los Angeles Times*, November 2, 1993, pp. C1 ff.

Chapter 15
The Peculiar Theory of Pollution

1. *Chicago Tribune*, April 19, 1970, p. 19.
2. Tarbell 1939/1985, p. 12.
3. Segal 1991 (newspaper story).
4. *Wall Street Journal*, May 30, 1991, p. B1.
5. Logan 1976, p. 332.
6. The study was by Bernhard Metzger of Arthur D. Little, for the OECD. My information about it comes from Cross 1992, and I found it just before sending the typescript to the publisher; I regret that I did not have time to obtain and examine the original, and therefore cannot vouch for the accuracy of this description.
7. Keeney 1990; Wildavsky, personal discussion.
8. Krupnick and Portney 1991, p. 524.
9. Hall et al. 1992.
10. Clark 1989.
11. Ehrlich 1981, p. 45.
12. Raven 1988, p. 229.
13. *ZPG Reporter*, September 1991, p. 1.
14. Nordhaus and Tobin 1972.
15. "News and Comment," *Science*, July 6, 1990, pp. 18–19.
16. Daly 1991.

Chapter 16
Whither the History of Pollution?

1. H. B. Creswell, quoted by Jane Jacobs in *Architectural Review*, December 1958, p. 19.
2. Quoted by Alfred Friendly 1970.
3. *U.S. News and World Report*, December 15, 1969, p. 77.

4. *Statistical Bulletin* of the Metropolitan Life Insurance Company, May 1977, p. 9.

5. Ames, in Simon 1995.

6. Holen, in Simon 1995.

7. Winslow 1980, pp. 244–5.

8. Tarbell 1985, p. 9.

9. Winter 1982, p. 116.

10. *Courier Gazette*, Rockland, Maine, Thursday, April 9, 1992, page unknown.

Chapter 17
Pollution Today: Specific Trends and Issues

1. Baumol and Oates 1984, p. 442. See Brimblecombe and Rodhe 1988 for additional history of air pollution.

2. Schwartz 1991, p. 212.

3. *Statistical Abstract* 1991, table 360.

4. Both from *Science*, "News and Comment," August 26, 1988, p. 26.

5. *NWI Resource*, vol. 2, June 1991, p. 10.

6. *Washington Post*, May 21, 1991, pp. A1, 15.

7. Kornai 1980; Bernstam, n.d.

8. In Elsom 1987, p. 236.

9. *Wall Street Journal*, May 2, 1990, ed page.

10. World Resource Institute 1990, table 24.5, p. 351.

11. UNEP 1987, table 1–12, p. 18.

12. Herfindahl and Kneese 1965, p. 2.

13. *New York Times*, February 6, 1977, page unknown.

14. *Time*, November 30, 1979, p. 44. See also Goldman 1970, pp. 294–307.

15. Waters 1990, p. 51.

16. *Science*, "News and Comment," August 26, 1988, p. 26.

17. *World Resources*, 1990–1991, table 22–2.

18. *Washington Post*, January 3, 1990, p. B8.

19. *Washington Post*, July 29, 1993, p. A3.

20. *Washington Post*, July 30, 1993, p. B3.

21. Quoted by Alfred Friendly 1970.

22. *Newsweek*, November 16, 1970, p. 67.

23. *Statistical Abstract of the U.S.*, various years; the quote is from "News of the Week in Review," *New York Times*, October 10, 1976, p. 4.

24. *Wall Street Journal*, September 15, 1977, p. 1. For the classic ecologists' analysis of Lake Erie, see Barry Commoner 1972, pp. 91–108. In fairness, I must add that Commoner noted that the total fish catch had not declined in the fashion Ehrlich and others charged (p. 93).

Chapter 18
Bad Environmental and Resource Scares

1. Barrons 1981, p. 97.

2. Tierney 1988, p. 35, adapted from Doll and Peto.

3. Ibid.

4. Ibid.

5. Whelan 1985.

6. Morgan 1990.

7. *San Francisco Chronicle*, September 11, 1992, p. A13.

8. *Washington Post*, December 17, 1992, p. A11.

9. *Wall Street Journal*, November 13, 1992, p. B2.

10. Maurice and Smithson 1984, chapter 9.

11. Leakey 1981, p. 151.

12. Raymond 1984, chapter 3.

13. Maurice and Smithson 1984, chapter 8.

14. Mazur 1981, p. 1.

15. Maurice and Smithson 1984, chapter 3.

16. Ibid.

17. Maddox 1972.

18. Mellanby 1989.

19. General references: Harrison, Whelan, Claus, George, and Karen Bolander, *Ecological Sanity* (New York: David McKay, 1977). Malaria cases in Ceylon in Whelan 1985.

20. Whelan 1985 and the host of references therein; Jukes 1992b. Re food chain and DDT, see Edwards 1992.

21. American Council on Science and Health 1982/1988.

22. Mazur 1981.

23. Lehr 1992, p. 86; Ray and Guzzo 1990, chapter 7.

24. Williams 1992.

25. *Washington Post*, January 26, 1993, Health p. 5.

26. Singer 1992.

27. Gosline 1987, personal correspondence.

28. Ibid.

29. Whelan, correspondence, January 22, 1993.

30. Whelan and Stare 1992, pp. 112–13.

31. *Newsweek*, May 11, 1992, p. 69.

32. Whelan 1985, p. 111.

33. Ibid., p. 109.

34. Ibid., p. 187–90; Ray and Guzzo 1990, chapter 7.

35. *Science*, vol. 257, September 4, 1992, p. 1335.

36. Whelan p. 94.

37. Ray and Guzzo 1990, p. 83. Bennett 1991; Ross 1992.

38. Schiager 1992.

39. The work was bad beyond ordinary scientific error. After much inquiry, the Office of Research Integrity of the U.S. Department of Health and Human Services decided that though it was entirely flawed, and correction should be published, "no scientific misconduct was found." *Washington Post*, March 9, 1994, p. A7.

40. Feinstein 1988, p. 1259; Orient 1992. *Washington Post*, February 3, 1993, p. A2.

41. *Wall Street Journal*, January 7, 1991, p. A14, cited by Tullock and Brady 1992.

42. Whelan 1985, pp. 185–86.

43. Ibid. pp. 120ff.

44. ACSH News Release.

45. Feinstein 1988, p. 1259.

46. *Wall Street Journal*, March 22, 1993, p. A1.

47. Whelan 1989.

48. Gosline 1987.

49. Whelan correspondence, January 22, 1993.

50. Whelan 1985; Ray and Guzzo, 1990, pp. 78–79.

51. Hobbs and Radke, 1992.

52. *Washington Post*, June 25, 1991, p. A3.

53. Adelman 1993.

54. *Washington Post*, February 14, 1993, p. A5.

55. Ibid., p. C6; *Newsweek*, February 8, 1993, p. 24.

56. "A statistician," *Readers Digest*, December 1989, p. 63.

57. Ralph Nader, quoted in *Wall Street Journal*, September 20, 1977, p. 20.

58. Ray and Guzzo 1990, chapter 5.

59. Brookes 1990, p. 2.

60. Ibid.

61. From Bray 1991.

62. *New York Times* Staff, 1975, p. 170.

63. *Washington Post*, May 19, 1992, p. A3.

64. Penner, Dickinson, and O'Neill 1992.

65. For reliable scholarly assessments which provide the full background to these propositions, please see Landsberg 1984; Michaels 1992, in Simon 1995; Balling 1992; Ellsaesser forthcoming; and Idso 1989. For some economic analyses of the consequences even if global warming were to occur, see Dornbush and Poterba 1991.

66. *Washington Times*, November 3, 1989, article by Cheryl Wetzstein.

67. For additional skeptical climatological discussion concerning global warming, see Jastrow 1992; Balling 1992; and Michaels 1992. For additional economic views of greenhouse effects, see Nordhaus 1992; Schelling 1992; and Lave, forthcoming; they discuss the wisdom of various policies given various assumptions about climatology.

68. *Time*, February 17, 1992, quoted in *MediaWatch*, March 1992, p. 1.

69. Singer 1989.

70. Elsom, 1987, p. 122.

71. *MediaWatch*, March 1992, p. 1.

72. Ray, n.d.

73. Singer 1989; forthcoming.

74. Ellsaesser 1990.

75. Hayden, forthcoming.

76. *Washington Post*, Washington Business, January 4, 1992, p. 5.

77. *Washington Post*, February 13, 1993, p. E1.

78. *Washington Post*, June 1, 1993, p. A1.

Chapter 19
Will Our Consumer Wastes Bury Us?

1. *Wall Street Journal*, article by Anne Nichols and Michael Allen, n.d.

2. Rathje and Murphy 1992, p. 162.

3. Ibid., pp. 114–15.

4. O'Neill 1991.

5. Environmental Research Associates, *The Environmental Report: The Power of Children*, reported in *Public Opinion*, U.S. Council for Energy Awareness, November, 1992.

6. David A. Hindin, November 25, 1989, p. A22.

7. Rathje 1989, p. 101.

8. Wiseman 1991a, p. 5.

9. Rathje 1989, p. 101.

10. Ibid.

11. Adapted from Wiseman 1991b.

12. Wiseman 1991b.

13. Scarlett 1991a, b, and c.

14. *Wall Street Journal*, August 31, 1989, p. B1.

15. Barnes 1991.

16. Rathje and Murphy 1992a, p. 35.

17. *Wall Street Journal*, June 2, 1992, pp. A1, 8.

18. *Wall Street Journal*, October 21, 1992, p. B4.

19. *Chicago Sun-Times*, February 26, 1993.

20. *Wall Street Journal*, August 1, 1993, p. A2.

21. *Newsweek*, January 28, 1974, p. 83.

22. *Time*, December 2, 1974, p. 59.

23. *Newsweek*, November 27, 1989, p. 63.

Chapter 20
Should We Conserve Resources for Others' Sakes?

1. *Washington Post*, July 10, 1991, p. B1.

2. O'Neill 1991.

3. Eric Kaufman, *The Daily Record,* April 21, 1990.

4. Weidenbaum 1991, reprint with no page number.

5. Van Hise 1910, p. 363.

6. Smith 1990, and Anderson and Leal 1989, give many such examples.

7. *Washington Post,* December 27, 1993, p. A3.

8. *Champaign-Urbana News Gazette*, October 16, 1977, p. 52-C.

9. *Wall Street Journal*, April 24, 1991, p. A1.

10. *Washington Post*, February 23, 1991, p. C1.

11. Johnson 1974b, pp. 35–37.

12. Ibid., p. 35, quoting from *Hearings on U.S. and World Food Situation*, 93rd Congress, 1st session, October 1973, p. 103.

13. Steven Conwin, letter to editor, *New York Times Magazine*, June 30, 1974, p. 20.

14. *The Humanist*, April 1975, p. 20.

15. Study described in *Daily Illini*, October 20, 1977, page unknown.

16. *New York Times*, October 9, 1977, p. 48.

17. The measurement of the average is complex statistically and definitionally, and need not be addressed here. See U.S. OTA 1991.

18. Crandall and Graham 1989, p. 118; *Consumers Research*, April 1991, p. 18.

19. Joan Claybrook, president of Public Citizen, quoted in *Washington Post*, July 5, 1991, p. A17.

20. *Champaign-Urbana News Gazette*, March 15, 1977, p. 2.

21. *Champaign-Urbana Caravan*, December 10, 1975, p. 3.
22. *The End of Starvation*, n.d., p. 6.
23. *Champaign-Urbana News Gazette*, March 18, 1973, p. 9.
24. *Washington Post*, December 6, 1989, p. A3.
25. Houthakker 1976, p. 122 (italics added).
26. Barnett and Morse 1963, p. 249.
27. *Newsweek*, September 30, 1974, p. 52.
28. *Wall Street Journal*, February 11, 1977, p. 8.

Chapter 21
Coercive Recycling, Forced Conservation, and Free-Market Alternatives

1. Lord 1983.
2. *Los Angeles Times*, April 19, 1989, part 5, pp. 1–2.
3. Ehrlich Debate, p. 9.
4. Garfield 1992.
5. Postrel and Scarlett 1991, p. 25.
6. Ibid., p. 24; Levin 1988.
7. Postrel and Scarlett 1991, p. 24.
8. July 23, 1991, p. C5.
9. *Wall Street Journal*, January 12, 1993, p. B1.
10. Logomasini 1991, p. 3; *Green Market Watch*, Citizens for the Environment, April 1992.
11. *Wall Street Journal*, May 11, 1992, p. B1.
12. *Wall Street Journal*, November 3, 1977, p. 1.
13. *Wall Street Journal*, January 25, 1989, p. B4.
14. *Wall Street Journal*, June 19, 1992, p. B1.
15. Anderson and Leal 1989, pp. 16–17.
16. May 22, 1992, p. A4.
17. See Barnum 1981.
18. Smith 1990, p. 26.
19. Anderson 1988.
20. Shaw and Stroup 1988.
21. Cited in Anderson and Leal 1989, p. 5.
22. *Washington Post*, May 8, 1992, p. D1.
23. *Washington Post*, July 17, 1991, p. D1.
24. For example, Anderson and Leal 1989.

Chapter 22
Standing Room Only? The Demographic Facts

1. Fichter 1972, pp. 24–25.
2. London 1984.
3. Ibid., p. 38.
4. Harrison Brown 1954, p. 221, quoted in Barnett and Morse 1963, p. 30.
5. No date, chapter 4.
6. Genesis 13:6–9.

7. Quoted by C. L. Sulzberger, *New York Times*, December 18, 1977, pp. iv–19.

8. Spengler 1978.

9. Quoted by Kleinman 1980, p. 231.

10. Ibid.

11. G. Myrdal 1968, p. 974.

12. *Statistical Yearbook of Indonesia*, Biro: Jakarta, 1990.

13. Annabelle Desmond, "How Many People Have Ever Lived on Earth?" *Population Bulletin 18: 1–19*. Reprinted in Kenneth C. W. Kammeyer, ed., *Population Studies*, 2nd ed. Chicago: Rand McNally, 1975.

14. Deevey 1960, in Ehrlich, Holdren, and Holm 1971, p. 49.

15. Cook and Borah 1971, p. 199.

16. Fogel, in Simon 1995.

17. *Wall Street Journal*, April 9, 1991, p. B1.

18. Bernstam and Carlson, n.d.

19. Eberstadt 1992/1995, pp. 53, 68.

20. Bernstam and Carlson, n.d., table 6.

21. Cover story, *Washington Post* Health section.

Chapter 23
What Will Future Population Growth Be?

1. Petty 1899, p. 464.

2. *Recent Social Trends in the United States*, vol. 1, *Report of the President's Research Committee on Social Trends* 1933, p. xx, quoted in Price 1967, p. 12.

3. U.S. Department of State 1969, p. 2.

4. *Time*, April 1, 1974, p. 40.

5. Lester R. Brown, McGrath, and Stoker 1976, p. 3.

6. *New York Times*, July 28, 1978.

7. Phone cite from UN World Population Chart 1990, doc. ST/ESA/SER.A/116/rev.

8. Elliot R. Morss and Ritchie H. Reed, eds., *Economic Aspects of Population Change* (Washington, D.C., 1972), p. 4, as quoted by Larry Neal, *Illinois Business Review*, March 1978, vol. 35, no. 2.

9. *Washington Post*, December 4, 1992, p. A10; *Wall Street Journal*, December 4, 1992, p. B1.

10. *Washington Post*, August 2, 1990, p. D3.

11. Ascher 1978; Armstrong 1978.

12. Miller 1992.

13. Wolfers 1971, p. 227.

14. Communication from Agnes Loo, Hong Kong Ministry of Labor, October 20, 1986.

15. DeGregori 1990.

16. Keyfitz and Flieger 1990, pp. 210, 279.

17. 1975 data, courtesy of Paul Handler and PLATO, University of Illinois.

18. *Historical Statistics of the United States* 1976, p. 16.

19. Latter forecasts from Keyfitz and Flieger 1990, p. 201.

20. Ibid., p. 210 for Bangladesh, assuming male proportion same as total.

21. *Wall Street Journal*, April 24, 1991, p. A1.
22. CEQ 1986, table 7–9, p. C-123.
23. *New York Times*, December 25, 1990, p. 7.
24. *Wall Street Journal*, April 18, 1991, p. B9.

Chapter 24
Do Humans Breed Like Flies? Or Like Norwegian Rats?

1. Vogt 1948, p. 228.
2. Sax 1960, p. 23.
3. Quoted by Howard Rusk in *New York Times*, August 4, 1968, p. 71.
4. 1989, p. 236.
5. Calhoun 1962.
6. Price 1967, p. 4.
7. van Vleck 1970.
8. Price 1967, p. 4.
9. Malthus 2d. ed. 1803, p. 203.
10. Gregg 1955a, p. 74, quoted by Barnett and Morse 1963, p. 31.
11. Gregg 1955b, p. 682.
12. Kirk 1969, p. 79.
13. Malthus, 2d ed., 1803, p. 3.
14. Ibid., pp. 3, 9.
15. Arensberg 1968, pp. 107–8.
16. Banfield 1958, p. 45.
17. Ibid., pp. 111–12.
18. See Stys data analyzed in Simon 1974; David, Mroz, and Wachter 1985; David and Mroz 1986.
19. Krzywicki 1934, p. 216; Nag 1962, p. 142.
20. Firth 1939/1965, pp. 36–37.
21. Firth 1936, p. 491.
22. Carr-Saunders 1922, p. 230.
23. Ibid., p. 124.
24. Ford 1952, p. 773.
25. Ibid., pp. 765–66.
26. Blake 1972.
27. Williams and Pratt 1990.
28. Stuart 1958, p. 99.
29. Freeman 1992, p. 25.
30. See Simon, 1973.
31. *Champaign-Urbana Courier*, January 20, 1971, p. 1.
32. Rainwater 1965, pp. 162–73.
33. Whelpton, Campbell, and Patterson 1966, p. 55.
34. Repetto 1976; Mueller 1976.
35. William Borders, "Indian Sees Benefits in His 8 Children," *New York Times*, May 30, 1976, p. 18.
36. Mamdani 1973, p. 109.

37. Carl E. Taylor 1965, pp. 482–83.

38. Ben-Porath 1976; Schultz 1976; Knodel 1968; and Knodel and Van De Walle 1967.

39. Malthus, 5th ed., 1817/1963, p. 12.

40. For me, one of the great mysteries of the intellectual world is the continued re-publication of Malthus's first edition—even by scholars of the first rank whose intellectual honesty is beyond question, such as Kenneth Boulding, who wrote an introduction to a re-publication of the first edition—though Malthus essentially repudiated his simple first-edition theorizing in later editions.

Chapter 25
Population Growth and the Stock of Capital

1. Johnson and Lee 1987.
2. Alonso and Fajans 1970, summarizing Mera 1970, and Fuchs 1967.
3. Alonso 1970, p. 439.
4. Stevens 1978, summarizes previous literature and presents an analysis of bank rates.
5. Edward K. Hawkins, in Wilson et al. 1966, p. 2.
6. L. J. Zimmerman 1965, p. 113.
7. Lebergott 1984, p. 91.
8. Clark and Hasswell 1967, p. 189.
9. Owen 1964, pp. 23–24.
10. Clark and Haswell 1967, p. 179.
11. Lebergott 1984, pp. 91, 92.
12. U.S., the White House 1967, 2:582.
13. Segal 1976, shows that this is true for the United States.
14. Habakkuk 1963, p. 615.
15. Wilson et al. 1966.
16. Angle 1954, pp. 102–3.
17. Boyd 1991.

Chapter 26
Population's Effects on Technology and Productivity

1. This first answer is largely definitional because the average worker's output per day is the same as the average worker's income per day, and aside from differences in the proportion of the population that works and the number of work days per year, average output per worker arithmetically equals per capita income.
2. Solow 1957; Denison 1962.
3. *Washington Post*, July 10, 1990, p. E7.
4. *Wall Street Journal*, September 20, 1990, p. B1.
5. Hofstadter 1985, p. 128.
6. Ibid.
7. *Science*, Research News, vol. 240, November 3, 1989, p. 580.
8. *Washington Post*, November 18, 1991, p. A3.
9. Petty 1899, p. 474.

10. Kuznets 1960. Just to make it a bit harder to criticize this basic idea by impugning its source, let us note that this general point of view has been stated by William Petty, the seventeenth-century English statistician who had no ideological axe to grind; by Colin Clark, who is indeed a Roman Catholic as "charged" by so many antinatalists; by Simon Kuznets, a non-Catholic non-Communist Nobel prize winner, who, economists agree, knows the broad factual outlines of economic-statistical history better than anyone who ever lived; and by Friedrich Engels, Marx's co-worker, who stated the argument most cogently and completely. If this point of view represents some sort of plot, the plotters obviously are a peculiar set of bedfellows.

11. Lester Brown 1974, p. 149.

12. Raymond 1984.

13. Miller, ed., in Hume 1985, pp. 115, 118.

14. Ibid., p. 118.

15. Ibid., p. 119.

16. Ibid., p. 120.

17. Ibid., p. 122.

18. 1951, p. 10.

19. Raymond 1984, pp. 141–42.

20. *Champaign-Urbana News Gazette*, June 17, 1978, p. A-4.

21. Bethe 1976, p. 2.

22. Mohr 1969, p. 112.

23. See Simon and Sullivan 1989, or Simon 1992.

24. Observation of this phenomenon by economists goes back to von Thunen in the nineteenth century (1966) and was demonstrated theoretically and empirically by Chayanov (1966). But Boserup (1965) has explored this idea most thoroughly and has presented a large quantity of supporting data. In the last decade anthropologists have found that this idea fits a great many of their observations in a variety of cultures; for a valuable integration and summary, see Mark Cohen (1977).

Evidence for the working of this process in Mesopotamia was presented by Smith and Young (1972; 1983). McCorriston and Hole (1991) provide evidence on the technical preconditions, including diversity of habitat, seasonal stress due to climatic change, social organization, and technological change. The contributions to the relevant theory may be distinguished as follows: Schmookler focused on induced invention for new knowledge induced by income and industrial growth but not population. Boserup focused on *adoption*, induced by population growth, of known inventions. Petty and Kuznets referred to the *supply of new inventors*. Barnett focused on *demand for new knowledge* induced by diminishing supplies of natural resources.

25. Elsewhere (1977, chapter 8, and 1978) I have studied the distinction between these two types of inventions both theoretically and with historical examples. See Simon 1992, chapter 10.

26. See also Simon and Steinmann 1991, reprinted in Simon 1992; Maurice and Smithson 1984.

27. *Science and Industry in the Nineteenth Century* (1953/1970), p. 131.

28. Ibid., pp. 129, 125.

29. See also Simon and Sullivan 1989 in this connection.

30. Ibid., pp. 130–31.

31. *Wall Street Journal*, February 1, 1982, p. 15.

32. Solow 1957, p. 320.

33. Fellner 1970, pp. 11–12.

34. Productivity measured broadly has not done so well in the 1970s in the United States. The reasons for this are not clearly understood, nor is it clear how much of this regression is due to such one-time factors as an increase in women, and a big cohort of youths, in the labor force. In my judgment, however, based on the long-run past, this is more likely to be a pause rather than a change in trend. For more information see Denison 1962.

35. 1993.

36. Love and Pashute 1978.

37. See Simon 1986; 1992, chapter 3, and references therein; Romer 1986.

38. Peterson 1990, pp. 4, 5.

39. Raymond 1984.

40. David Hume, 1777/1987, p. 115.

41. For a more formal theory and additional data, see Simon 1986, especially chapters 2 and 3, and Simon 1992, especially chapters 3 and 16 (Sullivan).

42. 1967, p. 22.

43. Jorgensen and Griliches 1967.

44. *Business Week*, May 7, 1966, pp. 164–65; see also Scherer 1970, p. 349.

45. Griliches 1958, p. 419. For a summary of other studies, all of which also arrive at estimates of a very high rate of return to society on investment in agricultural research, see Hayami and Ruttan 1971.

46. It is not possible in principle to quantitatively compare the amounts of overall knowledge created in two periods; see Simon 1988.

Chapter 27
Economies of Scope and Education

1. Petty 1899, p. 473.

2. The basic paper on learning by doing by an economist is that of Alchian 1963. In it he refers to the Rand Study he did just after World War II, and to the earlier engineering literature. More general data and discussion are found in Hirsch 1956. Since then the theoretical and empirical literature on the subject is large, but to my knowledge has not been well summarized.

3. For the theory, see Simon and Steinmann 1984; or chapters 5–7 in Simon 1987.

4. Sheffer 1970; Alonso and Fajans 1970; Haworth and Rasmussen 1973. Of course clean air is not included in these comparisons of cities of different sizes. But then, neither is the wider variety of cultural and entertainment opportunities in larger cities, and a whole host of other negative and positive factors.

5. Love 1978, and Simon and Love 1990.

6. Simon and Pilarski 1979. See also Winegarden 1975. T. P. Schultz 1987; Simon and Pilarski 1979/1992.

7. Becker 1981.

8. Gomes 1984.

9. The data presented in this chapter should be qualified by the observation that they mostly do not pertain to "Socialist" countries. And another qualification: The effect

of a country's population on its productive efficiency depends, of course, on its physical and political circumstances. One such factor is the extent to which a country is economically integrated with its neighboring countries. If the borders do not much restrict the flow of trade and if transportation is good and cheap, then the size of the country itself is less important. Monaco does not suffer from lack of division of labor, because it is so well integrated with its region; Israel's situation is quite different. Another factor affecting the absolute size of population required for efficiency is the stage of economic development. The less advanced is a society, the fewer specialties at which different people can work. That is, smallness may have less of a depressing effect on a very backward country that on a country further along in industrialization, all else equal (or it may *not* have; we don't have evidence.

Chapter 28
Population Growth, Natural Resources, and Future Generations

1. After Fischman and Landsberg, in Ridker 1972, p. 81.
2. The process is analyzed graphically, with simulation, and with the calculus, for the case of land as a protypical natural resource in Simon and Steinman 1991; see also chapter 3 of Simon 1992.
3. U.S. ERDA 1976.
4. *American Demographics*, September 1990, pp. 52–53.
5. See Simon 1988.
6. Feiss 1963–65, p. 117.
7. *Wall Street Journal*, August 12, 1992, p. B2.
8. Singer 1973, pp. 4–11.

Chapter 29
Population Growth and Land

1. *Smithsonian Magazine*, December 1976, quoted in *The Other Side*, April 1977, p. 1, italics in original.
2. Letter in *The Other Side*, ibid.
3. Takashi Oka, "Can the Spread of Deserts Be Halted?" *Christian Science Monitor*, November 12, 1976, p. 16, quoted in *The Other Side*, ibid.
4. 1957–1958, p. 127.
5. *Washington Post*, July 12, 1992, p. A1.
6. Clark and Haswell 1967, chapter 7.
7. Malthus 1830/1960, p. 15.
8. Compare the view of a conservationist: "Every grain of wheat and rye, every sugar beet, every egg, and piece of meat, every spoonful of olive oil, every glass of wine, depends on an irreducible minimum of earth to produce it. The earth is not made of rubber; it cannot be stretched. As the number of human beings increases, the relative amount of productive earth decreases by the amount" (William Vogt in *Reader's Digest*, January 1949, p. 141; quoted by Zimmerman 1951/1965, p. 815).
9. Connell 1965, pp. 430–31.
10. Ibid., p. 423.

11. Perkins 1969, p. 240.

12. Ibid., p. 77.

13. Ibid.

14. Slicher van Bath 1963, pp. 195–239.

15. Abel 1980, p. 25.

16. Ibid., p. 26.

17. Slicher van Bath 1963, p. 231.

18. Ohkawa 1970, pp. 11, 18, 22.

19. Furnivall 1957, p. 48.

20. Andrus 1948, p. 235.

21. Simon 1975b.

22. Revelle 1974, p. 170.

23. Lele and Mellor 1964, p. 20.

24. UN, Food and Agriculture Organization 1975, p. 24.

25. William Preter, AP story in *Champaign-Urbana News Gazette*, March 21, 1977, p. 5-A.

26. This is the pattern described by von Thunen 1966; Slicher van Bath 1963; and especially recently by Boserup 1965. See Simon 1977, chapter 8, and 1978c.

27. Reference lost.

28. See Sedjo and Clawson 1984, and forthcoming.

29. *Wall Street Journal*, n.d.

30. 1938, p. 376ff.

31. Reid and Lyon 1972, preface.

32. 1980, pp. 39–40.

33. Wright 1968, p. 463.

Chapter 30
Are People an Environmental Pollution?

1. Edwin L. Dale, Jr., "The Economics of Pollution," *New York Times Magazine*, April 19, 1970, pp. 29ff.

2. Commoner 1972, e.g., Shaw 1989.

3. The difference in mortality by income is not merely a matter of higher incomes buying better nutrition. The poorest person in the United States can buy a nutritious diet of soybeans, milk, and dog food. The fact that poor people do not eat such diets speaks to the complexity of the income-health relationship. See Wildavsky 1988, for data.

4. Ridker 1972, p. 25.

5. Birdsall and Griffin 1991, abstract.

6. Kolsrud and Torrey 1991.

7. An interesting account of the logic of sit-tight is found in Nathan Leopold's description of prison (1958):

Penitentiaries are hidebound institutions, regulated down to their tiniest detail by tradition. There is tremendous inertia to overcome in effecting any change. A compelling reason for doing anything in a given way is that it has always been done that way. Obvious improvements, easier ways of doing something are rejected simply

ace to oneself at sea. But the ship did not seem oppressively crowded when we
port. And if the ship's living quarters had included the space devoted to arma-
I think it would have been quite comfortable—for bachelors.
1973, p. 162.
. 136.
974.
Eberstadt 1992/1995, pp. 68–69.
Choldin 1978, p. 109.

33
Economic Picture: Population Growth and Living Standards

w York Times Magazine, May 14, 1967, p. 121.
omas Hardy, The Mayor of Casterbridge (New York: New Am. Lib., Signet,
89.
ovsky 1966, p. 38.
on 1977, p. 56. The calculation was for 1960; it may be a bit more now.
reviews, see Simon 1977, chapter 3; 1989; Chesnais 1985; Lee 1983; Kelley
burg 1987.
nets 1967; Easterlin 1967; Chesnais and Sauvy 1973.
on 1987; National Research Council 1986; for related discussion of LDCs, see
apter.
y 1969, p. 195.
, p. 16.
discussion of an earlier form of this model may be found in Simon 1977,
6. This model is described in Steinmann and Simon (forthcoming) and in
ecent technical papers available from the author on request.
National Research Council 1986.
r 1971, p. 73.
the White House 1972, p. 53.
rlin 1972, p. 45.
week, April 24, 1978, p. 94.
ington Post, July 23, 1992, p. A30.
h and Harriman 1971, pp. 36–67.
–103.
t, p. 89.
1989.

re II: LDCs

1973, p. 15.
124.
d Hoover 1958, p. 275.
1967; Easterlin 1967; Chesnais and Sauvy 1973; Simon and Gobin
rences in endnote 5 in chapter 33.

because they are new. In the management of the prison itself, especially with regard
to custodial matters, there is a certain amount of justification for this conservatism.
The smallest change in routine may involve angles not immediately apparent—not
thought of by the administration. But you can bank on it that there are always three
thousand active brains engaged in watching attentively for the slightest loophole.
And in such matters one mistake is one mistake too many. It is often better, as it is
always safer, to stick by the tried and true.

8. For information on that subject, which is beyond our scope here, see Olson and
Lansberg 1973.
9. *Wall Street Journal*, December 22, 1977, p. 1.

Chapter 31
Are Humans Causing Species Holocaust?

1. Diamond 1990, p. 55.
2. 1991, p. 761.
3. U.S. 1980, I, p. 3.
4. U.S. 1980, II, p. 331.
5. U.S. 1980, table 13–30, p. 331.
6. 1979, pp. 4–5.
7. Holden 1974, ppl 646–47.
8. U.S. 1980, II, p. 328.
9. 1989, p. 28.
10. 1989, p. 102.
11. 1989.
12. 1989, p. 43.
13. Lebergott 1984, p. 427.
14. Labandeira and Sepkoski 1993.
15. Edited by Whitmore and Sayer 1992.
16. Reid 1992, p. 55.
17. Simberloff 1992, p. 85.
18. Heywood and Stuart 1992, p. 93.
19. Ibid., p. 94.
20. Ibid., p. 96.
21. Ibid., p. 102.
22. Brown and Brown 1992, p. 127.
23. Ibid., p. 128.
24. Reid 1992, p. 55.
25. Heywood and Stuart 1992, p. 95.
26. Reid 1992, p. 56.
27. Ibid., p. 57.
28. Ibid.
29. Heywood and Stuart 1992, p. 93.
30. *Science* "News and Comment," written by Charles C. Mann and Mark L. Plum-
mer, June 25, 1993, p. 1868.
31. Ibid., p. 1869.

32. 1989, p. 103.
33. 1961.
34. 1989, p. 30.
35. Ibid., pp. 28 and 29.
36. Ibid., p. 30.
37. 1989, p. 42.
38. *Newsweek*, April 2, 1990, p. 51.
39. *Jerusalem Post*, week ending May 22, 1993, p. A5.
40. 1989, 37.
41. 1990, p. 59.
42. 1987, p. 199.
43. Quoted in Iker 1982, p. 29.
44. *New York Times*, March 8, 1990, p. A1.
45. Diamond 1990, p. 59.
46. 1988, p. 229.
47. Diamond 1990, p. 58.
48. Olson 1989, p. 5.
49. *New York Times*, November 29, 1990, p. A7.
50. 1988, p. 212.
51. 1992, pp. 228–29.
52. *Washington Post*, August 25, 1993, pp. A1, A14.
53. Raven and Wilson 1992, p. 1099.
54. *Science*, November 10, 1989, p. 757.
55. *Wall Street Journal*, August 5, 1993, pp. 1, 14.
56. *Science*, May 17, 1991, pp. 912–13.
57. *Newsweek*, September 9, 1991, p. 55.
58. Photo in *Reason*, December 1990, p. 37.
59. Lebergott 1984, pp. 428–29.

Chapter 32
A Greater Population Does Not Damage Health or Psychological and Social Well-Being

1. Glass 1964, quoted in Bogue 1969, p. 606.
2. Dublin, et al. 1949, p. 73. A peculiarity of the data, however (p. 342): 1939 U.S. life expectancy for white females was 54.6 for "cities of 100,000 or more" but only 51.1 for "other urban places." This does not jibe with lower life expectancy being associated with higher density. But it may be due to selective migration.
3. Glass 1964, in Bogue 1969, p. 606.
4. 1989 UN *Demographic Yearbook*, New York, 1991, table 18.
5. Kitagawa and Hauser 1973, p. 119.
6. Joseph Carter, University of Texas, quoted and described in *Washington Post*, November 16, 1992.
7. For completeness, we should note that, at the *very lowest* population densities, there may be too few people to maintain a chain of malarial and other parasitic infections, and an increase in density may then *increase* the incidence of these diseases. But

this applies only to people living at densities that were (were i stages of human history, and in a few extraordinary si more information, see McNeill 1977, chapter 2.

8. Gourou 1966, pp. 8, 9, 14, 98.
9. Ibid., p. 10.
10. Frederikson, in Heer, 1968, pp. 70–71.
11. Gourou 1966, p. 10.
12. Buer 1968, p. 219.
13. Lebergott 1964, p. 250.
14. Leonard 1979.
15. R. B. Gupta and Dr. K. Gupta, eds., *Internat* October 1979, p. 7.
16. Harrison 1978.
17. Commoner 1972.
18. B. H. Kean quoted in Harold M. Schmeck, ing on Humanity," *New York Times*, Education Sec
19. Huxley 1953, pp. 137–38.
20. Stephen J. Gould, review of Konrad Lor February 27, 1977, p. 2.
21. Hawley 1972; Choldin 1978; Winsborou 1972.
22. Booth and Edwards 1976, p. 308.
23. 1972.
24. Webb 1975, cited by Choldin 1978, p.
25. Ibid.
26. Freedman 1975.
27. Wattenberg 1974, p. 175; Rector 1995
28. 1989.
29. Dorn, p. 557.
30. Nobel winner William Shockley, quot
31. 1952.
32. The interested reader may consult Lindert 1980, in Easterlin 1980; and King
33. Zajonc 1976. The range is three an And interestingly, in the data that Zajonc Scholarship Qualification Test of 1965— dren in two-child families, (b) the first and (c) the first child in the largest families for sets reviewed by Zajonc—a Scotch study French and Scotch data, later-born child dren, just the opposite of the United Sta unwise to attach any meaning, or to ba small in real differences as these.
34. Reid and Lyon 1972, preface. Ha men on a Navy destroyer 390 feet long on three 100 by 50 foot home lots—I k

more s
were i
ments,
    35.
    36.
    37.
    38.
    39.

Chapter
The Big
in MDC

1. *Ne*
2. Th
1962),
3. Kar
4. Sim
5. For
1988; Ahl
6. Kuz
7. Sim
the next c
8. Sauv
9. 1965
10. Full
chapters 4-
a series of
11. See
12. Lade
13. U.S.
14. Easte
15. *News*
16. *Wash*
17. Ehrli
18. Pp. 8
19. Knigh
20. Simo

Chapter 34
The Big Pict

1. Piotrow
2. Ibid., p.
3. Coale a
4. Kuznets
1979. See refe

5. Simon and Gobin 1979.
6. Stryker 1977.
7. *Washington Post*, October 9, 1988, pp. A29, A36; by Blaine Harden.
8. Keyfitz 1985.
9. Ibid., p. 699.
10. Ibid., p. 697.
11. Ibid., p. 696.
12. Ibid., p. 701.
13. Full details are in Simon 1976; or 1992, chapter 8.
14. Kuznets 1965, p. 29 (italics added).
15. Boyd 1972.
16. *New York Times*, April 14, 1976; *Global 2000* II, p. 613.
17. *Time*, April 26, 1976, p. 56.

Chapter 36
The Rhetoric of Population Control: Does the End Justify the Means?

1. H. F. Wollenberg IV, "Davis, Borchers Clash over Vasectomies," *Champaign-Urbana News Gazette*, May 10, 1973, p. 2.
2. Kingsley Davis 1970, p. 33.
3. Sanger 1938, p. 347.
4. Davis 1968, quoted in Elliott et al. 1970.
5. Ehrlich 1968, p. xi.
6. Quoted by Nelson 1990, p. 57.
7. Wertham 1969, chapter 6.
8. Carey, in Carey and Simon 1978.
9. Day and Day 1964, p. 134; Parsons 1971, p. 298; Ehrlich, Ehrlich, and Holdren 1977, p. 807.
10. Silverman 1970.
11. Ibid.
12. L. Brown 1977, p. 148; Ehrlich 1968, p. 36; idem, 1968, p. 41; William P. Bundy, "Learning to Walk," *Newsweek*, February 25, 1972, p. 35.
13. *Newsweek*, March 30, 1970, p. 87.
14. John Stuart Mill's *On Liberty* (1859/1910) discusses this matter with great insight and high passion.
15. Silverman 1970.
16. I mention these facts about Stuart's publication (1958) not to dismiss the book—I think we should try to look beyond the cover of the book to evaluate it—but to show that *despite* its inauspicious start in life the book could obtain so much more interest than could Mather's and the well-known Harpers publishing firm.
17. Testimony before Congressional Subcommittee on Science, Research, and Development, July 21, 1970, quoted by Wolman 1971, p. 97 (italics added).
18. 1972, p. 3.
19. Roszak 1992.
20. Donor card accompanying a PP/WP brochure.
21. Faye Wattleton in fund-raising letter and leaflet accompanying brochure.
22. Paul Ehrlich, "Eco-Catastrophe," *Ramparts* 7: 24–28, 1969.

Chapter 37
The Reasoning behind the Rhetoric

1. Daniel E. Koshland, Jr., July 3, 1987, p. 9.

2. January 17, 1992, p. 265.

3. Borlaug 1971, pp. 8–9: "the frightening power of human reproduction must also be curbed; otherwise, the success of the green revolution will be ephemeral only." Wilson quoted in *Time*, August 1, 1977, p. 58: "It would be foolish, he says, to rear as many healthy children as possible in today's crowded world." Asimov in *Jewish News*, September 23, 1975, p. 32: "natural resources are being haphazardly drained and the population is allowed to grow unchecked . . . the population is increasing faster than the capacity to provide material and food for the growing numbers of people." Gell-Mann, "The Population Crisis: Rising Concern at Home," *Science*, November 7, 1969, p. 723: "We are all of us appalled at man's ravaging of his environment. The problem comes about as a product of three factors: population, the propensity for each individual to destroy the environment, and his capacity to do so through being armed with technology. All of these are increasing; all must be worked on in an effort to find some way to control the trend and ultimately make it level off or reverse." Andrei Sakharov 1978, p. 6. Wilt Chamberlain and David Shaw 1973, *Wilt* (New York: Warner Paperback): "I was especially hoping I would convince Richard [Nixon!] to take the lead in trying to solve the overpopulation problem—probably the biggest problem in the world today, as I see it. I figured that if he would throw the prestige of his office and the power of this country behind some sweeping birth-control programs in the more backward countries, we might make some real progress in that area." Landers, *Chicago Sun-Times*, June 23, 1970, p. 40: "Dear Ann Landers: It is now abundantly clear to even the most emptyheaded fools that something drastic must be done within the next decade to limit the size of families or we are all doomed." The writer then called for sterilization as a remedy. Landers replied, "Yes, I'm with you." "Dear Abby," *Champaign-Urbana News Gazette*, May 9, 1974, p. 34: "When the writers of the Good Book implored us to go forth and multiply, the world needed more people. Not so today. Quite the contrary." Rockefeller in *Newsweek*, March 30, 1970, p. 87 Raffi, *Sic*; *Washington Post*, May 32, 1992 p. G1. *Hammond World Atlas*, 1976, p. E-14. Leontief, Population-Environment Balance, fund-raising letter, no date. Gore, *Washington Post*, July 17, 1992, p. A28; *AmStat News*, February 1991, p. 6.

4. Mowrer 1961, p. 6; Bandura 1986, p. 45; Klerman 1987, p. 17.

5. Letter to a newspaper on a "world without population curbs" in *Des Moines Register*, July 12, 1972, p. 8.

6. Musson 1974.

7. Littlewood 1977, p. 6.

8. Hardin 1974.

9. Stuart 1958, p. 9.

10. Mayer, personal communication, 1980.

11. Love and Pashute [Simon], 1978. This study was originally published under a pseudonym. My purpose was not to hide these views behind the pen name, and in fact the study originally but unsuccessfully sought publication under my real name. It was published under a pseudonym to avoid the impression that the volume in which it was published, which I edited, contained too much of my own material.

12. This is similar to the finding of Kammeyer, Yetman, and McClendon 1972, who used county data.

13. I do not mean to suggest that southern family-planning clinics are bad. Rather, I think that such clinics are good because, like all aids to contraception, they help the individual achieve the kind of family and way of life that he or she wishes. Nevertheless, it seems to me that we should try to understand the motivations that lie behind such clinics, in order that we may meet truthfully and successfully with political objections to the extension of such clinics in the United States and elsewhere. Had the eugenicists Burch, Vogt, and Osborn had their way—which is what Zero Population Growth wants now—about immigration policy, my grandmother could not have entered the United States, and she and her descendants would have perished in Europe during World War II, as did her relatives who remained.

14. New York: Penguin, 1986.

15. Raphael Kazmann, *Modern Hydrology*, cited in Reisner 1986, p. 494.

16. Pp. 498–505, passim.

17. Quoted by Chase 1977, p. 55. I have not been able to verify the exact wording of the old Planned Parenthood slogan, despite perhaps ten phone calls to local and national PP/WP offices, and to their library in New York. At some point even the dedicated researcher must trust his/her memory and get on with the work.

18. Ibid.

19. 1938, p. 375.

20. Ibid., pp. 376–77.

21. If such laws had been on the books in the past, they would have been used against the immigrant ancestors of many of us. If an IQ test indicates a score of 70 or lower the person is designated "feeble-minded or mentally retarded." Administration of the IQ test "to steerage immigrants at Ellis Island [New York] in 1912 showed that, *according to the scores they made on these tests*, more than 80 percent of all Jewish, Italian, Hungarian, Russian, Polish and other non-Nordic people tested were feeble-minded defectives" (Chase 1977, pp. xix, 16). The results of such IQ tests were brought before Congress by the eugenics movement when lobbying to achieve the restrictive U.S. Immigration Act of 1924. The dedication of my 1977 technical book on population is as follows: "For my grandmother, Fanny Goodstein, who never went to school, but whose life made her family and community richer, economically and spiritually." Since I wrote that dedication I have learned (Chase 1977) that predecessors of the leaders of today's population organizations (going back through Guy Burch, director of the Population Reference Bureau, and key intellectual adviser to the environmental movement's early best-selling writers such as Vogt and Osborn) considered people like my grandmother to be mentally incompetent; like other Jewish immigrants from eastern Europe at the turn of the century, she would have scored abysmally low on the IQ test they considered a valid measure of her mental competence; eight out of ten of her sort of immigrant were rated as "feeble-minded defectives" (Chase 1977, p. xix).

22. Littlewood 1977, pp. 107–8.

23. Ibid., p. 80.

24. AP, *Daily Illini*, February 23, 1980, p. 3.

25. *Annual Review of Population Law* 1976, pp. 38–39.

26. *Newsweek*, March 10, 1980; AP, *Champaign-Urbana News Gazette*, March 1, 1980, p. 1.

27. Let me go further. Some of the people involved with these organizations are among the most unselfish and dedicated people that I have ever met. Take, for example, P. who set up a population-relation private enterprise partly to diffuse contraception and partly to create a dependable source of funding for innova tive fertility-reduction programs. He is almost saintly in turning over to nonprofit ventures almost all the profits from the private business that, in the highest conscience, he could have divided among himself and the other stockholders.

28. Daniel Koshland, editor of *Science*, writes: June 5, 1987, quoted in *Wall Street Journal*, July 28, 1987, p. 32.

Chapter 38
Ultimately—What Are Your Values?

1. David M. Graber (National Park Service research biologist), review in the *Los Angeles Times*, quoted by Virginia Postrel in "the Environmental Movement: A Skeptical View," *Vital Speeches* 1990, 732, quoted in "Population, the Environment, and Development—Reference Quotations," Perspectives on Population for UNCED, Office of Representative Chris Smith 5/6/92.

2. I am grateful to Thomas Wonnacott for sending me Dr. Seuss's book.

3. *Washington Post*, April 30, 1992, p. C3.

4. Dasgupta 1969.

5. Mailing piece received August 1980.

6. See Beisner 1988, 1990; and Nelson, 1990

7. Kates, Robert W., and Ian Burton, ed., *Geography, Resources, and Environment*, vol. 1, Selected Writings of Gilbert F. White (Chicago: The University of Chicago Press), 1986.

8. Garden City: Garden City Books, 1917/1936.

9. *Newsweek*, August 12, 1991, p. 44.

10. See her autobiography; Chase 1977; Gould 1981; Kevles 1985; and Proctor 1988, for history of the movement.

11. This information comes from a publication entitled *The Dismal Scientists: Eugenics from 1907–1990* for which no publisher is given, and which arrived in my mail with no cover letter or further identification. There is no doubt of the authenticity of the material, however; a partial list of members of the Eugenics Society, along with extensive bibliographic material on many of them was included in the typescript.

12. Chase 1977, p. 366.

13. Ibid., see chapter 16 for quotes.

14. Proctor 1988, p. 178.

15. Ibid., p. 177.

16. Meade 1955; see also Dasgupta 1969.

17. 1989, p. 76.

18. In Koch and Peden 1944, p. 327.

19. Ronald Reagan in CEQ *Annual Report*, 1986, p. iii.

20. In Raymond 1984, p. 177.

21. *Washington Post Magazine*, October 15, 1989, p. 10.

22. Singh 1989, pp. 2, 4.

23. Cited by Nelson 1990.

24. *Earth First Newsletter*, quoted by Ray 1990, p. 168.

25. July 13, 1992, p. 36.

26. Quoted by Ray 1990.

27. Quoted by Train 1991 in the context of discussion of "Religion and the Environment."

28. Nelson 1990.

Chapter 39
The Key Values

1. Stewart M. Ogilvy (honorary president of Friends of the Earth), "Population," in *Progress As If Survival Mattered: A Handbook for a Conserver Society*, Hugh Nash, ed. (San Francisco: Friends of the Earth, 1981), p. 71. Quoted in "Population, the Environment, and Development—Reference Quotations," Perspectives on Population for UNCED, Office of Representative Chris Smith 5/6/92.

2. Dr. Edward Chasteen, "The Case for Compulsory Birth Control," in *The American Population Debate*, Daniel Callahan, ed. (Garden City, New York: Doubleday, 1971), p. 276. Quoted in "Population, the Environment, and Development—Reference Quotations," Perspectives on Population for UNCED, Office of Representative Chris Smith 5/6/92.

3. Ehrlich 1968, p. 15.

4. *Science*, March 15, 1991.

5. Ehrlich 1968, pp. 197–98.

6. "Protecting the Environment Is a Top Priority," *Wall Street Journal*, November 8, 1989, p. A8.

7. *Washington Post*, Aug 9, 1991, p. A8.

8. *Washington Post*, June 28, 1991, p. B1.

9. *Science*, "News and Comment," January 18, 1991, p. 265.

10. David Berreby correspondence, about 1991.

11. *Washington Post*, March 31, 1991, p. A3.

12. Christensen 1991.

13. *Wall Street Journal*, March 18, 1992, p. B1.

14. *Washington Post*, March 20, 1991, pp. B1, 4.

15. *Washington Post*, March 24, 1991, *Book World*, p. 4.

16. *Wall Street Journal*, letters, October 7, 1992, p. A17.

17. *Washington Post*, June 30, 1992, p. A3.

18. *Washington Post*, September 3, 1992, p. A2.

19. Wolfers 1971, p. 229.

20. Ehrlich 1968, prologue.

21. In Reid and Lyon 1972, p. 197.

22. Willing 1971, p. 161.

23. Kingsley Davis 1968, from Elliott et al. 1970, p. ix.

24. Wattenberg 1974, p. 228.

25. International Advisory Committee on Population and Law 1977, pp. 26, 174.

26. Salaff and Wong 1978.

27. *The Washington Post*, December 22, 1993, pp. A1 and A28.

28. The December 1993 proposal was sufficiently outrageous that it induced newspaper editorials against it in the United States and elsewhere, and China had backed off somewhat at the time of writing this note in press in January 1994. But I have read of no protest by population or women's organizations.

29. Maduro and Schauerhammer 1992, pp. viii, ix.

30. Quoted by Ray 1990, p. 167.

31. *CEI Update*, April 1992, p. 4.

32. Easterbrook 1992, p. 24.

33. Quoted by Jonathan Schell, "Our Fragile Earth," *Discover*, October 1989, p. 47.

34. *Newsweek*, May 4, 1992, p. 68.

35. David Finkel, "Bay Blues," *Washington Post Magazine*, July 7, 1991, p. 10.

36. *Washington Post*, October 13, 1992, p. E1.

37. Chase 1986.

38. 1990, p. 152.

39. Ibid., p. 153.

40. Ibid., p. 160.

41. Ibid., p. 167.

42. Miller 1991.

43. In Hayek 1960.

Conclusion
The Ultimate Resource

1. Wigner 1967/1979.

2. Maurice and Smithson 1984, p. 121.

3. Mazur 1981.

4. Balling 1992, p. 151.

5. David Hume, "The Rise of Arts and Sciences," p. 113, in *Essays: Moral, Political, and Literary* (Indianapolis: Liberty Classics, 1985).

6. 1992.

7. For example, Williamson 1945, pp. 97, 109.

Epilogue
My Critics and I

1. I have analyzed the reasons why biologists think this way in a paper available upon request.

2. November 30, 1993, p. A22.

3. 1961, p. 107.

4. Perhaps I can claim priority in this with my 1977 book (chapter 6) and my 1986 book, which reproduces earlier journal articles on the subject, though the recent body of work seems to have developed independently of my formal work (much of it together with Steinmann).

5. "Chapter on Environmental Destruction," unpublished, received in letter from Wayburn dated November 28, 1990, 2638 Yorktown, Apt. 294, Houston, TX 77056.

6. 1994.

7. November 24, 1993.

8. Wayburn. See endnote 1.

9. This comment and several others to follow that are not endnoted are in Tierney 1990.

10. In an Earth Day meeting across the street which was publicized as well as could be, my colleagues and I spoke to an audience of about 20. Hardin and Ehrlich frequently complain about how the media and the public are hugely attracted to our utterances. Of course we sometimes do better than this meeting, but the doomsayers are hardly thrust out of public attention by us.

11. Tierney, p. 81.

12. *St. Louis Post-Dispatch*, December 13, 1993, pp. D1, 4.

13. Ehrlich 1981, cited in Simon 1990, p. 374.

14. Theirs is the only such commentary on an essay in this college text of readings on the environment. And of course my essay is the only one that does not sing in the environmentalist chorus, undoubtedly being included for "balance." As is often the case, the editor feels it necessary to follow me with a damage-control squad, lest I mislead innocent minds.

15. A. Ehrlich and P. Ehrlich 1994, p. 26.

16. Manuscript of George D. Moffett, The Woodrow Wilson Center, November 17, 1993.

17. "Turning Dreams Into Reality," *People*, vol. 1, no. 4, 1989, p. 16.

18. Quoted in Tierney.

19. Ehrlich and Ehrlich 1991, p. 229.

20. P. Ehrlich and A. Ehrlich 1995, p. 22.

21. *The Red and Black* (University of Georgia), April 9, 1991.

22. Tierney.

23. In *Social Science Quarterly*, reproduced in Simon 1990, p. 379.

24. *The Red and The Black*, April 9, 1991.

25. *Dodging Doomsday*, in the Horizon series, June 1, 1992.

26. Moffett.

27. Tierney, p. 81.

28. Myers and Simon 1994.

29. Abernethy 1991. The author, who teaches in a department of psychiatry, is the editor of the journal in which this article appeared. It purports to be an economic argument, but I cannot follow enough of it to criticize it.

30. Ehrlich and Ehrlich 1991, p. 228.

31. 1993, p. 385.

32. Ehrlich and Ehrlich 1990, p. 20 of galley proofs. Or see their 1991, p. 228: "Julian Simon, a specialist in mail-order marketing."

33. BBC Horizon, p. 18.

34. Professor William R. Hawkins, *AICF Special Report*, April 1991.

35. "Population and Development Within the Ecosphere: A Bibliographic Essay," xerox, December 1990.

36. Anderton 1988.

37. Simon 1989.

38. *Wall Street Journal*, September 14, 1992, p. A10.

39. 1925/1959, p. 12.

40. Ibid., p. 19.

41. "Editorial: The Dismal Science," in a magazine of which Asimov was the editor. I possess only the photocopy of this page.

42. 1993, pp. 377, 378, 379.

43. *Washington Post*, December 14, 1990, p. A27.

44. Sirageldin and Kantner, 1982, p. 172.

45. Mark Plotkin, World Wildlife Fund, Cox Newspapers.

46. Garrett Hardin in *The New Republic*.

47. Cited in Simon 1990, p. 396.

48. Letter from Peter Samuels, June 28, 1992.

49. Cited by Tierney 1990.

50. Ehrlich and Ehrlich 1991, p. 229. There is a certain irony in Ehrlich's frequent lament that I do not understand science, given that I am the author of a text on research methods in social science that has gone through three successful editions (the first being the bestseller for a while); basic methods in social science are much the same as research methods in other sciences. Ehrlich also taxes me with lack of quantitative understanding—for example, "count to 20" in the quote preceding this endnote—when I can fairly claim to be the main inventor of the resampling (Monte Carlo) approach to statistics (including the first publication of the bootstrap technique) which is now revolutionizing all of that subject; see that same book (Simon 1969; third edition with P. Burstein 1985, and other publications on request).

51. For full details on this incident, see Simon 1990, selection 54.

52. See previous footnote.

53. Sanford Thatcher 1994.

54. More of the Mellon letter and about the incident may be found in Simon 1990, selection 57.

55. Rae 1965, pp. 126–27.

56. Mill 1859/1910, p. 112.

References

Books of special interest to the lay reader are marked with one, two, or three asterisks, according to their likely value to such a reader.

Abel, Wilhelm. 1980. *Agricultural Fluctuations in Europe*. New York: St. Martins.

Abelson, Philip H. 1972. "Limits to Growth" (editorial). *Science* 175.

————, ed. 1974. *Energy: Use, Conservation and Supply*. Washington, D.C.: AAAS.

————. 1975. *Food: Politics, Economics, Nutrition, and Research*. Washington, D.C.: AAAS.

Abelson, Philip H. 1991. "Radon Today—The Role of Flimflam in Public Policy." *Regulation* (Fall): 95–100.

Abercrombie, Keith, and Arthur McCormack. 1976. "Population Growth and Food Supplies in Different Time Perspectives." *Population and Development Review* 2 (September/December):479–98.

Abernethy, Virginia. 1991. "How Julian Simon Could Win the Bet and Still Be Wrong." *Population and Environment* 13 (Fall):3–7.

Adams, Richard P. 1974. "On the Necessity of Literature." *AAUP Bulletin* (Spring):24–26.

Adams, Robert M. 1965. *Land behind Baghdad*. Chicago: University of Chicago Press.

————. 1976. "From Sites to Patterns." *University of Chicago Magazine* 19 (March).

Adelman, Irma. 1963. "An Econometric Analysis of Population Growth." *American Economic Review* 53:314–19.

Adelman, Ken. "Surmounting the Fear-Mongers," *Washington Times*, July 30, 1993, editorial.

Adelman, Morris A. 1995. "Trends in the Price and Supply of Oil." In Simon, ed. 1995.

* Adler, Cy A. 1973. *Ecological Fantasies*. New York: Green Eagle Press (241 W. 97th St., NY 10025, 212–663–2167).

Adler, Jonathan. 1992. "Little Green Lies." *Policy Review* (Summer):18–26.

Ahlburg, Dennis A. 1987. "The Impact of Population Growth on Economic Growth in Developing Nations: The Evidence from Macroeconomic-Demographic Models." In Johnson and Lee, pp. 479–522.

Aird, John S. 1982. "Population Studies and Population Policy in China." *Population and Development Review* 8, no. 2 (June):268.

* ————. 1990. *Slaughter of the Innocents*. Washington, D.C.: The AEI Press.

Akins, James E. 1975. "The Oil Crisis: This Time the Wolf Is Here." In *Economics of Energy*, edited by Leslie E. Grayson, pp. 268–90. Princeton, N.J.: The Darwin Press.

Alchian, A. A. 1963. "Reliability of Progress Curves in Airframe Production." *Econometrica* 31:679–93.

Alonso, William (with Michael Fajans). 1970. "The Cost of Living and Income by Urban Size." Working Paper #128, Institute of Urban and Regional Development, University of California, Berkeley.

————. 1971. "The Economics of Urban Size." *Papers of the Regional Science Association* 26.

Alvarez, Luis W. 1987. *Adventures of a Physicist*. New York: Basic Books.

American Council on Science and Health. 1987. "E.P.A. Erred in Report on Lead in Drinking Water." News release in *ACSH News & Views* 8, no. 2 (March/April).

———. 1988. "Irradiated Foods." 3d ed. December.

* Anderson, Terry L. 1983a. *Water Crisis: Ending the Policy Drought*. Baltimore: Johns Hopkins University Press.

* ———. 1983b. *Water Rights: Scarce Resource Allocation, Bureaucracy, and the Environment*. Cambridge, Mass.: Ballinger Press.

———. 1995. "Water, Water Everywhere, But Not a Drop to Sell." In Simon, ed., 1995.

Anderson, Terry L., and Donald R. Leal. 1989. "Insider Our Outdoor Policy." *Cato Institute Policy Analysis*, September 29.

* ———. 1991. *Free Market Environmentalism*. San Francisco: Pacific Research Institute for Public Policy and Westview Press.

Anderton, Douglas. 1988. Review of Simon 1986. *Contemporary Sociology* (July):506–7.

———. 1989. Response to Simon 1989. *Contemporary Sociology* (March):170.

Andrus, J. Russell. 1948. *Burmese Economic Life*. Stanford: Stanford University Press.

Angle, Paul, ed. 1954. *The Lincoln Reader*. New York: Pocket Books.

Arensberg, Conrad M. 1968. *The Irish Countryman*. 2d ed. New York: Macmillan.

Armstrong, Scott. 1978. *Long-Range Forecasting: From Crystal Ball to Computer*. New York: Wiley.

* Arnold, Andrea. *Fear of Food*. 1990. Bellevue, Washington: Free Enterprise Press.

* Arnold, Ron. 1987. *Ecology Wars*. Bellevue, Washington: Free Enterprise Press.

Ascher, William. 1978. *Forecasting: An Appraisal for Policy Makers and Planners*. Baltimore: Johns Hopkins University Press.

Ashton, Basil, Kennith Hill, Alan Piazza, and Robin Zeitz. 1984. "Famine in China, 195–1961." *Population and Development Review* 10 (December) 613–45.

Atack, Jeremy. 1995. "Long Trends in Productivity." In Simon, ed. 1995.

Atkinson, Ian. 1989. "Introduced Animals and Extinctions." In *Conservation for the Twenty-first Century*, edited by David Western and Mary C. Pearl. New York, Oxford: Oxford University Press.

Bachrach, Peter, and Elihu Bergman. 1973. *Power and Choice: The Formulation of American Population Policy*. Lexington, Mass.: Lexington Books.

* Back, Kurt W. 1989. *Family Planning and Population Control*. Boston: Twayne Publishers.

Bacon, Francis. 1605/1944. *Advancement of Learning and Novum Organum*. New York: Wiley.

* Baden, John. 1984. *The Vanishing Farmland Crisis*. Lawrence: University of Kansas Press.

* Baden, John, and Richard L. Stroup. 1981. *Bureaucracy vs. Environment: The Environmental Costs of Bureaucratic Governance*. Ann Arbor: University of Michigan Press.

** Baden, John, and Donald Leal, eds. 1990. *The Yellowstone Primer: Land and Resource Management in the Greater Yellowstone Ecosystem*. San Francisco: Pacific Research Institute for Public Policy.

** Bailey, Ronald. 1993. *Ecoscam: The False Prophets of Ecological Apocalypse*. New York: St. Martins Press.

Baker, David B., and R. Peter Richards. 1992. "Herbicide Concentrations in Ohio's

Drinking Water Supplies: A Quantitative Exposure Assessment." In Lehr, pp. 84–100.

** Balling, Robert. C., Jr. 1992. *The Heated Debate*. San Francisco: Pacific Research Institute.

Bandura, Albert. 1986. *Social Foundations of Thought and Action—A Social Cognitive Theory*. Englewood Cliffs, N.J.: Prentice Hall.

Banfield, Edward. 1958. *The Moral Basis of a Backward Society*. Chicago: Free Press.

Banks, Ferdinand E. 1976. *The Economies of Natural Resources*. New York: Plenum Press.

Barkai, Haim. 1977. Reflections on the Political Economy of Energy Conservation in the United States. Mimeo. Research report 100, Department of Economics, Hebrew University of Jerusalem. Mimeo.

Barlowe, Raleigh. 1972. *Land Resource Economics: The Economics of a Real Property*. 2d ed. Englewood Cliffs, N.J.: Prentice Hall.

Barnes, John A. 1991. "Learning to Love the Dump Next Door." *Wall Street Journal*. June 25, p. A22.

Barnett, Harold J. 1971. "Population Problems—Myths and Realities." *Economic Development and Cultural Change* 19 (July).

*** Barnett, Harold, and Chandler Morse. 1963. *Scarcity and Growth*. Baltimore: Johns Hopkins Press.

Barnum, P. T. 1855–1869/1981. *Struggles and Triumphs* New York: Penguin.

Baron, Galo Wittmayer. 1952. *A Social and Religious History of the Jews*. New York: Columbia University Press.

** Barrons, Keith C. 1981. *Are Pesticides Really Necessary?* Chicago: Regnery. (This excellent book delves into a variety of subjects related to the present volume but for which there is no space.)

Barrow, John D., and Frank J. Tipler. 1988. *The Anthropic Cosmological Principle*. New York: Oxford University Press.

Bass, Frank M. 1978. "The Relationship between Diffusion Rates, Experience Curves, and Demand Elasticities for Consumer Durable Technological Innovations." Paper no. 660, Institute for Research in the Behavioral, Economic and Management Schools, Purdue University, Lafayette, Ohio. Mimeo.

Bass, Frank M., Trichy V. Krishnan, and Dipak C. Jain. 1994. "Why the Bass Model Fits without Decision Variables." *Management Science* vol. 3, no. 3 (Summer): pp. 203ff.

Bauer, Peter T. 1976. *Dissent on Development*. London: Weidenfeld and Nicholson.

Baumol, William. 1986. "On the Possibility of Continuing Expansion of Finite Resources," *Kyklos* 39 (Fasc. 2): 167–79.

Baumol, William J., and Wallace E. Oates. 1984. "Long-Run Trends in Environmental Quality." In *The Resourceful Earth*, edited by Julian L. Simon and Herman Kahn, pp. 439–75.

** Baxter, William F. 1974. *People or Penguins: The Case for Optimal Pollution*. New York: Columbia University Press. (An excellent short introduction to the relevant theory.)

Becker, Gary S. 1981. *A Treatise on the Family*. Cambridge: Harvard University Press.

* Beckerman, Wilfred. 1974. *In Defense of Economic Growth*. London: Jonathan Cape.

** Beckmann, Peter. 1976. *The Health Hazards of Not Going Nuclear*. Boulder, Colo: Golem Press.

Beckmann, Petr. 1984. "Solar Energy and Other 'Alternative' Energy Sources." In *The Resourceful Earth*, edited by Julian L. Simon and Herman Kahn, pp. 415–27.

———. 1992. "Electromagnetic Fields and VDT-itis." In Lehr, pp. 253–66.

* Beisner, E. Calvin. 1988. *Prosperity and Poverty: The Compassionate Use of Resources in a World of Scarcity*. Westchester, Ill: Crossway Books.

* ———. 1990. *Prospects for Growth: A Biblical View of Population, Resources, and the Future*. Westchester, Ill: Crossway Books.

———. 1992. *Centesimus Annus, The Nature of Man, and the Human Economy*. Mimeo.

Bell, David E., Howard Raiffa, and Amos Tversky, ed. 1988. *Decision Making*. Cambridge: Cambridge University Press.

** Bennett, Michael J. 1991. *The Asbestos Racket*, Washington: Free Enterprise Press.

* Bennett, M. K. 1954. *The World's Food*. New York: Harper & Brothers.

Ben-Porath, Yoram. 1976. "Fertility Response to Child Mortality: Microdata from Isreal." *Journal of Political Economy* 84:S168–78.

* Bernal, J. D. 1953/1970. *Science and Industry in the Nineteenth Century*. London: Routledge and Kegan Paul.

Bernstam, Michael S. 1995. "Comparative Trends in Resource Use and Pollution in Market and Socialist Economies." In Simon, ed. 1995.

Bernstam, Mikhail S. 1990. "The Wealth of Nations and the Environment." Xerox.

Bernstam, Mikhail S., with Elwood Carlson. n.d. "Productivity of Resources, Economic System, Population and the Environment: Is the Invisible Hand Too Short or Crippled?" Xerox.

Bethe, Hans A. 1969. "Atomic Power: The Quality of Life." Edited by Cornell University Faculty Members. Ithaca, N.Y.: Cornell University Press.

———. 1976. "The Necessity of Fission Power." *Scientific American* 234:16ff.

Bills, Nelson L., and Ralph E. Heimlich. 1984. "Assessing Erosion on U.S. Cropland—Land Management and Physical Features." U.S. Department of Agriculture, Agricultural Economic Report Number 513, July.

Birdsall, Nancy, and Charles Griffin. 1991. "Population Growth: Externalities and Poverty." The World Bank, February.

Bisson, Robert A., and Farouk El-Baz. n.d. *Megawatersheds Exploration Model*. Laconia, N.H.: BCI Geonetics.

Blainey, Geoffrey. 1973. *The Causes of War*. Glencoe: Free Press.

Blake, Judith, and Prithwis Das Gupta. 1972. "The Fallacy of the Five Million Women: A Re-Estimate." *Demography* 9, no. 4 (November): 569–88.

** Block, Walter E., ed. 1990. *Economics and the Environment: A Reconciliation*. Vancouver, B.C.: Fraser Institute.

Bloom, David G., and Neil G. Bennett. 1989. "Future Shock." *The New Republic* (June 19) 18–21.

Bloomgarden, Kathy. 1983. "Managing the Environment: The Public's View." In *Public Opinion* (February/March): 47ff.

Bogorad, Lawrence. n.d. "Overview of the Potential and Prospects in Genetic Engineering of Plants." In *Chemistry and World Food Supplies: The New Frontiers CHEMRAWN II*, edited by L. W. Shemilt, pp. 553–62. New York: Pergamon.

Bogue, Donald. 1969. *Principles of Demography*. New York: Wiley.

Booth, Alan, and John N. Edwards. 1976. "Crowding and Family Relations." *American Sociological Review* 41:308–21.

Borlaug, Norman E. 1971. We Must Expand Population Research Now to Slow World Population Growth. In Population Crisis Committee, *Mankind's Greatest Needs: Population Research*. Washington, D.C.: Population Crisis Committee.

Boserup, Ester. 1965. *The Conditions of Agricultural Growth*. London: Allen & Unwin.

Bourgeois-Pichat, J. 1989. "From the 20th to the 21st Century: Europe and Its Population after the Year 2000." *Population*, English selection no. 1 (September): 57–90.

Bovard, James. 1989. *The Farm Fiasco*. San Francisco: Institute for Contemporary Studies.

Boyd, Robert. 1972. "World Dynamics: A Note." *Science* 177:516–19.

Boyd, William Young II. 1991. "Not Another Panama Canal Treaty—Another Panama Canal," *Wall Street Journal*, September 6, p. A9.

Bray, Anna J. 1991. "The Ice Age Cometh." *Policy Review* (Fall): 82–84.

Brimblecombe, Peter. 1987. *The Big Smoke*. London: Methuen.

Brimblecombe, Peter, and Henning Rodhe. 1988. "Air Pollution—Historical Trends." *Durability of Building Materials* 5:291–308.

Brobst, Donald. 1979. "Fundamental Concepts for the Analysis of Resource Availability." In Vincent Kerry Smith, ed., 1979, pp. 106–42.

Brookes, Warren T. 1990. "Acid Rain: The $140 Billion Fraud?" *Consumer Comments* 14 (November). (Publication of Consumer Alert.)

Brown, Gardner M., Jr., and Barry C. Field. 1978. "Implications of Alternative Measures of Natural Resource Scarcity." *Journal of Political Economy* 86:229.

Brown, Harrison, James Bonner, and John Weir. 1963. *The Next Hundred Years*. New York: Viking Press.

Brown, K. S., and G. G. Brown. 1992. "Habitat Alteration and Species Loss in Brazilian Forests." In T. C. Whitmore and J. A. Sayer, pp. 119–42.

Brown, Lester, 1974. *In the Human Interest: A Strategy to Stabilize World Population*. New York: Norton.

———. 1978. *The Twenty Ninth Day*. New York: W. W. Norton.

Brown, Lester R., William U. Chandler, Alan Durning, Christopher Flavin, Lori Heise, Jodi Jacobson, Sandra Postel, Cynthia Pollock Shea, Linda Starke, and Edward C. Wolf. 1988. *State of the World—1988*. New York: W. W. Norton.

Brown, Lester R., Christopher Flavin, and Sandra Postel. *Saving the Planet*. 1991. New York: W. W. Norton.

Brown, Lester, Patricia L. McGrath, and Bruce Stoker. 1976. *Twenty-two Dimensions of the Population Problem*. Washington, D.C.: Worldwatch Institute.

Buer, M. C. 1968. *Health, Wealth, and Population in the Early Days of the Industrial Revolution*. Repr. of 1926 ed. London: Routledge.

Bugbee, Bruce G., and Fank B. Salisbury. 1988. "Exploring the Limits of Crop Productivity." *Plant Physiology* 91:869–78.

Burnett, W. M., and S. D. Ban. 1989. "Changing Prospects for Natural Gas in the United States." *Science* 244 (April 21): 305–10.

Cambel, A. B. 1993. *Applied Chaos Theory—A Paradigm for Complexity*. San Diego: Academic Press.

Campbell, Jeremy. 1982. *Grammatical Man*. New York: Simon and Schuster.

Carey, James W., and Julian L. Simon. 1978. "The Church's Responsibility to Teach the Value of Life: A Surprising Dialogue between Catholic and Jew." Univeristy of Illinois, Urbana, Dept. of Economics. Mimeo.

Carlson, Allan C. (undated correspondence) quoting Richard Neuhaus, *In Defense of People*. New York: MacMillan, 1971, p. 187, quoting Hardin.

Carlson, Elwood, and Mikhail S. Bernstam. n.d. "Population and Resources Under the Socialist Economic System." Xerox.

Carr-Saunders, A. M. 1922. *The Population Problem: A Study in Human Evolution*. Oxford: Oxford University Press.

Cerf, Christopher, and Victor Navasky. 1984. *The Experts Speak*. New York: Pantheon.

Chase, Allan. 1977. *The Legacy of Malthus*. New York: Alfred A. Knopf.

Chase, Alston. 1986. *Playing God in Yellowstone: The Destruction of America's First National Park*. New York: Atlantic Monthly Press.

Chayanov, A. V. 1966. *The Theory of Peasant Economy*. Edited by D. Thorner et al. Homewood, Ill.: Irwin.

Chesnais, Jean-Claude. 1985. "Progres Economique et Transition Demographique dans les Pays Pauvres: Trente Ans d'Experience (1950–1980)." *Population* 40:11–28.

Chesnais, Jean-Claude, and Alfred Sauvy. 1973. "Progrès économique et accroissement de la population; une expérience commentée." *Population* 28: 843–57.

Cheyfitz, Edward T. 1944. "More For Less." *Fortune* 30, no. 6 (December): 130–31.

Childe, Gordon. 1950. *What Happened in History*. Baltimore: Penguin.

China Population Newsletter 1990. vol. 7, no. 1 (February).

Choldin, Harvey M. 1978. "Urban Density and Pathology." *Annual Review of Sociology* 4:91-113.

Choucri, Nazli. 1974. *Population Dynamics and International Violence*. Lexington, Mass: Lexington Books.

Christensen, Sally Thane. 1991. "Is a Tree Worth a Life?" *Newsweek* (August 5): pp. 9, 11.

* Clark, Colin. 1957. *Conditions of Economic Progress*, 3rd ed. New York: Macmillan.

* Clark, Colin 1967. *Population Growth and Land Use*. New York: St. Martin's Press.

Clark, Colin. 1978. "Population Growth and Productivity." In Julian L. Simon, 1978c.

* Clark, Colin, and Margaret Haswell. 1967. *The Economics of Subsistence Agriculture*. New York: St. Martin's Press.

Clark, Mary E. 1989. Letter to editor. *Science* 246 (October 6): 10.

Claus, George, and Karen Bolander. 1977. *Ecological Sanity*. New York: David McKay.

Cloud, Preston. 1969. "Mineral Resources from the Sea." In National Academy of Sciences. *Resources and Man: A Study and Recommendations*. San Francisco: W. H. Freeman.

———. 1971. "Resources, Population, and Quality of Life." In *Is There an Optimum Level of Population?* edited by S. Fred Singer. New York: McGraw-Hill.

Clough, Shepard B. 1951, 1957. *The Rise and Fall of Civilization*. New York: Columbia University Press.

Coale, Ansley, and Edgar M. Hoover. 1958. *Population Growth and Economic Development in Low-Income Countries*. Princeton, N.J.: Princeton University Press.

Cohen, Bernard L. 1980. "The Disposal of Radioactive Wastes from Fission Reactors." *Scientific American* (June). In *Energy and Environment: Readings from Scientific American*, edited by Raymond Silver. San Francisco: W. H. Freeman, 1980.

** Cohen, Bernard. 1983. *Before It's Too Late: A Scientist's Case for Nuclear Energy*. New York: Plenum Press.

————. 1984. "The Hazards of Nuclear Power." In *The Resourceful Earth*, edited by Julian L. Simon and Herman Kahn, pp. 545–65.

Cohen, Karl. 1984. "Nuclear Power." In *The Resourceful Earth*, edited by Julian L. Simon and Herman Kahn, pp. 387–414.

Cohen, Mark Nathan. 1977. *The Food Crisis in Prehistory*. New Haven, Conn. Yale University Press.

Cohn, Norman. 1970. *The Pursuit of the Millennium*. London: Granada Publishing.

Colinvaux, Paul A. 1989. "The Past and Future Amazon." *Scientific American* (May): 102–8.

Commoner, Barry. 1972. *The Closing Circle: Nature, Man, and Technology*. New York: Bantam.

Conable, Barber. 1988. In *Population and Development Review* 14 (December): 753–55.

Connell, K. H. 1965. "Land and Population in Ireland, 1750–1845." In *Population in History*, edited by D. V. Glass and D.E.C. Eversley. Chicago: Aldine.

Conquest, Robert. 1986. *The Harvest of Sorrow*. New York: Oxford University Press.

Consumer Alert. 1990. "Asbestos Rip-Out, Consumer Rip-Off." *Consumer Alert Comments* 14, no. 2 (March): 1.

Cook, Earl. 1976. "Limits to Exploitation of Non-Renewable Resources," *Science* 191 (February 20): 677–82.

Cook, Robert C. 1951. *Human Fertility: The Modern Dilemma*. New York: Sloane.

Cook, Robert C., and Jane Lecht, eds. 1973. *People!* Rev. ed. Washington, D.C.: Columbia Books.

Cook, Sherburne F., and Woodrow Borah. 1971. *Essays in Population History: Mexico and the Caribbean*. Berkeley: University of California Press, pp. viii–82.

Cornelius, Wayne A. 1977. "Illegal Migration to the United States: Recent Research Findings, Policy Implications, and Research Priorities." Center for International Studies, MIT. Mimeo.

Council on Environmental Quality. 1986. *Environment Quality—17th Annual Report*, p. iii.

Crandall, Robert W., and John D. Graham. 1989. "The Effect of Fuel Economy Standards on Automobile Safety." *Journal of Law & Economics* 32 (April): 97–118.

Crane, Barbara. 1989. "Policy Responses to Population Growth: A Global Perspective." In *Population and U.S. Policy*, Principia College, April 20–22.

Crane, Barbara, and Jason L. Finkle. 1989. "The United States, China, and the United Nations Population Fund." *Population and Development Review* 15 (March): 23–60.

Critchfield, Richard. 1981. *Villages*. Garden City, N.Y.: Anchor Press/Doubleday.

Cross, Frank B. 1992. "Environmental Protection and Economic Growth," *Kansas Journal of Law and Public Policy* 2 (Spring): 53–65.

Crosson, P. R., and A. T. Stout. 1983. *Productivity Effects of Cropland Erosion in the United States*. Washington, D.C.: Resources for the Future.

Cuhsan, Alfred G. Forthcoming. "Demographic Correlates of Political Instability in Latin America: The Impact of Population Growth, Density, and Urbanization." *Review of Latin American Studies*.

Daly, Herman, ed. 1973. *Toward a Steady-State Economy*. San Francisco: W. H. Freeman.

Daly, Herman E. 1977. *Steady-State Economics*. San Francisco: W. H. Freeman.

Daly, Herman E. 1991. Letter to editor. *Science* 254 (October 18): 358.

Daly, Herman E., and John B. Cobb, Jr. 1989. *For the Common Good*. Boston: Beacon Press.

Darmstadter, Joel. 1972. *Energy*. In Ridker 1972.

Darmstadter, Joel, et al. 1971. *Energy in the World Economy*. Baltimore: Johns Hopkins University Press.

Dasgupta, Partha. 1969. "On the Concept of Optimum Population." *The Review of Economic Studies* 36:295–318.

David, Paul A., Thomas A. Mroz, and Kennth W. Wachter. 1985. "Rational Strategies of Birth-Spacing and Fertility Regulation in Rural France during the Ancien Regime." Working Paper 14, Stanford Project on the History of Fertility Control, March. Xerox.

David, Paul A., and Thomas A. Mroz. 1986. "A Sequential Econometric Model of Birth-Spacing Behavior Among Rural French Villagers, 1749–1789." Working Paper no. 19, Stanford Project on the History of Fertility Control, January. Xerox.

Davidson, Cliff I. 1979. "Air Pollution in Pittsburgh: A Historical Perspective." *Journal of the Air Pollution Control Association* 29 (October): 1031–40.

Davis, Joseph S. 1953. "The Population Urge and the American Economy, 1945–80." *Journal of Political Economy* 61:369–88.

Davis, Kingsley. 1970. "The Climax of Population Growth: Past and Future Perspective." *California Medicine* 113, no. 5, 33–39.

Day, Lincoln H., and Alice Day. 1964. *Too Many Americans*. New York: Houghton Mifflin.

* Deacon, Robert T., and M. Bruce Johnson, eds. 1985. *Forestlands: Public and Private*. San Francisco: Pacific Institute for Public Policy Research.

De Beijer, J. R. 1979. "Brazil." *World Wood Review* (July): 38–39.

Deevey, Edward S. 1960. "The Human Population." *Scientific American* 203:195–204. In Ehrlich, Holdren, and Holm 1971.

DeGregori, Thomas R. 1990. "Ehrlichs and the Population 'Bomb' that Didn't Explode." Review of *The Population Explosion*, in the *Houston Chronicle*, July 8.

Demeny, Paul. 1986. "Population and the Invisible Hand." *Demography* 23 (November): 473–88.

———. 1989. "Demography and the Limits to Growth." *Population and Development Review*.

Denison, Edward F. 1962. *The Sources of Economic Growth in the United States and the Alternatives Before Us*. New York: Committee for Economic Development.

Desowitz, Robert S. 1991. *The Malaria Capers*. New York: W. W. Norton.

Diamond, Jared. 1989. "Overview of Recent Extinctions." In *Conservation for the Twenty-first Century*, edited by David Western and Mary C. Pearl. New York, Oxford: Oxford University Press.

———. 1990. "Playing Dice with Megadeath." *Discover* (April): 55–59.

DiLorenzo, Thomas, and James Bennett. 1991. *Distrust of Energy Markets Leads to Policy Failures*. St. Louis: Center for the Study of American Business.

Dixon, Bernard. 1973. *What Is Science For?* New York: Harper.

* Donaldson, Peter J. 1990. *Nature against Us*. Chapel Hill: The University of North Carolina Press.

Dorn, Harold F. 1956. "Present Knowledge Concerning the Effects of Differential Fertility." In *Demographic Analysis: Selected Readings*, edited by Joseph J. Spengler and Otis Dudley Duncan, pp. 552–58. New York: Free Press.

————. 1963. "World Population Growth." In *The Population Dilemma*, edited by Philip M. Hauser. Englewood Cliffs, N.J.: Prentice Hall.

Dornbusch, Rudiger, and James M. Poterba, eds. 1991. *Global Warming*. Cambridge, Mass.: The MIT Press.

Dr. Seuss. 1959. *Happy Birthday to You!* New York: Random House.

Driessen, Paul K. 1987. "Pumping Oil—and Growing Fish." *Hispanic Times* (March/April).

Dublin, Louis I., Alfred J. Lotka, and Mortimer Spiegelman. 1949. *Length of Life: A Study of the Life Table*. Rev. ed. New York: Ronald Press.

Duncan, Otis Dudley. 1956. "Is the Intelligence of the General Population Declining?" In *Demographic Analysis: Selected Readings*, edited by Joseph J. Spengler and Otis Dudley Duncan, pp. 577–83. New York: Free Press.

Dunford, Richard W. 1983. "An Overview of the Farmland Retention Issue." Congressional Research Service, December 9.

Dunlap, Riley E. 1987. "Public Opinion on the Environment in the Reagan Era." *Environment* (July/August).

————. 1991. Untitled article. *Environment* (October): 10ff.

Dunlap, Riley E., and Rik Scarce. 1991. "The Polls—Poll Trends." *Public Opinion Quarterly* 55: 651–72.

Dyson, Freeman. 1988. *Infinite in All Directions*. New York: Harper and Row.

Earth-Works Group. 1989. *50 Simple Things You Can Do to Save the Earth*. Berkeley, Calif.: Earthworks Press.

Easterbrook, Gregg. 1986. "Vanishing Farmland Reappears." *Atlantic Monthly* (July): 17–20.

————. 1992. "Green Cassandras." *The New Republic* (July 6): 23–25.

————. 1995. *A Moment on the Earth*. New York: Viking Press.

Easterlin, Richard A. 1955. "The Theory of International Economic Policy," vol. 2. *Trade and Welfare*. London: Oxford University Press.

————. 1967. "Effects of Population Growth in the Economic Development of Developing Countries." *The Annals of the American Academy of Political and Social Science* 369:98–108.

————. 1972. "Comment on Allen C. Kelley, Demographic Changes and American Economic Development: Past, Present and Future." In U.S. Commission on Population Growth and the American Future, *Economic Aspects of Population Change*, edited by Elliot R. Morse and Ritchie H. Reeds, 2:45. Washington, D.C.: GPO.

————, ed. 1980. "Population and Economic Change in Developing Countries." Chicago: University of Chicago Press.

Eaton, Jonathan. 1988. "Foreign-Owned Land." *American Economic Review* 78 (March): 76–88.

Eberstadt, Nicholas. 1988. *The Poverty of Communism*, Transaction.

————. 1992/1995. *The Tyranny of Numbers*. Washington: AEI Press.

————. 1994. "Demographic Shocks in Eastern Germany, 1989–1993." *Europe-Asia Studies* 46, no. 3:519–34.

Eckholm, Erik P. 1976. *Losing Ground: Environmental Stress and World Food Prospects*. New York: W. W. Norton.

Edwards, J. Gordon. 1992a. "DDT Effects on Bird Abundance and Reproduction." In Lehr 1992, pp. 195–216.

————. 1992b. "The Myth of Food-Chain Biomagnification." In Lehr 1992, pp. 125–34.

** Efron, Edith. 1984. *The Apocalyptics: How Environmental Politics Controls What We Know about Cancer*. New York: Simon and Schuster.

Ehrlich, Paul R. 1968. *The Population Bomb*. New York: Ballantine.

————. 1975. *An Ecologist's Perspective on Nuclear Power*. Federation of American Scientists. Cited by Karl Cohen 1984, p. 410. (Source of "machine gun" quote).

————. 1981. "An Economist in Wonderland," *Social Science Quarterly* 62 (March): 45–49.

————. 1982. "That's Right—You Should Check It Out for Yourself." *Social Science Quarterly*, 63 (June): 385–86.

————. 1985. Review of *The Resourceful Earth*. *Bulletin of the Atomic Scientists* (February): 44.

Ehrlich, Paul R., and Anne H. Ehrlich. 1970/1972. *Population, Resources, Environment: Issues in Human Ecology*. 2d ed. San Francisco: W. H. Freeman.

————. 1974. *The End of Affluence: A Blueprint for Your Future*. New York: Ballantine.

————. 1981. *Extinction*. New York: Random House.

————. 1990. *The Population Explosion*. New York: Simon and Schuster.

————. 1991. *Healing the Planet*. Reading, Mass., Menlo Park, Calif., New York: Addison-Wesley.

————. 1995. "Simple Simon Environmental Analysis." In *Environmental Science: Working with the Earth*, 5th ed., edited by G. Tyler Miller, Jr., pp. 22–24. Belmont: Calif.: Wadsworth.

Ehrlich, Paul R., Anne H. Ehrlich, and John P. Holdren. 1977. *Ecoscience: Population, Resources, Environment*. 2d ed. San Francisco: W. H. Freeman.

Ehrlich, Paul R., and Richard L. Harriman. 1971. *How to Be a Survivor: A Plan to Save Spaceship Earth*. New York: Ballantine.

Ehrlich, Paul R., John P. Holdren, and Richard W. Holm, eds. 1971. *Man and the Ecosphere*. San Francisco: W. H. Freeman.

Ehrlich, Paul, and Stephen Schneider. 1995. Op-ed articles, *San Francisco Chronicle*, May 18.

Ehrlich, Paul, and Edward O. Wilson. 1991. "Biodiversity Studies: Science and Policy." *Science* 253 (August 16): 758–62.

Einstein, Albert. 1954. *Ideas and Opinions*. (Based on *Mein Weltbild*, ed. by Carl Seelig, and other sources.) New translations and revisions by Sonja Bargmann. New York: Bonanza Books.

Eliot, Johan W. 1966. "The Development of Family Planning Services by State and Local Health Departments in the United States." In *American Journal of Public Health*, Supplement edited by S. Polgar and W. Cowles (January) 56:6–16.

Elliott, Robin, Lynn C. Landman, Richard Lincoln, and Theodore Tsuruoka. 1971. U.S. Population Growth and Family Planning: A Review of the Literature." In *The American Population Debate*, edited by Daniel Callahan, p. 206. New York: Anchor Books.

Ellsaesser, Hugh W. 1988. "Global 2000 Revisited II." February. Xerox.

————. 1990a. "The Holes in the 'Ozone Hole.'" *21st Century* (Summer): 8–11.

————. 1990b. "Plant Earth: Are Scientists Undertakers or Caretakers?" August. Xerox.

————. 1992. "An Atmosphere of Paradox: From Acid Rain to Ozone." In Lehr 1992, pp. 546–56.

** Elsom, Derek. 1987. *Atmospheric Pollution*. Oxford: Blackwell.

————. 1995. "Atmospheric Pollution Trends in the United Kingdom." In Simon, ed. 1995.

* Engels, Frederick. 1953. "The Myth of Overpopulation." From *Outlines of a Critique of Political Economy* reprinted in *Marx and Engels on Malthus*, edited by Ronald L. Meek. London: Lawrence and Wishart.

Epstein, Trude Scarlett. 1965. "Economic Change and the Differentiation in New Britain." *Economic Record* 41:173–92.

Ericsson, Neil R., and Peter Morgan. 1978. "The Economic Feasibility of Shale Oil: An Activity Analysis." *Bell Journal of Economics* 9:457ff.

est. n.d. *The End of Starvation*. Brochure of The Hunger Project.

* Everett, Alexander H. 1826 / 1970. *New Ideas in Population*. New York: A. M. Kelley.

Eversley, D.E.C. 1965. "Population, Economy and Society." In *Population in History*, edited by D. Glass and D. E. C. Eversley. Chicago: Aldine.

Feinstein, Alvan R. 1988. "Scientific Standards in Epidemiologic Studies of the Menace of Daily Life." *Science* 242 (December 2): 1257–63.

Feiss, Julian W. 1963–65. Minerals. In *Scientific American* eds., *Technology and Economic Development*. Harmondsworth, England: Penguin, in association with Chatto & Windus.

Fellner, William. 1970. "Trends in the Activities Generating Technological Progress." *American Economic Review* 60:1–29.

Ferguson, Adam. 1995. *An Essay on the History of Civil Society*. New Brunswick, N.J.: Transaction Publishers.

Feshbach, Murray. 1995. "Mortality and Health in the Soviet Union." In Simon 1995.

Feynman, Richard P. 1994a. *Six Easy Pieces*. Reading, Mass.: Helix Books, Addison-Wesley.

————. 1994b. *The Character of Physical Law*. New York: Modern Library.

Fichter, George S. 1972. *The Golden Stamp Book of Earth and Ecology*. Racine, Wis.: Western.

Field, Roger. 1988. "Old Macdonald Had a Factory." *Discover* (December): 46–51.

Firth, Raymond W. 1936. *We, the Tikopia*. London: Allen & Unwin.

————. 1939/1965. *Primitive Polynesian Economy*. London: Routledge.

Fischel, William A. 1988. "Discussion: Why Not Disown NALS?" *Land Use Transition in Urbanizing Areas*. Proceedings, June 6–7, pp. 199–205.

Fischman, Leonard L., and Hans H. Landsberg. 1972. "Adequacy of Nonfuel Minerals and Forest Resources." In Ridker 1972.

Fisher, W. Holden. 1971. "The Anatomy of Inflation: 1953–1975." *Scientific American* 225:15–22.

Flesch, Rudolf. 1951. *The Art of Clear Thinking*. New York: Harper.

Flexner, James Thomas. 1969. *Washington—The Indispensable Man*. New York: New American Library.

Flynn, Leonard T. 1992. "Pesticides: Helpful or Harmful?" In Lehr 1992, pp. 61–72.

Folsom, Burt. 1988. "John D. Rockefeller and the Oil Industry." *The Freeman* (October): 402–12.

Fogel, Robert. 1995. "The Contribution of Improved Nutrition to the Decline in Mortality Rates in Europe and America." In Simon 1995.

Ford, Clellan S. 1952. "Control of Conception in Crosscultural Perspective." *World Population Problems and Birth Control. Annals of the New York Academy of Sciences* 54:763–68.

Fornos, Werner. 1984. "A Time for Action." *Populi* 11, no. 1:32–35.

Frederick, Kenneth D., and Roger A. Sedjo, eds. 1991. *America's Renewable Resources: Historical Trends and Current Challenges*. Washington, D.C.: Resources for the Future, Inc.

Frederiksen, Harald. 1968. "Elimination of Malaria and Mortality Decline." In Heer 1968.

Freedman, Jonathan L. 1975. *Crowding and Behavior*. New York: Viking Press.

Freedman, Ronald, and Bernard Berelson. 1974. "The Human Population." *Scientific American* 231:30–39.

Freeman, Derek. 1992. "Paradigms in Collision: The Far-reaching Controversy over the Samoan Researches of Margaret Mead and Its Significance for the Human Sciences." *Academic Questions* (Summer): 5, no. 3: 23–33.

Frey, Thomas H. 1973. *Major Uses of Land in the United States: Summary for 1969*. Agricultural Economic Report no. 247. Economic Research Service. U.S. Department of Agriculture. Washington, D.C.: GPO.

———. 1975. *Cropland for Today and Tomorrow*. Agricultural Economic Report no. 291. Economic Research Service. U.S. Department of Agriculture. Washington, D.C.: GPO.

———. 1995. "Land Use Trends in the United States." In Simon, ed. 1995.

Frieden, Bernard. 1979. "Middle Class, Go Home!" *The Wharton Magazine* 3 (Spring): 24.

Friedman, David. 1972. *Laissez-Faire in Population*. An Occasional Paper of the Population Council.

Friendly, Alfred. 1970. "British Stand Fast in Battle against Pollution of Environment." *Washington Post*. February 5, p. A10.

Fuchs, Victor R. 1967. *Differentials in Hourly Earning by Region and City Size, 1959*. New York: Columbia University Press.

Fuller, Buckminster. 1969. *Utopia or Oblivion: The Prospect for Humanity*. New York: Bantam.

** Fumento, Michael. 1993. *Science Under Siege: Balancing Technology and the Environment*. New York: Morrow.

Furnivall, J. S. 1957. *An Introduction to the Political Economy of Burma*. 3rd ed. Rangoon: Peoples Literature.

Fyfe, W. S. 1981. "The Environmental Crisis: Quantifying Geosphere Interactions." *Science* 213 (July 3): 105–10.

Galle, Omer R., Walter R. Gove, and J. Miller McPherson. 1972. "Population Density and Pathology: What Are the Relations for Man?" *Science* 176 (April 7): 23–30.

Gardner, Bruce. 1979. *Optimal Stockpiling of Grain*. Lexington, Mass: Lexington Books.

———. 1981. *The Governing of Agriculture*. Lawrence: University of Kansas Press.

Garfield, Bob. 1992. "The Sultan of Slag." *The Washington Post Magazine*. June 28, pp. 18–22, 28–30.

Gasser, Charles S., and Robert T. Fraley. 1989. "Genetically Engineering Plants for Crop Improvement." *Science* 244 (June 16): 1293–1306.

George, Henry. 1879/1979. *Progress and Poverty*. New York: Robert Schalkenbach Foundation.

Georgescu-Roegen, Nicholas. 1966. *Analytical Economics*. Cambridge, Mass.: Harvard University Press.

———. 1971. *The Entropy Law and the Economic Process*. Cambridge, Mass.: Harvard University Press.

———. 1979. "Comments on the Papers by Daly and Stiglitz." In *Scarcity and Growth Revisited*, edited by Kevin V. Smith, pp. 95–105. Baltimore: Johns Hopkins University Press.

Ghosh, Palash R. 1990. "Latest Studies Do Not Support Link between Cancer Mortality and Radiation Discharges." *The Journal of Nuclear Medicine* 31, 11 (November): 11A–18A, 25A.

Gilbert, Dennis, A. n.d. *Compendium of American Public Opinion*. New York: Facts on File.

** Gilder, George. 1984. *The Spirit of Enterprise*. New York: Simon and Schuster.

Gillroy, John M., and Robert Y. Shapiro. 1986. "The Polls: Environmental Protection." *Public Opinion Quarterly* 50: 270–79.

Givens, Ron, Karen Springen, and Timothy Noah. 1989. "A Scare in the Corn Belt." *Newsweek*. March 6, p. 70.

** Glasner, David. 1985. *Politics, Prices, and Petroleum*. San Francisco: Pacific Institute.

Glass, Donald V. 1964. "Some Indicators of Differences between Urban and Rural Mortality in England and Wales and Scotland." *Population Studies* 17:263–67.

Glover, Donald, and Julian L. Simon. 1975. "The Effects of Population Density upon Infra-structure: The Case of Road Building." *Economic Development and Cultural Change* 23:453–68.

Godfriaux, Bruce L. 1987. "Net Primary Production: The Tomato Example," *Science* 235 (January 3): 15.

Goeller, H. E., and A. M. Weinberg. 1976. "The Age of Substitutability." *Science* 191, no. 4428: 683–89.

Goldman, Marshall I. 1970. "The Convergence of Environmental Disruption." *Science* 170:37–42. Reproduced in *Economics of the Environment: Selected Readings*, edited by Robert Dorfman and Nancy S. Dorfman. New York: W. W. Norton.

———. 1971. "Ecological Facelifting in the U.S.S.R. or Improving on Nature." In *Maison des Sciences de L'Homme Symposium, 1971, Political Economy of Environment: Problems of Method*, with an introduction by Ignacy Sach. Paris: Mouton.

Goldsmith, Raymond W. 1985. *Comparative National Balance Sheets*. Chicago: University of Chicago Press.

Gomes, Melba. 1984. "Family Size and Educational Attainment in Kenya." *Population and Development Review* 10, no. 4 (December): 647–56.

Goodall, Rae. 1975. *The Visible Scientists*. Boston: Little, Brown.

Gorer, Albert. 1992. *Earth in the Balance*. Boston: Houghton-Mifflin.

Gosline, Carl A. undated. "The History of Environmental Scares." Xerox.

———. 1970. "Doing Something With Really New Ideas." *Les Nouvelle* 5, no. 5 (November).

Gould, Stephen Jay. 1981. *The Mismeasure of Man*. New York: W. W. Norton.

Gourou, Pierre. 1966. *The Tropical World, Its Social and Economic Conditions and Its Future Status*. New York: Wiley.

Graham, George E., 1991. "Mothers, Not Malnutrition, Cause Infant Mortality." *Wall Street Journal*. April 2, p. A20.

Grantham, George. 1995. "Agricultural Productivity before the Green Revolution." In Simon, ed. 1995.

Gray, Paul E. 1989. "Nuclear Reactors Everyone Will Love." *Wall Street Journal*. August 17, p. A14.

Gregg, Alan. 1955a. "Hidden Hunger at the Summit." *Population Bulletin* 11, no. 5: 65–69.

Gregg, Alan. 1955b. "A Medical Aspect of the Population Problem. *Science* 121:681–82.

Grene, David, and Richmond Lattimore, eds. 1959, *The Complete Greek Tragedies*, vol. 1, *Aeschylus*. Chicago: University of Chicago Press.

* Greve, Michael S., and Fred L. Smith, eds. 1992. *Environmental Politics: Public Costs, Private Rewards*. New York: Praeger.

Griliches, Zvi. 1958. "Research Costs and Social Returns: Hybrid Corn and Related Innovation. *Journal of Political Economy* 66:419–31.

Grossman, Gene M., and Elhanan Helpman. 1990. "Comparative Advantage and Long-Run Growth." *The American Economic Review* (September): 796ff.

Guest, Edgar A. 1946. *Collected Verse of Edgar A. Guest*. Chicago: The Reilly & Lee Co.

Gurr, Ted Robert. 1985. "On the Political Consequences of Scarcity and Economic Decline." *International Studies Quarterly* 29: 51–75.

Habakkuk, John. 1963. "Population Problems and European Economic Development in the Late Eighteenth and Nineteenth Centuries." *American Economic Review* 53: 607–18.

Hagen, Everett E. 1975. *The Economics of Development*. Homewood, Ill.: Irwin.

Haines, Michael. 1995. "Disease and Health through the Ages." In Simon 1995.

Hall, Jane V., Arthur M. Winer, Michael T. Kleinman, Frederick W. Lurmann, Victor Bajer, Steven D. Colome. 1992. "Valuing the Health Benefits of Clean Air." *Science* 255 (September 14): 812–16.

Hamburg, David A. 1984. "Population Growth and Development." *Science* 226, no. 4676 (November 16).

Handler, Philip. 1970. Testimony before the Congressional Subcommittee on Science, Research and Development. July 21. Quoted by Wolman 1971.

Hardin, Garrett. 1972. "The Tragedy of the Commons." In *Population Crisis—An Interdisciplinary Perspective*, edited by Reid, Sue Titus, and David L. Lyon, pp. 192–200. Glenview, Ill.: Scott, Foresman.

———. 1974. "Living in a Lifeboat." *Bioscience* 24:561–67.

———. 1981. *The New Republic*. October 28. pp. 31–34.

———. 1993. "The Global Threat of Unchecked Population Growth." *The World & I* (June): 377–96.

Harlan, Jack R. 1976. "The Plants and Animals That Nourish Man." *Scientific American* 235, no. 3 (September): 89–97.

Harper, A. E. 1984. "Nutrition and Health in the Changing Environment." In *The Resourceful Earth*, edited by Julian L. Simon and Herman Kahn, pp. 490–527.

Harris, Louis and Associates, Inc. 1988. "American Attitudes to International Family Planning and Population Issues." A survey conducted for The Population Crisis Committee and The Planned Parenthood Federation of America, Fieldwork: May, Study No. 884004.

Harrison, Gordon. 1978. *Mosquitoes, Malaria, and Man*. New York: EP Dutton.

Hart, John Fraser. 1984. "Cropland Change in the United States, 1944–78." In *The Resourceful Earth*, edited by Julian L. Simon and Herman Kahn, pp. 224–49.

Havemeyer, Loomis, ed. 1910. *Conservation of Our Natural Resources*. New York: Macmillan.

Hawking, Stephen W. 1988. *A Brief History of Time*. New York: Bantam.

Hawkins, E. K. 1962. *Roads and Road Transport in an Underdeveloped Country*. London: Colonial Office.

Hawley, Amost H. 1972. "Population Density and the City." *Demography* 9: 521–30.

Haworth, C. T., and D. W. Rasmussen. 1973. "Determinants of Metropolitan Cost of Living Variations." *Southern Economic Journal* 40:183–92.

Hayami, Yujiro, and Vernon W. Ruttan. 1971. *Agricultural Development: An International Perspective*. Baltimore: Johns Hopkins University Press.

Hayden, Howard C. Forthcoming. "Ozone Depletion: What's Hidden Behind the Mask of Science?" *EGAD Quarterly* 1 no. 3 (University of Arizona).

* Hayek, Friedrich. 1952. *The Counter-Revolution of Science*. Glencoe: The Free Press.

———. 1960. *The Constitution of Liberty*. Chicago: University of Chicago Press. See excellent chapters on natural resources, along with the rest of the book.

———. 1967. "The Theory of Complex Phenomena." In *Studies in Philosophy, Politics, and Economics*, pp. 22–42. Chicago: University of Chicago Press.

* ———. 1973, 1976, 1979. *Law, Legislation, and Liberty*, vols 1–3. Chicago: University of Chicago Press.

*** ———. 1991. *The Fatal Conceit*. Chicago: University of Chicago Press.

Hayward, Steven. 1991. "Muddy Waters." *Reason* (July): 46–47.

*** Hazlitt, Henry. 1962. *Economics in One Lesson*, 2d ed. New York: Arlington House.

Heer, David M. 1968. *Readings in Population*. Englewood Cliffs, N.J.: Prentice Hall.

Heilbrun, Deborah. 1975. "Calls Lower Birth Rate Key to World Survival." *Jewish Notes* 23:32.

Heimlich, Ralph E. 1991. "Soil Erosion and Conservation Policies in the United States." In *Farming and the Countryside: An Economic Analysis of External Costs and Benefits*, edited by Nick Hanley, pp. 59–90. C.A.B. International.

Henderson, J. Vernon. 1987. "Industrialization and Urbanization: International Experience." In Johnson and Lee, pp. 189–224.

Herfindahl, Orris C., and Allen V. Kneese. 1965. *Quality of the Environment*. Baltimore: Johns Hopkins University Press.

Herrnstein, R. J. 1989. "IQ and Falling Birth Rates." *The Atlantic Monthly* (May): 72–76, 78–79.

Heywood, V. H., and S. N. Stuart. 1992. "Species Extinctions in Tropical Forests." In T. C. Whitmore and J. A. Sayer, pp. 91–118.

Hibbs, Douglas A., Jr. 1973. *Mass Political Violence: A Cross-National Causal Analysis*. New York: Wiley.

Hickel, Walter J. 1991. "Guest Column." *NWI Resource* 2 (Fall): p. 2.

Hirsch, Werner Z. 1956. "Firm Progress Ratios." *Econometrica* 24:136–43.

Hirschi, Travis, and Hanan C. Selvin. 1973. *Principles of Survey Analysis*. New York: Free Press.

Hirshleifer, Jack. 1985. "The Expanding Domain of Economics." *The American Economic Review* 75 (December).

Hirst, Eric, and John C. Moyers. 1974. "Efficiency of Energy Use in the United States." In Abelson 1974.

Hitler, Adolph. 1939. *Mein Kampf*. New York: Reynal & Hitchcock.

Hobbs, Peter V., and Lawrence F. Radke. 1992. "Airborne Studies of the Smoke from the Kuwait Oil Fires." *Science* 256 (May 15): 987–91.

Hoche, Alfred, and Karl Binding. 1920. *Release and Destruction of Lives Not Worth Living*. Cited by Proctor 1988, p. 178.

Hodgson, Dennis. 1988. "Orthodoxy and Revisionism in American Demography," *Population and Development Review* 14 (December): 541–70.

Hofstadter, Douglas R. 1985. *Metamagical Themas: Questing for the Essence of Mind and Pattern*. New York: Basic Books.

Holden, Constance. 1974. "Scientists Talk of the Need for Conservation and an Ethic of Biotic Diversity to Slow Species Extinction." *Science* (May): 647–48.

———. 1986. "A Revisionist Look at Population and Growth." *Science* 231 (March 28): 1493–94.

Holen, Arlene. 1995. "The History of Accident Rates in the United States." In Simon, ed. 1995.

Hollingsworth, Thomas Henry. 1969. *Historical Demography*. London: Hodder & Stoughton.

Holton, Gerald. 1973. *Thematic Origins of Scientific Thought*. Cambridge: Harvard University Press.

Horlacher, David E., and F. Landis MacKellar. 1987. "Population Growth versus Economic Growth (?)." Xerox.

Hoselitz, Bert P. 1957–1958. "Population Pressure, Industrialization, and Social Mobility." *Population Studies* 11: 123ff.

Houthakker, Hendrik S. 1976. "The Economics of Nonrenewable Resources." *Beihefte der Konjurkturpolitick* 23:115–24.

Howe, Charles W. 1979. *Natural Resource Economics*. New York: Wiley.

Hoyle, Fred, and Geoffrey Hoyle. 1980. *Commonsense in Nuclear Energy*. San Francisco: W. H. Freeman.

* Hume, David. 1777/1985. *Essays: Moral, Political, and Literary*. Edited by Eugene F. Miller. Indianapolis: Liberty Classics.

———. "Of Commerce." In *Essays*, pp. 253–67.

———. "Of the Rise and Progress of the Arts and Sciences." In *Essays*, pp. 111–37.

Huxley, Julian. 1953. *Evolution in Action*. Harmondsworth, England: Penguin, in association with Chatto & Windus.

** Idso, Sherwood B. 1989. *Carbon Dioxide and Global Change: Earth in Transition*. Tempe, Ariz.: IBR Press.

Iker, Sam. 1982. "Islands of Life In a Forest Sea." *Mosaic* (September/October): 24–29.

Instituto Brasiliero Desinuol. 1980. "Brazil." *World Wood Review* (July): 56–57.

International Advisory Committee on Population and Law. 1977. *Annual Review of Population Law 1976: Constitutions, Legislation, Regulations, Legal Opinions and Judicial Decisions*. Law and population book series no. 20. Medford, Mass.: Tufts University.

International Economic Report of the President. 1974. Transmitted to Congress February 1974. Washington, D.C.: GPO.

** Isaacs, Rael Jean, and Erich Isaacs. 1983. *The Coercive Utopians.* Chicago: Regner.

Ise, John. 1924. *The United States Forest Policy.* New Haven, Conn.: Yale University Press.

Jablon, S., and H. Kato. 1970. "Childhood Cancer in Relation to Prenatal Exposure to Atomic Bomb Radiation." *The Lancet,* November 14.

Jacobs, Jane. 1961. *The Death and Life of Great American Cities.* New York: Random House.

Jaffe, Frederick S. 1969. Activities Relevant to the Study of Population Policy for the U.S. Memo to Bernard Berelson, March 11. In Elliott et al. 1970.

Jaffe, Frederick S., cited in Simon 1981, taken from Robin Elliott, Lynn C. Landman, Richard Lincoln, and Theodore Tsuruoka 1970. "U.S. Population Growth and Family Planning: A Review of the Literature." In *Family Planning Perspectives,* vol. 2, repr. in Daniel Callahan, ed., *The American Population Debate.* New York: Anchor Books, 1971, p. 206.

James, Jeffrey. 1987. "Population and Technical Change in the Manufacturing Sector of Developing Countries." In Johnson and Lee, pp. 225–58.

Jastrow, Robert. 1992. "What Happened to the Greenhouse Effect?" In xerox of The Heritage Lectures, July 31.

* Jastrow, Robert, William Nierenberg, and Frederick Seitz. 1990. *Scientific Perspectives on the Greenhouse Problem.* Ottawa, Ill.: Jameson Books.

Jefferson, Thomas. 1904. *The Works of Thomas Jefferson.* Edited by Paul Leicester Ford, p. 123. New York: G.P. Putnam's Sons.

Jevons, W. Stanley. 1865. *The Coal Question.* London: Macmillan.

Jha, L. K. 1988. "Indo-US Relations: Changing Perspectives." *Darshan* 5 (March): 1–4.

Jo Kwong. 1990. *Protecting the Environment: Old Rhetoric, New Imperatives.* Washington, D.C.: Capital Research Center.

Johnson, D. Gale. 1970. "Famine." *Encyclopaedia Britannica.*

———. 1973. "World Food Problems and Prospects." Washington, D.C.: Am. Enterprise. Mimeo.

———. 1974a. "Population, Food and Economic Development." *American Statistician* 28: 89–93.

———. 1974b. *World Food Problems and Prospects.* Washington, D.C.: Am. Enterprise.

———. 1976. "Food for the Future: A Perspective." *Population and Development Review* (March) 2:1–20.

———. 1980. "The World Food Situation: Developments during the 1970's and Prospects for the 1980's." Office of Agricultural Economics Paper no. 80. University of Chicago. March 5. Mimeo.

———. 1984. "World Food and Agriculture." In *The Resourceful Earth,* edited by Julian L. Simon and Herman Kahn, pp. 67–112.

* ———. 1990. *The People's Republic of China.* San Francisco: ICS Press.

Johnson, D. Gale, and Ronald D. Lee. 1987. *Population Growth and Economic Development: Issues and Evidence.* Madison, Wis.: University of Wisconsin Press.

Johnson, Ronald, and Gary Libecap. 1980. "Efficient Markets and the Great Lakes Timber: A Conservation Issue Revisited." *Explorations in Economic History* 17: 372–

85. Discussed by T. J. Ijima and Jane S. Shaw, "The Great 19th Century Timber Heist Revisited," in *PERC VIEWPOINTS*, September, 1989.

* Jones, Eric L. 1981. *The European Miracle*. New York: Cambridge University Press.

Jones, K., and A. D. Smith. 1970. *The Economic Impact of Commonwealth Immigration*. Cambridge: Cambridge University Press.

Jorgensen, Dale, and Zvi Griliches. 1967. "The Explanation of Productivity Change. *Review of Economic Studies* 34:249–83.

Jukes, Thomas H. 1992a. "The Hazards of Biotechnology: Facts and Fancy." In Lehr, pp. 135–44.

Jukes, Thomas H. 1992b. "The Tragedy of DDT" In Lehr, pp. 217–22.

Juskevitch, Judith C., and C. Greg Guyer. 1990. "Bovine Growth Hormone: Human Food Safety Evaluation." *Science* 249, (August 24): 875–84.

Kahn, Herman, William Brown, and Leon Martel, with the assistance of the staff of the Hudson Institute. 1976. *The Next 200 Years: A Scenario for America and the World*. New York: Morrow.

Kahneman, Daniel, Paul Slovic, and Amos Tversky, eds. 1982. *Judgment under Uncertainty: Heuristics and Biases*. Cambridge: Cambridge University Press.

Kaminskaya, Dina. 1982. *Final Judgment: My Life as a Soviet Defense Attorney*. New York: Simon and Schuster.

Kammeyer, Kenneth C. W., Norma R. Yetman, and McKee J. McClendon. 1972. "Family Planning Services and Redistribution of Black Americans." In *Population Studies: Selected Essays*, edited by Kenneth C. W. Kammeyer. Chicago: Rand McNally, 1975.

Kanovsky, Eliyahu. 1966. *The Economy of the Israeli Kibbutz*. Cambridge: Harvard University Press.

Kantner, John F. 1982. "Population Policy and Political Atavism." *Demography* 19 (November): 429–38.

Kasun, Jacqueline R. 1986. *The War Against Population: The Economics and Ideology of World Population Control*. Ottawa, Ill: Jameson Books.

** ———. 1988. *The War on Population*. San Francisco: Ignatius Press.

Kauppi, Pekka E., Kari Mielkainen, and Kullervo Kuusela. 1992. "Biomass and Carbon Budget of European Forests, 1971 to 1990." *Science* 256 (April): 70–74.

Keeney, Ralph L. 1990. "Mortality Risks Induced by Economic Expenditures." *Risk Analysis* 10, no. 1: 147–59.

Kelley, Allen C. n.d. "Revisionism Revisited: An Essay on the Population Debate in Historical Perspective." Xerox.

———. 1972. "Scale Economies, Inventive Activity, and the Economics of American Population Growth." *Explorations in Economic History* (Fall): 35–72.

———. 1976. "Demographic Change and the Size of the Government Sector." *Southern Economic Journal* 43, no. 2 (October).

———. 1986. "The National Academy of Sciences Report on Population Growth and Economic Development." April 10. Xerox.

———. 1988. "Economic Consequences of Population Change in the Third World." *Journal of Economic Literature* (December): 1685–1728.

Kelley, Allen, and Robert Schmidt. 1994. "Population and Income Change." *World Bank Discussion Paper* 249.

* Kevles, Daniel J. 1985. *In the Name of Eugenics*. Berkeley: University of California Press.

Keyfitz, Nathan. 1966. "Population Density and the Style of Social Life." *BioScience* 16:868–73. In Reid and Lyon 1972.

————. 1985. "An East Javanese Village in 1953 and 1985: Observations on Development." *Population and Development Review* 11, no. 4 (December): 695–719.

Keyfitz, Nathan, and Wilhelm Flieger. 1990. *World Population Growth and Aging*. Chicago: University of Chicago Press.

Keynes, John Maynard. 1920. *The Economic Consequences of the Peace*. New York: Harcourt, Brace.

King, Elizabeth M. 1987. "The Effect of Family Size on Family Welfare: What Do We Know?" In Johnson and Lee, pp. 373–412.

Kirk, Dudley. 1969. "Natality in the Developing Countries, Recent Trends and Prospects." In *Fertility and Family Planning: A World View*, edited by S. J. Behrman, Leslie Corsa, and Ronald Freedman. Ann Arbor: University of Michigan Press.

Kiser, Clyde V. 1970. "Changing Fertility Patterns in the United States." *Social Biology* 17:312–15.

Kitagawa, Evelyn M., and Philip M. Hauser. 1973. *Differential Mortality in the United States: A Study in Socioeconomic Epidemiology*. Cambridge, Mass.: Harvard University Press.

* Kleinman, David S. 1980. *Human Adaptation and Population Growth*. New York: Universe.

Klerman, Gerald L. 1987. "The Nature of Depression—Mood, Symptom, Disorder." Reprinted from *The Measurement of Depression*, edited by Marsella, Hirschfeld, and Katz.

Knight, G. Wilson. 1955. *The Mutual Flame*. London: Methuen.

Knodel, John. 1968. "Infant Mortality and Fertility in Three Bavarian Villages: An Analysis of Family Histories from the 19th Century." *Population Studies* 2 (November): 297–318.

Knodel, John, and Etienne Van De Walle. 1967. Breast Feeding, Fertility and Infant Mortality: An Analysis of some Early German Data. *Population Studies* 21:109–31.

Koch, Adrienne, and William Peden, eds. 1944. *The Life and Selected Writings Of Thomas Jefferson*. New York: Random House.

Kolsrud, Gretchen, and Barbara Boyle Torrey. 1991. "The Importance of Population Growth in Future Commercial Energy Consumption." Paper presented to AAAS in 1991.

Kornai, Janos. 1980. *Economics of Shortage*. Amsterdam: New Holland.

Korns, Alex. 1977. "Coverage Issues Raised by Comparisons between CPS and Establishment Employment." *American Stat. Assn. Proceedings*, Social Stat. section.

* Kristol, Irving. 1978. *Two Cheers for Capitalism*. New York: Basic Books.

Krug, Edward C. 1992. "The Great Acid Rain Flimflam." In Lehr, pp. 35–43.

Krupnick, Alan J., and Paul R. Portney. 1991. "Controlling Urban Air Pollution: A Benefit-Cost Assessment," *Science* 252 (April 26): 522–28.

Krzywicki, Ludwik. 1934. *Primitive Society and Its Vital Statistics*. London: Macmillan.

Kumar, Joginder. 1973. *Population and Land in World Agriculture*. Berkeley: University of California Press.

Kunz, Philip R., and Evan T. Peterson, 1972. "Family Size and Academic Achievement." In *Population, Resources, and the Future: Non-Malthusian Perspectives*, edited by Howard M. Bahr, Bruce A. Chadwick, and Darwin L. Thomas. Provo: Brigham Young University Press.

Kuznets, Simon. 1960. "Population Change and Aggregate Out-put." In *Demographic and Economic Change in Developed Countries*. Princeton, N.J.: Princeton University Press.

————. 1965. "Demographic Aspects of Modern Economic Growth." Paper presented at World Population Conference, Belgrade. September.

————. 1967. "Population and Economic Growth." *Proceedings of the American Philosophical Society* 11:170–93.

————. 1971. *Economic Growth of Nations*. Cambridge, Mass.: Harvard University Press.

** Kwong, Jo Ann. n.d. *Myths about Environmental Policy*. Washington, D.C.: Citizens for the Environment.

* ————. 1990. *Market Environmentalism: Lessons for Hong Kong*. Hong Kong: The Chinese University Press.

Laarman, Jan, and Roger Sedjo. 1992. *Global Forests: Issues for Six Billion People*. New York: McGraw-Hill.

Labandeira, Conrad C., and J. John Sepkoski, Jr. 1993. "Insect Diversity in the Fossil Record." *Science* (July 16): 310–14.

Lader, Lawrence. 1971. *Breeding Ourselves to Death*. New York: Ballantine.

————. 1973. *The Margaret Sanger Story, the Fight for Birth Control*. Repr. of 1955 ed. Westport, Conn.: Greenwood.

Lal, Deepak. Forthcoming. *Cultural Stability and Economic Stagnation: India, 1500 B.C.–1980 A.D.* London and New York: Oxford University Press.

Lancaster, Clarise, and Frederick J. Schewen. 1977. "Counting the Uncountable Illegals: Some Initial Statistical Speculation Employing Capture-Recapture Technique." Paper given at Am. Stat. Assn.

Landsberg, Hans H. 1964. *Natural Resources for U.S. Growth: A Look Ahead to the Year 2000*. Baltimore: Johns Hopkins University Press. Published for Resources for the Future, Inc.

————. 1974. "Low-Cost, Abundant Energy: Paradise Lost?" In Abelson 1974.

————. 1984. "Global Climatic Trends." In *The Resourceful Earth*, edited by Julian L. Simon and Herman Kahn, pp. 272–315.

Lapp, Ralph E. 1973. The Logarithmic Century Charting Future Shock. Englewood Cliffs, N.J.: Prentice Hall.

Layzer, David. 1990. *Cosmogenesis: Growth of Order in the Universe*. New York: Oxford University Press.

Leakey, Richard E. 1981. *The Making of Mankind*. New York: E. P. Dutton.

Lebergott, Stanley. 1964. *Manpower in Economic Growth*. New York: McGraw-Hill.

* ————. 1984. *The Americans: An Economic Record*. New York: W. W. Norton.

Lee, Ronald. 1983. "Economic Consequences of Population Size, Structure and Growth," International Union for the Scientific Study of Population, *Newsletter* no. 17 (January–April): 43–59.

————. 1985. Review of *World Development Report 1984*, *Population and Development Review* 11 (March): pp. 127–30.

Lee, W. R., ed. 1979. *European Demography and Economic Development.* New York: St. Martin's Press.

*** Lehr, Jay. 1992. *Rational Readings on Environmental Concerns.* New York: Van Nostrand.

Leibenstein, Harvey. 1972. "The Impact of Population Growth on the American Economy." In *The Report of the Commissions on Population Growth and American Future,* vol. 2: *Economic Aspects of Population Change.* Washington, D.C.: GPO.

Lele, Uma J., and John W. Mellor. 1964. "Estimates of Change and Causes of Change in Food Grains Production: India 1949–50 to 1960–61." *Cornell University Agricultural Development Bulletin 2.*

Leonard, Jonathon A. 1979. "The 'Queen of Diseases' Strikes Back." *Harvard Magazine* (July–August): 20–24.

Leopold, Luna B. 1991. "Ethos, Equity, and the Water Resource," *Geotimes* (December): 6, 7.

Leopold, Nathan F., Jr. 1958. *Life Plus 99 Years.* New York: Popular Lib.

Lesko Associates. 1975. Basic Data and Guidance Required to Implement a Major Illegal Alien Study during Fiscal Year 1976. Paper submitted to INS, October 15.

Levin, Michael H. 1988. "The Trash Mess Won't Be Easily Disposed Of." *Wall Street Journal,* December 15, p. A18.

Lewis, H. W. 1990. *Technological Risk.* New York: W. W. Norton.

Lindert, Peter H. 1980. "Child Costs and Economic Development." In Easterlin 1980.
———. 1978. *Fertility and Scarcity in America.* Princeton, N.J.: Princeton University Press.

Lindzen, Richard S. 1992. "Global Warming: The Origin and Nature of Alleged Scientific Consensus." March 11. Xerox.

Lipset, Seymour Martin, and William Schneider. 1987. *The Confidence Gap—Business, Labor, and Government in the Public Mind,* rev. ed. Baltimore: Johns Hopkins University Press.

Lipson, Gerald, and Dianne Wolman. 1972. "Polling Americans on Birth Control and Population. *Family Planning Perspectives* 4:39–42.

Littlewood, Thomas. 1977. *The Politics of Population Control.* South Bend: University of Notre Dame Press.

Logan, Joshua. 1976. *Josh—My Up and Down, In and Out Life.* New York: Delacorte Press.

Logomasini, Angela. 1991. "How to Manage America's Trash: Private Solutions to a Public Problem." *Environmental Perspectives.* Washington, D.C.: Citizens for the Environment.

** London, Herbert I. 1984. *Why Are They Lying to Our Children?* New York: Stein and Day.

Lord, Bette Bao. 1983. *Eighth Moon.* New York: Avon Books.

Love, Douglas. 1978. City Sizes and Prices. Ph.D. dissertation, University of Illinois.

Love, Douglas, and Lincoln Pashute [Julian L. Simon]. 1978. "The Effect of Population Size and Concentration upon Scientific Productivity." In Julian L. Simon 1978c.

Lovins, Amory B. 1977. *Soft Energy Paths.* Cambridge: Ballinger.

Lowdermilk, W. C. 1953. "Conquest of the Land through Seven Thousand Years." Agriculture Information Bulletin no. 99. U.S. Department of Agriculture, SCS.

Lugo, Ariel E., ed. 1989. "Diversity of Tropical Species." In *Biology International,* special issue.

Lunch, William, and Stanley Rothman. 1995. "American Public Opinion: The Environment and Energy." In Simon, ed. 1995.

* Luttrell, Clifford B. 1989. *The High Cost of Farm Welfare*. Washington, D.C.: Cato Institute.

Lynd, Lee R., Janet H. Cushman, Roberta J. Nichols, and Charles E. Wyman. 1991. "Fuel Ethanol from Cellulosic Biomass." *Science* 251 (March 15): 1318–22.

Lyons, Gene. 1990. "Playing Games at *Newsweek*." In *The Yellowstone Primer*, edited by John A. Baden and Donald Leal, pp. 151–67. San Francisco: Pacific Research Institute for Public Policy.

** MacCracken, Samuel. 1982. *The War Against the Atom*. New York: Basic Books.

Maddison, Angus. 1982. *Phases of Capitalitst Development*. New York: Oxford.

* Maddox, John. 1972. *The Doomsday Syndrome*. London: Macmillan.

Madigan, Russel T. 1981. *Of Minerals and Man* (Parkville, Victoria, Australia: Australasian Institute of Mining and Metallurgy, 1981).

* Maduro, Rogelio A., and Ralf Schauerhammer. 1992. *The Holes in the Ozone Scare*. Washington, D.C.: 21st Century Science Associates.

Malthus, Thomas R. 1803. "Essay on Population." *An Essay on the Principle of Population, or a View of Its Past and Present Effects on Human Happiness*. London: J. Johnson. A new ed., very thick, enlarged.

———. 1817/1963. *Principles of Population*. 5th ed. Homewood, Ill.: Irwin.

———. 1830/1960. *On Population: Three Essays by Thomas Malthus, Julian Huxley, and Frederick Osborn*. New York: New American Lib., Mentor Books.

Mamdani, Mahmood. 1973. *The Myth of Population Control (Family, Caste, and Class in an Indian Village)*. New York and London: Monthly Review Press.

Mandeville, Bernard. 1705 / 1962. *The Fable of the Bees, or Private Vices, Publick Benefits*. New York: Capricorn.

Manpower and Immigration. 1974. *Three Years in Canada*. Ottawa: Information Canada.

Marsh and McLennan. 1980. *Risk in a Complex Society: A Marsh & McLennan Public Opinion Survey*. New York: Louis Harris.

Marshall, L. E. 1972. "Sees Hazards in Overpopulation." Letter to the editor. *Des Moines Register*. July 12, p. 8.

Mason, Andrew. 1987. "National Saving Rates and Population Growth: A New Model and New Evidence." In Johnson and Lee, pp. 523–60.

* Mather, Kirtley. 1940. "The Future of Man as an Inhabitant of the Earth." *Sigma Xi Quarterly* 28 (Spring).

* ———. 1944. *Enough and to Spare*. 2d ed. New York: Harper.

** Maurice, Charles, and Charles W. Smithson. 1984. *The Doomsday Myth*. Stanford: Hoover Institution.

Mayer, Leo V. 1982. "Farm Exports and Soil Conservations." *Proceedings of the Academy of Political Science* 34: 99–111. Quoted by Schultz 1984.

* Mazur, Allan. 1981. *Dynamics of Technical Controversy*. Washington, D.C.: Communications Press.

McCorriston, Joy, and Frank Hole. 1991. "The Ecology of Seasonal Stress and the Origins of Agriculture in the Near East." *American Anthropologist* 93, no. 1 (March): 46–69.

McEvedy, Colin, and Richard Jones. 1978. *Atlas of World Population Histostory*. New York: Penguin.

McKelvey, Vincent E. 1973. "Mineral Resource Estimates and Public Policy." *Summary of United States mineral resources*. U.S. Department of the Interior. Washington, D.C.: GPO.

* McKenzie, Richard B., and Dwight R. Lee. 1991. *Quicksilver Capital*. New York: Free Press.

McKetta, John J. 1992. "Acid Rain—The Whole Story to Date." In Lehr, pp. 44–60.

McNamara, Robert S. 1973. *One Hundred Countries, Two Billion People: The Dimensions of Development*. New York: Praeger.

McNeill, William H. 1977. *Plagues and Peoples*. Garden City, N.Y.: Anchor Books.

McNicholl, Geoffrey. 1984. "Consequences of Rapid Population Growth: An Overview and Assessment." *Population and Development Review* 10 (June): 177–240.

Meade, James E. 1937. *An Introduction to Economic Analysis and Policy*. London: Oxford University Press.

———. 1955. *The Theory of International Economic Policy*. Vol. 2: *Trade and Welfare*. London: Oxford University Press.

———. 1961. "Mauritius: A Case Study in Malthusian Economics." *Economic Journal* 71: 521–34.

———. 1967. "Population Explosion, the Standard of Living and Social Conflict." *Economic Journal* 77: 233–55.

Meadows, Dennis L., William W. Behrens, III, Donella H. Meadows, Roger F. Naill, Jorgen Randers, and Erich K. O. Zahn. 1974. *Dynamics of Growth in a Finite World*. Cambridge, Mass.: Wright-Allen.

Meadows, Donella H., Dennis L. Meadows, and Jorgen Randers. 1992. *Beyond the Limits*. Post Mills, Vt.: Chelsea Green.

Meadows, Donella H., Dennis L. Meadows, Jorgen Randers, and William W. Behrens III. 1972. *The Limits to Growth*. New York: Potomac Associates.

Meek, Ronald. 1953. *Marx and Engels on Malthus*. Delhi: People's Publishing.

Meguire, Philip. 1993. Correspondence, August 26.

Mellanby, Kenneth. 1989. "With Safeguards, DDT Should Still Be Used." *Wall Street Journal*. September 12, p. A26.

Mera, K. 1970. "Urban Agglomeration and Economic Efficiency." *Economic Development and Cultural Change* 21:309–21.

Merklein, Helmut A., and W. Carey Hardy. 1977. *Energy Economics*. Houston: Gulf Pub.

Mesle, France. 1991. "La mortalité dans les pays d'Europe de l'est." *Population* 3, 612.

Metz, William D. 1974. "Oil Shale: A Huge Resource of Low-Grade Fuel." In Abelson 1974.

Metzger, Mary, and Cinthya P. Whittaker. 1991. *This Planet Is Mine*. New York: Simon and Schuster.

** Michaels, Patrick. 1992. *Sound and Fury: The Science and Politics of Global Warming*. Washington, D.C.: Cato Institute.

Middle East Information Series. 1974. (Spring/Summer): 26–27.

Mill, John Stuart. 1859/1948. "On Liberty." In *Utilitarianism, Liberty, and Representative Government* New York: Dent.

Miller, James A. 1991. *Population Research Institute Review* 1 (March/April and May/June).

———. 1992. "Nigeria's Population Bomb Fizzles Out." *Wall Street Journal*. May 12, p. A24.

Mills, Stephanie. 1991. "Population—Red-Hot Realities for a Finite Planet." *Garbage* (May–June): 46–51.

Mitchell, Edward J. 1974. *U.S. Energy Policy: A Primer*. Washington, D.C.: American Enterprise.

Mitra, Barun S. 1993. "Facts, not Fiction." Self-published, 96/10 Pushp Vihar -1, Saket, New Delhi, 110017.

Mitra, Barun. n.d. "The Debate on Environment—An Economic Perspective." Xerox.

Mohr, L. B. 1969. "Determinants of Innovation in Organizations." *American Political Science Review* 63:111–26.

Monnier, Alain. 1990. "The Effects of Family Policies in the GDR." *Population* (English selection) 2: 127–40.

Morawetz, David. 1978. *Twenty-Five Years of Economic Development: 1950 to 1975*. Baltimore: Johns Hopkins University Press.

Morgan, M. Granger. 1990. Review of *Currents of Death: Power Lines, Computer Terminals, and the Attempt to Cover Up Their Threat to Your Health*, by Paul Brodeur. In *Scientific American* (April): 118–23.

* Mosher, Steven, W. 1983. *Broken Earth: The Rural Chinese*. New York: Free Press.

Mowrer, O. Hobart. 1961. *The Crisis in Psychiatry and Religion*. New York: D. Van Nostrand.

Mueller, Eva. 1976. "The Economic Value of Children in Peasant Agriculture." In Ridker 1976.

Muggeridge, Malcolm. 1972. *Chronicles of Wasted Time*, vol 1: *The Green Stick*. New York: William Morrow.

Musson, Carole. 1974. "Local Attitudes to Population Control in South Buckinghamshire." In *Population and Its Problems: A Plain Man's Guide*, edited by H. B. Parry. Oxford: Clarendon Press.

Myers, Norman. 1979. *The Sinking Ark*. New York: Pergamon.

———. 1989. "A Major Extinction Spasm: Predictable and Inevitable?" In *Conservation for the Twenty-first Century*, edited by David Western and Mary C. Pearl. New York, Oxford: Oxford University Press.

Myers, Ramon H. 1970. *The Chinese Peasant Economy: Agricultural Development in Hopei and Shantung, 1890–1949*. Cambridge: Harvard University Press.

Myrdal, Alva. 1941/1968. *Nation and Family*. Cambridge: MIT Press.

Myrdal, Gunnar. 1940. *Population: A Problem for Democracy*. Cambridge: Harvard University Press.

———. 1968. *Asian Drama: An Inquiry into the Poverty of Nations*. vol. 1. New York: Pantheon.

Nag, Meni. 1962. *Factors Affecting Fertility in Non-industrial Societies: A Cross-Cultural Study*. New Haven, Conn.: Yale University Publishers in Anthropology.

National Academy of Sciences. 1965. *The Growth of U.S. Population: Analysis of the Problems and Recommendations for Research, Training, and Service*. Report by the Committee on Population. Washington, D.C.: National Research Council.

———. 1971. *Rapid Population Growth: Consequences and Policy Implications*. Baltimore: Johns Hopkins University Press.

————. 1975. *Mineral Resources and the Environment*. Report by the Committee on Mineral Resources and the Environment (COMRATE). Commission on Natural Resources. Washington, D.C.: National Research Council.

————. 1979. *Energy in Transition: 1985–2010*. San Francisco: W. H. Freeman.

* National Center for Policy Analysis. 1991. *Progressive Environmentalism: A Pro-Human, Pro-Science, Pro-Free Enterprise Agenda for Change*. Dallas: NPCA.

National Commission on Materials Policy. 1973. *Material Needs and the Environment Today and Tomorrow*. Washington, D.C.: GPO.

*** National Research Council, Committee on Population, and Working Group on Population Growth and Economic Development. 1986. *Population Growth and Economic Development: Policy Questions*. Washington, D.C.: National Academy Press.

————. 1990b. "Tom Hayden, Meet Adam Smith and Thomas Aquinas." *Forbes* (October 29): 94–97.

Nelson, Robert H. 1990a. "Unoriginal Sin." *Policy Review* (Summer): 52–59.

————. 1995. "Availability and Usage of Outdoor Recreation." In Simon, ed. 1995.

Nerlove, Marc, and Lakshmi K. Raut. 1994. "Growth Models with Endogenous Population: A General Framework." Xerox.

New Scientist. 1992. Comment page, "No Shortages, Yet." (May 30): 3.

New York Times Staff. 1975. *Give Us This Day*. New York: Arno Press.

Nordhaus, William D. 1974. "Resources as a Constraint on Growth." *American Economic Review* 64:22–26.

————. 1992. "An Optimal Transition Path for Controlling Greenhouse Gases." *Science* 258 (November 20): 1315–19.

Nordhaus, William D., and James Tobin. 1972. *Is Growth Obsolete?* New York: NBER.

North, David S., and Marian F. Houstoun. 1976. *The Characteristics and Role of Illegal Aliens in the U.S. Labor Market: An Exploratory Study*. Washington, D.C.: Linton and Co.

* North, Douglass C. 1981. "Structure and Change in Economic History." New York: W. W. Norton.

Novick, David, with Kurt Bleicken, W. E. Depay, Jr., Stanley A. Hutchins, J. W. Noah, and Mary B. Novick. 1976. *A World of Scarcities: Critical Issues in Public Policy*. New York: Wiley.

Ogaya, Naohira, and Noriko O. Tsuya. 1988. "Demographic Change and Human Resources Development in Asia and the Pacific: An Overall View." Nihon University Population Research Institute, March.

Ohkawa, K. 1970. "Phases of Agricultural Development and Economic Growth. In *Agricultural and Economic Growth, Japan's Experience*, edited by K. Ohkawa, B. Johnston, and H. Kaneda. Princeton, N.J.: Princeton University Press.

Oka, Takashi. 1976. "Can the Spread of Deserts Be Halted?" *Christian Science Monitor*. November 12, p. 16. Quoted in *The Other Side*, April 1977.

Oldenburg, Don. 1987. "Whistle Blower's Anguish." *Washington Post*. March 31, p. C5.

Olson, Mancur, Jr. 1965. *The Logic of Collective Action*. Cambridge, Mass.: Harvard University Press.

Olson, Mancur, Jr., and Hans H. Landsberg, eds. 1973. *The No-Growth Society*. Special issue of *Daedalus* (Fall) 102.

** Olson, Sherry H. 1971. *The Depletion Myth: History of Railroad Use of Timber*. Cambridge, Mass.: Harvard University Press.

Olson, Storrs L. 1989. "Extinction on Islands: Man as a Catastrophe." In *Conservation for the Twenty-first Century*, edited by David Western and Mary C. Pearl. New York, Oxford: Oxford University Press.

O'Neill, Catherine. 1991. "Seek a Solution to Pollution." *Washington Post*. August 6, Health, p. 18.

Opportunity Systems, Inc. 1975–77. *First, Second, Third, Fourth Wave Reports: Vietnam Resettlement Operational Feedback.*Washington, D.C.: Opportunity Systems.

Orient, Jane M. 1992. "Worried about TCE? Have Another Cup of Coffee." In Lehr, pp. 186–88.

Ortega y Gasset, José. 1961. *The Revolt of the Masses*. London: Unwin.

Osborn, Fairfield. 1953. *Limits of the Earth*. Boston: Little, Brown.

*** Osterfeld, David. 1992. *Prosperity versus Planning*. New York: Oxford.

Othmer, Donald F., and Oswald A. Roels. 1974. "Power, Fresh Water, and Food from Cold, Deep Sea Water. In Abelson 1974.

Owen, Wilfred. 1964. *Strategy for Mobility*. Washington, D.C.: Brookings.

Owens, William. 1986. *This Stubborn Soil*. New York: Vintage.

Paddock, William, and Paul Paddock. 1967. *Famine—1975! America's Decision: Who Will Survive?* Boston: Little, Brown.

Parsons, Jack. 1971. *Population Versus Liberty*. London: Pemberton.

Patoski, Joe Nick. 1992. "All's Fair in Love and Catfish." *Texas Monthly* (July): 96, 118–19.

Paul, William. 1986. "World Development Report 1984—Two Years Later." April. Xerox.

Pavlik, Zdenek. 1991. "Les tendances demographiques longues en Europe de l'est." *Population* 3, 463–78.

Penner, Joyce E., Robert E. Dickinson, and Christine A. O'Neill. 1992. "Effects of Aerosol from Biomass Burning on the Global Radiation Budget." *Science* 256 (June 5): 1432–33.

Penrose, Roger. 1989. *The Emperor's New Mind*. New York: Oxford University Press.

Pequet, Gary M. 1990. "Crop Controls and Indian Raids in Colonial Virginia." *The Freeman* (February): 59–60.

Perez, Margarita Delgado, and Massimo Livi-Baci. 1992. "Fertility in Italy and Spain, the Lowest in the World." *Family Planning Perspectives*, vol. 24, no. 4: 163.

Perkins, Dwight. 1969. *Agricultural Development in China, 1368-1968*. Chicago: Aldine.

Persson, R. 1974. *World Forest Resources*. Stockholm: Royal College.

Peterson, Ivars. 1990. *Island of Truth*. New York: W. H. Freeman.

Peto, Richard. 1984. "Why Cancer?" In *The Resourceful Earth*, edited by Julian L. Simon and Herman Kahn, pp. 528–44.

Petty, William. 1676/1899. *The Economic Writings of Sir William Petty*, edited by Charles Henry Hull. 2 vols. Cambridge: Cambridge University Press.

Piel, Gerard. 1984. "Let Them Eat Cake." *Science* 226, no. 4673 (October 26).

Pingali, Prabhu L., and Hans P. Binswanger. 1987. "Population Density and Agricultural Intensification: A Study of the Evolution of Technologies in Tropical Agriculture." In Johnson and Lee, pp. 27–56.

* Piotrow, Phyllis Tilson. 1973. *World Population Crisis: The United States' Response*. New York: Praeger.

Poleman, T. T. 1975. "World Food: A Perspective." In Abelson 1975.

Polit, Denise F. 1989. "Effects of a Comprehensive Program for Teenage Parents: Five

Years after Project Redirection." *Family Planning Perspectives* 21, no. 4 (July/August): 164ff.

Population and Family Planning Section American Public Health Association. Undated. Memo to "All US Citizens, Members and Attendees at the IUSSP Conference."

Postrel, Virginia I., and Lynn Scarlett. 1991. "Talking Trash." *Reason* (August/September): 22–31.

Prentice, S. D. 1893. "Natural Gas and Oil Production." *Cassier's Magazine* (April): 413–15.

Preston, Samuel H. 1980. "Causes and Consequences of Mortality Declines in Less Developed Countries during the Twentieth Century." In Easterlin 1980.

———. 1982. "Review of *The Ultimate Resource.*" *Population and Development Review* 8, no. 1 (March).

———. 1987. "The Social Sciences and the Population Problem." *Sociological Forum* 2 (Fall): 619–44.

———. 1995. "Human Mortality throughout History and Pre-history." In Simon, ed. 1995.

Price, Daniel O., ed. 1967. *The 99th hour*. Chapel Hill: University of North Carolina Press.

Price, Derek de Solla. 1961. *Science since Babylon*. New Haven, Conn.: Yale University Press.

Proctor, Robert. 1988. *Racial Hygiene: Medicine under the Nazis*. Cambridge, Mass.: Harvard University Press.

Quinn, James F., and Alan Hastings. 1987. "Extinction in Subdivided Habitats." *Conservation Biology* 1, no. 3 (October): 198–208.

Rae, John. 1965. *Life of Adam Smith*. New York: Augustus M. Kelley.

Rainwater, Lee. 1965. *Family Design: Marital Sexuality, Family Size, and Contraception*. Chicago: Aldine.

Rathje, William L. 1989. "Rubbish." *The Atlantic Monthly* (December): 99–109.

** Rathje, William, and Cullen Murphy. 1992a. *Rubbish! The Archaeology of Garbage*. New York: HarperCollins.

———. 1992b. "Five Major Myths about Garbage, and Why They're Wrong." *Smithsonian* (July): 113–22

Raven, Peter. 1983. Director of the Missouri Botanical Garden. Commencement Address at Knox College, June 4.

———. 1988. "The Cause and Impact of Deforestation." In *Earth '88—Changing Geographic Perspectives*, pp. 212–29.

Raven, Peter H., and Edward G. Wilson. 1992. "A Fifty-Year Plan for Biodiversity Surveys." *Science* 258, no. 13 (November): 1099.

Ray, Dixie Lee, quoted in Jo Kwong. n.d. *Myths about Environmental Policy*. Washington, D.C.: Citizens for the Environment.

** Ray, Dixie Lee, with Lou Guzzo. 1990. *Trashing the Planet*. Chicago: Regnery Gateway.

* Raymond, Robert. 1984. *Out of the Fiery Furnace*. Australia: Macmillan.

Reed, T. B., and R. M. Lerner. 1974. *Methanol: A Versatile Fuel for Immediate Use*. In Abelson 1974.

Reid, Sue Titus, and David L. Lyon, eds. 1972. *Population Crisis—An Interdisciplinary Perspective*. Glenview, Ill: Scott, Foresman.

Reid, W. V. 1992. "How Many Species Will There Be?" In T. C. Whitmore, and J. A. Sayer, pp. 55–74.

Reid, Walter V., and Kenton R. Miller. 1989. *Keeping Options Alive: The Scientific Basis for Conserving Biodiversity*. World Resources Institute, October.

Reisner, Marc. 1986. *Cadillac Desert*. New York: Viking.

Repetto, Robert G. 1976. "Direct Economic Costs and Value of Children." In Ridker 1976.

———. 1985. "Why Doesn't Julian Simon Believe His Own Research?" Letter to the editor. *Washington Post*. November 2, p. A21.

Report on the Limits to Growth. 1972. Washington, D.C.: International Bank for Reconstruction and Development.

Rescher, N. 1978. *Scientific Progress*. Pittsburgh: University of Pittsburgh Press. Originally from M. Stanley Livingston, "Particle Accelerators: A Brief History," Cambridge, 1969, p. 111.

Revelle, Roger. 1974. "Food and Population." *Scientific American* 231:160–71.

Ridker, Ronald. 1972. "Resource and Environmental Consequences of Population Growth and the American Future." In *Population, Resources, and the Environment*, vol. 3, edited by Ronald Ridker. The Commission on Population Growth and the American Future. Washington, D.C.: GPO.

———, ed. 1976. *Population and Development: The Search for Selective Interventions*. Baltimore: Resources for the Future and Johns Hopkins.

Rifkin, Jeremy. 1989. *Entropy: Into the Greenhouse World*. Rev. ed. New York: Bantam.

Roberts, Royston M. 1989. *Serendipity*. New York: Wiley.

Robinson, J. Gregory. 1979. Estimating the Approximate Size of the Illegal Alien Population in the United States by the Comparative Trend Analysis of Age-Specific Death Rates. Paper given at PAA.

Robson, Geoffrey R. 1974. "Geothermal Electricity Production." In Abelson 1974.

Rohter, Larry. 1979. "Amazon Basin's Forests Going Up in Smoke." *Washington Post*. January 5, p. A14.

Romer, Paul M. 1986. "Increasing Returns and Long-Run Growth." *Journal of Political Economy* 94 (October): 1002–37.

Romer, Paul M., and Hiroo Sasaki. 1985. "Monotonically Decreasing Natural Resource Prices under Perfect Foresight." University of Rochester, February. Xerox.

Rose, David J. 1974. "Nuclear Electric Power." In Abelson 1974.

Rosenberg, Nathan. 1969. "The Direction of Technological Change: Inducement Mechanisms and Focusing Devices." *Economic Development and Cultural Change* 18, part 1 (October): 1–24.

Rosenberg, Nathan. 1972. *Technology and American Economic Growth*. New York: Harper.

Ross, Edward A. 1927. *Standing Room Only*. New York: Century.

Ross, Malcolm. 1992. "Minerals and Health: The Asbestos Problem." In Lehr, pp. 101–14.

Ross, Marc. 1989. "Improving the Efficiency of Electricity Use in Manufacturing," *Science* 244 (April 21): 311–17.

Roszak, Theodore. 1992. "Green Guilt and Ecological Overload." *New York Times*. June 9, Op-Ed page.

Rothwell, Geoffrey. 1992. "Can Nuclear Power Compete?" *Regulation* (Winter): pp. 66–74.

Roush, Gar A. 1930. "The Mineral Resources." In *Conservation of our Natural Resources*, edited by Loomis Havemeyer. New York: Macmillan. (Based on van Hise's 1910 book.)

Roush, G. Jon. 1989. "The Disintegrating Web: The Causes and Consequences of Extinction." *The Nature Conservancy Magazine* (November/December): 4–15.

Russell, Bertrand. 1925/1959/1985. *The ABC of Relativity*. New York: Mentor.

———. 1929. *Marriage and Morals*. New York: Horace Liveright.

———. 1953. *The Impact of Science on Society*. New York: Simon and Schuster.

** Rydenfelt, Sven. 1984. *A Pattern for Failure* San Diego/New York: Harcourt Brace.

Sagan, Leonard A. 1989. "On Radiation, Paradigms, and Hormesis." *Science* 245 (August 11): 574 and 621.

Sakharov, Andreid. 1978. *Alarm & Hope*. New York: Vintage Books.

Salaff, Janet, and Aline K. Wong. 1978. "Are Disincentives Coercive? The View from Singapore." *International Family Planning Perspectives and Digest* 4:50–55.

Samuelson, Paul A. 1966. "Foreword" to Georgescu-Roegen.

———. 1973. *The Samuelson Sampler*. Glen Ridge, N.J.: Thomas Horton and Daughters.

Sanderson, F. H. 1975. "The Great Food Fumble." In Abelson 1975.

Sanger, Margaret. 1938. *Margaret Sanger: An Autobiography*. New York: W. W. Norton.

———. 1971. *An Autobiography*. New York: Dover Publications.

* Sauvy, Alfred. 1963. *Fertility and Survival*. New York: Collier Books.

———. 1969. *General Theory of Population*. New York: Basic Books.

———. 1976. *Zero Growth*. Trans. by A. Maguire. New York: Praeger.

Sax, Karl. 1960. *Standing Room Only: The World's Exploding Population*. 2d ed. Boston: Beacon Press.

Scarlett, Lynn. 1991a. "The True Cost of Trash." *NY: The City Journal* (Spring): 5.

———. 1991b. "Trash Glut Overrated; Recycling Is Too Costly." *USA Today*, February 19, editorial page.

———. 1991c. "Make Your Environment Dirtier—Recycle." *Wall Street Journal*, January 14, editorial page.

* Schall, James V. 1977. *Welcome, Number 4,000 000 000!* Canfield, Ohio: Alba House Communications.

Schecter, Mordecai, and Robert C. Lucas. 1978. *Simulation of Recreational Use for Park and Wilderness Managment*. Cited by Lebergott 1984.

Schelling, Thomas C. 1992. "Some Economics of Global Warming." *The American Economic Review* 82, no. 1 (March): 1–14.

Scherer, Frederic H. 1970. *Industrial Market Structures and Economic Performance*. Chicago: Rand McNally.

Schiager, Keith J. 1992. "Radon—Risk and Reason." In Lehr, pp. 619–26.

Schlesinger, William H., et al. 1990. "Biological Feedbacks in Global Desertification." *Science* 247 (March 3): 1043–48.

Schmeck, Harold M., Jr. 1975. "Changing Climates Threaten Food Supplies." *New York Times Staff*, pp. 171–78.

Schmidt, Ronald H. 1988. "Hotelling's Rule Repealed? An Examina tion of Exhaustible Resource Pricing." *Federal Reserve Bank of San Francisco Economic Review* (Fall): 41–54.

Schmookler, Jacob. 1966. *Invention and Economic Growth*. Cambridge, Mass.: Harvard University Press.

Schneider, Stephen. 1976. *The Genesis Strategy*. New York: Plenum Press.

* Schoeck, Helmut. 1969. *Envy.* Indianapolis: Liberty Press.

Schran, Peter. 1969. *The Development of Chinese Agriculture 1950–1959.* Urbana: University of Illinois Press.

* Schuettinger, Robert, and Eamonn Butler. 1979. *Forty Years of Price Controls.* Washington: Heritage.

Schultz, T. Paul. 1976. "Interrelationships between Mortality and Fertility." In Ridker 1976.

————. 1987. "School Expenditures and Enrollments, 1960–80: The Effects of Income, Prices, and Population Growth." In Johnson and Lee, pp. 413–78.

Schultz, Theodore W. 1951. "The Declining Economic Importance of Land." *Economic Journal* (December): 725–40.

* ————. 1981. *Investing in People.* Chicago: University of Chicago Press.

Schultz, Theodore. 1984. "The Dynamics of Soil Erosion in the United States." In Baden, pp. 45–57.

Schulze, E. -D. 1989. "Air Pollution and Forest Decline in a Spruce (Picea abies) Forest." *Science* 244 (May 19): 776–83.

Schumpeter, Joseph A. 1954. *History of Economic Analysis.* New York: Oxford University Press.

Schwartz, Joel. 1991. Quoted in *Science News.* April 6, p. 212.

Scully, Gerald W. 1988. "The Institutional Framework and Economic Development." *Journal of Political Economy* 96, no. 3 (June): 652–62.

Sedjo, Roger A. 1980. "Forest Plantations in Brazil and Their Possible Effects on World Pulp Markets." *Journal of Forestry* 78 (November): 702–4.

Sedjo, Roger A., and Marion Clawson. 1984. "Global Forests." In *The Resourceful Earth,* edited by Julian L. Simon and Herman Kahn, pp. 128–70.

————. 1995. "Global Forests Revisited." In Simon, ed. 1995.

Segal, David. 1976. "Are There Returns to Scale in City Size?" *Review of Economic Statistics* 58:339–50.

Sen, Amartya. 1987. *The Standard of Living.* Cambridge, Mass.: Cambridge University Press.

Shapiro, Leo J. 1991. "Leveraging Our Luck." *Contingencies* (Nov./Dec.): 26–32.

Shaw, Jane R., and Richard L. Stroup. 1988. "Gone Fishin'." *Reason* (Aug./Sept.): 34–37.

Shaw, R. Paul. 1989. "Rapid Population Growth and Environmental Degradatation: Ultimate versus Proximate Factors." *Environmental Conservation* 16 (Autumn): 199–208.

Sheffer, Daniel. 1970. "Comparable Living Costs and Urban Size: A Statistical Analysis." *American Institute of Planners Journal* 36:417–21.

Sherman, Stratford P. 1990. "How High School Kids See the 1990s." *Fortune* (March 26): p. 226.

Shewhart, W. A. 1931. *Economic Control of Quality of Manufactured Product.* New York: D. Van Nostrand.

Shoji, Kobe. 1977. "Drip Irrigation." *Scientific American* 237: 15ff.

Silverman, Paul. 1970. Speech delivered at the University of Illinois at Champaign-Urbana, Earth Day.

Simberloff, D. 1992. "Do Species-Area Curves Predict Extinction in Fragmented Forest?" In T. C. Whitmore and J. A. Sayer, pp. 75–90.

Simon, Judith. 1989. Memo concerning superior court decisions using economic-demographic arguments. October 3.

Simon, Julian L. 1970. "The Concept of Causality in Economics." *Kyklos* 23 (Fasc. 2): 226–54.

———. 1975a. *Applied Managerial Economics.* Englewood Cliffs, N.J.: Prentice Hall.

———. 1975b. "The Positive Effect of Population on Agricultural Savings in Irrigation Systems." *Review of Economics and Statistics* 57:71–79.

———. 1977. *The Economics of Population Growth.* Princeton, N.J.: Princeton University Press.

———. 1978a. *Basic Research Methods in Social Science.* 2d ed. New York: Random House.

———. 1978b. "An Integration of the Invention-Pull and Population-Push Theories of Economic-Demographic History. In Simon 1978c.

———. 1978c. *Research in Population Economics.* vol. 1. Greenwich, Conn.: JAI Press.

———. 1980a. "Resources, Population, Environment: An Over-supply of False Bad News." *Science* 208 (June 27): 1431–37.

———. 1980b. "Reply." *Science* 210, no. 4476 (December 19): 1296–1308.

———. 1980c. What Immigrants Take From, and Give to, the Public Coffers. Report to the Select Commission on Immigration and Refugee Policy, August 15.

*** ———. 1981. *The Ultimate Resource.* Princeton, N.J.: Princeton University Press.

———. 1986a. *Theory of Population and Economic Growth.* Oxford: Great Britain: Basil Blackwell.

———. 1986b. "Implications for U.S. Policy of the NAS Report on Population Growth and Economic Development: Policy Questions." March 6. Xerox.

———. 1986c. "Disappearing Species, Deforestation, and Data." *New Scientist* (May 15): 60–63.

———. 1987. *Effort, Opportunity, and Wealth.* New York: Basil Blackwell.

———. 1988. "Paradoxes and Difficulties in the Evaluation of Progress and Technological Advance, Past and Future." *Technology in Society* 10: 425–32; reprinted in Simon 1992.

———. 1989a. Reply to Anderton 1988. *Contemporary Sociology* (March): 169–70.

———. 1989b. "On Aggregate Empirical Studies Relating Population Variables to Economic Development." *Population and Development Review* 15, no. 2 (June): 323–32.

*** ———. 1990a. *Population Matters: People, Resources, Environment, Immigration.* New Brunswick, N.J.: Transaction Press.

———. 1990b. "Economic Thought About Population Consequences: Some Reflections." Xerox.

———. 1990c. "The Phony Farmland Scare." *Washington Journalism Review* (May): 27–33 .

———. 1990d. "The Population Establishment, Corruption, and Reform." In *Population Policy: Contemporary Issues,* edited by G. Roberts. Reprinted in Simon 1990b.

———. 1992a. *Population and Development in Poor Countries.* Princeton, N.J.: Princeton University Press.

———. 1992b. "Modern Economics and Population Growth." Xerox.

———. 1993. *Good Mood: The New Psychology of Overcoming Depression.* Chicago: Open Court.

** ———, ed. 1995. *The State of Humanity.* Boston and Oxford: Basil Blackwell.

Simon, Julian L. Forthcoming. "The Really Important Effects of Immigrants upon Natives' Incomes." In *Conference on Immigration*, edited by Barry Chiswick. Washington, D.C.: AEI.

Simon, Julian L., and Paul Burstein. 1985. *Basic Research Methods in Social Science*. 3rd ed. New York: Random House.

Simon, Julian L., and Roy Gobin. 1979. "The Relationship between Population and Economic Growth in LDC's." In *Research in Population Economics*, vol. 2, edited by Julian L. Simon and Julie deVanzo. Greenwich, Conn.: JAI Press.

Simon, Julian L., and Douglas O. Love. 1990. "City Size, Prices, and Efficiency for Individual Goods and Services." *The Annals of Regional Science* 24: 163–75.

Simon, Julian L. (with Norman Myers). *Scarcity of Abundance? A Debate on the Environment*. New York: W. W. Norton. Forthcoming in Italian.

Simon, Julian L., and Adam M. Pilarski. 1979. "The Effect of Population Growth upon the Quantity of Education Children Receive. *Review of Economics and Statistics* 61:572–84.

Simon, Julian L. (with Gunter Steinmann). 1984. "The Economic Implications of Learning-by-Doing for Population Size and Growth." *European Economic Review* 26: 167–85.

Simon, Julian (with Gunter Steinmann). 1985. "On the Optimum Theoretical Rate of Population Growth." *Jahrbucher fur Nationalokonomie und Statistik*. (Stuttgart: Gustav Fischer Verlag), vol. 200/5, pp. 508–31.

———. 1991. "Population Growth, Farmland, and the Long-Run Standard of Living." *Journal of Population Economics*.

Simon, Julian L., and Richard Sullivan. 1989. "Population Size, Knowledge Stock, and Other Determinants of Agricultural Publication and Patenting. England, 1541–1850." *Explorations in Economic History* 26: 21–44.

Simon, Julian L. (with Guenter Weinrauch and Stephen Moore). 1994. "The Reserves of Extracted Resources: Historical Data." *Non-Renewable Resources* (Summer).

Simon, Julian L., and Aaron Wildavsky. 1984. "On Species Loss, the Absence of Data, and Risks to Humanity." In *The Resourceful Earth*, edited by Julian L. Simon and Herman Kahn, pp. 171–83.

Simon, Rita James. 1971. "Public Attitudes Toward Population and Pollution." *Public Opinion Quarterly* 35:95–101.

Singer, Isaac Bashevis. 1973. *The Fools of Chelm and Their History*. New York: Farrar, Straus and Giroux.

Singer, Max. 1981. "How the Scarcity Error Hurts America." *Washington Quarterly*, (Spring).

** ———. 1988. *Passage to a Human World*. New Brunswick, N.J.: Transaction Press.

** Singer, S. Fred. 1989. *Global Climate Change*. New York: Paragon House.

———. 1992. "My Adventures in the Ozone Layer." In Lehr, pp. 535–45.

Singh, Karan. 1989. "Man & Nature." In *Darshan* 6, no. 6 (June): 1–4.

Sirageldin, Ismail, and John F. Kantner. 1982. "Review." *Population and Development Review* (March): 169–73.

Slade, Margaret E. 1982. "Trends in Natural-Resource Commodity Prices: An Analysis of the Time Domain." *Journal of Environmental Economics and Management* 9: 122–37.

———. 1987. "Natural Resources, Population Growth, and Economic Well-Being." In Johnson and Lee, pp. 331–72.

Slicher van Bath, B. H. 1963. *The Agrarian History of Western Europe,* A.D. 500–1850. London: Arnold.

Slovic, Paul, Nancy Kraus, and Vincent T. Covello. 1990. "What *Should* We Know about Making Risk Comparisons?" *Risk Analysis* 10, no. 3: 389–92.

Smith, Adam. 1937. *An Inquiry into the Nature and Causes of the Wealth of Nations,* edited by Edwin Cannan. New York: Modern Lib.

Smith, Barton, and Robert Newman. 1977. "Depressed Wages along the U.S.-Mexican Border: An Empirical Analysis." *Economic Inquiry* 15:56–66.

Smith, Fred L. Jr. 1990a. "The Liberating Effects of the Auto." *Reason* (Aug./Sept.): 22–26.

———. 1990b. "Free Market Environmentalism: Using Property Rights to Protect the Environment." Washington: Competitive Enterprise Institute.

Smith, Kathleen, and David Loveland. 1988. "Natural Resources—Energy Concerns in the 1990s." *Environment,* vol. 30, no. 8 (October): 2–4.

Smith, P.E.L., and T. C. Young, Jr. 1972. "The Evolution of Early Agriculture and Culture in Greater Mesopotamia: A Trial Model." In *Population Growth: Anthropological Implications,* edited by B. J. Spooner, pp. 1–59. Cambridge, Mass.: Massachusetts Institute of Technology Press.

———. "The Force of Numbers: Population Pressure in the Central Western Zagros 12,000–4500 B.C." In *The Hilly Flanks and Beyond: Essays on the Prehistory of Southwestern Asia Presented to Robert J. Braidwood,* edited by T. Cuyler Young, Jr., Philip E. L. Smith and Peder Mortensen, pp. 141–56. Chicago: The Oriental Institute of the University of Chicago, Studies in Ancient Oriental Civilization no. 36.

Smith, V. Kerry, ed. 1979. *Scarcity and Growth Revisited.* Baltimore: Resources for the Future and Johns Hopkins.

Smithsonian Institute Board of Regents. 1941. *Annual Report Showing the Operations, Expenditures, and Conditions of the Institution for the Year Ending June 30, 1940.* Washington, D.C.: GPO.

Sobo, Elizabeth. 1991a. *Unconventional Warfare and The Theory of Competitive Reproduction—A Study of U.S. Intervention & Covert Action in the Developing World.* Washington, D.C.: self-published.

———. 1991b. *Population Control and National Security—A Review of U.S. National Security Policy on Population Issues 1970–1988.* Washington, D.C.: self-published.

Solow, Robert. 1957. "Technical Change and the Aggregate Production Function." *The Review of Economics and Statistics* 39:312–20.

Sommer, Adrian. 1976. "Attempt at an Assessment of the World's Tropical Mist Forests." *Unasylva* 28: 5–27.

Sorokin, Pitinim. 1937/1978. *Social and Cultural Dynamics.* 4 vols. Boston: Little, Brown.

Sowell, Thomas. 1983. *The Economics and Politics of Race.* New York: William Morrow.

———. 1987. *A Conflict of Visions.* New York: Quill.

Spengler, Joseph J. 1978. "Population Phenomena and Population Theory." In Simon 1978c.

Srinivasan, T. N. 1987a. "Population and Food." In Johnson and Lee, pp. 3–26.

———. 1987b. "Population Growth and Economic Development." August. Xerox.

Starkey, Marion L. 1981. *The Devil in Massachusetts.* Garden City, N.Y.: Dolphin Books.

Steinmann, Gunter, and Julian L. Simon. 1980. Phelps' Technical Progress Model Generalized." *Economic Letters* 5: 177–82.

Stevens, Jerry. 1978. "Demographic Market Structure and Bank Performance. Dept. of Economics, University of Illinois. Mimeo.

Stevens, William K. 1991. "Dry Climate May Have Forced Invention of Agriculture." *The New York Times.* April 2, pp. C1, C7.

* Stroup, Richard L. and John Baden. 1983. *Natural Resources: Bureaucratic Myths and Environmental Management.* Cambridge, Mass.: Ballinger Press.

Stryker, J. Dirck. 1977. "Optimum Population in Rural Areas: Empirical Evidence from the Franc Zone. *The Quarterly Journal of Economics* 91:177–93.

Stuart, Alexander. 1958. *Overpopulation: Twentieth Century Nemesis.* New York: Exposition Press.

Stys, W. 1957. "The Influence of Economic Conditions on the Fertility of Peasant Women." *Population Studies* 11:136–48.

Sullivan, Richard J. 1995. "Trends in the Agricultural Labor Force." In Simon, ed. 1995.

Sveikauskas, Leo. 1975. "The Productivity of Cities." *The Quarterly Journal of Economics* 89:343–413.

Swanson, Earl R., and Earl O. Heady. 1984. "Soil Erosion in the United States." In *The Resourceful Earth,* edited by Julian L. Simon and Herman Kahn, pp. 202–23.

Talmon, J. L. 1961. *The Origins of Totalitarian Democracy.* New York: Praeger.

Tarbell, Ida M. 1939/1985. *All in a Day's Work: An Autobiography by Ida M. Tarbell.* New York: Macmillan.

Taylor, Carl E. 1965. "Health and Population." *Foreign Affairs* 43:475–86.

Taylor, Gordon Rattray. 1970. *The Doomsday Book.* London: Thames & Hudson.

Taylor, John J. 1989. "Improved and Safer Nuclear Power." *Science* 244 (April 21): 318–25.

Terhune, Kenneth W. 1975. *A Review of the Actual and Expected Consequences of Family Size.* National Institutes of Health Publication No. 75–779. Public Health Service. HEW. Washington, D.C.: GPO.

Thatcher, Sanford G. 1994. "Listbuilding at University Presses." In *Editors as Gatekeepers,* edited by Rita J. Simon and James J. Fyfe. Lanham, Md.: Rowman and Littlefield.

Thomas, Dorothy S. 1941. *Social and Economic Aspects of Swedish Population Movements.* New York: Macmillan.

Tierney, John. 1988. "Not To Worry." In *Hippocrates* (January/February): 29–32, 34, 37–38.

———. 1990. "Betting the Planet." *New York Times Magazine,* December 2, pp. 52–81.

Tiffen, Mary, and Michael Mortimore. 1992. "Environment, Population Growth and Productivity in Kenya: A Case Study of Machakos District." *Development Policy Review* 10: 359–87.

Tilton, John E. 1977. *The Future of Nonfuel Minerals.* Washington, D.C.: Brookings.

Tipler, Frank. 1992. "The Ultimate Fate of Life in Universes Which Undergo Inflation." *Physics Letters* B286: 36–43.

Train, Russell E. 1991. "Religion and the Environment." *Journal of Forestry* (September): 12–15.

Tullock, Gordon, and Gordon Brady. 1992. "The Risk of Crying Wolf." In *Predicting Ecosystem Risk,* edited by Cairns, Niederlehner, and Orvos. Princeton Scientific.

United Nations. Department of Economic and Social Affairs. 1956. *The Aging of Populations and Its Economic and Social Implications.* Population Studies, no. 26. New York: UN.

United Nations Environment Programme. 1987. *Environmental Data Report*, Prepared for UNEP by the Monitoring and Assessment Research Centre, London, UK. London: Basil Blackwell.

United Nations, Expert Group. 1989. "Consequences of Rapid Population Growth in Developing Countries." 1989. June. Xerox.

———. Food and Agriculture Organization. Various years. *Production Yearbook*. New York: UN.

———. Fund for Population Activities. 1975. *Annual Report*. New York: UN.

U.S. Congress. 1973. *Hearings on U.S. and World Food Situation*. 93rd Cong. 1st sess. October.

U.S. Congress, Office of Technology Assessment. 1991. *Improving Automobile Fuel Economy: New Standards, New Approaches*, OTA-E-504. Washington, D.C.: U.S. October, p. 21.

U.S. Council of Economic Advisers Economic Report of the President. Various years. Washington, D.C.

U.S. Council on Environmental Quality. 1975. *Sixth Annual Report*. Washington, D.C.: GPO.

———. 1976. *Seventh Annual Report*. Washington, D.C.: GPO.

U.S. CEQ and Department of State. 1980. *The Global 2000 Report to the President*, vol. 2. Washington, D.C.: GPO.

———. 1981. *Global Future: Time to Act*. Washington, D.C.: GPO.

U.S. Dept. of Agriculture. Economic Research Service. 1974. *Our Land and Water Resources: Current and Prospective Supplies and Uses*. Miscellaneous Publication no. 1290. Washington, D.C.: GPO.

U.S. Department of Agriculture, Economic Research Service. 1981. *Economic Indicators of the Farm Sector*, Statistic Bulletin 674. Washington, D.C.: GPO.

U.S. Department of Commerce. Various years. *Statistical Abstract of the United States*. Washington, D.C.: GPO.

U.S. Department of Commerce, Bureau of the Census. Various Years. *Statistical abstract of the United States*. Washington, D.C.: GPO.

———. Various years. *Population Reports*. Washington, D.C.: GPO.

U.S. Department of State. 1969. *Bulletin*, August 11. Washington, D.C.: GPO.

U.S. ERDA. 1976. *Energy and the Environment*. Washington, D.C.: GPO.

U.S. Forest Service. 1982. *An Analysis of the Timber Situation in the United States, 1952–2030*. Forest Resource Report 23. Washington, D.C.: GPO.

U.S. General Accounting Office. 1978. *Reducing Population Growth through Social and Economic Change in Developing Countries—A New Direction for U.S. Assistance*. Report to the Congress of the U.S. Washington, D.C.: GPO.

———. 1990. "Report to the Chairman: Foreign Assistance—AID's Population Program." Subcommittee on Foreign Operations, Committee on Appropriations, U.S. Senate, May.

U.S. National Security Council. 1974. *Implications of Worldwide Population Growth for U.S. Security and Overseas Interests*, December 10.

———. 1976. *U.S. International Population Policy, First Annual Report*. Prepared by the Interagency Task Force On Population Policy, May.

———. 1977. *First Annual Report on U.S. International Population Policy 1976*, January 3. Signed by Brent Scowcroft.

U.S. The White House. 1933. *Recent Social Trends in the United States*. vol. 1: *The President's Research Committee on Social Trends*. Washington, D.C.: GPO.

———. 1952. *Resources for Freedom*. 4 vols. The President's Materials Policy Commission (The Paley Commission). Washington, D.C.: GPO. June.

———. 1967. *The World Food Problem*. Vols. 1–2. Washington, D.C.: GPO.

———. 1972. Population and the American Future. *The Report of the Commission on Population Growth and the American Future*. New York: Signet.

Vajk, J. Peter. 1978. *Doomsday Has Been Cancelled*. Culver City, Calif.: Peace Press.

van Hise, Charles R. 1910. *The Conservation of Natural Resources in the United States*. New York: Macmillan.

Van Vleck, David B. 1970. "A Biologist Urges Stabilizing U.S. Population Growth." *University: A Princeton Quarterly* (Spring): 16–18.

Villalpondo, M. Vic et al. 1977. *A Study of the Socio-economic Impact of Illegal Aliens, County of San Diego*. San Diego: Human Resources Agency, County of San Diego. January.

Vitousek, Peter M., Paul Ehrlich, and Anne Ehrlich. 1987. "Net Primary Production: Original Calculations." *Science* 235 (February 13): 730.

Vogt, William. 1948. *Road to Survival*. New York: Sloane.

Vogt, William. 1960. *People! Challenge to Survival*. New York: Sloane.

* von Mises, Ludwig. 1972. *The Anti-Capitalist Mentality*. (South Holland, Ill., Libertarian Press.

von Thunen, Johann H. 1966. *The Isolated State*. New York: Pergamon.

Wade, Nicholas. 1974. "Windmills: The Resurrection of an Ancient Energy Technology." In Abelson 1974.

Wagret, Paul. 1968. *Polderlands*. London: Methuen.

Waldrop, M. Mitchell. 1981. "Wood: Fuel of the Future?" *Science* (February 27): 914.

Ware, Helen. 1978. Personal correspondence, March 20.

** Warwick, Donald P. 1982. *Bitter Pills: Population Policies and Their Implementation in Eight Developing Countries*. Cambridge: Cambridge University Press.

———. 1986. "The Indonesian Family Planning Program: Government Influence and Client Choice." *Population and Development Review* 12 (September): 453–90.

Waters, Tom. 1990. "Ecoglasnost." *Discover* (April): 51–53.

Watson, Andrew. 1988. "The Reform of Agricultural Marketing in China since 1978." *China Quarterly* (March): 1–28.

* Wattenberg, Ben J. 1974. *The Real America*. Garden City, N.Y.: Doubleday.

*** ———. 1987. *The Birth Dearth*. New York: Pharos Books.

** Weber, James A. 1977. *Grow or Die!* New Rochelle, N.Y.: Arlington House.

Weidenbaum, Murray. 1991. "Slight Reading." *Reason* (March): 42–43.

Wells, H. G. 1962. *Experiment in Autobiography*. Boston: Little, Brown.

Wertham, Frederick. 1969. *A Sign for Cain: An Exploration of Human Violence*. New York: Warner.

West, E. C. 1971. *Canada-United States Price and Productivity Differences in Manufacturing Industries, 1963*. Ottawa: Economic Council of Canada.

Western, David. 1989. "Conservation Biology." In *Conservation for the Twenty-first Century*, edited by David Western and Mary C. Pearl. New York, Oxford: Oxford University Press.

Westoff, Charles F. 1988. "Is the KAP-Gap Real?" *Population and Development Review* 14, no. 2 (June): 225–32.

*** Whelan, Elizabeth M. 1985. *Toxic Terror: The Truth Behind the Cancer Scare*. Jameson Books.

Whelan, Elizabeth M. 1989a. "Apple Dangers Are Just So Much Applesauce." *Wall Street Journal*. March 14, p. A24.

———. 1989b. "Don't Ban Red Dye; It's No Health Risk." *USA Today*. August 16, p. 8A.

* Whelan, Elizabeth M., and Fredrick J. Stare. 1992. In *Panic in the Pantry*, edited by Stephen Barrett. Buffalo, N.Y.: Prometheus Books.

Whelpton, P. K., A. Campbell Arthur, and J. E. Patterson. 1966. *Fertility and Family Planning in the United States*. Princeton, N.J.: Princeton University Press.

White, Gilbert F. 1984. "Water Resource Adequacy: Illusion and Reality." In *The Resourceful Earth*, edited by Julian L. Simon and Herman Kahn. pp. 250–66.

Whitmore, T. C., and J. A. Sayer, eds. 1992. *Tropical Deforestation and Species Extinction*. New York: Chapman and Hall.

Whittaker, R. H., and G. E. Likens. 1975. "The Biosphere and Man." In *Primary Productivity of the Biosphere*, edited by H. Lieth and R. H. Whittaker. New York: Springer.

Wiener, Norbert. 1950. *The Human Use Of Human Beings*. New York: Avon Books.

Wigner, Eugene P. 1967/1979. *Symmetries and Reflections*. Woodbridge, Conn.: Oxbow Press.

Wildavsky, Aaron. 1980. "Richer Is Safer." *The Public Interest* (Summer): 23–29.

*** ———. 1988. *Searching for Safety*. New Brunswick, N.J.: Transaction Press.

Williams, Linda B., and William F. Pratt. 1990. "Wanted and Unwanted Childbearing in the United States: 1973–88." In *Advance Data* (U. S. Department of Health and Human Services publication), no. 189 (September 26).

Williams, Walter. 1992. "Environmental Update." *The Reporter* (September 21).

Williamson, Francis S. L. 1969. "Population Pollution." *Bio-Science* 19:979–83. In Reid and Lyon 1972.

Williamson, Harold F. 1945. "Natural Resources and International Policy—Prophecies of Scarcity or Exhaustion of Natural Resources in the United States." *American Economic Review* (May): 97–109.

Willing, Martha Kent. 1971. *Beyond Conception: Our Children's Children*. Boston: Gambit.

Wilson, Edward O. 1992. *The Diversity of Life*. Cambridge, Mass.: Harvard University Press.

Wilson, Francis, and Mamphela Ramphele. 1989. *Uprooting Poverty in South Africa*. New York: The Global Hunger Project.

Wilson, George W., Barbara R. Bergmann, Leon V. Hinser, and Martin S. Klein. 1966. *The Impact of Highway Investment on Development*. Washington, D.C.: Brookings.

Winegarden, C. R. 1975. "Educational Expenditure and School Enrollments in Less-Developed Countries: A Simultaneous-Equation Method. *The Eastern Economic Journal* 2:77–87.

Wing, Steve. 1991. Referred to in "New Cancer Data from Oak Ridge," edited by Constance Holden. *Science* 252 (April 5): 34.

Winsborough, Hal H. 1965. "The Social Consequences of High Population Density." *Law and Contemporary Problems* 30, no. 1 (Winter).

Winsche, W. E., K. C. Hoffman, and F. J. Salzano. 1974. "Hydrogen: Its Future Role in the Nation's Energy Economy." In Abelson 1974.

Winter, J. M. 1982. "The Decline of Mortality in Britain 1870–1950." In *Population and Society in Britain 1850–1980*, edited by Theo Barker and Michael Drake, pp. 100–20.

Wise, John P. 1984. "The Future of Food from the Sea." In *The Resourceful Earth*, edited by Julian L. Simon and Herman Kahn, pp. 113–27.

———. 1991. "Dumping: Less Wasteful Than Recycling." *Wall Street Journal*, July 18, p. A10.

Wiseman, Clark. 1991a. "Government and Recycling: Are We Promoting Waste?" Gonzaga University, June. Xerox.

Wolf, Martin. 1974. "Solar Energy Utilization by Physical Methods." In Abelson 1974.

Wolfers, David. 1971. "The Case against Zero Growth." *International Journal of Environmental Studies* 1:227–32.

Wolff, Sheldon. 1989. "Are Radiation-Induced Effects Hormetic?" *Science* 245 (August 11): 575 and 621.

Wolfson, Margaret. 1983. *Profiles in Population Assistance*. Development Centre of the Organization for Economic Co-operation and Development.

Wolman, Abel. 1971. Review of Paul R. Ehrlich and Anne H. Ehrlich, *Population, Resources, Environment*. In *Milbank Memorial Fund Quarterly* 49 (January), part I: 93–97.

World Food Supply: PSAC Panel Warns of Impending Famine. 1967. *Science* 156: 1578.

World Resources Institute. 1990. *World Resources*. New York: Oxford.

Wright, Quincy. 1968. "War: The Study of War." In *International Encyclopedia of the Social Sciences*, edited by David Sills. New York: Macmillan-Free Press.

Wrigley, Henry E. 1881–1882. "The Amount of Oil Remaining in Pennsylvania and New York." Transactions of the American Institute of Mining Engineers, vol. 10, pp. 354–60.

Yaari, Shmuel. 1974. "World Over a Barrel." *Jerusalem Post Magazine* 4:4.

Yasuba, Yasukichi. 1962. *Birth Rates of the White Population in the United States, 1800–1860: An Economic Study*. Baltimore: Johns Hopkins University Press.

Young, Arthur. 1774/1967. *Political Arithmetic*. New York: Augustus M. Kelley.

Zajonc, R. B. 1976. "Family Configuration and Intelligence." *Science* 192: 227–36.

Zimmerman, Erich W. 1951/1965. *World Resources and Industries*. 2d ed. New York: Harper.

Zimmerman, L. J. 1965. *Poor Lands, Rich Lands*. New York: Random House.

Zinsmeister, Karl. 1989. "Harvest." *Reason* (November): 23–30.

Zonis, Marvinvin. 1976. "Petroleum and Politics in the Persian Gulf." *University of Chicago Magazine* (March): 14ff.

Zuk, Gary. 1985. "National Growth and International Conflict: A Reevaluation of Choucri and North's Thesis." *The Journal of Politics* 47: 269–81.

Index

Page numbers in boldface type indicate figures or tables.